SECOND EDITION

Learning Java™

Patrick Niemeyer and Jonathan Knudsen

Beijing · Cambridge · Farnham · Köln · Paris · Sebastopol · Taipei · Tokyo

Learning Java™, Second Edition
by Patrick Niemeyer and Jonathan Knudsen

Published by O'Reilly & Associates, Inc., 1005 Gravenstein Highway North, Sebastopol, CA 95472.

O'Reilly & Associates books may be purchased for educational, business, or sales promotional use. An online edition of this book is also available (*safari.oreilly.com*). For more information, contact our corporate/institutional sales department: (800) 998-9938 or *corporate@oreilly.com*.

Editor:	Debra Cameron
Production Editor:	Mary Anne Weeks Mayo
Cover Designer:	Hanna Dyer
Interior Designer:	Melanie Wang

Printing History:

November 2000:	First Edition.
June 2002:	Second Edition.

ISBN: 0-596-00285-8
[M]

Table of Contents

Preface

This book is about the Java™ language and programming environment. Whether you are a software developer or just someone who's been active on the Internet in the past few years, you've undoubtedly heard a lot about Java. Its introduction was one of the most exciting developments in the history of the Internet. Java became the darling of the Internet programming community as soon as the alpha version was released in 1995. Immediately, thousands of people were writing Java applets to add to their web pages. Since then Java has grown up and traveled far from its browser-based roots. Java is now, arguably, the most popular programming language in the world, used by millions. In recent years Java has surpassed languages such as C++ and Visual Basic in terms of developer demand and become the de facto language for new development—especially for web-based applications and services. Most universities are now using Java in their introductory courses, alongside the other important modern languages. Perhaps you are using this text in one of your classes right now!

What, then, is Java? Java is a new kind of programming language that was developed by Sun Microsystems to work on myriads of computing devices and to thrive in networked applications. It's widely used to create interactive web pages and web services. However, we have still seen only the start. The Java language and environment are rich enough to support new kinds of applications, such as dynamically extensible web browsers and mobile agents. Entirely new kinds of computer platforms have been and are being developed around Java; these include handheld devices and network computers that download all their software dynamically over the network. In the coming years, we'll see even more of what Java can do. Fancy web pages are fun and interesting, but they certainly aren't the end of the story. The success of Java is changing the way we think about computing in fundamental ways.

This book gives you a thorough grounding in Java fundamentals. *Learning Java*, Second Edition, attempts to live up to its name by mapping out the Java language, its class libraries, programming techniques, and idioms. We'll dig deep into interesting areas and at least scratch the surface of the rest. Other titles from O'Reilly &

Associates pick up where we leave off and provide more comprehensive information on specific areas and applications of Java.

Whenever possible, we provide compelling, realistic and examples and avoid merely cataloging features. The examples are simple but hint at what can be done. We won't be developing the next great "killer app" in these pages, but we hope to give you a starting point for many hours of experimentation and inspired tinkering that will lead you to learn more on your own.

New Developments

This book, *Learning Java*, is actually the fourth edition—reworked and retitled—of our original popular *Exploring Java*. With each edition we've taken great care not only to add new material covering additional features, but to thoroughly revise and update the existing content to synthesize the coverage and add years of real world perspective and experience to these pages.

One noticeable change in recent editions is that we've deemphasized the use of applets, reflecting their somewhat static role over the past couple of years in creating interactive web pages. And in this edition we've greatly expanded our coverage of web applications and services, which are now mature technologies. We've also included a chapter on working with XML and XSL, which are important new technologies.

We cover the most interesting features of Sun's newest release of Java, officially called Java 2 Standard Edition SDK Version 1.4. (In the old days, it would have been called JDK for Java Development Kit; Sun now uses the term SDK for Software Development Kit.) Sun coined the term "Java 2" to cover the major new features introduced in Java Version 1.2. When it's necessary to mention versions, we'll simply refer to them as Java 1.x.

New features in Java 1.4 include important improvements for servlets and web applications, regular expressions, Swing enhancements, new language features such as assertions and chained exceptions, logging and preferences APIs and a completely new I/O facility.

Another important change in recent Java history (Version 1.2) was the ascendancy of Java Swing as the main API for graphical user interface programming. All the material in this book relating to AWT, Java's original GUI programming interface, has been recast and updated in terms of the Swing facilities.

New in This Edition

This edition of the book has been significantly reworked to be as complete and up to date as possible. New topics in this edition include:

- Language assertions and exception chaining (Chapter 4)
- Regular expressions (Chapter 9)
- The new preferences and logging APIs (Chapter 10)
- The NIO package for scaleable I/O (Chapters 11 and 12)
- Full coverage of the servlet and web applications API (Chapter 14)
- Swing updates including formatted text and the new focus system (Chapters 15 through 17)
- JavaBeans examples using the NetBeans IDE (Chapter 21)
- Information on the Java Plug-in and applet signing (Chapter 22)
- Full coverage of XML including SAX, DOM, DTDs, XSL/XSLT, and the new JavaBeans XMLEncoder (Chapter 23)

Audience

This book is for computer professionals, students, technical people, and Finnish hackers. It's for everyone who has a need for hands-on experience with the Java language with an eye toward building real applications. This book could also be considered a crash course in object-oriented programming; as you learn about Java, you'll also learn a powerful and practical approach to object-oriented software development.

Superficially, Java looks like C or C++, so you'll have a head start in using this book if you have some experience with one of these languages. If you do not however, don't worry. Don't make too much of the syntactic similarities between Java and C or C++. In many respects, Java acts like more dynamic languages such as Smalltalk and Lisp. Knowledge of another object-oriented programming language should certainly help, although you may have to change some ideas and unlearn a few habits. Java is considerably simpler than languages like C++ and Smalltalk. If you learn well from good, concise examples and personal experimentation, we think you'll like this book.

Although we encourage you to take a broad view, you would have every right to be disappointed if we ignored the Web. A substantial part of this book does discuss Java in the context of web applications, so you should be familiar with the basic ideas behind web browsers, servers, and documents.

Using This Book

This book is organized roughly as follows:

- Chapter 1, *Yet Another Language?* and Chapter 2, *A First Application*, provide a basic introduction to Java concepts and a tutorial to give you a jump start on Java programming.

- Chapter 3, *Tools of the Trade*, discusses tools for developing with Java (the compiler, the interpreter, and the JAR file package). It also covers important concepts such as embedding Java code in HTML support and object signing.

- Chapter 4, *The Java Language*, through Chapter 8, *Threads*, describe the Java language itself. Chapter 8 covers the language's thread facilities, which should be of particular interest to advanced programmers.

- Chapter 9, *Working with Text*, covers basic string utilities and the powerful Regular Expressions API.

- Chapter 10, *Core Utilities*, and Chapter 11, *Input/Output Facilities*, cover much of the core API. Chapter 10 describes basic utilities, and Chapter 11 covers I/O facilities.

- Chapter 12, *Network Programming*, and Chapter 13, *Programming for the Web*, cover Java networking including sockets and NIO, URLs, and remote method invocation (RMI).

- Chapter 14, *Servlets and Web Applications*, covers web applications using servlets, servlet filters, and WAR files.

- Chapter 15, *Swing*, through Chapter 20, *Working with Images and Other Media*, cover the Abstract Window Toolkit (AWT) and Swing, which provide graphical user interface (GUI) and image support.

- Chapter 21, *JavaBeans*, covers the JavaBeans™ component architecture.

- Chapter 22, *Applets*, covers applets, the area in which Java saw its initial success.

- Chapter 23, *XML*, covers the Java APIs for working with XML and XSLT.

If you're like us, you don't read books from front to back. If you're really like us, you usually don't read the Preface at all. However, on the off chance that you will see this in time, here are a few suggestions:

- If you are an experienced programmer who has to learn Java in the next five minutes, you are probably looking for the examples. You might want to start by glancing at the tutorial in Chapter 2. If that doesn't float your boat, you should at least look at the information in Chapter 3, which tells how to use the compiler and interpreter, and gives the basics of a standalone Java application. This should get you started.

- Chapters 12 through 14 are essential if you are interested in writing advanced networked or web-based applications. This is one of the more interesting and important parts of Java.

- Chapters 15 though 21 discuss Java's graphics features and component architecture. You should read this if you are interested in writing graphical Java applications or applets.

- Chapter 22 covers the Applet API, including the Java Plug-in for guaranteed browser compatibility and signed applets for advanced applications.

- Chapter 23 covers the Java APIs for working with XML, including SAX, DOM, DTDs, and using XSL to render output for the Web. XML technology is becoming key to cross-platform development.

On the CD-ROM

The accompanying CD-ROM provides all you need to start working with Java immediately. Open source software on the CD-ROM includes:

- Java 2 Standard Edition SDK (Version 1.4.0)
- NetBeans (Version 3.3.1), a visual IDE for working with JavaBeans
- Ant (Version 1.4.1), a Java servlet engine from the Jakarta Project
- Tomcat (Version 4.0.3), a Java servlet engine from the Jakarta Project
- BeanShell (Version 1.2), a simple Java scripting language

Online Resources

There are many online sources for information about Java. Sun Microsystems's official web site for Java topics is *http://java.sun.com*; look here for the latest news, updates, and Java releases. This is where you'll find the Java SDK, which includes the compiler, the interpreter, and other tools (the SDK is also on the CD-ROM that comes with this book).

You should also visit O'Reilly & Associates' Java site at *http://java.oreilly.com*. There you'll find information about other O'Reilly Java books, and a pointer to the home page for *Learning Java*, *http://www.oreilly.com/catalog/learnjava2/*, where you'll find the source code examples for this book.

The *comp.lang.java* newsgroup can be a good source of information and announcements, and a place to ask intelligent questions.

Conventions Used in This Book

The font conventions used in this book are quite simple.

Italic is used for:

- Unix pathnames, filenames, and program names
- Internet addresses, such as domain names and URLs
- New terms where they are defined
- GUI buttons and menus, and threads
- Program names, compilers, interpreters, utilities, and commands

`Constant width` *is used for:*

- Anything that might appear in a Java program, including method names, variable names, and class names
- Command lines and options that should be typed verbatim on the screen
- Tags that might appear in an HTML or XML document
- Keywords, objects, and environment variables

`Constant width bold` *is used for:*

- Text that is typed by the user in code examples

`Constant width italic` *is used for:*

- Replaceable items in code

 This icon designates a note, which is an important aside to the nearby text.

 This icon designates a warning relating to the nearby text.

In the main body of text, we always use a pair of empty parentheses after a method name to distinguish methods from variables and other creatures.

In the Java source listings, we follow the coding conventions most frequently used in the Java community. Class names begin with capital letters; variable and method names begin with lowercase. All the letters in the names of constants are capitalized. We don't use underscores to separate words in a long name; following common practice, we capitalize individual words (after the first) and run the words together. For example: `thisIsAVariable`, `thisIsAMethod()`, `ThisIsAClass`, and `THISISACONSTANT`. Also, note that we differentiate between static and nonstatic methods when we refer to them. Unlike some books, we never write `Foo.bar()` to mean the `bar()` method of `Foo` unless `bar()` is actually static.

How to Contact Us

Please address comments and questions concerning this book to the publisher:

O'Reilly & Associates, Inc.
1005 Gravenstein Highway North
Sebastopol, CA 95472
(800) 998-9938 (in the United States or Canada)
(707) 829-0515 (international or local)
(707) 829-0104 (fax)

We have a web page for this book, where we list errata, examples, or any additional information. You can access this page at:

http://www.oreilly.com/catalog/learnjava2

To comment or ask technical questions about this book, send email to:

bookquestions@oreilly.com

For more information about our books, conferences, Resource Centers, and the O'Reilly Network, see our web site at:

http://www.oreilly.com

Acknowledgments

Many people have contributed to putting this book together, both in its *Exploring Java* incarnation and in its current form as *Learning Java*. Foremost we would like to thank Tim O'Reilly for giving us the opportunity to write this book. Special thanks to Mike Loukides, the series editor, whose endless patience and experience got us through the difficult parts. Paula Ferguson and John Posner contributed their organizational and editing abilities to get the material into final form. We could not have asked for a more skillful or responsive team of people with whom to work.

Speaking of borrowings, the original version of the glossary came from David Flanagan's book, *Java in a Nutshell*. We also borrowed the class hierarchy diagrams from David's book. These diagrams were based on similar diagrams by Charles L. Perkins. His original diagrams are available at *http://rendezvous.com/java/*.

Thanks also to Marc Wallace and Steven Burkett for reading the original work in progress and for the support of our friends at Washington University. A big thanks to Deb Cameron who edited this edition of the book and kept me from getting too far behind schedule (thanks for all the hard work Deb!). Thanks to all those who reviewed or answered questions for the latest edition: Jim Elliott and Brian Cole for Swing, Jack Shirazi for NIO, Tim Boudreau for NetBeans, Ed Howland for XML, and Ian Darwin for regular expressions. (Check out Ian's O'Reilly *Java Cookbook* for more examples.) Thanks also to Ray O'Leary, Mario Aquino, and Mark Volkmann for their reviews. Finally, special thanks to Song Fang for putting up with me through all this work.

Yet Another Language?

The greatest challenges and most exciting opportunities for software developers today lie in harnessing the power of networks. Applications created today, whatever their intended scope or audience, will almost certainly be run on machines linked by a global network of computing resources. The increasing importance of networks is placing new demands on existing tools and fueling the demand for a rapidly growing list of completely new kinds of applications.

We want software that works—consistently, anywhere, on any platform—and that plays well with other applications. We want dynamic applications that take advantage of a connected world, capable of accessing disparate and distributed information sources. We want truly distributed software that can be extended and upgraded seamlessly. We want intelligent applications—such as autonomous agents that can roam the Net for us, ferreting out information and serving as electronic emissaries. We know, to some extent, what we want. So why don't we have it?

The problem, historically, has been that the tools for building these applications have fallen short. The requirements of speed and portability have been, for the most part, mutually exclusive, and security has been largely ignored or misunderstood. There are truly portable languages, but they are mostly bulky, interpreted, and slow. These languages are popular as much for their high-level functionality as for their portability. And there are fast languages, but they usually provide speed by binding themselves to particular platforms, so they can meet the portability issue only half-way. There are even a few recent safe languages, but they are primarily offshoots of the portable languages and suffer from the same problems.

Enter Java

The Java™ programming language, developed at Sun Microsystems under the guidance of Net luminaries James Gosling and Bill Joy, is designed to be a machine-independent programming language that is both safe enough to traverse networks and powerful enough to replace native executable code. Java addresses the issues raised here and may help us start building the kinds of applications we want.

Initially, most of the enthusiasm for Java centered around its capabilities for building embedded applications for the Web called *applets*. Applets can be independent programs in and of themselves, or serve as sophisticated frontends to programs running on a server. More recently, interest has shifted to other areas. In Version 1.2, Java introduced Swing, one of the most sophisticated toolkits for building graphical user interfaces in any language. This development allowed Java to become a popular platform for developing traditional client-side application software. Java has also become the premier platform for web applications, using the *servlet* interface, and for enterprise applications using technologies such as Enterprise JavaBeans™. Java network portability makes it the platform of choice for modern distributed applications. This book shows you how to use Java to accomplish real programming tasks, such as building networked applications and creating functional user interfaces.

Java's Origins

The seeds of Java were planted in 1990 by Sun Microsystems patriarch and chief researcher, Bill Joy. Since Sun's inception in the early '80s, it has steadily pushed one idea: "The network is the computer." At the time though, Sun was competing in a relatively small workstation market, while Microsoft was beginning its domination of the more mainstream, Intel-based PC world. When Sun missed the boat on the PC revolution, Joy retreated to Aspen, Colorado, to work on advanced research. He was committed to the idea of accomplishing complex tasks with simple software and founded the aptly named Sun Aspen Smallworks.

Of the original members of the small team of programmers assembled in Aspen, James Gosling is the one who will be remembered as the father of Java. Gosling first made a name for himself in the early '80s as the author of Gosling Emacs, the first version of the popular Emacs editor that was written in C and ran under Unix. Gosling Emacs became popular but was soon eclipsed by a free version, GNU Emacs, written by Emacs' original designer. By that time, Gosling had moved on to design Sun's NeWS window system, which briefly contended with the X Window System for control of the Unix graphical user interface (GUI) desktop in 1987. While some people would argue that NeWS was superior to X, NeWS lost out because Sun kept it proprietary and didn't publish source code, while the primary developers of X formed the X Consortium and took the opposite approach.

Designing NeWS taught Gosling the power of integrating an expressive language with a network-aware windowing GUI. It also taught Sun that the Internet programming community will ultimately refuse to accept proprietary standards, no matter how good they may be. The seeds of Java's remarkably permissive licensing scheme were sown by NeWS's failure. Gosling brought what he had learned to Bill Joy's nascent Aspen project, and in 1992, work on the project led to the founding of the

Sun subsidiary, FirstPerson, Inc. Its mission was to lead Sun into the world of consumer electronics.

The FirstPerson team worked on developing software for information appliances, such as cellular phones and personal digital assistants (PDAs). The goal was to enable the transfer of information and real-time applications over cheap infrared and packet-based networks. Memory and bandwidth limitations dictated small and efficient code. The nature of the applications also demanded they be safe and robust. Gosling and his teammates began programming in C++, but they soon found themselves confounded by a language that was too complex, unwieldy, and insecure for the task. They decided to start from scratch, and Gosling began working on something he dubbed "C++ minus minus."

With the foundering of the Apple Newton, it became apparent that the PDA's ship had not yet come in, so Sun shifted FirstPerson's efforts to interactive TV (ITV). The programming language of choice for ITV set-top boxes was to be the near ancestor of Java, a language called Oak. Even with its elegance and ability to provide safe interactivity, Oak could not salvage the lost cause of ITV at that time. Customers didn't want it, and Sun soon abandoned the concept.

At that time, Joy and Gosling got together to decide on a new strategy for their language. It was 1993, and the explosion of interest in the Internet, and the Web in particular, presented a new opportunity. Oak was small, robust, architecture-independent, and object-oriented. As it happens, these are also the requirements for a universal, network-savvy programming language. Sun quickly changed focus, and, with a little retooling, Oak became Java.

Future Buzz?

It would not be overdoing it to say that Java has caught on like wildfire. Even before its first official release, while Java was still a nonproduct, nearly every major industry player had jumped on the Java bandwagon. Java licensees included Microsoft, Intel, IBM, and virtually all major hardware and software vendors. That's not to say that everything has come up roses. Even with all this support, Java has taken a lot of knocks and had some growing pains during its first few years.

An ongoing lawsuit between Sun and Microsoft over the distribution of Java with Internet Explorer has hampered its deployment on the world's most common operating system—Windows. Microsoft's involvement with Java has also become one focus of a larger federal lawsuit over serious anticompetitive practices at the company, with court testimony revealing concerted efforts by the software giant to undermine Java's future by introducing incompatibilities in its version of Java. Meanwhile, Microsoft has introduced their own Java-like language called C# (C-sharp) as part of their .NET initiative. This can only be interpreted as an indication of the success of the Java architecture.

As we begin looking at the Java architecture, you'll see that much of what is exciting about Java comes from the self-contained, virtual machine environment in which Java applications run. Java has been carefully designed so that this supporting architecture can be implemented either in software, for existing computer platforms, or in customized hardware, for new kinds of devices. Sun and other industry giants are producing fast Java chips and microprocessors tailored to run media-rich Java applications. Hardware implementations of Java are currently used in smart cards and other embedded systems. They are also planned for larger devices such as network terminals and web pads. Software implementations of Java are available for all modern computer platforms down to portable computing devices such as the popular Palm PDA. Java is also shipping now with many new cell phones.

Many people see Java as part of a trend toward cheap, Internet-based, "operating system-less" appliances that will weave the Net into more and more consumer-related areas. The first attempts at marketing "network computers" as alternatives to the standard PC have not gone very well. (The combination of Windows and cheap PC hardware create a formidable barrier.) But the desktop is only one corner of the network. Only time will tell what people will do with Java, but it's probably worth at least a passing thought that the applet you write today might well be running on someone's wristwatch tomorrow. If that seems too futuristic, remember that you can already get "smart cards" and "wearable" devices such as rings and dog tags that have Java interpreters embedded in them. These devices are capable of doing everything from financial transactions (paying a hotel bill) to unlocking a door (the door to your hotel room) to rerouting phone calls (so your hotel room receives your business calls). The hardware is already here; it can't be long before the rest of the software infrastructure begins to take advantage of it. A Java wristwatch is not a silly notion.

A Virtual Machine

Java is both a compiled and an interpreted language. Java source code is turned into simple binary instructions, much like ordinary microprocessor machine code. However, whereas C or C++ source is refined to native instructions for a particular model of processor, Java source is compiled into a universal format—instructions for a *virtual machine*.

Compiled Java *byte code* is executed by a Java runtime interpreter. The runtime system performs all the normal activities of a real processor, but it does so in a safe, virtual environment. It executes a stack-based instruction set and manages a storage heap. It creates and manipulates primitive data types, and loads and invokes newly referenced blocks of code. Most importantly, it does all this in accordance with a strictly defined open specification that can be implemented by anyone who wants to produce a Java-compliant virtual machine. Together, the virtual machine and language definition provide a complete specification. There are no features of the base

Java language left undefined or implementation-dependent. For example, Java specifies the sizes of all its primitive data types, rather than leaving it up to the platform implementation.

The Java interpreter is relatively lightweight and small; it can be implemented in whatever form is desirable for a particular platform. On most systems, the interpreter is written in a fast, natively compiled language such as C or C++. The interpreter can be run as a separate application, or it can be embedded in another piece of software, such as a web browser.

Put together this means that Java code is implicitly portable. The same Java application byte code can run on any platform that provides a Java runtime environment, as shown in Figure 1-1. You don't have to produce alternative versions of your application for different platforms, and you don't have to distribute source code to end users.

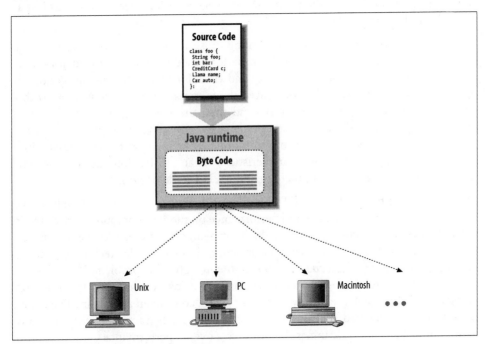

Figure 1-1. The Java runtime environment

The fundamental unit of Java code is the *class*. As in other object-oriented languages, classes are application components that hold executable code and data. Compiled Java classes are distributed in a universal binary format that contains Java byte code and other class information. Classes can be maintained discretely and stored in files or archives locally or on a network server. Classes are located and loaded dynamically at runtime as they are needed by an application.

In addition to the platform-specific runtime system, Java has a number of fundamental classes that contain architecture-dependent methods. These *native methods* serve as the gateway between the Java virtual machine and the real world. They are implemented in a natively compiled language on the host platform and provide low-level access to resources such as the network, the windowing system, and the host filesystem. The rest of Java is written entirely in Java and is therefore portable. This includes fundamental Java tools such as the Java compiler and web browser components, which are also written in Java and are therefore available on all Java platforms.

Historically, interpreters have been considered slow, but because the Java interpreter runs compiled byte code, Java is a relatively fast interpreted language. More importantly, Java has also been designed so that software implementations of the runtime system can optimize their performance by compiling byte code to native machine code on the fly. This is called just-in-time (JIT) or dynamic compilation. Sun claims that with just-in-time compilation, Java code can execute nearly as fast as native compiled code and maintain its transportability and security.

This is an often misunderstood point among those who want to compare language performance. There is only one intrinsic performance hit that compiled Java code suffers at runtime for the sake of security and virtual machine design—array bounds checking. Everything else can be optimized down to native code just as it can with a statically compiled language. Going beyond that, the Java language includes more structural information than many other languages, providing more room for optimizations. Also remember that these optimization can be made at runtime, taking into account the actual application characteristics. What can be done at compile time that can't be done better at runtime? Well, there is a trade-off: time.

The problem with a traditional JIT compilation is that optimizing code takes time and is extremely important for good performance on modern computer hardware. So a JIT compiler can produce decent results but may not be able to take the time necessary to do a good job of optimization up front. Sun's compiler technology, called HotSpot, uses a trick called *adaptive compilation* to solve this problem. If you look at what programs actually spend their time doing, it turns out that they spend almost all their time executing a relatively small part of the code again and again. The chunk of code that is executed repeatedly may only be a small fraction of the total program, but its behavior determines the program's overall performance.

To take advantage of this fact, HotSpot starts out as a normal Java byte code interpreter, but with a difference: it measures (profiles) the code as it is executing, to see what parts are being executed repeatedly. Once it knows which parts of the code are crucial to performance, HotSpot compiles those sections—and only those sections—into true machine code. Since it compiles only a small portion of the program into machine code, it can afford to take the time necessary to optimize those portions. The rest of the program may not need to be compiled at all—just interpreted—saving memory and time. In fact Sun's default Java VM can run in one of two modes:

client and server, which tell it whether the emphasize quick start-up time and memory conservation or flat out performance.

The technology for doing this is complex, but the idea is essentially simple: optimize the parts of the program that need to go fast, and don't worry about the rest. Another advantage of using an adaptive compiler at runtime is that it can make novel kinds of optimizations that a static (compile-time only) compiler cannot dream of.

Java Compared with Other Languages

Java is a new language, but it draws on many years of programming experience with other languages in its choice of features. Much can be said in comparing and contrasting Java with other languages. There are at least three pillars necessary to support a universal language for network programming today: portability, speed, and security. Figure 1-2 shows how Java compares to other languages.

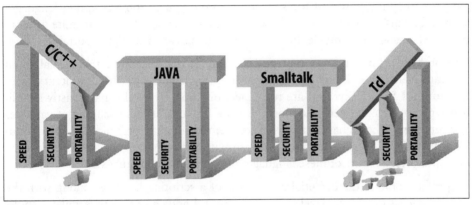

Figure 1-2. Programming languages compared

You may have heard that Java is a lot like C or C++, but that's really not true, except at a superficial level. When you first look at Java code, you'll see that the basic syntax looks like C or C++. But that's where the similarities end. Java is by no means a direct descendant of C or a next-generation C++. If you compare language features, you'll see that Java actually has more in common with languages such as Smalltalk and Lisp. In fact, Java's implementation is about as far from native C as you can imagine.

The surface-level similarities to these languages are worth noting, however. Java borrows heavily from C and C++ syntax, so you'll see lots of familiar language constructs, including an abundance of curly braces and semicolons. Java also subscribes to the C philosophy that a good language should be compact; in other words, it should be sufficiently small and regular so a programmer can hold all the language's capabilities in his or her head at once. Just as C is extensible with libraries, packages of Java classes can be added to the core language components.

C has been successful because it provides a reasonably featureful programming environment, with high performance and an acceptable degree of portability. Java also tries to balance functionality, speed, and portability, but it does so in a very different way. C trades functionality for portability; Java trades speed for portability. Java also addresses security issues while C doesn't.

In the early days, before JIT and adaptive compilation, Java was considerably slower than compiled languages. But as we described in the previous section, Java's performance is now comparable to C or C++ for equivalent tasks.

Scripting languages, such as Perl, Python, and Ruby, are becoming very popular, and for good reason. There's no reason a scripting language can't be suitable for safe, networked applications. But most scripting languages are not designed for serious, large-scale programming. The attraction to scripting languages is that they are dynamic; they are powerful tools for rapid prototyping. Some scripting languages such as Perl also provide powerful tools for text-processing tasks that more general-purpose languages find unwieldy. Scripting languages are also highly portable.

One problem with scripting languages, however, is that they are rather casual about program structure and data typing. Most scripting languages (with a hesitant exception for Perl 5.0 and Python) are not object-oriented. They also have vastly simplified type systems and generally don't provide for sophisticated scoping of variables and functions. These characteristics make them unsuitable for building large, modular applications. Speed is another problem with scripting languages; the high-level, fully interpreted nature of these languages often makes them quite slow.

Java offers some of the essential advantages of a scripting language, along with the added benefits of a lower-level language. Java 1.4 adds a complete Regular Expression API that makes it as powerful as Perl for working with text.

However, don't confuse Java with JavaScript! JavaScript is an object-based scripting language being developed by Netscape and others. It serves as a glue and an "in the document" language for dynamic, interactive HTML-based applications. JavaScript takes its name from its intended integration with Java. You can currently interact with Java applets embedded in HTML using JavaScript. There have been a few portable implementations of JavaScript that would promote it to the level of a general scripting language. For more information on JavaScript, check out *JavaScript: The Definitive Guide* by David Flanagan (O'Reilly & Associates).

Incremental development with object-oriented components, combined with Java's simplicity, make it possible to develop applications rapidly and change them easily. Many studies have found that development in Java is 10 times faster than in C or C++, strictly based on language features. Java also comes with a large base of core classes for common tasks such as building GUIs and doing network communications.

But along with these features, Java has the scalability and software-engineering advantages of more static languages. It provides a safe structure on which to build higher-level frameworks (and even other languages).

As we've already said, Java is similar in design to languages such as Smalltalk and Lisp. However, these languages are currently used mostly as research vehicles, rather than for developing large-scale systems. One reason is that they never developed a standard portable binding to operating-system services, such as the C standard library or the Java core classes. Smalltalk is compiled to an interpreted bytecode format, and it can be dynamically compiled to native code on the fly, just like Java. But Java improves on the design by using a bytecode verifier to ensure the correctness of compiled Java code. This verifier gives Java a performance advantage over Smalltalk because Java code requires fewer runtime checks. Java's bytecode verifier also helps with security issues, something that Smalltalk doesn't address. Smalltalk is a mature language, though, and Java's designers took lessons from many of its features.

Throughout the rest of this chapter, we'll present a bird's-eye view of the Java language. We'll explain what's new and what's not-so-new about Java, how it differs from other languages, and why.

Safety of Design

You have no doubt heard a lot about the fact that Java is designed to be a safe language. But what do we mean by safe? Safe from what or whom? The security features that attract the most attention for Java are those features that make possible new types of dynamically portable software. Java provides several layers of protection from dangerously flawed code, as well as more mischievous things such as viruses and Trojan horses. In the next section, we'll take a look at how the Java virtual machine architecture assesses the safety of code before it's run, and how the Java *class loader* (the bytecode loading mechanism of the Java interpreter) builds a wall around untrusted classes. These features provide the foundation for high-level security policies that can allow or disallow various kinds of activities on an application-by-application basis.

In this section, though, we'll look at some general features of the Java programming language. Perhaps more important than the specific security features, although often overlooked in the security din, is the safety that Java provides by addressing common design and programming problems. Java is intended to be as safe as possible from the simple mistakes we make ourselves, as well as those we inherit from legacy software. The goal with Java has been to keep the language simple, provide tools that have demonstrated their usefulness, and let users build more complicated facilities on top of the language when needed.

Syntactic Sweet 'n' Low

Java is parsimonious in its features; simplicity rules. Unlike C++, Java doesn't allow programmer-defined operator overloading. (The string concatenation operator + is the only system-defined, overloaded operator in Java.). Java doesn't have a preprocessor, so it doesn't have macros, #define statements, or conditional source compilation. These constructs exist in other languages primarily to support platform dependencies, so in that sense they should not be needed in Java. Conditional compilation is also commonly used for debugging purposes. Debugging code can be included directly in your Java source code by making it conditional on a constant (we'll talk about those in Chapter 4). The Java compiler is smart enough to remove this code when it determines that it won't be called.

Java provides a well-defined *package* structure for organizing class files. The package system allows the compiler to handle some of the functionality of the traditional *make* utility (a tool for building executables from source code). The compiler also works with compiled Java classes because all type information is preserved; there is no need for "header" files, as in C/C++. All this means that Java code requires less context to read. Indeed, you may sometimes find it faster to look at the Java source code than to refer to class documentation.

Java replaces some features that have been troublesome in other languages. For example, Java supports only a single inheritance class hierarchy but allows multiple inheritance of interfaces. An *interface*, like an abstract class in C++, specifies some of the behavior of an object without defining its implementation, a powerful mechanism borrowed from Objective C. It allows a class to implement the behavior of the interface, without needing to be a subclass of anything in particular. Interfaces in Java eliminate the need for multiple inheritance of classes, without causing the problems associated with multiple inheritance. As you'll see in Chapter 4, Java is a simple, yet elegant, programming language.

Type Safety and Method Binding

One attribute of a language is the kind of type checking it uses. Generally, when we categorize a language as *static* or *dynamic,* we are referring to the amount of information about variable types that is known at compile time versus what is determined while the application is running.

In a strictly statically typed language such as C or C++, data types are etched in stone when the source code is compiled. The compiler benefits from having enough information to enforce usage rules, so that it can catch many kinds of errors before the code is executed, such as storing a floating-point value in an integer variable. The code then doesn't require runtime type checking, so it can be compiled to be small and fast. But statically typed languages are inflexible. They don't support high-level constructs such as lists and collections as naturally as languages with dynamic type checking, and they make it impossible for an application to safely import new data types while it's running.

In contrast, a dynamic language such as Smalltalk or Lisp has a runtime system that manages the types of objects and performs necessary type checking while an application is executing. These kinds of languages allow for more complex behavior and are in many respects more powerful. However, they are also generally slower, less safe, and harder to debug.

The differences in languages have been likened to the differences among kinds of automobiles.* Statically typed languages such as C++ are analogous to a sports car— reasonably safe and fast—but useful only if you're driving on a nicely paved road. Highly dynamic languages such as Smalltalk are more like an off-road vehicle: they afford you more freedom but can be somewhat unwieldy. It can be fun (and sometimes faster) to go roaring through the back woods, but you might also get stuck in a ditch or mauled by bears.

Another attribute of a language is the way it binds method calls to their definitions. In an language such as C or C++, the definitions of methods are normally bound at compile time, unless the programmer specifies otherwise. Smalltalk, on the other hand, is called a "late-binding" language because it locates the definitions of methods dynamically at runtime. Early-binding is important for performance reasons; an application can run without the overhead incurred by searching method tables at runtime. But late-binding is more flexible. It's also necessary in an object-oriented language, where a subclass can override methods in its superclass, and only the runtime system can determine which method to run.

Java provides some of the benefits of both C++ and Smalltalk; it's a statically typed, late-binding language. Every object in Java has a well-defined type that is known at compile time. This means the Java compiler can do the same kind of static type checking and usage analysis as C++. As a result, you can't assign an object to the wrong type of variable or call nonexistent methods on an object. The Java compiler goes even further and prevents you from using uninitialized variables (see Chapter 4).

However, Java is fully runtime-typed as well. The Java runtime system keeps track of all objects and makes it possible to determine their types and relationships during execution. This means you can inspect an object at runtime to determine what it is. Unlike C or C++, casts from one type of object to another are checked by the runtime system, and it's possible to use new kinds of dynamically loaded objects with a level of type safety. And since Java is a late-binding language, all methods are like *virtual methods* in C++. This means that it's possible for a subclass to override methods in its superclass, even a subclass loaded at runtime.

* The credit for the car analogy goes to Marshall P. Cline, author of the C++ FAQ.

Incremental Development

Java carries all data-type and method-signature information with it from its source code to its compiled bytecode form. This means that Java classes can be developed incrementally. Your own Java classes can also be used safely with classes from other sources your compiler has never seen. In other words, you can write new code that references binary class files, without losing the type safety you gain from having the source code.

A common irritation with C++ is the "fragile base class" problem. In C++, the implementation of a base class can be effectively frozen by the fact that it has many derived classes; changing the base class may require recompilation of the derived classes. This is an especially difficult problem for developers of class libraries. Java avoids this problem by dynamically locating fields within classes. As long as a class maintains a valid form of its original structure, it can evolve without breaking other classes that are derived from it or that make use of it.

Dynamic Memory Management

Some of the most important differences between Java and C or C++ involve how Java manages memory. Java eliminates ad hoc pointers and adds garbage collection and true arrays to the language. These features eliminate many otherwise insurmountable problems with safety, portability, and optimization.

Garbage collection alone should save countless programmers from the single largest source of programming errors in C or C++: explicit memory allocation and deallocation. In addition to maintaining objects in memory, the Java runtime system keeps track of all references to those objects. When an object is no longer in use, Java automatically removes it from memory. You can simply ignore objects you no longer use, with confidence that the interpreter will clean them up at an appropriate time.

Java uses a sophisticated garbage collector that runs intermittently in the background, which means that most garbage collecting takes place during idle times, between I/O pauses, mouse clicks, or keyboard hits. Next-generation runtime systems such as HotSpot have even more advanced garbage collection that can even differentiate the usage patterns of objects (such as short-lived versus long-lived) and optimize their collection. Once you get used to garbage collection, you won't go back. Being able to write air-tight C code that juggles memory without dropping any on the floor is an important skill, but once you become addicted to Java, you can reallocate some of those brain cells to new tasks.

You may hear people say that Java doesn't have pointers. Strictly speaking, this statement is true, but it's also misleading. What Java provides are references—a safe kind of pointer—and Java is rife with them. A reference is a strongly typed handle for an object. All objects in Java, with the exception of primitive numeric types, are accessed through references. If necessary, you can use references to build all the normal kinds of data structures you're accustomed to building with pointers, such as linked lists, trees, and so forth. The only difference is that with references you have to do so in a type-safe way.

Another important difference between a reference and a pointer is that you can't do pointer arithmetic with references (they can point only to specific objects or elements of an array). A reference is an atomic thing; you can't manipulate the value of a reference except by assigning it to an object. References are passed by value, and you can't reference an object through more than a single level of indirection. The protection of references is one of the most fundamental aspects of Java security. It means that Java code has to play by the rules; it can't peek into places it shouldn't.

Unlike C or C++ pointers, Java references can point only to class types. There are no pointers to methods. People sometimes complain about this missing feature, but you will find that tasks that call for pointers to methods can be accomplished more cleanly using interfaces and adapter classes instead. We should also mention that Java has a sophisticated "reflection" API that actually allows you to reference and invoke individual methods. However this is not the normal way of doing things. We discuss reflection in Chapter 6.

Finally, arrays in Java are true, first-class objects. They can be dynamically allocated and assigned like other objects. Arrays know their own size and type, and although you can't directly define or subclass array classes, they do have a well-defined inheritance relationship based on the relationship of their base types. Having true arrays in the language alleviates much of the need for pointer arithmetic like that in C or C++.

Error Handling

Java's roots are in networked devices and embedded systems. For these applications, it's important to have robust and intelligent error management. Java has a powerful exception-handling mechanism, somewhat like that in newer implementations of C++. Exceptions provide a more natural and elegant way to handle errors. Exceptions allow you to separate error-handling code from normal code, which makes for cleaner, more readable applications.

When an exception occurs, it causes the flow of program execution to be transferred to a predesignated "catcher" block of code. The exception carries with it an object that contains information about the situation that caused the exception. The Java compiler requires that a method either declare the exceptions it can generate or catch and deal with them itself. This promotes error information to the same level of importance as argument and return typing. As a Java programmer, you know precisely what exceptional conditions you must deal with, and you have help from the compiler in writing correct software that doesn't leave them unhandled.

Threads

Applications today require a high degree of parallelism. Even a very single-minded application can have a complex user interface—which requires concurrent activities. As machines get faster, users become more sensitive to waiting for unrelated tasks that seize control of their time. Threads provide efficient multiprocessing and distribution of tasks for both client and server applications. Java makes threads easy to use because support for them is built into the language.

Concurrency is nice, but there's more to programming with threads than just performing multiple tasks simultaneously. In many cases, threads need to be synchronized, which can be tricky without explicit language support. Java supports synchronization based on the *monitor* and *condition* model developed by C.A.R. Hoare—a sort of lock and key system for accessing resources. The keyword synchronized designates methods for safe, serialized access within an object. Only one synchronized method within the object may run at a given time. There are also simple, primitive methods for explicit waiting and signaling between threads interested in the same object.

Learning to program with threads is an important part of learning to program in Java. See Chapter 8 for a discussion of this topic. For complete coverage of threads, refer to *Java Threads* by Scott Oaks and Henry Wong (O'Reilly).

Scalability

At the lowest level, Java programs consist of *classes*. Classes are intended to be small, modular components. They can be separated physically on different systems, retrieved dynamically, stored in a compressed format, and even cached in various distribution schemes. Over classes, Java provides *packages*, a layer of structure that groups classes into functional units. Packages provide a naming convention for organizing classes and a second level of organizational control over the visibility of variables and methods in Java applications.

Within a package, a class is either publicly visible or protected from outside access. Packages form another type of scope that is closer to the application level. This lends itself to building reusable components that work together in a system. Packages also help in designing a scalable application that can grow without becoming a bird's nest of tightly coupled code.

Safety of Implementation

It's one thing to create a language that prevents you from shooting yourself in the foot; it's quite another to create one that prevents others from shooting you in the foot.

Encapsulation is a technique for hiding data and behavior within a class; it's an important part of object-oriented design. It helps you write clean, modular software. In most languages, however, the visibility of data items is simply part of the relationship between the programmer and the compiler. It's a matter of semantics, not an assertion about the actual security of the data in the context of the running program's environment.

When Bjarne Stroustrup chose the keyword private to designate hidden members of classes in C++, he was probably thinking about shielding you from the messy details of a class developer's code, not the issues of shielding that developer's classes and objects from attack by someone else's viruses and Trojan horses. Arbitrary casting and pointer arithmetic in C or C++ make it trivial to violate access permissions on classes without breaking the rules of the language. Consider the following code:

```
// C++ code
class Finances {
    private:
        char creditCardNumber[16];
        ...
};

main( ) {
    Finances finances;

    // Forge a pointer to peek inside the class
    char *cardno = (char *)&finances;
    printf("Card Number = %s\n", cardno);
}
```

In this little C++ drama, we have written some code that violates the encapsulation of the Finances class and pulls out some secret information. This sort of shenanigan—abusing an untyped pointer—is not possible in Java. If this example seems unrealistic, consider how important it is to protect the foundation (system) classes of the runtime environment from similar kinds of attacks. If untrusted code can corrupt the components that provide access to real resources, such as the filesystem, the network, or the windowing system, it certainly has a chance at stealing your credit-card numbers.

In Visual BASIC, it's also possible to compromise the system by peeking, poking, and, under DOS, installing interrupt handlers.

If a Java application is to dynamically download code from an untrusted source on the Internet and run it alongside applications that might contain confidential information, protection has to extend very deep. The Java security model wraps three layers of protection around imported classes, as shown in Figure 1-3.

At the outside, application-level security decisions are made by a security manager. A security manager controls access to system resources such as the filesystem, network ports, and the windowing environment. A security manager relies on the ability of a

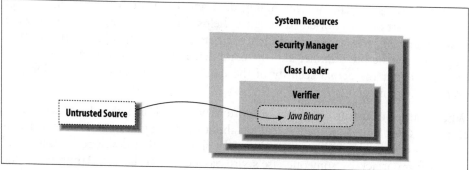

Figure 1-3. The Java security model

class loader to protect basic system classes. A class loader handles loading classes from the network. At the inner level, all system security ultimately rests on the Java verifier, which guarantees the integrity of incoming classes.

The Java bytecode verifier is a fixed part of the Java runtime system. Class loaders and security managers (or *security policies* to be more precise), however, are components that may be implemented differently by different applications that load byte code, such as applet viewers and web browsers. All three of these pieces need to be functioning properly to ensure security in the Java environment.*

The Verifier

Java's first line of defense is the *bytecode verifier*. The verifier reads byte code before it is run and makes sure it is well-behaved and obeys the basic rules of the Java language. A trusted Java compiler won't produce code that does otherwise. However, it's possible for a mischievous person to deliberately assemble bad code. It's the verifier's job to detect this.

Once code has been verified, it's considered safe from certain inadvertent or malicious errors. For example, verified code can't forge references or violate access permissions on objects. It can't perform illegal casts or use objects in unintended ways. It can't even cause certain types of internal errors, such as overflowing or underflowing the operand stack. These fundamental guarantees underlie all of Java's security.

You might be wondering, isn't this kind of safety implicit in lots of interpreted languages? Well, while it's true that you shouldn't be able to corrupt the interpreter with bogus BASIC code, remember that the protection in most interpreted languages

---

* You may have seen reports about various security flaws in Java. While these weaknesses are real, it's important to realize that they have been found in the various implementations of components, namely Sun's, Netscape's, and Microsoft's Java virtual machines, not in the basic security model itself. One of the reasons Sun has released the source code for Java is to encourage people to search for weaknesses so that they can be removed.

happens at a higher level. Those languages are likely to have heavyweight interpreters that do a great deal of runtime work, so they are necessarily slower and more cumbersome.

By comparison, Java byte code is a relatively light, low-level instruction set. The ability to statically verify the Java byte code before execution lets the Java interpreter run at full speed with full safety, without expensive runtime checks.

The verifier is a type of mathematical "theorem prover." It steps through the Java byte code and applies simple, inductive rules to determine certain aspects of how the byte code will behave. This kind of analysis is possible because compiled Java byte code contains a lot more type information than the object code of other languages of this kind. The byte code also has to obey a few extra rules that simplify its behavior. First, most bytecode instructions operate only on individual data types. For example, with stack operations, there are separate instructions for object references and for each of the numeric types in Java. Similarly, there is a different instruction for moving each type of value into and out of a local variable.

Second, the type of object resulting from any operation is always known in advance. There are no bytecode operations that consume values and produce more than one possible type of value as output. As a result, it's always possible to look at the next instruction and its operands and know the type of value that will result.

Because an operation always produces a known type, by looking at the starting state it's possible to determine the types of all items on the stack and in local variables at any point in the future. The collection of all this type information at any given time is called the *type state* of the stack; this is what Java tries to analyze before it runs an application. Java doesn't know anything about the actual values of stack and variable items at this time, just what kind of items they are. However, this is enough information to enforce the security rules and to ensure that objects are not manipulated illegally.

To make it feasible to analyze the type state of the stack, Java places an additional restriction on how Java bytecode instructions are executed: all paths to the same point in the code have to arrive with exactly the same type state.[*]

---

[*] The implications of this rule are of interest mainly to compiler writers. The rule means that Java byte code can't perform certain types of iterative actions within a single frame of execution. A common example would be looping and pushing values onto the stack. This is not allowed because the path of execution would return to the top of the loop with a potentially different type state on each pass, and there is no way that a static analysis of the code can determine whether it obeys the security rules. This restriction makes it possible for the verifier to trace each branch of the code just once and still know the type state at all points. Thus, the verifier can ensure that instruction types and stack value types always correspond, without actually following the execution of the code. For a more thorough explanation of all this, see *The Java Virtual Machine* by Jon Meyer and Troy Downing (O'Reilly).

Class Loaders

Java adds a second layer of security with a *class loader*. A class loader is responsible for bringing the byte code for one or more Java classes into the interpreter. Every application that loads classes from the network must use a class loader to handle this task.

After a class has been loaded and passed through the verifier, it remains associated with its class loader. As a result, classes are effectively partitioned into separate namespaces based on their origin. When a loaded class references another class name, the location of the new class is provided by the original class loader. This means that classes retrieved from a specific source can be restricted to interact only with other classes retrieved from that same location. For example, a Java-enabled web browser can use a class loader to build a separate space for all the classes loaded from a given URL.

The search for classes always begins with the built-in Java system classes. These classes are loaded from the locations specified by the Java interpreter's classpath (see Chapter 3). Classes in the classpath are loaded by the system only once and can't be replaced. This means that it's impossible for an applet to replace fundamental system classes with its own versions that change their functionality.

Security Managers

Finally, a *security manager* is responsible for making application-level security decisions. A security manager is an object that can be installed by an application to restrict access to system resources. The security manager is consulted every time the application tries to access items such as the filesystem, network ports, external processes, and the windowing environment; the security manager can allow or deny the request.

A security manager is most useful for applications that run untrusted code as part of their normal operation. Since a Java-enabled web browser can run applets that may be retrieved from untrusted sources on the Net, such a browser needs to install a security manager as one of its first actions. This security manager then restricts the kinds of access allowed after that point. This lets the application impose an effective level of trust before running an arbitrary piece of code. And once a security manager is installed, it can't be replaced.

In recent versions of Java, the security manager works in conjunction with an access controller that lets you implement security policies by editing a file. Access policies can be as simple or complex as a particular application warrants. Sometimes it's sufficient simply to deny access to all resources or to general categories of services such as the filesystem or network. But it's also possible to make sophisticated decisions based on high-level information. For example, a Java-enabled web browser could use an access policy that lets users specify how much an applet is to be trusted or that allows or denies access to specific resources on a case-by-case basis. Of course, this assumes that the browser can determine which applets it ought to trust. We'll see how this problem is solved shortly.

The integrity of a security manager is based on the protection afforded by the lower levels of the Java security model. Without the guarantees provided by the verifier and the class loader, high-level assertions about the safety of system resources are meaningless. The safety provided by the Java bytecode verifier means that the interpreter can't be corrupted or subverted and that Java code has to use components as they are intended. This, in turn, means that a class loader can guarantee that an application is using the core Java system classes and that these classes are the only way to access basic system resources. With these restrictions in place, it's possible to centralize control over those resources with a security manager.

Application and User-Level Security

There's a fine line between having enough power to do something useful and having all the power to do anything you want. Java provides the foundation for a secure environment in which untrusted code can be quarantined, managed, and safely executed. However, unless you are content with keeping that code in a little black box and running it just for its own benefit, you will have to grant it access to at least some system resources so that it can be useful. Every kind of access carries with it certain risks and benefits. For example, in the web browser environment, the advantages of granting an untrusted (unknown) applet access to your windowing system are that it can display information and let you interact in a useful way. The associated risks are that the applet may instead display something worthless, annoying, or offensive. Since most people can accept that level of risk, graphical applets and the Web in general are possible.

At one extreme, the simple act of running an application gives it a resource—computation time—that it may put to good use or burned frivolously. It's difficult to prevent an untrusted application from wasting your time or even attempting a "denial of service" attack. At the other extreme, a powerful, trusted application may justifiably deserve access to all sorts of system resources (e.g., the filesystem, process creation, network interfaces); a malicious application could wreak havoc with these resources. The message here is that important and sometimes complex security issues have to be addressed.

In some situations, it may be acceptable to simply ask the user to "okay" requests. Sun's HotJava web browser can pop up a dialog box and ask the user's permission for an applet to access an otherwise restricted file. However, we can put only so much burden on our users. An experienced person will quickly grow tired of answering questions; an inexperienced user may not be able to answer the questions correctly. Is it okay for me to grant an applet access to something if I don't understand what that is?

Making decisions about what is dangerous and what is not can be difficult. Even ostensibly harmless access, such as displaying a window, can become a threat when paired with the ability of an untrusted application to communicate from your host. The Java Security Manager provides an option to flag windows created by an untrusted application with a special, recognizable border to prevent it from impersonating another application and perhaps tricking you into revealing your password or your secret recipe collection. There is also a grey area, in which an application can do devious things that aren't quite destructive. An applet that can mail a bug report can also mail-bomb your boss. The Java language provides the tools to implement whatever security policies you want. However, what these policies will be ultimately depends on who you are, what you are doing, and where you are doing it.

Signing Classes

Web browsers that run Java applets, such as Sun's HotJava, start by defining a few rules and some coarse levels of security that restrict where applets may come from and what system resources they may access. These rules are sufficient to keep the waving Duke applet from clutching your password file, but they aren't sufficient for applications you'd like to trust with sensitive information. To fully exploit the power of Java, we need to have some nontechnical basis on which to make reasonable decisions about what a program can be allowed to do. This nontechnical basis is trust; basically, you trust certain entities not to do anything that's harmful to you. For a home user, this may mean that you trust the "Bank of Boofa" to distribute applets that let you transfer funds between your accounts, or you may trust L.L. Bean to distribute an applet that debits your Visa account. For a company, this may mean you trust applets originating behind your firewall and perhaps applets from a few high-priority customers, to modify internal databases. In all these cases, you don't need to know in detail what the program is going to do and give it permission for each operation. You only need to know that you trust your local bank.

This doesn't mean that there isn't a technical aspect to the problem of trust. Trusting your local bank when you walk up to the ATM means one thing; trusting some web page that claims to come from your local bank means something else entirely. It would be very difficult to impersonate the ATM two blocks down the street (though it has been known to happen), but, depending on your position on the Net, it's not all that difficult to impersonate a web site or to intercept data coming from a legitimate web site and substitute your own.

That's where cryptography comes in. Digital signatures, together with certificates, are techniques for verifying that data truly comes from the source it claims to have come from and hasn't been modified en route. If the Bank of Boofa signs its checkbook applet, your browser can verify that the applet actually came from the bank, not an imposter, and hasn't been modified. Therefore, you can tell your browser to trust applets that have the Bank of Boofa's signature. Java supports digital signatures; the details are covered in Chapter 3.

Java and the Web

The application-level safety features of Java make it possible to develop new kinds of applications that were not feasible before. A web browser that uses the Java runtime system can incorporate Java applets as executable content inside documents. This means that web pages can contain not only static hypertext information but also full-fledged interactive applications. The added potential for use of the Web is enormous. A user can retrieve and use software simply by navigating with a web browser. Formerly static information can be paired with portable software for interpreting and using the information. Instead of just providing some data for a spreadsheet, for example, a web document might contain a fully functional spreadsheet application embedded within it that allows users to view and manipulate the information.

In addition to applets, a more recent model for Internet downloadable application content is Java Web Start. The Web Start API allows your web browser to install applications locally, with stringent security still enforced by the Java runtime system. This system can also automatically update the software when it is used. We'll discuss this more in Chapter 22.

Applets

The term "applet" is used to mean a small, subordinate, or embeddable application. By "embeddable," we mean it's designed to be run and used within the context of a larger system. In that sense, most programs are embedded within a computer's operating system. An operating system manages its native applications in a variety of ways: it starts, stops, suspends, and synchronizes applications; it provides them with certain standard resources; and it protects them from one another by partitioning their environments.

As far as the web browser model is concerned, an applet is just another type of object to display; it's embedded into an HTML page with a special tag. Java-enabled web browsers can execute applets directly, in the context of a particular document, as shown in Figure 1-4. Browsers can also implement this feature using Sun's Java Plug-in, which runs Java just like other browser plug-ins display other kinds of content.

A Java applet is a compiled Java program, composed of classes just like any Java program. While a simple applet may consist of only a single class, most large applets should be broken into many classes. Classes may be stored in separate files on the server, allowing them to be retrieved as needed, but more generally are packaged together into archives. Java defines a standard archive format—the JAR file—which is built on the common ZIP archive format.

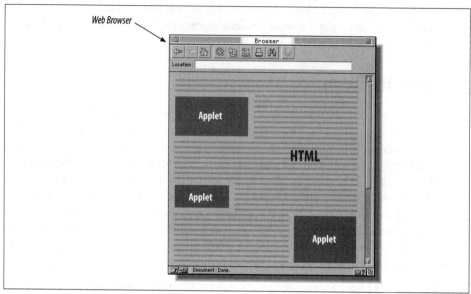

Figure 1-4. Applets in a web document

An applet has a four-part life cycle. When an applet is initially loaded by a web browser, it's asked to initialize itself. The applet is then informed each time it's displayed and each time it's no longer visible to the user. Finally, the applet is told when it's no longer needed, so that it can clean up after itself. During its lifetime, an applet may start and suspend itself, do work, communicate with other applications, and interact with the web browser.

Applets are autonomous programs, but they are confined within the walls of a web browser or applet viewer, and have to play by its rules. We'll be discussing the details of what applets can and can't do as we explore features of the Java language. However, under the most conservative security policies, an applet can interact only with the user and can communicate over the network only with the host from which it originated. Other types of activities, such as accessing files or interacting directly with outside applications, are typically prevented by the security manager that is part of the web browser or applet viewer. But aside from these restrictions, there is no fundamental difference between a Java applet and a standalone Java application.

New Kinds of Media

When it was first released, Java quickly achieved a reputation for multimedia capabilities. Frankly, this wasn't really deserved. At that point, Java provided facilities for doing simple animations and playing audio (which was leaps and bounds beyond static web pages). You could animate and play audio simultaneously, though you couldn't synchronize the two. Still, this was a significant advance for the Web, and people thought it was pretty impressive.

Java's multimedia capabilities have now taken shape. Java now has CD-quality sound, 3D animation, media players that synchronize audio and video, speech synthesis and recognition, and more. The Java Media Framework now supports most common audio and video file formats; the Java Sound API (part of the core classes) can record sound from a computer's microphone.

New Software Development Models

For many years, people have been using integrated development environments (IDEs) to create user interfaces. These environments let you generate applications by moving components around on the screen, connecting components to each other, and so on. In short, designing a user interface becomes a lot more like drawing a picture than like writing code. (Usually these tools also help you write code in the more traditional sense as well.)

For visual development environments to work well, you need to be able to create reusable software components. That's what the JavaBeans architecture is all about: it defines a way to package software as reusable building blocks. A graphical development tool can figure out a component's capabilities, customize the component, and connect it to other components to build applications. JavaBeans takes the idea of graphical development a step further. JavaBeans components, called Beans, aren't limited to visible, user interface components: you can have Beans that are entirely invisible and whose job is purely computational. For example, you can have a Bean that does database access; you can connect this to a Bean that lets the user request information from the database; and you can use another Bean to display the result. You can also have a set of Beans that implement the functions in a mathematical library; you can then do numerical analysis by connecting different functions to each other. In either case, you can create programs without writing a single line of code using Beans from a variety of sources. Granted, someone would have to write the Beans in the first place, but that's a different kind of task.

The JavaBeans APIs are a set of naming and design patterns that work with other Java capabilities—*reflection* and *serialization*—to allow tools to discover the capabilities of components and hook them together. The JavaBeans standard also specifies ways for individual beans to provide explicit information for these builder tools, including user friendly names and appearance information.

Visual development tools that support JavaBeans include Sun's Forte for Java—a commercial product that is also available in an open source version called NetBeans (*http://www.netbeans.org/*), IBM's VisualAge, Inprise's JBuilder (*http://www.inprise. com*), and WebGain's Visual Cafe (*http://www.webgain.com*). By using a "bridge," JavaBeans can also function inside ActiveX components, which are used by many IDEs.

Java as a General Application Language

Java was introduced to the world through the web browser and the Java applet API. However, Java is more than just a tool for building multimedia applications. Java is a powerful, general-purpose programming language that just happens to be safe and architecture-independent. Standalone Java applications are not subject to the restrictions placed on applets; they can perform the same jobs as do programs written in languages such as C and C++.

Any software that implements the Java runtime system can run Java applications. Applications written in Java can be large or small, standalone or component-like, as in other languages. Java applets are different from other Java applications only in that they expect to be managed by a larger application. They are also normally considered untrusted code. In this book, we will build examples of both applets and standalone Java applications. With the exception of the few things untrusted applets can't do, such as access files, all the tools we examine in this book apply to both applets and standalone Java applications.

A Java Road Map

With everything that's going on, it's hard to keep track of what's available now, what's promised, and what has been around for some time. The following sections comprise a road map that imposes some order on Java's past, present, and future.

The Past: Java 1.0–Java 1.3

Java 1.0 provided the basic framework for Java development: the language itself plus packages that let you write applets and simple applications. Although 1.0 is officially obsolete, there are still a lot of applets in existence that conform to its API.

Java 1.1 superseded 1.0, incorporating major improvements in the AWT package (Java's original GUI facility), a new event pattern, new language facilities such as reflection and inner classes, and many other critical features. Java 1.1 remains important, because it is supported natively by most versions of Netscape Navigator and Microsoft Internet Explorer browsers. For various political reasons, the future of the browser world has been frozen in this condition for many years; to execute applets using any features of Java after Version 1.1, you need to use the Java Plug-in, which allows Netscape and IE to use an up-to-date Java implementation. The latest version of Netscape (6.x) also supports Java 1.3.

Java 1.2, dubbed "Java 2" by Sun, was a major release in December 1998. It provided many improvements and additions, mainly in terms of the set of APIs that were bundled into the standard distributions. The most notable additions were the inclusion of the Swing GUI package as a core API and a new, full-fledged 2D drawing API. Swing is Java's advanced user interface toolkit with capabilities far exceeding the old

AWT's. (Swing, AWT, and some other packages have been variously called the JFC, or Java Foundation Classes.) Java 1.2 also added a proper Collections API to Java.

Java 1.3, released in early 2000, added minor features but was primarily focused on performance. With Version 1.3, Java got significantly faster on many platforms and Swing got many bug fixes. In this timeframe, Java enterprise APIs such as Servlets and Enterprise JavaBeans also matured.

The Present: Java 1.4

This book includes all the latest and greatest improvements through the final release of Java 1.4. This release provides many important and long-awaited features including language assertions, regular expressions, preferences and logging APIs, a new I/O system for high-volume applications, standard support for XML, fundamental improvements in AWT and Swing, and a greatly matured Java Servlets API for web applications.

Here's a brief overview of the most important features of the current core Java API:

JDBC (Java Database Connectivity)
> A general facility for interacting with databases. (Introduced in Java 1.1.)

RMI (Remote Method Invocation)
> Java's distributed objects system. RMI lets you call methods on objects hosted by a server running somewhere else on the network. (Introduced in Java 1.1.)

Java Security
> A facility for controlling access to system resources, combined with a uniform interface to cryptography. Java Security is the basis for signed classes, which were discussed earlier.

JFC (Java Foundation Classes)
> A catch-all for a number of new features, including the Swing user interface components; "pluggable look-and-feel," which means the ability of the user interface to adapt itself to the "look-and-feel" of the platform you're using; drag and drop; and accessibility, which means the ability to integrate with special software and hardware for people with disabilities.

Java 2D
> Part of JFC; enables high-quality graphics, font manipulation, and printing.

Internationalization
> The ability to write programs that adapt themselves to the language the user wants to use; the program automatically displays text in the appropriate language. (Introduced in Java 1.1.)

JNDI (Java Naming and Directory Interface)
> A general service for looking up resources. JNDI unifies access to directory services such as LDAP, Novell's NDS, and others.

The following "standard extension" APIs aren't part of the core Java distribution; you may have to download them separately.

JavaMail
> A uniform API for writing email software.

Java 3D
> A facility for developing applications with 3D graphics.

Java Media
> Another catch-all that includes Java 2D, Java 3D, the Java Media Framework (a framework for coordinating the display of many different kinds of media), Java Speech (for speech recognition and synthesis), Java Sound (high-quality audio), Java TV (for interactive television and similar applications), and others.

Java Servlets
> A facility that lets you write server-side web applications in Java.

Java Cryptography
> Actual implementations of cryptographic algorithms. (This package was separated from Java Security for legal reasons.)

JavaHelp
> A facility for writing help systems and incorporating them in Java programs.

Enterprise JavaBeans
> A component architecture for building distributed server-side applications.

Jini
> An extremely interesting catch-all that is designed to enable massively distributed computing, including computing on common household appliances. In a few years, your stereo may be able to execute Java programs.

Java Card
> A version of Java for very small (i.e., credit card-sized) devices, which have severe limitations on speed and memory.

In this book, we'll try to give you a taste of as many features as possible; unfortunately for us (but fortunately for Java software developers), the Java environment has become so rich that it's impossible to cover everything in a single book.

The Future

You can think of the first four years of Java development as a "big bang," followed by an "inflationary" phase as Sun added new features and improved old features, at an incredible rate. Things seem to be slowing down now: new APIs aren't being announced as often, and those that are announced tend to be more specialized. At least for the moment, the Java world is stabilizing. This is especially good news for the business world, which is rapidly building a new infrastructure based on Java APIs.

Probably the most exciting front for Java now is in the area of small devices. The Java "Java 2 Micro Edition" or J2ME is a subset of Java designed to fit on devices with limited capabilities. The reference platform for the J2ME architecture is the Palm PDA. Java is also now beginning to ship in cell phones, allowing downloadable applications and media.

Availability

You have several choices for Java development environments and runtime systems. Sun's Java software development kit is available for Solaris, Linux, and Windows. Visit Sun's Java web site at *http://java.sun.com* for more information about obtaining the latest Java SDK (Version 1.4 is included on the accompanying CD-ROM). There are also Java ports for other platforms, including NetWare, HP-UX, OSF/1 (including Digital Unix), Silicon Graphics' IRIX, and various IBM operating systems (including AIX, OS/2, OS/390, and OS/400). For more information, see the web pages maintained by the vendor you're interested in. Sun maintains a web page summarizing porting efforts at *http://java.sun.com/cgi-bin/java-ports.cgi*. Another good source for current information is the Java FAQ from the *comp.lang.java* newsgroup.

Most versions of Netscape Navigator and Microsoft Internet Explorer come with their own Java runtime system that runs Java applets and supports Java 1.1. Neither supports later Java releases at present, although Netscape 6 does support Java 1.3. To ameliorate the problem in general, Sun has released a Java Plug-in that allows you to specify and install the latest versions of Java; it is distributed with the Java development kit (SDK) and runtime systems (JRE) for Windows.

CHAPTER 2
A First Application

Before diving into our full discussion of the Java language, let's get our feet wet by jumping into some working code and splashing around a bit. In this chapter, we'll build a friendly little application that illustrates a number of concepts used throughout the book. We'll take this opportunity to introduce general features of the Java language and of Java applications. Look to subsequent chapters for more details.

This chapter also serves as a brief introduction to the object-oriented and multithreaded aspects of Java. If these concepts are new to you, we hope that encountering them here in Java for the first time will be a straightforward and pleasant experience. If you have worked with another object-oriented or multithreaded programming environment, you should especially appreciate Java's simplicity and elegance. This chapter is intended to give you a bird's eye view of the Java language and a feel for how it is used. If you have trouble with any of the concepts introduced here, rest assured they will be covered in greater detail later in the book.

We can't stress enough the importance of experimentation as you learn new concepts here and throughout the book. Don't just read the examples—run them. Copy the source code from the accompanying CD-ROM or from our web site at *http://www.oreilly.com/catalog/learnjava2*. Compile the programs on your machine, and try them. Then, turn our examples into your examples: play with them, change their behavior, break them, fix them, and hopefully have some fun along the way.

HelloJava

In the tradition of introductory programming texts, we begin with Java's equivalent of the archetypal "Hello World" application, HelloJava.

We'll end up taking four passes at this example before we're done (HelloJava, HelloJava2, etc.), adding features and introducing new concepts along the way. But let's start with the minimalist version:

```
public class HelloJava {
  public static void main( String[] args ) {
    System.out.println("Hello, Java!");
  }
}
```

This five-line program declares a class called HelloJava and a method called main(). It uses a predefined method called println() to write some text as output. It is a *command-line program*, which means that it runs in a shell or DOS window and prints its output there. That's a bit old-school for our taste, so before we go any further, we're going to give HelloJava a *graphical user interface* (GUI). Don't worry about the code too much yet; just follow along with the progression here, and we'll come back for explanations in a moment.

In place of the line containing the println() method, we're going to use something called a JFrame object to put a window on the screen. We can start by replacing the println line with the following three lines:

```
JFrame frame = new JFrame( "Hello Java!" );
frame.setSize( 300, 300 );
frame.setVisible( true );
```

This snippet creates a JFrame object with the title "Hello Java!" The JFrame is a graphical window. To display it, we simply configure its size on the screen using the setSize() method and make it visible by calling the setVisible() method.

If we stopped here, we would see an empty window on the screen with our "Hello Java!" banner as its title. But we'd like our message inside the window, not just scrawled on the top of it. To put something in the window, we need a couple more lines. The following, complete example adds a JLabel object to display the text centered in our window. The additional line at the top is necessary to tell Java where to find the JFrame and JLabel classes (the definitions of the JFrame and JLabel objects that we're using).

```
import javax.swing.*;

public class HelloJava {
  public static void main( String[] args ) {
    JFrame frame = new JFrame( "Hello Java!" );
    JLabel label = new JLabel("Hello Java!", JLabel.CENTER );
    frame.getContentPane( ).add( label );
    frame.setSize( 300, 300 );
    frame.setVisible( true );
  }
}
```

Now that we've got something presentable, let's take a moment to compile and run this example. Place the text in a file called *HelloJava.java*.

Now compile this source using the Java compiler, *javac*:

```
% javac HelloJava.java
```

This produces the Java bytecode binary class file *HelloJava.class*.

You can run the application with the Java virtual machine by specifying the class name (not the filename) as an argument:

```
% java HelloJava
```

You should see the proclamation shown in Figure 2-1. Congratulate yourself: you have written your first application! Take a moment to bask in the glow of your monitor.

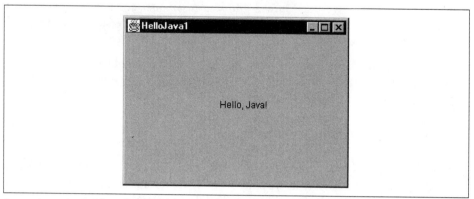

Figure 2-1. The HelloJava application

Be aware that when you click on the window's close box, the window goes away, but your program is still running. To stop Java and return control to the command line, type Ctrl-C or whatever key sequence stops a running application on your platform. We'll remedy this shortcoming in a later version of the example.

HelloJava may be a small program, but there is quite a bit going on behind the scenes. Those few lines represent the tip of an iceberg. What lies under the surface are the layers of functionality provided by the Java language and its foundation class libraries. Remember that in this chapter, we're going to cover a lot of ground quickly in an effort to show you the big picture. We'll try to offer enough detail for a good understanding of what is happening in each example, deferring full explanations until the appropriate chapters. This holds for both elements of the Java language and the object-oriented concepts that apply to them. Later chapters provide more detailed cataloging of Java's syntax, components, and object-oriented features.

Classes

The previous example defines a class named HelloJava.

```
public class HelloJava {
    ...
```

Classes are the fundamental building blocks of most object-oriented languages. A *class* is a group of data items, with associated functions that can perform operations on that data. The data items in a class are called *variables* or sometimes *fields*; in Java, functions are called *methods*. The primary benefits of an object-oriented language are this association between data and functionality in class units and also the ability of classes to *encapsulate* or hide details, freeing the developer from worrying about low-level details.

In an application, a class might represent something concrete, such as a button on a screen or the information in a spreadsheet, or it could be something more abstract, such as a sorting algorithm or perhaps the sense of ennui in a character in a role-playing game. A class representing a spreadsheet might, for example, have variables that represent the values of its individual cells and methods that perform operations on those cells, such as "clear a row" or "compute values."

Our HelloJava class is an entire Java application in a single class. It defines just one method, main(), which holds the body of our program:

```
public class HelloJava {
    public static void main( String[] args ) {
    ...
```

It is this main() method that is called first, when the application is started. The bit labeled String [] args allows us to pass command-line arguments to the application. We'll walk through the main() method in the next section. Finally, we'll note that although this version of HelloJava does not define any variables as part of its class, it does use two variables, frame and label, inside its main() method. We'll have more to say about variables soon as well.

The main() Method

As we saw when we ran our example, running a Java application means picking a particular class and passing it as an argument to the Java virtual machine. When we did this, the java command looked in our HelloJava class to see if it contained the special method named main() of just the right form. It did, and so it was executed. If it had not been there we would have received an error message. The main() method is the entry point for applications. Every standalone Java application includes at least one class with a main() method that performs the necessary actions to start the rest of the program.

Our main() method sets up a window (a JFrame) that will contain the visual output of the HelloJava class. Right now, it's doing all the work in the application. But in an object-oriented application, we normally delegate responsibilities to many different classes. In the next incarnation of our example we're going to perform just such a split—creating a second class—and we'll see that as the example subsequently evolves, the main() method remains more or less the same, simply holding the startup procedure.

Let's quickly walk through our main() method, just so we know what it does. First, main() creates a JFrame, the window that will hold our example:

```
JFrame frame = new JFrame("Hello Java!");
```

The word new in this line of code is very important: JFrame is the name of a class that represents a window on the screen. But the class itself is just a template, like a building plan. The new keyword tells Java to allocate memory and actually create a particular JFrame object. In this case, the argument inside the parentheses tells the JFrame what to display in its title bar. We could have left out the "Hello Java" text and used empty parentheses to create a JFrame with no title.

When frame windows are first created, they are very small. So before we show the JFrame, we set its size to something reasonable:

```
frame.setSize( 300, 300 );
```

This is an example of invoking a method on a particular object. In this case the setSize() method is defined by the JFrame class, and it affects the particular JFrame object we've placed in the variable frame. Like the frame, we also create an instance of JLabel to hold our text inside the window:

```
JLabel label = new JLabel("Hello Java!", JLabel.CENTER );
```

JLabel is much like a physical label. It holds some text at a particular position, in this case on our frame. This is a very object-oriented concept: using an object to hold some text, instead of simply invoking some method to "draw" the text and moving on. The rationale for this will become clearer later.

Next we have to place the label into the frame we created:

```
frame.getContentPane().add( label );
```

Here we're calling a method named getContentPane() and using the result to attach our label. You can think of the JFrame as having several "pages" to it, and this effectively causes our label to be placed on top.

main()'s final task is to show the frame window and its contents, which otherwise would be invisible. An invisible window makes for a pretty boring application.

```
frame.setVisible( true );
```

That's the whole main() method. As we progress through the examples in this chapter, it will remain mostly unchanged as the HelloJava class evolves around it.

Garbage Collection

We've told you how to create a new object with the new operator, but we haven't said anything about how to get rid of an object when you are done with it. If you are a C programmer, you may be wondering why not. The reason is that you don't have to do anything to get rid of objects when you are done with them.

The Java runtime system uses a *garbage collection* mechanism to deal with objects no longer in use. The garbage collector sweeps up objects not referenced by any variables and removes them from memory. Garbage collection is one of the most important features of Java. It frees you from the error-prone task of having to worry about details of memory allocation and deallocation. Now back to elaborating on our HelloJava class.

Classes and Objects

A class is a blueprint for a part of an application; it holds methods and variables that make up that component. Many individual working copies of a given class can exist while an application is active. These individual incarnations are called *instances* of the class or *objects*. Two instances of a given class may contain different data, but they always have the same methods.

As an example, consider a Button class. There is only one Button class, but an application can create many different Button objects, each one an instance of the same class. Furthermore, two Button instances might contain different data, perhaps giving each a different appearance and performing a different action. In this sense, a class can be considered a mold for making the object it represents, something like a cookie cutter stamping out working instances of itself in the memory of the computer. As you'll see later, there's a bit more to it than that—a class can in fact share information among its instances—but this explanation suffices for now. Chapter 5 has the whole story on classes and objects.

The term *object* is very general and in some other contexts is used almost interchangeably with *class*. Objects are the abstract entities all object-oriented languages refer to in one form or another. We will use "object" as a generic term for an instance of a class. We might, therefore, refer to an instance of the Button class as a Button, a Button object, or, indiscriminately, as an object.

The main() method in the previous example creates a single instance of the JLabel class and shows it in an instance of the JFrame class. You could modify main() to create many instances of JLabel, perhaps each in a separate window.

Variables and Class Types

In Java, every class defines a new *type* (data type). A variable can be declared to be of this type and then hold instances of that class. A variable could, for example, be of type Button and hold an instance of the Button class, or of type SpreadSheetCell and hold a SpreadSheetCell object, just as it could be any of the simpler types such as int or float representing numbers. The fact that variables have types and cannot simply hold any kind of object is another important feature of the language that ensures safety and correctness of code.

Ignoring the variables used inside the main() method for the moment, there is only one other variable declared our simple HelloJava example. It's found in the declaration of the main() method itself:

```
public void main( String [] args ) {
```

Just like functions in other languages, a method in Java declares a list of variables that it accepts as *arguments* or *parameters*, and it specifies the types of those variables. In this case the main method is requiring that when it is invoked, it be passed a list of String objects in the variable named args. The String is the fundamental object representing text in Java. As we hinted earlier, Java uses the args parameter to pass any command-line arguments supplied to the VM into your application. (We don't use them here.)

To this point we have loosely referred to variables as holding objects. In reality, variables that have class types don't so much contain objects as point to them. Class-type variables are references to objects. A *reference* is a pointer to or a name for an object. If you declare a class-type variable without assigning it an object, it doesn't point to anything. It's assigned the default value of null, meaning "no value." If you try to use a variable with a null value as if it were pointing to a real object, a runtime error, NullPointerException, occurs.

Of course, object references have to come from somewhere. In our example, we created two objects using the new operator. We'll examine object creation in more detail a little later in the chapter.

HelloComponent

Thus far our HelloJava example has contained itself in a single class. In fact, because of its simple nature it has really served as just a single large method. Although we have used a couple of objects to display our GUI message, our own code does not illustrate any object-oriented structure. Well, we're going to correct that right now by adding a second class. To give us something to build on throughout this chapter we're going to take over the job of the JLabel class (bye bye JLabel!) and replace it with our own graphical class: HelloComponent. Our HelloComponent class will start simple, just displaying our "Hello Java!" message at a fixed position. We'll add capabilities later.

The code for our new class is very simple, just a few more lines:

```
import java.awt.*;

class HelloComponent extends JComponent {
  public void paintComponent( Graphics g ) {
    g.drawString( "Hello, Java!", 125, 95 );
  }
}
```

You can add this text to the *HelloJava.java* file, or you can place it in its own file called *HelloComponent.java*. If you put it in the same file, you must move the new import statement to the top of the file, along with the other one. To use our new class in place of the JLabel, simply replace the two lines referencing the label with:

```
HelloComponent hello = new HelloComponent( );
frame.getContentPane( ).add( hello );
```

This time when you compile *HelloJava.java,* you will see two binary class files: *Hello-Java.class* and *HelloComponent.class.* Running the code should look much like the JLabel version, but if you resize the window, you'll notice that our class does not automatically adjust to center the code.

So what have we done, and why have we gone to such lengths to insult the perfectly good JLabel component?! We've created our new HelloComponent class, *extending* a generic graphical class called JComponent. To extend a class simply means to add functionality to an existing class, creating a new one. We'll get into that in the next section. Here we have created a new kind of JComponent that contains a method called paintComponent( ), responsible for drawing our message. Our paintComponent( ) method takes one argument named (somewhat tersely) g, which is of type Graphics. When the paintComponent( ) method is invoked, a Graphics object is assigned to g, which we use in the body of the method. We'll say more about paintComponent( ) and the Graphics class in a moment. As for why, you'll see when we add all sorts of new features to our new component later on.

Inheritance

Java classes are arranged in a parent-child hierarchy in which the parent and child are known as the *superclass* and *subclass*, respectively. We'll explore these concepts fully in Chapter 6. In Java, every class has exactly one superclass (a single parent), but possibly many subclasses. The only exception to this rule is the Object class, which sits atop the entire class hierarchy; it has no superclass.

The declaration of our class in the previous example uses the keyword extends to specify that HelloComponent is a subclass of the JComponent class:

```
public class HelloComponent extends JComponent {
```

A subclass may inherit some or all the variables and methods of its superclass. Through inheritance, the subclass can use those variables and methods as if it has declared them itself. A subclass can add variables and methods of its own, and it can also *override* or change the meaning of inherited variables and methods. When we use a subclass, overridden variables and methods are hidden (replaced) by the sub-class's own versions of them. In this way, inheritance provides a powerful mechanism whereby a subclass can refine or extend the functionality of its superclass.

For example, the hypothetical spreadsheet class might be subclassed to produce a new scientific spreadsheet class with extra mathematical functions and special built-in constants. In this case, the source code for the scientific spreadsheet might declare methods for the added mathematical functions and variables for the special constants, but the new class automatically has all the variables and methods that constitute the normal functionality of a spreadsheet; they are inherited from the parent spreadsheet class. This also means the scientific spreadsheet maintains its identity as a spreadsheet, and we can use it anywhere the simpler spreadsheet is used. That last sentence has profound implications, which we'll explore throughout the book. It means that specialized objects can be used in place of more generic objects, customizing their behavior without changing the underlying application.

Our HelloComponent class is a subclass of the JComponent class and inherits many variables and methods not explicitly declared in our source code. This is what allows our tiny class to serve as a component in a JFrame, with just a few customizations.

The JComponent Class

The JComponent class provides the framework for building all kinds of user interface components. Particular components, such as buttons, labels, and list boxes, are implemented as subclasses of JComponent.

We override methods in such a subclass to implement the behavior of our particular component. This may sound restrictive, as if we are limited to some predefined set of routines, but that is not the case at all. Keep in mind that the methods we are talking about are ways to interact with the windowing system. We don't have to squeeze our whole application in there. A realistic application might involve hundreds or thousands of classes, with legions of methods and variables and many threads of execution. The vast majority of these are related to the particulars of our job (these are called *domain objects*). The JComponent class and other predefined classes serve only as a framework on which to base code that handles certain types of user interface events and displays information to the user.

The paintComponent() method is an important method of the JComponent class; we override it to implement the way our particular component displays itself on the screen. The default behavior of paintComponent() doesn't do any drawing at all. If we hadn't overridden it in our subclass, our component would simply have been invisible. Here, we're overriding paintComponent() to do something only slightly more interesting. We don't override any of the other inherited members of JComponent because they provide basic functionality and reasonable defaults for this (trivial) example. As HelloJava grows, we'll delve deeper into the inherited members and use additional methods. We will also add some application-specific methods and variables just for the needs of HelloComponent.

JComponent is really the tip of another iceberg called Swing. Swing is Java's user interface toolkit, represented in our example by the import statement at the top; we'll discuss it in some detail in Chapters 15 through 18.

Relationships and Finger Pointing

We can correctly refer to HelloComponent as a JComponent because subclassing can be thought of as creating an "is a" relationship, in which the subclass is a kind of its superclass. HelloComponent is therefore a kind of JComponent. When we refer to a kind of object, we mean any instance of that object's class or any of its subclasses. Later, we will look more closely at the Java class hierarchy and see that JComponent is itself a subclass of the Container class, which is further derived from a class called Component, and so on, as shown in Figure 2-2.

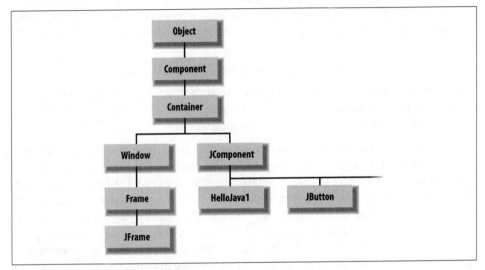

Figure 2-2. Part of the Java class hierarchy

In this sense, a HelloComponent object is a kind of JComponent, which is a kind of Container, and each of these can ultimately be considered to be a kind of Component. It's from these classes that HelloComponent inherits its basic GUI functionality and (as we'll discuss later) the ability to have other graphical components embedded within it as well.

Component is a subclass of the top-level Object class, so all these classes are types of Objects. Every other class in the Java API inherits behavior from Object, which defines a few basic methods, as you'll see in Chapter 7. We'll continue to use the word object (lowercase o) in a generic way to refer to an instance of any class; we'll use Object to refer specifically to that class.

Package and Imports

We mentioned earlier that the first line of our example tells Java where to find some of the classes that we've been using:

```
import javax.swing.*;
```

Specifically, it tells the compiler that we are going to be using classes from the Swing GUI toolkit (in this case, JFrame, JLabel, and JComponent). These classes are organized into a package called javax.swing. A Java *package* is a group of classes that are related by purpose or by application. Classes in the same package have special access privileges with respect to one another and may be designed to work together closely.

Packages are named in a hierarchical fashion with dot-separated components, such as java.util and java.util.zip. Classes in a package must follow conventions about where they are located in the classpath. They also take on the name of the package as part of their "full name" or, to use the proper terminology, their *fully qualified name*. For example, the fully qualified name of the JComponent class is javax.swing. JComponent. We could have referred to it by that name directly, in lieu of using the import statement:

```
public class HelloComponent extends javax.swing.JComponent {...}
```

The statement import javax.swing.* enables us to refer to all the classes in the javax. swing package by their simple names. So we don't have to use fully qualified names to refer to the JComponent, JLabel, and JFrame classes.

As we saw when we added our second example class, there may be one or more import statements in a given Java source file. The imports effectively create a "search path" that tells Java where to look for classes that we refer to by their simple, unqualified names. The imports we've seen use the dot star (.*) notation to indicate that the entire package should be imported. But you can also specify just a single class. For example, our current example uses only the Graphics class from the java.awt package. So we could have used import java.awt.Graphics instead of using the wildcard * to import all the AWT package's classes. However, we are anticipating using several more classes from this package later.

The java. and javax. package hierarchies are special. Any package that begins with java. is part of the core Java API and is available on any platform that supports Java. The javax. package normally denotes a standard extension to the core platform, which may or may not be installed. However in recent years many standard extensions have been added to the core Java API without renaming them. The javax.swing package is an example; it is part of the core API in spite of its name. Figure 2-3 illustrates some of the core Java packages, showing a representative class or two from each.

java.lang contains fundamental classes needed by the Java language itself; this package is imported automatically and that is why we didn't need an import statement to use class names such as String or System in our examples. The java.awt package contains classes of the older, graphical Abstract Window Toolkit; java.net contains the networking classes.

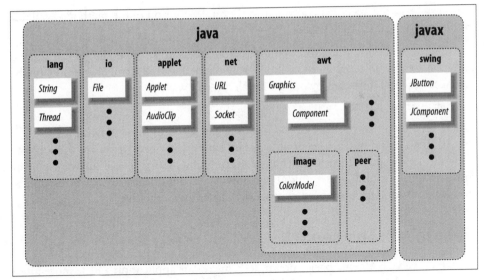

Figure 2-3. Some core Java packages

The paintComponent( ) Method

The source for our HelloComponent class defines a method, paintComponent(), that overrides the paintComponent() method of the JComponent class:

```
public void paintComponent( Graphics g ) {
    g.drawString( "Hello, Java!", 125, 95 );
}
```

The paintComponent() method is called when it's time for our example to draw itself on the screen. It takes a single argument, a Graphics object, and doesn't return any type of value (void) to its caller.

Modifiers are keywords placed before classes, variables, and methods to alter their accessibility, behavior, or semantics. paintComponent() is declared as public, which means it can be invoked (called) by methods in classes other than HelloComponent. In this case, it's the Java windowing environment that is calling our paintComponent() method. A method or variable declared as private is only inaccessible from inside its own class.

The Graphics object, an instance of the Graphics class, represents a particular graphical drawing area. (It is also called a *graphics context*.) It contains methods that can be used to draw in this area, and variables that represent characteristics such as clipping or drawing modes. The particular Graphics object we are passed in the paintComponent() method corresponds to our HelloComponent's area of the screen, inside our frame.

The Graphics class provides methods for rendering shapes, images, and text. In HelloComponent, we invoke the drawString() method of our Graphics object to scrawl our message at the specified coordinates. (For a description of the methods available in the Graphics class, see Chapter 19.)

As we've seen earlier, a method of an object is accessed by appending a dot (.) and its name to the object that holds it. We invoked the drawString() method of the Graphics object (referenced by our g variable) in this way:

```
g.drawString( "Hello, Java!", 125, 95 );
```

It may be difficult to get used to the idea that our application is drawn by a method that is called by an outside agent at arbitrary times. How can we do anything useful with this? How do we control what gets done and when? These answers will be forthcoming. For now, just think about how you would begin to structure applications that respond on command instead of by their own initiative.

HelloJava2: The Sequel

Now that we've got some basics down, let's make our application a little more interactive. The following minor upgrade, HelloJava2, allows us to drag the message text around with the mouse.

We'll call this example HelloJava2 rather than cause confusion by continuing to expand the old one. But the primary changes here and further on will be in adding capabilities to the HelloComponent class and simply making the corresponding changes to the names to keep them straight, e.g., HelloComponent2, HelloComponent3, etc. Having just seen inheritance at work, you might wonder why we aren't creating a subclass of HelloComponent and exploiting inheritance to build upon our previous example and extend its functionality. Well, in this case, that would not provide much advantage, and for clarity we will simply start over.

Here is HelloJava2:

```
//file: HelloJava2.java
import java.awt.*;
import java.awt.event.*;
import javax.swing.*;

public class HelloJava2
{
  public static void main( String[] args ) {
    JFrame frame = new JFrame( "HelloJava2" );
    frame.getContentPane( ).add( new HelloComponent2("Hello Java!") );
    frame.setDefaultCloseOperation( JFrame.EXIT_ON_CLOSE );
    frame.setSize( 300, 300 );
    frame.setVisible( true );
  }
}

class HelloComponent2 extends JComponent
    implements MouseMotionListener
```

```
{
  String theMessage;
  int messageX = 125, messageY = 95; // Coordinates of the message

  public HelloComponent2( String message ) {
    theMessage = message;
    addMouseMotionListener(this);
  }

  public void paintComponent( Graphics g ) {
    g.drawString( theMessage, messageX, messageY );
  }

  public void mouseDragged(MouseEvent e) {
    // Save the mouse coordinates and paint the message.
    messageX = e.getX( );
    messageY = e.getY( );
    repaint( );
  }

  public void mouseMoved(MouseEvent e) { }
}
```

Two slashes in a row indicates that the rest of the line is a comment. We've added a few comments to HelloJava2 to help you keep track of everything.

Place the text of this example in a file called *HelloJava2.java* and compile it as before. You should get new class files, *HelloJava2.class* and *HelloComponent2.class* as a result.

Run the example as before:

```
% java HelloJava2
```

Feel free to substitute your own salacious comment for the "Hello, Java!" message and enjoy many hours of fun, dragging the text around with your mouse. Notice that now when you click the window's close button, the application exits; we'll explain that later when we talk about events.

Instance Variables

We have added some variables to the HelloComponent2 class in our example:

```
int messageX = 125, messageY = 95;
String theMessage;
```

messageX and messageY are integers that hold the current coordinates of our movable message. We have crudely initialized them to default values that should place the message somewhere near the center of the window. Java integers are 32-bit signed numbers, so they can easily hold our coordinate values. The variable theMessage is of type String and can hold instances of the String class.

You should note that these three variables are declared inside the braces of the class definition, but not inside any particular method in that class. These variables are called *instance variables,* and they belong to the class as a whole. Specifically, copies of them appear in each separate instance of the class. Instance variables are always visible to (and usable by) all the methods inside their class. Depending on their modifiers, they may also be accessible from outside the class.

Unless otherwise initialized, instance variables are set to a default value of zero, false, or null, depending on their type. Numeric types are set to zero, boolean variables are set to false, and class type variables always have their value set to null, which means "no value." Attempting to use an object with a null value results in a runtime error.

Instance variables differ from method arguments and other variables that are declared inside the scope of a particular method. The latter are called *local variables.* They are effectively private variables that can be seen only by code inside the method. Java doesn't initialize local variables, so you must assign values yourself. If you try to use a local variable that has not yet been assigned a value, your code generates a compile-time error. Local variables live only as long as the method is executing and then disappear, unless something else saves their value. Each time the method is invoked, its local variables are recreated and must be assigned values.

We have used the new variables to make our previously stodgy paintComponent() method more dynamic. Now all the arguments in the call to drawString() are determined by these variables.

Constructors

The HelloJava2 class includes a special kind of a method called a *constructor.* A constructor is called to set up a new instance of a class. When a new object is created, Java allocates storage for it, sets instance variables to their default values, and calls the constructor method for the class to do whatever application-level setup is required.

A constructor always has the same name as its class. For example, the constructor for the HelloJava2 class is called HelloJava2(). Constructors don't have a return type, but you can think of them as creating an object of their class's type. Like other methods, constructors can take arguments. Their sole mission in life is to configure and initialize newly born class instances, possibly using information passed to them in these parameters.

An object is created with the new operator specifying the constructor for the class and any necessary arguments. The resulting object instance is returned as a value. In our example, a new HelloComponent2 instance is created in the main() method by this line:

```
frame.getContentPane( ).add( new HelloComponent2("Hello, Java!") );
```

This line actually does three things. We could write them as three separate lines which are a little easier to understand:

```
HelloJava2 newobj = new HelloComponent2("Hello, Java!");
Container content = frame.getContentPane();
content.add( newobj );
```

The first line is the important one, where a new `HelloComponent2` object is created. The `HelloComponent2` constructor takes a `String` as an argument and, as we have arranged it, uses it to set the message that is displayed in the window. With a little magic from the Java compiler, quoted text in Java source code is turned into a `String` object. (See Chapter 9 for a complete discussion of the `String` class.) The second and third lines simply take our new component and add it to the frame to make it visible, as we did in the previous examples.

While we're on the topic, if you'd like to make our message configurable, you can change the constructor line to the following:

```
HelloJava2 newobj = new HelloComponent2( args[0] );
```

Now you can pass the text on the command line when you run the application:

```
% java HelloJava2 "Hello Java!"
```

`args[0]` refers to the first command-line parameter. Its meaning will be clearer when we discuss arrays later in the book.

`HelloJava2`'s constructor then does two things: it sets the text of the `Message` instance variable and calls `addMouseMotionListener()`. This method is part of the event mechanism, which we discuss next. It tells the system, "Hey, I'm interested in anything that happens involving the mouse."

```
public HelloJava2(String message) {
    theMessage = message;
    addMouseMotionListener( this );
}
```

The special, read-only variable called `this` is used to explicitly refer to our object in the call to `addMouseMotionListener()`. A method can use `this` to refer to the instance of the object that holds it. The following two statements are therefore equivalent ways of assigning the value to the `Message` instance variable:

```
theMessage = message;
```

or:

```
this.theMessage = message;
```

We'll normally use the shorter, implicit form to refer to instance variables. But we'll need `this` when we have to explicitly pass a reference to our object to a method in another class. We often do this so that methods in other classes can invoke our public methods (a *callback*, explained later in this chapter) or use our public variables.

Events

The last two methods of `HelloJava2`, `mouseDragged()` and `mouseMoved()`, let us get information from the mouse. Each time the user performs an action, such as pressing a key on the keyboard, moving the mouse, or perhaps banging his or her head against a touch screen, Java generates an *event*. An event represents an action that has occurred; it contains information about the action, such as its time and location. Most events are associated with a particular GUI component in an application. A keystroke, for instance, can correspond to a character being typed into a particular text entry field. Pressing a mouse button can activate a particular button on the screen. Even just moving the mouse within a certain area of the screen can trigger effects such as highlighting or changing the cursor's shape.

To work with these events we've imported a new package, `java.awt.event`, which provides specific `Event` objects that we use to get information from the user. (Notice that importing `java.awt.*` doesn't automatically import the event package. Packages don't really contain other packages, even if the hierarchical naming scheme would imply that they do.)

There are many different event classes, including `MouseEvent`, `KeyEvent`, and `ActionEvent`. For the most part, the meaning of these events is fairly intuitive. A `MouseEvent` occurs when the user does something with the mouse, a `KeyEvent` occurs when the user presses a key, and so on. `ActionEvent` is a little special; we'll see it at work later in this chapter in our third version of `HelloJava`. For now, we'll focus on dealing with `MouseEvents`.

GUI components in Java generate events for specific kinds of user actions. For example, if you click the mouse inside a component, the component generates a mouse event. Objects can ask to receive the events from one or more components by registering a *listener* with the event source. For example, to declare that a listener wants to receive a component's mouse-motion events, you invoke that component's `addMouseMotionListener()` method, specifying the listener object as an argument. That's what our example is doing in its constructor. In this case, the component is calling its own `addMouseMotionListener()` method, with the argument `this`, meaning "I want to receive my own mouse-motion events."

That's how we register to receive events. But how do we actually get them? That's what the two "mouse" related methods in our class are for. The `mouseDragged()` method is called automatically on a listener to receive the events generated when the user drags the mouse—that is, moves the mouse with any button pressed. The `mouseMoved()` method is called whenever the user moves the mouse over the area without pressing a button. In this case, we've placed these methods in our `HelloComponent2` class and had it register itself as the listener. This is entirely appropriate for our new "text dragging" component. But more generally good design usually dictates that event listeners be implemented as *adapter classes* that provide better separation of GUI and "business logic." We'll discuss that in detail later in the book.

So, our `mouseMoved()` method is boring: it doesn't do anything. We ignore simple mouse motions and reserve our attention for dragging. `mouseDragged()` has a bit more meat to it. This method is called repeatedly by the windowing system to give us updates on the position of the mouse. Here it is:

```
public void mouseDragged( MouseEvent e ) {
  messageX = e.getX( );
  messageY = e.getY( );
  repaint( );
}
```

The first argument to `mouseDragged()` is a `MouseEvent` object, e, that contains all the information we need to know about this event. We ask the `MouseEvent` to tell us the x and y coordinates of the mouse's current position by calling its `getX()` and `getY()` methods. We save these in the `messageX` and `messageY` instance variables for use elsewhere.

The beauty of the event model is that you have to handle only the kinds of events you want. If you don't care about keyboard events, you just don't register a listener for them; the user can type all she wants, and you won't be bothered. If there are no listeners for a particular kind of event, Java won't even generate it. The result is that event handling is quite efficient.*

While we're discussing events we should mention another small addition we slipped into HelloJava2:

```
frame.setDefaultCloseOperation( JFrame.EXIT_ON_CLOSE );
```

This line tells the frame to exit the application when its close button is pressed. It's called the "default" close operation because this operation, like almost every other GUI interaction, is governed by events. We could register a window listener to get notification of when the user pushes the close button and take whatever action we like. But this convenience method handles the common cases.

Finally, we've danced around a couple of questions here: how does the system know that our class contains the necessary `mouseDragged()` and `mouseMoved()` methods (where do these names come from)? And why do we have to supply a `mouseMoved()` method that doesn't do anything? The answer to these questions has to do with interfaces. We'll discuss interfaces after clearing up some unfinished business with `repaint()`.

---

* Event handling in Java 1.0 was a very different story. Early on, Java did not have a notion of event listeners and all event handling happened by overriding methods in base GUI classes. This was both inefficient and led to poor design with a proliferation of highly specialized components.

The repaint( ) Method

Since we changed the coordinates for the message (when we dragged the mouse), we would like HelloJava2 to redraw itself. We do this by calling repaint(), which asks the system to redraw the screen at a later time. We can't call paintComponent() directly, even if we wanted to, because we don't have a graphics context to pass to it.

We can use the repaint() method of the JComponent class to request that our component be redrawn. repaint() causes the Java windowing system to schedule a call to our paintComponent() method at the next possible time; Java supplies the necessary Graphics object, as shown in Figure 2-4.

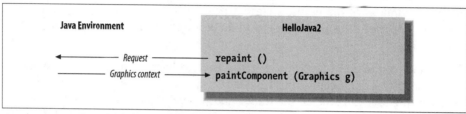

Figure 2-4. Invoking the repaint() method

This mode of operation isn't just an inconvenience brought about by not having the right graphics context handy. The foremost advantage to this mode of operation is that the repainting behavior is handled by someone else while we are free to go about our business. The Java system has a separate, dedicated thread of execution that handles all repaint() requests. It can schedule and consolidate repaint() requests as necessary, which helps to prevent the windowing system from being overwhelmed during such painting-intensive situations as scrolling. Another advantage is that all the painting functionality must be encapsulated in our paintComponent() method; we aren't tempted to spread it throughout the application.

Interfaces

Now it's time to face the question we avoided earlier: how does the system know to call mouseDragged() when a mouse event occurs? Is it simply a matter of knowing that mouseDragged() is some magic name that our event handling method must have? Not quite; the answer to the question touches on the discussion of interfaces, which are one of the most important features of the Java language.

The first sign of an interface comes on the line of code that introduces the HelloComponent2 class: we say that the class implements the MouseMotionListener interface.

```
class HelloComponent2 extends JComponent
    implements MouseMotionListener
{
```

Essentially, an interface is a list of methods that the class must have; this particular interface requires our class to have methods called mouseDragged() and mouseMoved(). The interface doesn't say what these methods have to do; indeed, mouseMoved() doesn't do anything. But it does say that the methods must take a MouseEvent as an argument and return void (i.e., no return value).

An interface is a contract between you, the code developer, and the compiler. By saying that your class implements the MouseMotionListener interface, you're saying that these methods will be available for other parts of the system to call. If you don't provide them, a compilation error will occur.

But that's not the only way interfaces impact this program. An interface also acts like a class. For example, a method could return a MouseMotionListener or take a MouseMotionListener as an argument. When you refer to an object by an interface name in this way it means that you don't care about the object's actual class; the only requirement is that the class implements that interface. addMouseMotionListener() is such a method: its argument must be an object that implements the MouseMotionListener interface. The argument we pass is this, the HelloComponent2 object itself. The fact that it's an instance of JComponent is irrelevant; it could be a Cookie, an Aardvark, or any other class we dream up. What's important is that it implements MouseMotionListener, and thus declares that it will have the two named methods. That's why we need a mouseMoved() method, even though the one we supplied doesn't do anything: the MouseMotionListener interface says we have to have one.

The Java distribution comes with many interfaces that define what classes have to do. This idea of a contract between the compiler and a class is very important. There are many situations like the one we just saw where you don't care what class something is, you just care that it has some capability, such as listening for mouse events. Interfaces give us a way of acting on objects based on their capabilities without knowing or caring about their actual type. They are a tremendously important concept in how we use Java as an object-oriented language, and we'll talk about them in detail in Chapter 4.

We'll also see shortly that interfaces provide a sort of escape clause to the Java rule that any new class can extend only a single class ("single inheritance"). A class in Java can extend only one class but can implement as many interfaces as it wants; our next example implements two interfaces, and the final example in this chapter implements three. In many ways, interfaces are almost like classes, but not quite. They can be used as data types, can extend other interfaces (but not classes) and can be inherited by classes (if class A implements interface B, subclasses of A also implement B). The crucial difference is that classes don't actually inherit methods from interfaces; the interfaces merely specify the methods the class must have.

HelloJava3: The Button Strikes!

Now we can move on to some fun stuff. HelloJava3 brings us a new graphical interface component: the JButton.* In this example we will add a JButton component to our application that changes the color of our text each time the button is pressed. The draggable-message capability is still there, too. Our new code looks like this:

```java
//file: HelloJava3.java
import java.awt.*;
import java.awt.event.*;
import javax.swing.*;

public class HelloJava3
{
  public static void main( String[] args ) {
    JFrame frame = new JFrame( "HelloJava3" );
    frame.getContentPane().add( new HelloComponent3("Hello Java!") );
    frame.setDefaultCloseOperation( JFrame.EXIT_ON_CLOSE );
    frame.setSize( 300, 300 );
    frame.setVisible( true );
  }
}

class HelloComponent3 extends JComponent
    implements MouseMotionListener, ActionListener
{
  String theMessage;
  int messageX = 125, messageY = 95;   // Coordinates of the message

  JButton theButton;

  int colorIndex;   // Current index into someColors
  static Color[] someColors = {
    Color.black, Color.red, Color.green, Color.blue, Color.magenta };

  public HelloComponent3( String message ) {
    theMessage = message;
    theButton = new JButton("Change Color");
    setLayout( new FlowLayout() );
    add( theButton );
    theButton.addActionListener( this );
    addMouseMotionListener( this );
  }

  public void paintComponent( Graphics g ) {
    g.drawString(theMessage, messageX, messageY);
```

---

* Why isn't it just called a Button? Button is the name that was used in Java's original GUI toolkit, the Abstract Window Toolkit (AWT). AWT had some significant shortcomings, so it was extended and essentially replaced by Swing in Java 2. Since AWT already took the reasonable names such as Button and MenuBar and mixing them in code could be confusing, Swing user interface components have names that are prefixed with "J", such as JButton and JMenuBar.

```
      }

      public void mouseDragged( MouseEvent e ) {
        messageX = e.getX( );
        messageY = e.getY( );
        repaint( );
      }

      public void mouseMoved( MouseEvent e ) {}

      public void actionPerformed( ActionEvent e ) {
        // Did somebody push our button?
        if (e.getSource( ) == theButton)
          changeColor( );
      }

      synchronized private void changeColor( ) {
        // Change the index to the next color, awkwardly.
        if (++colorIndex == someColors.length)
          colorIndex = 0;
        setForeground( currentColor( ) ); // Use the new color.
        repaint( );
      }

      synchronized private Color currentColor( ) {
        return someColors[colorIndex];
      }
    }
```

Compile HelloJava3 in the same way as the other applications. Run the example, and you should see the display shown in Figure 2-5. Drag the text. Each time you press the button the color should change. Call your friends! Test yourself for color-blindness!

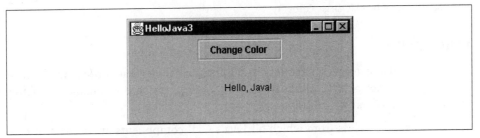

Figure 2-5. The HelloJava3 application

So what have we added this time? Well, for starters we have a new variable:

```
JButton theButton;
```

The theButton variable is of type JButton and is going to hold an instance of the javax.swing.JButton class. The JButton class, as you might expect, represents a graphical button, like other buttons in your windowing system.

Three additional lines in the constructor create the button and display it:

```
theButton = new JButton("Change Color");
setLayout( new FlowLayout( ) );
add( theButton );
```

In the first line, the new keyword creates an instance of the JButton class. The next line affects the way our component will be used as a container to hold the button. It tells HelloComponent3 how it should arrange components that are added to it for display—in this case to use a scheme called a FlowLayout (more on that coming up). Finally, it adds the button to our component, just like we added the HelloComponent3 to the content pane of the JFrame in the main() method.

Method Overloading

JButton has more than one constructor. A class can have multiple constructors, each taking different parameters and presumably using them to do different kinds of setup. When there are multiple constructors for a class, Java chooses the correct one based on the types of arguments used with them. We call the JButton constructor with a String argument, so Java locates the constructor method of the JButton class that takes a single String argument and uses it to set up the object. This is called *method overloading*. All methods in Java, not just constructors, can be overloaded; this is one aspect of the object-oriented programming principle of *polymorphism*.

Overloaded constructors generally provide a convenient way to initialize a new object. The JButton constructor we've used sets the text of the button as it is created:

```
theButton = new JButton("Change Color");
```

This is shorthand for creating the button and setting its label, like this:

```
theButton = new JButton( );
theButton.setText("Change Color");
```

Components

We have used the terms *component* and *container* somewhat loosely to describe graphical elements of Java applications. But these terms are the names of actual classes in the java.awt package.

Component is a base class from which all Java's GUI components are derived. It contains variables that represent the location, shape, general appearance, and status of the object, as well as methods for basic painting and event handling. javax.swing. JComponent extends the base Component class and refines it for the Swing toolkit. The paintComponent() method we have been using in our example is inherited from the JComponent class. HelloComponent is a kind of JComponent and inherits all its public members, just as other GUI components do.

The JButton class is also derived from JComponent and therefore shares this functionality. This means that the developer of the JButton class had methods such as paintComponent() available with which to implement the behavior of the JButton object, just as we did when creating our example. What's exciting is that we are perfectly free to further subclass components such as JButton and override their behavior to create our own special types of user-interface components. JButton and HelloJava3 are, in this respect, equivalent types of things.

Containers

The Container class is an extended type of Component that maintains a list of child components and helps to group them. The Container causes its children to be displayed and arranges them on the screen according to a particular layout strategy.

Because a Container is also a Component, it can be placed alongside other Component objects in other Containers, in a hierarchical fashion, as shown in Figure 2-6. Our HelloComponent3 class is a kind of Container (by virtue of the JComponent class) and can therefore hold and manage other Java components and containers such as buttons, sliders, text fields, and panels.

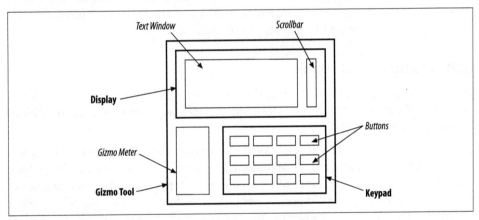

Figure 2-6. Layout of Java containers and components

In Figure 2-6, the italicized items are Components, and the bold items are Containers. The keypad is implemented as a container object that manages a number of keys. The keypad itself is contained in the GizmoTool container object.

Since JComponent descends from Container, it can be both a component and a container. In fact, we've already used it in this capacity in the HelloComponent3 example. It does its own drawing and handles events, just like a component. But it also contains a button, just like a container.

Layout

Having created a `JButton` object, we need to place it in the container (`HelloComponent3`), but where? An object called a `LayoutManager` determines the location within the `HelloJava3` container at which to display the `JButton`. A `LayoutManager` object embodies a particular scheme for arranging components on the screen and adjusting their sizes. You'll learn more about layout managers in Chapter 18. There are several standard layout managers to choose from, and we can, of course, create new ones. In our case, we specify one of the standard managers, a `FlowLayout`. The net result is that the button is centered at the top of the `HelloJava3` container.

To add the button to the layout, we invoke the `add()` method that `HelloJava3` inherits from `Container`, passing the `JButton` object as a parameter:

```
add( theButton );
```

`add()` is a method inherited by our class from the `Container` class. It appends our `JButton` to the list of components the `HelloJava3` container manages. Thereafter, `HelloJava3` is responsible for the `JButton`: it causes the button to be displayed and it determines where in its window the button should be placed. Unlike the more complex `JFrame`, a regular `JComponent` doesn't require the `getContentPane()` method; it has only a single container, and we use the simple `add()` method.

Subclassing and Subtypes

If you look up the `add()` method of the `Container` class, you'll see that it takes a `Component` object as an argument. But in our example we've given it a `JButton` object. What's going on?

As we've said, `JButton` is a subclass of the `Component` class. Because a subclass is a kind of its superclass and has, at minimum, the same public methods and variables, Java allows us to use an instance of a subclass anywhere we could use an instance of its superclass. This is a very important concept, and it's another aspect of the object-oriented principle of polymorphism. `JButton` is a kind of `Component`, so any method that expects a `Component` as an argument will accept a `JButton`.

More Events and Interfaces

Now that we have a `JButton`, we need some way to communicate with it, that is, to get the events it generates. We could just listen for mouse clicks within the button and act accordingly. But that would require customization, via subclassing of the `JButton`, and we would be giving up the advantages of using a pre-fab component. Instead, we have the `HelloComponent3` object listen for higher level events, corresponding to button presses. A `JButton` generates a special kind of event called an

ActionEvent when someone clicks on it with the mouse. To receive these events, we have added another method to the HelloComponent3 class:

```
public void actionPerformed( ActionEvent e ) {
  if ( e.getSource( ) == theButton )
    changeColor( );
}
```

If you followed the previous example, you shouldn't be surprised to see that HelloComponent3 now declares that it implements the ActionListener interface in addition to MouseMotionListener. ActionListener requires us to implement an actionPerformed() method that is called whenever an ActionEvent occurs. You also shouldn't be surprised to see that we added a line to the HelloJava3 constructor, registering itself (this) as a listener for the button's action events:

```
theButton.addActionListener( this );
```

Note that this time we're registering our component as a listener with a different object—the button—whereas previously we were asking for our own events.

The actionPerformed() method takes care of any action events that arise. First, it checks to make sure that the event's source (the component generating the event) is what we think it should be: theButton. This may seem superfluous; after all there is only one button, what else could possibly generate an action event? In this application, nothing. But it's a good idea to check because another application may have many buttons, and you may need to figure out which one has been clicked. Or you may add a second button to this application later, and you don't want it to break something. To check this, we call the getSource() method of the ActionEvent object, e. We then use the == operator to make sure the event source matches theButton.

 In Java, == is a test for identity, not equality; it is true if the event source and theButton are the same object. The distinction between equality and identity is important. We would consider two String objects to be equal if they have the same characters in the same sequence. However, they might not be the same object. In Chapter 7 we'll look at the equals( ) method, which tests for equality.

Once we establish that the event e comes from the right button, we call our changeColor() method, and we're finished.

You may be wondering why we don't have to change mouseDragged() now that we have a JButton in our application. The rationale is that the coordinates of the event are all that matter for this method. We are not particularly concerned if the event happens to fall within an area of the screen occupied by another component. This means you can drag the text right through the JButton: try it and see! In this case, the arrangement of containers means that the button is on top of our component, so the text is dragged beneath it.

Color Commentary

To support HelloJava3's colorful side, we have added a couple of new variables and two helpful methods. We create and initialize an array of Color objects representing the colors through which we cycle when the button is pressed. We also declare an integer variable that serves as an index into this array, specifying the position of the current color:

```
int colorIndex;
static Color[] someColors = { Color.black, Color.red,
    Color.green, Color.blue, Color.magenta };
```

A number of things are going on here. First let's look at the Color objects we are putting into the array. Instances of the java.awt.Color class represent colors; they are used by all classes in the java.awt package that deal with basic color graphics. Notice that we are referencing variables such as Color.black and Color.red. These look like examples of an object's instance variables, but Color is not an object, it's a class. What is the meaning of this? We'll discuss that next.

Static Members

A class can contain variables and methods that are shared among all instances of the class. These shared members are called *static variables* and *static methods*. The most common use of static variables in a class is to hold predefined constants or unchanging objects that all the instances can use.

There are two advantages to this approach. The more obvious advantage is that static members take up space only in the class; the members are not replicated in each instance. But more importantly, static members can be accessed even if no instances of the class exist. In this example, we use the static variable Color.red without having to create an instance of the Color class.

An instance of the Color class represents a visible color. For convenience, the Color class contains some static, predefined objects with friendly names such as green, red, and (the happy color) magenta. The variable green, for example, is a static member in the Color class. The data type of the variable green is Color. Internally, in Java-land it is initialized like this:

```
public final static Color green = new Color(0, 255, 0);
```

The green variable and the other static members of Color cannot be modified (after they've been initialized), so they are effectively constants and can be optimized as such by the Java VM. The alternative to using these predefined colors is to create a color manually by specifying its red, green, and blue (RGB) components using a Color class constructor.

Arrays

Next, we turn our attention to the array. We have declared a variable called someColors, which is an array of Color objects. In Java, arrays are *first-class* objects. This means that an array is, itself, a type of object—one that knows how to hold an indexed list of some other type of object. An array is indexed by integers; when you index an array, the resulting value is an object reference—that is, a reference to the object that is located in the array's specified slot. Our code uses the colorIndex variable to index someColors. It's also possible to have an array of simple primitive types, such as floats, rather than objects.

When we declare an array, we can initialize it using the familiar C-like curly brace construct. Specifying a comma-separated list of elements inside curly braces is a convenience that instructs the compiler to create an instance of the array with those elements and assign it to our variable. Alternatively, we could have just declared our someColors variable and, later, allocated an array object for it and assigned individual elements to that array's slots. See Chapter 5 for a complete discussion of arrays.

Our Color Methods

Now we have an array of Color objects and a variable with which to index the array. Two private methods do the actual work for us. The private modifier on these methods specifies that they can be called only by other methods in the same instance of the class. They cannot be accessed outside the object that contains them. We declare members to be private to hide the detailed inner workings of a class from the outside world. This is called *encapsulation* and is another tenet of object-oriented design, as well as good programming practice. Private methods are created as helper functions for use solely in the class implementation.

The first method, currentColor(), is simply a convenience routine that returns the Color object representing the current text color. It returns the Color object in the someColors array at the index specified by our colorIndex variable:

```
synchronized private Color currentColor( ) {
    return someColors[colorIndex];
}
```

We could just as readily have used the expression someColors[colorIndex] everywhere we use currentColor(); however, creating methods to wrap common tasks is another way of shielding ourselves from the details of our class. In an alternative implementation, we might have shuffled off details of all color-related code into a separate class. We could have created a class that takes an array of colors in its constructor and then provided two methods: one to ask for the current color and one to cycle to the next color (just some food for thought).

The second method, changeColor(), is responsible for incrementing the colorIndex variable to point to the next Color in the array. changeColor() is called from our actionPerformed() method whenever the button is pressed:

```
synchronized private void changeColor( ) {
    // Change the index to the next color, awkwardly.
    if ( ++colorIndex == someColors.length )
        colorIndex = 0;
    setForeground( currentColor( ) ); // Use the new color.
    repaint( );
}
```

Here we increment colorIndex and compare it to the length of the someColors array. All array objects have a variable called length that specifies the number of elements in the array. If we have reached the end of the array, we wrap around to the beginning by resetting the index to zero. We've flagged this with a comment to indicate that we're doing something fishy here. But we'll come back to that in a moment. After changing the currently selected color, we do two things. First, we call the component's setForeground() method, which changes the color used to draw text in our component. Then we call repaint() to cause the component to be redrawn with the new color for the draggable message.

What is the synchronized keyword that appears in front of our currentColor() and changeColor() methods? Synchronization has to do with threads, which we'll examine in the next section. For now, all you need know is that the synchronized keyword indicates these two methods can never be running at the same time. They must always run one after the other.

The reason for this is related to the fishy way we increment out index. Notice that in changeColor(), we increment colorIndex before testing its value. Strictly speaking, this means that for some brief period of time while Java is running through our code, colorIndex can have a value that is past the end of our array. If our currentColor() method happened to run at that same moment, we would see a runtime "array out of bounds" error. Now, it would be easy for us to fix the problem in this case with some simple arithmetic before changing the value, but this simple example is representative of more general synchronization issues we need to address. We'll use it to illustrate the use of the synchronized keyword. In the next section, you'll see that Java makes dealing with these problems relatively easy through language-level synchronization support.

HelloJava4: Netscape's Revenge

We have explored quite a few features of Java with the first three versions of the HelloJava application. But until now, our application has been rather passive; it has been completely *event-driven*, waiting patiently for events to come its way and responding to the whims of the user. Now our application is going to take some initiative—HelloJava4 will blink! Here is the code for our latest version:

```java
//file: HelloJava4.java
import java.awt.*;
import java.awt.event.*;
import javax.swing.*;

public class HelloJava4
{
  public static void main( String[] args ) {
    JFrame frame = new JFrame( "HelloJava4" );
    frame.getContentPane().add( new HelloComponent4("Hello Java!") );
    frame.setDefaultCloseOperation( JFrame.EXIT_ON_CLOSE );
    frame.setSize( 300, 300 );
    frame.setVisible( true );
  }
}

class HelloComponent4 extends JComponent
    implements MouseMotionListener, ActionListener, Runnable
{
  String theMessage;
  int messageX = 125, messageY = 95; // Coordinates of the message

  JButton theButton;

  int colorIndex; // Current index into someColors.
  static Color[] someColors = {
    Color.black, Color.red, Color.green, Color.blue, Color.magenta };

  boolean blinkState;

  public HelloComponent4( String message ) {
    theMessage = message;
    theButton = new JButton("Change Color");
    setLayout( new FlowLayout() );
    add( theButton );
    theButton.addActionListener( this );
    addMouseMotionListener( this );
    Thread t = new Thread( this );
    t.start();
  }

  public void paintComponent( Graphics g ) {
    g.setColor(blinkState ? getBackground() : currentColor( ));
    g.drawString(theMessage, messageX, messageY);
  }

  public void mouseDragged(MouseEvent e) {
    messageX = e.getX();
    messageY = e.getY();
    repaint();
  }
```

```
public void mouseMoved(MouseEvent e) { }

public void actionPerformed( ActionEvent e ) {
  if ( e.getSource() == theButton )
    changeColor();
}

synchronized private void changeColor() {
  if (++colorIndex == someColors.length)
    colorIndex = 0;
  setForeground( currentColor() );
  repaint();
}

synchronized private Color currentColor(  ) {
  return someColors[colorIndex];
}

public void run( ) {
  try {
    while(true) {
      blinkState = !blinkState; // Toggle blinkState.
      repaint(); // Show the change.
      Thread.sleep(300);
    }
  } catch (InterruptedException ie) { }
}
}
```

Compile and run this version of HelloJava just like the others. You'll see that the text does in fact blink. Our apologies if you find this annoying—we're not overly fond of it either.

Threads

All the changes we've made in HelloJava4 have to do with setting up a separate thread of execution to make the text blink. Java is a *multithreaded* language, which means there can be many paths of execution, effectively running at the same time. A *thread* is a separate flow of control within a program. Conceptually, threads are similar to processes, except that unlike processes, multiple threads share the same program space, which means that they can share variables and methods (but also have their own local variables). Threads are also quite lightweight in comparison to processes, so it's conceivable for a single application to be running many (perhaps hundreds or thousands) of threads concurrently.

Multithreading provides a way for an application to handle many different tasks at the same time. It's easy to imagine multiple things going on at the same time in an application like a web browser. The user could be listening to an audio clip while scrolling an image; at the same time, the browser can be downloading an image.

Multithreading is especially useful in GUI-based applications because it improves the interactive performance of these applications.

Unfortunately for us, programming with multiple threads can be quite a headache. The difficulty lies in making sure routines are implemented so they can be run concurrently, by more than one thread at a time. If a routine changes the value of multiple state variables, for example, then it may be important that those changes happen together, without overlapping changes affecting each other. Later in this section, we'll examine briefly the issue of coordinating multiple threads' access to shared data. In other languages, synchronization of threads can be extremely complex and error-prone. You'll see that Java gives you a few simple tools that help you deal with many of these problems. Java threads can be started, interrupted, and assigned priorities. Threads are preemptive, so a higher priority thread can interrupt a lower priority thread when vying for processor time. See Chapter 8 for a complete discussion of threads.

The Java runtime system creates and manages a number of threads. (Exactly how varies with the implementation.) We've already mentioned the repaint thread, which manages repaint() requests and event processing for GUI components that belong to the java.awt and javax.swing packages. Our example applications have done most of their work in one thread. Methods such as mouseDragged() and actionPerformed() are invoked by the windowing thread and run by its thread, on its time. Similarly, our HelloComponent constructor runs as part of the main application thread (the main() method). This means we are somewhat limited in the amount of processing we do within these methods. If we were, for instance, to go into an endless loop in our constructor, our application would never appear, as it would never finish initializing. If we want an application to perform any extensive processing, such as animation, a lengthy calculation, or communication, we should create separate threads for these tasks.

The Thread Class

As you might have guessed, threads are created and controlled as Thread objects. An instance of the java.lang.Thread class corresponds to a single thread. It contains methods to start, control, and interrupt the thread's execution. Our plan here is to create a Thread object to handle our blinking code. We call the Thread's start() method to begin execution. Once the thread starts, it continues to run until it completes its work, we interrupt it, or we stop the application.

So how do we tell the thread which method to run? Well, the Thread object is rather picky; it always expects to execute a method called run() to perform the action of the thread. The run() method can, however, with a little persuasion, be located in any class we desire.

We specify the location of the run() method in one of two ways. First, the Thread class itself has a method called run(). One way to execute some Java code in a separate thread is to subclass Thread and override its run() method to do our bidding. Invoking the start() method of the subclass object causes its run() method to execute in a separate thread.

It's not usually desirable to create a subclass of Thread to contain our run() method. The Thread class has a constructor that takes an object as its argument. If we create a Thread object using this constructor and call its start() method, the Thread executes the run() method of the argument object, rather than its own. In order to accomplish this, Java needs a guarantee that the object we are passing it does indeed contain a compatible run() method. We already know how to make such a guarantee: we use an interface. Java provides an interface named Runnable that must be implemented by any class that wants to become a Thread.

The Runnable Interface

We've used the second technique in the HelloJava4 example. To create a thread, the HelloComponent4 object passes itself (this) to the Thread constructor. This means that HelloComponent4 must implement the Runnable interface, by implementing the run() method. This method is called automatically when the runtime system needs to start the thread.

We indicate that the class implements the interface in our class declaration:

```
public class HelloComponent4
    extends JComponent
    implements MouseMotionListener, ActionListener, Runnable {...}
```

At compile time, the Java compiler checks to make sure we abide by this statement. We have carried through by adding an appropriate run() method to HelloComponent4. It takes no arguments and returns no value. Our run() method accomplishes blinking by changing the color of our text a few times a second. It's a very short routine, but we're going to delay looking at it until we tie up some loose ends in dealing with the Thread itself.

Starting the Thread

We want the blinking to begin when the application starts. So we'll start the thread in the initialization code in HelloComponent4's constructor. It takes only two lines:

```
Thread t = new Thread(this);
t.start( );
```

First, the constructor creates a new instance of Thread, passing it the object that contains the run() method to the constructor. Since HelloComponent4 itself contains our run() method, we pass the special variable this to the constructor. this always refers to our object. After creating the new Thread, we call its start() method to begin execution. This, in turn, invokes HelloComponent4's run() method in the new thread.

Running Code in the Thread

Our run() method does its job by setting the value of the variable blinkState. We have added blinkState, a boolean variable which can have the value true or false, to represent whether we are currently blinking on or off:

```
boolean blinkState;
```

A setColor() call has been added to our paintComponent() method to handle blinking. When blinkState is true, the call to setColor() draws the text in the background color, making it disappear:

```
g.setColor(blinkState ? getBackground( ) : currentColor( ));
```

Here we are being very terse, using the C-language-style ternary operator to return one of two alternative color values based on the value of blinkState. If blinkState is true, the value is the value returned by the getBackground() method. If it is false, the value is the value returned by currentColor().

Finally, we come to the run() method itself:

```
public void run( ) {
  try {
    while( true ) {
      blinkState = !blinkState;
      repaint( );
      Thread.sleep(300);
    }
  }
  catch (InterruptedException ie) {}
}
```

Basically, run() is an infinite while loop, which means the loop will run continuously until the thread is terminated by the application exiting.

The body of the loop does three things on each pass:

- Flips the value of blinkState to its opposite value using the not operator (!)
- Calls repaint() to redraw the text
- Sleeps for 300 milliseconds (about a third of a second)

sleep() is a static method of the Thread class. The method can be invoked from anywhere and has the effect of putting the currently running thread to sleep for the specified number of milliseconds. The effect here is to give us approximately three blinks per second. The try/catch construct, described in the next section, traps any errors in the call to the sleep() method of the Thread class.

Exceptions

The try/catch statement in Java handles special conditions called *exceptions*. An exception is a message that is sent, normally in response to an error, during the execution of a statement or a method. When an exceptional condition arises, an object is created that contains information about the particular problem or condition. Exceptions act somewhat like events. Java stops execution at the place where the exception occurred, and the exception object is said to be *thrown* by that section of code. Like an event, an exception must be delivered somewhere and handled. The section of code that receives the exception object is said to *catch* the exception. An exception causes the execution of the instigating section of code to stop abruptly and transfers control to the code that receives the exception object.

The try/catch construct allows you to catch exceptions for a section of code. If an exception is caused by any statement inside a try clause, Java attempts to deliver the exception to the appropriate catch clause. A catch clause looks like a method declaration with one argument and no return type.

```
try {
  ...
} catch ( SomeExceptionType e ) {
  ...
}
```

If Java finds a catch clause with an argument type that matches the type of the exception, that catch clause is invoked. A try clause can have multiple catch clauses with different argument types; Java chooses the appropriate one in a way that is analogous to the selection of overloaded methods. You can catch multiple types of exceptions from a block of code. Depending on the type of exception thrown, the appropriate catch clause is executed.

If there is no try/catch clause surrounding the code, or a matching catch clause is not found, the exception is thrown up to the calling method. If the exception is not caught there, it's thrown up another level, and so on until the exception is handled, or the Java VM prints an error and exits. This provides a very flexible error-handling mechanism so that exceptions in deeply nested calls can bubble up to the surface of the call stack for handling. As a programmer, you need to know what exceptions a particular statement can generate. For this reason, methods in Java are required to declare the exceptions they can throw. If a method doesn't handle an exception itself, it must specify that it can throw that exception so that its calling method knows that it may have to handle it. See Chapter 4 for a complete discussion of exceptions and the try/catch clause.

So, why do we need a try/catch clause in the run() method? What kind of exception can Thread's sleep() method throw and why do we care about it when we don't seem to check for exceptions anywhere else? Under some circumstances, Thread's sleep() method can throw an InterruptedException, indicating that it was

---

interrupted by another thread. Since the `run()` method specified in the `Runnable` interface doesn't declare it can throw an `InterruptedException`, we must catch it ourselves, or the compiler will complain. The `try/catch` statement in our example has an empty `catch` clause, which means that it handles the exception by ignoring it. In this case, our thread's functionality is so simple it doesn't matter if it's interrupted (and it won't be anyway). All the other methods we have used either handle their own exceptions or throw only general-purpose exceptions called `RuntimeExceptions` that are assumed to be possible everywhere and don't need to be explicitly declared.

Synchronization

At any given time we can have lots of threads running in an application. Unless we explicitly coordinate them, these threads will be executing methods without any regard for what the other threads are doing. Problems can arise when these methods share the same data. If one method is changing the value of some variables at the same time another method is reading these variables, it's possible that the reading thread might catch things in the middle and get some variables with old values and some with new. Depending on the application, this situation could cause a critical error.

In our HelloJava examples, both our `paintComponent()` and `mouseDragged()` methods access the `messageX` and `messageY` variables. Without knowing more about the implementation of the Java environment, we have to assume that these methods could conceivably be called by different threads and run concurrently. `paintComponent()` could be called while `mouseDragged()` is in the midst of updating `messageX` and `messageY`. At that point, the data is in an inconsistent state and if `paintComponent()` gets lucky, it could get the new x value with the old y value. Fortunately, Swing does not allow this to happen in this case because all event activity is handled by a single thread, and we probably would not even notice if it were to happen in this application anyway. We did, however, see another case, in our `changeColor()` and `currentColor()` methods, where there is the potential for a more serious "out of bounds" error.

The synchronized modifier tells Java to acquire a *lock* for the object that contains the method before executing that method. Only one method in the object can have the lock at any given time, which means that only one synchronized method in that object can be running at a time. This allows a method to alter data and leave it in a consistent state before a concurrently running method is allowed to access it. When the method is done, it releases the lock on the class.

Unlike synchronization in other languages, the `synchronized` keyword in Java provides locking at the language level. This means there is no way that you can forget to unlock a class. Even if the method throws an exception or the thread is terminated, Java will release the lock. This feature makes programming with threads in Java much easier than in other languages. See Chapter 8 for more details on coordinating threads and shared data.

Whew! Well, it's time to say goodbye to HelloJava. We hope that you have developed a feel for the major features of the Java language and that this will help you as you explore the details of programming with Java. If you are a bit bewildered by some of the material presented here, take heart. We'll be covering all the major topics presented here again in their own chapters throughout the book. This tutorial was meant to be something of a "trial by fire" to get the important concepts and terminology into your brain so that the next time you hear them you'll have a head start.

Tools of the Trade

There are many options for Java development environments, from the traditional text-editor-and-command-line tools to full blown IDEs such as Sun's Forte for Java, WebGain's Visual Café, and Inprise's JBuilder. The examples in this book were developed using the Solaris and Windows versions of the standard Java Software Development Kit (SDK), so we will describe those tools here. When we refer to the compiler or interpreter, we'll be referring to the command-line versions of these tools, so the book is a bit biased toward those of you who are working in a Unix or DOS-like environment with a shell and filesystem. However, the basic features we'll be describing for Sun's Java interpreter and compiler should be applicable to other Java environments as well.

In this chapter, we'll describe the tools you'll need to compile and run Java applications. The last part of the chapter discusses how to pack Java class files into Java archives (JAR files). Chapter 22 also describes the ability to "sign" classes within a JAR file and to give greater privileges to classes with a signature that you trust.

The Java Interpreter

A Java interpreter is software that implements the Java virtual machine and runs Java applications. It can be a standalone application like the *java* program that comes with the SDK or part of a larger application like a browser. It's likely the interpreter itself is written in a native, compiled language for a particular platform. Other tools, such as Java compilers and IDEs, are often being implemented directly in Java to maximize their portability. Sun's Forte for Java (called NetBeans in the open source version included on this book's CD-ROM) is one example of a pure-Java IDE.

The Java interpreter performs all the activities of the Java runtime system. It loads Java class files and interprets the compiled String. It verifies compiled classes loaded from untrusted sources. In an implementation that supports dynamic, or just-in-time, compilation, the interpreter also serves as a specialized compiler that turns Java String into native machine instructions.

Throughout most of this book, we'll be building standalone Java programs, but we'll make frequent references to Java applets as well. Both are kinds of Java applications run by a Java interpreter. The difference is that a standalone Java application has all its parts; it's a complete program that runs independently. An applet is more like an embeddable program module. The Java interpreter can't run an applet directly because it is used as part of a larger application. To run an applet, you can use a web browser or the appletviewer tool that comes with the SDK. HotJava, a web browser written in Java, and the appletviewer are standalone Java applications run directly by the Java interpreter; these programs implement the additional structure needed to run Java applets.

For a standalone Java application, there must be at least one class that contains a method called main(), which contains the statements to be executed upon startup. To run the application, start the interpreter, specifying that class as an argument.You can also specify options to the interpreter as well as arguments to be passed to the application. Sun's Java interpreter is called java:

```
% java [interpreter options] class_name [program arguments]
```

The class should be specified as a fully qualified class name, including the package name, if any. Note, however, that you don't include the *.class* file extension. Here are a few examples:

```
% java animals.birds.BigBird
% java MyTest
```

The interpreter searches for the class in the *classpath*, a list of directories where packages of classes are stored. We'll discuss the classpath in detail in the next section. The classpath is typically specified by an environment variable, which you can override with the command-line option -classpath.

After loading the class specified on the command line, the interpreter executes the class's main() method. From there, the application can start additional threads, reference other classes, and create its user interface or other structures, as shown in Figure 3-1.

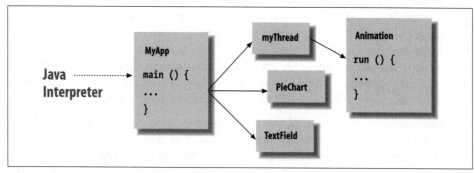

Figure 3-1. Starting a Java application

The main() method must have the right *method signature*. A method signature is the set of information that defines the method. It includes the method's name, arguments and return type, as well as type and visibility modifiers. The main() method must be a public, static method that takes an array of String objects as its argument and does not return any value (void):

```
public static void main ( String [] myArgs )
```

Because main() is a public and static method, it can be accessed directly from another class using the name of the class that contains it. We'll discuss the implications of visibility modifiers such as public and the meaning of static in Chapters 4 through 6.

The main() method's single argument, the array of String objects, holds the command-line arguments passed to the application. The name that we give the parameter doesn't matter; only the type is important. In Java, the content of myArgs is a true array. There's no need for an argument count parameter because myArgs knows how many arguments it contains and can happily provide that information:

```
int argc = myArgs.length;
```

myArgs[0] is the first command-line argument, and so on. Note that this differs from C/C++, where argument zero is the name of the application. If you're accustomed to parsing C command-line arguments, you'll need to be careful not to trip over this difference.

The Java interpreter continues to run until the main()method of the initial class file returns and until any threads that it starts are complete. Special threads designated as "daemon" threads are silently killed when the rest of the application has completed.

System Properties

Java does not directly provide access to "environment variables" from the host operating system. But it does allow any number of *system property* values to be passed to the application when the interpreter is started. System properties are simply name-value string pairs that are available to the application through the static System.getProperty() method. You can use these properties as an alternative to command-line arguments to pass configuration information to your application at runtime. Each value is passed to the interpreter using the -D option followed by *name=value*. For example:

```
% java -Dstreet=sesame -Dscene=alley animals.birds.BigBird
```

The value of the street property is then accessible this way:

```
String street = System.getProperty("street");
```

The Classpath

The concept of a *path* should be familiar to anyone who has worked on a DOS or Unix platform. It's an environment variable that provides an application with a list of places to look for some resource. The most common example is a path for executable programs. In a Unix shell, the PATH environment variable is a colon-separated list of directories that are searched, in order, when the user types the name of a command. The Java CLASSPATH environment variable, similarly, is a list of locations that can be searched for packages containing Java class files. Both the Java interpreter and the Java compiler use CLASSPATH when searching for packages and classes on the local host.

An element of the classpath can be a directory name or the name of an *archive file*. Java supports archives of class files in its own Java archive (JAR) format, and in the conventional ZIP format. JAR and ZIP are really the same format, but JAR archives include extra files that describe each archive's contents. JAR files are created with the Java development kit's *jar* utility; many tools for creating ZIP archives are publicly available. The archive format enables large groups of classes and their resources to be distributed in a single file; the Java interpreter automatically extracts individual class files from an archive, as needed.

The precise means and format for setting the classpath vary from system to system. On a Unix system, you set the CLASSPATH environment variable with a colon-separated list of directories and class archive files:

```
CLASSPATH=/home/vicky/Java/classes:/home/josh/oldstuff/foo.jar:.
export CLASSPATH
```

This example specifies a classpath with three locations: a directory in the user's home, a JAR file in another user's directory, and the current directory, which is always specified with a dot (.). The last component of the classpath, the current directory, is useful when tinkering with classes, but as a general rule, it's bad practice to put the current directory in any kind of path.

On a Windows system, the CLASSPATH environment variable is set with a semicolon-separated list of directories and class archive files:

```
set CLASSPATH=D:\users\vicky\Java\classes;.
```

The Java interpreter and the other command-line tools also know how to find the core classes, which are the classes included in every Java installation. The classes in the java.lang, java.io, java.net, and javax.swing packages, for example, are all core classes. You don't need to include these classes in your classpath; the Java interpreter and the other tools can find them by themselves.

To find other classes, the Java interpreter searches the locations on the classpath in order. The search combines the path location and the fully qualified class name. For example, consider a search for the class animals.birds.BigBird. Searching the classpath directory */usr/lib/java* means the interpreter looks for an individual class file at */usr/lib/java/animals/birds/BigBird.class*. Searching a ZIP or JAR archive on the classpath, say */home/vicky/Java/utils/classutils.jar*, means that the interpreter looks for component file *animals/birds/BigBird.class* in that archive.

For the Java interpreter, *java*, and the Java compiler, *javac*, the classpath can also be specified with the -classpath option:

```
% javac -classpath /pkg/sdk/lib/classes.zip:/home/pat/java:. Foo.java
```

If you don't specify the CLASSPATH environment variable, it defaults to the current directory (.); this means that the files in your current directory are normally available. If you change the classpath and don't include the current directory, these files will no longer be accessible.

javap

A useful tool to know about is the *javap* command. With *javap*, you can print a description of a compiled class. You don't have to have the source code, and you don't even have to know exactly where it is, only that it is in your classpath. For example:

```
% javap java.util.Stack
```

prints the information about the java.util.Stack class:

```
Compiled from Stack.java
public class java.util.Stack extends java.util.Vector {
    public java.util.Stack();
    public java.lang.Object push(java.lang.Object);
    public synchronized java.lang.Object pop();
    public synchronized java.lang.Object peek();
    public boolean empty();
    public synchronized int search(java.lang.Object);
}
```

This is very useful if you don't have other documentation handy and can also be helpful in debugging classpath issues. If you are feeling really adventurous you can try *javap* with the -c option, which causes it to also print the JVM instructions for each method in the class!

Policy Files

One of the truly novel things about Java is that security is built into the language. As described in Chapter 1, the Java VM can verify class files and Java's security manager can impose limits on what classes do. In early versions of Java, it was necessary to implement security policies *programmatically* by writing a Java security manager class and using it in your application. A major shift occurred in Java 1.2, when a new *declarative* security system was added. This system allows you to write *policy files—*

text-based descriptions of permissions—which are much simpler and don't require code changes. These policy files tell the security manager what to allow and disallow and for whom.

With security policies you can answer questions such as: "If I download a program from somewhere on the Internet, how can I prevent it from stealing information on my computer and sending it back to someone else?" "How can I prevent a malicious program from disabling my computer or erasing data on my disk?" Most computing platforms have no answer for these questions.

In early versions of Java, much of the buzz had to do with the security of applets. Applets generally run with security restrictions that prevent them from doing questionable things such as reading from or writing to the disk or contacting arbitrary computers on the network. With security policy files, it's just as easy to apply applet-style security to any application without modifying it. Furthermore, it's easy to fine-tune the access you grant. For example, you can allow an application to access the disk, but only in a specific directory, or you can allow network access to certain addresses.

Understanding security and security policies is important, so we'll cover it here. However, in practice, you probably won't use this facility yourself, unless you are writing a framework for running applications from many unknown sources. The Java Web Start facility is an example of such a framework. It installs and updates Java applications over the Web with user-definable security restrictions.

The Default Security Manager

By default, no security manager is installed when you launch a Java application locally. You can turn on security using an option of the *java* interpreter to install a default security manager. The default security policy enforces many of the same rules as for applets. To see how this works, let's write a little program that does something questionable, making a network connection to some computer on the Internet. (We cover the specifics of network programming in Chapters 12 and 13.)

```
//file: EvilEmpire.java
import java.net.*;

public class EvilEmpire {
  public static void main(String[] args) throws Exception{
    try {
      Socket s = new Socket("207.46.131.13", 80);
      System.out.println("Connected!");
    }
    catch (SecurityException e) {
      System.out.println("SecurityException: could not connect.");
    }
  }
}
```

If you run this program with the Java interpreter, it makes the network connection:

```
C:\> java EvilEmpire
Connected!
```

But since this program is "evil," let's install the default security manager, like this:

```
C:\> java -Djava.security.manager EvilEmpire
SecurityException: could not connect.
```

That's better, but suppose that the application actually has a legitimate reason to make its network connection. We'd like to leave the default security manager in place, just to be safe, but we'd like to grant this application permission to make a network connection.

The policytool Utility

To permit our EvilEmpire example to make a network connection, we need to create a *policy file* that contains the appropriate permission. A handy utility called *policytool*, included with the SDK, helps make policy files. Fire it up from a command line like this:

```
C:\> policytool
```

You may get an error message when *policytool* starts up about not finding a default policy file. Don't worry about this; just click *OK* to make the message go away.

We now add a network permission for the EvilEmpire application. The application is identified by its origin, also called a *codebase*, described by a URL. In this case, it is a file: URL that points to the location of the EvilEmpire application on your disk.

If you started up *policytool*, you should be looking at its main window, shown in Figure 3-2. Click on *Add Policy Entry*. Another window pops up, like the one shown in Figure 3-3 (but with the fields empty).

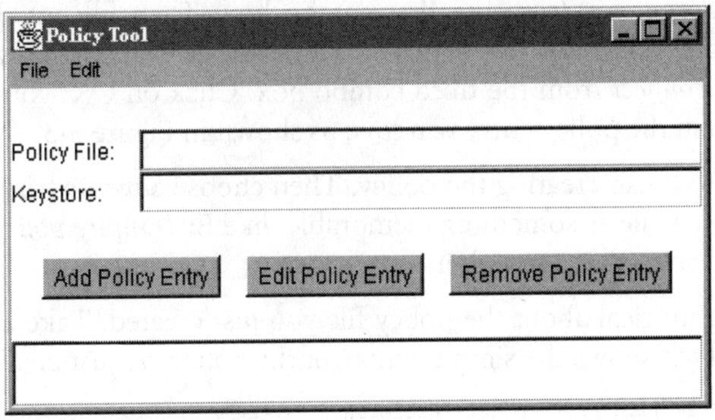

Figure 3-2. The policytool window

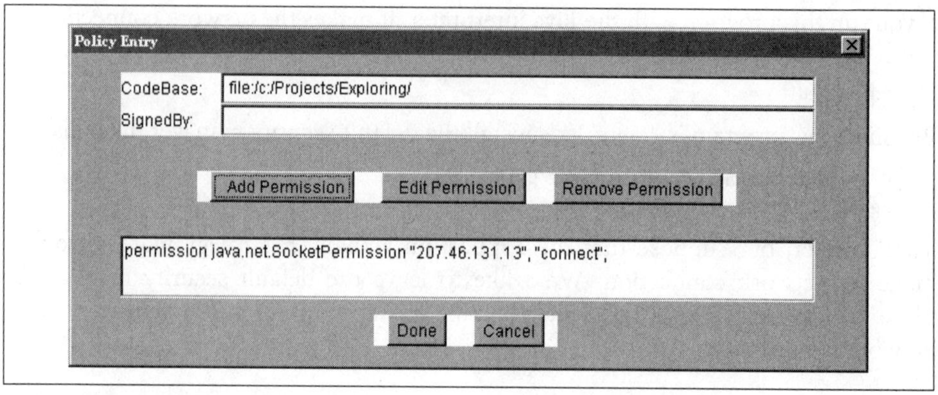

Figure 3-3. Adding a policy entry

First, fill in the codebase with the URL of the directory containing `EvilEmpire` as shown in the figure. Then click on *Add Permission*. Yet another window pops up, shown in Figure 3-4.

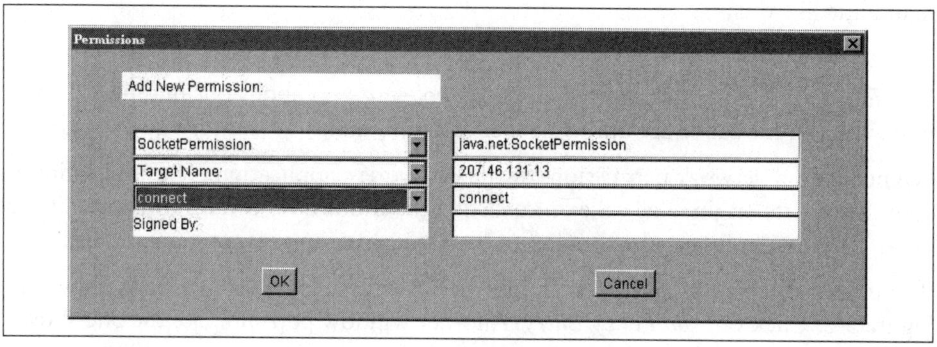

Figure 3-4. Creating a new permission

Choose *SocketPermission* from the first combo box. Then fill out the second text field on the right side with the network address that `EvilEmpire` will connect to. Finally, choose *connect* from the third combo box. Click on *OK*; you should see the new permission in the policy entry window, as shown in Figure 3-3.

Click on *Done* to finish creating the policy. Then choose *Save As* from the *File* menu and save the policy file as something memorable, like *EvilEmpire.policy*. You can quit *policytool* now; we're all done with it.

There's nothing magical about the policy file you just created. Take a look at it with a text editor, which shows the simple syntax of the policy we just created:

```
grant codeBase "file:/c:/Projects/Exploring/" {
  permission java.net.SocketPermission "207.46.131.13", "connect";
};
```

You can eschew *policytool* entirely and just create policy files with a text editor, if you're more comfortable that way.

Using a Policy File with the Default Security Manager

Now that we've gone to the trouble of creating a policy file, let's use it. You can tell the default security manager to use the policy file with another command-line option to the java interpreter:

```
C:\> java -Djava.security.manager -Djava.security.policy=EvilEmpire.policy EvilEmpire
Connected!
```

EvilEmpire can now make its socket connection because we have explicitly granted it permission with a policy file. The default security manager still protects us in other ways, however. EvilEmpire cannot write or read files on the disk except in the directory it came from, and it cannot make connections to any other network addresses except the one we specified. Take a moment and bask in this warm fuzzy feeling.

Later, in Chapter 22, you'll see *policytool* again when we explain signed applets. In this chapter, codebases are identified by URLs, which isn't the most secure option. Through tricky network shenanigans, a clever forger may be able to give you code that appears to be from somewhere it's not. Cryptographically signed code is even more trustworthy; see Chapter 22 for details.

The Java Compiler

In this section, we'll say a few words about *javac*, the Java compiler in the SDK. (If you are happily working in another development environment, you may want to skip ahead to the next section.) The *javac* compiler is written entirely in Java, so it's available for any platform that supports the Java runtime system.

javac turns Java source code into a compiled class that contains Java virtual machine String. By convention, source files are named with a *.java* extension; the resulting class files have a *.class* extension. Each source code file is a single compilation unit. As you'll see in Chapter 6, classes in a given compilation unit share certain features, such as package and import statements.

javac allows one public class per file and insists the file have the same name as the class. If the filename and class name don't match, *javac* issues a compilation error. A single file can contain multiple classes, as long as only one of the classes is public. Avoid packing many classes into a single source file. Including nonpublic classes in a *.java* file is one easy way to tightly couple such classes to a public class. But you might also consider using inner classes (see Chapter 6).

Now for an example. Place the following source code in file *BigBird.java*:

```
package animals.birds;

public class BigBird extends Bird {
    ...
}
```

Now compile it with:

```
% javac BigBird.java
```

Unlike the Java interpreter, which takes just a class name as its argument, *javac* needs a filename to process. The previous command produces the class file *BigBird. class* in the same directory as the source file. While it's useful to have the class file in the same directory as the source for testing a simple example, for most real applications, you need to store the class file in an appropriate place in the classpath.

You can use the -d option to javac to specify an alternative directory for storing the class files it generates. The specified directory is used as the root of the class hierarchy, so *.class* files are placed in this directory or in a subdirectory below it, depending on whether the class is contained in a package. (The compiler creates intermediate subdirectories automatically, if necessary.) For example, we can use the following command to create the *BigBird.class* file at */home/vicky/Java/classes/animals/birds/BigBird.class*:

```
% javac -d /home/vicky/Java/classes BigBird.java
```

You can specify multiple *.java* files in a single *javac* command; the compiler creates a class file for each source file. But you don't need to list source files for other classes your class references, as long as the other classes have already been compiled. During compilation, Java resolves other class references using the classpath. If our class refers to other classes in animals.birds or other packages, the appropriate paths should be listed in the classpath at compile time, so that javac can find the appropriate class files.

The Java compiler is more intelligent than your average compiler, replacing some of the functionality of a *make* utility. For example, *javac* compares the modification times of the source and class files for all referenced classes and recompiles them as necessary. A compiled Java class remembers the source file from which it was compiled, so as long as the source file is in the same directory as the class file, javac can recompile the source if necessary. If, in the previous example, class BigBird references another class, animals.furry.Grover, *javac* looks for the source file *Grover.java* in an animals.furry package and recompiles it if necessary to bring the *Grover.class* class file up to date.

By default, however, javac checks only source files that are referenced directly from other source files. This means that if you have an out-of-date class file that is referenced only by an up-to-date class file, it may not be noticed and recompiled. You can force *javac* to walk the entire graph of objects using the -depend option, but this can increase compilation time significantly. And this technique still won't help if you want to keep class libraries or other collections of classes up to date even if they aren't being referenced at all. For that you should consider a *make* utility.

Finally, it's important to note that *javac* can compile an application even if only the compiled versions of referenced classes are available. You don't need source code for all your objects. Java class files contain all the data type and method signature information that source files contain, so compiling against binary class files is as type-safe (and exception-safe) as compiling with Java source code.

Java Archive (JAR) Files

Java archive files (JAR files) are Java's suitcases. They are the standard and portable way to pack up all the parts of your Java application into a compact bundle for distribution or installation. You can put whatever you want into a JAR file: Java class files, serialized objects, data files, images, sounds, etc. As we'll see in Chapter 22, a JAR file can carry one or more digital signatures that attest to its integrity and authenticity. A signature can be attached to the file as a whole or to individual items in the file.

The Java runtime system understands JAR files and can load class files directly from an archive. So you can pack your application's classes in a JAR file and place it in your CLASSPATH, as described earlier. You can do the equivalent for applets by listing the JAR file in the ARCHIVE attribute of the HTML <APPLET> tag. Nonclass files (data, images, etc.) contained in your JAR file can also be retrieved from the classpath using the getResource() method (described in Chapter 11). Using this facility your code doesn't have to know whether any resource is in a plain file or a member of a JAR archive. Whether a given class or data file is an item in a JAR file, an individual file on the classpath, or an applet on a remote server, you can always refer to it in a standard way and let Java's class loader resolve the location.

File Compression

Items stored in JAR files are compressed with the standard ZIP file compression.[*] Compression makes downloading classes over a network much faster. A quick survey of the standard Java distribution shows that a typical class file shrinks by about 40% when it is compressed. Text files such as arbitrary HTML or ASCII containing English words often compress by as much as 75%—to one-quarter their original size. (On the other hand, image files don't get smaller when compressed; most of the common image formats have compression built in.)

---

[*] JAR files are completely compatible with the ZIP archives familiar to Windows users. You could even use tools like *pkzip* to create and maintain simple JAR files. But *jar*, the Java archive utility, can do a bit more, as we'll see.

Compression is not the only advantage that a JAR file has for transporting files over a network. Placing all the classes in a single JAR file enables them to be downloaded in a single transaction. Eliminating the overhead of making HTTP requests is likely to be a big savings, since individual class files tend to be small, and a complex applet could easily require many of them. On the downside, startup time could be increased if a large JAR file must be downloaded over a slow connection before the applet can start up.

The jar Utility

The *jar* utility provided with the SDK is a simple tool for creating and reading JAR files. Its user interface isn't particularly friendly. It mimics the Unix *tar* (tape archive) command. If you're familiar with *tar*, you'll recognize the following incantations:

jar -cvf *jarFile path* [*path*] [.. .]
   Create *jarFile* containing *path*(s)

jar -tvf *jarFile* [*path*] [...]
   List the contents of *jarFile*, optionally showing just *path*(s)

jar -xvf *jarFile* [*path*] [...]
   Extract the contents of *jarFile*, optionally extracting just *path*(s)

In these commands, the letters c, t, and x tell *jar* whether it is creating an archive, listing an archive's contents, or extracting files from an archive. The f means that the next argument will be the name of the JAR file on which to operate. The v tells *jar* to be more verbose when displaying information about files. In verbose mode, you can get information about file sizes, modification times, and compression ratios.

Subsequent items on the command line (i.e., anything aside from the letters telling *jar* what to do and the file on which *jar* should operate) are taken as names of archive items. If you're creating an archive, the files and directories you list are placed in it. If you're extracting, only the filenames you list are extracted from the archive. (If you don't list any files, *jar* extracts everything in the archive.)

For example, let's say we have just completed our new game, *spaceblaster*. All the files associated with the game are in three directories. The Java classes themselves are in the *spaceblaster/game* directory, *spaceblaster/images* contains the game's images, and *spaceblaster/docs* contains associated game data. We can pack all this in an archive with this command:

```
% jar cvf spaceblaster.jar spaceblaster
```

Because we requested verbose output, *jar* tells us what it is doing:

```
adding:spaceblaster/ (in=0) (out=0) (stored 0%)
adding:spaceblaster/game/ (in=0) (out=0) (stored 0%)
adding:spaceblaster/game/Game.class (in=8035) (out=3936) (deflated 51%)
adding:spaceblaster/game/Planetoid.class (in=6254) (out=3288) (deflated 47%)
adding:spaceblaster/game/SpaceShip.class (in=2295) (out=1280) (deflated 44%)
```

```
adding:spaceblaster/images/ (in=0) (out=0) (stored 0%)
adding:spaceblaster/images/spaceship.gif (in=6174) (out=5936) (deflated 3%)
adding:spaceblaster/images/planetoid.gif (in=23444) (out=23454) (deflated 0%)
adding:spaceblaster/docs/ (in=0) (out=0) (stored 0%)
adding:spaceblaster/docs/help1.html (in=3592) (out=1545) (deflated 56%)
adding:spaceblaster/docs/help2.html (in=3148) (out=1535) (deflated 51%)
```

jar creates the file *spaceblaster.jar* and adds the directory *spaceblaster*, in turn adding the directories and files within *spaceblaster* to the archive. In verbose mode, *jar* reports the savings gained by compressing the files in the archive.

We can unpack the archive with this command:

% jar xvf spaceblaster.jar

Likewise, we can extract an individual file or directory with:

% jar xvf spaceblaster.jar *filename*

But you normally don't have to unpack a JAR file to use its contents; Java tools know how to extract files from archives automatically. We can list the contents of our JAR with the command:

% jar tvf spaceblaster.jar

Here's the output; it lists all the files, their sizes, and creation times:

```
    0 Thu May 15 12:18:54 PDT 1997 META-INF/
 1074 Thu May 15 12:18:54 PDT 1997 META-INF/MANIFEST.MF
    0 Thu May 15 12:09:24 PDT 1997 spaceblaster/
    0 Thu May 15 11:59:32 PDT 1997 spaceblaster/game/
 8035 Thu May 15 12:14:08 PDT 1997 spaceblaster/game/Game.class
 6254 Thu May 15 12:15:18 PDT 1997 spaceblaster/game/Planetoid.class
 2295 Thu May 15 12:15:26 PDT 1997 spaceblaster/game/SpaceShip.class
    0 Thu May 15 12:17:00 PDT 1997 spaceblaster/images/
 6174 Thu May 15 12:16:54 PDT 1997 spaceblaster/images/spaceship.gif
23444 Thu May 15 12:16:58 PDT 1997 spaceblaster/images/planetoid.gif
    0 Thu May 15 12:10:02 PDT 1997 spaceblaster/docs/
 3592 Thu May 15 12:10:16 PDT 1997 spaceblaster/docs/help1.html
 3148 Thu May 15 12:10:02 PDT 1997 spaceblaster/docs/help2.html
```

JAR manifests

Note that the *jar* command automatically adds a directory called *META-INF* to our archive. The *META-INF* directory holds files describing the contents of the JAR file. It always contains at least one file: *MANIFEST.MF*. The *MANIFEST.MF* file can contain a "packing list" naming the files in the archive along with a user-definable set of attributes for each entry.

The manifest is a text file containing a set of lines in the form *keyword: value*. In Java 1.2 and later, the manifest is by default empty and contains only JAR file version information:

```
Manifest-Version: 1.0
Created-By: 1.2.1 (Sun Microsystems Inc.)
```

In Chapter 22, we'll discuss *signed* JAR files. When you sign a JAR file with a digital signature digest (checksum) information is added to the manifest for each item in the archive. It looks like this:

```
Name: com/oreilly/Test.class
SHA1-Digest: dF2GZt8G11dXY2p4olzzIc5RjP3=
...
```

In the case of a signed JAR, the *META-INF* directory holds digital signature files for items in the archive. In Java 1.1, digest information was always added to the JAR. But since it's really necessary only for signed JAR files, it is omitted by default when you create an archive in Java 1.2 and later.

You can add your own information to the manifest descriptions by specifying your own, supplemental, manifest file when you create the archive. This is a good place to store other simple kinds of attribute information about the files in the archive, perhaps version or authorship information.

For example, we can create a file with the following keyword: value lines:

```
Name: spaceblaster/images/planetoid.gif
RevisionNumber: 42.7
Artist-Temperament: moody
```

To add this information to the manifest in our archive, place it in a file called *myManifest.mf* and give the following *jar* command:

```
% jar -cvmf myManifest.mf spaceblaster.jar spaceblaster
```

We included an additional option with the command, m, which specifies that *jar* should read additional manifest information from the file given on the command line. How does *jar* know which file is which? Because m is before f, it expects to find the manifest information before the name of the JAR file it will create. If you think that's awkward, you're right; get the names in the wrong order, and *jar* will do the wrong thing. Be careful.

Although these attributes aren't automatically available to the application code, it's easy to retrieve them from a JAR file using the java.util.jar.Manifest class.

We'll see more examples of adding information to the JAR manifest later in Chapter 21. The JavaBeans APIs use manifest information to designate which classes are "beans" using a Java-Bean attribute. This information is used by IDEs which work with JavaBeans and load them from the JAR files.

Making a JAR file runnable

Aside from attributes, there are a few special values you can put in the manifest file. One of these, Main-Class, allows you to specify the class containing the primary main() method for an application contained in the JAR:

```
Main-Class: com.oreilly.Game
```

If you add this to your JAR file manifest (using the m option described earlier), you can run the application directly from the JAR:

```
% java -jar spaceblaster.jar
```

More importantly, under Windows and other GUI environments you can simply click on the JAR file to launch the application. The interpreter looks for the Main-Class value in the manifest. It then loads the named class as the application's initial class.

## CHAPTER 4

The Java Language

In this chapter, we introduce the framework of the Java language and some of its fundamental facilities. We don't try to provide a full language reference here; instead, we'll lay out the basic structures of Java with special attention to how it differs from other languages. For example, we'll take a close look at arrays in Java, because they are significantly different from those in some other languages. We won't, on the other hand, spend too much time explaining basic language constructs such as loops and control structures. Nor will we talk much about Java's object-oriented side here, as that's covered in detail in Chapters 5 through 7. As always, we'll try to provide meaningful examples to illustrate how to use Java in everyday programming tasks.

Text Encoding

Java is a language for the Internet. Since the people of the Net speak and write in many different human languages, Java must be able to handle a large number of languages as well. One of the ways in which Java supports international access is through Unicode character encoding. Unicode uses a 16-bit character encoding; it's a worldwide standard that supports the scripts (character sets) of most languages.*

Java source code can be written using the Unicode character encoding and stored either in its full 16-bit form or with ASCII-encoded Unicode character values. This makes Java a friendly language for non-English-speaking programmers who can use their native alphabet for class, method, and variable names.

The Java char type and String objects also support Unicode. But if you're concerned about having to labor with two-byte characters, you can relax. The String API makes the character encoding transparent to you. Unicode is also ASCII-friendly; the first

---

* For more information about Unicode, see *http://www.unicode.org*. Ironically, one of the scripts listed as "obsolete and archaic" and not currently supported by the Unicode standard is Javanese—a historical language of the people of the Island of Java.

256 characters are defined to be identical to the first 256 characters in the ISO8859-1 (Latin-1) encoding; if you stick with these values, there's really no distinction between the two.

Most platforms can't display all currently defined Unicode characters. As a result, Java programs can be written with special Unicode escape sequences. A Unicode character can be represented with this escape sequence:

```
\uxxxx
```

xxxx is a sequence of one to four hexadecimal digits. The escape sequence indicates an ASCII-encoded Unicode character. This is also the form Java uses to output Unicode characters in an environment that doesn't otherwise support them.

Java stores and manipulates characters and strings internally as Unicode values. Java also comes with classes to read and write Unicode-formatted character streams.

Comments

Java supports both C-style block comments delimited by /* and */ and C++ - style line comments indicated by //:

```
/*  This is a
        multiline
            comment.    */

// This is a single-line comment
// and so // is this
```

As in C, block comments can't be nested. Single-line comments are delimited by the end of a line; extra // indicators inside a single line have no effect. Line comments are useful for short comments within methods; they don't conflict with wrapping block comment indicators around large chunks of code during development.

javadoc Comments

By convention, a block comment beginning with /** indicates a special *doc comment*. A doc comment is designed to be extracted by automated documentation generators, such as the Java SDK's *javadoc* program. A doc comment is terminated by the next */, just as with a regular block comment. Leading spacing and the first * on each line is ignored; lines beginning with @ are interpreted as special tags for the documentation generator.

Here's an example:

```
/**
 * I think this class is possibly the most amazing thing you will
 * ever see. Let me tell you about my own personal vision and
 * motivation in creating it.
 * <p>
```

```
 * It all began when I was a small child, growing up on the
 * streets of Idaho. Potatoes were the rage, and life was good...
 *
 * @see PotatoPeeler
 * @see PotatoMasher
 * @author John 'Spuds' Smith
 * @version 1.00, 19 Dec 1996
 */
```

javadoc creates HTML documentation for classes by reading the source code and pulling out the embedded comments. The author and version information is presented in the output, and the @see tags make hypertext links to the appropriate class documentation.

The compiler also looks at the doc comments; in particular, it is interested in the @deprecated tag, which means that the method has been declared obsolete and should be avoided in new programs. The fact that a method is deprecated is noted in the compiled class file so a warning message can be generated whenever you use a deprecated feature in your code (even if the source isn't available).

Doc comments can appear above class, method, and variable definitions, but some tags may not be applicable to all of these. For example, a variable declaration can contain only a @see tag. Table 4-1 summarizes the tags used in doc comments.

Table 4-1. Doc comment tags

Tag	Description	Applies to
@see	Associated class name	Class, method, or variable
@author	Author name	Class
@version	Version string	Class
@param	Parameter name and description	Method
@return	Description of return value	Method
@exception	Exception name and description	Method
@deprecated	Declares an item to be obsolete	Class, method, or variable

Types

The type system of a programming language describes how its data elements (variables and constants) are associated with actual storage. In a statically typed language, such as C or C++, the type of a data element is a simple, unchanging attribute that often corresponds directly to some underlying hardware phenomenon, such as a register or a pointer value. In a more dynamic language such as Smalltalk or Lisp, variables can be assigned arbitrary elements and can effectively change their type throughout their lifetime. A considerable amount of overhead goes into validating what happens in these languages at runtime. Scripting languages such as Perl achieve ease of use by providing drastically simplified type systems in which only certain data elements can be stored in variables, and values are unified into a common representation, such as strings.

Java combines the best features of both statically and dynamically typed languages. As in a statically typed language, every variable and programming element in Java has a type that is known at compile time, so the runtime system doesn't normally have to check the type validity of assignments while the code is executing. Unlike C or C++, Java also maintains runtime information about objects and uses this to allow truly safe runtime polymorphism and casting (using an object as a type other than its declared type).

Java data types fall into two categories. *Primitive types* represent simple values that have built-in functionality in the language; they are fixed elements, such as literal constants and numbers. *Reference types* (or class types) include objects and arrays; they are called reference types because they are passed "by reference," as we'll explain shortly.

Primitive Types

Numbers, characters, and boolean values are fundamental elements in Java. Unlike some other (perhaps more pure) object-oriented languages, they are not objects. For those situations where it's desirable to treat a primitive value as an object, Java provides "wrapper" classes (see Chapter 10). One major advantage of treating primitive values as such is that the Java compiler can more readily optimize their usage.

Another important portability feature of Java is that primitive types are precisely defined. For example, you never have to worry about the size of an int on a particular platform; it's always a 32-bit, signed, two's complement number. Table 4-2 summarizes Java's primitive types.

Table 4-2. Java primitive data types

Type	Definition
boolean	true or false
char	16-bit Unicode character
byte	8-bit signed two's complement integer
short	16-bit signed two's complement integer
int	32-bit signed two's complement integer
long	64-bit signed two's complement integer
float	32-bit IEEE 754 floating-point value
double	64-bit IEEE 754 floating-point value

Those of you with a C background may notice that the primitive types look like an idealization of C scalar types on a 32-bit machine, and you're absolutely right. That's how they're supposed to look. The 16-bit characters were forced by Unicode, and ad hoc pointers were deleted for other reasons. But overall, the syntax and semantics of Java primitive types are meant to fit a C programmer's mental habits.

Floating-point precision

Floating-point operations in Java follow the IEEE 754 international specification, which means that the result of floating-point calculations is normally the same on different Java platforms. However, since Version 1.3, Java has allowed for extended precision on platforms that support it. This can introduce extremely small-valued and arcane differences in the results of high-precision operations. Most applications would never notice this, but if you want to ensure that your application produces exactly the same results on different platforms, use the special keyword strictfp as a class modifier on the class containing the floating-point manipulation.

Variable declaration and initialization

Variables are declared inside of methods or classes in C style. For example:

```
int foo;
double d1, d2;
boolean isFun;
```

Variables can optionally be initialized with an appropriate expression when they are declared:

```
int foo = 42;
double d1 = 3.14, d2 = 2 * 3.14;
boolean isFun = true;
```

Variables that are declared as instance variables in a class are set to default values if they aren't initialized. (In this case, they act much like static variables in C or C++.) Numeric types default to the appropriate flavor of zero, characters are set to the null character (\0), and boolean variables have the value false. Local variables declared in methods, on the other hand, must be explicitly initialized before they can be used.

Integer literals

Integer literals can be specified in octal (base 8), decimal (base 10), or hexadecimal (base 16). A decimal integer is specified by a sequence of digits beginning with one of the characters 1–9:

```
int i = 1230;
```

Octal numbers are distinguished from decimal numbers by a leading zero:

```
int i = 01230;            // i = 664 decimal
```

As in C, a hexadecimal number is denoted by the leading characters 0x or 0X (zero "x"), followed by digits and the characters a–f or A–F, which represent the decimal values 10–15:

```
int i = 0xFFFF;           // i = 65535 decimal
```

Integer literals are of type int unless they are suffixed with an L, denoting that they are to be produced as a long value:

```
long l = 13L;
long l = 13;        // equivalent: 13 is converted from type int
```

(The lowercase character l ("el") is also acceptable but should be avoided because it often looks like the numeral 1.)

When a numeric type is used in an assignment or an expression involving a type with a larger range, it can be promoted to the larger type. For example, in the second line of the previous example, the number 13 has the default type of int, but it's promoted to type long for assignment to the long variable. Certain other numeric and comparison operations also cause this kind of arithmetic promotion. A numeric value can never be assigned to a type with a smaller range without an explicit (C-style) cast, however:

```
int i = 13;
byte b = i;         // Compile-time error, explicit cast needed
byte b = (byte) i;  // OK
```

Conversions from floating-point to integer types always require an explicit cast because of the potential loss of precision.

Floating-point literals

Floating-point values can be specified in decimal or scientific notation. Floating-point literals are of type double unless they are suffixed with an f or F denoting that they are to be produced as a float value:

```
double d = 8.31;
double e = 3.00e+8;
float f = 8.31F;
float g = 3.00e+8F;
```

Character literals

A literal character value can be specified either as a single-quoted character or as an escaped ASCII or Unicode sequence:

```
char a = 'a';
char newline = '\n';
char smiley = '\u263a';
```

Reference Types

In Java, as in other object-oriented languages, you create new complex data types from primitives by creating a class that defines a new type in the language. For instance, if we create a new class called Foo in Java, we are also implicitly creating a new type called Foo. The type of an item governs how it's used and where it's assigned. An item of type Foo can, in general, be assigned to a variable of type Foo or passed as an argument to a method that accepts a Foo value.

In an object-oriented language like Java, a type is not necessarily just a simple attribute. Reference types are related in the same way as the classes they represent. Classes exist in a hierarchy, where a subclass is a specialized kind of its parent class. The corresponding types have the same relationship, where the type of the child class is considered a subtype of the parent class. Because child classes always extend their parents and have, at a minimum, the same functionality, an object of the child's type can be used in place of an object of the parent's type. For example, if you create a new class, Cat, that extends Animal, there is a new type Cat that is considered a subtype of Animal. Objects of type Cat can then be used anywhere an object of type Animal can be used; an object of type Cat is said to be assignable to a variable of type Animal. This is called *subtype polymorphism* and is one of the primary features of an object-oriented language. We'll look more closely at classes and objects in Chapter 5.

Primitive types in Java are used and passed "by value." In other words, when a primitive value is assigned or passed as an argument to a method, it's simply copied. Reference types, on the other hand, are always accessed "by reference." A *reference* is simply a handle or a name for an object. What a variable of a reference type holds is a reference to an object of its type (or of a subtype, as described earlier). A reference is like a pointer in C or C++, except that its type is strictly enforced and the reference value itself is a primitive entity that can't be examined directly. A reference variable can't be created or changed other than through assignment to an appropriate object. When references are assigned or passed to methods, they are copied by value. If you are familiar with C, you can think of a reference as a pointer type that is automatically dereferenced whenever it's mentioned.

Let's run through an example. We specify a variable of type Foo, called myFoo, and assign it an appropriate object:*

```
Foo myFoo = new Foo( );
Foo anotherFoo = myFoo;
```

myFoo is a reference-type variable that holds a reference to the newly constructed Foo object. (For now, don't worry about the details of creating an object; we'll cover that in Chapter 5.) We create a second Foo type variable, anotherFoo, and assign it to the same object. There are now two identical references: myFoo and anotherFoo. If we change things in the state of the Foo object itself, we see the same effect by looking at it with either reference.

---

* The comparable code in C++ would be:
```
Foo& myFoo = *(new Foo( ));
Foo& anotherFoo = myFoo;
```

We can pass an object to a method by specifying a reference-type variable (in this case, either `myFoo` or `anotherFoo`) as the argument:

```
myMethod( myFoo );
```

An important, but sometimes confusing, distinction to make at this point is that the reference itself is passed by value. That is, the argument passed to the method (a local variable from the method's point of view) is actually a third copy of the reference. The method can alter the state of the `Foo` object itself through that reference, but it can't change the caller's notion of the reference to `myFoo`. That is, the method can't change the caller's `myFoo` to point to a different `Foo` object; it can change only its own. For those occasions when we want a method to have the side effect of changing a reference passed to it, we have to wrap that reference in another object to provide a layer of indirection.

Reference types always point to objects, and objects are always defined by classes. However, two special kinds of reference types specify the type of object they point to in a slightly different way. Arrays in Java have a special place in the type system. They are a special kind of object automatically created to hold a series of some other type of object, known as the *base type*. Declaring an array-type reference implicitly creates the new class type, as you'll see in the next section.

Interfaces are a bit sneakier. An interface defines a set of methods and a corresponding type. Any object that implements all methods of the interface can be treated as an object of that type. Variables and method arguments can be declared to be of interface types, just like class types, and any object that implements the interface can be assigned to them. This allows Java to cross the lines of the class hierarchy in a type-safe way.

A Word About Strings

Strings in Java are objects; they are therefore a reference type. `String` objects do, however, have some special help from the Java compiler that makes them look more like primitive types. Literal string values in Java source code are turned into `String` objects by the compiler. They can be used directly, passed as arguments to methods, or assigned to `String` type variables:

```
System.out.println( "Hello World..." );
String s = "I am the walrus...";
String t = "John said: \"I am the walrus...\"";
```

The + symbol in Java is overloaded to provide string concatenation as well as numeric addition. Along with its sister +=, this is the only overloaded operator in Java:

```
String quote = "Four score and " + "seven years ago,";
String more = quote + " our" + " fathers" +  " brought...";
```

Java builds a single String object from the concatenated strings and provides it as the result of the expression. We discuss the String class in Chapter 9.

Statements and Expressions

Although Java's means of declaring methods is quite different from C++, Java's statement and expression syntax is similar to C. Again, the creators of Java came from this background, and the intention was to make the low-level details of Java easily accessible to C programmers. Java *statements* appear inside methods and classes; they describe all activities of a Java program. Variable declarations and assignments, such as those in the previous section, are statements, as are basic language structures such as conditionals and loops. *Expressions* produce values; an expression is evaluated to produce a result, to be used as part of another expression or in a statement. Method calls, object allocations, and, of course, mathematical expressions are examples of expressions. Technically, since variable assignments can be used as values for further assignments or operations (in somewhat questionable programming style), they can be considered to be both statements and expressions.

One of the tenets of Java is to keep things simple and consistent. To that end, when there are no other constraints, evaluations and initializations in Java always occur in the order in which they appear in the code—from left to right, top to bottom. We'll see this rule used in the evaluation of assignment expressions, method calls, and array indexes, to name a few cases. In some other languages, the order of evaluation is more complicated or even implementation-dependent. Java removes this element of danger by precisely and simply defining how the code is evaluated. This doesn't mean you should start writing obscure and convoluted statements, however. Relying on the order of evaluation of expressions is a bad programming habit, even when it works. It produces code that is hard to read and harder to modify. Real programmers, however, are not made of stone, and you may catch us doing this once or twice when we can't resist the urge to write terse code.

Statements

As in C or C++, statements and expressions in Java appear within a *code block*. A code block is syntactically a series of statements surrounded by an open curly brace ({) and a close curly brace (}). The statements in a code block can contain variable declarations:

```
{
    int size = 5;
    setName("Max");
    ...
}
```

Methods, which look like C functions, are in a sense code blocks that take parameters and can be called by their names, for example, SetUpDog:

```
setUpDog( String name ) {
    int size = 5;
    setName( name );
    ...
}
```

Variable declarations are limited in scope to their enclosing code block. That is, they can't be seen outside of the nearest set of braces:

```
{
    int i = 5;
}
```

```
i = 6;            // Compile-time error, no such variable i
```

In this way, code blocks can be used to arbitrarily group other statements and variables. The most common use of code blocks, however, is to define a group of statements for use in a conditional or iterative statement.

Since a code block is itself collectively treated as a statement, we define a conditional like an if/else clause as follows:

```
if ( condition )
    statement;
[ else
    statement; ]
```

Thus, the if clause has the familiar (to C/C++ programmers) functionality of taking two different forms. Here's one:

```
if ( condition )
    statement;
```

Here's the other:

```
if ( condition )  {
    [ statement; ]
    [ statement; ]
    [ ... ]
}
```

The *condition* is a boolean expression. You can't use an integer expression or a reference type like you can in C. In other words, while i==0 is legitimate, i is not (unless i itself is boolean).

In the second form, the statement is a code block, and all its enclosed statements are executed if the conditional succeeds. Any variables declared within that block are visible only to the statements within the successful branch of the condition. Like the if/else conditional, most of the remaining Java statements are concerned with controlling the flow of execution. They act for the most part like their namesakes in other languages.

The do and while iterative statements have the familiar functionality; their conditional test is also a boolean expression:

```
while ( condition )
    statement;

do
    statement;
while ( condition );
```

The for statement also looks like it does in C:

```
for ( initialization; condition; incrementor )
    statement;
```

The variable initialization expression can declare a new variable which is then limited to the scope of the for statement:

```
for (int i = 0; i < 100; i++ ) {
    System.out.println( i )
    int j = i;
    ...
}
```

Java does not in general support the C comma operator, which groups multiple expressions into a single expression. However, you can use multiple comma-separated expressions in the initialization and increment sections of the for loop. For example:

```
for (int i = 0, j = 10; i < j; i++, j-- ) {
    ...
}
```

The Java switch statement takes an integer type (or an argument that can be automatically promoted to an integer type) and selects among a number of alternative case branches:

```
switch ( int expression ) {
    case int expression :
        statement;
    [ case int expression
        statement;
    ...
    default :
        statement;   ]
}
```

No two of the case expressions can evaluate to the same value. As in C, an optional default case can be specified to catch unmatched conditions. Normally, the special statement break is used to terminate a branch of the switch:

```
switch ( retVal ) {
    case myClass.GOOD :
        // something good
        break;
```

```
         case myClass.BAD :
             // something bad
             break;
         default :
             // neither one
             break;
    }
```

The Java break statement and its friend `continue` perform unconditional jumps out of a loop or conditional statement. They differ from the corresponding statements in C by taking an optional label as an argument. Enclosing statements, such as code blocks and iterators, can be labeled with identifier statements:

```
one:
    while ( condition ) {
        ...
        two:
            while ( condition ) {
                ...
                // break or continue point
            }
            // after two
    }
    // after one
```

In this example, a break or continue without argument at the indicated position would have the normal, C-style effect. A break would cause processing to resume at the point labeled "after two"; a continue would immediately cause the two loop to return to its condition test.

The statement break two at the indicated point would have the same effect as an ordinary break, but break one would break both levels and resume at the point labeled "after one." Similarly, continue two would serve as a normal continue, but continue one would return to the test of the one loop. Multilevel break and continue statements remove the remaining justification for the evil goto statement in C/C++.

There are a few Java statements we aren't going to discuss right now. The try, catch, and finally statements are used in exception handling, as we'll discuss later in this chapter. The synchronized statement in Java is used to coordinate access to statements among multiple threads of execution; see Chapter 8 for a discussion of thread synchronization.

Unreachable statements

On a final note, we should mention that the Java compiler flags "unreachable" statements as compile-time errors. An unreachable statement is one that the compiler determines won't be called at all. Of course there may be many methods that are actually never called in your code, but the compiler detects only those that it can "prove" will never be called simply by simple checking at compile time. For example, a method with an unconditional return statement in the middle of it causes a compile-time error. So does a method with something like this:

```
if (1 < 2)
return;
// unreachable statements
```

Expressions

An expression produces a result, or value, when it is evaluated. The value of an expression can be a numeric type, as in an arithmetic expression; a reference type, as in an object allocation; or the special type void, which is the declared type of a method that doesn't return a value. In the last case, the expression is evaluated only for its *side effects*, that is, the work it does aside from producing a value. The type of an expression is known at compile time. The value produced at runtime is either of this type or, in the case of a reference type, a compatible (assignable) subtype.

Operators

Java supports almost all standard C operators. These operators also have the same precedence in Java as they do in C, as shown in Table 4-3.

Table 4-3. Java operators

Precedence	Operator	Operand type	Description
1	++, —	Arithmetic	Increment and decrement
1	+, -	Arithmetic	Unary plus and minus
1	~	Integral	Bitwise complement
1	!	Boolean	Logical complement
1	(type)	Any	Cast
2	*, /, %	Arithmetic	Multiplication, division, remainder
3	+, -	Arithmetic	Addition and subtraction
3	+	String	String concatenation
4	<<	Integral	Left shift
4	>>	Integral	Right shift with sign extension
4	>>>	Integral	Right shift with no extension
5	<, <=, >, >=	Arithmetic	Numeric comparison
5	instanceof	Object	Type comparison
6	==, !=	Primitive	Equality and inequality of value
6	==, !=	Object	Equality and inequality of reference
7	&	Integral	Bitwise AND
7	&	Boolean	Boolean AND
8	^	Integral	Bitwise XOR

Table 4-3. Java operators (continued)

Precedence	Operator	Operand type	Description
8	^	Boolean	Boolean XOR
9	|	Integral	Bitwise OR
9	|	Boolean	Boolean OR
10	&&	Boolean	Conditional AND
11	||	Boolean	Conditional OR
12	?:	NA	Conditional ternary operator
13	=	Any	Assignment
13	*=, /=, %=, +=, -=, <<=, >> =, >>>=, &=, ^=, |=	Any	Assignment with operation

There are a few operators missing from the standard C collection. As we said, Java doesn't support the comma operator for combining expressions, although the for statement allows you to use it in the initialization and increment sections. Java doesn't allow direct pointer manipulation, so it doesn't support the reference (&), dereference (*), and sizeof operators that are familiar to C/C++ programmers. We should also note that the percent (%) operator is not strictly a modulo, but a remainder, and it can have a negative value.

Java also adds some new operators. As we've seen, the + operator can be used with String values to perform string concatenation. Because all integral types in Java are signed values, the >> operator performs a right-arithmetic-shift operation with sign extension. The >>> operator treats the operand as an unsigned number and performs a right-arithmetic-shift with no sign extension. The new operator, as in C++, is used to create objects; we will discuss it in detail shortly.

Assignment

While variable initialization (i.e., declaration and assignment together) is considered a statement, with no resulting value, variable assignment alone is also an expression:

```java
int i, j;        // statement
i = 5;           // both expression and statement
```

Normally, we rely on assignment for its side effects alone, but, as in C, an assignment can be used as a value in another part of an expression:

```java
j = ( i = 5 );
```

Again, relying on order of evaluation extensively (in this case, using compound assignments in complex expressions) can make code very obscure and hard to read. Do so at your own peril.

The null value

The expression `null` can be assigned to any reference type. It has the meaning of "no reference." A `null` reference can't be used to reference anything and attempting to do so generates a `NullPointerException` at runtime.

Variable access

The dot (.) operator has multiple meanings. It can retrieve the value of an instance variable (of some object) or a static variable (of some class). It can also specify a method to be invoked on an object or class. Using the dot (.) to access a variable in an object is an expression that results in the value of the variable accessed. This can be either a numeric type or a reference type:

```
int i;
String s;
i = myObject.length;
s = myObject.name;
```

A reference-type expression can be used in further evaluations, by selecting variables or calling methods within it:

```
int len = myObject.name.length( );
int initialLen = myObject.name.substring(5, 10).length( );
```

Here we have found the length of our `name` variable by invoking the `length()` method of the `String` object. In the second case, we took an intermediate step and asked for a substring of the `name` string. The `substring` method of the `String` class also returns a `String` reference, for which we ask the length. Compounding operations like this is also called "chaining," which we'll mention again later.

Method invocation

A method invocation is essentially a function call: an expression that results in a value. The value's type is the return type of the method. Thus far, we have seen methods invoked by name:

```
System.out.println( "Hello World..." );
int myLength = myString.length( );
```

Here we invoked the methods `println()` and `length()` on different objects. Selecting which method is invoked, however, can be more complicated than it appears, because Java allows method overloading and overriding (multiple methods with the same name); the details are discussed in Chapter 5.

Like the result of any expression, the result of a method invocation can be used in further evaluations, as we saw earlier. You can allocate intermediate variables to make it absolutely clear what your code is doing, or you can opt for brevity where appropriate; it's all a matter of coding style. The two following code snippets are equivalent:

```
int initialLen = myObject.name.substring(5, 10).length( );

String temp1 = myObject.name;
String temp2 = temp1.substring(5, 10);
int initialLen = temp2.length( );
```

Object creation

Objects in Java are allocated with the new operator:

```
Object o = new Object( );
```

The argument to new is the constructor for the class. The *constructor* is a method that always has the same name as the class. The constructor specifies any required parameters to create an instance of the object. The value of the new expression is a reference of the type of the created object. Objects always have one or more constructors, though they may not always be accessible to you.

We'll look at object creation in detail in Chapter 5. For now, just note that object creation is a type of expression and that the resulting object reference can be used in general expressions. In fact, because the binding of new is "tighter" than that of dot (.), you can easily create a new object and invoke a method in it, without assigning the object to a reference type variable:

```
int hours = new Date( ).getHours( );
```

The Date class is a utility class that represents the current time. Here we create a new instance of Date with the new operator and call its getHours() method to retrieve the current hour as an integer value. The Date object reference lives long enough to service the method call and is then cut loose and garbage-collected at some point in the future.

Calling methods in object references in this way is, again, a matter of style. It would certainly be clearer to allocate an intermediate variable of type Date to hold the new object and then call its getHours() method. However, combining operations like this is common.

The instanceof operator

The instanceof operator can be used to determine the type of an object at run-time. It compares an object against a particular type. instanceof returns a boolean value that indicates whether an object is an instance of a specified class or a subclass of that class:

```
Boolean b;
String str = "foo";
b = ( str instanceof String );    // true
```

```
b = ( str instanceof Object );    // also true
b = ( str instanceof Date );      // false, not a Date or subclass
```

instanceof also correctly reports if the object is of the type of an array or a specified interface (as we'll discuss later):

```
if ( foo instanceof byte[] )
    ...
```

It is also important to note that the value null is not considered an instance of any object. So the following test returns false, no matter what the declared type of the variable:

```
String s = null;
if ( s instanceof String )
    // false, won't happen
```

Exceptions

Java's roots are in embedded systems—software that runs inside specialized devices such as hand-held computers, cellular phones, and fancy toasters. In those kinds of applications, it's especially important that software errors be handled robustly. Most users would agree that it's unacceptable for their phone to simply crash or for their toast (and perhaps their house) to burn because their software failed. Given that we can't eliminate the possibility of software errors, it's a step in the right direction to recognize and deal with anticipated application-level errors in a methodical way.

Dealing with errors in a language such as C is entirely the responsibility of the programmer. There is no help from the language itself in identifying error types, and there are no tools for dealing with them easily. In C, a routine generally indicates a failure by returning an "unreasonable" value (e.g., the idiomatic -1 or null). As the programmer, you must know what constitutes a bad result and what it means. It's often awkward to work around the limitations of passing error values in the normal path of data flow.* An even worse problem is that certain types of errors can legitimately occur almost anywhere, and it's prohibitive and unreasonable to explicitly test for them at every point in the software.

Java offers an elegant solution to these problems through *exceptions*. (Java exception handling is similar to, but not quite the same as, exception handling in C++.) An *exception* indicates an unusual condition or an error condition. Program control becomes unconditionally transferred or "thrown" to a specially designated section of code where it's caught and handled. In this way, error handling is orthogonal to (or outside) the normal flow of the program. We don't have to have special return values

---

* The somewhat obscure setjmp( ) and longjmp( ) statements in C can save a point in the execution of code and later return to it unconditionally from a deeply buried location. In a limited sense, this is the functionality of exceptions in Java.

for all our methods; errors are handled by a separate mechanism. Control can be passed long distance from a deeply nested routine and handled in a single location when that is desirable, or an error can be handled immediately at its source. There are still some standard methods that return -1 as a special value, but these are generally limited to situations where we are expecting a special value.*

A Java method is required to specify the exceptions it can throw (i.e., the ones that it doesn't catch itself); this means that the compiler can make sure we handle them. In this way, the information about what errors a method can produce is promoted to the same level of importance as its argument and return types. You may still decide to punt and ignore obvious errors, but in Java you must do so explicitly.

Exceptions and Error Classes

Exceptions are represented by instances of the class java.lang.Exception and its subclasses. Subclasses of Exception can hold specialized information (and possibly behavior) for different kinds of exceptional conditions. However, more often they are simply "logical" subclasses that serve only to identify a new exception type. Figure 4-1 shows the subclasses of Exception in the java.lang package. It should give you a feel for how exceptions are organized. Most other packages define their own exception types, which usually are subclasses of Exception itself or of its important subclass RuntimeException.

Another important exception class is IOException in the package java.io. The IOException class has many subclasses for typical I/O problems (such as FileNotFoundException) and networking problems (such as MalformedURLException). Network exceptions belong to the java.net package. Another important descendant of IOException is RemoteException, which belongs to the java.rmi package. It is used when problems arise during remote method invocation (RMI). Throughout this book we'll mention the exceptions you need to be aware of as we run into them.

An Exception object is created by the code at the point where the error condition arises. It can be designed to hold whatever information is necessary to describe the exceptional condition and also includes a full stack trace for debugging. (A *stack trace* is the list of all the methods called in order to reach the point where the exception was thrown). The Exception object is passed as an argument to the handling block of code, along with the flow of control. This is where the terms "throw" and "catch" come from: the Exception object is thrown from one point in the code and caught by the other, where execution resumes.

---

* For example, the getHeight( ) method of the Image class returns -1 if the height isn't known yet. No error has occurred; the height will be available in the future. In this situation, throwing an exception would be inappropriate.

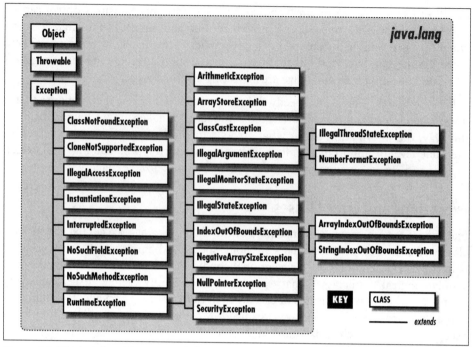

Figure 4-1. The java.lang.Exception subclasses

The Java API also defines the java.lang.Error class for unrecoverable errors. The subclasses of Error in the java.lang package are shown in Figure 4-2. A notable Error type is AssertionError, which is used by the Java assert language statement to indicate a failure. We'll talk about that a bit later. A few other packages define their own subclasses of Error, but subclasses of Error are much less common (and less useful) than subclasses of Exception. You generally needn't worry about these errors in your code (i.e., you do not have to catch them); they are intended to indicate fatal problems or virtual machine errors. An error of this kind usually causes the Java interpreter to display a message and exit. You are actively discouraged from trying to catch or recover from them because they are supposed to indicate a fatal program bug, not a routine condition.

Both Exception and Error are subclasses of Throwable. Throwable is the base class for objects which can be "thrown" with the Java language throw statement. In general you should extend only Exception, Error or one of their subclasses.

Exception Handling

The try/catch guarding statements wrap a block of code and catch designated types of exceptions that occur within it.

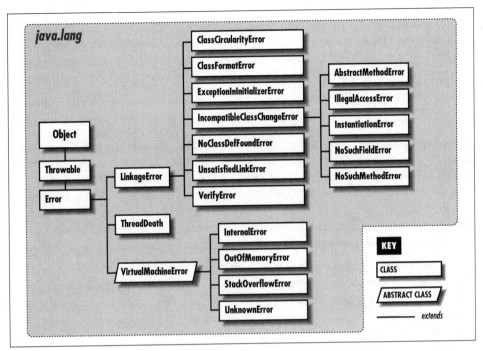

Figure 4-2. The java.lang.Error subclasses

```
try {
    readFromFile("foo");
    ...
}
catch ( Exception e ) {
    // Handle error
    System.out.println( "Exception while reading file: " + e );
    ...
}
```

In this example, exceptions that occur within the body of the try portion of the statement are directed to the catch clause for possible handling. The catch clause acts like a method; it specifies an argument of the type of exception it wants to handle and, if it's invoked, it receives the Exception object as an argument. Here we receive the object in the variable e and print it along with a message.

A try statement can have multiple catch clauses that specify different types (subclasses) of Exception:

```
try {
    readFromFile("foo");
    ...
}
catch ( FileNotFoundException e ) {
    // Handle file not found
    ...
```

```
    }
    catch ( IOException e ) {
        // Handle read error
        ...
    }
    catch ( Exception e ) {
        // Handle all other errors
        ...
    }
```

The catch clauses are evaluated in order, and the first possible (assignable) match is taken. At most, one catch clause is executed, which means that the exceptions should be listed from most specific to least. In the previous example, we'll anticipate that the hypothetical readFromFile() can throw two different kinds of exceptions: one for a file not found and another for a more general read error. Any subclass of Exception is assignable to the parent type Exception, so the third catch clause acts like the default clause in a switch statement and handles any remaining possibilities.

One beauty of the try/catch scheme is that any statement in the try block can assume that all previous statements in the block succeeded. A problem won't arise suddenly because a programmer forgot to check the return value from some method. If an earlier statement fails, execution jumps immediately to the catch clause; later statements are never executed.

Bubbling Up

What if we hadn't caught the exception? Where would it have gone? Well, if there is no enclosing try/catch statement, the exception pops to the top of the method in which it appeared and is, in turn, thrown from that method up to its caller. If that point in the calling method is within a try clause, control passes to the corresponding catch clause. Otherwise the exception continues propagating up the call stack, from one method to its caller. In this way, the exception bubbles up until it's caught, or until it pops out of the top of the program, terminating it with a runtime error message. There's a bit more to it than that because, in this case, the compiler might have reminded us to deal with it, but we'll get back to that in a moment.

Let's look at another example. In Figure 4-3, the method getContent() invokes the method openConnection() from within a try/catch statement. In turn, openConnection() invokes the method sendRequest(), which calls the method write() to send some data.

In this figure, the second call to write() throws an IOException. Since sendRequest() doesn't contain a try/catch statement to handle the exception, it's thrown again from the point where it was called in the method openConnection(). Since openConnection() doesn't catch the exception either, it's thrown once more. Finally it's caught by the try statement in getContent() and handled by its catch clause.

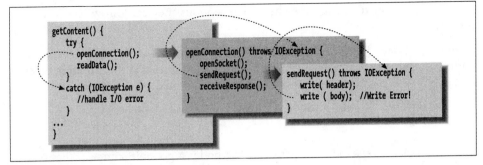

```
getContent() {
    try {
        openConnection();
        readData();
    }
    catch (IOException e) {
        //handle I/O error
    }
    ...
}
```

```
openConnection() throws IOException {
    openSocket();
    sendRequest();
    receiveResponse();
}
```

```
sendRequest() throws IOException {
    write( header);
    write ( body);  //Write Error!
}
```

Figure 4-3. Exception propagation

Exception Stack Traces

Since an exception can bubble up quite a distance before it is caught and handled, we may need a way to determine exactly where it was thrown. All exceptions can dump a *stack trace* that lists their method of origin and all the nested method calls it took to arrive there. Most commonly the user sees this when it is printed using the printStackTrace() method.

```
try {
    // complex task
} catch ( Exception e ) {
    // dump information about exactly where the exception occurred
    e.printStackTrace( System.err );
    ...
}
```

Java 1.4 introduces methods that allow you to retrieve the stack trace information programmatically, using the Throwable getStackTrace() method. This method returns an array of StackTraceElement objects, each of which represents a method call on the stack. You can ask a StackTraceElement for details about that method's location using the methods getFileName(), getClassName(), getMethodName(), and getLineNumber().

Checked and Unchecked Exceptions

We explained earlier how Java forces us to be explicit about our error handling. But it's not realistic to require that every conceivable type of error be handled in every situation. So Java exceptions are divided into two categories: *checked* and *unchecked*. Most application-level exceptions are checked, which means that any method that throws one, either by generating it itself (as we'll discuss later) or by ignoring one that occurs within it, must declare that it can throw that type of exception in a special throws clause in its method declaration. We haven't yet talked in detail about declaring methods; we'll cover that in Chapter 5. For now all you need to know is that methods have to declare the checked exceptions they can throw or allow to be thrown.

Again in Figure 4-3, notice that the methods openConnection() and sendRequest() both specify that they can throw an IOException. If we had to throw multiple types of exceptions, we could declare them separated with commas:

```
void readFile( String s ) throws IOException, InterruptedException {
    ...
}
```

The throws clause tells the compiler that a method is a possible source of that type of checked exception and that anyone calling that method must be prepared to deal with it. The caller may use a try/catch block to catch it, or it may declare that it can throw the exception itself.

In contrast, exceptions that are subclasses of either the class java.lang. RuntimeException or the class java.lang.Error are unchecked. See Figure 4-1 for the subclasses of RuntimeException. (Subclasses of Error are generally reserved for serious class loading or runtime system problems.) It's not a compile-time error to ignore the possibility of these exceptions; methods don't have to declare they can throw them. In all other respects, unchecked exceptions behave the same as other exceptions. We are free to catch them if we wish; we simply aren't required to.

Checked exceptions are intended to cover application-level problems such as missing files and unavailable hosts. As good programmers (and upstanding citizens), we should design software to recover gracefully from these kinds of conditions. Unchecked exceptions include problems such as "out of memory" and "array index out of bounds." While these may indicate application-level programming errors, they can occur almost anywhere and usually aren't possible to recover from. Fortunately, because there are unchecked exceptions, you don't have to wrap every one of your array-index operations in a try/catch statement.

To sum up, checked exceptions are problems a reasonable application should try to handle gracefully; unchecked exceptions (runtime exceptions or errors) are problems from which we would not normally expect our software to recover. Error types are those explicitly intended to be conditions that we should never try to handle or recover from.

Throwing Exceptions

We can throw our own exceptions: either instances of Exception or one of its existing subclasses, or our own specialized exception classes. All we have to do is create an instance of the Exception and throw it with the throw statement:

```
throw new Exception( );
```

Execution stops and is transferred to the nearest enclosing try/catch statement. (There is little point in keeping a reference to the Exception object we've created here.) An alternative constructor lets us specify a string with an error message:

```
throw new Exception("Something really bad happened");
```

You can retrieve this string by using the Exception object's getMessage() method. Often, though, you can just refer to the object itself; in the first example in the earlier section, "Exception Handling," an exception's string value is automatically provided to the println() method.

By convention, all types of Exception have a String constructor like this. The earlier String message is somewhat facetious and vague. Normally you won't be throwing a plain old Exception but a more specific subclass. For example:

```
public void checkRead( String s ) {
    if ( new File(s).isAbsolute( ) || (s.indexOf("..") != -1) )
        throw new SecurityException(
            "Access to file : "+ s +" denied.");
}
```

In this code, we partially implement a method to check for an illegal path. If we find one, we throw a SecurityException, with some information about the transgression.

Of course, we could include whatever other information is useful in our own specialized subclasses of Exception. Often, though, just having a new type of exception is good enough because it's sufficient to help direct the flow of control. For example, if we are building a parser, we might want to make our own kind of exception to indicate a particular kind of failure:

```
class ParseException extends Exception {
    ParseException( ) {
        super( );
    }
    ParseException( String desc ) {
        super( desc );
    }
}
```

See Chapter 5 for a full description of classes and class constructors. The body of our Exception class here simply allows a ParseException to be created in the conventional ways we've created exceptions previously (either generically or with a simple string description). Now that we have our new exception type, we can guard like so:

```
// Somewhere in our code
...
try {
    parseStream( input );
} catch ( ParseException pe ) {
    // Bad input...
} catch ( IOException ioe ) {
    // Low-level communications problem
}
```

As you can see, although our new exception doesn't currently hold any specialized information about the problem (it certainly could), it does let us distinguish a parse error from an arbitrary I/O error in the same chunk of code.

Chaining exceptions

Sometimes you'll want to take some action based on an exception and then turn around and throw a new exception in its place. This is common when building frameworks, where low-level detailed exceptions are handled and represented by higher level exceptions that can be managed more easily. For example you might want to catch an IOException in a communication package, possibly perform some cleanup, and ultimately throw a higher level exception of your own, maybe something like LostServerConnection.

You can do this in the obvious way by simply catching the exception and then throwing a new one. But then you lose important information, including the stack trace of the original "causal" exception. To deal with this, you can use the technique of exception *chaining*. This means that you include the causal exception in the new exception that you throw. Java 1.4 adds explicit support for exception chaining. Base exception types can be constructed with an exception as an argument or the standard String message and an exception:

```
throw new Exception( "Here's the story...", causalException );
```

You can get access to this exception later with the getCause() method, which returns the causal exception. More importantly, Java automatically prints both exceptions and their respective stack traces if you print the exception or if it is shown to the user.

You can add this kind of constructor to your own exception subclasses as well (delegating to the parent constructor). However, since this is (at least formally) a recent addition to Java, many preexisting exception types do not provide this kind of constructor. You can still take advantage of this pattern by using the Throwable method initCause() to set the causal exception explicitly after constructing your exception and before throwing it:

```
Try {
  // ...
} catch ( IOException cause ) {
  Exception e =
    new IOException("What we have here is a failure to communicate...");
  e.initCause( cause );
  throw e;
}
```

try Creep

The try statement imposes a condition on the statements that it guards. It says that if an exception occurs within it, the remaining statements are abandoned. This has consequences for local variable initialization. If the compiler can't determine whether a local variable assignment we placed inside a try/catch block will happen, it won't let us use the variable:

```
void myMethod( ) {
    int foo;

    try {
        foo = getResults( );
    }
    catch ( Exception e ) {
        ...
    }

    int bar = foo;  // Compile-time error -- foo may not have been initialized
```

In this example, we can't use foo in the indicated place because there's a chance it was never assigned a value. One obvious option is to move the assignment inside the try statement:

```
try {
    foo = getResults( );

    int bar = foo;  // Okay because we get here only
                    // if previous assignment succeeds
}
catch ( Exception e ) {
    ...
}
```

Sometimes this works just fine. However, now we have the same problem if we want to use bar later in myMethod(). If we're not careful, we might end up pulling everything into the try statement. The situation changes if we transfer control out of the method in the catch clause:

```
try {
    foo = getResults( );
}
catch ( Exception e ) {
    ...
    return;
}

int bar = foo;  // Okay because we get here only
                // if previous assignment succeeds
```

The compiler is smart enough to know that if an error had occurred in the try clause we wouldn't have reached the bar assignment. Your code will dictate its own needs; you should just be aware of the options.

The finally Clause

What if we have some cleanup to do before we exit our method from one of the catch clauses? To avoid duplicating the code in each catch branch and to make the cleanup more explicit, use the finally clause. A finally clause can be added after a try and any associated catch clauses. Any statements in the body of the finally clause are guaranteed to be executed, no matter why control leaves the try body (whether an exception was thrown or not):

```
try {
    // Do something here
}
catch ( FileNotFoundException e ) {
    ...
}
catch ( IOException e ) {
    ...
}
catch ( Exception e ) {
    ...
}
finally {
    // Clean up here
}
```

In this example, the statements at the cleanup point are executed eventually, no matter how control leaves the try. If control transfers to one of the catch clauses, the statements in finally are executed after the catch completes. If none of the catch clauses handles the exception, the finally statements are executed before the exception propagates to the next level.

If the statements in the try execute cleanly, or if we perform a return, break, or continue, the statements in the finally clause are executed. To perform cleanup operations, we can even use try and finally without any catch clauses:

```
try {
    // Do something here
    return;
}
finally {
    System.out.println("Whoo-hoo!");
}
```

Exceptions that occur in a catch or finally clause are handled normally; the search for an enclosing try/catch begins outside the offending try statement.

Performance Issues

We mentioned at the beginning of this section that there are methods in the core Java APIs that still return "out of bounds" values such as -1 or null instead of throwing Exceptions. Why is this? Well, for some it is simply a matter of convenience;

where a special value is easily discernible, we may not want to have to wrap those methods in try/catch blocks.

But there is also a performance issue. Because of the way the Java virtual machine is implemented, guarding against an exception being thrown (using a try) is free. It doesn't add any overhead to the execution of your code. However, throwing an exception is not free. When an exception is thrown, Java has to locate the appropriate try/catch block and perform other time-consuming activities at runtime.

The result is that you should throw exceptions only in truly "exceptional" circumstances and try to avoid using them for expected conditions, especially when performance is an issue. For example, if you have a loop, it may be better to perform a small test on each pass and avoid throwing the exception, rather than throwing it frequently. On the other hand, if the exception is thrown only one in a gazillion times, you may want to eliminate the overhead of the test code and not worry about the cost of throwing that exception.

Assertions

An assertion is a simple pass/fail test of some condition, performed while your application is running. Assertions can be used to check the "sanity" of your code, anywhere you believe certain conditions are guaranteed by correct program behavior. They are distinct from other kinds of tests because they check conditions that should never be violated: if the assertion fails, the application is to be considered broken and generally halts with an appropriate error message. Assertions are supported directly by the Java language so that they can be turned on or off at runtime to remove any performance penalty of including them in your code.

Using assertions to test for the correct behavior of your application is a simple but powerful technique for ensuring software quality. It fills a gap between those aspects of software that can be checked automatically by the compiler and those more generally checked by "unit tests" and human testing. Assertions test assumptions about program behavior and make them guarantees (at least while they are activated).

Explicit support for assertions was added in Java 1.4. However, if you've written much code in any language, you have probably used assertions in some form. For example, you may have written something like the following:

```
if ( !condition )
    throw new AssertionError("fatal error: 42");
```

An assertion in Java is equivalent to this example but performed with the assert language keyword. It takes a boolean condition and an optional expression value. If the assertion fails, an AssertionError is thrown, which usually causes Java to bail out of the application.

The optional expression may evaluate to either a primitive or object type. Either way, its sole purpose is to be turned into a string and shown to the user if the assertion fails; most often you'll use a string message explicitly. Here are some examples:

```
assert false;
assert ( array.length > min );
assert a > 0 : a
assert foo != null :  "foo is not null!"
```

In the event of failure, the first two assertions print only a generic message whereas the third prints the value of a and the last prints the foo is not null! message.

Again, the important thing about assertions is not just that they are more terse than the equivalent if condition but that they can be enabled or disabled when you run the application. Disabling assertions means that their test conditions are not even evaluated, so there is no performance penalty for including them in your code (other than, perhaps, space in the class files when they are loaded).

Assertions are supported only in Java 1.4 and (for now) require passing a special switch to the compiler so it recognizes the assert keyword. So to use the assert examples, you'll have to compile using the -source compiler switch and specify 1.4 as the language version. For example:

```
% javac -source 1.4 MyApplication.java
```

Assertions were implemented this way to provide some migration time for existing applications with their own methods named assert, which will now be illegal. In some future release, assertions will be recognized by default.

Enabling and Disabling Assertions

Assertions are turned on or off at runtime. When disabled, assertions still exist in the class files but are not executed and consume no time. You can enable and disable assertions for an entire application or on a package-by-package or even class-by-class basis. By default, assertions are turned off in Java 1.4. To enable them for your code, use the Java flag -ea or -enableassertions:

```
% java -ea MyApplication
```

To turn on assertions for a particular class, append the class name like so:

```
% java -ea:com.oreilly.examples.Myclass
```

To turn on assertions just for particular packages append the package name with trailing ellipses (three dots) like so:

```
% java -ea:com.oreilly.examples...
```

When you enable assertions for package, Java also enables all subordinate package names (e.g., *com.oreilly.examples.text*). However you can become more selective by using the corresponding -da or -disableassertions flag to negate individual packages or classes. You can combine all this to achieve arbitrary groupings like this:

```
% java -ea:com.oreilly.examples... -da:com.oreilly.examples.text
    -ea:com.oreilly.examples.text.MonkeyTypewriters  MyApplication
```

This example enables assertions for the com.oreilly.examples package as a whole, excludes the package com.oreilly.examples.text, then turns exceptions on for just one class, MonkeyTypewriters, in that package.

Using Assertions

An assertion enforces a rule about something that should be unchanging in your code and would otherwise go unchecked. You can use an assertion for added safety anywhere you want to verify your assumptions about program behavior that can't be checked by the compiler.

A common situation that cries out for an assertion is testing for multiple conditions or values where one should always be found. In this case, a failing assertion as the default or "fall through" behavior indicates the code is broken. For example, suppose we have a value called direction that should always contain either the constant value LEFT or RIGHT:

```
if ( direction == LEFT )
    doLeft();
else if ( direction == RIGHT )
    doRight()
else
    assert false : "bad direction";
```

The same applies to the default case of a switch:

```
switch ( direction ) {
    case LEFT:
        doLeft();
        break;
    case RIGHT:
        doRight();
        break;
    default:
        assert false;
}
```

In general, you should not use assertions for checking the validity of arguments to methods because you want that behavior to be part of your application, not just a test for quality control that can be turned off. The validity of input to a method is called its *pre-conditions,* and you should usually throw an exception if they are not met; this elevates the preconditions to part of the method's "contract" with the user. However, checking the results of your methods before returning them is always valid; these are called *post-conditions.*

Sometimes determining what is or is not a pre-condition depends on your point of view. For example, when a method is used internally within a class, pre-conditions may already be guaranteed by the methods that call it. Public methods of the class should probably throw exceptions when their pre-conditions are violated, but a private method might use assertions because its callers are always closely related code that should obey the correct behavior.

Finally, note that assertions can not only test simple expressions but perform complex validation as well. Remember that anything you place in the condition expression of an assert statement is not evaluated when assertions are turned off. You can make helper methods for your assertions, containing arbitrary amounts of code. And, although it suggests a dangerous programming style, you can even use assertions that have side effects to capture values for use by later assertions—all of which will be disabled when assertions are turned off. For example:

```
int savedValue;
assert ( savedValue = getValue( )) != -1;
// Do work...
assert checkValue( savedValue );
```

Here, in the first assert, we use helper method getValue() to retrieve some information and save it for later. Then after doing some work, we check the saved value using another assertion, perhaps comparing results. When assertions are disabled we'll no longer save or check the data. Note that it's necessary for us to be somewhat cute and make our first assert condition into a boolean by checking for a known value. Again, using assertions with side effects is a bit dangerous because you have to be careful that those side effects are only seen by other assertions. Otherwise, you'll be changing your application behavior when you turn them off.

Arrays

An array is a special type of object that can hold an ordered collection of elements. The type of the elements of the array is called the *base type* of the array; the number of elements it holds is a fixed attribute called its *length*. Java supports arrays of all primitive and reference types.

The basic syntax of arrays looks much like that of C or C++. We create an array of a specified length and access the elements with the index operator, [ ]. Unlike other languages, however, arrays in Java are true, first-class objects. An array is an instance of a special Java array class and has a corresponding type in the type system. This means that to use an array, as with any other object, we first declare a variable of the appropriate type and then use the new operator to create an instance of it.

Array objects differ from other objects in Java in three respects:

- Java implicitly creates a special array class type for us whenever we declare an array type variable. It's not strictly necessary to know about this process in order to use arrays, but it helps in understanding their structure and their relationship to other objects in Java.

- Java lets us use the [ ] operator to access array elements, so that arrays look as we expect. We could implement our own classes that act like arrays, but we would have to settle for having methods such as get() and put() instead of using the special [ ] notation.

- Java provides a corresponding special form of the new operator that lets us construct an instance of an array and specify its length with the [ ] notation or initialize it from a structured list of values.

Array Types

An array-type variable is denoted by a base type followed by the empty brackets, [ ]. Alternatively, Java accepts a C-style declaration, with the brackets placed after the array name.

The following are equivalent:

```
int [] arrayOfInts;
int arrayOfInts [];
```

In each case, arrayOfInts is declared as an array of integers. The size of the array is not yet an issue, because we are declaring only the array-type variable. We have not yet created an actual instance of the array class, with its associated storage. It's not even possible to specify the length of an array when declaring an array-type variable.

An array of objects can be created in the same way:

```
String [] someStrings;
Button someButtons [];
```

Array Creation and Initialization

The new operator is used to create an instance of an array. After the new operator, we specify the base type of the array and its length, with a bracketed integer expression:

```
arrayOfInts = new int [42];
someStrings = new String [ number + 2 ];
```

We can, of course, combine the steps of declaring and allocating the array:

```
double [] someNumbers = new double [20];
Component widgets [] = new Component [12];
```

As in C, array indices start with zero. Thus, the first element of someNumbers[] is 0, and the last element is 19. After creation, the array elements are initialized to the default values for their type. For numeric types, this means the elements are initially zero:

```
int [] grades = new int [30];
grades[0] = 99;
```

```
    grades[1] = 72;
    // grades[2] == 0
```

The elements of an array of objects are references to the objects, not actual instances of the objects. The default value of each element is therefore `null`, until we assign instances of appropriate objects:

```
    String names [] = new String [4];
    names [0] = new String( );
    names [1] = "Boofa";
    names [2] = someObject.toString( );
    // names[3] == null
```

This is an important distinction that can cause confusion. In many other languages, the act of creating an array is the same as allocating storage for its elements. In Java, a newly allocated array of objects actually contains only reference variables, each with the value `null`.* That's not to say that there is no memory associated with an empty array; there is memory needed to hold those references (the empty "slots" in the array). Figure 4-4 illustrates the names array of the previous example.

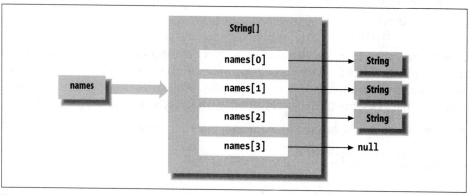

Figure 4-4. A Java array

names is a variable of type `String[]` (i.e., a string array). This particular `String[]` object contains four `String` type variables. We have assigned `String` objects to the first three array elements. The fourth has the default value `null`.

Java supports the C-style curly braces {} construct for creating an array and initializing its elements:

```
    int [] primes = { 1, 2, 3, 5, 7, 7+4 };    // primes[2] == 3
```

---

* The analog in C or C++ is an array of pointers to objects. However, pointers in C or C++ are themselves two- or four-byte values. Allocating an array of pointers is, in actuality, allocating the storage for some number of those pointer objects. An array of references is conceptually similar, although references are not themselves objects. We can't manipulate references or parts of references other than by assignment, and their storage requirements (or lack thereof) are not part of the high-level Java language specification.

An array object of the proper type and length is implicitly created, and the values of the comma-separated list of expressions are assigned to its elements.

We can use the {} syntax with an array of objects. In this case, each expression must evaluate to an object that can be assigned to a variable of the base type of the array, or the value null. Here are some examples:

```
String [] verbs = { "run", "jump", someWord.toString( ) };
Button [] controls = { stopButton, new Button("Forwards"),
    new Button("Backwards") };
// All types are subtypes of Object
Object [] objects = { stopButton, "A word", null };
```

The following are equivalent:

```
Button [] threeButtons = new Button [3];
Button [] threeButtons = { null, null, null };
```

Using Arrays

The size of an array object is available in the public variable length:

```
char [] alphabet = new char [26];
int alphaLen = alphabet.length;              // alphaLen == 26

String [] musketeers = { "one", "two", "three" };
int num = musketeers.length;                 // num == 3
```

length is the only accessible field of an array; it is a variable, not a method. (Don't worry, the compiler tells you when you accidentally use parentheses, as if it were a method; everyone does now and then.)

Array access in Java is just like array access in C; you access an element by putting an integer-valued expression between brackets after the name of the array. The following example creates an array of Button objects called keyPad and then fills the array with Button objects:

```
Button [] keyPad = new Button [ 10 ];
for ( int i=0; i < keyPad.length; i++ )
    keyPad[ i ] = new Button( Integer.toString( i ) );
```

Attempting to access an element that is outside the range of the array generates an ArrayIndexOutOfBoundsException. This is a type of RuntimeException, so you can either catch and handle it yourself, if you really expect it, or ignore it, as we've already discussed:

```
String [] states = new String [50];

try {
    states[0] = "California";
    states[1] = "Oregon";
    ...
    states[50] = "McDonald's Land";   // Error: array out of bounds
}
```

```
catch ( ArrayIndexOutOfBoundsException err ) {
    System.out.println( "Handled error: " + err.getMessage( ) );
}
```

It's a common task to copy a range of elements from one array into another. Java supplies the arraycopy() method for this purpose; it's a utility method of the System class:

```
System.arraycopy(source,sourceStart,destination,destStart,length);
```

The following example doubles the size of the names array from an earlier example:

```
String [] tmpVar = new String [ 2 * names.length ];
System.arraycopy( names, 0, tmpVar, 0, names.length );
names = tmpVar;
```

A new array, twice the size of names, is allocated and assigned to a temporary variable tmpVar. The arraycopy() method is then used to copy the elements of names to the new array. Finally, the new array is assigned to names. If there are no remaining references to the old array object after names has been copied, it is garbage-collected on the next pass.

Anonymous Arrays

Often it is convenient to create "throw-away" arrays, arrays that are used in one place and never referenced anywhere else. Such arrays don't need to have a name because you never need to refer to them again in that context. For example, you may want to create a collection of objects to pass as an argument to some method. It's easy enough to create a normal, named array; but if you don't actually work with the array (if you use the array only as a holder for some collection), you shouldn't have to. Java makes it easy to create "anonymous" (i.e., unnamed) arrays.

Let's say you need to call a method named setPets(), which takes an array of Animal objects as arguments. Provided Cat and Dog are subclasses of Animal, here's how to call setPets() using an anonymous array:

```
Dog pokey = new Dog ("gray");
Cat boojum = new Cat ("grey");
Cat simon = new Cat ("orange");
setPets ( new Animal [] { pokey, boojum, simon });
```

The syntax looks just like the initialization of an array in a variable declaration. We implicitly define the size of the array and fill in its elements using the curly-brace notation. However, since this is not a variable declaration, we have to explicitly use the new operator to create the array object.

You can use anonymous arrays to simulate variable-length argument lists (called VARARGS in C), a feature of many programming languages that Java doesn't provide. The advantage of anonymous arrays over variable-length argument lists is that the former allow stricter type checking; the compiler always knows exactly what arguments are expected, and therefore it can verify that method calls are correct.

Multidimensional Arrays

Java supports multidimensional arrays in the form of arrays of array type objects. You create a multidimensional array with C-like syntax, using multiple bracket pairs, one for each dimension. You also use this syntax to access elements at various positions within the array. Here's an example of a multidimensional array that represents a chess board:

```
ChessPiece [][] chessBoard;
chessBoard = new ChessPiece [8][8];
chessBoard[0][0] = new ChessPiece( "Rook" );
chessBoard[1][0] = new ChessPiece( "Pawn" );
...
```

Here chessBoard is declared as a variable of type ChessPiece[][] (i.e., an array of ChessPiece arrays). This declaration implicitly creates the type ChessPiece[] as well. The example illustrates the special form of the new operator used to create a multidimensional array. It creates an array of ChessPiece[] objects and then, in turn, makes each element into an array of ChessPiece objects. We then index chessBoard to specify values for particular ChessPiece elements. (We'll neglect the color of the pieces here.)

Of course, you can create arrays with more than two dimensions. Here's a slightly impractical example:

```
Color [][][] rgbCube = new Color [256][256][256];
rgbCube[0][0][0] = Color.black;
rgbCube[255][255][0] = Color.yellow;
...
```

As in C, we can specify a partial index of a multidimensional array to get an array-type object with fewer dimensions. In our example, the variable chessBoard is of type ChessPiece[][]. The expression chessBoard[0] is valid and refers to the first element of chessBoard, which, in Java, is of type ChessPiece[]. For example, we can create a row for our chess board:

```
ChessPiece [] startRow =  {
    new ChessPiece("Rook"), new ChessPiece("Knight"),
    new ChessPiece("Bishop"), new ChessPiece("King"),
    new ChessPiece("Queen"), new ChessPiece("Bishop"),
    new ChessPiece("Knight"), new ChessPiece("Rook")
};

chessBoard[0] = startRow;
```

We don't necessarily have to specify the dimension sizes of a multidimensional array with a single new operation. The syntax of the new operator lets us leave the sizes of some dimensions unspecified. The size of at least the first dimension (the most significant dimension of the array) has to be specified, but the sizes of any number of trailing, less significant array dimensions may be left undefined. We can assign appropriate array-type values later.

We can create a checkerboard of boolean values (which is not quite sufficient for a real game of checkers) using this technique:

```
boolean [][] checkerBoard;
checkerBoard = new boolean [8][];
```

Here, checkerBoard is declared and created, but its elements, the eight boolean[] objects of the next level, are left empty. Thus, for example, checkerBoard[0] is null until we explicitly create an array and assign it, as follows:

```
checkerBoard[0] = new boolean [8];
checkerBoard[1] = new boolean [8];
...
checkerBoard[7] = new boolean [8];
```

The code of the previous two examples is equivalent to:

```
boolean [][] checkerBoard = new boolean [8][8];
```

One reason we might want to leave dimensions of an array unspecified is so that we can store arrays given to us by another method.

Note that since the length of the array is not part of its type, the arrays in the checkerboard do not necessarily have to be of the same length. That is, multidimensional arrays don't have to be rectangular. Here's a defective (but perfectly legal, to Java) checkerboard:

```
checkerBoard[2] = new boolean [3];
checkerBoard[3] = new boolean [10];
```

And here's how you could create and initialize a triangular array:

```
int [][] triangle = new int [5][];
for (int i = 0; i < triangle.length; i++) {
    triangle[i] = new int [i + 1];
    for (int j = 0; j < i + 1; j++)
        triangle[i][j] = i + j;
}
```

Inside Arrays

We said earlier that arrays are instances of special array classes in the Java language. If arrays have classes, where do they fit into the class hierarchy and how are they related? These are good questions; however, we need to talk more about the object-oriented aspects of Java before answering them. That's the subject of the next chapter. For now, take it on faith that arrays fit into the class hierarchy.

CHAPTER 5

Objects in Java

In this chapter, we get to the heart of Java and explore the object-oriented aspects of the language. The term *object-oriented design* refers to the art of decomposing an application into some number of objects, self-contained application components that work together. The goal is to break your problem down into a number of smaller problems that are simpler and easier to handle and maintain. Object-based designs have proven themselves over the years, and object-based languages such as Java provide a strong foundation for writing very small to very large applications. Java was designed from the ground up to be an object-oriented language, and all the Java APIs and libraries are built around solid object-based design patterns.

An object design "methodology" is a system or a set of rules created to help you break down your application into objects. Often this means mapping real-world entities and concepts (sometimes called the "problem domain") into application components. Various methodologies attempt to help you factor your application into a good set of reusable objects. This is good in principle, but the problem is that good object-oriented design is still more art than science. While you can learn from the various off-the-shelf design methodologies, none of them will help you in all situations. The truth is that there is no substitute for experience.

We won't try to push you into a particular methodology here; there are shelves full of books to do that.[*]

Instead, we'll just provide some common sense hints to get you started. The following general design guidelines will hopefully make more sense after you've read this and the next chapter.

---

[*] Once you have some experience with basic object-oriented concepts, you might want to take a look at *Design Patterns: Elements of Reusable Object-Oriented Software* by Gamma, Helm, Johnson, and Vlissides (Addison-Wesley). This book catalogs useful object-oriented designs that have been refined over the years by experience. Many appear in the design of the Java APIs.

- Hide as much of your implementation as possible. Never expose more of the internals of an object than you have to. This is key to building maintainable, reusable code. Avoid public variables in your objects, with the possible exception of constants. Instead define *accessor* methods to set and return values (even if they are simple types). Later, when you need to, you'll be able to modify and extend the behavior of your objects without breaking other classes that rely on them.

- Specialize objects only when you have to—use *composition* instead of *inheritance*. When you use an object in its existing form, as a piece of a new object, you are *composing* objects. When you change or refine the behavior of an object (by *subclassing*), you are using *inheritance*. You should try to reuse objects by composition rather than inheritance whenever possible, because when you compose objects, you are taking full advantage of existing tools. Inheritance involves breaking down the barrier of an object and should be done only when there's a real advantage. Ask yourself if you really need to inherit the whole public interface of an object (do you want to be a "kind" of that object) or if you can just delegate certain jobs to the object and use it by composition.

- Minimize relationships between objects and try to organize related objects in packages. Objects that work closely together can be grouped using Java packages, which can hide those that are not of general interest. Think about how much work it would take to make your objects generally useful, outside of your current application. You may save yourself a lot of time later.

Classes

Classes are the building blocks of a Java application. A *class* can contain methods (functions), variables, initialization code, and, as we'll discuss later on, even other classes. It serves as a blueprint for making class *instances*, which are runtime objects that implement the class structure. You declare a class with the `class` keyword. Methods and variables of the class appear inside the braces of the class declaration:

```
class Pendulum {
    float mass;
    float length = 1.0;
    int cycles;

    float getPosition ( float time ) {
        ...
    }
    ...
}
```

The `Pendulum` class contains three variables: `mass`, `length`, and `cycles`. It also defines a method called `getPosition()`, which takes a `float` value as an argument and returns a `float` value as a result. Variables and method declarations can appear in any order, but variable initializers can't make "forward references" to other variables that appear later. Once we've defined the Pendulum class, we can create a Pendulum object (an instance of that class) as follows:

```
Pendulum p;
p = new Pendulum( );
```

Recall that our declaration of the variable p doesn't create a Pendulum object; it simply creates a variable that refers to an object of type Pendulum. We still have to create the object, using the new keyword. Now that we've created a Pendulum object, we can access its variables and methods, as we've already seen many times:

```
p.mass = 5.0;
float pos = p.getPosition( 1.0 );
```

Two kinds of variables can be defined in a class: *instance variables* and *static variables*. Every object instance has its own set of instance variables; the values of these variables in one object can differ from the values in another object. We'll talk about static variables later, which, in contrast, are shared among all instances of an object. In either case, if you don't initialize a variable when you declare it, it's given a default value appropriate for its type (null, zero, or false).

Figure 5-1 shows a hypothetical TextBook application that uses two instances of Pendulum through the reference-type variables bigPendulum and smallPendulum. Each of these Pendulum objects has its own copy of mass, length, and cycles. As with variables, methods defined in a class may be *instance methods* or *static methods*. An instance method is associated with an instance of the class, but the relationship isn't quite as simple as for variables. Instance methods are accessed through an object instance, but the object doesn't have its own copy of the methods (there is no duplication of code). Instead, the association means that instance methods can "see" and operate on the values of the instance variables of the object. As you'll see in Chapter 6 when we talk about subclassing; there's more to learn about how methods see variables. In that chapter we'll also discuss how instance methods can be "overridden" in child classes—a very important feature of object-oriented design. Both aspect differ from static methods, which we'll see later are really more like global functions—associated with a class by name only.

Accessing Fields and Methods

Inside a class, we can access variables and call methods of the class directly by name. Here's an example that expands upon our Pendulum:

```
class Pendulum {
    ...
    void resetEverything( ) {
        mass = 1.0;
        length = 1.0;
        cycles = 0;
        ...
```

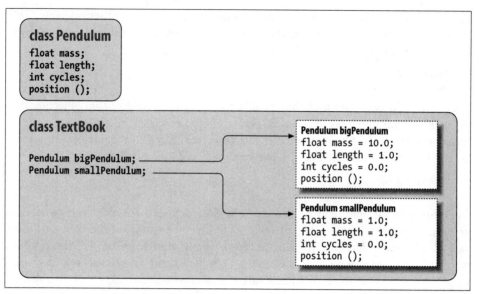

Figure 5-1. Instances of the Pendulum class

```
        float startingPosition = getPosition( 0.0 );
    }
    ...
}
```

Other classes access members of an object through a reference, using the (C-style) dot notation:

```
class TextBook {
    ...
    void showPendulum( ) {
        Pendulum bob = new Pendulum( );
        ...
        int i = bob.cycles;
        bob.resetEverything( );
        bob.mass = 1.01;
        ...
    }
    ...
}
```

Here we have created a second class, TextBook, that uses a Pendulum object. It creates an instance in showPendulum() and then invokes methods and accesses variables of the object through the reference bob.

Several factors affect whether class members can be accessed from "outside" the class (from another class). You can use the visibility modifiers public, private, and protected to control access; classes can also be placed into a *package*, which affects their scope. The private modifier, for example, designates a variable or method for use only by other members of the class itself. In the previous example, we could change the declaration of our variable cycles to private:

```
class Pendulum {
    ...
    private int cycles;
    ...
```

Now we can't access cycles from TextBook:

```
class TextBook {
    ...
    void showPendulum( ) {
        ...
        int i = bob.cycles;  // Compile time error
```

If we still need to access cycles in some capacity, we might add a public getCycles() method to the Pendulum class. We'll take a detailed look at packages, access modifiers, and how they affect the visibility of variables and methods in Chapter 6.

Static Members

As we've said, instance variables and methods are associated with and accessed through an instance of the class—i.e., through a particular object. In contrast, members that are declared with the static modifier live in the class and are shared by all instances of the class. Variables declared with the static modifier are called *static variables* or *class variables*; similarly, these kinds of methods are called *static methods* or *class methods*. We can add a static variable to our Pendulum example:

```
class Pendulum {
    ...
    static float gravAccel = 9.80;
    ...
```

We have declared the new float variable gravAccel as static. That means if we change its value in any instance of a Pendulum, the value changes for all Pendulum objects, as shown in Figure 5-2.

Static members can be accessed like instance members. Inside our Pendulum class, we can refer to gravAccel, like an instance variable:

```
class Pendulum {
    ...
    float getWeight ( ) {
        return mass * gravAccel;
    }
    ...
}
```

However, since static members exist in the class itself, independent of any instance, we can also access them directly through the class. We don't need a Pendulum object

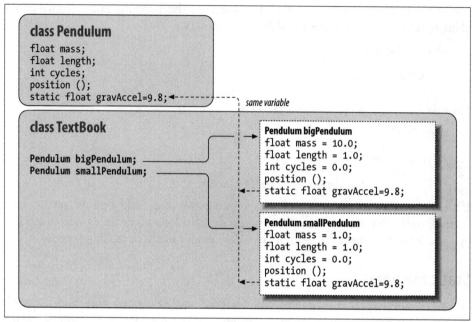

Figure 5-2. Static variables shared by all instances of a class

to set the variable gravAccel; instead we can use the class name in place of a reference-type variable:

```
Pendulum.gravAccel = 8.76;
```

This changes the value of gravAccel for any current or future instances. Why would we want to change the value of gravAccel? Well, perhaps we want to explore how pendulums would work on different planets. Static variables are also very useful for other kinds of data shared among classes at runtime. For instance, you can create methods to register your objects so that they can communicate, or you can keep track of references to them. It's also common to use static variables to define constant values. In this case, we use the static modifier along with the final modifier. So, if we cared only about pendulums under the influence of the Earth's gravitational pull, we could change Pendulum as follows:

```
class Pendulum {
    ...
    static final float EARTH_G = 9.80;
    ...
```

We have followed a common convention and named our constant with capital letters. Now the value of EARTH_G is a constant; it can be accessed by any instance of Pendulum (or anywhere, for that matter), but its value can't be changed at runtime.

It's important to use the combination of static and final only for things that are really constant. That's because the compiler is allowed to "inline" such values within classes that reference them. This means that if you change a static final variable you may have to recompile all code that uses that class (this is really the only case where you have to do that in Java). Static members are useful as flags and identifiers, which can be accessed from anywhere. They are especially useful for values needed in the construction of an instance itself. In our example, we might declare a number of static values to represent various kinds of Pendulum objects:

```
class Pendulum {
    ...
    static int SIMPLE = 0, ONE_SPRING = 1, TWO_SPRING = 2;
    ...
```

We might then use these flags in a method that sets the type of a Pendulum or, more likely, in a special constructor, as we'll discuss shortly:

```
Pendulum pendy = new Pendulum( );
pendy.setType( Pendulum.ONE_SPRING );
```

Again, inside the Pendulum class, we can use static members directly by name, as well; there's no need for the Pendulum. prefix:

```
class Pendulum {
    ...
    void resetEverything( ) {
        setType ( SIMPLE );
        ...
    }
    ...
}
```

Methods

Methods appear inside class bodies. They contain local variable declarations and other Java statements that are executed by a calling thread when the method is invoked. Method declarations in Java look like ANSI C-style function declarations with two restrictions: a method in Java always specifies a return type (there's no default). The returned value can be a primitive type, a reference type, or the type void, which indicates no returned value. Next, a method always has a fixed number of arguments. The combination of method overloading and true arrays reduces the need for a variable number of arguments, as offered in some languages.

Here's a simple example:

```
class Bird {
    int xPos, yPos;

    double fly ( int x, int y ) {
        double distance = Math.sqrt( x*x + y*y );
        flap( distance );
        xPos = x;
        yPos = y;
```

```
        return distance;
    }
    ...
}
```

In this example, the class Bird defines a method, fly(), that takes as arguments two integers: x and y. It returns a double type value as a result, using the return keyword.

Local Variables

The fly() method declares a local variable called distance, which it uses to compute the distance flown. A local variable is temporary; it exists only within the scope of its method. Local variables are allocated and initialized when a method is invoked; they are normally destroyed when the method returns. They can't be referenced from outside the method itself. If the method is executing concurrently in different threads, each thread has its own copies of the method's local variables. A method's arguments also serve as local variables within the scope of the method.

An object created within a method and assigned to a local variable may or may not persist after the method has returned. As with all objects in Java, it depends on whether any references to the object remain. If an object is created, assigned to a local variable, and never used anywhere else, that object is no longer referenced when the local variable is destroyed, so garbage collection removes the object. If, however, we assign the object to an instance variable, pass it as an argument to another method, or pass it back as a return value, it may be saved by another variable holding its reference. We'll discuss object creation and garbage collection in more detail shortly.

Shadowing

If a local variable and an instance variable have the same name, the local variable *shadows* or hides the name of the instance variable within the scope of the method. In the following example, the local variables xPos and yPos hide the instance variables of the same name:

```
class Bird {
    int xPos, yPos;
    int xNest, yNest;
    ...
    double flyToNest( ) {
        int xPos = xNest;
        int yPos = yNest:
        return ( fly( xPos, yPos ) );
    }
    ...
}
```

When we set the values of the local variables in flyToNest(), it has no effect on the values of the instance variables.

The "this" reference

You can use the special reference this any time you need to refer explicitly to the current object. Often you don't need to use this, because the reference to the current object is implicit; such is the case when using unambiguously named instance variables inside a class. But we can use this to refer explicitly to instance variables in our object, even if they are shadowed. The following example shows how we can use this to allow argument names that shadow instance variable names. This is a fairly common technique, because it saves your having to make up alternative names. Here's how we could implement our fly() method with shadowed variables:

```java
class Bird {
    int xPos, yPos;

    double fly ( int xPos, int yPos ) {
        double distance = Math.sqrt( xPos*xPos + yPos*yPos );
        flap( distance );
        this.xPos = xPos;
        this.yPos = yPos;
        return distance;
    }
    ...
}
```

In this example, the expression this.xPos refers to the instance variable xPos and assigns it the value of the local variable xPos, which would otherwise hide its name. The only reason we need to use this in the previous example is because we've used argument names that hide our instance variables, and we want to refer to the instance variables. You can also use the this reference any time you want to pass a reference to your object to some other method; we'll show examples of that later.

Static Methods

Static methods (class methods), like static variables, belong to the class and not to an individual instance of the class. What does this mean? Well, foremost, a static method lives outside of any particular class instance. It can be invoked by name, through the class name, without any objects around. Because it is not bound to a particular object instance, a static method can directly access only other static members of the class. It can't directly see any instance variables or call any instance methods, because to do so we'd have to ask, "on which instance?" Static methods can be called from instances, just like instance methods, but the important thing is that they can also be used independently.

Our fly() method uses a static method: Math.sqrt(), which is defined by the java.lang.Math class; we'll explore this class in detail in Chapter 10. For now, the important thing to note is that Math is the name of a class and not an instance of a Math object. (It so happens that you can't even make an instance of the Math class.) Because static methods can be invoked wherever the class name is available, class methods are closer to C-style functions. Static methods are particularly useful for utility methods that perform work that is useful either independently of instances or in creating instances. For example, in our `Bird` class, we could enumerate all types of birds that can be created:

```
class Bird {
    ...
    static String [] getBirdTypes( ) {
     String [] types;
     // Create list...
         return types;
    }
    ...
}
```

Here we've defined a static method getBirdTypes(), which returns an array of strings containing bird names. We can use getBirdTypes() from within an instance of `Bird`, just like an instance method. However, we can also call it from other classes, using the `Bird` class name as a reference:

```
String [] names = Bird.getBirdTypes( );
```

Perhaps a special version of the `Bird` class constructor accepts the name of a bird type. We could use this list to decide what kind of bird to create.

Static methods also play an important role in various design patterns, where you limit the use of the new operator for a class to one method, a static method called a *factory method*. We'll talk more about object construction later. But suffice it to say that it's common to see usage like this:

```
Bird bird = Bird.getBird( "pigeon" );
```

Initializing Local Variables

In the flyToNest() example, we made a point of initializing the local variables xPos and yPos. Unlike instance variables, local variables must be initialized before they can be used. It's a compile-time error to try to access a local variable without first assigning it a value:

```
void myMethod( ) {
    int foo = 42;
    int bar;

    bar += 1;  // compile-time error, bar uninitialized

    bar = 99;
    bar += 1;  // OK here
}
```

Notice that this doesn't imply local variables have to be initialized when declared, just that the first time they are referenced must be in an assignment. More subtle possibilities arise when making assignments inside conditionals:

```
void myMethod {
  int foo;
  if ( someCondition ) {
    foo = 42;
    ...
  }
  foo += 1;    // Compile-time error, foo may not be initialized
}
```

In this example, foo is initialized only if someCondition is true. The compiler doesn't let you make this wager, so it flags the use of foo as an error. We could correct this situation in several ways. We could initialize the variable to a default value in advance or move the usage inside the conditional. We could also make sure the path of execution doesn't reach the uninitialized variable through some other means, depending on what makes sense for our particular application. For example, we could return from the method abruptly:

```
int foo;
...
if ( someCondition ) {
    foo = 42;
    ...
} else
    return;

foo += 1;
```

In this case, there's no chance of reaching foo in an uninitialized state, so the compiler allows the use of foo after the conditional.

Why is Java so picky about local variables? One of the most common (and insidious) sources of errors in C or C++ is forgetting to initialize local variables, so Java tries to help us out. If it didn't, Java would suffer the same potential irregularities as C or C++.[*]

Argument Passing and References

Let's consider what happens when you pass arguments to a method. All primitive data types (e.g., int, char, float) are passed by value. By now you're probably used to the idea that reference types (i.e., any kind of object, including arrays and strings) are used through references. An important distinction is that the references themselves (the pointers to these objects) are actually primitive types and are passed by value too.

---

[*] As with malloc'ed storage in C or C++, Java objects and their instance variables are allocated on a heap, which allows them default values once, when they are created. Local variables, however, are allocated on the Java virtual machine stack. As with the stack in C and C++, failing to initialize these could mean successive method calls could receive garbage values, and program execution might be inconsistent or implementation-dependent.

Consider the following piece of code:

```
...
    int i = 0;
    SomeKindOfObject obj = new SomeKindOfObject( );
    myMethod( i, obj );
    ...
void myMethod(int j, SomeKindOfObject o) {
    ...
}
```

The first chunk of code calls myMethod(), passing it two arguments. The first argument, i, is passed by value; when the method is called, the value of i is copied into the method's parameter, j. If myMethod() changes the value of j, it's changing only its copy of the local variable.

In the same way, a copy of the reference to obj is placed into the reference variable o of myMethod(). Both references refer to the same object, so any changes made through either reference affect the actual (single) object instance. If we change the value of, say, o.size, the change is visible either as o.size (inside myMethod()) or as obj.size (in the calling method). However, if myMethod() changes the reference o itself—to point to another object—it's affecting only its local variable reference. It doesn't affect the caller's variable obj, which still refers to the original object. In this sense, passing the reference is like passing a pointer in C and unlike passing by reference in C++.

What if myMethod() needs to modify the calling method's notion of the obj reference as well (i.e., make obj point to a different object)? The easy way to do that is to wrap obj inside some kind of object. For example, we could wrap the object up as the lone element in an array:

```
SomeKindOfObject [] wrapper = new SomeKindOfObject [] { obj };
```

All parties could then refer to the object as wrapper[0] and would have the ability to change the reference. This is not aesthetically pleasing, but it does illustrate that what is needed is the level of indirection.

Another possibility is to use this to pass a reference to the calling object. In that case, the calling object serves as the wrapper for the reference. Let's look at a piece of code that could be from an implementation of a linked list:

```
class Element {
    public Element nextElement;

    void addToList( List list ) {
        list.addToList( this );
    }
}
class List {
    void addToList( Element element ) {
        ...
```

```
        element.nextElement = getNextElement( );
    }
}
```

Every element in a linked list contains a pointer to the next element in the list. In this code, the Element class represents one element; it includes a method for adding itself to the list. The List class itself contains a method for adding an arbitrary Element to the list. The method addToList() calls addToList() with the argument this (which is, of course, an Element). addToList() can use the this reference to modify the Element's nextElement instance variable. The same technique can be used in conjunction with interfaces to implement callbacks for arbitrary method invocations.

Method Overloading

Method overloading is the ability to define multiple methods with the same name in a class; when the method is invoked, the compiler picks the correct one based on the arguments passed to the method. This implies that overloaded methods must have different numbers or types of arguments. (In Chapter 6, we'll look at *method overriding*, which occurs when we declare methods with identical signatures in different classes.)

Method overloading (also called *ad-hoc polymorphism*) is a powerful and useful feature. The idea is to create methods that act in the same way on different types of arguments. This creates the illusion that a single method can operate on any of the types. The print() method in the standard PrintStream class is a good example of method overloading in action. As you've probably deduced by now, you can print a string representation of just about anything using this expression:

```
System.out.print( argument )
```

The variable out is a reference to an object (a PrintStream) that defines nine different, "overloaded" versions of the print() method. The versions take arguments of the following types: Object, String, char[], char, int, long, float, double, and boolean.

```
class PrintStream {
    void print( Object arg ) { ... }
    void print( String arg ) { ... }
    void print( char [] arg ) { ... }
    ...
}
```

You can invoke the print() method with any of these types as an argument, and it's printed in an appropriate way. In a language without method overloading, this requires something more cumbersome, such as a uniquely named method for printing each type of object. Then it's your responsibility to remember what method to use for each data type.

In the previous example, print() has been overloaded to support two reference types: Object and String. What if we try to call print() with some other reference type? Say, perhaps, a Date object? When there's not an exact type match, the compiler searches for an acceptable, *assignable* match. Since Date, like all classes, is a subclass of Object, a Date object can be assigned to a variable of type Object. It's therefore an acceptable match, and the Object method is selected.

What if there's more than one possible match? Say, for example, we tried to print a subclass of String called MyString. (The String class is final, so it can't be subclassed, but please allow this brief transgression for purposes of explanation.) MyString is assignable to either String or to Object. Here the compiler makes a determination as to which match is "better" and selects that method. In this case, it's the String method.

The intuitive explanation is that the String class is closer to MyString in the inheritance hierarchy. It is a *more specific* match. A more rigorous way of specifying it would be to say that a given method is more specific than another method if the argument types of the first method are all assignable to the argument types of the second method. In this case, the String method is more specific to a subclass of String than the Object method because type String is assignable to type Object. The reverse is not true.

If you're paying close attention, you may have noticed we said that the compiler resolves overloaded methods. Method overloading is not something that happens at runtime; this is an important distinction. It means that the selected method is chosen once, when the code is compiled. Once the overloaded method is selected, the choice is fixed until the code is recompiled, even if the class containing the called method is later revised and an even more specific overloaded method is added. This is in contrast to *overridden* methods, which are located at runtime and can be found even if they didn't exist when the calling class was compiled. We'll talk about method overriding later in the chapter.

One last note about overloading. In earlier chapters, we've pointed out that Java doesn't support programmer-defined overloaded operators and that + is the only system-defined overloaded operator. If you've been wondering what an overloaded operator is, we can finally clear up that mystery. In a language like C++, you can customize operators such as + and * to work with objects that you create. For example, you could create a class Complex that implements complex numbers and then overload methods corresponding to + and * to add and multiply Complex objects. Some people argue that operator overloading makes for elegant and readable programs, while others say it's just "syntactic sugar" that makes for obfuscated code. The Java designers clearly espoused the latter opinion when they chose not to support programmer-defined overloaded operators.

Object Creation

Objects in Java are allocated on a system "heap" memory space, much like that in C or C++. Unlike in C or C++, however, we needn't manage that memory ourselves. Java takes care of memory allocation and deallocation for you. Java explicitly allocates storage for an object when you create it with the new operator. More importantly, objects are removed by garbage collection when they're no longer referenced.

Constructors

Objects are allocated with the new operator using an *object constructor*. A constructor is a special method with the same name as its class and no return type. It's called when a new class instance is created, which gives the class an opportunity to set up the object for use. Constructors, like other methods, can accept arguments and can be overloaded (they are not, however, inherited like other methods; we'll discuss inheritance in Chapter 6).

```
class Date {
    long time;

    Date( ) {
        time = currentTime( );
    }

    Date( String date ) {
        time = parseDate( date );
    }
    ...
}
```

In this example, the class Date has two constructors. The first takes no arguments; it's known as the *default constructor*. Default constructors play a special role: if we don't define any constructors for a class, an empty default constructor is supplied for us. The default constructor is what gets called whenever you create an object by calling its constructor with no arguments. Here we have implemented the default constructor so that it sets the instance variable time by calling a hypothetical method, currentTime(), which resembles the functionality of the real java.util.Date class. The second constructor takes a String argument. Presumably, this String contains a string representation of the time that can be parsed to set the time variable. Given the constructors in the previous example, we create a Date object in the following ways:

```
Date now = new Date( );
Date christmas = new Date("Dec 25, 2002");
```

In each case, Java chooses the appropriate constructor at compile time based on the rules for overloaded method selection.

If we later remove all references to an allocated object, it'll be garbage-collected, as we'll discuss shortly:

```
christmas = null;          // fair game for the garbage collector
```

Setting this reference to null means it's no longer pointing to the "Dec 25, 2002" object. (So would setting christmas to any other value.) Unless that object is referenced by another variable, it's now inaccessible and can be garbage-collected.

A few more notes: constructors can't be declared abstract, synchronized, or final (we'll define the rest of those terms later). Constructors can, however, be declared with the visibility modifiers public, private, or protected to control their accessibility. We'll talk in detail about visibility modifiers in the next chapter.

Working with Overloaded Constructors

A constructor can refer to another constructor in the same class or the immediate superclass using special forms of the this and super references. We'll discuss the first case here, and return to that of the superclass constructor after we have talked more about subclassing and inheritance. A constructor can invoke another, overloaded constructor in its class using the reference this() with appropriate arguments to select the desired constructor. If a constructor calls another constructor, it must do so as its first statement:

```
class Car {
    String model;
    int doors;

    Car( String m, int d ) {
        model = m;
        doors = d;
        // other, complicated setup
        ...
    }

    Car( String m ) {
        this( m, 4 );
    }
    ...
}
```

In this example, the class Car has two constructors. The first, more explicit one, accepts arguments specifying the car's model and its number of doors. The second constructor takes just the model as an argument and, in turn, calls the first constructor with a default value of four doors. The advantage of this approach is that you can have a single constructor do all the complicated setup work; other auxiliary constructors simply feed the appropriate arguments to that constructor.

The call to this() must appear as the first statement in our second constructor. The syntax is restricted in this way because there's a need to identify a clear chain of command in the calling of constructors. At one end of the chain, Java invokes the constructor of the superclass (if we don't do it explicitly) to ensure that inherited members are initialized properly before we proceed.

There's also a point in the chain, just after the constructor of the superclass is invoked, where the initializers of the current class's instance variables are evaluated. Before that point, we can't even reference the instance variables of our class. We'll explain this situation again in complete detail after we have talked about inheritance.

For now, all you need to know is that you can invoke a second constructor only as the first statement of another constructor. For example, the following code is illegal and causes a compile-time error:

```
Car( String m ) {
    int doors = determineDoors( );
    this( m, doors );   // Error: constructor call
                        // must be first statement
}
```

The simple model name constructor can't do any additional setup before calling the more explicit constructor. It can't even refer to an instance member for a constant value:

```
class Car {
    ...
    final int default_doors = 4;
    ...

    Car( String m ) {
        this( m, default_doors ); // Error: referencing
                                  // uninitialized variable
    }
    ...
}
```

The instance variable defaultDoors is not initialized until a later point in the chain of constructor calls, so the compiler doesn't let us access it yet. Fortunately, we can solve this particular problem by using a static variable instead of an instance variable:

```
class Car {
    ...
    static final int DEFAULT_DOORS = 4;
    ...

    Car( String m ) {
        this( m, DEFAULT_DOORS );  // Okay now
    }
    ...
}
```

The static members of a class are initialized when the class is first loaded, so it's safe to access them in a constructor.

Static and Nonstatic Initializer Blocks

It's possible to declare a block of code (some statements within curly braces) directly within the scope of a class. This code block doesn't belong to any method; instead, it's executed once, at the time the object is constructed, or, in the case of a code block marked static, at the time the class is loaded. These blocks can be used to do additional setup for the class or an object instance and are sometimes called initializer blocks.

Instance initializer blocks can be thought of as extensions of instance variable initialization. They're called at the time the instance variable's initializers are evaluated (after superclass construction), in the order that they appear in the Java source:

```
class MyClass {
    Properties myProps = new Properties( );
    // set up myProps
    {
        myProps.put("foo", "bar");
        myProps.put("boo", "gee");
    }
    int a = 5;
    ...
```

Normally this kind of setup could be done just as well in the object's constructor. A notable exception is in the case of an anonymous inner class (see Chapter 6).

Similarly, you can use static initializer blocks to set up static class members. This allows the static members of a class to have complex initialization just like objects do with constructors:

```
class ColorWheel {
    static Hashtable colors = new Hashtable( );

    // set up colors
    static {
        colors.put("Red", Color.red );
        colors.put("Green", Color.green );
        colors.put("Blue", Color.blue );
        ...
    }
    ...
}
```

The class ColorWheel provides a variable colors that maps the names of colors to Color objects in a Hashtable. The first time the class ColorWheel is referenced and loaded, the static components of ColorWheel are evaluated, in the order they appear in the source. In this case, the static code block simply adds elements to the colors Hashtable.

Object Destruction

Now that we've seen how to create objects, it's time to talk about their destruction. If you're accustomed to programming in C or C++, you've probably spent time hunting down memory leaks in your code. Java takes care of object destruction for you; you don't have to worry about memory leaks, and you can concentrate on more important programming tasks.

Garbage Collection

Java uses a technique known as *garbage collection* to remove objects that are no longer needed. The garbage collector is Java's grim reaper. It lingers, usually in a low-priority thread, stalking objects and awaiting their demise. It finds them and watches them, periodically counting references to them to see when their time has come. When all references to an object are gone, and it's no longer accessible, the garbage-collection mechanism declares the object *unreachable* and reclaims its space back to the available pool of resources. An unreachable object is one that cannot be found through any references in the running application.

There are many different algorithms for garbage collection; the Java virtual machine architecture doesn't require a particular scheme. It's worth noting, however, by way of example, how some implementations of Java accomplish this task. Under a scheme called "mark and sweep," Java first walks through the tree of all accessible object references and marks them as alive. Then Java scans the heap looking for identifiable objects that aren't marked. In this scenario, Java is able to find objects on the heap because they are stored in a characteristic way and have a particular signature of bits in their handles unlikely to be reproduced naturally. This kind of algorithm doesn't become confused by the problem of cyclic references, in which detached objects can mutually reference each other and appear alive (and that behavior is guaranteed by Java). It did, however, slow Java's execution and so in Java 1.3, Sun implemented a new garbage collection method.

As of Java 1.3, garbage collection effectively runs continuously in a very efficient way that should never cause a significant delay in execution. Java garbage collectors use state-of-the-art techniques to balance efficiency of collection with performance and to minimize interruption of your application. The improvement in Java's garbage collection since the early releases has been remarkable and is one of the reasons that Java is now competitive with traditional compiled languages in terms of speed.

In general you do not have to concern yourself with the garbage-collection process. But there is one method that can be useful for debugging. You can prompt the garbage collector to make a sweep explicitly by invoking the System.gc() method. This method is somewhat implementation-dependent but could be used if you want to guarantee that Java has cleaned up before you do some activity.

Finalization

Before an object is removed by garbage collection, its `finalize()` method is invoked to give it a last opportunity to clean up its act and free other kinds of resources it may be holding. While the garbage collector can reclaim memory resources, it may not take care of things such as closing files and terminating network connections as gracefully or efficiently as could your code. That's what the `finalize()` method is for. An object's `finalize()` method is called once and only once before the object is garbage-collected. However, there's no guarantee when that will happen. Garbage collection may, in theory, never run on a system that is not short of memory. It is also interesting to note that finalization and collection occur in two distinct phases of the garbage-collection process. First items are finalized; then they are collected. It is therefore possible that finalization can (intentionally or unintentionally) create a lingering reference to the object in question, postponing its garbage collection. The object is, of course, subject to collection later, if the reference goes away, but its `finalize()` method isn't called again.

The `finalize()` methods of superclasses are not invoked automatically for you. If you need to invoke the finalization routine of your parent classes, you should invoke the `finalize()` method of your superclass, using `super.finalize()`. We discuss inheritance and overridden methods in Chapter 6.

Weak and Soft References

In general, as we've described, Java's garbage collector reclaims objects when they are unreachable. An unreachable object, again, is one that is no longer referenced by any variables within your application, one that is not reachable through any chain of references by any running thread. Such an object cannot be used by the application any longer and is therefore a clear case where the object should be removed.

There are, however, situations where it is advantageous to have Java's garbage collector work with your application to decide when it is time to remove a particular object. For these cases, Java allows you to hold an object reference indirectly through a special wrapper object, a type of `java.lang.ref.Reference`. If Java then decides to remove the object, the reference the wrapper holds turns to `null` automatically. But while the reference exists, you may continue to use it in the ordinary way and if you wish, assign it elsewhere (using normal references), preventing its garbage collection.

There are two types of `Reference` wrappers that implement different schemes for deciding when to let their target references be garbage-collected. The first is called a `WeakReference`. Weak references are eligible for garbage collection immediately; they do not prevent garbage collection the way that ordinary "strong" references do. This means that if you have a combination of strong references and references contained in `WeakReference` wrappers in your application, the garbage collector waits until only `WeakReferences` remain and then collects the object. This is an essential feature that allows garbage collection to work with certain kinds of caching schemes. Often you'll want to cache an object reference for performance (to avoid creating it or looking it up). But unless you take specific action to remove unneeded objects from your cache, the cache keeps those objects alive forever by maintaining live references to them. By using weak references, you can implement a cache that automatically throws away references when the object would normally be garbage-collected. In fact, an implementation of HashMap called WeakHashMap is provided that does just this (see Chapter 10 for details).

The second type of reference wrapper is called SoftReference. A soft reference is similar to a weak reference, but it tells the garbage collector to be less aggressive about reclaiming its contents. Soft-referenced objects are collected only when and if Java runs short of memory. This is useful for a slightly different kind of caching where you want to keep some content around unless there is a need to get rid of it. For example, a web browser can use soft references to cache images or HTML strings internally, thus keeping them around as long as possible until memory constraints come into play. (A more sophisticated application might also use its own scheme based on "least recently used" marking of some kind.)

The java.lang.ref package contains the WeakReference and SoftReference wrappers, as well as a facility called ReferenceQueue that allows your application to receive a list of references that have been collected. It's important that your application use the queue or some other checking mechanism to remove the Reference objects themselves after their contents have been collected; otherwise your cache will soon fill up with empty Reference object wrappers.

## CHAPTER 6

Relationships Among Classes

So far, in our exploration of Java we have seen how to create Java classes and objects, which are instances of those classes. But by themselves objects would be little more than a convention for organizing code. It is in the relationships between objects—their connections and privileges with respect to one another—that the power of an object-oriented language is really expressed.

That's what we'll cover in this chapter. In particular, we'll be looking at several kinds of relationships:

Inheritance relationships
> How a class inherits methods and variables from its parent class

Interfaces
> How to declare that a class supports certain behavior and define a type to refer to that behavior

Packaging
> How to organize objects into logical groups

Inner classes
> A generalization of classes that lets you nest a class definition inside another class definition

Subclassing and Inheritance

Classes in Java exist in a hierarchy. A class in Java can be declared as a *subclass* of another class using the extends keyword. A subclass *inherits* variables and methods from its *superclass* and can use them as if they were declared within the subclass itself:

```
class Animal {
    float weight;
    ...
    void eat( ) {
        ...
```

```
    }
    ...
}

class Mammal extends Animal {
    int heartRate;
    // inherits weight
    ...
    void breathe( ) {
        ...
    }
    // inherits eat( )
}
```

In this example, an object of type Mammal has both the instance variable weight and the method eat(). They are inherited from Animal.

A class can extend only one other class. To use the proper terminology, Java allows *single inheritance* of class implementation. Later in this chapter we'll talk about interfaces, which take the place of *multiple inheritance* as it's primarily used in C++.

A subclass can be further subclassed. Normally, subclassing specializes or refines a class by adding variables and methods (you cannot remove or hide variables or methods by subclassing). For example:

```
class Cat extends Mammal {
    boolean longHair;
    // inherits weight and heartRate
    ...
    void purr( ) {
        ...
    }
    // inherits eat( ) and breathe( )
}
```

The Cat class is a type of Mammal that is ultimately a type of Animal. Cat objects inherit all the characteristics of Mammal objects and, in turn, Animal objects. Cat also provides additional behavior in the form of the purr() method and the longHair variable. We can denote the class relationship in a diagram, as shown in Figure 6-1.

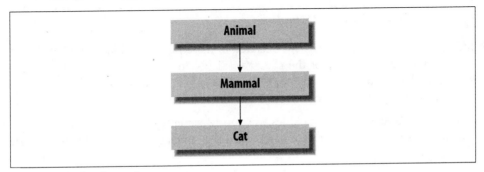

Figure 6-1. A class hierarchy

A subclass inherits all members of its superclass not designated as private. As we'll discuss shortly, other levels of visibility affect what inherited members of the class can be seen from outside of the class and its subclasses, but at a minimum, a subclass always has the same set of visible members as its parent. For this reason, the type of a subclass can be considered a *subtype* of its parent, and instances of the subtype can be used anywhere instances of the supertype are allowed. Consider the following example:

```
Cat simon = new Cat( );
Animal creature = simon;
```

The Cat instance simon in this example can be assigned to the Animal type variable creature because Cat is a subtype of Animal.

Shadowed Variables

In the section "Methods" in Chapter 5, we saw that a local variable of the same name as an instance variable *shadows* (hides) the instance variable. Similarly, an instance variable in a subclass can shadow an instance variable of the same name in its parent class, as shown in Figure 6-2.

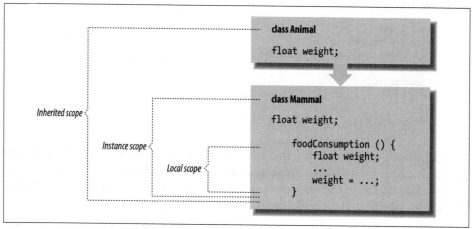

Figure 6-2. The scope of shadowed variables

In Figure 6-2, the variable weight is declared in three places: as a local variable in the method foodConsumption() of the class Mammal, as an instance variable of the class Mammal, and as an instance variable of the class Animal. The actual variable selected depends on the scope in which we are working.

In the previous example, all variables were of the same type. Just about the only reason to declare a variable with the same type in a subclass is to provide an alternate initializer.

A more important use of shadowed variables involves changing their types. We could, for example, shadow an int variable with a double variable in a subclass that needs decimal values instead of integer values. We can do this without changing the existing code because, as its name suggests, when we shadow variables, we don't replace them but instead mask them. Both variables still exist; methods of the superclass see the original variable, and methods of the subclass see the new version. The determination of what variables the various methods see occurs at compile time.

Here's a simple example:

```
class IntegerCalculator {
    int sum;
    ...
}

class DecimalCalculator extends IntegerCalculator {
    double sum;
    ...
}
```

In this example, we shadow the instance variable sum to change its type from int to double.* Methods defined in the class IntegerCalculator see the integer variable sum, while methods defined in DecimalCalculator see the floating-point variable sum. However, both variables actually exist for a given instance of DecimalCalculator, and they can have independent values. In fact, any methods that DecimalCalculator inherits from IntegerCalculator actually see the integer variable sum.

Since both variables exist in DecimalCalculator, we need to reference the variable inherited from IntegerCalculator. We do that using the super reference:

```
int s = super.sum;
```

Inside of DecimalCalculator, the super keyword used in this manner refers to the sum variable defined in the superclass. We'll explain the use of super more fully in a bit.

Another important point about shadowed variables has to do with how they work when we refer to an object by way of a less derived type. For example, we can refer to a DecimalCalculator object as an IntegerCalculator. If we do so and then access the variable sum, we get the integer variable, not the decimal one:

```
DecimalCalculator dc = new DecimalCalculator( );
IntegerCalculator ic = dc;

int s = ic.sum;        // accesses IntegerCalculator sum
```

After this detailed explanation, you may still be wondering what shadowed variables are good for. Well, to be honest, the usefulness of shadowed variables is limited, but

---

* Note that a better way to design our calculators would be to have an abstract Calculator class with two subclasses: IntegerCalculator and DecimalCalculator.

it's important to understand the concepts before we talk about doing the same thing with methods. We'll see a different and more dynamic type of behavior with method shadowing, or to use the correct terminology, *method overriding*.

Overriding Methods

In Chapter 5, we saw that we could declare *overloaded methods* (i.e., methods with the same name but a different number or type of arguments) within a class. Overloaded method selection works in the way we described on all methods available to a class, including inherited ones. This means that a subclass can define some overloaded methods that augment the overloaded methods provided by a superclass.

But a subclass can do more than that; it can define a method that has exactly the *same* method signature (arguments and return type) as a method in its superclass. In that case, the method in the subclass *overrides* the method in the superclass and effectively replaces its implementation, as shown in Figure 6-3. Overriding methods to change the behavior of objects is called *subtype polymorphism*. It's the usage most people think of when they talk about the power of object-oriented languages.

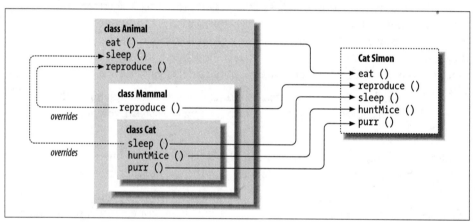

Figure 6-3. Method overriding

In Figure 6-3, Mammal overrides the reproduce() method of Animal, perhaps to specialize the method for the peculiar behavior of mammals' giving live birth.[*] The Cat object's sleeping behavior is also overridden to be different from that of a general Animal, perhaps to accommodate cat naps. The Cat class also adds the more unique behaviors of purring and hunting mice.

From what you've seen so far, overridden methods probably look like they shadow methods in superclasses, just as variables do. But overridden methods are actually

---

[*] We'll ignore the platypus, which is an obscure nonovoviviparous mammal.

more powerful than that. When there are multiple implementations of a method in the inheritance hierarchy of an object, the one in the "most derived" class (the lowest one in the hierarchy) always overrides the others, even if we refer to the object by way of a less derived type.*

For example, if we have a Cat instance assigned to a variable of the more general type Animal, and we call its sleep() method, we still get the sleep() method implemented in the Cat class, not the one in Animal:

```
Cat simon = new Cat( );
Animal creature = simon;
    ...
creature.sleep( );        // accesses Cat sleep( );
```

In other words, a Cat acts like a Cat, regardless of whether you know specifically that you have that kind of animal or not. In other respects, the variable creature looks like an Animal. For example, access to a shadowed variable would find the implementation in the Animal class, not the Cat class. However, because methods are searched for in subclasses first, the appropriate method in the Cat class can be located, even though we are dealing with an Animal object. This means we can deal with specialized objects as if they were more general types of objects and still take advantage of their specialized implementations of behavior.

One note before we move on: A common programming error in Java is to accidentally overload a method when trying to override it. Any difference in the number or type of arguments produces two overloaded methods instead of a single, overridden method. Make it a habit to look twice when overriding methods.

Overridden methods and dynamic binding

In a previous section, we mentioned that *overloaded* methods are selected by the compiler at compile time. *Overridden* methods, on the other hand, are selected dynamically at runtime. Even if we create an instance of a subclass, our code has never seen before (perhaps a new object type loaded from the network), any overriding methods that it contains are located and used at runtime, replacing those that existed when we last compiled our code.

In contrast, if we load a new class that implements an additional, more specific overloaded method, our code continues to use the implementation it discovered at compile time. Another effect of this is that casting (i.e., explicitly telling the compiler to treat an object as one of its assignable types) affects the selection of overloaded methods but not overridden methods.

---

* An overridden method in Java acts like a virtual method in C++.

Static method binding

Static methods don't belong to any object instance; they are accessed directly through a class name, so they are not dynamically selected at runtime like instance methods. That is why static methods are called "static";they are always bound at compile time.

A static method in a superclass can be shadowed by another static method in a subclass, as long as the original method was not declared final. However, you can't override a static method with a non-static method. In other words, you can't change a static method in a superclass into an instance method in a subclass.

final methods and performance

In languages like C++, the default is for methods to act like shadowed variables, so you have to declare explicitly the methods you want to be dynamic (or, as C++ terms them, *virtual*). In Java, instance methods are, by default, dynamic. But you can use the final modifier to declare that an instance method can't be overridden in a subclass, and it won't be subject to dynamic binding.

We have seen final used with variables to effectively make them constants. When applied to a method, final means that its implementation is constant; no overriding allowed. final can also be applied to an entire class, which means the class can't be subclassed.

In the old days, dynamic method binding came with a significant performance penalty, and some people are still inclined to use the final modifier to guard against this. But runtime systems such as Sun's HotSpot should eliminate the need for this kind of fudging. A profiling runtime can determine which methods are not being overridden and "optimistically" inline them, treating them as if they were final until it becomes necessary to do otherwise.

Compiler optimizations

In some versions of Java, the *javac* compiler can be run with a -0 switch, which tells it to perform certain optimizations. With optimizations turned on, the compiler can inline final methods to improve performance (while slightly increasing the size of the resulting class file). private methods, which are effectively final, can also be inlined, and final classes may also benefit from more powerful optimizations. Note that the -0 compiler switch will probably gradually go away in favor of smarter runtime systems. We mention it here mainly for completeness.

Another kind of optimization allows you to include debugging code in your Java source without a size penalty. Java doesn't have a preprocessor to explicitly control what source is included, but you can get some of the same effects by making a block of code conditional on a constant (i.e., static and final) variable. The Java compiler is smart enough to remove this code when it determines that it won't be called. For example:

```
static final boolean DEBUG = false;
...
final void debug (String message) {
    if (DEBUG) {
        System.err.println(message);
        // do other stuff
        ...
    }
}
```

In this case, the compiler can recognize that the condition on the DEBUG variable is always false, and the body of the debug() method will be optimized away. But that's not all: because debug() itself is also final, it can be inlined, and an empty inlined method generates no code at all. So when we compile with DEBUG set to false, calls to the debug() method generate no residual code at all.

Method selection revisited

By now you should have a good, intuitive feel for how methods are selected from the pool of potentially overloaded and overridden method names of a class. If, however, you are dying for a dry definition, we'll provide one now. If you are satisfied with your understanding, you may wish to skip this little exercise in logic.

In a previous section, we offered an inductive rule for overloaded method resolution. It said that a method is considered more specific than another if its arguments are assignable to the arguments of the second method. We can now expand this rule to include the resolution of overridden methods by adding the following condition: to be more specific than another method, the type of the class containing the method must also be assignable to the type of the class holding the second method.

What does that mean? Well, the only classes whose types are assignable are classes in the same inheritance hierarchy. So, what we're talking about now is the set of all methods of the same name in a class or any of its parent or child classes. Since sub-class types are assignable to superclass types, but not vice versa, the resolution is pushed, in the way that we expect, down the chain, toward the subclasses. This effectively adds a second dimension to the search, in which resolution is pushed down the inheritance tree towards more refined classes and, simultaneously, toward the most specific overloaded method within a given class.

Exceptions and overridden methods

When we talked about exception handling in Chapter 4, we didn't mention an important restriction that applies when you override a method. When you override a method, the new method (the overriding method) must adhere to the throws clause of the method it overrides. In other words, if an overridden method declares that it can throw an exception, the overriding method must also specify that it can throw the same kind of exception or a subtype of that exception. By allowing the exception to be a subtype of the one specified by the parent, the overriding method can refine the type of exception thrown to go along with its new behavior. For example:

```
class MeatInedibleException extends InedibleException {
    ...
}

class Animal {
    void eat( Food f ) throws InedibleException {
        ...
    }
}
class Herbivore extends Animal {
    void eat( Food f ) throws InedibleException {
        if ( f instanceof Meat )
            throw new MeatInedibleException( );
        ...
    }
}
```

In this code, Animal specifies that it can throw an InedibleException from its eat() method. Herbivore is a subclass of Animal, so its eat() method must also be able to throw an InedibleException. However, Herbivore's eat() method actually throws a more specific exception: MeatInedibleException. It can do this because MeatInedibleException is a subtype of InedibleException (remember that exceptions are classes, too). Our calling code's catch clause can therefore be more specific:

```
Animal creature = ...
try {
    creature.eat( food );
} catch ( MeatInedibleException ) {
    // creature can't eat this food because it's meat
} catch ( InedibleException ) {
    // creature can't eat this food
}
```

However, if we don't care why the food is inedible, we're free to catch InedibleException alone because a MeatInedibleException is also an InedibleException.

 The eat() method in the Herbivore class could have declared that it throws a MeatInedibleException, not a plain old InedibleException. But it should do so only if it throws this subtype of the exception (if eating meat is the only cause of herbivore indigestion).

Special References: this and super

The special references this and super allow you to refer to the members of the current object instance or to members of the superclass, respectively. We have seen this used elsewhere to pass a reference to the current object and to refer to shadowed instance variables. The reference super does the same for the parents of a class. You can use it to refer to members of a superclass that have been shadowed or overridden. A common arrangement is for an overriding method in a subclass to do some preliminary work and then defer to the overridden method of the superclass to finish the job:

```
class Animal {
    void eat( Food f ) throws InedibleException {
        // consume food
    }
}

class Herbivore extends Animal {
    void eat( Food f ) throws MeatInedibleException {
        // check if edible
        ...
        super.eat( f );
    }
}
```

In this example, our Herbivore class overrides the Animal eat() method to first do some checking on the food object. After doing its job, it uses super.eat() to call the (otherwise overridden) implementation of eat() in its superclass.

super prompts a search for the method or variable to begin in the scope of the immediate superclass rather than the current class. The inherited method or variable found may reside in the immediate superclass or in a more distant one. The usage of the super reference when applied to overridden methods of a superclass is special; it tells the method resolution system to stop the dynamic method search at the superclass instead of at the most derived class (as it otherwise does). Without super, there would be no way to access overridden methods.

Casting

A *cast* explicitly tells the compiler to change the apparent type of an object reference. In Java (unlike C++), casts are checked both at compile time and at runtime to make sure they are legal. Attempting to cast an object to an incompatible type at runtime results in a ClassCastException. Only casts between objects in the same inheritance hierarchy (and as we'll see later, to appropriate interfaces) are legal in Java and pass the scrutiny of the compiler and the runtime system.

Casts in Java affect only the treatment of references; they never change the form of the actual object. This is an important rule to keep in mind. You never change the object pointed to by a reference by casting it; you change only the compiler's (or runtime system's) notion of it.

A cast can be used to *narrow* the type of a reference—to make it more specific. Often, we'll do this when we have to retrieve an object from a more general type of collection or when it has been previously used as a less derived type. (The prototypical example is using an object in a Vector or Hashtable, as you'll see in Chapter 10.) Continuing with our Cat example:

```
Animal creature;
Cat simon;
// ...

creature = simon;        // OK
// simon = creature;      // Compile time error, incompatible type
simon = (Cat)creature;    // OK
```

We can't reassign the reference in creature to the variable simon even though we know it holds an instance of a Cat (Simon). We have to perform the indicated cast. This is called *downcasting* the reference.

Note that an implicit cast was performed when we went the other way to *widen* the reference simon to type Animal during the first assignment. In this case, an explicit cast would have been legal but superfluous.

If casting seems complicated, here's a simple way to think about it. Basically, you can't lie about what an object is. If you have a Cat object, you can cast it to a less derived type (i.e., a type above it in the class hierarchy) such as Animal or even Object, because all Java classes are a subclass of Object. If you have an Object you know is a Cat, you can downcast the Object to be an Animal or a Cat. However, if you aren't sure if the Object is a Cat or a Dog at runtime, you should check it with instanceof before you perform the cast. If you get the cast wrong, the runtime system throws a ClassCastException.

As we mentioned earlier, casting can affect the selection of compile-time items such as variables and overloaded methods, but not the selection of overridden methods. Figure 6-4 shows the difference. As shown in the top half of the diagram, casting the reference simon to type Animal (widening it) affects the selection of the shadowed variable weight within it. However, as the lower half of the diagram indicates, the cast doesn't affect the selection of the overridden method sleep().

Using Superclass Constructors

When we talked earlier about constructors, we discussed how the special statement this() invokes an overloaded constructor upon entry to another constructor. Similarly, the statement super() explicitly invokes the constructor of a superclass. Of course, we also talked about how Java makes a chain of constructor calls that includes the superclass's constructor, so why use super() explicitly? When Java makes an implicit call to the superclass constructor, it calls the default constructor. So, if we want to invoke a superclass constructor that takes arguments, we have to do so explicitly using super().

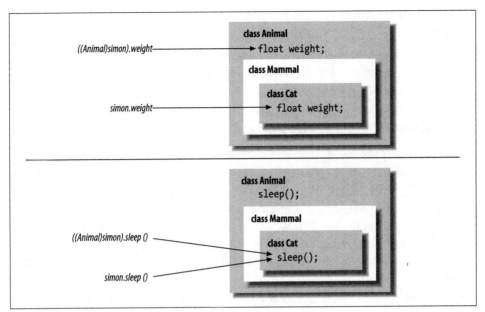

Figure 6-4. Casting and selection of methods and variables

If we are going to call a superclass constructor with super(), it must be the first statement of our constructor, just as this() must be the first call we make in an overloaded constructor. Here's a simple example:

```
class Person {
    Person ( String name ) {
        //  setup based on name
        ...
    }
    ...
}

class Doctor extends Person {
    Doctor ( String name, String specialty ) {
        super( name );
        // setup based on specialty
        ...
    }
    ...
}
```

In this example, we use super() to take advantage of the implementation of the superclass constructor and avoid duplicating the code to set up the object based on its name. In fact, because the class Person doesn't define a default (no arguments) constructor, we have no choice but to call super() explicitly. Otherwise, the compiler would complain that it couldn't find an appropriate default constructor to call. In other words, if you subclass a class whose constructors all take arguments, you have to invoke one of the superclass's constructors explicitly from your subclass constructor.

Instance variables of the class are initialized upon return from the superclass constructor, whether that's due to an explicit call to super() or an implicit call to the default superclass constructor.

Full Disclosure: Constructors and Initialization

We can now tell the full story of how constructors are chained together and when instance variable initialization occurs. The rule has three parts and is applied repeatedly for each successive constructor invoked.

- If the first statement of a constructor is an ordinary statement—i.e., not a call to this() or super()—Java inserts an implicit call to super() to invoke the default constructor of the superclass. Upon returning from that call, Java initializes the instance variables of the current class and proceeds to execute the statements of the current constructor.

- If the first statement of a constructor is a call to a superclass constructor via super(), Java invokes the selected superclass constructor. Upon its return, Java initializes the current class's instance variables and proceeds with the statements of the current constructor.

- If the first statement of a constructor is a call to an overloaded constructor via this(), Java invokes the selected constructor, and upon its return, simply proceeds with the statements of the current constructor. The call to the superclass's constructor has happened within the overloaded constructor, either explicitly or implicitly, so the initialization of instance variables has already occurred.

Abstract Methods and Classes

A method in Java can be declared with the abstract modifier to indicate that it's just a prototype. An abstract method has no body; it's simply a signature declaration followed by a semicolon. You can't directly use a class that contains an abstract method; you must instead create a subclass that implements the abstract method's body.

```
abstract void vaporMethod( String name );
```

In Java, a class that contains one or more abstract methods must be explicitly declared as an abstract class, also using the abstract modifier:

```
abstract class vaporClass {
    ...
    abstract void vaporMethod( String name );
    ...
}
```

An abstract class can contain other nonabstract methods and ordinary variable declarations, but it can't be instantiated. To be used, it must be subclassed, and its abstract methods must be overridden with methods that implement a body. Not all abstract methods have to be implemented in a single subclass, but a subclass that doesn't override all its superclass's abstract methods with actual, concrete implementations must also be declared `abstract`.

Abstract classes provide a framework for classes that are to be "filled in" by the implementer. The `java.io.InputStream` class, for example, has a single abstract method called `read()`. Various subclasses of `InputStream` implement `read()` in their own ways to read from their own sources. The rest of the `InputStream` class, however, provides extended functionality built on the simple `read()` method. A subclass of `InputStream` inherits these nonabstract methods to provide functionality based on the simple `read()` method that the subclass implements.

Interfaces

Java expands on the concept of abstract methods with *interfaces*. It's often desirable to specify a group of abstract methods defining some behavior for an object without tying it to any implementation at all. In Java, this is called an *interface*. An interface defines a set of methods that a class must implement. A class in Java can declare that it *implements* an interface if it implements the required methods. Unlike extending an abstract class, a class implementing an interface doesn't have to inherit from any particular part of the inheritance hierarchy or use a particular implementation.

Interfaces are kind of like Boy Scout or Girl Scout merit badges. A scout who has learned to build a birdhouse can walk around wearing a little sleeve patch with a picture of one. This says to the world, "I know how to build a birdhouse." Similarly, an *interface* is a list of methods that define some set of behavior for an object. Any class that implements each method listed in the interface can declare at compile time that it implements the interface and wear, as its merit badge, an extra type—the interface's type.

Interface types act like class types. You can declare variables to be of an interface type, you can declare arguments of methods to accept interface types, and you can specify that the return type of a method is an interface type. In each case, what is meant is that any object that implements the interface (i.e., wears the right merit badge) can fill that role. In this sense, interfaces are orthogonal to the class hierarchy. They cut across the boundaries of what kind of object an item *is* and deal with it only in terms of what it can *do*. A class can implement as many interfaces as it desires. In this way, interfaces in Java replace much of the need for multiple inheritance in other languages (and all its messy complications).

An interface looks, essentially, like a purely abstract class (i.e., a class with only abstract methods). You define an interface with the interface keyword and list its methods with no bodies, just prototypes (signatures):

```
interface Driveable {
    boolean startEngine( );
    void stopEngine( );
    float accelerate( float acc );
    boolean turn( Direction dir );
}
```

The previous example defines an interface called Driveable with four methods. It's acceptable, but not necessary, to declare the methods in an interface with the abstract modifier; we haven't done that here. More importantly, the methods of an interface are always considered public, and you can optionally declare them as so. Why public? Well, the user of the interface wouldn't necessarily be able to see them otherwise, and interfaces are generally intended to describe the behavior of an object, not its implementation.

Interfaces define capabilities, so it's common to name interfaces after their capabilities. Driveable, Runnable, and Updateable are good interface names. Any class that implements all the methods can then declare it implements the interface by using a special implements clause in its class definition. For example:

```
class Automobile implements Driveable {
    ...
    public boolean startEngine( ) {
        if ( notTooCold )
            engineRunning = true;
        ...
    }

    public void stopEngine( ) {
        engineRunning = false;
    }

    public float accelerate( float acc ) {
        ...
    }

    public boolean turn( Direction dir ) {
        ...
    }
    ...
}
```

Here, the class Automobile implements the methods of the Driveable interface and declares itself Driveable using the implements keyword.

As shown in Figure 6-5, another class, such as Lawnmower, can also implement the Driveable interface. The figure illustrates the Driveable interface being implemented by two different classes. While it's possible that both Automobile and Lawnmower could derive from some primitive kind of vehicle, they don't have to in this scenario. This is a significant advantage of interfaces over standard multiple inheritance, as implemented in languages such as C++.

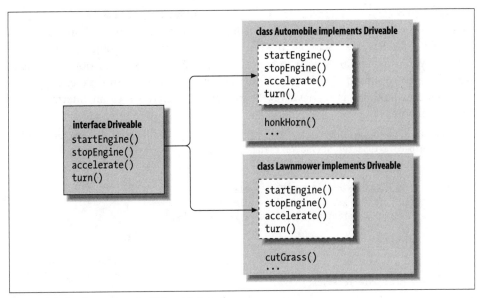

Figure 6-5. Implementing the Driveable interface

After declaring the interface, we have a new type, Driveable. We can declare variables of type Driveable and assign them any instance of a Driveable object:

```
Automobile auto = new Automobile( );
Lawnmower mower = new Lawnmower( );
Driveable vehicle;

vehicle = auto;
vehicle.startEngine( );
vehicle.stopEngine( );

vehicle = mower;
vehicle.startEngine( );
vehicle.stopEngine( );
```

Both Automobile and Lawnmower implement Driveable, so they can be considered of that type.

Interfaces as Callbacks

Interfaces can be used to implement "callbacks" in Java. This is when an object effectively passes a reference to one or more of its methods to another object. The callback occurs when the other object subsequently invokes one of the methods. In C or C++, this is prime territory for function pointers; Java uses interfaces instead. More generally, this concept is extended in Java to the idea of *events* in which listener objects register with even sources. But we'll cover that concept in great detail in later chapters.

Consider two classes: a TickerTape class that displays data and a TextSource class that provides an information feed. We'd like our TextSource to send any new text data. We could have TextSource store a reference to a TickerTape object, but then we could never use our TextSource to send data to any other kind of object. Instead, we'd have to proliferate subclasses of TextSource that dealt with different types. A more elegant solution is to have TextSource store a reference to an interface type, TextUpdateable:

```
interface TextUpdateable {
    void doTextUpdate( String text );
}

class TickerTape implements TextUpdateable {
    public void doTextUpdate( String text ) {
        System.out.println("TICKER:\n" + text + "\n");
    }
}

class TextSource {
    TextUpdateable receiver;

    TextSource( TextUpdateable r ) {
        receiver = r;
    }

    public void sendText( String s ) {
        receiver.doTextUpdate( s );
    }
}
```

The only thing the TextSource really cares about is finding the right method to invoke in order to output some text. Using an interface establishes a "well-known" name, doTextUpdate, for that method.

When the TextSource is constructed, a reference to the TickerTape (which implements the interface) is stored in an instance variable. This "registers" the TickerTape as the TextSource's "output device." Whenever it needs to output data, the TextSource calls the output device's doTextUpdate() method.

Interface Variables

Although interfaces mostly allow us to specify behavior without implementation, there's one exception. An interface can contain constants (static final variables), which appear in any class that implements the interface. This feature enables pre-defined parameters for use with the methods:

```
interface Scaleable {
    static final int BIG = 0, MEDIUM = 1, SMALL = 2;
    void setScale( int size );
}
```

The Scaleable interface defines three integers: BIG, MEDIUM, and SMALL. All variables defined in interfaces are implicitly final and static; you don't have to use the modifiers, but, for clarity, we recommend you do. A class that implements Scaleable sees these variables:

```
class Box implements Scaleable {

    void setScale( int size ) {
        switch( size ) {
            case BIG:
                ...
            case MEDIUM:
                ...
            case SMALL:
                ...
        }
    }
    ...
}
```

Flag and empty interfaces

Sometimes, interfaces are created just to hold constants; anyone who implements the interfaces can see the constant names, as if they were included directly in their class. This is a somewhat degenerate, but acceptable, use of interfaces.

More often, completely empty interfaces are used to serve as a marker that a class has a special property. The java.io.Serializeable interface is a good example. Classes that implement Serializable don't add any methods or variables. Their additional type simply identifies them to Java as classes that want to be able to be serialized.

Subinterfaces

An interface can extend another interface, just as a class can extend another class. Such an interface is called a *subinterface*. For example:

```
interface DynamicallyScaleable extends Scaleable {
    void changeScale( int size );
}
```

The interface DynamicallyScaleable extends our previous Scaleable interface and adds an additional method. A class that implements DynamicallyScaleable must implement all the methods of both interfaces.

Note here that we are using the term *extends* and not *implements* to subclass the interface. Interfaces can't implement anything! But an interface is allowed to extend as many interfaces as it wants. If you want to extend two or more interfaces, list them after the extends keyword, separated by commas:

```
interface DynamicallyScaleable extends Scaleable, SomethingElseable {
    ...
}
```

Keep in mind that although Java supports multiple inheritances of interfaces, each class can extend only a single parent class.

Packages and Compilation Units

A *package* is a name for a group of related classes and interfaces. In Chapter 3 we discussed how Java uses package names to locate classes during compilation and at runtime. In this sense, packages are somewhat like libraries; they organize and manage sets of classes. Packages provide more than just source-code-level organization though. They also create an additional level of scope for their classes and the variables and methods within them. We'll talk about the visibility of classes later in this section. In the next section, we'll discuss the effect that packages have on access to variables and methods among classes.

Compilation Units

The source code for a Java class is organized into *compilation units*. A simple compilation unit contains a single class definition and is named for that class. The definition of a class named MyClass, for instance, would appear in a file named *MyClass.java*. For most of us, a compilation unit is just a file with a *.java* extension, but in theory in an integrated development environment, it could be an arbitrary entity. For brevity here, we'll refer to a compilation unit simply as a file.

The division of classes into their own compilation units is important because the Java compiler assumes much of the responsibility of a *make* utility. The compiler relies on the names of source files to find and compile dependent classes. It's possible to put more than one class definition into a single file, but there are some restrictions we'll discuss shortly.

A class is declared to belong to a particular package with the package statement. The package statement must appear as the first statement in a compilation unit. There can be only one package statement, and it applies to the entire file:

```
package mytools.text;

class TextComponent {
    ...
}
```

In this example, the class TextComponent is placed in the package mytools.text.

Package Names

Package names are constructed in a hierarchical way, using a dot-separated naming convention. Package-name components construct a unique path for the compiler and runtime systems to locate files; however, they don't create relationships between packages in any other way. There is no such thing as a "subpackage"; the package namespace is, in actuality, flat—not hierarchical. Packages under a particular part of a package hierarchy are related only by convention. For example, if we create another package called mytools.text.poetry (presumably for text classes specialized in some way to work with poetry), those classes won't be part of the mytools.text package; they won't have the access privileges of package members. In this sense, the package-naming convention can be misleading. One minor deviation from this notion is that assertions, which we described in Chapter 4, can be turned on or off for a package and all packages "under" it. But that is really just a convenience and not represented in the code structure.

Class Visibility

By default, a class is accessible only to other classes within its package. This means that the class TextComponent is available only to other classes in the mytools.text package. To be visible elsewhere, a class must be declared as public:

```
package mytools.text;

public class TextEditor {
    ...
}
```

The class TextEditor can now be referenced anywhere. There can be only a single public class defined in a compilation unit; the file must be named for that class.

By hiding unimportant or extraneous classes, a package builds a *subsystem* that has a well-defined interface to the rest of the world. Public classes provide a *facade* for the operation of the system. The details of its inner workings can remain hidden, as shown in Figure 6-6. In this sense, packages can hide classes in the way classes hide private members.

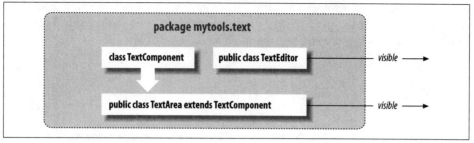

Figure 6-6. Packages and class visibility

Figure 6-6 shows part of the hypothetical mytools.text package. The classes TextArea and TextEditor are declared public, so they can be used elsewhere in an application. The class TextComponent is part of the implementation of TextArea and is not accessible from outside of the package.

Importing Classes

Classes within a package can refer to each other by their simple names. However, to locate a class in another package, we have to be more specific. Continuing with the previous example, an application can refer directly to our editor class by its *fully qualified name* of mytools.text.TextEditor. But we'd quickly grow tired of typing such long class names, so Java gives us the import statement. One or more import statements can appear at the top of a compilation unit, after the package statement. The import statements list the fully qualified names of classes and packages to be used within the file.

Like a package statement, an import statement applies to the entire compilation unit. Here's how you might use an import statement:

```
package somewhere.else;
import mytools.text.TextEditor;

class MyClass {
    TextEditor editBoy;
    ...
}
```

As shown in this example, once a class is imported, it can be referenced by its simple name throughout the code.

It is also possible to import all the classes in a package using the * wildcard notation:

```
import mytools.text.*;
```

Now we can refer to all public classes in the mytools.text package by their simple names.

Obviously, there can be a problem with importing classes that have conflicting names. If two different packages contain classes that use the same name, you just have to fall back to using fully qualified names to refer to those classes. You can either use the fully qualified name directly, or you can add an additional import statement that disambiguates the class name. Other than the potential for naming conflicts, there's no penalty for importing classes. Java doesn't carry extra baggage into the compiled class files. In other words, Java class files don't contain other class definitions; they only reference them.

One note about conventions: in our efforts to keep our examples short we'll often import entire packages (.*) even when we only use a class or two from it. In practice, it's always better to be specific when possible and list individual, fully qualified class imports. Some people avoid using package imports entirely, choosing to list every imported class individually, but that's an extreme.

The Unnamed Package

A class that is defined in a compilation unit that doesn't specify a package falls into the large, amorphous, unnamed package. Classes in this nameless package can refer to each other by their simple names. Their path at compile time and runtime is considered to be the current directory, so package-less classes are useful for experimentation and testing (and for brevity in examples in books about Java).

Visibility of Variables and Methods

One of the most important aspects of object-oriented design is *data hiding*, or *encapsulation*. By treating an object in some respects as a "black box" and ignoring the details of its implementation, we can write stronger, simpler code with components that can be easily reused.

Basic Access Modifiers

By default, the variables and methods of a class are accessible to members of the class itself and to other classes in the same package. To borrow from C++ terminology, classes in the same package are *friendly*. We'll call this the default level of visibility. As you'll see as we go on, the default visibility lies in the middle of the range of restrictiveness that can be specified.

The modifiers public and private, on the other hand, define the extremes. As we mentioned earlier, methods and variables declared as private are accessible only within their class. At the other end of the spectrum, members declared as public are accessible from any class in any package, provided the class itself can be seen. (The class that contains the methods must be public to be seen outside of its package, as we discussed previously.) The public members of a class should define its most general functionality—what the black box is supposed to do.

Figure 6-7 illustrates the four simplest levels of visibility, continuing the example from the previous section. Public members in TextArea are accessible from anywhere. Private members are not visible from outside the class. The default visibility allows access by other classes in the package.

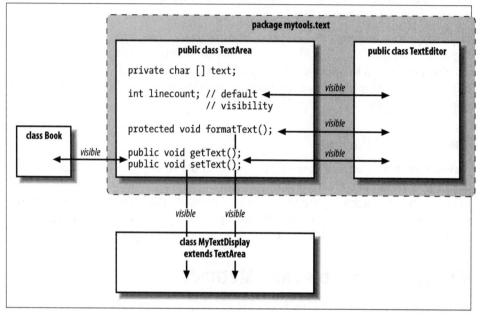

Figure 6-7. Private, default, protected, and public visibility

The protected modifier allows special access permissions for subclasses. Contrary to how it might sound, protected is slightly less restrictive than the default level of accessibility. In addition to the default access afforded classes in the same package, protected members are visible to subclasses of the class, even if they are defined in a different package. If you are a C++ programmer and so are used to more restrictive meanings, this may rub you the wrong way.*

Table 6-1 summarizes the levels of visibility available in Java; it runs generally from most restrictive to least. Methods and variables are always visible within a declaring class itself, so the table doesn't addresses that scope.

---

* Early on, the Java language allowed for certain combinations of modifiers, one of which was private protected. The meaning of private protected was to limit visibility strictly to subclasses (and remove package access). This was later deemed confusing and overly complex. It is no longer supported.

Table 6-1. Visibility modifiers

Modifier	Visibility
Private	None
None (default)	Classes in the package
Protected	Classes in package and subclasses inside or outside the package
Public	All classes

Subclasses and Visibility

Subclasses add two important (but unrelated) complications to the topic of visibility. First, when you override methods in a subclass, the overriding method must be at least as visible as the overridden method. While it is possible to take a private method and override it with a public method in a subclass, the reverse is not possible; you can't override a public method with a private method. This restriction makes sense if you realize that subtypes have to be usable as instances of their supertype (e.g., a Mammal is a subclass of Animal and therefore must be usable as an Animal). If we could override a method with a less visible method, we would have a problem: our Mammal might not be able to do all the things an Animal can. However, we can reduce the visibility of a variable. In this case, the variable acts like any other shadowed variable; the two variables are distinct and can have separate visibilities in different classes.

The next complication is a bit harder to follow: the protected variables of a class are visible to its subclasses, but only through objects of the subclass's type or its subtypes. In other words, a subclass can see a protected variable of its superclass as an inherited variable, but it can't access that same variable in a separate instance of the superclass itself. This statement may be confusing because we often forget that visibility modifiers don't restrict access between instances of the same class in the same way they restrict access between instances of different classes. Two instances of the same type of object can normally access all each other's members, including private ones. Said another way: two instances of Cat can access all each other's variables and methods (including private ones), but a Cat can't access a protected member in an instance of Animal unless the compiler can prove that the Animal is a Cat. That is, Cats have the special privileges of being an Animal only with respect to other Cats, not just any Animal. If you find this hard to follow, don't worry too much. You shouldn't run into these issues very often (if ever).

Interfaces and Visibility

Interfaces behave like classes within packages. An interface can be declared public to make it visible outside its package. Under the default visibility, an interface is visible only inside its package. Like classes, there can be only one public interface declared in a compilation unit.

Arrays and the Class Hierarchy

At the end of Chapter 4, we mentioned that arrays have a place in the Java class hierarchy, but we didn't give you any details. Now that we've discussed the object-oriented aspects of Java, we can give you the whole story.

Array classes live in a parallel Java class hierarchy under the Object class. If a class is a direct subclass of Object, then an array class for that base type also exists as a direct subclass of Object. Arrays of more derived classes are subclasses of the corresponding array classes. For example, consider the following class types:

```
class Animal { ... }
class Bird extends Animal { ... }
class Penguin extends Bird { ... }
```

Figure 6-8 illustrates the class hierarchy for arrays of these classes. Arrays of the same dimension are related to one another in the same manner as their base type classes. In our example, Bird is a subclass of Animal, which means that the Bird[] type is a subtype of Animal[]. In the same way a Bird object can be used in place of an Animal object, a Bird[] array can be assigned to a variable of type Animal[]:

```
Animal [][] animals;
Bird [][] birds = new Bird [10][10];
birds[0][0] = new Bird( );

// make animals and birds reference the same array object
animals = birds;
observe( animals[0][0] );          // processes Bird object
```

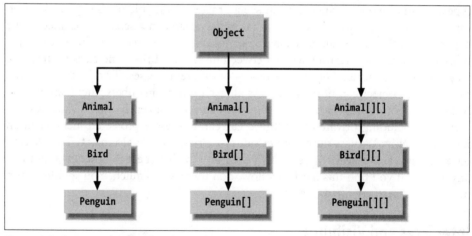

Figure 6-8. Arrays in the Java class hierarchy

Because arrays are part of the class hierarchy, we can use instanceof to check the type of an array:

```
if ( birds instanceof Animal[][] )      // true
```

An array is a subtype of `Object` and so can be assigned to `Object` type variables:

```
Object something;
something = animals;
```

Since Java knows the actual type of all objects, you can also cast back if appropriate:

```
animals = (Animal [][])something;
```

Under unusual circumstances, Java may not be able to check the types of objects you place into arrays at compile time. In those cases, it's possible to receive an `ArrayStoreException` if you try to assign the wrong type of object to an array element. Consider the following:

```
class Dog { ... }
class Poodle extends Dog { ... }
class Chihuahua extends Dog { ... }

Dog [] dogs;
Poodle [] poodles = new Poodle [10];

dogs = poodles;
dogs[3] = new Chihuahua( );  // runtime error, ArrayStoreException
```

Both `Poodle` and `Chihuahua` are subclasses of `Dog`, so an array of `Poodle` objects can therefore be assigned to an array of `Dog` objects. The problem is that an object assignable to an element of an array of type `Dog[]` may not be assignable to an element of an array of type `Poodle[]`. A `Chihuahua` object, for instance, can be assigned to a `Dog` element because it's a subtype of `Dog`, but not to a `Poodle` element.*

Inner Classes

Java 1.1 added to the language a large heap of syntactic sugar called *inner classes*. Simply put, classes in Java can be declared at any level of scope. That is, you can declare a class within any set of curly braces (i.e., almost anywhere that you could put any other Java statement), and its visibility is limited to that scope in the same way that the name of a variable or method would be. Inner classes are a powerful and aesthetically pleasing facility for structuring code. Their even sweeter cousins, *anonymous inner classes*, are another powerful shorthand that make it seem as if you can create classes dynamically within Java's statically typed environment.

However, if you delve into the inner workings of Java, inner classes are not quite as aesthetically pleasing or dynamic. We said that they are syntactic sugar; this means

---

* In some sense, this could be considered a hole in the Java type system. It doesn't occur elsewhere in Java—only with arrays. This is because array objects exhibit *covariance* in overriding their assignment and extraction methods. Covariance allows array subclasses to override methods with arguments or return values that are subtypes of the overridden methods, where the methods would normally be overloaded or prohibited. This allows array subclasses to operate on their base types with type safety, but also means that subclasses have different capabilities than their parents, leading to the problem shown earlier.

that they let you leverage the compiler by writing a few lines of code that trigger a lot of behind-the-scenes work somewhere between the compiler's front end and the bytecode. Inner classes rely on code generation; they are a feature of the Java language, but not of the Java virtual machine. As a programmer you may never need be aware of this; you can simply rely on inner classes like any other language construct. However, you should know a little about how inner classes work to better understand the results and a few potential side effects.

To this point, all our classes have been *top-level* classes. We have declared them, freestanding, at the package level. Inner classes are essentially nested classes, like this:

```
Class Animal {
    Class Brain {
        ...
    }
}
```

Here the class Brain is an inner class: it is a class declared inside the scope of class Animal. Although the details of what that means require a fair bit of explanation, we'll start by saying that the Java language tries to make the meaning, as much as possible, the same as for the other Java entities (methods and variables) living at that level of scope. For example, let's add a method to the Animal class:

```
Class Animal {
    Class Brain {
        ...
    }
    void performBehavior( ) { ... }
}
```

Both the inner class Brain and the method performBehavior() are within the scope of Animal. Therefore, anywhere within Animal we can refer to Brain and performBehavior() directly, by name. Within Animal, we can call the constructor for Brain (new Brain()) to get a Brain object or invoke performBehavior() to carry out that method's function. But neither Brain nor performBehavior() are generally accessible outside of the class Animal without some additional qualification.

Within the body of the Brain class and the body of the performBehavior() method, we have direct access to all the other methods and variables of the Animal class. So, just as the performBehavior() method could work with the Brain class and create instances of Brain, code within the Brain class can invoke the performBehavior() method of Animal as well as work with any other methods and variables declared in Animal.

That last bit has important consequences. From within Brain we can invoke the method performBehavior(); that is, from within an instance of Brain we can invoke the performBehavior() method of an instance of Animal. Well, which instance of Animal? If we have several Animal objects around (say, a few Cats and Dogs), we need to know whose `performBehavior()` method we are calling. What does it mean for a class definition to be "inside" another class definition? The answer is that a `Brain` object always lives within a single instance of `Animal`: the one that it was told about when it was created. We'll call the object that contains any instance of `Brain` its *enclosing instance*.

A `Brain` object cannot live outside of an enclosing instance of an `Animal` object. Anywhere you see an instance of `Brain`, it will be tethered to an instance of `Animal`. Although it is possible to construct a `Brain` object from elsewhere (i.e., another class), `Brain` always requires an enclosing instance of `Animal` to "hold" it. We'll also say now that if `Brain` is to be referred to from outside of `Animal`, it acts something like an `Animal.Brain` class. And just as with the `performBehavior()` method, modifiers can be applied to restrict its visibility. There is even an interpretation of the `static` modifier, which we'll talk about a bit later.

Although we'd probably never find a need to do it, we can construct an instance of `Brain` from outside the class by referencing an instance of `Animal`. To do this requires that the inner class `Brain` be accessible and that we use a special form of the `new` operator designed just for inner classes:

```
Animal monkey = new Animal();
Animal.Brain monkeyBrain = monkey.new Brain();
```

Here the `Animal` instance `monkey` is used to qualify the `new` operator on `Brain`. Again, this is not a very common thing to do. Static inner classes are more useful. We'll talk about them a bit later.

Inner Classes as Adapters

A particularly important use of inner classes is to make *adapter classes*. An adapter class is a "helper" class that ties one class to another in a very specific way. Using adapter classes, you can write your classes more naturally, without having to anticipate every conceivable user's needs in advance. Instead, you provide adapter classes that marry your class to a particular interface. As an example, let's say that we have an `EmployeeList` object:

```
public class EmployeeList {
    private Employee [] employees = ... ;
    ...
}
```

`EmployeeList` holds information about a set of employees. Let's say that we would like to have `EmployeeList` provide its elements via an iterator. An iterator is a simple, standard interface to a sequence of objects. The `java.util.Iterator` interface has several methods:

```
public interface Iterator {
    boolean hasMore ( );
    Object next( );
```

```
    void remove( );
}
```

It lets us step through its elements, asking for the next one and testing to see if more remain. The iterator is a good candidate for an adapter class because it is an interface that our EmployeeList can't readily implement itself. Why can't the list implement the iterator directly? Because an iterator is a "one-way," disposable view of our data. It isn't intended to be reset and used again. It may also be necessary for there to be multiple iterators walking through the list at different points. We must therefore keep the iterator implementation separate from the EmployeeList itself. This is crying out for a simple class to provide the iterator capability. But what should that class look like?

Well, before we knew about inner classes, our only recourse would have been to make a new "top-level" class. We would probably feel obliged to call it EmployeeListIterator:

```
class EmployeeListIterator implements Iterator {
    // lots of knowledge about EmployeeList
    ...
}
```

Here we have a comment representing the machinery that the EmployeeListIterator requires. Think for just a second about what you'd have to do to implement that machinery. The resulting class would be completely coupled to the EmployeeList and unusable in other situations. Worse, to function it must have access to the inner workings of EmployeeList. We would have to allow EmployeeListIterator access to the private array in EmployeeList, exposing this data more widely than it should be. This is less than ideal.

This sounds like a job for inner classes. We already said that EmployeeListIterator was useless without an EmployeeList; this sounds a lot like the "lives inside" relationship we described earlier. Furthermore, an inner class lets us avoid the encapsulation problem because it can access all the members of its enclosing instance. Therefore, if we use an inner class to implement the iterator, the array employees can remain private, invisible outside the EmployeeList. So let's just shove that helper class inside the scope of our EmployeeList:

```
public class EmployeeList {
    private Employee [] employees = ... ;
    ...

    class Iterator implements java.util.Iterator {
        int element = 0;

        boolean hasMore( ) {
            return  element < employees.length ;
        }

        Object next( ) {
```

```
            if ( hasMoreElements( ) )
                return employees[ element++ ];
            else
                throw new NoSuchElementException( );
        }

        void remove( ) {
            throw new UnsupportedOperationException( );
        }
    }
}
```

Now EmployeeList can provide a method like the following to let other classes work with the list:

```
Iterator getIterator( ) {
        return new Iterator( );
    }
```

One effect of the move is that we are free to be a little more familiar in the naming of our iterator class. Since it is no longer a top-level class, we can give it a name that is appropriate only within the EmployeeList. In this case, we've named it Iterator to emphasize what it does, but we don't need a name like EmployeeIterator that shows the relationship to the EmployeeList class because that's implicit. We've also filled in the guts of the Iterator class. As you can see, now that it is inside the scope of EmployeeList, Iterator has direct access to its private members, so it can directly access the employees array. This greatly simplifies the code and maintains compile-time safety.

Before we move on, we should note that inner classes can have constructors, even though we didn't need one in this example. They are in all respects real classes.

Inner Classes Within Methods

Inner classes may also be declared within the body of a method. Returning to the Animal class, we can put Brain inside the performBehavior( ) method if we decide that the class is useful only inside that method:

```
Class Animal {
    void performBehavior( ) {
        Class Brain {
            ...
        }
    }
}
```

In this situation, the rules governing what Brain can see are the same as in our earlier example. The body of Brain can see anything in the scope of performBehavior( ) and above it (in the body of Animal). This includes local variables of performBehavior( ) and its arguments. But because of the ephemeral (fleeting) nature of a method invocation, there are a few limitations and additional restrictions, as described in the following sections. If you are thinking that inner classes within methods sounds a bit arcane, bear with us until we talk about anonymous inner classes, which are tremendously useful.

Limitations on inner classes in methods

performBehavior() is a method, and methods have limited lifetimes. When they exit, their local variables normally disappear into the abyss. But an instance of Brain (like any object) lives on as long as it is referenced. So Java must make sure that any local variables used by instances of Brain created within an invocation of performBehavior() also live on. Furthermore, all the instances of Brain that we make within a single invocation of performBehavior() must see the same local variables. To accomplish this, the compiler must be allowed to make copies of local variables. Thus, their values cannot change once an inner class has seen them. This means that any of the method's local variables that are referenced by the inner class must be declared final. The final modifier means that they are constant once assigned. This is a little confusing and easy to forget, but the compiler will graciously remind you.

Static inner classes

We mentioned earlier that the inner class Brain of the class Animal can in some ways be considered an Animal.Brain class. That is, it is possible to work with a Brain from outside the Animal class, using just such a qualified name: Animal.Brain. But given that our Animal.Brain class always requires an instance of an Animal as its enclosing instance, it's not as common to work with them directly in this way.

But there is another situation in which we might use inner classes by name. An inner class that lives within the body of a top-level class (not within a method or another inner class) can be declared static. For example:

```
class Animal  {
    static class MigrationPattern {
        ...
    }
    ...
}
```

A static inner class such as this acts just like a new top-level class called Animal.MigrationPattern. We can use it just like any other class, without regard to any enclosing instances. Although this may seem strange, it is not inconsistent, since a static member never has an object instance associated with it. The requirement that the inner class be defined directly inside a top-level class ensures that an enclosing instance won't be needed. If we have permission, we can create an instance of the class using the qualified name:

```
Animal.MigrationPattern stlToSanFrancisco =
    new Animal.MigrationPattern( );
```

As you see, the effect is that `Animal` acts something like a minipackage, holding the `MigrationPattern` class. Here we have used the fully qualified name, but we could also import it like any other class:

```
import Animal.MigrationPattern;
```

This enables us to refer to it simply as `MigrationPattern`. We can use all the standard visibility modifiers on inner classes, so a static inner class can have `private`, `protected`, default, or `public` visibility.

Here's another example. The Java 2D API uses static inner classes to implement specialized shape classes. For example, the `java.awt.geom.Rectangle2D` class has two inner classes, `Float` and `Double`, that implement two different precisions. These shape classes are actually very simple subclasses; it would have been sad to have to multiply the number of top-level classes in that package by three to accommodate all of them.

Anonymous inner classes

Now we get to the best part. As a general rule, the more deeply encapsulated and limited in scope our classes are, the more freedom we have in naming them. We saw this in our previous iterator example. This is not just a purely aesthetic issue. Naming is an important part of writing readable and maintainable code. We generally want to use the most concise and meaningful names possible. A corollary to this is that we prefer to avoid doling out names for purely ephemeral objects that are going to be used only once.

Anonymous inner classes are an extension of the syntax of the `new` operation. When you create an anonymous inner class, you combine a class declaration with the allocation of an instance of that class, creating effectively a "one time only" class and a class instance in one operation. After the `new` keyword, you specify either the name of a class or an interface, followed by a class body. The class body becomes an inner class, which either extends the specified class or, in the case of an interface, is expected to implement the specified interface. A single instance of the class is created and returned as the value.

For example, we could do away with the declaration of the `Iterator` class in the `EmployeeList` example by using an anonymous inner class in the `getIterator()` method:

```
Iterator getIterator( ) {
    return new Iterator( ) {
        int element = 0;
        boolean hasMore( ) {
            return  element < employees.length ;
        }
        Object next( ) {
            if ( hasMoreElements( ) )
                return employees[ element++ ];
```

```
        else
            throw new NoSuchElementException( );
    }
    void remove( ) {
        throw new UnsupportedOperationException( );
    }
    };
}
```

Here we have simply moved the guts of Iterator into the body of an anonymous inner class. The call to new implicitly creates a class that implements the Iterator interface and returns an instance of the class as its result. Note the extent of the curly braces and the semicolon at the end. The getIterator() method contains a single statement, the return statement.

But the previous code certainly does not improve readability. Inner classes are best used when you want to implement a few lines of code, when the verbiage and conspicuousness of declaring a separate class detracts from the task at hand.

Here's a better example. Suppose that we want to start a new thread to execute the performBehavior() method of our Animal:

```
new Thread( ) {
    public void run( ) { performBehavior( );  }
}.start( );
```

Here we have gone over to the terse side. We've allocated and started a new Thread, using an anonymous inner class that extends the Thread class and invokes our performBehavior() method in its run() method. The effect is similar to using a method pointer in some other language. However, the inner class allows the compiler to check type consistency, which would be more difficult (or impossible) with a true method pointer. At the same time, our anonymous adapter class with its three lines of code is much more efficient and readable than creating a new, top-level adapter class named AnimalBehaviorThreadAdapter.

While we're getting a bit ahead of the story, anonymous adapter classes are a perfect fit for event handling (which we'll cover fully in Chapter 15). Skipping a lot of explanation, let's say you want the method handleClicks() to be called whenever the user clicks the mouse. You would write code like this:

```
addMouseListener(new MouseInputAdapter( ) {
    public void mouseClicked(MouseEvent e) { handleClicks(e); }
});
```

In this case, the anonymous class extends the MouseInputAdapter class by overriding its mouseClicked() method to call our method. A lot is going on in a very small space, but the result is clean, readable code. You get to assign method names that are meaningful to you, while allowing Java to do its job of type checking.

Scoping of the "this" reference

Sometimes an inner class may want to get a handle on its "parent" enclosing instance. It might want to pass a reference to its parent or to refer to one of the parent's variables or methods that has been hidden by one of its own. For example:

```
class Animal {
    int size;
    class Brain {
        int size;
    }
}
```

Here, as far as `Brain` is concerned, the variable `size` in `Animal` is hidden by its own version.

Normally an object refers to itself using the special `this` reference (implicitly or explicitly). But what is the meaning of `this` for an object with one or more enclosing instances? The answer is that an inner class has multiple `this` references. You can specify which `this` you want by prefixing it with the name of the class. So, for instance (no pun intended), we can get a reference to our `Animal` from within `Brain` like so:

```
class Brain {
    Animal ourAnimal = Animal.this;
    ...
}
```

Similarly, we could refer to the `size` variable in `Animal`:

```
class Brain {
    int animalSize = Animal.this.size;
    ...
}
```

How do inner classes really work?

Finally, we'll get our hands dirty and take a look at what's really going on when we use an inner class. We've said that the compiler is doing all the things that we had hoped to forget about. Let's see what's actually happening. Try compiling this trivial example:

```
class Animal {
    class Brain {
    }
}
```

What you'll find is that the compiler generates two *.class* files: *Animal.class* and *Animal$Brain.class*.

The second file is the class file for our inner class. Yes, as we feared, inner classes are really just compiler magic. The compiler has created the inner class for us as a normal, top-level class and named it by combining the class names with a dollar sign.

The dollar sign is a valid character in class names but is intended for use only by automated tools. (Please don't start naming your classes with dollar signs.) Had our class been more deeply nested, the intervening inner-class names would have been attached in the same way to generate a unique top-level name.

Now take a look at it with the SDK's *javap* utility (don't quote the argument on a Windows system):

```
% javap 'Animal$Brain'
class Animal$Brain extends java.lang.Object {
    Animal$Brain(Animal);
}
```

You'll see that the compiler has given our inner class a constructor that takes a reference to an `Animal` as an argument. This is how the real inner class gets the handle on its enclosing instance.

The worst thing about these additional class files is that you need to know they are there. Utilities such as *jar* don't automatically find them; when you're invoking a such a utility, you need to specify these files explicitly or use a wildcard that finds them.

Security implications

Given what we just saw—that the inner class really does exist as an automatically generated top-level class—how does it get access to private variables? The answer, unfortunately, is that the compiler is forced to break the encapsulation of your object and insert accessor methods so that the inner class can reach them. The accessor methods are given package-level access, so your object is still safe within its package walls, but it is conceivable that this difference could be meaningful if people were allowed to create new classes within your package.

The visibility modifiers on inner classes also have some problems. Current implementations of the virtual machine do not implement the notion of a `private` or `protected` class within a package, so giving your inner class anything other than `public` or default visibility is only a compile-time guarantee. It is difficult to conceive of how these security issues could be abused, but it is interesting to note that Java is straining a bit to stay within its original design.

Working with Objects and Classes

In the previous two chapters, we came to know Java objects and their interrelationships. We will now climb the scaffolding of the Java class hierarchy to the very top and finish our study of the core language at the summit. In this chapter we'll talk about the Object class itself, which is the "grandmother" of all classes in Java. We'll also describe the even more fundamental Class class (the class named "Class") that represents Java classes in the Java virtual machine. We'll discuss what you can do with these objects in their own right. Finally, this will lead us to a more general topic: the Java Reflection API, which lets a Java program inspect and interact with (possibly unknown) objects on the fly.

The Object Class

java.lang.Object is the ancestor of all objects; it's the primordial class from which all other classes are ultimately derived. Methods defined in Object are therefore very important because they appear in every instance of every class, throughout all of Java. At last count, there were nine public methods in Object. Five of these are versions of wait() and notify() that are used to synchronize threads on object instances, as we'll discuss in Chapter 8. The remaining four methods are used for basic comparison, conversion, and administration.

Every object has a toString() method that can be called when it's to be represented as a text value. PrintStream objects use toString() to print data, as discussed in Chapter 11. toString() is also used implicitly when an object is referenced in a string concatenation. Here are some examples:

```
MyObj myObject = new MyObj( );
Answer theAnswer = new Answer( );

System.out.println( myObject );
String s = "The answer is: " + theAnswer ;
```

To be friendly, a new kind of object should override toString() and implement its own version that provides appropriate printing functionality. Two other methods, equals() and hashCode(), may also require specialization when you create a new class.

Equality and Equivalence

equals() determines whether two objects are equivalent. Precisely what that means for a particular class is something that you'll have to decide for yourself. Two String objects, for example, are considered equivalent if they hold precisely the same characters in the same sequence:

```
String userName = "Joe";
...
if ( userName.equals( suspectName ) )
    arrest( userName );
```

Using equals() is *not* the same as:

```
if ( userName == suspectName )      // Wrong!
```

This code line tests whether the two reference variables, userName and suspectName, refer to the same object. It is a test for *identity*, not equality. Two variables that are identical (point to the same object) will of course test equal, but the converse is not always true.

A class should override the equals() method if it needs to implement its own notion of equality. If you have no need to compare objects of a particular class, you don't necessarily need to override equals().

Watch out for accidentally overloading equals() when you mean to override it. With overloading, the method signatures differ; with overriding, they must be the same. The equals() method signature specifies an Object argument and a boolean return value. You'll probably want to check only objects of the same type for equivalence. But in order to override (not overload) equals(), the method must specify its argument to be an Object.

Here's an example of correctly overriding an equals() method in class Shoes with an equals() method in subclass Sneakers. Using its own method, a Sneakers object can compare itself with any other object:

```
class Sneakers extends Shoes {
    public boolean equals( Object arg ) {
        if ( (arg != null) && (arg instanceof Sneakers) ) {
            // compare arg with this object to check equivalence
            // If comparison is okay...
            return true;
        }
```

```
        return false;
    }
    ...
}
```

If we specified public boolean equals(Sneakers arg) ... in the Sneakers class, we'd overload the equals() method instead of overriding it. If the other object happens to be assigned to a non-Sneakers variable, the method signature won't match. The result: superclass Shoes's implementation of equals() is called, which may or may not be what you intended.

Hashcodes

The hashCode() method returns an integer that is a hashcode for the object. A *hashcode* is like a signature or checksum for an object; it's a random-looking identifying number that is usually generated from the contents of the object. The hashcode should always be different for instances of the class that contain different data, but should be the same for instances that compare "equal" with the equals() method. Hashcodes are used in the process of storing objects in a Hashtable or a similar kind of collection. The hashcode helps the Hashtable optimize its storage of objects by serving as an identifier for distributing them into storage evenly and locating them quickly later.

The default implementation of hashCode() in Object assigns each object instance a unique number. If you don't override this method when you create a subclass, each instance of your class will have a unique hashcode. This is sufficient for some objects. However, if your classes have a notion of equivalent objects (if you have overridden equals()), and you want equal objects to serve as equivalent keys in a Hashtable, you should override hashCode() so that your equivalent objects generate the same hashcode value.

Cloning Objects

Objects can use the clone() method of the Object class to make copies of themselves. A copied object is a new object instance, separate from the original. It may or may not contain exactly the same state (the same instance variable values) as the original; that is controlled by the object being copied. Just as important, the decision as to whether the object allows itself to be cloned at all is up to the object.

The Java Object class provides the mechanism to make a simple copy of an object including all of its state—a *bitwise* copy. But by default this capability is turned off. (We'll hit upon why in a moment.) To make itself cloneable, an object must implement the java.lang.Cloneable interface. This is a flag interface indicating to Java that the object wants to cooperate in being cloned (the interface does not actually contain any methods). If the object isn't cloneable, the clone() method throws a CloneNotSupportedException.

clone( ) is a protected method, so by default it can be called only by an object on itself, an object in the same package, or another object of the same type or a subtype. If we want to make an object cloneable by everyone, we have to override its clone( ) method and make it public.

Here is a simple, cloneable class—Sheep:

```
import java.util.Hashtable;

public class Sheep implements Cloneable {
    Hashtable flock = new Hashtable( );

    public Object clone( ) {
        try {
            return super.clone( );
        } catch (CloneNotSupportedException e ) {
            throw new Error("This should never happen!");
        }
    }
}
```

Sheep has one instance variable, a Hashtable called flock (which the sheep uses to keep track of its fellow sheep). Our class implements the Cloneable interface, indicating that it is okay to copy Sheep, and it has overridden the clone( ) method to make it public. Our clone( ) simply returns the object created by the superclass's clone( ) method—a copy of our Sheep. Unfortunately, the compiler is not smart enough to figure out that the object we're cloning will never throw the CloneNotSupportedException, so we have to guard against it anyway. Our sheep is now cloneable. We can make copies like so:

```
Sheep one = new Sheep( );
Sheep anotherOne = (Sheep)one.clone( );
```

The cast is necessary here because the return type of clone( ) is Object.*

We now have two sheep instead of one. A properly implemented equals( ) method would tell us that the sheep are equivalent, but == tells us that they aren't the same; that is, they are two distinct objects. Java has made a *shallow copy* of our Sheep. What's so shallow about it? Java has simply copied the values of our variables. That means that the flock instance variable in each of our Sheep still holds the same information—that is, both sheep have a reference to the same Hashtable. The situation looks like that shown in Figure 7-1.

This may or may not be what you intended. If we instead want our Sheep to have separate copies of all its variables (or something in between), we can take control

---

* You might think that we could override the clone( ) method in our objects to refine the return type of the clone( ) method. However this is currently not possible in Java. You can't override methods and change their return types. Technically this would be called *covariant return typing*. It's something that may find its way into the language eventually.

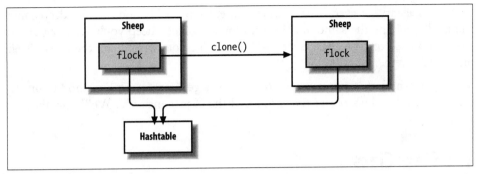

Figure 7-1. Shallow copy of an object

ourselves. In the following example, DeepSheep, we implement a "deep" copy, duplicating our own flock variable:

```
public class DeepSheep implements Cloneable {
    Hashtable flock = new Hashtable( );

    public Object clone( ) {
        try {
            DeepSheep copy = (DeepSheep)super.clone( );
            copy.flock = (Hashtable)flock.clone( );
            return copy;
        } catch (CloneNotSupportedException e ) {
            throw new Error("This should never happen!");
        }
    }
}
```

Our clone() method now clones the Hashtable as well. Now, when a DeepSheep is
cloned, the situation looks more like that shown in Figure 7-2.

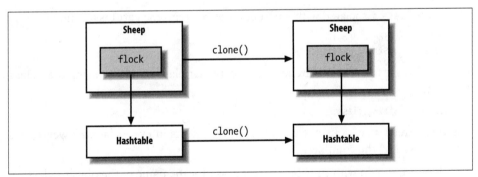

Figure 7-2. Deep copy of an object

Each DeepSheep now has its own hashtable. You can see now why objects are not cloneable by default. It would make no sense to assume that all objects can be sensibly
duplicated with a shallow copy. Likewise, it makes no sense to assume that a deep

copy is necessary, or even correct. In this case, we probably don't need a deep copy; the flock contains the same members no matter which sheep you're looking at, so there's no need to copy the Hashtable. But the decision depends on the object itself and its requirements.

The last method of Object we need to discuss is getClass(). This method returns a reference to the Class object that produced the Object instance. We'll talk about it next.

The Class Class

A good measure of the complexity of an object-oriented language is the degree of abstraction of its class structures. We know that every object in Java is an instance of a class, but what exactly is a class? In languages like C++, objects are formulated by and instantiated from classes, but classes are really just artifacts of the compiler. Thus, in those languages you see classes mentioned only in source code, not at runtime. By comparison, classes in Smalltalk are real, runtime entities in the language that are themselves described by "metaclasses" and "metaclass classes." Java strikes a happy medium between these two languages with what is effectively a two-tiered system that uses Class objects.

Classes in Java source code are represented at runtime by instances of the java.lang. Class class. There's a Class object for every class you use; this Class object is responsible for producing instances of its class. But you don't have to worry about that unless you are interested in loading new kinds of classes dynamically at runtime. The Class object is also the basis for "reflecting" on a class to find its methods and other properties, allowing you to find out about an object's structure at runtime. We'll discuss reflection in the next section.

We get the Class associated with a particular object with the getClass() method:

```
String myString = "Foo!"
Class c = myString.getClass( );
```

We can also get the Class reference for a particular class statically, using the .class notation:

```
Class c = String.class;
```

The .class reference looks like a static field that exists in every class. However, it is really resolved by the compiler.

One thing we can do with the Class object is ask for the name of the object's class:

```
String s = "Boofa!";
Class myclass= s.getClass( );
System.out.println( myclass.getName( ) );   // "java.lang.String"
```

Another thing that we can do with a `Class` is to ask it to produce a new instance of its type of object. Continuing with the previous example:

```
try {
    String s2 = (String)strClass.newInstance( );
}
catch ( InstantiationException e ) { ... }
catch ( IllegalAccessException e ) { ... }
```

`newInstance()` has a return type of `Object`, so we have to cast it to a reference of the appropriate type. (`newInstance()` has to be able to return any kind of constructed object.) A couple of exceptions can be thrown here. An `InstantiationException` indicates we're trying to instantiate an abstract class or an interface. `IllegalAccessException` is a more general exception that indicates we can't access a constructor for the object. Note that `newInstance()` can create only an instance of a class that has an accessible default constructor. It doesn't allow us to pass any arguments to a constructor. (But see the later section "Accessing Constructors," where we'll learn how to do just that.)

All this becomes more meaningful when we add the capability to look up a class by name. `forName()` is a static method of `Class` that returns a `Class` object given its name as a `String`:

```
try {
    Class sneakersClass = Class.forName("Sneakers");
}
catch ( ClassNotFoundException e ) { ... }
```

A `ClassNotFoundException` is thrown if the class can't be located.

Combining these tools, we have the power to load new kinds of classes dynamically. When combined with the power of interfaces, we can use new data types by name in our applications:

```
interface Typewriter {
    void typeLine( String s );
    ...
}

class Printer implements Typewriter {
    ...
}

class MyApplication {
    ...
    String outputDeviceName = "Printer";

    try {
        Class newClass = Class.forName( outputDeviceName );
        Typewriter device = (Typewriter)newClass.newInstance( );
        ...
```

```
            device.typeLine("Hello...");
        }
        catch ( Exception e ) { ... }
    }
```

Here we have an application loading a class implementation (Printer, which imple-ments the Typewriter interface) knowing only its name. Imagine the name was entered by the user or looked up from a configuration file. This kind of class loading is the basis for many kinds of configurable systems in Java.

Reflection

In this section, we'll take a look at the Java Reflection API, supported by the classes in the java.lang.reflect package. As its name suggests, reflection is the ability for a class or object to examine itself. Reflection lets Java code look at an object (more pre-cisely, the class of the object) and determine its structure. Within the limits imposed by the security manager, you can find out what constructors, methods, and fields a class has, as well as their attributes. You can even change the value of fields, dynami-cally invoke methods, and construct new objects, much as if Java had primitive pointers to variables and methods. And you can do all this on objects that your code has never even seen before.

We don't have room here to cover the Reflection API fully. As you might expect, the reflect package is complex and rich in details. But reflection has been designed so that you can do a lot with relatively little effort; 20% of the effort gives you 80% of the fun.

The Reflection API is used by JavaBeans to determine the capabilities of objects at runtime. It's also used at a lower level by object serialization to tear apart and build objects for transport over streams or into persistent storage. Obviously, the power to pick apart objects and see their internals must be zealously guarded by the security manager. The general rule is that your code is not allowed to do anything with the Reflection API that it couldn't do with static (ordinary, compiled) Java code. In short, reflection is a powerful tool, but it isn't an automatic loophole. By default, an object can't use it to work with fields or methods that it wouldn't normally be able to access (for example, another object's private fields), although those privileges can be granted, as we'll discuss later.

The three primary features of a class are its fields (variables), methods, and construc-tors. For purposes of describing or accessing an object, these three features are repre-sented by separate classes in the Reflection API: java.lang.reflect.Field, java.lang.reflect.Method, and java.lang.reflect.Constructor. We can look up these members of a class using the Class object.

The Class class provides two pairs of methods for getting at each type of feature. One pair allows access to a class's public features (including those inherited from its superclasses) while the other pair allows access to any public or nonpublic item declared directly within the class (but not features that are inherited), subject to security considerations. Some examples:

- `getFields()` returns an array of `Field` objects representing all a class's public variables, including those it inherits.
- `getDeclaredFields()` returns an array representing all the variables declared in the class, regardless of their access modifiers (not including variables the security manager won't let you see), but not including inherited variables.
- For constructors, the distinction between "all constructors" and "declared constructors" is not meaningful (classes do not inherit constructors), so `getConstructors()` and `getDeclaredConstructors()` differ only in that the former returns public constructors, while the latter returns all the class's constructors.

Each pair of methods includes a method for listing all the items at once (for example, `getFields()`) and a method for looking up a particular item by name and—for methods and constructors—by signature (for example, `getField()`, which takes the field name as an argument).

The following listing shows the methods in the `Class` class:

`Field [] getFields();`
> Get all public variables, including inherited ones.

`Field getField(String name);`
> Get the specified public variable, which may be inherited.

`Field [] getDeclaredFields();`
> Get all public and nonpublic variables declared in this class (not including those inherited from superclasses).

`Field getDeclaredField(String name);`
> Get the specified variable, public or nonpublic, declared in this class (inherited variables not considered).

`Method [] getMethods();`
> Get all public methods, including inherited ones.

`Method getMethod(String name, Class [] argumentTypes);`
> Get the specified public method whose arguments match the types listed in `argumentTypes`. The method may be inherited.

`Method [] getDeclaredMethods();`
> Get all public and nonpublic methods declared in this class (not including those inherited from superclasses).

`Method getDeclaredMethod(String name, Class [] argumentTypes);`
> Get the specified method, public or nonpublic, whose arguments match the types listed in `argumentTypes`, and which is declared in this class (inherited methods not considered).

```
Constructor [] getConstructors( );
```
   Get all public constructors of this class.
```
Constructor getConstructor(Class [] argumentTypes);
```
   Get the specified public constructor of this class whose arguments match the types listed in argumentTypes.
```
Constructor [] getDeclaredConstructors( );
```
   Get all public and nonpublic constructors of this class.
```
Constructor getDeclaredConstructor(Class [] argumentTypes);
```
   Get the specified constructor, public or nonpublic, whose arguments match the types listed in argumentTypes.

As a quick example, we'll show how easy it is to list all the public methods of the java.util.Calendar class:

```
Method [] methods = Calendar.class.getMethods( );
for (int i=0; i < methods.length; i++)
    System.out.println( methods[i] );
```

Here we have used the .class notation to get a reference to the Class of Calendar. Remember the discussion of the Class class; the reflection methods don't belong to a particular instance of Calendar itself; they belong to the java.lang.Class object that describes the Calendar class. If we wanted to start from an instance of Calendar (or, say, an unknown object), we could have used the getClass() method of the object instead:

```
Method [] methods = myUnknownObject.getClass( ).getMethods( );
```

Security

Access to the Reflection API is governed by a security manager. A fully trusted application has access to all the previously discussed functionality; it can gain access to members of classes at the level of restriction normally granted code within its scope. It is, however, possible to grant special access to code so that it can use the Reflection API to gain access to private and protected members of other classes in a way that the Java language ordinarily disallows.

The Field, Method, and Constructor classes all extend from a base class called AccessibleObject. The AccessibleObject class has one important method called setAccessible(), which allows you to deactivate normal security when accessing that particular class member. That may sound too easy. It is indeed simple, but whether that method allows you to disable security or not is a function of the Java security manager and security policy. You can do this in a normal Java application running without any security policy.

Accessing Fields

The class java.lang.reflect.Field represents static variables and instance variables. Field has a full set of overloaded accessor methods for all the base types (for example, getInt() and setInt(), getBoolean() and setBoolean()) and get() and set() methods for accessing members that are object references. Let's consider this class:

```
class BankAccount {
    public int balance;
}
```

With the Reflection API, we can read and modify the value of the public integer field balance:

```
BankAccount myBankAccount = ...;
...
try {
    Field balanceField = BankAccount.class.getField("balance");
    // read it
    int mybalance = balanceField.getInt( myBankAccount );
    // change it
    balanceField.setInt( myBankAccount, 42 );
} catch ( NoSuchFieldException e ) {
    ... // there is no "balance" field in this class
} catch ( IllegalAccessException e2) {
    ... // we don't have permission to access the field
}
```

In this example, we are assuming that we already know the structure of a BankAccount object. But in general we could gather that information from the object itself.

All the data access methods of Field take a reference to the particular object instance that we want to access. In the code shown earlier, the getField() method returns a Field object that represents the balance of the BankAccount class; this object doesn't refer to any specific BankAccount. Therefore, to read or modify any specific BankAccount, we call getInt() and setInt() with a reference to myBankAccount, which is the particular account we want to work with. An exception occurs if we try to access a field that doesn't exist, or if we don't have the proper permission to read or write to the field. If we make balance a private field, we can still look up the Field object that describes it, but we won't be able to read or write its value.

Therefore, we aren't doing anything that we couldn't have done with static code at compile time; as long as balance is a public member of a class that we can access, we can write code to read and modify its value. What's important is that we're accessing balance at runtime, and we could just as easily use this technique to examine the balance field in a class that was dynamically loaded.

Accessing Methods

The class java.lang.reflect.Method represents a static or instance method. Subject to the normal security rules, a Method object's invoke() method can be used to call the underlying object's method with specified arguments. Yes, Java does have something like a method pointer!

As an example, we'll write a Java application called Invoke that takes as command-line arguments the name of a Java class and the name of a method to invoke. For simplicity, we'll assume that the method is static and takes no arguments:

```
//file: Invoke.java
import java.lang.reflect.*;

class Invoke {
  public static void main( String [] args ) {
    try {
      Class c = Class.forName( args[0] );
      Method m = c.getMethod( args[1], new Class [] { } );
      Object ret = m.invoke( null, null );
      System.out.println(
          "Invoked static method: " + args[1]
          + " of class: " + args[0]
          + " with no args\nResults: " + ret );
    } catch ( ClassNotFoundException e ) {
      // Class.forName( ) can't find the class
    } catch ( NoSuchMethodException e2 ) {
      // that method doesn't exist
    } catch ( IllegalAccessException e3 ) {
      // we don't have permission to invoke that method
    } catch ( InvocationTargetException e4 ) {
      // an exception occurred while invoking that method
      System.out.println(
          "Method threw an: " + e4.getTargetException( ) );
    }
  }
}
```

We can run invoke to fetch the value of the system clock:

```
% java Invoke java.lang.System currentTimeMillis
Invoked static method: currentTimeMillis of class:
java.lang.System with no args
Results: 861129235818
```

Our first task is to look up the specified Class by name. To do so, we call the forName() method with the name of the desired class (the first command-line argument). We then ask for the specified method by its name. getMethod() has two arguments: the first is the method name (the second command-line argument), and the second is an array of Class objects that specifies the method's signature. (Remember that any method may be overloaded; you must specify the signature to make it clear which version you want.) Since our simple program calls only methods with no arguments, we create an anonymous empty array of Class objects. Had we wanted to invoke a method that takes arguments, we would have passed an array of the classes of their respective types, in the proper order. For primitive types we would have used the standard wrappers (Integer, Float, Boolean, etc.) to hold the values. The classes of primitive types in Java are represented by special static TYPE fields of their respective wrappers; for example, use Integer.TYPE for the class of an int.

Once we have the Method object, we call its invoke() method. This calls our target method and returns the result as an Object. To do anything nontrivial with this object, you have to cast it to something more specific. Presumably, since you're calling the method, you know what kind of object to expect. If the returned value is a primitive type such as int or boolean, it will be wrapped in the standard wrapper class for its type. (Wrappers for primitive types are discussed in Chapter 10.) If the method returns void, invoke() returns a java.lang.Void object. This is the wrapper class that represents void return values.

The first argument to invoke() is the object on which we would like to invoke the method. If the method is static, there is no object, so we set the first argument to null. That's the case in our example. The second argument is an array of objects to be passed as arguments to the method. The types of these should match the types specified in the call to getMethod(). Because we're calling a method with no arguments, we can pass null for the second argument to invoke(). As with the return value, you must use wrapper classes for primitive argument types.

The exceptions shown in the previous code occur if we can't find or don't have permission to access the method. Additionally, an InvocationTargetException occurs if the method being invoked throws some kind of exception itself. You can find what it threw by calling the getTargetException() method of InvocationTargetException.

Accessing Constructors

The java.lang.reflect.Constructor class represents an object constructor that accepts arguments. You can use it, subject to the security manager of course, to create a new instance of an object. Recall that you can create instances of a class with Class.newInstance(), but you cannot specify arguments with that method. This is the solution to that problem, if you really need to do it.

Here we'll create an instance of java.util.Date,[*] passing a string argument to the constructor:

```
try {
    Constructor c =
        Date.class.getConstructor(new Class [] { String.class } );
    Object o = c.newInstance( new Object [] { "Jan 1, 2000" } );
```

---

[*] This Date constructor is deprecated but will serve us for this example.

```
        Date d = (Date)o;
        System.out.println(d);
    } catch ( NoSuchMethodException e ) {
        // getConstructor( ) couldn't find the constructor we described
    } catch ( InstantiationException e2 ) {
        // the class is abstract
    } catch ( IllegalAccessException e3 ) {
        // we don't have permission to create an instance
    } catch ( InvocationTargetException e4 ) {
        // the construct threw an exception
    }
```

The story is much the same as with a method invocation; after all, a constructor is really no more than a method with some strange properties. We look up the appropriate constructor for our Date class—the one that takes a single String as its argument—by passing getConstructor() an array containing the String class as its only element. (If the constructor required more arguments, we would put additional objects in the array, representing the class of each argument.) We can then invoke newInstance(), passing it a corresponding array of argument objects. Again, to pass primitive types, we would wrap them in their wrapper types first. Finally, we cast the resulting object to a Date and print it.

The exceptions from the previous example apply here, too, along with IllegalArgumentException and InstantiationException. The latter is thrown if the class is abstract and therefore can't be instantiated.

What About Arrays?

The Reflection API allows you to create and inspect arrays of base types using the java.lang.reflect.Array class. The process is very much the same as with the other classes, so we won't cover it in detail. The primary feature is a static method of Array called newInstance(), which creates an array, allowing you to specify a base type and length. You can also use it to construct multidimensional array instances, by specifying an array of lengths (one for each dimension). For more information, look in your favorite Java language reference.

Dynamic Interface Adapters

Ideally, Java reflection would allow us to do everything at runtime that we can do at compile time (without forcing us to generate and compile source into bytecode). But that is not entirely the case. Although we can dynamically load and create instances of objects at runtime using the Class.forName() method, there is no general way to create new types of objects—for which no class files preexist—on the fly.

In Java 1.3, the java.lang.reflect.Proxy class was added, which takes a step towards solving this problem by allowing the creation of adapter objects that implement arbitrary interfaces. The Proxy class is a factory that can generate an adapter class implementing any interface (or interfaces) you want. When methods are invoked on the adapter class, they are delegated to a designated InvocationHandler object. You can use this to create implementations of any kind of interface at runtime and handle the method calls anywhere you want. This is particularly important for tools that work with JavaBeans, which must dynamically register event listeners. (We'll mention this again in Chapter 21.)

In the following snippet, we take an interface name and construct a proxy implementing the interface. It outputs a message whenever any of the interface's methods is invoked:

```
import java.lang.reflect.*;

InvocationHandler handler =
    new InvocationHandler( ) {
        invoke( Object proxy, Method method, Object[] args ) {
            System.out.println( "Method: "+ method.getName( ) +"( )"
                                +" of interface: "+ interfaceName
                                + " invoked on proxy." );
            return null;
        }
    };

Class clas = Class.forName( MyInterface );

MyInterface interfaceProxy =
    (MyInterface)Proxy.newProxyInstance(
        clas.getClassLoader( ), new Class[] { class }, handler );
```

The resulting object, interfaceProxy, is cast to the type of the interface we want. It will call our handler whenever any of its methods are invoked.

First we make an implementation of InvocationHandler. This is an object with an invoke() method that takes as its argument the Method being called and an array of objects representing the arguments to the method call. Then we fetch the class of the interface that we're going to implement using Class.forName(). Finally we ask the proxy to create an adapter for us, specifying the types of interfaces (you can specify more than one) that we want implemented and the handler to use. invoke() is expected to return an object of the correct type for the method call. If it returns the wrong type, a special runtime exception is thrown. Any primitive types in the arguments or in the return value should be wrapped in the appropriate wrapper class. (The runtime system unwraps the return value, if necessary.)

What Is Reflection Good for?

In Chapter 21 we'll learn how reflection is used to dynamically discover capabilities and features of JavaBean objects. But these are somewhat behind-the-scenes applications. What can reflection do for us in everyday situations?

Well, we could use reflection to go about acting as if Java had dynamic method invocation and other useful capabilities; in Chapter 21, we'll also develop a dynamic adapter class using reflection. But as a general coding practice, dynamic method invocation is a bad idea. One of the primary features of Java is its strong typing and safety. You abandon much of that when you take a dip in the reflecting pool. And although the performance of the Reflection API is very good, it is not as fast as compiled method invocations in general.

More appropriately, you can use reflection in situations where you need to work with objects that you can't know about in advance. Reflection puts Java on a higher plane of programming languages, opening up possibilities for new kinds of applications. As we hinted earlier, one of the most important uses for reflection is in integrating Java with scripting languages. With reflection, you can write a source code interpreter in Java that can access the full Java APIs, create objects, invoke methods, modify variables and do all the other things a Java program can do at compile time, while it is running. In fact someone has done this—one of the authors of this book!

The BeanShell scripting language

I (Pat) can't resist inserting a plug here for BeanShell—my free, open source, lightweight Java scripting language. BeanShell is just what I alluded to in the previous section—a Java application that uses the Reflection API to execute Java statements and expressions dynamically. You can use BeanShell interactively to quickly try out some of the examples in this book (although you can't create classes per se). BeanShell exercises the Java Reflection API to its fullest and serves as a demonstration of how dynamic the Java runtime environment really is.

You can find a copy of BeanShell on the CD-ROM that accompanies this book and the latest release and documentation at its web site, *http://www.beanshell.org*. In recent years BeanShell has become quite popular. It is now distributed with Emacs as part of the JDE and bundled with popular application environments including BEA's WebLogic server, NetBeans, and Sun's Forte for Java IDE. See Appendix B for more information on getting started. I hope you find it both interesting and useful!

Threads

At the heart of designing computer systems and software lies the problem of managing time, specifically, scheduling what to do and when to do it. We take for granted that modern computer systems such as desktop computers can manage many applications running concurrently and produce the effect that the software is running simultaneously. Of course we know that, for the most part, our single processor computers can do only one thing at a time. The magic is performed by slight of hand in the operating system, which juggles applications and turns its attention from one to the next so quickly that they appear to run at once.

In the old days, the unit of concurrency for such systems was the application or *process*. To the OS, a process was more or less a black box that decided what do to on its own. If an application required greater concurrency, it could get it only by running multiple processes and communicating between them, but this was a heavy-weight approach and not very elegant. Later, the concept of threads was introduced. Threads provide fine-grained concurrency within a process, under the application's own control. Threads have existed for a long time but have historically been tricky to use. In Java, support for threading is built right into the language, which means it's easier to work with threads. It also means that Java's APIs take full advantage of threading. So it's important that you become familiar with threads early in your exploration of Java.

Threads are integral to the design of many Java APIs. For example, when we look at GUI programming later in this book, you'll see that a component's paint() method isn't called directly by the application but rather by a separate master thread within the Java runtime system. At any given time, there may be many such background threads, performing activities in parallel with your application. In fact, it's easy to get half a dozen or more threads running in an application without even trying, simply by loading images, updating the screen, playing audio, and so on. But these things happen behind the scenes; you don't normally have to worry about them. In this chapter, we'll talk about writing applications that create and use their own threads explicitly.

Introducing Threads

Conceptually, a *thread* is a flow of control within a program. A thread is similar to the more familiar notion of a process, except that multiple threads within the same application share much of the same state—in particular, they run in the same address space. It's not unlike a golf course, which many golfers use at the same time. Sharing the same address space means that threads share a working area. They have access to the same objects including static and instance variables within their application. However, threads have their own copies of local variables, just as players share the golf course, but not personal things like clubs and balls.

Multiple threads in an application have the same problems as the golfers—in a word, synchronization. Just as you can't have two sets of players blindly playing the same green at the same time, you can't have several threads trying to access the same variables without some kind of coordination. Someone is bound to get hurt. A thread can reserve the right to use an object until it's finished with its task, just as a golf party gets exclusive rights to the green until it's done. And a thread that is more important can raise its priority, asserting its right to play through.

The devil is in the details, of course, and those details have historically made threads difficult to use. Fortunately Java makes creating, controlling, and coordinating threads simpler by integrating some of these concepts directly into the language.

It is common to stumble over threads when you first work with them because creating a thread exercises many of your new Java skills all at once. You can avoid confusion by remembering there are always two players involved in running a thread: a Java language object that represents the thread itself and an arbitrary target object that contains the method the thread is to execute. Later, you will see that it is possible to play some sleight of hand and combine these two roles, but that special case just changes the packaging, not the relationship.

The Thread Class and the Runnable Interface

A new thread is born when we create an instance of the java.lang.Thread class. The Thread object represents a real thread in the Java interpreter and serves as a handle for controlling and coordinating with its execution. With it, we can start the thread, wait for it to complete, cause it to sleep for a time, or interrupt its activity. The constructor for the Thread class accepts information about where the thread should begin its execution. Conceptually, we would like to simply tell it what method to run, but since there are no pointers to methods in Java (not in this sense anyway), we can't specify one directly. Instead, we have to take a short detour and use the java.lang.Runnable interface to create an object that contains a "runnable" method. Runnable defines a single, general-purpose method.

```
public interface Runnable {
    abstract public void run( );
}
```

Every thread begins its life by executing the run() method in a Runnable object, the "target object" that was passed to the thread's constructor. The run() method can contain any code, but it must be public, take no arguments, have no return value, and throw no checked exceptions.

Any class that contains an appropriate run() method can declare that it implements the Runnable interface. An instance of this class is then a runnable object that can serve as the target of a new thread. If you don't want to put the run() method directly in your object (and very often you don't), you can always make an adapter class that serves as the Runnable for you. The adapter's run() method can then call any method it wants after the thread is started. We'll show examples of these options later.

Creating and starting threads

A newly born thread remains idle until we give it a figurative slap on the bottom by calling its start() method. The thread then wakes up and proceeds to execute the run() method of its target object. start() can be called only once in the lifetime of a thread. Once a thread starts, it continues running until the target object's run() method returns (or throws an unchecked exception of some kind). The start() method has a sort of evil twin method called stop(), which kills the thread permanently. However, this method is deprecated and should no longer be used. We'll explain why and give some examples of a better way to stop your threads later in this chapter. We will also look at some other methods you can use to control a thread's progress while it is running.

Now let's look at an example. The following class, Animation, implements a run() method to drive its drawing loop:

```
class Animation implements Runnable {
    public void run( ) {
        while ( true ) {
            // draw Frames
            ...
        }
    }
}
```

To use it, we create a Thread object, passing it an instance of Animation as its target object, and invoke its start() method. We can perform these steps explicitly:

```
Animation happy = new Animation("Mr. Happy");
Thread myThread = new Thread( happy );
myThread.start( );
```

Here we have created an instance of our Animation class and passed it as the argument to the constructor for myThread. When we call the start() method, myThread begins to execute Animation's run() method. Let the show begin!

This situation is not terribly object-oriented. More often, we want an object to handle its own threads, as shown in Figure 8-1, which depicts a Runnable object that creates and starts its own thread. We'll show our Animation class performing these actions in its constructor, although in practice it might be better to place them in a more explicit controller method (e.g., startAnimation()).

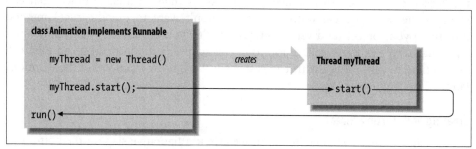

Figure 8-1. Interaction between Animation and its thread

```
class Animation implements Runnable {
    Thread myThread;
    Animation (String name) {
        myThread = new Thread( this );
        myThread.start( );
    }
    ...
}
```

In this case, the argument we pass to the Thread constructor is this, the current object (which is a Runnable). We keep the Thread reference in the instance variable myThread in case we want to interrupt the show or exercise some other kind of control later.

A natural-born thread

The Runnable interface lets us make an arbitrary object the target of a thread, as we did in the previous example. This is the most important general usage of the Thread class. In most situations in which you need to use threads, you'll create a class (possibly a simple adapter class) that implements the Runnable interface.

However we'd be remiss not to show you the other technique for creating a thread. Another design option is to make our target class a subclass of a type that is already runnable. As it turns out, the Thread class itself conveniently implements the

Runnable interface; it has its own run() method, which we can override directly to do our bidding:

```
class Animation extends Thread {
    public void run( ) {
        while ( true ) {
            // draw Frames
            ...
        }
    }
}
```

The skeleton of our Animation class looks much the same as before, except that our class is now a subclass of Thread. To go along with this scheme, the default constructor of the Thread class makes itself the default target. That is, by default, the Thread executes its own run() method when we call the start() method, as shown in Figure 8-2. So now our subclass can just override the run() method in the Thread class. (Thread itself defines an empty run() method.)

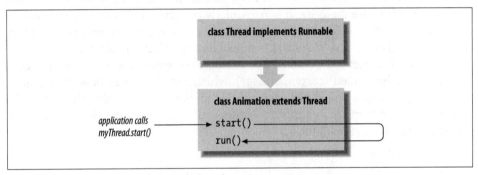

Figure 8-2. Animation as a subclass of Thread

Now we create an instance of Animation and call its start() method (which it also inherited from Thread):

```
Animation bouncy = new Animation("Bouncy");
bouncy.start( );
```

Alternatively, we can have the Animation object start its thread when it is created, as before:

```
class Animation extends Thread {

    Animation (String name) {
        start( );
    }
    ...
}
```

Here our Animation object just calls its own start() method when an instance is created. (Again, it's probably better form to start and stop our objects explicitly after they're created rather than starting threads as a hidden side effect of object creation. But this serves the example well.)

Subclassing Thread may seem like a convenient way to bundle a thread and its target run() method. However, this approach often isn't the best design. If you subclass Thread to implement a thread, you are saying you need a new type of object that is a kind of Thread, which exposes all of the public API of the Thread class. While there is something very satisfying about taking an object that's primarily concerned with performing a task and making it a Thread, the actual situations where you'll want to create a subclass of Thread should not be very common. In most cases, it is more natural to let the requirements of your program dictate the class structure. If you find you're subclassing Thread a lot, you may want to examine whether you are falling into the design trap of making objects that are really glorified functions.

Using an adapter

Finally, as we have suggested, we can build an adapter class to give us more control over how to structure the code. It is particularly convenient to create an anonymous inner class that implements Runnable and invokes an arbitrary method in our object. This almost gives the feel of starting a thread and specifying an arbitrary method to run, as if we had method pointers. For example, suppose that our Animation class provides a method called startAnimating(), which performs setup (loads the images, etc.) and then starts a thread to perform the animation. We'll say that the actual guts of the animation loop are in a private method called drawFrames(). We could use an adapter to run drawFrames() for us:

```
class Animation {

    public void startAnimating( ) {
        // do setup, load images, etc.
        ...
        // start a drawing thread
        Thread myThread = new Thread ( new Runnable( ) {
            public void run() { drawFrames( ); }
        } );
        myThread.start( );
    }

    private void drawFrames( ) {
        // do animation ...
    }
}
```

In this code, the anonymous inner class implementing Runnable is generated for us by the compiler. We create a thread with this anonymous object as its target and have its run() method call our drawFrames() method. We have avoided implementing a generic run() method in our application code at the expense of generating an extra class.

Note that we could be even more terse in the previous example by simply having our anonymous inner class extend `Thread` rather than implement `Runnable`. We could also start the thread without saving a reference to it if we won't be using it later.

```
new Thread( ) {
    public void run( ) { drawFrames( ); }
}.start( );
```

Controlling Threads

We have seen the `start()` method used to bring a newly created thread to life. Several other instance methods let us explicitly control a thread's execution:

- The `sleep()` method causes the current thread to wait for a designated period of time, without consuming much (or possibly any) CPU time.
- The methods `wait()` and `join()` coordinate the execution of two or more threads. We'll discuss them in detail when we talk about thread synchronization later in this chapter.
- The `interrupt()` method wakes up a thread that is sleeping in a `sleep()` or `wait()` operation or is otherwise blocked on a long I/O operation.[*]

Deprecated methods

We should also mention that there are three deprecated thread control methods: `stop()`, `suspend()`, and `resume()`. The `stop()` method complements `start()`; it destroys the thread. `start()`, and the deprecated `stop()` method, can be called only once in the life cycle of a thread. By contrast, the deprecated `suspend()` and `resume()` methods were used to arbitrarily pause and then restart the execution of a thread.

Although these deprecated methods still exist in the latest version of Java (and will probably be there forever), they shouldn't be used in new code development. The problem with both `stop()` and `suspend()` is that they seize control of a thread's execution in an uncoordinated and harsh way. This makes programming difficult; it's not always easy for an application to anticipate and properly recover from being interrupted at an arbitrary point in its execution. Moreover, when a thread is seized using one of these methods, the Java runtime system must release all its internal locks used for thread synchronization. This can cause unexpected behavior and, in the case of `suspend()`, can easily lead to deadlock.

A better way to affect the execution of a thread—which requires just a bit more work on your part—is by creating some simple logic in your thread's code to use monitor variables (flags), possibly in conjunction with the `interrupt()` method, which allows you to wake up a sleeping thread. In other words, you should cause your thread to

---

[*] `interrupt()` does not work in versions of Java prior to 1.1 and, historically, has not worked consistently in all Java implementations.

stop or resume what it is doing by asking it nicely rather than by pulling the rug out from under it unexpectedly. The thread examples in this book use this technique in one way or another.

The sleep( ) method

We often need to tell a thread to sit idle, or "sleep," for a fixed period of time. While a thread is asleep, or otherwise blocked on input of some kind, it doesn't consume CPU time or compete with other threads for processing. For this, we can either call the thread's sleep() instance method or use the static convenience method Thread. sleep(), which affects the currently executing thread. In either case, the call causes the thread to go idle for a specified number of milliseconds:

```
try {
    // The current thread
    Thread.sleep( 1000 );
    // particular thread
    someThread.sleep( 500 );
} catch ( InterruptedException e ) {
    // someone woke us up prematurely
}
```

The sleep() method may throw an InterruptedException if it is interrupted by another thread via the interrupt() method. As you see in the previous code, the thread can catch this exception and take the opportunity to perform some action— such as checking a variable to determine whether or not it should exit—or perhaps just perform some housekeeping and then go back to sleep.

The join( ) method

Finally, if you need to coordinate your activities with another thread by waiting for the other thread to complete its task, you can use the join() method. Calling a thread's join() method causes the caller to block until the target thread completes. Alternatively, you can poll the thread by calling join() with a number of milliseconds to wait. This is a very coarse form of thread synchronization. Later in this chapter, we'll look at a much more general and powerful mechanism for coordinating the activities of threads: wait() and notify().

The interrupt( ) method

Earlier we described the interrupt() method as a way to wake up a thread that is idle in a sleep(), wait(), or lengthy I/O operation. This is indeed the prescribed functionality of the method. However, historically, this has been a weak spot, and Java implementations have had trouble getting it to work correctly in all cases. In early Java VMs (prior to Version 1.1), interrupt did not work at all. In more recent versions there are still problems with interrupting I/O calls. By an I/O call we mean when an application is blocked in a read() or write() method, moving bytes to or from a source such as a file or the network. In this case Java is supposed to throw an `InterruptedIOException` when the `interrupt()` is performed. However this has never been reliable across all Java implementations. To address this in Java 1.4, a new I/O framework (java.nio) was introduced with one of its goals being to specifically address these problems. When the thread associated with an NIO operation is interrupted, the thread wakes up and the I/O stream (called a "channel") is automatically closed. (See Chapter 11 for more about the NIO package.)

Death of a Thread

A thread continues to execute until one of the following things happens:

- It explicitly returns from its target `run()` method.
- It encounters an uncaught runtime exception.
- The evil and nasty deprecated `stop()` method is called.

So what happens if none of these things occurs, and the `run()` method for a thread never terminates? The answer is that the thread can live on, even after what is ostensibly the part of the application that created it has finished. This means we have to be aware of how our threads eventually terminate, or an application can end up leaving orphaned threads that unnecessarily consume resources.

In many cases, we really want to create background threads that do simple, periodic tasks in an application. The `setDaemon()` method can be used to mark a thread as a daemon thread that should be killed and discarded when no other application threads remain. Normally, the Java interpreter continues to run until all threads have completed. But when daemon threads are the only threads still alive, the interpreter will exit.

Here's a devilish example using daemon threads:

```
class Devil extends Thread {
    Devil( ) {
        setDaemon( true );
        start( );
    }
    public void run( ) {
        // perform evil tasks
    }
}
```

In this example, the `Devil` thread sets its daemon status when it is created. If any `Devil` threads remain when our application is otherwise complete, the runtime system kills them for us. We don't have to worry about cleaning them up.

Daemon threads are primarily useful in standalone Java applications and in the implementation of the Java runtime system itself, but not component applications such as applets. Since an applet runs inside another Java application, any daemon threads it creates can continue to live until the controlling application exits—probably not the desired effect. A browser or any other application can use ThreadGroups to contain all the threads created by subsystems of an application and then clean them up if necessary.

One final note about killing threads gracefully. A very common problem new developers encounter the first time they create an application using an AWT or Swing component is that their application never exits; the Java VM just seems to hang indefinitely after everything is finished. This is because when working with graphics, Java has created an AWT thread to process input and painting events. The AWT thread is not a daemon thread so it doesn't exit automatically when other application threads have completed, and the developer must call System.exit() explicitly. (If you think about it, this makes sense. Since most GUI applications are event-driven and simply wait for user input, they would otherwise simply exit after their startup code completed.)

Threading an Applet

Applets are embeddable Java applications that are expected to start and stop themselves on command. Applets may be asked to start and stop themselves any number of times. A Java-enabled web browser normally starts an applet when the applet is displayed and stops it when the user moves to another page or (in theory) when the user scrolls the applet out of view. To conform to the semantics of the API, we would like an applet to cease its nonessential activity when it is stopped and resume it when started again. (If you're not familiar with applets, you may want to take a look at Chapter 22 at this point.)

In this section, we will build UpdateApplet, a simple base class for an applet that maintains a thread to automatically update its display at regular intervals. Although we're building an applet here, the general techniques are important for all threaded applications.

UpdateApplet handles the basic starting and stopping behavior for us:

```
//file: UpdateApplet.java
public class UpdateApplet extends java.applet.Applet
    implements Runnable
{
    private Thread updateThread;
    int updateInterval = 1000;

    public void run( ) {
        while ( updateThread != null ) {
            try {
                Thread.sleep( updateInterval );
            } catch (InterruptedException e ) {
                return;
            }
            repaint( );
```

```
        }
    }

    public void start( ) {
        if ( updateThread == null ) {
            updateThread = new Thread(this);
            updateThread.start( );
        }
    }
    public void stop( ) {
        if ( updateThread != null ) {
            Thread runner = updateThread;
            updateThread = null;    // flag to quit
            runner.interrupt( );    // wake up if asleep
        }
    }
}
```

UpdateApplet is a Runnable object that alternately sleeps and calls its repaint() method. (There's nothing to paint, though, so running this applet is kind of boring. Later in this section, we'll subclass it to implement a digital clock.) It has two other public methods: start() and stop(). These are methods of the Applet class we are overriding; don't confuse them with the similarly named methods of the Thread class. These start() and stop() methods are called by the web browser or applet viewer to tell the applet when it should and should not be running.

UpdateApplet illustrates an environmentally friendly way to deal with threads in a simple applet. UpdateApplet simply dismisses its thread each time the applet is stopped and recreates it if the applet is restarted. When UpdateApplet's start() method is called, we first check to make sure there is no currently executing updateThread. We then create one to begin our execution. When our applet is subsequently asked to stop, we set a flag indicating that it should stop and then make sure it is awake by invoking its interrupt() method. In our stop() method, we set updateThread to null, which serves three purposes: it allows the garbage collector to clean up the dead Thread object; it indicates to UpdateApplet's start() method that the thread is gone so that another one can be started when necessary; and it serves as the flag to indicate to the running thread that it is time to quit. If you feel that we have overburdened this variable, you might consider using a separate boolean variable for the flag condition.

One thing about Applets: in truth, an Applet's start() and stop() methods are guaranteed to be called in sequence. As a result, we shouldn't have to check for the existence of updateThread in start(). (It should always be null.) However, it's good programming practice to perform the test. If we didn't, and for some reason stop() were to fail at its job, we might inadvertently start a lot of threads.

With UpdateApplet doing all the work for us, we can now create the world's simplest clock applet with just a few lines of code. Figure 8-3 shows our Clock. (This might be a good one to run on your Java wristwatch.)

Sat Apr 21 09:37:51 MDT 2002

Figure 8-3. The Clock applet

Here's the code:

```
//file: Clock.java
public class Clock extends UpdateApplet {
    public void paint( java.awt.Graphics g ) {
        g.drawString( new java.util.Date( ).toString( ), 10, 25 );
    }
}
```

The `java.util.Date().toString()` method creates a string that contains the current time.

Our `Clock` applet provides a good example of a simple thread; we don't mind throwing it away and subsequently rebuilding it if the user should happen to wander on and off our web page a few times. But what if the task that our thread handles isn't so simple? What if, for instance, we have to open a socket and establish a connection with another system? This isn't strictly a function of the thread of course. But a more general solution might be to have the thread set a timer for itself and clean up at some point in the future.

Now if you're concerned about being so cavalier in creating and discarding `Thread` objects, you might also ask if we couldn't simply do a little more logic and save our thread. Perhaps we could teach the applet's `start()` method to have the existing thread start up again rather than having to create a new thread. It should be apparent how to go about this using the `wait()` and `notify()` methods after you read the next section on thread synchronization.

However, an issue with applets is that we have no control over how a user navigates web pages. For example, say a user scrolls our applet out of view, and we pause our thread. Now we have no way of ensuring that the user will bring the applet back into view before moving to another page. And actually, the same situation would occur if the user simply moves on to another page and never comes back. That's not a problem in this simple example, but there may be cases in which we need to do some application cleanup before we die. For this situation the Applet API gives us the `destroy()` method. `destroy()` is called by the Java runtime system when the applet is going to be removed (often from a cache). It provides a place at which we can free up any resources the applet is holding.

Synchronization

Every thread has a life of its own. Normally, a thread goes about its business without any regard for what other threads in the application are doing. Threads may be time-sliced, which means they can run in arbitrary spurts and bursts as directed by the operating system. On a multiprocessor system, it is even possible for many different threads to be running simultaneously on different CPUs. This section is about coordinating the activities of two or more threads so that they can work together and not collide in their use of the same address space (coordinating their play on the golf course).

Java provides a few simple structures for synchronizing the activities of threads. They are all based on the concept of monitors, a widely used synchronization scheme (developed by C.A.R. Hoare). You don't have to know the details about how monitors work to be able to use them, but it may help you to have a picture in mind.

A monitor is essentially a lock. The lock is attached to a resource that many threads may need to access, but that should be accessed by only one thread at a time. It's very much like a restroom with a door that locks. If the resource is not being used, the thread can acquire the lock and access the resource. By the same token, if the restroom is unlocked, you can enter and lock the door. When the thread is done, it relinquishes the lock, just as you unlock the door and leave it open for the next person. However, if another thread already has the lock for the resource, all other threads have to wait until the current thread finishes and releases the lock. This is just like when the restroom is locked when you arrive: you have to wait until the current occupant is done and unlocks the door.

Fortunately, Java makes the process of synchronizing access to resources quite easy. The language handles setting up and acquiring locks; all you have to do is specify which resources require locks.

Serializing Access to Methods

The most common need for synchronization among threads in Java is to serialize their access to some resource (an object)—in other words, to make sure that only one thread at a time can manipulate an object or variable.* In Java, every object has a lock associated with it. To be more specific, every class and every instance of a class has its own lock. The synchronized keyword marks places where a thread must acquire the lock before proceeding.

---

* Don't confuse the term "serialize" in this context with Java object serialization, which is a mechanism for making objects persistent. But the underlying meaning (to place one thing after another) does apply to both. In the case of object serialization, it is the object's data which is laid out, byte for byte, in a certain order.

For example, say we implemented a SpeechSynthesizer class that contains a say() method. We don't want multiple threads calling say() at the same time, or we wouldn't be able to understand anything being said. So we mark the say() method as synchronized, which means that a thread has to acquire the lock on the SpeechSynthesizer object before it can speak:

```
class SpeechSynthesizer {
    synchronized void say( String words ) {
        // speak
    }
}
```

Because say() is an instance method, a thread has to acquire the lock on the SpeechSynthesizer instance it is using before it can invoke the say() method. When say() has completed, it gives up the lock, which allows the next waiting thread to acquire the lock and run the method. Note that it doesn't matter whether the thread is owned by the SpeechSynthesizer itself or some other object; every thread has to acquire the same lock, that of the SpeechSynthesizer instance. If say() were a class (static) method instead of an instance method, we could still mark it as synchronized. But in this case because there is no instance object involved, the lock is on the class object itself.

Often, you want to synchronize multiple methods of the same class so that only one method modifies or examines parts of the class at a time. All static synchronized methods in a class use the same class object lock. By the same token, all instance methods in a class use the same instance object lock. In this way, Java can guarantee that only one of a set of synchronized methods is running at a time. For example, a SpreadSheet class might contain a number of instance variables that represent cell values, as well as some methods that manipulate the cells in a row:

```
class SpreadSheet {
    int cellA1, cellA2, cellA3;

    synchronized int sumRow( ) {
        return cellA1 + cellA2 + cellA3;
    }

    synchronized void setRow( int a1, int a2, int a3 ) {
        cellA1 = a1;
        cellA2 = a2;
        cellA3 = a3;
    }
    ...
}
```

In this example, both methods setRow() and sumRow() access the cell values. You can see that problems might arise if one thread were changing the values of the variables in setRow() at the same moment another thread was reading the values in sumRow(). To prevent this, we have marked both methods as *synchronized*. When threads are synchronized, only one is run at a time. If a thread is in the middle of executing setRow() when another thread calls sumRow(), the second thread waits until the first one is done executing setRow() before it gets to run sumRow(). This synchronization allows us to preserve the consistency of the SpreadSheet. And the best part is that all this locking and waiting is handled by Java; it's transparent to the programmer.

In addition to synchronizing entire methods, the synchronized keyword can be used in a special construct to guard arbitrary blocks of code. In this form it also takes an explicit argument that specifies the object for which it is to acquire a lock:

```
synchronized ( myObject ) {
    // Functionality that needs to be synced
}
```

This code block can appear in any method. When it is reached, the thread has to acquire the lock on myObject before proceeding. In this way, we can synchronize methods (or parts of methods) in different classes in the same way as methods in the same class.

A synchronized instance method is, therefore, equivalent to a method with its statements synchronized on the current object. Thus:

```
synchronized void myMethod ( ) {
    ...
}
```

is equivalent to:

```
void myMethod ( ) {
    synchronized ( this ) {
        ...
    }
}
```

Accessing instance variables

In the SpreadSheet example, we guarded access to a set of instance variables with a synchronized method, which we did mainly so that we wouldn't change one of the variables while someone was reading the rest of them. We wanted to keep them coordinated. But what about individual variable types? Do they need to be synchronized? Normally the answer is no. Almost all operations on primitives and object reference types in Java happen *atomically*: they are handled by the virtual machine in one step, with no opportunity for two threads to collide. You can't be in the middle of changing a reference and be only part way done when another thread looks at the reference.

But watch out—we did say almost. If you read the Java virtual machine specification carefully, you will see that the double and long primitive types are not guaranteed to be handled atomically. Both of these types represent 64-bit values. The problem has to do with how the Java VM's stack handles them. It is possible that this specification will be beefed up in the future. But for now, if you have any fears, synchronize access to your `double` and `long` instance variables through accessor methods.

Reentrant locking

The locks acquired by Java upon entering a synchronized method or block of code are reentrant. This means that the thread holding onto the lock may acquire the same lock again any number of times and will never block waiting for itself. In most cases this just means that the code behaves as you'd expect; a thread can call a synchronized method recursively, for example, and can itself call upon other synchronized methods within the same object.

The wait( ) and notify( ) Methods

With the `synchronized` keyword, we can serialize the execution of complete methods and blocks of code. The `wait()` and `notify()` methods of the `Object` class extend this capability. Every object in Java is a subclass of `Object`, so every object inherits these methods. By using `wait()` and `notify()`, a thread can effectively give up its hold on a lock at an arbitrary point and then wait for another thread to give it back before continuing.* All of the coordinated activity still happens inside synchronized blocks, and still only one thread is executing at a given time.

By executing `wait()` from a synchronized block, a thread gives up its hold on the lock and goes to sleep. A thread might do this if it needs to wait for something to happen in another part of the application, as we'll see shortly. Later, when the necessary event happens, the thread that is running it calls `notify()` from a block synchronized on the same object. Now the first thread wakes up and begins trying to acquire the lock again.

When the first thread manages to reacquire the lock, it continues from the point it left off. However, the thread that waited may not get the lock immediately (or perhaps ever). It depends on when the second thread eventually releases the lock and which thread manages to snag it next. Note also that the first thread won't wake up from the `wait()` unless another thread calls `notify()`. There is an overloaded version of `wait()`, however, that allows us to specify a timeout period. If another thread doesn't call `notify()` in the specified period, the waiting thread automatically wakes up.

Let's look at a simple scenario to see what's going on. In the following example, we'll assume there are three threads—one waiting to execute each of the three

---

* In actuality, they don't really pass the lock around; the lock becomes available and, as we'll describe, a thread that is scheduled to run acquires it.

synchronized methods of the MyThing class. We'll call them the *waiter*, *notifier*, and *related* threads. Here's a code fragment to illustrate:

```
class MyThing {
    synchronized void waiterMethod( ) {
        // do some stuff
        wait( );    // now wait for notifier to do something
        // continue where we left off
    }
    synchronized void notifierMethod( ) {
        // do some stuff
        notify( ); // notify waiter that we've done it
        // continue doing stuff
    }
    synchronized void relatedMethod( ) {
        // do some related stuff
    }
    ...
}
```

Let's assume *waiter* gets through the gate first and begins executing waiter-Method( ). The two other threads are initially blocked, trying to acquire the lock for the MyThing object. When waiter executes the wait() method, it relinquishes its hold on the lock and goes to sleep. Now there are now two viable threads waiting for the lock. Which thread gets it depends on several factors, including chance and the priorities of the threads. (We'll discuss thread scheduling in the next section.)

Let's say that *notifier* is the next thread to acquire the lock, so it begins to run notifierMethod(). *waiter* continues to sleep, and *related* languishes, waiting for its turn. When *notifier* executes the call to notify(), the runtime system prods the *waiter* thread, effectively telling it something has changed. *waiter* then wakes up and rejoins *related* in vying for the MyThing lock. Note that it doesn't receive the lock automatically; it just changes from saying, "Leave me alone" to "I want the lock."

At this point, *notifier* still owns the lock and continues to hold it until the synchronized notifierMethod() returns—or perhaps executes a wait() itself. At that point, the other two methods get to fight over the lock. *waiter* would like to continue executing waiterMethod() from the point it left off, while *related*, which has been patient, would like to get started. We'll let you choose your own ending for the story.

For each call to notify(), the runtime system wakes up just one method that is asleep in a wait() call. If there are multiple threads waiting, Java picks a thread on an arbitrary basis, which may be implementation-dependent. The Object class also provides a notifyAll() call to wake up all waiting threads. In most cases, you'll probably want to use notifyAll() rather than notify(). Keep in mind that notify() really means, "Hey, something related to this object has changed. The condition you are waiting for may have changed, so check it again." In general, there is no reason to assume only one thread at a time is interested in the change or able to act upon it. Different threads might look upon whatever has changed in different ways.

Often, our *waiter* thread is waiting for a particular condition to change, and we will want it to sit in a loop like the following:

```
while ( condition != true )
    wait( );
```

Other synchronized threads call `notify()` or `notifyAll()` when they have modified the environment so that *waiter* can check the condition again. Using wait conditions like this is the civilized alternative to polling and sleeping, as you'll see in the following section.

Passing Messages

Now we'll illustrate a classic interaction between two threads: a `Producer` and a `Consumer`. A producer thread creates messages and places them into a queue while a consumer reads and displays them. To be realistic, we'll give the queue a maximum depth. And to make things really interesting, we'll have our consumer thread be lazy and run much more slowly than the producer. This means that `Producer` occasionally has to stop and wait for `Consumer` to catch up. Here are the `Producer` and `Consumer` classes:

```
import java.util.*;

public class Consumer implements Runnable {
    Producer producer;

    Consumer( Producer producer ) {
        this.producer = producer;
    }

    public void run() {
        while ( true ) {
            String message = producer.getMessage();
            System.out.println("Got message: " + message);
            try {
                Thread.sleep( 2000 );
            } catch ( InterruptedException e ) { }
        }
    }

    public static void main(String args[]) {
        Producer producer = new Producer();
        new Thread( producer ).start();
        Consumer consumer = new Consumer( producer );
        new Thread( consumer ).start();
    }
}

public class Producer implements Runnable{
    static final int MAXQUEUE = 5;
    private List messages = new ArrayList();
```

```
public void run( ) {
    while ( true ) {
        putMessage( );
        try {
            Thread.sleep( 1000 );
        } catch ( InterruptedException e ) { }
    }
}

private synchronized void putMessage( )
{
    while ( messages.size( ) >= MAXQUEUE )
        try {
            wait( );
        } catch( InterruptedException e ) { }

    messages.add( new java.util.Date().toString( ) );
    notify( );
}

// called by Consumer
public synchronized String getMessage( )
{
    while ( messages.size( ) == 0 )
        try {
            notify( );
            wait( );
        } catch( InterruptedException e ) { }
    String message = (String)messages.remove(0);
    notify( );
    return message;
}
}
```

For convenience, we have included a main() method in the Consumer class that runs the complete example. It creates a Consumer that is tied to a Producer and starts the two classes. You can run the example as follows:

% **java Consumer**

This produces the timestamp messages created by the Producer:

```
Got message: Sun Dec 19 03:35:55 CST 1999
Got message: Sun Dec 19 03:35:56 CST 1999
Got message: Sun Dec 19 03:35:57 CST 1999
...
```

The timestamps initially show a spacing of one second, although they appear every two seconds. Our Producer runs faster than our Consumer. Producer would like to generate a new message every second, while Consumer gets around to reading and displaying a message only every two seconds. Can you see how long it will take the message queue to fill up? What will happen when it does?

Let's look at the code. We are using a few new tools here. Producer and Consumer implement the Runnable interface, and each has a thread associated with it. The Producer and Consumer classes pass messages through an instance of a java.util.List object. We haven't discussed the List class yet. Think of this one as a queue: we simply add and remove elements in first-in, first-out order.

The important activity is in the synchronized methods: putMessage() and getMessage(). Although one of the methods is used by the Producer thread and the other by the Consumer thread, they both live in the Producer class so that we can coordinate them simply by declaring them synchronized. Here they both implicitly use the Producer object's lock. If the queue is empty, the Consumer blocks in a call in the Producer, waiting for another message.

Another design option would implement the getMessage() method in the Consumer class and use a synchronized code block to synchronize explicitly on the Producer object. In either case, synchronizing on the Producer enables us to have multiple Consumer objects that feed on the same Producer. We'll do that later in this section.

putMessage()'s job is to add a new message to the queue. It can't do this if the queue is already full, so it first checks the number of elements in messages. If there is room, it stuffs in another timestamp message. If the queue is at its limit, however, putMessage() has to wait until there's space. In this situation, putMessage() executes a wait() and relies on the consumer to call notify() to wake it up after a message has been read. Here we have putMessage() testing the condition in a loop. In this simple example, the test probably isn't necessary; we could assume that when putMessage() wakes up, there is a free spot. However, this test is another example of good programming practice. Before it finishes, putMessage() calls notify() itself to prod any Consumer that might be waiting on an empty queue.

getMessage() retrieves a message for the Consumer. It enters a loop like that of putMessage(), waiting for the queue to have at least one element before proceeding. If the queue is empty, it executes a wait() and expects the Producer to call notify() when more items are available. Notice that getMessage() makes its own calls to notify(). It does this any time the queue is empty, to prod a producer that might be sleeping and also after it consumes a message, to give the producer the go ahead to fill the queue again. These scenarios are more plausible if there are more consumers, as we'll see next.

Now let's add another consumer to the scenario, just to make things really interesting. Most of the necessary changes are in the Consumer class; here's the code for the modified class, now called NamedConsumer:

```
public class NamedConsumer implements Runnable
{
    Producer producer;
    String name;

    NamedConsumer(String name, Producer producer) {
```

```
            this.producer = producer;
            this.name = name;
        }

        public void run() {
            while ( true ) {
                String message = producer.getMessage();
                System.out.println(name + " got message: " + message);
                try {
                    Thread.sleep( 2000 );
                } catch ( InterruptedException e ) { }
            }
        }

        public static void main(String args[]) {
            Producer producer = new Producer();
            new Thread( producer ).start();

            NamedConsumer consumer = new NamedConsumer( "One", producer );
            new Thread( consumer ).start();
            consumer = new NamedConsumer( "Two", producer );
            new Thread( consumer ).start();
        }
    }
```

The NamedConsumer constructor takes a string name to identify each consumer. The run() method uses this name in the call to println() to identify which consumer received the message.

The only required modification to the Producer code is to change the notify() calls to notifyAll() calls in putMessage() and getMessage(). (We could have used notifyAll() in the first place.) Now, instead of the consumer and producer playing tag with the queue, we can have many players waiting for the condition of the queue to change. We might have a number of consumers waiting for a message, or we might have the producer waiting for a consumer to take a message. Whenever the condition of the queue changes, we prod all the waiting methods to reevaluate the situation by calling notifyAll().

Here is some sample output when there are two NamedConsumers running, as in the main() method shown previously:

```
One got message: Sat Mar 20 20:00:01 CST 1999
Two got message: Sat Mar 20 20:00:02 CST 1999
One got message: Sat Mar 20 20:00:03 CST 1999
Two got message: Sat Mar 20 20:00:04 CST 1999
One got message: Sat Mar 20 20:00:05 CST 1999
Two got message: Sat Mar 20 20:00:06 CST 1999
One got message: Sat Mar 20 20:00:07 CST 1999
Two got message: Sat Mar 20 20:00:08 CST 1999
...
```

We see nice, orderly alternation between the two consumers as a result of the calls to sleep() in the various methods. Interesting things would happen, however, if we were to remove all calls to sleep() and let things run at full speed. The threads would compete, and their behavior would depend on whether the system is using time-slicing. On a time-sliced system, there should be a fairly random distribution between the two consumers while on a nontime-sliced system, a single consumer could monopolize the messages. And since you're probably wondering about time-slicing, let's talk about thread priority and scheduling.

ThreadLocal Objects

A common issue that arises is the need to maintain some information or state on a per-thread basis. For example, we might want to carry some context with the current thread as it executes our application. Or we might simply want to have a value that is different for different threads. Java supports this through the ThreadLocal class. A ThreadLocal is an object wrapper that automatically maintains a separate value for any thread calling it. For example:

```
ThreadLocal userID = new ThreadLocal();
userID.set("Pat");  // called by thread 1
userID.set("Bob"); // called by thread 2
userID.get(); // thread 1 gets "Pat"
userID.get(); // thread 2 gets "Bob"
```

You can use an instance of ThreadLocal anywhere you might use a static or instance variable to automatically maintain separate values for each thread.

Scheduling and Priority

Java makes few guarantees about how it schedules threads. Almost all of Java's thread scheduling is left up to the Java implementation and, to some degree, the application. Although it might have made sense (and would certainly have made many developers happier) if Java's developers had specified a scheduling algorithm, a single scheduling algorithm isn't necessarily suitable for all the roles that Java can play. Instead, Sun decided to put the burden on you to write robust code that works whatever the scheduling algorithm, and let the implementation tune the algorithm for whatever is best.[*]

Therefore, the priority rules that we'll describe next are carefully worded in the Java language specification to be a general guideline for thread scheduling. You should be able to rely on this behavior overall (statistically), but it is not a good idea to write

---

[*] A notable alternative to this is the "real-time" Java specification which defines specialized thread behavior for certain types of applications. It is being developed under the Java community process and can be found at *http://www.rtj.org/*.

code that relies on very specific features of the scheduler to work properly. You should instead use the control and synchronization tools that we have described in this chapter to coordinate your threads.*

Every thread has a priority value. If at any time a thread of a higher priority than the current thread becomes runnable (is started, stops sleeping, or is notified), it preempts the lower-priority thread and begins executing. By default, threads at the same priority are scheduled round-robin, which means once a thread starts to run, it continues until it does one of the following:

- Sleeps, by calling Thread.sleep() or wait()
- Waits for a lock, in order to run a synchronized method
- Blocks on I/O, for example, in a read() or accept() call
- Explicitly yields control, by calling yield()
- Terminates, by completing its target method or with a stop() call (deprecated)

This situation looks something like Figure 8-4.

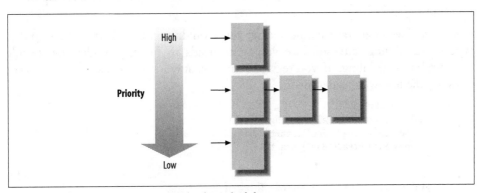

Figure 8-4. Priority preemptive, round-robin scheduling

Time-Slicing

In addition to prioritization, many systems implement time-slicing of threads.† In a time-sliced system, thread processing is chopped up, so that each thread runs for a short period of time before the context is switched to the next thread, as shown in Figure 8-5.

---

* *Java Threads* by Scott Oaks and Henry Wong (O'Reilly) includes a detailed discussion of synchronization, scheduling, and other thread-related issues.

† In the beginning, with Java's Release 1.0, Sun's Interpreter for Windows used time-slicing, as did the Netscape Navigator Java VM. Sun's Java 1.0 for Solaris didn't. All modern implementations using "real threads" should perform time-slicing, so this question is largely settled.

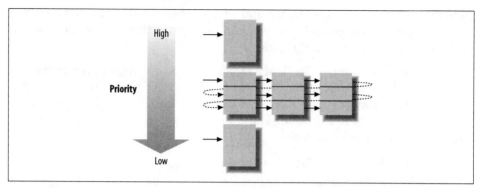

Figure 8-5. Priority preemptive, time-sliced scheduling

Higher-priority threads still preempt lower-priority threads in this scheme. The addition of time-slicing mixes up the processing among threads of the same priority; on a multiprocessor machine, threads may even be run simultaneously. This can introduce a difference in behavior for applications that don't use threads and synchronization properly.

Since Java doesn't guarantee time-slicing, you shouldn't write code that relies on this type of scheduling; any software you write needs to function under the default round-robin scheduling. If you're wondering what your particular flavor of Java does, try the following experiment:

```
public class Thready {
    public static void main( String args [] ) {
        new ShowThread("Foo").start(  );
        new ShowThread("Bar").start(  );
    }

    static class ShowThread extends Thread {
        String message;

        ShowThread( String message ) {
            this.message = message;
        }
        public void run(  ) {
            while ( true )
                System.out.println( message );
        }
    }
}
```

The Thready class starts up two ShowThread objects. ShowThread is a thread that goes into a hard loop (very bad form) and prints its message. Since we don't specify a priority for either thread, they both inherit the priority of their creator, so they have the same priority. When you run this example, you will see how your Java implementation does its scheduling. Under a round-robin scheme, only "Foo" should be printed;

"Bar" never appears. In a time-slicing implementation, you should occasionally see the "Foo" and "Bar" messages alternate (which is most likely what you will see).

Priorities

Now let's change the priority of the second thread:

```
class Thready {
    public static void main( String args [] ) {
        new ShowThread("Foo").start( );
        Thread bar = new ShowThread("Bar");
        bar.setPriority( Thread.NORM_PRIORITY + 1 );
        bar.start( );
    }
}
```

As you might expect, this changes how our example behaves. Now you may see a few "Foo" messages, but "Bar" should quickly take over and not relinquish control, regardless of the scheduling policy.

Here we have used the setPriority() method of the Thread class to adjust our thread's priority. The Thread class defines three standard priority values (they're integers): MIN_PRIORITY, NORM_PRIORITY, and MAX_PRIORITY.

If you need to change the priority of a thread, you should use one of these values, possibly with a small increment or decrement. Avoid using values near MAX_PRIORITY; if you elevate many threads to this priority level, priority will quickly become meaningless. A slight increase in priority should be enough for most needs. For example, specifying NORM_PRIORITY + 1 in our example is enough to beat out our other thread.

We should also note that in an applet environment you may not have access to maximum priority because you're limited by the maximum priority of the thread group in which you were created (see "Thread Groups" later in this chapter).

Finally, in our opinion, utilizing thread priorities should really be reserved more for system and framework development. It is not as useful or flexible in practice as simply implementing application-level control over processing using patterns like prioritized queues or pools.

User-Controlled Time-Slicing

There is a rough technique you can use to achieve an effect similar to time-slicing in a Java application, even if the Java runtime system does not support it directly. The idea is simply to create a high (maximum) priority thread that does nothing but repeatedly sleep for a short interval and then wake up. Since the higher-priority thread (in general) interrupts any lower-priority threads when it becomes runnable, you effectively chop up the execution time of your lower-priority threads, which should then execute in the standard round-robin fashion. We call this technique rough because of the weakness of the specification for Java threads with respect to their preemptiveness. If you use this technique, you should consider it only a potential optimization.

Yielding

Whenever a thread sleeps, waits, or blocks on I/O, it gives up its time slot, and another thread is scheduled. As long as you don't write methods that use hard loops, all threads should get their due. However, a thread can also signal that it is willing to give up its time voluntarily at any point with the yield() call. We can change our previous example to include a yield() on each iteration:

```
...
static class ShowThread extends Thread {
    ...
    public void run( ) {
        while ( true ) {
            System.out.println( message );
            yield( );
        }
    }
}
```

Now you should see "Foo" and "Bar" messages strictly alternating. If you have threads that perform very intensive calculations or otherwise eat a lot of CPU time, you might want to find an appropriate place for them to yield control occasionally. Alternatively, you might want to drop the priority of your compute-intensive thread so that more important processing can proceed around it.

Unfortunately the Java language specification is very weak with respect to yield(). It is another one of these things you should consider an optimization hint rather than a guarantee. In the worst case, the runtime system may simply ignore calls to yield().

Native Threads

We mentioned the possibility that different threads could run on different processors. This would be an ideal Java implementation. Unfortunately, many implementations don't even allow multiple threads to run in parallel with other processes running on the same machine. Older implementations of threading (known variously as "pthreads" or "green threads") effectively simulate threading within an individual process like the Java interpreter. One feature that you might want to confirm in choosing a Java implementation is called *native threads*. This means that the Java runtime system is able to use the real (native) threading mechanism of the host environment, which should perform better and, ideally, allow multiprocessor operation.

Thread Groups

The `ThreadGroup` class allows us to deal with threads wholesale: we can use it to arrange threads in groups and deal with the groups as a whole. A thread group can contain other thread groups, in addition to individual threads, so our arrangements can be hierarchical. Thread groups are particularly useful when we want to start a task that might create many threads of its own. By assigning the task a thread group, we can later identify and control all the task's threads. Thread groups are also the subject of restrictions that can be imposed by the Java Security Manager. So we can restrict a thread's behavior according to its thread group. For example, we can forbid threads in a particular group from interacting with threads in other groups. This is one way web browsers can prevent threads started by Java applets from stopping important system threads.

When we create a thread, it normally becomes part of the thread group to which the currently running thread belongs. To create a new thread group of our own, we can call the constructor:

```
ThreadGroup myTaskGroup = new ThreadGroup("My Task Group");
```

The `ThreadGroup` constructor takes a name, which a debugger can use to help you identify the group. (You can also assign names to the threads themselves.) Once we have a group, we can put threads in the group by supplying the `ThreadGroup` object as an argument to the `Thread` constructor:

```
Thread myTask = new Thread( myTaskGroup, taskPerformer );
```

Here, `myTaskGroup` is the thread group, and `taskPerformer` is the target object (the Runnable object that performs the task). Any additional threads that `myTask` creates also belong to the `myTaskGroup` thread group.

Working with the ThreadGroup Class

Creating thread groups isn't interesting unless you do things with them. The `ThreadGroup` class exists so that you can control threads in batches. It has methods that parallel the basic `Thread` control methods—even the deprecated `stop()`, `suspend()`, and `resume()`. These methods in the thread group operate on all the threads they contain. You can also mark a thread group as a "daemon"; a daemon thread group is automatically removed when all its children are gone. If a thread group isn't a daemon, you have to call `destroy()` to remove it when it is empty.

We can set the maximum priority for threads created in a thread group by calling `setMaximumPriority()`. Thereafter, no threads can be created in the thread group with a priority higher than the maximum; threads that change their priority can't set their new priority higher than the maximum.

Finally, you can get a list of all threads in a group. The method `activeCount()` tells you how many threads are in the group; the method `enumerate()` gives you a list of them. The argument to enumerate() is an array of Threads, which enumerate() fills in with the group's threads. (Use activeCount() to make an array of the right size.) Both activeCount() and enumerate() operate recursively on all thread groups the group contains.

It is also the responsibility of the ThreadGroup to handle uncaught runtime exceptions thrown by the run() methods of its threads. You can override the uncaughtException() method of ThreadGroup when making your own thread groups to control this behavior.

Thread Performance

The way that applications use threads and the associated costs and benefits have greatly impacted the design of many Java APIs. We will discuss some of the issues in detail in other chapters of this book. But it is worth mentioning briefly here some aspects of thread performance and how the use of threads has dictated the form and functionality of several recent Java packages.

The Cost of Synchronization

The act of acquiring locks to synchronize threads, even when there is no contention, takes time. In older implementations of Java this time could be significant. With newer VMs, it is almost negligible.* However, unnecessary synchronization at a low level can still slow applications where legitimate concurrent access would be proper and could be more efficiently organized at a higher level of abstraction. Because of this, two important APIs were specifically crafted to avoid unnecessary synchronization, by placing it under the control of the developer: the Java Collections API and the Swing GUI API.

The java.util Collections API replaces earlier simple Java aggregate types—namely Vector and Hashtable—with more fully featured and, notably, unsynchronized types (List and HashMap). The Collections API allows application code to synchronize access to collections and provides special "fail fast" functionality to help detect concurrent access and throw an exception. It also provides synchronization "wrappers" that can provide safe access in the old style.

The Java Swing GUI, which grew out of AWT, has taken a different very approach to providing speed and safety. Swing dictates that modification of its components (with notable exceptions) must all be done by a single thread: the main event queue. Swing solves performance problems as well as nasty issues of determinism in ordering of

---

* In a completely naïve test (simple loop) using JDK 1.4.0 on a 400-MHz Sparc Ultra-60, we measured the cost of synchronization on an object to be about one-tenth of a microsecond. However, when the lock is contested it would surely be more expensive.

events by forcing a single super-thread to control the GUI. The application may access the event queue thread indirectly by pushing commands onto a queue through a simple interface.

Thread Resource Consumption

A fundamental pattern in Java, which we will see illustrated Chapters 11 and 12, is to start many threads to handle asynchronous external resources such as socket connections. For maximum efficiency, a web server might, for example, be tempted to create a thread for each client connection it is servicing. With each client having its own thread, I/O operations may block and restart as needed. But as efficient as this may be in terms of throughput, it is very inefficient in terms of server resources. Threads consume memory; each thread has its own "stack" for local variables, and switching between running threads (context switching) adds overhead to the CPU. While threads are relatively lightweight (in theory it is possible to have hundreds or perhaps thousands running on a large server) at a certain point the resources consumed by the threads themselves start defeating the purpose of starting more threads. Often this point is reached at only a few dozen threads. Creating a thread per client is not a very scaleable option.

An alternative approach is to create "thread pools" where a fixed number of threads pull tasks from a queue and return for more when they are finished. This recycling of threads makes for solid scalability, but it has historically been difficult to implement efficiently in Java because stream I/O (for things like sockets) has not fully supported nonblocking operations. This has changed with Java 1.4 and the introduction of the NIO (new I/O) package, java.nio. The NIO package introduces asynchronous I/O channels: nonblocking reads and writes along with the ability to "select" or test the readiness of streams for moving data. Channels can also be asynchronously closed, allowing threads to work gracefully. With the NIO package, it should be possible to create servers with much more sophisticated, scaleable thread patterns.

## CHAPTER 9

Working with Text

If you've been reading this book sequentially, you've read all about the core Java language constructs, including the object-oriented aspects of the language and the use of threads. Now it's time to shift gears and start talking about the Java Application Programming Interface (API), the collection of classes that comprise the standard Java packages and come with every Java implementation. Java's core packages are one of its most distinguishing features. Many other object-oriented languages have similar features, but none has as extensive a set of standardized APIs and tools as Java does. This is both a reflection of and a reason for Java's success. Table 9-1 lists the most important packages in the API and shows which chapters discuss each of the packages.

Table 9-1. Java API packages

Package	Contents	Chapter
java.applet	The Applet API	22
java.beans	JavaBeans API	21
java.io, java.nio	Input and output	11
java.lang, java.lang.ref	Basic language classes	4, 5, 6, 7, 8, 9
java.lang.reflect	Reflection	7
java.net, java.rmi	Networking and Remote Method Invocation classes	12
java.text, java.util.regex	International text classes and regular expressions	9
java.util	Utilities and collections classes	9, 10, 11
javax.swing, java.awt	Swing GUI and 2D graphics	15, 16, 17, 18, 19

As you can see in Table 9-1, we examined some classes in java.lang in earlier chapters on the core language constructs. Starting with this chapter, we throw open the Java toolbox and begin examining the rest of the API classes, starting with text-related utilities, because they are fundamental to all kinds of applications.

We begin our exploration with some of the fundamental language classes in java.lang concerning strings. Figure 9-1 shows the class hierarchy of the java.lang package.

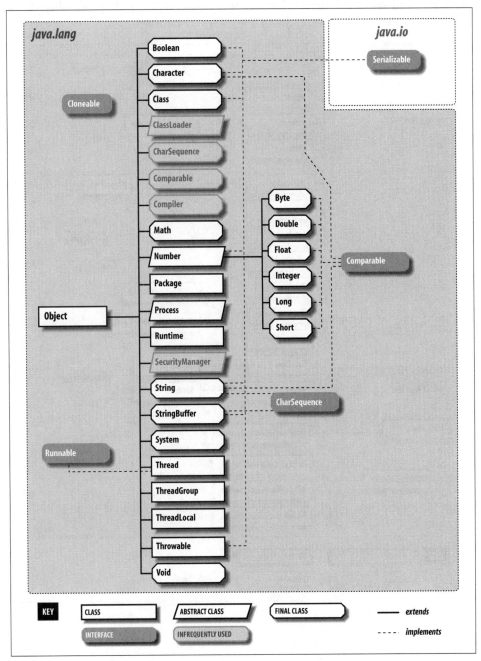

Figure 9-1. The java.lang package

We'll also look at some of the classes in java.util in this chapter, including locales for internationalization. We'll cover more classes in java.util, including classes that support math, date and time values, collections, and many more in Chapter 10. Figure 9-2 shows the class hierarchy of the java.util package.

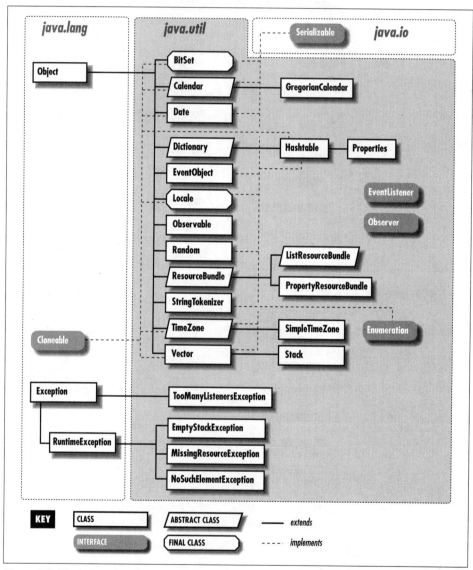

Figure 9-2. The java.util package

Other Text-Related APIs

In this chapter, we cover most of the special-purpose, text-related APIs in Java, including classes for simple parsing of words and numbers, text formatting, internationalization, and regular expressions. But since so much of what we do with computers is oriented around text, classifying some APIs as text-related can be somewhat arbitrary. Some of the text-related packages we cover in the next chapter include the Java Calendar API, the Properties and User Preferences APIs, and the Logging API. But probably the most important new tools in the text arena are those for working with the Extensible Markup Language, XML. In Chapter 23, we cover this topic in detail, along with the XSL/XSLT stylesheet language. Together they provide a powerful framework for rendering documents.

Strings

Now we take a closer look at the Java String class (or, more specifically, java.lang. String). Because strings are used so extensively, the Java String class has quite a bit of functionality. We'll test-drive most of the important features, but if you want to go deeper, you should refer to a Java class reference manual such as the *Java Fundamental Classes Reference* by Mark Grand and Jonathan Knudsen (O'Reilly).

A String object encapsulates a sequence of Unicode characters. Strings are immutable; once you create a String object, you can't change its value. Operations that appear to change the content or length of a string instead return a new String object that copies or internally references the needed characters of the original. Java implementations make an effort to consolidate identical strings and string literals in the same class into a shared-string pool.

String Constructors

Literal strings are allocated with double quotes and can be assigned to a String variable:

```
String quote = "To be or not to be";
```

Java automatically converts the literal string into a String object. If you're a C or C++ programmer, you may be wondering about the internal structure of this string; you don't have to worry about this with Java strings. We've said that the String class stores Unicode characters, and Java uses arrays internally to hold them. But the details are encapsulated in the String class, so you don't have to worry about them.

As always, arrays in Java are real objects that know their own length, so String objects in Java don't require special terminators. If you need to know the length of a String, use the length() method:

```
int length = quote.length( );
```

Strings can take advantage of the only overloaded operator in Java, the + operator, for string concatenation. The following code produces equivalent strings:

```
String name = "John " + "Smith";
String name = "John ".concat("Smith");
```

Literal strings can't span lines in Java source files, but we can concatenate lines to produce the same effect:

```
String poem =
    "'Twas brillig, and the slithy toves\n" +
    "   Did gyre and gimble in the wabe:\n" +
    "All mimsy were the borogoves,\n" +
    "   And the mome raths outgrabe.\n";
```

Embedding lengthy text in source code should now be a thing of the past, given that we can retrieve a String from anywhere on the planet via a URL. In Chapter 13, we'll see how to do things like this:

```
String poem = (String) new URL(
    "http://myserver/~dodgson/jabberwocky.txt").getContent( );
```

In addition to making strings from literal expressions, you can construct a String from an array of characters:

```
char [] data = new char [] { 'L', 'e', 'm', 'm', 'i', 'n', 'g' };
String lemming = new String( data );
```

You can also construct a String from an array of bytes:

```
byte [] data = new byte [] { (byte)97, (byte)98, (byte)99 };
String abc = new String(data, "ISO8859_1");
```

The second argument to the String constructor for byte arrays is the name of an encoding scheme. The String construct uses it to convert the given bytes to Unicode characters. Unless you know something about Unicode, you can use the form of the constructor that accepts a byte array only; the default encoding scheme on your system will be used.[*]

Conversely, the charAt() method of the String class lets you access the characters of a String in an array-like fashion:

```
String s = "Newton";
for ( int i = 0; i < s.length( ); i++ )
    System.out.println( s.charAt( i ) );
```

This code prints the characters of the string one at a time. Alternately, we can get the characters all at once with toCharArray(). Here's a way to save typing a bunch of single quotes:

```
char [] abcs = "abcdefghijklmnopqrstuvwxyz".toCharArray( );
```

---

[*] In Windows, the default encoding is CP1252; in Solaris, it's ISO8859_1.

Strings from Things

We can get the string representation of most things with the static String.valueOf() method. Various overloaded versions of this method give us string values for all of the primitive types:

```
String one = String.valueOf( 1 );
String two = String.valueOf( 2.384f );
String notTrue = String.valueOf( false );
```

All objects in Java have a toString() method, inherited from the Object class. For class-type references, String.valueOf() invokes the object's toString() method to get its string representation. If the reference is null, the result is the literal string "null":

```
String date = String.valueOf( new Date( ) );
System.out.println( date );        // "Sun Dec 19 05:45:34 CST 2002"

date = null;
System.out.println( date );        // "null"
```

Because string concatenation uses the valueOf() method internally, it's common to use the empty string and the plus operator (+) to get the string value of any object. For example:

```
String two = "" + 2.384f;
String today = "" + new Date( );
```

Comparing Strings

The standard equals() method can compare strings for *equality*; they contain exactly the same characters. You can use a different method, equalsIgnoreCase(), to check the equivalence of strings in a case-insensitive way:

```
String one = "FOO";
String two = "foo";

one.equals( two );             // false
one.equalsIgnoreCase( two );   // true
```

A common mistake for novice programmers in Java is to compare strings with the == operator when they mean to use the equals() method. Remember that strings are objects in Java, and == tests for object *identity*, that is, whether the two arguments being tested are the same object. In Java, it's easy to make two strings that have the same characters but are not the same string object. For example:

```
String foo1 = "foo";
String foo2 = String.valueOf( new char [] { 'f', 'o', 'o' } );

foo1 == foo2        // false!
foo1.equals( foo2 ) // true
```

This mistake is particularly dangerous, because it often works for the common case in which you are comparing literal strings (strings declared with double quotes right in the code). The reason for this is that Java tries to manage strings efficiently by combining them. At compile time, Java finds all the identical strings within a given class and makes only one object for them. This is safe because strings are immutable and cannot change. You can coalesce strings in this way at runtime using the String intern() method. Interning a string returns an equivalent string reference that is unique across the VM.

The compareTo() method compares the lexical value of the String to another String, determining whether it sorts alphabetically earlier than, the same as, or later than the target string. It returns an integer that is less than, equal to, or greater than zero:

```
String abc = "abc";
String def = "def";
String num = "123";

if ( abc.compareTo( def ) < 0 )        // true
if ( abc.compareTo( abc ) == 0 )       // true
if ( abc.compareTo( num ) > 0 )        // true
```

On some systems, the behavior of lexical comparison is complex, and obscure alternative character sets exist. Java avoids this problem by comparing characters strictly by their position in the Unicode specification.

The Collator class

The java.text package provides a sophisticated set of classes for comparing strings, even in different languages. German, for example, has vowels with umlauts and another character that resembles the Greek letter beta and represents a double "s." How should we sort these? Although the rules for sorting such characters are precisely defined, you can't assume that the lexical comparison we used earlier has the correct meaning for languages other than English. Fortunately, the Collator class takes care of these complex sorting problems.

In the following example, we use a Collator designed to compare German strings. You can obtain a default Collator by calling the Collator.getInstance() method with no arguments. Once you have an appropriate Collator instance, you can use its compare() method, which returns values just like String's compareTo() method. The following code creates two strings for the German translations of "fun" and "later," using Unicode constants for these two special characters. It then compares them, using a Collator for the German locale;* the result is that "fun" (Spaß) sorts before "later" (später).

---

* Locales help you deal with issues relevant to particular languages and cultures; we'll talk about them in the later section "Internationalization."

```
String fun = "Spa\u00df";
String later = "sp\u00e4ter";
Collator german = Collator.getInstance(Locale.GERMAN);
if (german.compare(fun, later) < 0) // true
```

Using collators is essential if you're working with languages other than English. In Spanish, for example, "ll" and "ch" are treated as separate characters and alphabetized separately. A collator handles cases like these automatically.

Searching

The String class provides several simple methods for finding fixed substrings within a string. The startsWith() and endsWith() methods compare an argument string with the beginning and end of the String, respectively:

```
String url = "http://foo.bar.com/";
if ( url.startsWith("http:") )         // true
```

The indexOf() method searches for the first occurrence of a character or substring and returns the starting character position:

```
String abcs = "abcdefghijklmnopqrstuvwxyz";
int i = abcs.indexOf( 'p' );           // 15
int i = abcs.indexOf( "def" );         // 3
```

Similarly, lastIndexOf() searches for the last occurrence of a character or substring in a target string.

For more complex searching, you can use the new Regular Expression API, which allows you to look for and parse complex patterns. We'll talk about regular expressions later in this chapter.

Editing

A number of methods operate on the String and return a new String as a result. While this is useful, you should be aware that creating lots of strings in this manner can affect performance. If you need to modify a string often, you should use the StringBuffer class, as we'll discuss shortly.

trim() is a useful method that removes leading and trailing whitespace (i.e., carriage return, newline, and tab) from the String:

```
String str = "   abc   ";
str = str.trim( );                     // "abc"
```

In this example, we have thrown away the original String (with excess whitespace), so it will be garbage-collected.

The `toUpperCase()` and `toLowerCase()` methods return a new `String` of the appropriate case:

```
String down = "FOO".toLowerCase( );     // "foo"
String up   = down.toUpperCase( );      // "FOO"
```

`substring()` returns a specified range of characters. The starting index is inclusive; the ending is exclusive:

```
String abcs = "abcdefghijklmnopqrstuvwxyz";
String cde = abcs.substring(2, 5);      // "cde"
```

As of Java 1.4, the `String` class adds two new methods that allow you to do pattern substitution: `replaceAll()` and `replaceFirst()`. We'll talk about these when we discuss regular expressions later in this chapter.

String Method Summary

Many people complain when they discover that the Java `String` class is final (i.e., it can't be subclassed). There is a lot of functionality in `String`, and it would be nice to be able to modify its behavior directly. The `String` class is final because of performance and security implications. With final classes, the Java VM can make implementation-dependent optimizations, and since strings are used ubiquitously throughout the Java APIs, subclassing at the very least needs to be scrutinized carefully for security issues. Table 9-2 summarizes the methods provided by the `String` class.

Table 9-2. String methods

Method	Functionality
charAt()	Gets a particular character in the string
compareTo()	Compares the string with another string
concat()	Concatenates the string with another string
copyValueOf()	Returns a string equivalent to the specified character array
endsWith()	Checks whether the string ends with a specified suffix
equals()	Compares the string with another string
equalsIgnoreCase()	Compares the string with another string, ignoring case
getBytes()	Copies characters from the string into a byte array
getChars()	Copies characters from the string into a character array
hashCode()	Returns a hashcode for the string
indexOf()	Searches for the first occurrence of a character or substring in the string
intern()	Fetches a unique instance of the string from a global shared-string pool
lastIndexOf()	Searches for the last occurrence of a character or substring in a string
length()	Returns the length of the string
regionMatches()	Checks whether a region of the string matches the specified region of another string

Table 9-2. String methods (continued)

Method	Functionality
replace()	Replaces all occurrences of a character in the string with another character
startsWith()	Checks whether the string starts with a specified prefix
substring()	Returns a substring from the string
toCharArray()	Returns the array of characters from the string
toLowerCase()	Converts the string to lowercase
toString()	Returns the string value of an object
toUpperCase()	Converts the string to uppercase
trim()	Removes leading and trailing whitespace from the string
valueOf()	Returns a string representation of a value
matches()	Determines if the whole string matches a regular expression pattern
replaceFirst()	Replaces the first occurrence of a regular expression pattern with a pattern
replaceAll()	Replaces all occurrences of a regular expression pattern with a pattern
split()	Splits the string into an array of strings using a regular expression pattern as a delimiter

The java.lang.StringBuffer Class

In contrast to the immutable string, the java.lang.StringBuffer class is a modifiable and expandable buffer for characters. It's an efficient alternative to code like this:

```
String ball = "Hello";
ball = ball + " there.";
ball = ball + " How are you?";
```

This example repeatedly produces new String objects. The character array must be copied over and over, which can adversely affect performance. A more economical alternative is to use a StringBuffer object and its append() method:

```
StringBuffer ball = new StringBuffer("Hello");
ball.append(" there.");
ball.append(" How are you?");
```

The StringBuffer class provides a number of overloaded append() methods for appending any type of data to the buffer.

We can get a String back from the StringBuffer with its toString() method:

```
String message = ball.toString( );
```

You can also retrieve part of a StringBuffer, as a String, using one of the substring() methods.

StringBuffer also provides a number of overloaded insert() methods for inserting various types of data at a particular location in the string buffer. Furthermore, you can remove a single character or a range of characters with the deleteCharAt() and delete() methods. Finally, you can replace part of the StringBuffer with the contents of a String using the replace() method.

The String and StringBuffer classes cooperate so that even in this last operation, no copy of the data has to be made. The string data is shared between the objects, unless and until we try to change it in the StringBuffer.

You should use a StringBuffer instead of a String any time you need to keep adding characters to a string; it's designed to handle such modifications efficiently. You still have to convert the StringBuffer to a String when you need to use any of the methods in the String class, but you can print a StringBuffer directly using System.out.println() because println() calls the toString()method for you.

Another thing you should know about StringBuffer methods is that they are thread-safe (like most methods in the Java APIs). This means that multiple threads can work on the same StringBuffer instance, and modifications happen sequentially (without interfering).

You might be interested to know that the compiler uses a StringBuffer to implement String concatenation. Consider the following expression:

```
String foo = "To " + "be " + "or";
```

It is equivalent to:

```
String foo = new
    StringBuffer( ).append("To ").append("be ").append("or").toString( );
```

The java.util.StringTokenizer Class

A common programming task involves parsing a string of text into words or "tokens" that are separated by some set of delimiter characters. The java.util. StringTokenizer class is a utility that does just this. Before we go on, we should mention that in Java 1.4 the String class itself, in conjunction with the new regular expression package, has added string-tokenizing capabilities that are more powerful and convenient to use than the simple StringTokenizer. So we'll cover this topic again when we talk about splitting strings using the String split() method in the section of this chapter on regular expressions.

Let's look at an example using StringTokenizer. The following snippet reads words from the string text:

```
String text = "Now is the time for all good men (and women)...";
StringTokenizer st = new StringTokenizer( text );

while ( st.hasMoreTokens( ) ) {
    String word = st.nextToken( );
    ...
}
```

First, we create a new `StringTokenizer` from the `String`. We invoke the `hasMoreTokens()` and `nextToken()` methods to loop over the words of the text. By default, the `StringTokenizer` class uses standard whitespace characters—carriage return, newline, and tab—as delimiters.

The `StringTokenizer` is an enumeration. It implements the `java.util.Enumeration` interface, which means that `StringTokenizer` also implements two more general methods for accessing elements: `hasMoreElements()` and `nextElement()`. These methods are defined by the `Enumeration` interface; they provide a standard way to return a sequence of values. The `Enumeration` interface is implemented by many items that return sequences or collections of objects. The advantage of `nextToken()` is that it returns a `String`, whereas `nextElement()` returns an `Object` type that must be cast. We'll talk about enumerations and iterators (another interface for the same concept) in the next chapter.

You can also specify your own set of delimiter characters in the `StringTokenizer` constructor, using another `String` argument to the constructor. Any contiguous combination of the specified characters that appears in the target string is treated as the equivalent of whitespace for tokenizing:

```
text = "http://foo.bar.com/";
tok = new StringTokenizer( text, "/:" );

if ( tok.countTokens( ) < 2 )
    ... // bad URL

String protocol = tok.nextToken( );   // "http"
String host = tok.nextToken( );       // "foo.bar.com"
```

This example parses a URL specification to get at the protocol and host components. The characters / and : are used as separators. The `countTokens()` method provides a fast way to see how many tokens will be returned by `nextToken()` without actually creating the `String` objects.

`StringTokenizer` can do a few more tricks. An overloaded form of `nextToken()` accepts a string that defines a new delimiter set for that and subsequent reads. The `StringTokenizer` constructor also accepts a flag that specifies that separator characters are to be returned individually as tokens themselves. By default, the delimiter characters are skipped over and not returned.

Again, we'll return to this topic when we talk about regular expressions and the `String` `split()` method later in this chapter.

Parsing and Formatting Text

Parsing and formatting text is a large and open-ended topic. So far in this chapter we've looked at only primitive operations on strings—creation, basic editing, searching, and simple tokenizing. Now we'd like to move on to more structured forms of text. Java has a rich set of APIs for parsing and printing formatted strings, including numbers, dates, times, and currency values. We'll cover most of these topics in this chapter, but we'll wait to discuss date and time formatting until Chapter 10.

In this section, we're going to talk about just one of the more common operations: parsing primitive numbers. Later in this chapter we'll delve into the java.text package, which provides full-blown parsing and formatting tools. We'll also look at the topic of internationalization to see how Java can help "localize" parsing and formatting of text, numbers, and dates for particular nationalities. Finally we'll take a detailed look at regular expressions, which are the newest and most powerful text-parsing tool Java offers. Regular expressions let you define your own patterns of arbitrary complexity, search for them, and parse them from text.

Parsing Primitive Numbers

In Java, numbers and booleans are primitive types—not objects. But for each primitive type, Java also defines a primitive wrapper class. Specifically, the java.lang package includes the following classes: Byte, Short, Integer, Long, Float, Double, and Boolean. We'll talk about these in detail in Chapter 10, but we bring them up now because these classes hold static utility methods that know how to parse their respective types from strings.

For example, the Integer and Long classes provide the static methods Integer.parseInt() and Long.parseLong() that read a String and return the corresponding primitive type:

```
int n = Integer.parseInt( "42" );
long l = Long.parseLong( "99999999999" );
```

The Float and Double classes provide the static methods Float.parseFloat()and Double.parseDouble() for parsing strings into floating-point primitives:

```
float f = Float.parseFloat( "4.2" );
double d = Double.parseDouble( "99.99999999" );
```

The Boolean class deviates from this a little. Instead of having a "parse" method, you must construct a Boolean wrapper object from your string and then ask it for its value:

```
boolean b = new Boolean("true").booleanValue( );
```

The reason for this will become clearer when we examine the other uses for the primitive wrappers. Primitive wrappers support many "value" methods that allow you to convert between types.

Working with alternate bases

It's easy to parse integer type numbers (byte, short, int, long) in alternate number bases. You can use the parse methods of the primitive wrapper classes, simply specifying the base as a second parameter:

```
long l = Long.parseLong( "CAFEBABE", 16 );  // l = 3405691582
byte b = Byte.parseByte ( "12", 8 ); // b = 10
```

You can also convert a long or integer value to a string value in a specified base using special static toString() methods of the Integer and Long classes:

```
String s = Long.toString( 3405691582L, 16 );  // s = "cafebabe"
```

For convenience, each class also has a static toHexString() method for working with base 16:

```
String s = Integer.toHexString( 255 ).toUpper();  // s = "FF";
```

We'll revisit numeric parsing and formatting later in this chapter when we cover the NumberFormat class of the java.text package.

Number formats

Although we can parse simple numbers in this way for simple cases, we are not taking into account the conventions used internationally. Let's pretend for a moment that we are programming Java in the rolling hills of Tuscany (some of you may not have to pretend). We would follow the local customs for representing numbers and write code like the following:

```
double d = Double.parseDouble("1.234,56");  // oops!
```

Unfortunately, this code throws a NumberFormatException, which is a runtime exception thrown whenever a number cannot be parsed. We'll see how to handle number formatting for different countries using the java.text package next.

Internationalization

The Java virtual machine lets us write code that executes in the same way on any Java platform. But in a global marketplace, that is only half the battle. A big question remains: will the application content and data be understandable to end users all over the world? Must users know English to use your application? The answer is that Java provides thorough support for customizing the language components of your application for most modern languages and dialects. In this section, we'll talk about the concepts of internationalization (often abbreviated "I18N") and the classes that support them.

The java.util.Locale Class

Internationalization programming revolves around the Locale class. The class itself is very simple; it encapsulates a country code, a language code, and a rarely used variant code. Commonly used languages and countries are defined as constants in the Locale class. (It's ironic that these names are all in English.) You can retrieve the codes or readable names, as follows:

```
Locale l = Locale.ITALIAN;
System.out.println(l.getCountry( ));            // IT
System.out.println(l.getDisplayCountry( ));     // Italy
System.out.println(l.getLanguage( ));           // it
System.out.println(l.getDisplayLanguage( ));    // Italian
```

The country codes comply with ISO 3166. You will find a complete list of country codes at *http://www.chemie.fu-berlin.de/diverse/doc/ISO_3166.html*. The language codes comply with ISO 639. A complete list of language codes is at *http://www.ics.uci.edu/pub/ietf/http/related/iso639.txt*. There is no official set of variant codes; they are designated as vendor-specific or platform-specific.

You can retrieve the default Locale for your location with the static Local.getDefault() method.

Various classes throughout the Java API use a Locale to decide how to represent themselves. We ran into one earlier when talking about sorting text with the Collator class. We'll also use them later in this chapter to format numbers and currency, and again in the next chapter with the DateFormat class, which uses Locales to determine how to format and parse dates and times.

Resource Bundles

If you're writing an internationalized program, you want all the text that is displayed by your application to be in the correct language or languages. Given what you have just learned about locales, you could customize your application by testing for the current locale and printing different messages. This would quickly get cumbersome, however, because the messages for all locales would be hardcoded in your source code. ResourceBundle and its subclasses offer a cleaner, more flexible solution.

A ResourceBundle is a collection of objects your application can access by name. It acts much like the Hashtable or Map collections we'll discuss in Chapter 10, looking up objects based on Strings that serve as keys. A ResourceBundle of a given name may be defined for many different Locales. To get a particular ResourceBundle, call the factory method ResourceBundle.getBundle(), which accepts the name of the ResourceBundle and a Locale. The following example gets the ResourceBundle named

"Message" for two Locales; from each bundle, it retrieves the message whose key is "HelloMessage" and prints the message:

```
//file: Hello.java
import java.util.*;

public class Hello {
  public static void main(String[] args) {
    ResourceBundle bun;
    bun = ResourceBundle.getBundle("Message", Locale.ITALY);
    System.out.println(bun.getString("HelloMessage"));
    bun = ResourceBundle.getBundle("Message", Locale.US);
    System.out.println(bun.getString("HelloMessage"));
  }
}
```

The getBundle() method throws the runtime exception MissingResourceException if an appropriate ResourceBundle cannot be located.

ResourceBundles are defined in three ways. They can be standalone classes, in which case they are either subclasses of ListResourceBundle or direct implementations of ResourceBundle. They can also be backed by a property file, in which case they are represented at runtime by a PropertyResourceBundle object. ResourceBundle. getBundle() returns either a matching class or an instance of PropertyResourceBundle corresponding to a matching property file. The algorithm used by getBundle() is based on appending the country and language codes of the requested Locale to the name of the resource. Specifically, it searches for resources in this order:

```
name_language_country_variant
name_language_country
name_language
name
name_default-language_default-country_default-variant
name_default-language_default-country
name_default-language
```

In this example, when we try to get the ResourceBundle named Message, specific to Locale.ITALY, it searches for the following names (no variant codes are in the Locales we are using):

```
Message_it_IT
Message_it
Message
Message_en_US
Message_en
```

Let's define the Message_it_IT ResourceBundle now, using the lowest level mechanism, a subclass of ListResourceBundle:

```
import java.util.*;

public class Message_it_IT extends ListResourceBundle {
  public Object[][] getContents( ) {
```

```
    return contents;
}

static final Object[][] contents = {
    {"HelloMessage", "Buon giorno, world!"},
    {"OtherMessage", "Ciao."},
};
}
```

ListResourceBundle makes it easy to define a ResourceBundle class; all we have to do is override the getContents() method. This method simply returns a two-dimensional array containing the names and values of its resources. In this example, contents[1][0] is the second key (OtherMessage), and contents [1][1] is the corresponding message (Ciao.).

Now let's define a ResourceBundle for Locale.US. This time, we'll take the easy way and make a property file. Save the following data in a file called Message_en_US. properties:

```
HelloMessage=Hello, world!
OtherMessage=Bye.
```

So what happens if somebody runs your program in Locale.FRANCE, and no ResourceBundle is defined for that Locale? To avoid a runtime MissingResourceException, it's a good idea to define a default ResourceBundle. In our example, you can change the name of the property file to Message.properties. That way, if a language- or country-specific ResourceBundle cannot be found, your application can still run.

The java.text Package

The java.text package includes, among other things, a set of classes designed for generating and parsing string representations of objects. In this section, we'll talk about three classes: NumberFormat, ChoiceFormat, and MessageFormat. In Chapter 10, we'll cover the DateFormat class.

The NumberFormat class can be used to format and parse currency, percentages, or plain old numbers. NumberFormat is an abstract class, but it has several useful factory methods that produce formatters for different types of numbers. For example, to format or parse currency strings, use getCurrencyInstance():

```
double salary = 1234.56;
String here =      // $1,234.56
    NumberFormat.getCurrencyInstance( ).format(salary);
String italy =     // L 1.234,56
    NumberFormat.getCurrencyInstance(Locale.ITALY).format(salary);
```

The first statement generates an American salary, with a dollar sign, a comma to separate thousands, and a period as a decimal point. The second statement presents the same string in Italian, with a lire sign, a period to separate thousands, and a comma

---

as a decimal point. Remember that NumberFormat worries about format only; it doesn't attempt to do currency conversion. (That would require, among other things, access to a dynamically updated table of exchange rates—a good opportunity for a JavaBean but too much to ask of a simple formatter.) We can go the other way and parse a formatted value using the parse() method, as we'll see in the next example.

Likewise, getPercentInstance() returns a formatter you can use for generating and parsing percentages. If you do not specify a Locale when calling a getInstance() method, the default Locale is used:

```
int progress = 44;
NumberFormat pf = NumberFormat.getPercentInstance( );
System.out.println(pf.format(progress));      // "44%"
try {
    System.out.println(pf.parse("77.2%"));    // "0.772"
}
catch (ParseException e) {}
```

And if you just want to generate and parse plain old numbers, use a NumberFormat returned by getInstance() or its equivalent, getNumberInstance():

```
NumberFormat guiseppe = NumberFormat.getInstance(Locale.ITALY);

// defaults to Locale.US
NumberFormat joe = NumberFormat.getInstance( );

try {
  double theValue = guiseppe.parse("34.663,252").doubleValue( );
  System.out.println(joe.format(theValue));  // "34,663.252"
}
catch (ParseException e) {}
```

We use guiseppe to parse a number in Italian format (periods separate thousands, comma is the decimal point). The return type of parse() is Number, so we use the doubleValue() method to retrieve the value of the Number as a double. Then we use joe to format the number correctly for the default (U.S.) locale.

Here's a list of the factory methods for text formatters in the java.text package. Again, we'll look at the DateFormat methods in the next chapter.

```
NumberFormat.getCurrencyInstance( )
NumberFormat.getCurrencyInstance(Locale inLocale)
NumberFormat.getInstance( )
NumberFormat.getInstance(Locale inLocale)
NumberFormat.getNumberInstance( )
NumberFormat.getNumberInstance(Locale inLocale)
NumberFormat.getPercentInstance( )
NumberFormat.getPercentInstance(Locale inLocale)
DateFormat.getDateInstance( )
DateFormat.getDateInstance(int style)
DateFormat.getDateInstance(int style, Locale aLocale)
DateFormat.getDateTimeInstance( )
```

```
DateFormat.getDateTimeInstance(int dateStyle, int timeStyle)
DateFormat.getDateTimeInstance(int dateStyle, int timeStyle, Locale aLocale)
DateFormat.getInstance( )
DateFormat.getTimeInstance( )
DateFormat.getTimeInstance(int style)
DateFormat.getTimeInstance(int style, Locale aLocale)
```

Thus far we've seen how to format numbers as text. Now we'll take a look at a class, ChoiceFormat, that maps numerical ranges to text. ChoiceFormat is constructed by specifying the numerical ranges and the strings that correspond to them. One constructor accepts an array of doubles and an array of Strings, where each string corresponds to the range running from the matching number up to (but not including) the next number in the array:

```
double[] limits = new double [] {0, 20, 40};
String[] labels = new String [] {"young", "less young", "old"};
ChoiceFormat cf = new ChoiceFormat(limits, labels);
System.out.println(cf.format(12)); // young
System.out.println(cf.format(26)); // less young
```

You can specify both the limits and the labels using a special string in an alternative ChoiceFormat constructor:

```
ChoiceFormat cf = new ChoiceFormat("0#young|20#less young|40#old");
System.out.println(cf.format(40)); // old
System.out.println(cf.format(50)); // old
```

The limit and value pairs are separated by vertical bars (|); the number sign (#) separates each limit from its corresponding value.

ChoiceFormat is most useful for handling pluralization in messages, enabling you to avoid hideous constructions such as, "you have one file(s) open". You can create readable error messages by using ChoiceFormat along with the MessageFormat class. To construct a MessageFormat, pass it a pattern string. A pattern string is a lot like the string you feed to the printf() function in C/C++, although the syntax is different. Arguments are delineated by curly brackets and may include information about how they should be formatted. Each argument consists of a number, an optional type, and an optional style, as summarized in Table 9-3.

Table 9-3. MessageFormat arguments

Type	Styles
Choice	Pattern
Date	short, medium, long, full, *pattern*
Number	integer, percent, currency, *pattern*
Time	short, medium, long, full, *pattern*

Let's use an example to clarify all this:

```
MessageFormat mf = new MessageFormat("You have {0} messages.");
Object[] arguments = {"no"};
System.out.println(mf.format(arguments)); // "You have no messages."
```

We start by constructing a MessageFormat object; the argument to the constructor is the pattern on which messages are based. The special incantation {0} means "use element zero from the array of arguments supplied to the format() method." When we generate a message by calling format(), we pass in values to replace the placeholders ({0}, {1}, ...) in the template. In this case, we pass the array arguments[] to mf. format; this substitutes arguments[0], yielding the result, You have no messages.

Let's try this example again, but this time, we'll format a number and a date instead of a string argument:

```
MessageFormat mf = new MessageFormat(
    "You have {0, number, integer} messages on {1, date, long}.");
Object[] arguments = {new Integer(93), new Date( )};

// "You have 93 messages on April 10, 2002."
System.out.println(mf.format(arguments));
```

In this example, we need to fill in two spaces in the template, so we need two elements in the arguments[] array. Element 0 must be a number and is formatted as an integer. Element 1 must be a Date and is printed in the long format. When we call format(), the arguments[] array supplies these two values.

This is still sloppy. What if there is only one message? To make this grammatically correct, we can embed a ChoiceFormat-style pattern string in our MessageFormat pattern string:

```
MessageFormat mf = new MessageFormat(
  "You have {0, number, integer} message{0, choice, 0#s|1#|2#s}.");
Object[] arguments = {new Integer(1)};

// "You have 1 message."
System.out.println(mf.format(arguments));
```

In this case, we use element 0 of arguments[] twice: once to supply the number of messages and once to provide input to the ChoiceFormat pattern. The pattern says to add an s if argument 0 has the value zero or is two or more.

Finally, a few words on how to be clever. If you want to write international programs, you can use resource bundles to supply not only the text of messages, but the strings for your MessageFormat objects, as well. Thus you can automatically format messages that are in the appropriate language with dates and other language-dependent fields handled appropriately.

In this context, it's helpful to realize that messages don't need to read elements from the array in order. In English, you would say, "Disk C has 123 files"; in some other language, you might say, "123 files are on Disk C." You could implement both messages with the same set of arguments:

```
MessageFormat m1 = new MessageFormat(
    "Disk {0} has {1, number, integer} files.");
MessageFormat m2 = new MessageFormat(
    "{1, number, integer} files are on disk {0}.");
Object[] arguments = {"C", new Integer(123)};
```

In real life, the code could be even more compact; you'd use only a single MessageFormat object, initialized with a string taken from a resource bundle.

Regular Expressions

Now it's time to take a brief detour on our trip through Java and enter the land of *regular expressions*. A regular expression, or regex for short, describes a text pattern. Regular expressions are used with many tools—including the java.util.regex package, text editors, and many scripting languages—to provide sophisticated text-searching and powerful string-manipulation capabilities.

If you are already familiar with the concept of regular expressions and how they are used with other languages, you may wish to simply skim this section. At minimum you'll need to look at "The java.util.regex API" section, which covers the Java package necessary to use them. On the other hand, if you've come to this point on your Java journey with a clean slate on this topic, and you're wondering exactly what regular expressions are, then pop open your favorite beverage and get ready. You are about to learn about the most powerful tool in the arsenal of text manipulation and what is, in fact, a tiny language within a language, all in the span of a few pages.

Regex Notation

A regular expression describes a pattern in text. By pattern, we mean just about any feature you can imagine identifying in text from the literal characters alone, without actually understanding their meaning. This includes features such as words, word groupings, lines and paragraphs, punctuation, case, and more generally, strings and numbers with a specific structure to them, such as phone numbers, email addresses, and quoted phrases. With regular expressions you can search the dictionary for all the words that have the letter "q" without its pal "u" next to it, or words that start and end with the same letter. Once you have constructed a pattern, you can use simple tools to hunt for it in text or to determine if a given string matches it. A regex can also be arranged to help you dismember specific parts of the text it matched, which you could then use as elements of replacement text if you wish.

Write once, run away

Before moving on, we should say a few words about regular expression syntax in general. At the beginning of this section, we casually mentioned that we would be discussing a new language. Regular expressions do, in fact, comprise a simple form of programming language. If you think for a moment about the examples we cited earlier, you can see that something like a language is going to be needed to describe even simple patterns—such as email addresses—that have some variation in form.

A computer science textbook would classify regular expressions at the bottom of the hierarchy of computer languages, in terms of both what they can describe and what you can do with them. They are still capable of being quite sophisticated, however. As with most programming languages, the elements of regular expressions are simple, but they can be built up in combination to arbitrary complexity. And that is where things start to get sticky.

Since regexes work on strings, it is convenient to have a very compact notation that can be easily wedged between characters. But compact notation can be very cryptic, and experience shows that it is much easier to write a complex statement than to read it again later. Such is the curse of the regular expression. You may find that in a moment of late-night, caffeine-fueled inspiration, you can write a single glorious pattern to simplify the rest of your program down to one line. When you return to read that line the next day, however, it may look like just so much Egyptian hieroglyphics to you. Simpler is generally better. If you can break your problem down and do it more clearly in several steps, maybe you should.

Escaped characters

Now that you're properly warned, we have to throw one more thing at you before we build you back up. Not only can the regex notation get a little hairy, but it is also somewhat ambiguous with ordinary Java strings. An important part of the notation is the escaped character, a character with a backslash in front of it. For example, the escaped d character, \d, is shorthand that matches any single digit character (0–9). However, you cannot simply write "\d" as part of a Java string, because Java uses the backslash for its own special characters and to specify Unicode character sequences. Fortunately, Java gives us a replacement: an escaped backslash, which is two backslashes (\\), means a literal backslash. The rule is that when you want a backslash to appear in your regex, you must escape it with an extra one:

```
"\\d" // Java string that yields backslash "d"
```

And just to make things crazier, because regex notation itself uses backslash to denote special characters, it must provide the same "escape hatch" as well—allowing you to double up backslashes if you want a literal backslash. If you want to specify a regular expression that includes a single literal backslash, it looks like this:

```
"\\\\"  // Java string yields two backslashes; regex yields one
```

Most of the "magic" operator characters you read about in this section operate on the character that precedes them, so these also must be escaped if you want their literal meaning. This includes such characters as .,*,+, braces {}, and parentheses ().

If you need to create part of an expression that has several literal characters in it, you might be able to use the special delimiters \Q and \E to help you. Any text appearing between \Q and \E is automatically escaped. (Note that you still need the Java String escapes—double backslashes for backslash, but not quadruple).

Beyond that, my only suggestion to help maintain your sanity when working with these examples is to keep two copies—a comment line showing the naked regular expression and the real Java string, where you must double up all backslashes.

Characters and character classes

Now let's dive into the actual regex syntax. The simplest form of a regular expression is just some plain, literal text, which means match exactly that text. This can be a single character or more. For example, in the following string, the pattern s can match the character s in the words rose and is:

```
"A rose is $1.99."
```

The pattern rose can match only the literal word rose. But this isn't very interesting. Let's crank things up a notch by introducing some special characters and the notion of character "classes."

Any character: dot (.)

The special character dot (.) matches any single character. The pattern .ose matches rose, nose, ose (space followed by ose) or any other character followed by the sequence ose. Two dots match any two characters, and so on. The dot operator is nondiscriminating. It normally stops only for an end-of-line character (and, optionally, you can tell it not to; we discuss that later).

We can consider "." to represent the group or class of all characters. And regexes define more interesting character classes as well.

Whitespace or nonwhitespace character: \s, \S

The special character \s matches a literal-space character or one of the following characters: \t (tab), \r (carriage return), \n (newline), \f (formfeed), and backspace. The corresponding special character \S does the inverse, matching any character except whitespace.

Digit or nondigit character: \d, \D

\d matches any of the digits 0–9. \D does the inverse, matching all characters but digits.

Word or nonword character: \w, \W

\w matches a "word" character, including upper- and lowercase letters A–Z, a–z, the digits 0–9, and the underscore character (_). \W matches everything except those characters.

Custom character classes

You can define your own character classes using the notation [...]. For example, the following class matches any of the characters a, b, c, x, y, or z:

```
[abcxyz]
```

The special x–y range notation can be used as shorthand for the alphabetic characters. The following example defines a character class containing all upper- and lowercase letters:

```
[A-Za-z]
```

Placing a caret (^) as the first character inside the brackets inverts the character class. For example:

```
[^A-F]   // G, H, I, ..., a, b, c, ... etc.
```

matches any character except uppercase A through F.

Nesting character classes simply adds them:

```
[A-F[G-Z]]   // A-Z
```

The && logical AND notation can be used to take the intersection (characters in common):

```
[a-p&&[l-z]]   // l, m, n, o, p
[A-Z&&[^P]]   // A through Z except P
```

Position markers

The pattern "[Aa] rose" (including an upper- or lowercase A) matches three times in the following phrase:

```
"A rose is a rose is a rose"
```

Position characters allow you to designate the relative location of a match. The most important are ^ and $, which match the beginning and end of a line, respectively:

```
^[Aa] rose   // matches "A rose" at the beginning of line
[Aa] rose$   // matches "a rose" at end of line
```

Actually, by default, ^ and $ match the beginning and end of "input," which is often a line. If you are working with multiple lines of text and wish to match the beginnings and endings of lines within a single large string, you can turn on "multiline" mode—see the later section "Special options."

The position markers \b and \B match a word boundary or nonword boundary, respectively. For example, the following pattern matches rose and rosemary, but not primrose:

```
\brose
```

Iteration (multiplicity)

Simply matching fixed character patterns would not get us very far. Next we look at operators that count the number of occurrences of a character (or more generally, of a pattern, as we'll see later).

Any (zero or more iterations): asterisk (*)

Placing an asterisk after a character or character class means "allow any number of that type of character"—in other words, zero or more. For example, the following pattern matches a digit with any number of leading zeros (possibly none):

```
0*\d   // match a digit with any number of leading zeros
```

Some (one or more iterations): plus sign (+)

The plus sign (+) means "one or more" iterations and is equivalent to XX* (pattern followed by pattern asterisk). For example, the following pattern matches a multiple-digit number with leading zeros:

```
0*\d+   // match a number (one or more digits) with leading zeros
```

It may seem redundant to match the zeros at the beginning of expression because zero is, of course, a digit and is matched by the \d+ portion of the expression anyway. However, we'll show later how you can pick apart the string using a regex and get at just the pieces you want. For example, in this case, you might want to strip off the leading zeros and keep just the digits.

Optional (zero or one iteration): question mark (?)

The question mark operator (?) allows exactly zero or one iteration. For example, the following pattern matches a credit-card expiration date, which may or may not have a slash in the middle:

```
\d\d/?\d\d   // match four digits with an optional slash in the middle
```

Range (between x and y iterations, inclusive): {x,y}

The {x,y} curly-brace range operator is the most general iteration operator. It specifies a precise range to match. A range takes two arguments: a lower bound and an upper bound, separated by a comma. This regex matches any word with five to seven characters, inclusive:

```
\b\w{5,7}\b   // match words with at least 5 and at most 7 letters
```

At least x or more iterations (y is infinite): {x,}

If you omit the upper bound, simply leaving a dangling comma in the range, the upper bound becomes infinite. This is a way to specify a minimum of occurrences with no maximum.

Grouping

Just as in logical or mathematical operations, parentheses can be used in regular expressions to make subexpressions or to put boundaries on parts of expressions.

This power lets us extend the operators we've talked about to work not only on characters, but on also words or other regular expressions. For example:

```
(yada)+
```

Here we are applying the + (one or more) operator to the whole pattern yada, not just one character. It matches yada, yadayada, yadayadayada, and so on.

Using grouping, we can start building more complex expressions. For example, while many email addresses have a three-part structure (e.g., *foo@bar.com*), the domain name portion can, in actuality, contain an arbitrary number of dot-separated components. To handle this properly, we can use an expression like this one:

```
\w+@\w+(\.\w)+    // Match an email address
```

This expression matches a word, followed by an @ symbol, followed by another word and then one or more literal dot-separated words, e.g., *pat@pat.net*, *bob@foo.bar.com*, or *mate@foo.bar.co.uk*.

Capture groups

In addition to basic grouping of operations, parentheses have an important, additional role: the text matched by each parenthesized subexpression can be separately retrieved. That is, you can isolate the text that matched each subexpression. There is then a special syntax for referring to each capture group within the regular expression by number. This important feature has two uses.

First, you can construct a regular expression that refers to the text it has already matched and uses this text as a parameter for further matching. This allows you to express some very powerful things. For example, we can now show the dictionary example we mentioned in the introduction. Let's find all the words that start and end with the same letter:

```
\b(\w)\w*\1\b // match words beginning and ending with the same letter
```

See the 1 in this expression? It's a reference to the first capture group in the expression, \w. References to capture groups take the form \n where *n* is the number of the capture group, counting from left to right. In this example, the first capture group matches a word character on a word boundary. Then we allow any number of word characters up to the special reference \1 (also followed by a word boundary). The \1 means "the value matched in capture group one." Since these characters must be the same, this regex matches words that start and end with the same character.

The second use of capture groups is in referring to the matched portions of text while constructing replacement text. We'll show you how to do that a bit later when we talk about the Regular Expression API.

Capture groups can contain more than one character, of course, and you can have any number of groups. You can even nest capture groups. Next, we discuss exactly how they are numbered.

Numbering

Capture groups are numbered, starting at 1, and moving from left to right, by counting the number of open parentheses it takes to reach them. The special group number 0 always refers to the entire expression match. For example, consider the following string:

```
one ((two) (three (four)))
```

This string creates the following matches:

```
Group 0: one two three four
Group 1: two three four
Group 2: two
Group 3: three four
Group 4: four
```

Before going on, we should note one more thing. So far in this section we've glossed over the fact that parentheses are doing double duty: creating logical groupings for operations and defining capture groups. What if the two roles conflict? Suppose we have a complex regex that uses parentheses to group subexpressions and to create capture groups? In that case, you can use a special noncapturing group operator (?:) to do logical grouping instead of using parentheses. You probably won't need to do this often, but it's good to know.

Alternation

The vertical bar (|) operator denotes the logical OR operation, also called alternation or choice. The | operator does not operate on individual characters but instead applies to everything on either side of it. It splits the expression in two unless constrained by parentheses grouping. For example, a slightly naïve approach to parsing dates might be the following:

```
\w+, \w+ \d+ \d+|\d\d/\d\d/\d\d  // pattern 1 or pattern 2
```

In this expression, the left side matches patterns such as Fri, Oct 12 2001, and the right matches 10/12/2001.

The following regex might be used to match email addresses with one of three domains (*net*, *edu*, and *gov*):

```
\w+@[\w\.]*\.(net|edu|gov)  // email address ending in .net, .edu, or .gov
```

Special options

There are several special options that affect the way the regex engine performs its matching. These options can be applied in two ways:

- You can pass in one or more flags during the Pattern.compile() step (discussed later in this chapter)
- You can include a special block of code in your regex

We show the latter approach. To do this, include one or more flags in a special block (?x) where x is the flag for the option we want to turn on. Generally, you do this at the beginning of the regex. You can also turn off flags by adding a minus sign (?-x), which allows you to apply flags to select parts of your pattern.

The following flags are available:

Case-insensitive: (?i)
The (?i) flag tells the regex engine to ignore case while matching, for example:

```
(?i)yahoo    // match Yahoo, yahoo, yah00, etc.
```

Dot all: (?s)
The (?s) flag turns on "dot all" mode, allowing the dot character to match anything, including end-of-line characters. It is useful if you are matching patterns that span multiple lines. The s stands for "single line mode," a somewhat confusing name derived from Perl.

Multiline: (?m)
By default, ^ and $ don't really match the beginning and ending of lines (as defined by carriage return or newline combinations); they instead match the beginning or ending of the entire input text. Turning on multiline mode with (?m) causes them to match the beginning and ending of every line as well as the beginning and end of input. Specifically, this means the spot before the first character, the spot after the last character, and the spots just after and just before line terminators inside the string.

Unix lines: (?d)
The (?d) flag changes the definition of the line terminator for the ^, $, and . special characters to Unix-style newline only (\n). By default, carriage return newline (\r\n) is also allowed.

Greediness

We've seen hints that regular expressions are capable of sorting out some complex patterns. But there are cases where what is matched is ambiguous (at least to you, though not in fact to the regex engine). Probably the most important example has to do with the number of characters the iterator operators consume before stopping. The .* operation best illustrates this. Consider the following string:

```
"Now is the time for <bold>action</bold>, not words."
```

Suppose we want to search for all the HTML-style tags (the parts between the < and > characters), perhaps because we want to remove them.

We might naïvely start with this regex:

```
</?.*>  // match <, optional /, and then anything up to >
```

We then get the following match, which is much too long:

```
<bold>action</bold>
```

The problem is that the .* operation, like all the iteration operators, is by default "greedy," meaning that it consumes absolutely everything it can, up until the last match for the terminating character (in this case >) in the file or line.

There are solutions for this problem. The first is to "say what it is," that is, to be more specific about what is allowed between the braces. The content of an HTML tag cannot actually include *anything*; for example, it cannot include a closing bracket (>). So we could rewrite our expression as:

```
</?\w*> // match <, optional /, any number of word characters, then >
```

But suppose the content is not so easy to describe. For example, we might be looking for quoted strings in text, which could include just about any text. In that case we can use a second approach and "say what it is not." We can invert our logic from the previous example and specify that anything *except* a closing bracket is allowed inside the brackets:

```
</?[^>]*>
```

This is probably the most efficient way to tell the regex engine what to do. It then knows exactly what to look for to stop reading. This approach has limitations, however. It is not obvious how to do this if the delimiter is more complex than a single character. It is also not very elegant.

Finally, we come to our general solution: the use of "reluctant" operators. For each of the iteration operators, there is an alternative, nongreedy form that consumes as few characters as possible, while still trying to get a match with what comes after it. This is exactly what we needed in our previous example.

Reluctant operators take the form of the standard operator with a "?" appended. (Yes, we know that's confusing.) We can now write our regex as:

```
</?.*?> // match <, optional /, minimum number of any chars, then >
```

Here we have appended ? to .* to cause .* to match as few characters as possible while still making the final match of >. The same technique (appending the ?) works with all the iteration operators, as in the two following examples:

```
.+?    // one or more, nongreedy
.{x,y}? // between x and y, nongreedy
```

Lookaheads and lookbehinds

In order to understand our next topic, let's return for a moment to the position marking characters (^, $, \b, and \B) that we discussed earlier. Think about what exactly these special markers do for us. We say, for example, that the \b marker matches a word boundary. But the word "match" here may be a bit too strong. In reality, it "requires" a word boundary to appear at the specified point in the regex. Suppose we didn't have \b; how could we construct it? Well, we could try constructing a regex that matches the word boundary. It might seem easy, given the word and nonword character classes (\w and \W):

```
\w\W|\W\w  // match the start or end of a word
```

But now what? We could try inserting that pattern into our regular expressions wherever we would have used \b, but it's not really the same. Now we're actually matching those characters not just requiring them. This regular expression matches the two characters comprising the word boundary in addition to whatever else matches afterwards, whereas the \b operator simply *requires* the word boundary but doesn't match any text. The distinction is that \b isn't a matching pattern but a lookahead. A *lookahead* is a pattern that is required to match next in the string, but which is not consumed by the regex engine. When a lookahead pattern succeeds, the pattern moves on, and the characters are left in the stream for the next part to use. If the lookahead fails, the match fails (or it backtracks and tries a different approach).

We can make our own lookaheads with the lookahead operator (?=). For example, to match the letter X at the end of a word we could use:

```
(?=\w\W)X  // Find X at the end of a word
```

Here the regex engine requires the \W\w pattern to match but not consume the characters, leaving them for the next part of the pattern. This effectively allows us to write overlapping patterns (like the previous example). For instance, we can match the word "Pat" only when it's part of the word "Patrick," like so:

```
(?=Patrick)Pat  // Find Pat only in Patrick
```

Another operator (?!)—the *negative lookahead*—requires that the pattern not match. We can find all the occurrences of Pat not inside of a Patrick with this:

```
(?!Patrick)Pat  // Find Pat never in Patrick
```

It's worth noting that we could have written all of these examples in other ways, by simply matching a larger amount of text. For instance, in the first example we could have matched the whole word "Patrick". But that is not as precise, and if we wanted to use capture groups to pull out the matched text or parts of it later, we'd have to play games to get what we want. For example, suppose we wanted to substitute something for Pat (say, change the font). We'd have to use an extra capture group and replace the text with itself. Using lookaheads is much more elegant.

In addition to looking ahead in the stream, we can use the (?<=) and (?<!) *lookbehind* operators to look backwards in the stream. For example, we can find my last name, but only when it refers to me:

```
(?<=Pat )Niemeyer  // Niemeyer, only when preceded by Pat
```

Or we can find the string "bean" when it is not part of the phrase "Java bean":

```
(?<!Java *)bean   // The word bean, not preceded by Java
```

In these cases, the lookbehind and the matched text didn't overlap because the lookbehind was before the matched text. But you can place a lookahead or lookbehind at either point—before or after the match; for example, we could also match Pat Niemeyer like this:

```
Niemeyer(?<=Pat Niemeyer)
```

The java.util.regex API

Now that we've covered the theory of how to construct regular expressions, the hard part is over. All that's left is to investigate the Java API for applying regexes: searching for them in strings, retrieving captured text, and replacing matches with substitution text.

Pattern

As we've said, the regex patterns that we write as strings are, in actuality, little programs describing how to match text. At runtime, the Java regex package compiles these little programs into a form that it can execute against some target text. Several simple convenience methods accept strings directly to use as patterns. More generally however, Java allows you to explicitly compile your pattern and encapsulate it in an instance of a `Pattern` object. This is the most efficient way to handle patterns that are used more than once, because it eliminates needlessly recompiling the string. To compile a pattern, we use the static method `Pattern.compile()`:

```
Pattern urlPattern = Pattern.compile("\\w+://[\\w/]*");
```

Once you have a `Pattern`, you can ask it to create a `Matcher` object, which associates the pattern with a target string:

```
Matcher matcher = urlPattern.matcher( myText );
```

The matcher is what actually executes the matches. We'll talk about it next. But before we do, we'll just mention one convenience method of `Pattern`. The static method `Pattern.matches()` simply takes two strings—a regex and a target string—and determines if the target matches the regex. This is very convenient if you just want to do a quick test once in your application. For example:

```
Boolean match = Pattern.matches( "\\d+\\.\\d+f?", myText );
```

The previous line of code can test if the string myText contains a Java-style floating-point number such as "42.0f". Note that the string must match completely, to the end, to be considered a match.

The Matcher

A `Matcher` associates a pattern with a string and provides tools for testing, finding, and iterating over matches of the pattern against it. The `Matcher` is "stateful." For

---

example, the find() method tries to find the next match each time it is called. But you can clear the Matcher and start over by calling its reset() method.

If you're just interested in "one big match"—that is, you're expecting your string to either match the pattern or not—you can use matches() or lookingAt(). These correspond roughly to the methods equals() and startsWith() of the String class. The matches() method asks if the string matches the pattern in its entirety (with no string characters left over) and returns true or false. The lookingAt() method does the same, except that it asks only whether the string starts with the pattern and doesn't care if the pattern uses up all the string's characters.

More generally, you'll want to be able to search through the string and find one or more matches. To do this, you can use the find() method. Each call to find() returns true or false for the next match of the pattern and internally notes the position of the matching text. You can get the starting and ending character positions with the Matcher start() and end() methods, or you can simply retrieve the matched text with the group() method. For example:

```
import java.util.regex.*;

String text="A horse is a horse, of course of course...";
String pattern="horse|course";

Matcher matcher = Pattern.compile( pattern ).matcher( text );
while ( matcher.find( ) )
  System.out.println(
    "Matched: '"+matcher.group()+"' at position "+matcher.start( ) );
```

The previous snippet prints the starting location of the words "horse" and "course" (four in all):

```
Matched: 'horse' at position 2
Matched: 'horse' at position 13
Matched: 'course' at position 23
Matched: 'course' at position 33
```

The method to retrieve the matched text is called group() because it refers to capture group zero (the entire match). You can also retrieve the text of other numbered capture groups by giving the group() method an integer argument. You can determine how many capture groups you have with the groupCount() method:

```
for (int i=1; i < matcher.groupCount( ); i++)
System.out.println( matcher.group(i) );
```

Splitting strings

A very common need is to parse a string into a bunch of fields based on some delimiter, such as a comma. It's such a common problem that in Java 1.4, a method was added to the String class for doing just this. The static method String.split()

accepts a regular expression and returns an array of substrings broken around that pattern. For example:

```
String text = "Foo, bar ,    blah";
String [] fields = String.split( "\s*,\s*", text)
```

yields a String array containing Foo, bar, and blah. You can control the maximum number of matches and also whether you get "empty" strings (for text that might have appeared between two adjacent delimiters) using an optional limit field.

If you are going to use an operation like this more than a few times in your code, you should probably compile the pattern and use its split() method, which is identical to the version in String. The String.split() method is equivalent to:

```
Pattern.compile(pattern).split(string);
```

Replacing text

A common reason that you'll find yourself searching for a pattern in a string is to change it to something else. The regex package not only makes it easy to do this but also provides a simple notation to help you construct replacement text using bits of the matched text.

The most convenient form of this API is Matcher's replaceAll() method, which substitutes a replacement string for each occurrence of the pattern and returns the result. For example:

```
String text = "Richard Nixon's social security number is: 567-68-0515.";
Matcher matcher =
Pattern.compile("\\d\\d\\d-\\d\\d\-\\d\\d\\d\\d").matcher( text );
String output = matcher.replaceAll("XXX-XX-XXXX");
```

This code replaces all occurrences of U.S. government Social Security numbers with "XXX-XX-XXXX" (perhaps for privacy considerations).

Using captured text in a replacement. Literal substitution is nice, but we can make this even more powerful by using capture groups in our substitution pattern. To do this, we use the simple convention of referring to numbered capture groups with the notation $n, where n is the group number. For example, suppose we wanted to show just a little of the Social Security number in the above example, so that the user would know if we were talking about him. We could modify our regex to catch, for example, the last four digits like so:

```
\d\d\d-\d\d-(\d\d\d\d)
```

We can then use that in the substitution text:

```
String output = matcher.replaceAll("XXX-XX-$1");
```

Controlling the substitution. The `replaceAll()` method is useful, but you may want more control over each substitution. You may want to change each match to something different or base the change on the match in some programmatic way.

To do this, you can use the `Matcher` `appendReplacement()` and `appendTail()` methods. These methods can be used in conjunction with the `find()` method as you iterate through matches to build a replacement string. `appendReplacement()` and `appendTail()` operate on a `StringBuffer` that you supply. The `appendReplacement()` method builds a replacement string by keeping track of where you are in the text and appending all *nonmatched* text to the buffer for you as well as the substitute text that you supply. Each call to `find()` appends the intervening text from the last call, followed by your replacement, then skips over all the matched characters to prepare for the next one. Finally, when you have reached the last match, you should call `appendTail()`, which appends any remaining text after the last match. We'll show an example of this next, as we build a simple "template engine."

The simple template engine

Now let's tie together what we've discussed in a nifty example. A common problem that comes up in Java applications is working with bulky, multiline text. In general, you don't want to store text messages in your application code, because it makes them difficult to edit or internationalize. But when you move them to external files or resources, you need a way for your application to plug in information at runtime. The best example of this is in Java servlets; a generated HTML page is often 99% static text with only a few "variable" pieces plugged in. Technologies such as JSP and XSL were developed to address this. But these are big tools, and we have a simple problem. So let's create a simple solution—a template engine.

Our template engine reads text containing special template tags and substitutes values that we provide it. And since generating HTML or XML is one of the most important applications of this, we'll be friendly to those formats by making our tags conform to the style of an XML comment. Specifically, our engine searches the text for tags that look like this:

```
<!--TEMPLATE:name  This is the template for the user name -->
```

XML style comments start with `<!--` and can contain anything up to a closing `-->`. We'll add the convention of requiring a TEMPLATE:name field to specify the name of the value we want to use. But aside from that, we'll still allow any descriptive text the user wants to include. To be friendly (and consistent), we'll allow any amount of whitespace to appear in the tags, including multiline text in the comments. We'll also ignore the text case of the "TEMPLATE" identifier, just in case. Now, we could do this all with low level `String` commands, looping over whitespace and taking substrings a lot. But using the power of regexes, we can do it much more cleanly and with only about seven lines of relevant code. (We've rounded out the example with a few more to make it more useful).

```java
import java.util.*;
import java.util.regex.*;

public class Template
{
    Properties values = new Properties();
    Pattern templateComment =
        Pattern.compile("(?si)<!--\\s*TEMPLATE:(\\w+).*?-->");

    public void set( String name, String value ) {
        values.setProperty( name, value );
    }

    public String fillIn( String text ) {
        Matcher matcher = templateComment.matcher( text );

        StringBuffer buffer = new StringBuffer();
        while( matcher.find() ) {
            String name = matcher.group(1);
            String value = values.getProperty( name );
            matcher.appendReplacement( buffer, value );
        }
        matcher.appendTail( buffer );
        return buffer.toString();
    }
}
```

You'd use the Template class like this:

```java
String input = "<!-- TEMPLATE:name --> lives at "
    +"<!-- TEMPLATE:address -->";
Template template = new Template();
template.set("name", "Bob");
template.set("address", "1234 Main St.");
String output = template.fillIn( input );
```

In this code, input is a string containing tags for name and address. The set()
method provides the values for those tags.

Let's start by picking apart the regex, templatePattern, in the example:

```
(?si)<!--\s*TEMPLATE:(\w+).*?-->
```

It looks scary, but it's actually very simple. Just start reading from left to right. First,
we have the special flags declaration (?si) telling the regex engine that it should be
in single-line mode, with .* matching all characters including newlines (s), and
ignoring case (i). Next, there is the literal <!-- followed by any amount of
whitespace (\s) and the TEMPLATE: identifier. After the colon, we have a capture
group (\w+), which reads our name identifier and saves it for us to retrieve later. We
allow anything (.*) up to the -->, being careful to specify that .* should be nongreedy (.*?). We don't want .* to consume other opening and closing comment tags
all the way to the last one but instead to find the smallest match (one tag).

Our fillIn() method does the work, accepting a template string, searching it, and "replacing" the tag values with the values from set(), which we have stored in a Properties table. Each time fillIn() is called, it creates a Matcher to wrap the input string and get ready to apply the pattern. It then creates a temporary StringBuffer to hold the output and loops, using the Matcher find() method to get each tag. For each match, it retrieves the value of the capture group (group one) that holds the tag name. It looks up the corresponding value and replaces the tag with this value in the output string buffer using the appendReplacement() method. (Remember that appendReplacement() fills in the intervening text on each call, so we don't have to.) All that remains is to call appendTail() at the end to get the remaining text after the last match and return the string value. That's it!

Regular expressions aren't new, but they are new to Java (at least as a standard). We have shown you some of the power provided by these tools and (we hope) whetted your appetite for more. Regexes allow you to work in ways you may not have considered before. Especially now, when the software world is focused on textual representations of almost everything—from data to user interfaces—via XML and HTML, having powerful text-manipulation tools is fundamental. Just remember to keep those regexes simple so you can reuse them again and again..

## CHAPTER 10

Core Utilities

In this chapter we'll continue our look at the core Java APIs, covering more of the tools of the `java.util` package. The `java.util` package includes a wide range of utilities for mathematical operations, dates and times, structured collections of objects, stored user data, and logging I/O.

Math Utilities

Java supports integer and floating-point arithmetic directly in the language. Higher-level math operations are supported through the `java.lang.Math` class. As we'll discuss later, there are also wrapper classes for all primitive data types, so you can treat them as objects if necessary. These wrapper classes hold some methods for basic conversions. Java provides the `java.util.Random` class for generating random numbers.

First, a few words about built-in arithmetic in Java. Java handles errors in integer arithmetic by throwing an `ArithmeticException`:

```
int zero = 0;

try {
    int i = 72 / zero;
}
catch ( ArithmeticException e ) {
    // division by zero
}
```

To generate the error in this example, we created the intermediate variable zero. The compiler is somewhat crafty and would have caught us if we had blatantly tried to perform a division by a literal zero.

Floating-point arithmetic expressions, on the other hand, don't throw exceptions. Instead, they take on the special out-of-range values shown in Table 10-1.

Table 10-1. Special floating-point values

Value	Mathematical representation
POSITIVE_INFINITY	1.0/0.0
NEGATIVE_INFINITY	-1.0/0.0
NaN	0.0/0.0

The following example generates an infinite result:

```
double zero = 0.0;
double d = 1.0/zero;

if ( d == Double.POSITIVE_INFINITY )
    System.out.println( "Division by zero" );
```

The special value NaN indicates the result is "not a number." The value NaN has the special mathematical distinction of not being equal to itself (NaN != NaN evaluates to true). Use Float.isNaN() or Double.isNaN() to test for NaN.

The java.lang.Math Class

The java.lang.Math class provides Java's math library. All its methods are static and used directly; you don't have to (and you can't) instantiate a Math object. This kind of degenerate class is used when we really want methods to approximate global functions. It's not very object-oriented, but it provides a means of grouping some related utility functions in a single class and accessing them easily. Table 10-2 summarizes the methods in java.lang.Math.

Table 10-2. Methods in java.lang.Math

Method	Argument type(s)	Functionality
Math.abs(a)	int, long, float, double	Absolute value
Math.acos(a)	double	Arc cosine
Math.asin(a)	double	Arc sine
Math.atan(a)	double	Arc tangent
Math.atan2(a,b)	double	Angle part of rectangular-to-polar coordinate transform
Math.ceil(a)	double	Smallest whole number greater than or equal to a
Math.cos(a)	double	Cosine
Math.exp(a)	double	Math.E to the power a
Math.floor(a)	double	Largest whole number less than or equal to a
Math.log(a)	double	Natural logarithm of a
Math.max(a, b)	int, long, float, double	Maximum
Math.min(a, b)	int, long, float, double	Minimum
Math.pow(a, b)	double	a to the power b
Math.random()	None	Random-number generator

Table 10-2. Methods in java.lang.Math (continued)

Method	Argument type(s)	Functionality
Math.rint(a)	double	Converts double value to integral value in double format
Math.round(a)	float, double	Rounds to whole number
Math.sin(a)	double	Sine
Math.sqrt(a)	double	Square root
Math.tan(a)	double	Tangent

log(), pow(), and sqrt() can throw an ArithmeticException. abs(), max(), and min() are overloaded for all the scalar values, int, long, float, or double, and return the corresponding type. Versions of Math.round() accept either float or double and return int or long, respectively. The rest of the methods operate on and return double values:

```
double irrational = Math.sqrt( 2.0 );
int bigger = Math.max( 3, 4 );
long one = Math.round( 1.125798 );
```

For convenience, Math also contains the static final double values E and PI:

```
double circumference = diameter * Math.PI;
```

The java.math Package

If a long or a double just isn't big enough for you, the java.math package provides two classes, BigInteger and BigDecimal, that support arbitrary-precision numbers. These are full-featured classes with a bevy of methods for performing arbitrary-precision math. In the following example, we use BigDecimal to add two numbers:

```
try {
    BigDecimal twentyone = new BigDecimal("21");
    BigDecimal seven = new BigDecimal("7");
    BigDecimal sum = twentyone.add(seven);

    int answer= sum.intValue( );          // 28
}
catch (NumberFormatException nfe) { }
catch (ArithmeticException ae) { }
```

If you implement cryptographic or scientific algorithms for fun, BigInteger is crucial. But other than that, you're not likely to need these classes.

Wrappers for Primitive Types

In languages such as Smalltalk, numbers and other simple types are objects, which makes for an elegant language design but has trade-offs in efficiency and complexity. By contrast, there is a schism in the Java world between class types (i.e., objects) and primitive types (i.e., numbers, characters, and boolean values). Java accepts this trade-off simply for efficiency reasons. When you're crunching numbers, you want your computations to be lightweight; having to use objects for primitive types complicates performance optimizations. For the times you want to treat values as objects, Java supplies a wrapper class for each of the primitive types, as shown in Table 10-3.

Table 10-3. Primitive type wrappers

Primitive	Wrapper
void	java.lang.Void
boolean	java.lang.Boolean
char	java.lang.Character
byte	java.lang.Byte
short	java.lang.Short
int	java.lang.Integer
long	java.lang.Long
float	java.lang.Float
double	java.lang.Double

An instance of a wrapper class encapsulates a single value of its corresponding type. It's an immutable object that serves as a container to hold the value and let us retrieve it later. You can construct a wrapper object from a primitive value or from a String representation of the value. The following statements are equivalent:

```
Float pi = new Float( 3.14 );
Float pi = new Float( "3.14" );
```

Like the parsing methods we looked at in the previous chapter, the wrapper constructors throw a NumberFormatException when there is an error in parsing a string:

```
try {
    Double bogus = new Double( "huh?" );
} catch ( NumberFormatException e ) {     // bad number
}
```

Each of the numeric type wrappers implements the java.lang.Number interface, which provides "value" methods access to its value in all the primitive forms. You can retrieve scalar values with the methods doubleValue(), floatValue(), longValue(), intValue(), shortValue(), and byteValue():

```
Double size = new Double ( 32.76 );

double d = size.doubleValue( );     // 32.76
float f = size.floatValue( );       // 32.76
long l = size.longValue( );         // 32
int i = size.intValue( );           // 32
```

This code is equivalent to casting the primitive double value to the various types.

The most common need for a wrapper is when you want to use a primitive value in a situation that requires an object. For example, later in this chapter we'll look at the Java Collections API, which is a sophisticated set of classes for dealing with object groups such as lists, sets, and maps. All the Collections APIs work on object types, so you'll need to use wrappers to hold primitive numbers for them. As we'll see, a List is an extensible array of Objects. We can use wrappers to hold numbers in a List (along with other objects):

```
List myNumbers = new ArrayList( );
Integer thirtyThree = new Integer( 33 );
myNumbers.add( thirtyThree );
```

Here we have created an Integer wrapper object so that we can insert the number into the List, using addElement(). Later, when we are extracting elements from the List, we can recover the int value as follows:

```
Integer theNumber = (Integer)myNumbers.get(0);
int n = theNumber.intValue( );              // 33
```

Random Numbers

You can use the java.util.Random class to generate random values. It's a pseudo-random number generator that can be initialized with a 48-bit seed.[*] The default constructor uses the current time as a seed, but if you want a repeatable sequence, specify your own seed with:

```
long seed = mySeed;
Random rnums = new Random( seed );
```

This code creates a random-number generator. Once you have a generator, you can ask for random values of various types using the methods listed in Table 10-4.

Table 10-4. Random number methods

Method	Range
nextBoolean()	true or false
nextInt()	-2147483648 to 2147483647
nextInt(int n)	0 to (n - 1) inclusive
nextLong()	-9223372036854775808 to 9223372036854775807
nextFloat()	-1.0 to 1.0
nextDouble()	-1.0 to 1.0
nextGaussian()	Gaussian distribution, SD 1.0

---

[*] The generator uses a linear congruential formula. See *The Art of Computer Programming, Volume 2: Seminumerical Algorithms* by Donald Knuth (Addison-Wesley).

By default, the values are uniformly distributed. You can use the `nextGaussian()` method to create a Gaussian (bell curve) distribution of `double` values, with a mean of 0.0 and a standard deviation of 1.0.

The `static` method `Math.random()` retrieves a random `double` value. This method initializes a `private` random number generator in the `Math` class, using the default `Random` constructor. Thus every call to `Math.random()` corresponds to a call to `nextDouble()` on that random number generator.

Dates

Working with dates and times without the proper tools can be a chore.[*] In Java 1.1 and later, you get three classes that do all the hard work for you. The `java.util.Date` class encapsulates a point in time. The `java.util.GregorianCalendar` class, which descends from the abstract `java.util.Calendar`, translates between a point in time and calendar fields like month, day, and year. Finally, the `java.text.DateFormat` class knows how to generate and parse string representations of dates and times.[†]

The separation of the `Date` class and the `GregorianCalendar` class is analogous to having a class representing temperature and a class that translates that temperature to Celsius units. Conceivably, we could define other subclasses of `Calendar`, say `JulianCalendar` or `LunarCalendar`.

The default `GregorianCalendar` constructor creates an object that represents the current time, as determined by the system clock:

```
GregorianCalendar now = new GregorianCalendar( );
```

Other constructors accept values to specify the point in time. In the first statement in the following code, we construct an object representing August 9, 2001; the second statement specifies both a date and a time, which yields an object that represents 9:01 A.M., April 8, 2002.

```
GregorianCalendar daphne =
    new GregorianCalendar(2001, Calendar.AUGUST, 9);
GregorianCalendar sometime =
    new GregorianCalendar(2002, Calendar.APRIL, 8, 9, 1); // 9:01 AM
```

We can also create a `GregorianCalendar` by setting specific fields using the `set()` method. The `Calendar` class contains a torrent of constants representing both calendar fields and field values. The first argument to the `set()` method is a field constant; the second argument is the new value for the field.

---

[*] For a wealth of information about time and world time-keeping conventions, see *http://tycho.usno.navy.mil*, the U.S. Navy Directorate of Time. For a fascinating history of the Gregorian and Julian calendars, try this site: *http://www.magnet.ch/serendipity/hermetic/cal_stud/cal_art.htm*.

[†] In Java 1.0.2, the `Date` class performed all three functions. In Java 1.1 and later, most of its methods have been deprecated, so that the only purpose of the `Date` class is to represent a point in time.

```
GregorianCalendar kristen = new GregorianCalendar( );
kristen.set(Calendar.YEAR, 1972);
kristen.set(Calendar.MONTH, Calendar.MAY);
kristen.set(Calendar.DATE, 20);
```

A GregorianCalendar is created in the default time zone. Setting the time zone of the calendar is as easy as obtaining the desired TimeZone and giving it to the GregorianCalendar:

```
GregorianCalendar smokey = new GregorianCalendar( );
smokey.setTimeZone(TimeZone.getTimeZone("MST"));
```

Parsing and Formatting Dates

To represent a GregorianCalendar's date as a string, first create a Date object:

```
Date mydate = smokey.getTime( );
```

To create a string representing a point in time, create a DateFormat object and apply its format() method to a Date object. Like the NumberFormat object we looked at in the previous chapter, DateFormat itself is abstract, but it has several static ("factory") methods that return useful DateFormat subclass instances. To get a default DateFormat, simply call getInstance():

```
DateFormat plain = DateFormat.getInstance( );
String now = plain.format(new Date( ));          // 4/12/00 6:06 AM
```

You can generate a date string or a time string, or both, using the getDateInstance(), getTimeInstance(), and getDateTimeInstance() factory methods. The argument to these methods describes what level of detail you'd like to see. DateFormat defines four constants representing detail levels: they are SHORT, MEDIUM, LONG, and FULL. There is also a DEFAULT, which is the same as MEDIUM. The following code creates three DateFormat instances: one to format a date, one to format a time, and one to format a date and time together. Note that getDateTimeInstance() requires two arguments: the first specifies how to format the date, the second how to format the time:

```
// 12-Apr-00
DateFormat df  = DateFormat.getDateInstance(DateFormat.DEFAULT);

// 9:18:27 AM
DateFormat tf  = DateFormat.getTimeInstance(DateFormat.DEFAULT);

// Wednesday, April 12, 2000 9:18:27 o'clock AM EDT
DateFormat dtf =
   DateFormat.getDateTimeInstance(DateFormat.FULL, DateFormat.FULL);
```

We're showing only how to create the DateFormat objects here; to actually generate a String from a date, you'll need to call the format() method of these objects, passing a Date as an argument.

Formatting dates and times for other countries is just as easy. Overloaded factory methods accept a `Locale` argument:

```
// 12 avr. 00
DateFormat df =
  DateFormat.getDateInstance(DateFormat.DEFAULT, Locale.FRANCE);

// 9:27:49
DateFormat tf =
  DateFormat.getTimeInstance(DateFormat.DEFAULT, Locale.GERMANY);

// mercoledì 12 aprile 2000 9.27.49 GMT-04:00
DateFormat dtf =
    DateFormat.getDateTimeInstance(
        DateFormat.FULL, DateFormat.FULL, Locale.ITALY);
```

To parse a string representing a date, we use the parse() method of the `DateFormat` class. The result is a `Date` object. The parsing algorithms are finicky, so it's safest to parse dates and times that are in the same format produced by the `DateFormat`. The parse() method throws a `ParseException` if it doesn't understand the string you give it. All of the following calls to parse() succeed except the last; we don't supply a time zone, but the format for the time is `LONG`. Other exceptions are occasionally thrown from the parse() method. To cover all the bases, catch `NullPointerExceptions` and `StringIndexOutOfBoundsExceptions`, also.

```
try {
  Date d;
  DateFormat df;

  df = DateFormat.getDateTimeInstance(
          DateFormat.FULL, DateFormat.FULL);
  d = df.parse("Wednesday, April 12, 2000 2:22:22 o'clock PM EDT");

  df = DateFormat.getDateTimeInstance(
          DateFormat.MEDIUM, DateFormat.MEDIUM);
  d = df.parse("12-Apr-00 2:22:22 PM");

  df = DateFormat.getDateTimeInstance(
          DateFormat.LONG, DateFormat.LONG);
  d = df.parse("April 12, 2000 2:22:22 PM EDT");

  // throws a ParseException; detail level mismatch
  d = df.parse("12-Apr-00 2:22:22 PM");
}
catch (Exception e) { ... }
```

Timers

Java includes two handy classes for timed code execution. If you write a clock application, for example, you might want to update the display every second. Or you might want to play an alarm sound at some predetermined time. You could accomplish these tasks with multiple threads and calls to Thread.sleep(). But it's simpler to use the java.util.Timer and java.util.TimerTask classes.

Instances of Timer watch the clock and execute TimerTasks at appropriate times. You could, for example, schedule a task to run at a specific time like this:

```java
import java.util.*;

public class Y2K {
  public static void main(String[] args) {
    Timer timer = new Timer( );

    TimerTask task = new TimerTask( ) {
      public void run( ) {
        System.out.println("Y2K!");
      }
    };

    Calendar c = new GregorianCalendar(2000, Calendar.JANUARY, 1);
    timer.schedule(task, c.getTime( ));
  }
}
```

TimerTask implements the Runnable interface. To create a task, you can simply subclass TimerTask and supply a run( ) method. Here we've created a simple anonymous subclass of TimerTask that prints a message to System.out. Using the schedule() method of Timer, we've asked that the task be run on January 1, 2000. (Oops—too late! But you get the idea.)

There are some other varieties of schedule(); you can run tasks once or at recurring intervals. There are two kinds of recurring tasks—fixed delay and fixed rate. *Fixed delay* means that a fixed amount of time elapses between the end of the task's execution and the beginning of the next execution. *Fixed rate* means that the task should begin execution at fixed time intervals (the difference may be important if the time it takes to execute the command is substantial).

You could, for example, update a clock display every second with code like this:

```java
Timer timer = new Timer( );

TimerTask task = new TimerTask( ) {
    public void run( ) {
        repaint( ); // update the clock display
    }
};

timer.schedule(task, 0, 1000);
```

Timer can't really make any guarantees about exactly when things are executed; you'd need a real-time operating system for that kind of precision. However, Timer can give you reasonable assurance that tasks will be executed at particular times, provided the tasks are not overly complex; with a slow-running task, the end of one execution might spill into the start time for the next execution.

Collections

Collections are fundamental to all kinds of programming. Anywhere we need to keep a group of objects, we have some kind of collection. At the most basic level, Java supports collections in the form of arrays. But since arrays have a fixed length, they are awkward for groups of things that grow and shrink over the lifetime of an application. From the beginning, the Java platform has had two fundamental classes for managing groups of objects: the java.util.Vector class represents a dynamic list of objects, and the java.util.Hashtable class holds a map of key/value pairs. With Java 1.2 came a more comprehensive approach to collections called the Collections Framework. The Vector and Hashtable classes still exist, but they have now been brought into the framework (and have some eccentricities).

If you work with maps, dictionaries, or associative arrays in other languages, you understand how useful these classes are. If you have done a lot of work in C or another static language, you should find collections to be truly magical. They are part of what makes Java powerful and dynamic. Being able to work with groups of objects and make associations between them is an abstraction from the details of the types. It lets you think about the problems at a higher level and saves you from having to reproduce common structures every time you need them.

The Collections Framework is based around a handful of interfaces in the java.util package. These interfaces are divided into two hierarchies. The first hierarchy descends from the Collection interface. This interface (and its descendants) represents a container that holds other objects. The second hierarchy is based on the Map interface, which represents a group of key/value pairs.

The Collection Interface

The mother of all collections is an interface appropriately named Collection. It serves as a container that holds other objects, its *elements*. It doesn't specify exactly how the objects are organized; it doesn't say, for example, whether duplicate objects are allowed or whether the objects are ordered in some way. These kinds of details are left to child interfaces. Nevertheless, the Collection interface does define some basic operations:

public boolean add(Object *o*)
> This method adds the supplied object to this collection. If the operation succeeds, this method returns true. If the object already exists in this collection and the collection does not permit duplicates, false is returned. Furthermore, some collections are read-only. These collections throw an UnsupportedOperationException if this method is called.

```
public boolean remove(Object o)
```
This method removes the specified object from this collection. Like the add() method, this method returns true if the object is removed from the collection. If the object doesn't exist in this collection, false is returned. Read-only collections throw an UnsupportedOperationException if this method is called.

```
public boolean contains(Object o)
```
This method returns true if the collection contains the specified object.

```
public int size()
```
Use this method to find the number of elements in this collection.

```
public boolean isEmpty()
```
This method returns true if there are no elements in this collection.

```
public Iterator iterator()
```
Use this method to examine all the elements in this collection. This method returns an Iterator, which is an object you can use to step through the collection's elements. We'll talk more about iterators in the next section.

These methods are common to every Collection implementation. Any class that implements Collection or one of its child interfaces will have these methods.

Collections and arrays

Converting between collections and arrays is easy. As a special convenience, the elements of a collection can be placed into an array using the following methods:

```
public Object[] toArray()
public Object[] toArray(Object[] a)
```

The first method returns a plain Object array. With the second form, we can be more specific. If we supply our own array of the correct size, it will be filled in with the values. But there is a special feature; if the array is too short, a new array of the *same type* will be created, of the correct length, and returned to us. So it is idiomatic to pass in an empty array of the correct type just to specify the type of the array we want, like this:

```
String [] myStrings = (String [])myCollection( new String[0] );
```

You can convert an object type array to a List type collection with the static asList() method of the java.util.Arrays class:

```
List list = Arrays.asList( myStrings );
```

Working with Collections

A Collection is a dynamic container; it can grow to accommodate new items. For example, a List is a kind of Collection that implements a dynamic array. You can insert and remove elements at arbitrary positions within a `List`. `Collections` work directly with the type `Object`, so we can use `Collections` with instances of any class.[*]

We can even put different kinds of `Objects` in a `Collection` together; the `Collection` doesn't know the difference.

As you might guess, this is where things get tricky. To do anything useful with an `Object` after we take it back out of a `Collection`, we have to cast it back (narrow it) to its original type. This can be done safely in Java because the cast is checked at runtime. Java throws a `ClassCastException` if we try to cast an object to the wrong type. However, this need for casting means that your code must remember types or methodically test them with `instanceof`. That is the price we pay for having a completely dynamic collection class that operates on all types.

You might wonder if you can implement `Collection` to produce a class that works on just one type of element in a type-safe way. Unfortunately, the answer is no. We could implement `Collection`'s methods to make a `Collection` that rejects the wrong type of element at runtime, but this does not provide any new compile time, static type safety. In an upcoming version of Java, templates or generics will provide a safe mechanism for parameterizing types by restricting the types of objects used at compile time. For a glimpse at Java language work in this area, see:

    http://jcp.org/aboutJava/communityprocess/review/jsr014/

Iterators

An *iterator* is an object that lets you step through a sequence of values. This kind of operation comes up so often that it is given a generic interface: `java.util.Iterator`. The `Iterator` interface has only two primary methods:

`public Object next()`
> This method returns the next element of the associated collection.

`public boolean hasNext()`
> This method returns `true` if you have not yet stepped through all the `Collection`'s elements. In other words, it returns `true` if you can call `next()` to get the next element.

The following example shows how you could use an `Iterator` to print out every element of a collection:

```
public void printElements(Collection c, PrintStream out) {
    Iterator iterator = c.iterator( );
```

---

[*] In C++, where classes don't derive from a single `Object` class that supplies a base type and common methods, the elements of a collection would usually be derived from some common collectable class. This forces the use of multiple inheritance along with its associated problems.

```
    while (iterator.hasNext( ))
        out.println(iterator.next( ));
}
```

In addition to the traversal methods, Iterator provides the ability to remove an element from a collection:

public void remove()
> This method removes the last object returned from next() from the associated Collection.

But not all iterators implement remove(). It doesn't make sense to be able to remove an element from a read-only collection, for example. If element removal is not allowed, an UnsupportedOperationException is thrown from this method. If you call remove() before first calling next(), or if you call remove() twice in a row, you'll get an IllegalStateException.

java.util.Enumeration

Prior to the introduction of the Collections API there was another iterator interface: java.util.Enumeration. It used the slightly more verbose names: nextElement() and hasMoreElements() but accomplished the same thing. Many older classes provide Enumerations where they would now use Iterator. If you aren't worried about performance, you can convert your Enumeration into a List with a static convenience method of the java.util.Collections class:

```
    List list = Collections.list( enumeration );
```

Collection Types

The Collection interface has two child interfaces. Set represents a collection in which duplicate elements are not allowed, and List is a collection whose elements have a specific order.

Set has no methods besides the ones it inherits from Collection. It does, however, enforce the rule that duplicate elements are not allowed. If you try to add an element that already exists in a Set, the add() method returns false.

SortedSet adds only a few methods to Set. As you call add() and remove(), the set maintains its order. You can retrieve subsets (which are also sorted) using the subSet(), headSet(), and tailSet() methods. The first(), last(), and comparator() methods provide access to the first element, the last element, and the object used to compare elements (more on this later).

The last child interface of Collection is List. The List interface adds the ability to manipulate elements at specific positions in the list.

```
public void add(int index, Object element)
```
This method adds the given object at the supplied list position. If the position is less than zero or greater than the list length, an IndexOutOfBoundsException will be thrown. The element that was previously at the supplied position, and all elements after it are moved up by one index position.

```
public void remove(int index)
```
This method removes the element at the supplied position. All subsequent elements move down by one index position.

```
public Object get(int index)
```
This method returns the element at the given position.

```
public Object set(int index, Object element)
```
This method changes the element at the given position to the supplied object.

The Map Interface

The Collections Framework also includes the concept of a Map, which is a collection of key/value pairs. Another way of looking at a map is that it is a dictionary, similar to an associative array. Maps store and retrieve elements with key values; they are very useful for things like caches or minimalist databases. When you store a value in a map, you associate a key object with that value. When you need to look up the value, the map retrieves it using the key.

The java.util.Map interface specifies a map that, like Collection, operates on the type Object. A Map stores an element of type Object and associates it with a key, also of type Object. In this way, we can index arbitrary types of elements using arbitrary types as keys. As with Collection, casting is generally required to narrow objects back to their original type after pulling them out of a map.

The basic operations are straightforward:

```
public Object put(Object key, Object value)
```
This method adds the specified key/value pair to the map. If the map already contains a value for the specified key, the old value is replaced and returned as the result.

```
public Object get(Object key)
```
This method retrieves the value corresponding to key from the map.

```
public Object remove(Object key)
```
This method removes the value corresponding to key from the map. The value removed is returned.

```
public int size()
```
Use this method to find the number of key/value pairs in this map.

You can retrieve all the keys or values in the map:

`public Set keySet()`
> This method returns a Set that contains all the keys in this map.

`public Collection values()`
> Use this method to retrieve all the values in this map. The returned Collection can contain duplicate elements.

Map has one child interface, SortedMap. SortedMap maintains its key/value pairs in sorted order according to the key values. It provides the subMap(), headMap(), and tailMap() methods for retrieving sorted map subsets. Like SortedSet, it also provides a comparator() method that returns an object that determines how the map keys are sorted. We'll talk more about this later.

Finally, we should make it clear that although related, Map is not a type of Collection (Map does not extend the Collection interface). You might be wondering why. All of the methods of the Collection interface would appear to make sense for Map, except for iterator(). A Map, remember, has two sets of objects: keys and values and separate iterators for each.

One more note about maps: some map implementations (including Java's standard, HashMap) allow null to be used as a key or value, but others may not.

Implementations

Up until this point, we've talked only about interfaces. But you can't instantiate interfaces. The Collections Framework includes useful implementations of the collections interfaces. These implementations are listed by interface in Table 10-5.

Table 10-5. Collections framework implementation classes

Interface	Implementation
Set	HashSet
SortedSet	TreeSet
List	ArrayList, LinkedList, Vector
Map	HashMap, Hashtable, LinkedHashMap, IdentityHashMap
SortedMap	TreeMap

ArrayList offers good performance if you add to the end of the list frequently, while LinkedList offers better performance for frequent insertions and deletions. Vector has been around since Java 1.0; it's now retrofitted to implement the List methods. Vector's methods are synchronized by default, unlike the other Maps. The old Hashtable has been updated so that it now implements the Map interface. Its methods are also synchronized. As we'll discuss a bit later, there are other, more general ways to get synchronized collections.

Hashcodes and key values

The name `Hashtable` and `HashMap` refer to the fact that these map collections use object hashcodes in order to maintain their associations. Specifically, an element in a `Hashtable` or `HashMap` is not associated with a key strictly by the key object's identity but rather by the key's contents. This allows keys that are equivalent to access the same object. By "equivalent," we mean those objects that compare `true` with `equals()`. So, if you store an object in a `Hashtable` using one object as a key, you can use any other object that `equals()` tells you is equivalent to retrieve the stored object.

It's easy to see why equivalence is important if you remember our discussion of strings. You may create two `String` objects that have the same text in them but that come from different sources in Java. In this case, the `==` operator tells you that the objects are different, but the `equals()` method of the `String` class tells you that they are equivalent. Because they are equivalent, if we store an object in a `HashMap` using one of the `String` objects as a key, we can retrieve it using the other.

The hashcode of an object makes this association based on content. As we mentioned in Chapter 7, the hashcode is like a fingerprint of the object's data content. `HashMap` uses it to store the objects so that they can be retrieved efficiently. The hashcode is nothing more than a number (an integer) that is a function of the data. The number always turns out the same for identical data, but the hashing function is intentionally designed to generate as random a number as possible for different combinations of data. In other words, a very small change in the data should produce a big difference in the number. It is unlikely that two similar datasets would produce the same hashcode.

Internally, `HashMap` really just keeps a number of lists of objects, but it puts objects into the lists based on their hashcode. So when it wants to find the object again, it can look at the hashcode and know immediately how to get to the appropriate list. The `HashMap` still might end up with a number of objects to examine, but the list should be short. For each object it finds, it does the following comparison to see if the key matches:

```
if ((keyHashcode == storedKeyHashcode) && key.equals(storedKey))
    return object;
```

There is no prescribed way to generate hashcodes. The only requirement is that they be somewhat randomly distributed and reproducible (based on the data). This means that two objects that are not the same could end up with the same hashcode by accident. This is unlikely (there are 2^{32} possible integer values); moreover, it doesn't cause a problem because the `HashMap` ultimately checks the actual keys, as well as the hashcodes, to see if they are equal. Therefore, even if two objects have the same hashcode, they can still coexist in the `HashMap` as long as they don't test equal to one another as well.

Hashcodes are computed by an object's `hashCode()` method, which is inherited from the `Object` class if it isn't overridden. The default `hashCode()` method simply assigns each object instance a unique number to be used as a hashcode. If a class does not override this method, each instance of the class will have a unique hashcode. This goes along well with the default implementation of equals() in Object, which only compares objects for identity using ==.

You must override equals() in any classes for which equivalence of different objects is meaningful. Likewise, if you want equivalent objects to serve as equivalent keys, you need to override the hashCode() method as well to return identical hashcode values. To do this, you need to create some suitably complex and arbitrary function of the contents of your object. The only criterion for the function is that it should be almost certain to return different values for objects with different data, but the same value for objects with identical data.

Synchronized and Read-Only Collections

The java.util.Collections class is full of handy static methods that operate on Sets and Maps. (It's not the same as the java.util.Collection interface, which we've already talked about.) Since all the static methods in Collections operate on interfaces, they work regardless of the actual implementation classes you're using. There are lots of useful methods in here and we'll look at only a few now.

All the default collection implementations are not synchronized; that is, they are not safe for concurrent access by multiple threads. The reason for this is performance. In many applications there is no need for synchronization, so the Collections API does not provide it by default. Instead you can create a synchronized version of any collection using the following methods of the Collections class:

```
public static Collection synchronizedCollection(Collection c)
public static Set synchronizedSet(Set s)
public static List synchronizedList(List list)
public static Map synchronizedMap(Map m)
public static SortedSet synchronizedSortedSet(SortedSet s)
public static SortedMap synchronizedSortedMap(SortedMap m)
```

These methods create synchronized, thread-safe versions of the supplied collection, normally by wrapping them. We'll talk a little more about this later in this chapter.

Furthermore, you can use the Collections class to create read-only versions of any collection:

```
public static Collection unmodifiableCollection(Collection c)
public static Set unmodifiableSet(Set s)
public static List unmodifiableList(List list)
public static Map unmodifiableMap(Map m)
public static SortedSet unmodifiableSortedSet(SortedSet s)
public static SortedMap unmodifiableSortedMap(SortedMap m)
```

Sorting for Free

Collections includes other methods for performing common operations like sorting. Sorting comes in two varieties:

`public static void sort(List list)`
> This method sorts the given list. You can use this method only on lists whose elements implement the `java.lang.Comparable` interface. Luckily, many classes already implement this interface, including `String`, `Date`, `BigInteger`, and the wrapper classes for the primitive types (`Integer`, `Double`, etc.).

`public static void sort(List list, Comparator c)`
> Use this method to sort a list whose elements don't implement the `Comparable` interface. The supplied `java.util.Comparator` does the work of comparing elements. You might, for example, write an `ImaginaryNumber` class and want to sort a list of them. You would then create a `Comparator` implementation that knew how to compare two imaginary numbers.

Collections gives you some other interesting capabilities, too. If you're interested in learning more, check out the `min()`, `max()`, `binarySearch()`, and `reverse()` methods.

A Thrilling Example

Collections is a bread-and-butter topic, which means it's hard to make exciting examples about it. The example in this section reads a text file, parses all its words, counts the number of occurrences, sorts them, and writes the results to another file. It gives you a good feel for how to use collections in your own programs.

```java
//file: WordSort.java
import java.io.*;
import java.util.*;

public class WordSort {
  public static void main(String[] args) throws IOException {
    // get the command-line arguments
    if (args.length < 2) {
      System.out.println("Usage: WordSort inputfile outputfile");
      return;
    }
    String inputfile = args[0];
    String outputfile = args[1];

/* Create the word map. Each key is a word and each value is an
 * Integer that represents the number of times the word occurs
 * in the input file.
 */
    Map map = new TreeMap( );

    // read every line of the input file
    BufferedReader in =
```

```
      new BufferedReader(new FileReader(inputfile));

    String line;
    while ((line = in.readLine( )) != null) {
      // examine each word on the line
      StringTokenizer st = new StringTokenizer(line);
      while (st.hasMoreTokens( )) {
        String word = st.nextToken( );
        Object o = map.get(word);
        // if there's no entry for this word, add one
        if (o == null) map.put(word, new Integer(1));
        // otherwise, increment the count for this word
        else {
          Integer count = (Integer)o;
          map.put(word, new Integer(count.intValue( ) + 1));
        }
      }
    }
    in.close( );

    // get the map's keys
    List keys = new ArrayList(map.keySet( ));

    // write the results to the output file
    PrintWriter out = new PrintWriter(new FileWriter(outputfile));
    Iterator iterator = keys.iterator( );
    while (iterator.hasNext( )) {
      Object key = iterator.next( );
      out.println(key + " : " + map.get(key));
    }
    out.close( );
  }
}
```

Suppose, for example, that you have an input file named *Ian Moore.txt*:

```
Well it was my love that kept you going
Kept you strong enough to fall
And it was my heart you were breaking
When he hurt your pride

So how does it feel
How does it feel
How does it feel
How does it feel
```

You could run the example on this file using the following command line:

```
% java WordSort "Ian Moore.txt" count.txt
```

The output file, *count.txt*, looks like this:

```
And : 1
How : 3
Kept : 1
So : 1
```

```
Well : 1
When : 1
breaking : 1
does : 4
enough : 1
fall : 1
feel : 4
going : 1
he : 1
heart : 1
how : 1
hurt : 1
it : 6
kept : 1
love : 1
my : 2
pride : 1
strong : 1
that : 1
to : 1
was : 2
were : 1
you : 3
your : 1
```

The results are case-sensitive: "How" and "how" are recorded separately. You could modify this behavior by converting words to all lowercase after retrieving them from the StringTokenizer:

```
String word = st.nextToken( ).toLowerCase( );
```

Thread Safety and Iterators

Earlier we saw that the Collections class provides methods that create a thread-safe version of any Collection. There are methods for each subtype of Collection. The following example shows how to create a thread-safe List:

```
List list = new ArrayList( );
List syncList = Collections.synchronizedList(list);
```

Although synchronized collections are thread-safe, the Iterators returned from them are not. This is an important point. If you obtain an Iterator from a collection, you should do your own synchronization to ensure that the collection does not change as you're iterating through its elements. You can do this by convention by synchronizing on the collection itself with the synchronized keyword:

```
synchronized(syncList) {
    Iterator iterator = syncList.iterator( );
    // do stuff with the iterator here
}
```

WeakHashMap

In Chapter 5 we introduced the idea of weak references—object references that don't prevent their objects from being removed by the garbage collector. WeakHashMap is an implementation of Map that makes use of weak references in its keys and values. This means that you don't have to remove key/value pairs from a Map when you're finished with them. Normally if you removed all references to a key object in the rest of your application, the Map would still contain a reference and keep the object "alive." WeakHashMap changes this; once you remove references to a key object in the rest of the application, the WeakHashMap lets go of it too.

Properties

The java.util.Properties class is a specialized hashtable map for strings. Java uses a Properties object to hold environmental information in the way that environment variables are used in other programming environments. You can use a Properties table to hold arbitrary configuration information for an application in an easily accessible format. The Properties table can also load and store its information in text format using streams (see Chapter 11 for information on streams). In Java 1.4, a new Preferences API was introduced which is designed to take over much of the system configuration functionality of properties using XML files. We'll talk about that a bit later.

Any string values can be stored as key/value pairs in a Properties table. However, the convention is to use a dot-separated naming hierarchy to group property names into logical structures, as is done with X Window System resources on Unix systems.*

You can create an empty Properties table and add String key/value pairs just as you can with a Hashtable:

```
Properties props = new Properties( );
props.setProperty("myApp.xsize", "52");
props.setProperty("myApp.ysize", "79");
```

Thereafter, you can retrieve values with the getProperty() method:

```
String xsize = props.getProperty( "myApp.xsize" );
```

If the named property doesn't exist, getProperty() returns null. You can get an Enumeration of the property names with the propertyNames() method:

```
for ( Enumeration e = props.propertyNames( ); e.hasMoreElements; ) {
    String name = e.nextElement( );
    ...
}
```

---

* Unfortunately, this is just a naming convention right now, so you can't access logical groups of properties as you can with X resources.

When you create a `Properties` table, you can specify a second table for default property values:

```
Properties defaults;
...
Properties props = new Properties( defaults );
```

Now when you call getProperty(), the method searches the default table if it doesn't find the named property in the current table. An alternative version of getProperty() also accepts a default value; this value is returned instead of `null` if the property is not found in the current list or in the default list:

```
String xsize = props.getProperty( "myApp.xsize", "50" );
```

Loading and Storing

You can save a `Properties` table to an `OutputStream` using the save() method. The property information is output in a flat ASCII format. We'll talk about I/O in the next chapter, but bear with us for now. Continuing with the previous example, output the property information using the System.out stream as follows:

```
props.save( System.out, "Application Parameters" );
```

System.out is a standard output stream that prints to the console or command line of an application. We could also save the information to a file using a `FileOutputStream` as the first argument to save(). The second argument to save() is a `String` that is used as a header for the data. The previous code outputs something like the following to System.out:

```
#Application Parameters
#Mon Feb 12 09:24:23 CST 1999
myApp.ysize=79
myApp.xsize=52
```

The load() method reads the previously saved contents of a `Properties` object from an `InputStream`:

```
FileInputStream fin;
...
Properties props = new Properties( )
props.load( fin );
```

The list() method is useful for debugging. It prints the contents to an `OutputStream` in a format that is more human-readable but not retrievable by load(). It truncates long lines with an ellipsis (...).

System Properties

The java.lang.System class provides access to basic system environment information through the static System.getProperty() method. This method returns a `Properties` table that contains system properties. System properties take the place of environment variables in some programming environments. Table 10-6 summarizes system properties that are guaranteed to be defined in any Java environment.

Table 10-6. System properties

System property	Meaning
java.vendor	Vendor-specific string
java.vendor.url	URL of vendor
java.version	Java version
java.home	Java installation directory
java.class.version	Java class version
java.class.path	The classpath
os.name	Operating system name
os.arch	Operating system architecture
os.version	Operating system version
file.separator	File separator (such as / or \)
path.separator	Path separator (such as : or ;)
line.separator	Line separator (such as \n or \r\n)
user.name	User account name
user.home	User's home directory
user.dir	Current working directory

Applets are, by current web browser conventions, prevented from reading the following properties: java.home, java.class.path, user.name, user.home, and user.dir. As you'll see later, these restrictions are implemented by a SecurityManager object.

Your application can set system properties with the static method System. setProperty(). You can also set system properties when you run the Java interpreter, using the -D option:

```
% java -Dfoo=bar -Dcat=Boojum MyApp
```

Since it is common to use system properties to provide parameters such as numbers and colors, Java provides some convenience routines for retrieving property values and parsing them into their appropriate types. The classes Boolean, Integer, Long, and Color each come with a "get" method that looks up and parses a system property. For example, Integer.getInteger("foo") looks for a system property called foo and then returns it as an Integer. Color.getColor("foo") parses the property as an RGB value and returns a Color object.

The Preferences API

Java 1.4 introduced a Preferences API to accommodate the need to store both system and per user configuration data persistently across executions of the Java VM.

The Preferences API is like a portable version of the Windows registry, a mini database in which you can keep small amounts of information, accessible to all applications. Entries are stored as name/value pairs, where the values may be of several standard types including strings, numbers, booleans, and even short byte arrays. We should stress that the Preferences API is not intended to be used as a true database and you can't store large amounts of data in it. (That's not to say anything about how it's actually implemented).

Preferences are stored logically in a tree. A preferences object is a node in the tree located by a unique path. You can think of preferences as files in a directory structure; within the file are stored one or more name/value pairs. To store or retrieve items you ask for a preferences object for the correct path. Here is an example; we'll explain the node lookup shortly:

```
Preferences prefs = Preferences.userRoot( ).node("oreilly/learningjava");

prefs.put("author", "Niemeyer");
prefs.putInt("edition", 4);

String author = prefs.get("author", "unknown");
int edition = prefs.getInt("edition", -1);
```

In addition to the String and int type accessors, there are the following get methods for other types: getLong(), getFloat(), getDouble(), getByteArray(), and getBoolean(). Each of these get methods takes a key name and default value to be used if no value is defined. And of course for each get method, there is a corresponding "put" method that takes the name and a value of the corresponding type. Providing defaults in the get methods is mandatory. The intent is for applications to function even if there is no preference information or if the storage for it is not available, as we'll discuss later.

Preferences are stored in two separate trees: system preferences and user preferences. *System preferences* are shared by all users of the Java installation. But *user preferences* are maintained separately for each user; each user sees his or her own preference information. In our example, we used the static method userRoot() to fetch the root node (preference object) for the user preferences tree. We then asked that node to find the child node at the path *oreilly/learningjava*, using the node() method. The corresponding systemRoot() method provides the system root node.

The node() method accepts either a relative or an absolute path. A relative path asks the node to find the path relative to itself as a base. So we also could have gotten our node this way:

```
Preferences prefs =
    Preferences.userRoot( ).node("oreilly").node("learningjava");
```

But node() also accepts an absolute path, in which case the base node serves only to designate which tree the path is in. So we could use the absolute path */oreilly/learningjava* as the argument to any node() method and reach our preferences object.

Preferences for Classes

Java is an object-oriented language, and so it's natural to wish to associate preference data with classes. In Chapter 11, we'll see that Java provides special facilities for loading resource files associated with class files. The Preferences API follows this pattern by associating a node with each Java package. Its convention is simple: the node path is just the package name with the dots (.) converted to slashes (/). All classes in the package share the same node.

You can get the preference object node for a class using the static `Preferences.userNodeForPackage()` or `Preferences.systemNodeForPackage()` methods, which take a `Class` as an argument and return the corresponding package node for the user and system trees respectively. For example:

```
Preferences datePrefs = Preferences.systemNodeForPackage( Date.class );
Preferences myPrefs = Preferences.userNodeForPackage( MyClass.class );
Preferences morePrefs =
    Preferences.userNodeForPackage( myObject.getClass() );
```

Here we've used the `.class` construct to refer to the `Class` object for the `Date` class in the system tree and to our own `MyClass` class in the user tree. The `Date` class is in the `java.util` package, so we'll get the node */java/util* in that case. You can get the `Class` for any object instance using the `getClass()` method.

Preferences Storage

There is no need to "create" nodes. When you ask for a node you get a preferences object for that path in the tree. If you write something to it, that data is eventually placed in persistent storage, called the backing store. The *backing store* is the implementation-dependent storage mechanism used to hold the preference data. All the put methods return immediately, and no guarantees are made as to when the data is actually stored. You can force data to the backing store explicitly using the `flush()` method of the Preferences class. Conversely, you can use the `sync()` method to guarantee that a preferences object is up to date with respect to changes placed into the backing store by other applications or threads. Both `flush()` and `sync()` throw a `BackingStoreException` if data cannot be read or written for some reason.

You don't have to create nodes, but you can test for the existence of a data node with the `nodeExists()` method, and you can remove a node and all its children with the `removeNode()` method. To remove a data item from a node, use the `remove()` method, specifying the key; or you can remove all the data from a node with the `clear()` method (which is not the same as removing the node).

Although the details of the backing store are implementation-dependent, the Preferences API provides a simple import/export facility that can read and write parts of a preference tree to an XML file. (The format for the file is available at *http://java.sun. com/dtd/*). A preference object can be written to an output stream with the

---

exportNode() method. The exportSubtree() method writes the node and all its children. Going the other way, the static Preferences.importPreferences() method can read the XML file and populate the appropriate tree with its data. The XML file records whether it is user or system preferences, but user data is always placed into the current user's tree, regardless of who generated it.

It's interesting to note that since the import mechanism writes directly to the tree, you can't use this as a general data-to-XML storage mechanism; other current and forthcoming APIs play that role. Also, although we said that the implementation details are not specified, it's interesting to note how things really work in the current implementation. Java creates a directory hierarchy for each tree at *$JAVA_HOME/ jre/.systemPrefs* and *$HOME/.java/.userPrefs*, respectively. In each directory, there is an XML file called *prefs.xml* corresponding to that node.

Change Notification

Often your application should be notified if changes are made to the preferences while it's running. You can get updates on preference changes using the PreferenceChangeListener and NodeChangeListener interfaces. These interfaces are examples of *event listener* interfaces, and we'll see many examples of these in Chapters 15–17. We'll talk about the general pattern later, in the section "Observers and Observables." For now we'll just say that by registering an object that implements PreferenceChangeListener with a node you can receive updates on added, removed, and changed preference data for that node. The NodeChangeListener allows you to be told when child nodes are added to or removed from a specific node. Here is a snippet that prints all the data changes affecting our */oreilly/learningjava* node.

```
Preferences prefs =
    Preferences.userRoot( ).node("/oreilly/learningjava");

prefs.addPreferenceChangeListener( new PreferenceChangeListener( ) {
    public void preferenceChange(PreferenceChangeEvent e) {
        System.out.println("Value: " + e.getKey( )
            + " changed to "+ e.getNewValue( ) );
    }
} );
```

In brief, this example listens for changes to preferences and prints them. If this example isn't immediately clear, it should be after you've read about events in Chapter 15 and beyond.

The Logging API

Another feature introduced in Java 1.4 is the Logging API. The java.util.logging package provides a highly flexible and easy to use logging framework for system information, error messages, and fine-grained tracing (debugging) output. With the logging package you can apply filters to select log messages, direct their output to one or more destinations (including files and network services), and format the messages appropriately for their consumers.

Most importantly, much of this basic logging configuration can be set up externally at runtime through the use of a logging setup properties file or an external program. For example, by setting the right properties at runtime, you can specify that log messages are to be sent both to a designated file in XML format and also logged to the system console in a digested, human-readable form. Furthermore, for each of those destinations you can specify the level or priority of messages to be logged, ignoring those below a certain threshold of significance. By following the correct source conventions in your code, you can even make it possible to adjust the logging levels for specific parts of your application, allowing you to target individual packages and classes for detailed logging without being overwhelmed by too much output.

Overview

Any good logging API must have at least two guiding principles. First, performance should not inhibit the developer from using log messages freely. As with Java language assertions (discussed in Chapter 4), when log messages are turned off they should not consume any significant amount of processing time. This means there's no performance penalty for including logging statements as long as they're turned off. Second, although some users may want advanced features and configuration, a logging API must have some simple mode of usage that is convenient enough for time-starved developers to use in lieu of the old standby System.out.println(). Java's Logging API provides a simple model and many convenience methods that make it very tempting.

Loggers

The heart of the logging framework is the *logger*, an instance of java.util.logging. Logger. In most cases, this is the only class your code will ever have to deal with. A logger is constructed from the static Logger.getLogger() method, with a logger name as its argument. Logger names place loggers into a hierarchy, with a global, root logger at the top and a tree and children below. This hierarchy allows configuration to be inherited by parts of the tree so that logging can be automatically configured for different parts of your application. The convention is to use a separate logger instance in each major class or package and to use the dot-separated package and/or class name as the logger name. For example:

```
package com.oreilly.learnjava;
public class Book {
    static Logger log = Logger.getLogger("com.oreilly.learnjava.Book");
```

The logger provides a wide range of methods to log messages; some take very detailed information, and some convenience methods take only a string for ease of use. For example:

```
log.warning("Disk 90% full.");
log.info("New user joined chat room.");
```

We cover methods of the logger class in detail a bit later. The names warning and info are two examples of logging levels; there are seven levels ranging from SEVERE at the top to FINEST at the bottom. Distinguishing log messages in this way allows us to select the level of information that we want to see at runtime. Rather than simply logging everything and sorting through it later (with negative performance impact) we can tweak which messages are generated. We'll talk more about logging levels in the next section.

We should also mention that for convenience in very simple applications or experiments, a logger for the name "global" is provided in the static field Logger.global. You can use it as an alternative to the old standby System.out.println() for those cases where that is still a temptation:

```
Logger.global.info("Doing foo...")
```

Handlers

Loggers represent the client interface to the logging system, but the actual work of publishing messages to destinations (such as files or the console) is done by *handler* objects. Each logger may have one or more Handler objects associated with it, which includes several predefined handlers supplied with the Logging API: ConsoleHandler, FileHandler, StreamHandler, and SocketHandler. Each handler knows how to deliver messages to its respective destination. ConsoleHandler is used by the default configuration to print messages on the command line or system console. FileHandler can direct output to files using a supplied naming convention and automatically rotate the files as they become full. The others send messages to streams and sockets, respectively. There is one additional handler, MemoryHandler, that can hold a number of log messages in memory. MemoryHandler has a circular buffer, which maintains a certain number of messages until it is triggered to publish them to another designated handler.

As we said, loggers can be set to use one or more handlers. Loggers also send messages up the tree to each of their parent logger's handlers. In the simplest configuration this means that all messages end up distributed by the root logger's handlers. We'll see how to set up output using the standard handlers for the console, files, etc. shortly.

Filters

Before a logger hands off a message to its handlers or its parent's handlers, it first checks whether the logging level is sufficient to proceed. If the message doesn't meet the required level it is discarded at the source. In addition to level, you can implement arbitrary filtering of messages by creating Filter classes which examine the log message before it is processed. A Filter class can be applied to a logger externally, at runtime in the same way that the logging level, handlers, and formatters, discussed next, can be. A Filter may also be attached to an individual Handler to filter records at the output stage (as opposed to the source).

Formatters

Internally, messages are carried in a neutral format including all the source information provided. It is not until they are processed by a handler that they are formatted for output by an instance of a Formatter object. The logging package comes with two basic formatters: SimpleFormatter and XMLFormatter. The SimpleFormatter is the default used for console output. It produces short, human-readable, summaries of log messages. XMLFormatter encodes all the log message details into an XML record format. The DTD for the format can be found at *http://java.sun.com/dtd/*.

Logging Levels

Table 10-7 lists the logging levels from most significant to least significant.

Table 10-7. Logging API logging levels

Level	Meaning
SEVERE	Application failure
WARNING	Notification of potential problem
INFO	Messages of general interest to end users
CONFIG	Detailed system configuration information for administrators
FINE, FINER, FINEST	Successively more detailed application tracing information for developers

These levels fall into three camps: end user, administrator, and developer. Applications often default to logging only messages of the INFO level and above (INFO, WARNING, and SEVERE). These levels are generally seen by end users and messages logged to them should be suitable for general consumption. In other words, they should be written clearly so they make sense to an average user of the application. Often these kinds of message are presented to the end user on a system console or in a pop-up message dialog.

The CONFIG level should be used for relatively static but detailed system information that could assist an administrator or installer. This might include information about the installed software modules, host system characteristics, and configuration parameters. These details are important, but probably not as meaningful to an end user.

The FINE, FINER, and FINEST levels are for developers or people who have knowledge of the internals of the application. These should be used for tracing the application at successive levels of detail. You can define your own meanings for these. We'll suggest a rough outline in our example, coming up next.

A Simple Example

In the following (admittedly very contrived) example we use all the logging levels so that we can experiment with logging configuration. Although the sequence of messages is nonsensical, the text is representative of messages of that type.

```java
import java.util.logging.*;

public class LogTest {
    public static void main(String argv[])
    {
        Logger logger = Logger.getLogger("com.oreilly.LogTest");

        logger.severe("Power lost - running on backup!");
        logger.warning("Database connection lost, retrying...");
        logger.info("Startup complete.");
        logger.config("Server configuration: standalone, JVM version 1.4");
        logger.fine("Loading graphing package.");
        logger.finer("Doing pie chart");
        logger.finest("Starting bubble sort: value ="+42);
    }
}
```

There's not much to this example. We ask for a `logger` instance for our class using the static `Logger.getLogger()` method, specifying a class name. The convention is to use the fully qualified class name, so we'll pretend that our class is in a `com.oreilly` package.

Now run `LogTest`. You should see output like the following on the system console:

```
Jan 6, 2002 3:24:36 PM LogTest main
SEVERE: Power lost - running on backup!
Jan 6, 2002 3:24:37 PM LogTest main
WARNING: Database connection lost, retrying...
Jan 6, 2002 3:24:37 PM LogTest main
INFO: Startup complete.
```

We see the INFO, WARNING, and SEVERE messages, each identified with a date and timestamp and the name of the class and method (`LogTest main`) from which they came. Notice that the lower level messages did not appear. This is because the default logging level is normally set to INFO, meaning that only messages of severity INFO and above are logged. Also note that the output went to the system console and not to a log file somewhere; that's also the default. Now we'll describe where these defaults are set and how to override them at runtime.

Logging Setup Properties

As we said in the introduction, probably the most important feature of the Logging API is the ability to configure so much of it at runtime through the use of external properties or applications. The default logging configuration is stored in the file *jre/lib/logging.properties* in the directory where Java is installed. It's a standard Java properties file (of the kind we described earlier in this chapter).

The format of this file is simple. You can make changes to it, but you don't have to. Instead you can specify your own logging setup properties file on a case-by-case basis using a system property at runtime, as follows:

```
% java -Djava.util.logging.config.file=myfile.properties
```

In this command line, *myfile* is your properties file that contains directives we'll describe next. If you want to make this file designation more permanent, you can do so by setting the filename in the corresponding entry using the Java Preferences API described earlier in this chapter. You can go even further, and instead of specifying a setup file, supply a class that is responsible for setting up all logging configuration, but we won't get into that here.

A very simple logging properties file might look like this:

```
# Set the default logging level
.level = FINEST
# Direct output to the console
handlers = java.util.logging.ConsoleHandler
```

Here we have set the default logging level for the entire application using the `.level` (that's dot-level) property. We have also used the `handlers` property to specify that an instance of the `ConsoleHandler` should be used (just like the default setup) to show messages on the console. If you run our application again, specifying this properties file as the logging setup, you will now see all our log messages.

But we're just getting warmed up. Next let's look at a more complex configuration:

```
# Set the default logging level
.level = INFO

# Ouput to file and console
handlers = java.util.logging.FileHandler, java.util.logging.ConsoleHandler

# Configure the file output
java.util.logging.FileHandler.level = FINEST
java.util.logging.FileHandler.pattern = %h/Test.log
java.util.logging.FileHandler.limit = 25000
java.util.logging.FileHandler.count = 4
java.util.logging.FileHandler.formatter = java.util.logging.XMLFormatter

# Configure the console output
java.util.logging.ConsoleHandler.level = WARNING
```

```
# Levels for specific classes
com.oreilly.LogTest.level = FINEST
```

In this example, we have configured two log handlers: a ConsoleHandler with the logging level set to WARNING and also an instance of FileHandler that sends the output to an XML file. The file handler is configured to log messages at the FINEST level (all messages) and to rotate log files every 25,000 lines, keeping a maximum of four files.

The filename is controlled by the pattern property. Forward slashes in the filename are automatically localized to backslash (\) if necessary. The special symbol %h refers to the user home. You can use %t to refer to the system temporary directory. If filenames conflict, a number is appended automatically after a dot (starting at zero). Alternatively, you can use %u to indicate where a unique number should be inserted into the name. Similarly, when files rotate, a number is appended after a dot at the end. You can take control of where the rotation number is placed with the %g identifier.

In our example we specified the XMLFormatter class. We could also have used the SimpleFormatter class to send the same kind of simple output to the console. The ConsoleHandler also allows us to specify any formatter we wish, using the formatter property.

Finally, we promised earlier that you could control logging levels for parts of your applications. To do this, set properties on your application loggers using their hierarchical names:

```
# Levels for specific logger (class) names
com.oreilly.LogTest.level = FINEST
```

Here we've set the logging level for just our test logger, by name. The log properties follow the hierarchy, so we could set the logging level for all classes in the oreilly package with:

```
com.oreilly.level = FINEST
```

Logging levels are set in the order they are read in the properties file, so set the general ones first. Also note that the levels set on the handlers allow the file handler to filter only the messages being supplied by the loggers. So setting the file handler to FINEST won't revive messages squelched by a logger set to SEVERE (only the SEVERE messages will make it to the handler from that logger).

The Logger

In our example we used the seven convenience methods named for the various logging levels. There are also three groups of general methods that can be used to provide more detailed information. The most general are:

```
log(Level level, String msg)
log(Level level, String msg, Object param1)
```

```
log(Level level, String msg, Object params[])
log(Level level, String msg, Throwable thrown)
```

These methods accept as their first argument a static logging level identifier from the Level class, followed by a parameter, array, or exception type. The level identifier is one of Level.SEVERE, Level.WARNING, Level.INFO, and so on.

In addition to these four methods, there are four corresponding methods named logp() that also take a source class and method name as the second and third arguments. In our example, we saw Java automatically determine that information, so why would we want to supply it? Well, the answer is that Java may not always be able to determine the exact method name because of runtime dynamic optimization. The p in logp stands for "precise" and allows you to control this yourself.

There is yet another set of methods named logrb() (which probably should have been named "logprb()") that take both the class and method names and a resource bundle name. The resource bundle localizes the messages (see "Resource Bundles" in Chapter 9). More generally a logger may have a resource bundle associated with it when it is created, using another form of the getLogger method:

```
Logger.getLogger("com.oreilly.LogTest", "logMessages");
```

In either case, the resource bundle name is passed along with the log message and can be used by the formatter. If a resource bundle is specified, the standard formatters treat the message text as a key and try to look up a localized message. Localized messages may include parameters using the standard message format notation and the form of log(), which accepts an argument array.

Finally, there are convenience methods called entering(), exiting(), and throwing() which developers can use to log detailed trace information.

Performance

In the introduction we said that a priority of the Logging API is performance. To that end we've described that log messages are filtered at the source, using logging levels to cut off processing of messages early. This saves much of the expense of handling them. However it cannot prevent certain kinds of setup work that you might do before the logging call. Specifically, since we're passing things into the log methods, it's common to construct detailed messages or render objects to strings as arguments. Often this kind of operation is costly. To avoid unnecessary string construction, you should wrap expensive log operations in a conditional test using the Logger isLoggable() method to test whether you should carry out the operation:

```
if ( log.isLoggable( Level.CONFIG ) ) {
    log.config("Configuration: "+ loadExpensiveConfigInfo( ) );
}
```

Observers and Observables

The java.util.Observer interface and java.util.Observable class are relatively small utilities, but they provide a glimpse of a fundamental design pattern in Java. Observers and observables are part of the MVC (Model-View-Controller) framework. It is an abstraction that lets a number of client objects (the *observers*) be notified whenever a certain object or resource (the *observable*) changes in some way. We will see this pattern used extensively in Java's event mechanism, covered in Chapters 15 through 18.

The Observable object has a method an Observer calls to register its interest. When a change happens, the Observable sends a notification by calling a method in each of the Observers. The observers implement the Observer interface, which specifies that notification causes an Observer object's update() method to be called.

In the following example, we create a MessageBoard object that holds a String message. MessageBoard extends Observable, from which it inherits the mechanism for registering observers (addObserver()) and notifying observers (notifyObservers()). To observe the MessageBoard, we have Student objects that implement the Observer interface so that they can be notified when the message changes:

```java
//file: MessageBoard.java
import java.util.*;

public class MessageBoard extends Observable {
    private String message;

    public String getMessage( ) {
        return message;
    }
    public void changeMessage( String message ) {
        this.message = message;
        setChanged( );
        notifyObservers( message );
    }
    public static void main( String [] args ) {
        MessageBoard board = new MessageBoard( );
        Student bob = new Student( );
        Student joe = new Student( );
        board.addObserver( bob );
        board.addObserver( joe );
        board.changeMessage("More Homework!");
    }
} // end of class MessageBoard

class Student implements Observer {
    public void update(Observable o, Object arg) {
        System.out.println( "Message board changed: " + arg );
    }
}
```

Our MessageBoard object extends Observable, which provides a method called addObserver(). Each Student objects registers itself using this method and receives updates via its update() method. When a new message string is set, using the MessageBoard's changeMessage() method, the Observable calls the setChanged() and notifyObservers() methods to notify the observers. notifyObservers() can take as an argument an Object to pass along as an indication of the change. This object, in this case the String containing the new message, is passed to the observer's update() method, as its second argument. The first argument to update() is the Observable object itself.

The main() method of MessageBoard creates a MessageBoard and registers two Student objects with it. Then it changes the message. When you run the code, you should see each Student object print the message as it is notified.

You can imagine how you could implement the observer/observable relationship yourself using a List to hold the list of observers. In Chapter 15 and beyond, we'll see that the Java AWT and Swing event model extends this design pattern to use strongly typed observables and observers, called *events* and event listeners. But for now, we turn our discussion of core utilities to another fundamental topic: I/O.

Input/Output Facilities

In this chapter, we continue our exploration of the Java API by looking at many of the classes in the java.io and java.nio packages. These packages offer a rich set of tools for basic I/O and also provide the framework on which all file and network communication in Java is built.

Figure 11-1 shows the class hierarchy of these packages.

We'll start by looking at the stream classes in java.io, which are subclasses of the basic InputStream, OutputStream, Reader, and Writer classes. Then we'll examine the File class and discuss how you can interact with the filesystem using classes in java. io. We'll also take a quick look at the data compression classes provided in java. util.zip. Finally, we'll begin our investigation of the new java.nio package, introduced in Java 1.4. The NIO package adds significant new functionality for building high performance services.

Streams

Most fundamental I/O in Java is based on *streams*. A stream represents a flow of data, or a channel of communication with (at least conceptually) a *writer* at one end and a *reader* at the other. When you are working with the java.io package to perform terminal input and output, reading or writing files, or communicating through sockets in Java, you are using various types of streams. Later in this chapter we'll look at the NIO package, which introduces a similar concept called a *channel*. But for now we'll start by summarizing the available types of streams.

InputStream/OutputStream
> Abstract classes that define the basic functionality for reading or writing an unstructured sequence of bytes. All other byte streams in Java are built on top of the basic InputStream and OutputStream.

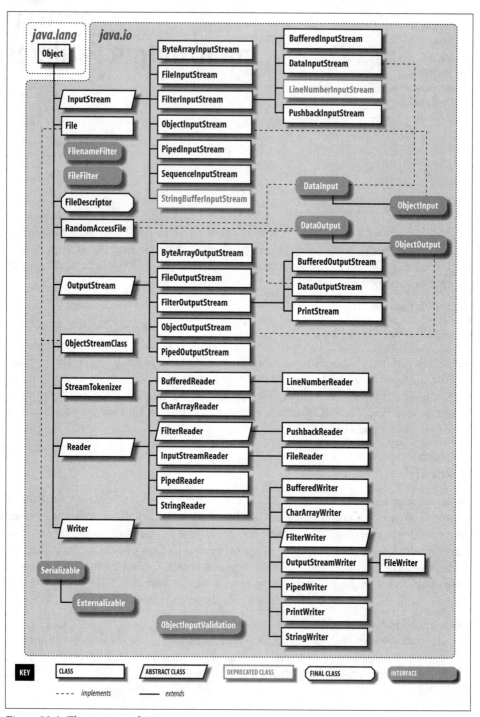

Figure 11-1. The java.io package

BUSINESS REPLY MAIL
FIRST CLASS MAIL   PERMIT NO. 80   SEBASTOPOL, CA

Postage will be paid by addressee

O'Reilly & Associates, Inc.
BOOK REGISTRATION
1005 GRAVENSTEIN HIGHWAY NORTH
SEBASTOPOL, CA 95472-9910

O'REILLY BOOK REGISTRATION

Register your book with O'Reilly by completing this card and receive a **FREE** copy of our latest catalog. Or register online at **register.oreilly.com** and, in addition to our catalog, we'll send you email notification of new editions of this book, information about new titles, and special offers available only to registered O'Reilly customers.

Which book(s) are you registering? Please include title and ISBN # (above bar code on back cover)

Title		ISBN #
Title		ISBN #
Title		ISBN #
Name	Company/Organization	
Address		
City	State	Zip/Postal Code	Country
Telephone	Email address	

www.oreilly.com

Part #10326

Reader/Writer

Abstract classes that define the basic functionality for reading or writing a sequence of character data, with support for Unicode. All other character streams in Java are built on top of Reader and Writer.

InputStreamReader/OutputStreamWriter

"Bridge" classes that convert bytes to characters and vice versa. Remember: in Unicode, a character is not a byte!

DataInputStream/DataOutputStream

Specialized stream filters that add the ability to read and write simple data types, such as numeric primitives and String objects, in a universal format.

ObjectInputStream/ObjectOutputStream

Specialized stream filters that are capable of writing whole serialized Java objects and reconstructing them.

BufferedInputStream/BufferedOutputStream/BufferedReader/BufferedWriter

Specialized stream filters that add buffering for additional efficiency.

PrintWriter

A specialized character stream that makes it simple to print text.

PipedInputStream/PipedOutputStream/PipedReader/PipedWriter

"Double-ended" streams that normally occur in pairs. Data written into a PipedOutputStream or PipedWriter is read from its corresponding PipedInputStream or PipedReader.

FileInputStream/FileOutputStream/FileReader/FileWriter

Implementations of InputStream, OutputStream, Reader, and Writer that read from and write to files on the local filesystem.

Streams in Java are one-way streets. The java.io input and output classes represent the ends of a simple stream, as shown in Figure 11-2. For bidirectional conversations, you'll use one of each type of stream.

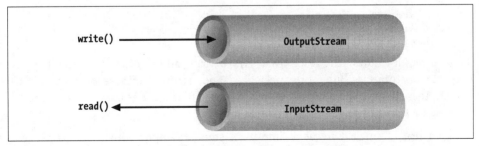

Figure 11-2. Basic input and output stream functionality

InputStream and OutputStream are abstract classes that define the lowest-level interface for all byte streams. They contain methods for reading or writing an unstructured flow of byte-level data. Because these classes are abstract, you can't create a generic input or output stream. Java implements subclasses of these for activities such as reading from and writing to files and communicating with sockets. Because all byte streams inherit the structure of InputStream or OutputStream, the various kinds of byte streams can be used interchangeably. A method specifying an InputStream as an argument can, of course, accept any subclass of InputStream. Specialized types of streams can also be layered to provide features, such as buffering, filtering, or handling larger data types.

Reader and Writer are very much like InputStream and OutputStream, except that they deal with characters instead of bytes. As true character streams, these classes correctly handle Unicode characters, which was not always the case with byte streams. Often, a bridge is needed between these character streams and the byte streams of physical devices such as disks and networks. InputStreamReader and OutputStreamWriter are special classes that use an *encoding scheme* to translate between character and byte streams.

We'll discuss all the interesting stream types in this section, with the exception of FileInputStream, FileOutputStream, FileReader, and FileWriter. We'll postpone the discussion of file streams until the next section, where we'll cover issues involved with accessing the filesystem in Java.

Terminal I/O

The prototypical example of an InputStream object is the *standard input* of a Java application. Like stdin in C or cin in C++, this is the source of input to a command-line (non-GUI) program. It is the input stream from the environment—usually a terminal window or the output of another command. The java.lang.System class, a general repository for system-related resources, provides a reference to standard input in the static variable System.in. It also provides streams for standard output and standard error in the out and err variables, respectively. The following example shows the correspondence:

```
InputStream stdin = System.in;
OutputStream stdout = System.out;
OutputStream stderr = System.err;
```

This example hides the fact that System.out and System.err aren't really OutputStream objects, but more specialized and useful PrintStream objects. We'll explain these later, but for now we can reference out and err as OutputStream objects, because they are a type of OutputStream as well.

We can read a single byte at a time from standard input with the InputStream's read() method. If you look closely at the API, you'll see that the read() method of the base InputStream class is an abstract method. What lies behind System.in is a particular implementation of InputStream; the subclass provides a real implementation of the read() method.

```
try {
    int val = System.in.read( );
    ...
}
catch ( IOException e ) {
    ...
}
```

Note that the return type of read() in this example is int, not byte as you'd expect. That's because Java's input stream read() method uses a convention of the C language. Although read() provides only a byte of information, its return type is int. This allows it to use the special return value of an integer -1, indicating that end of stream has been reached. You'll need to test for this condition when using the simple read() method. If an error occurs during the read, an IOException is thrown. All basic input and output stream commands can throw an IOException, so you should arrange to catch and handle them appropriately.

To retrieve the value as a byte, perform a cast:

```
byte b = (byte) val;
```

Be sure to check for the end-of-stream condition before you perform the cast.

An overloaded form of read() fills a byte array with as much data as possible up to the capacity of the array, and returns the number of bytes read:

```
byte [] buff = new byte [1024];
int got = System.in.read( buff );
```

We can also check the number of bytes available for reading on an InputStream with the available() method. Using that information, we could create an array of exactly the right size:

```
int waiting = System.in.available( );
if ( waiting > 0 ) {
    byte [] data = new byte [ waiting ];
    System.in.read( data );
    ...
}
```

However, the reliability of this technique depends on the ability of the underlying stream implementation to detect how much data can be retrieved. It generally works for files but should not be relied upon for all types of streams.

These read() methods block until at least some data is read (at least one byte). You must, in general, check the returned value to determine how much data you got and if you need to read more.

InputStream provides the skip() method as a way of jumping over a number of bytes. Depending on the implementation of the stream, skipping bytes may be more efficient than reading them. The close() method shuts down the stream and frees up any associated system resources. It's a good idea to close a stream when you are done using it.

Character Streams

Some `InputStream` and `OutputStream` subclasses of early versions of Java included methods for reading and writing strings, but most of them operated by naively assuming that a 16-bit Unicode character was equivalent to an 8-bit byte in the stream. Unfortunately, this works only for Latin-1 (ISO 8859-1) characters. To remedy this, the character stream classes `Reader` and `Writer` were introduced. Two special classes, `InputStreamReader` and `OutputStreamWriter`, bridge the gap between the world of character streams and the world of byte streams. These are character streams that are wrapped around an underlying byte stream. An encoding scheme is used to convert between bytes and characters. An encoding scheme name can be specified in the constructor of `InputStreamReader` or `OutputStreamWriter`. The default constructor can also be used; it uses the system's default encoding scheme. For example, let's parse a human-readable string from the standard input into an integer. We'll assume that the bytes coming from `System.in` use the system's default encoding scheme:

```
try {
    InputStreamReader converter = new InputStreamReader(System.in);
    BufferedReader in = new BufferedReader(converter);

    String text = in.readLine( );
    int i = NumberFormat.getInstance( ).parse(text).intValue( );
}
catch ( IOException e ) { }
catch ( ParseException pe ) { }
```

First, we wrap an `InputStreamReader` around `System.in`. This object converts the incoming bytes of `System.in` to characters using the default encoding scheme. Then, we wrap a `BufferedReader` around the `InputStreamReader`. `BufferedReader` gives us the `readLine()` method, which we can use to convert a full line of text into a `String`. The string is then parsed into an integer using the techniques described in Chapter 9.

We could have programmed the previous example using only byte streams, and it might have worked for users in the United States, at least. But character streams correctly support Unicode strings. Unicode was designed to support almost all the written languages of the world. If you want to write a program that works in any part of the world, in any language, you definitely want to use streams that don't mangle Unicode.

So how do you decide when you need a byte stream (`InputStream` or `OutputStream`) and when you need a character stream? If you want to read or write character strings, use some variety of `Reader` or `Writer`. Otherwise, a byte stream should suffice. Let's say, for example, that you want to read text from a file that was written by an earlier Java application. In this case, you could simply create a `FileReader`, which will convert the bytes in the file to characters using the system's default encoding scheme. If you have a file in a specific encoding scheme, you can create an `InputStreamReader` with the specified encoding scheme wrapped around a FileInputStream and read characters from it.

Another example comes from the Internet. Web servers serve files as byte streams. If you want to read Unicode strings with a particular encoding scheme from a file on the network, you'll need an appropriate InputStreamReader wrapped around the InputStream of the web server's socket (as we'll see in Chapter 12).

Stream Wrappers

What if we want to do more than read and write a sequence of bytes or characters? We can use a "filter" stream, which is a type of InputStream, OutputStream, Reader, or Writer that wraps another stream and adds new features. A filter stream takes the target stream as an argument in its constructor and delegates calls to it after doing some additional processing of its own. For example, you could construct a BufferedInputStream to wrap the system standard input:

```
InputStream bufferedIn = new BufferedInputStream( System.in );
```

The BufferedInputStream is a type of filter stream that reads ahead and buffers a certain amount of data. (We'll talk more about it later in this chapter.) The BufferedInputStream wraps an additional layer of functionality around the underlying stream. Figure 11-3 shows this arrangement for a DataInputStream.

As you can see from the previous code snippet, the BufferedInputStream filter is a type of InputStream. Because filter streams are themselves subclasses of the basic stream types, they can be used as arguments to the construction of other filter streams. This allows filter streams to be layered on top of one another to provide different combinations of features. For example, we could first wrap our System.in with a BufferedInputStream and then wrap the BufferedInputStream with a DataInputStream for reading special data types.

There are four superclasses corresponding to the four types of filter streams: FilterInputStream, FilterOutputStream, FilterReader, and FilterWriter. The first two are for filtering byte streams, and the last two are for filtering character streams. These superclasses provide the basic machinery for a "no op" filter (a filter that doesn't do anything) by delegating all their method calls to their underlying stream. Real filter streams subclass these and override various methods to add their additional processing. We'll make an example filter stream a little later in this chapter.

Data streams

DataInputStream and DataOutputStream are filter streams that let you read or write strings and primitive data types comprised of more than a single byte. DataInputStream and DataOutputStream implement the DataInput and DataOutput interfaces, respectively. These interfaces define the methods required for streams that

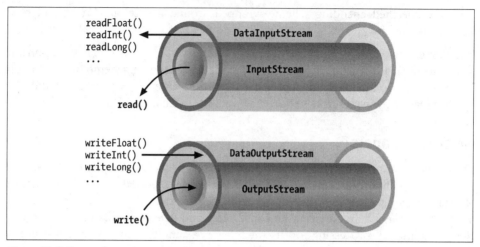

Figure 11-3. Layered streams

read and write strings and Java primitive numeric and boolean types in a machine-independent manner.

You can construct a `DataInputStream` from an `InputStream` and then use a method such as `readDouble()` to read a primitive data type:

```
DataInputStream dis = new DataInputStream( System.in );
double d = dis.readDouble( );
```

This example wraps the standard input stream in a `DataInputStream` and uses it to read a double value. `readDouble()` reads bytes from the stream and constructs a double from them. The `DataInputStream` methods expect the bytes of numeric data types to be in *network byte order*, a standard that specifies that the high-order bytes are sent first (also known as "big endian," as we'll discuss later).

The `DataOutputStream` class provides write methods that correspond to the read methods in `DataInputStream`. For example, `writeInt()` writes an integer in binary format to the underlying output stream.

The `readUTF()` and `writeUTF()` methods of `DataInputStream` and `DataOutputStream` read and write a Java `String` of Unicode characters using the UTF-8 "transformation format." UTF-8 is an ASCII-compatible encoding of Unicode characters commonly used for the transmission and storage of Unicode text. This differs from the `Reader` and `Writer` streams that can use arbitrary encodings that may not preserve all the Unicode characters.

We can use a `DataInputStream` with any kind of input stream, whether it be from a file, a socket, or standard input. The same applies to using a `DataOutputStream`, or, for that matter, any other specialized streams in `java.io`.

Buffered streams

The `BufferedInputStream`, `BufferedOutputStream`, `BufferedReader`, and `BufferedWriter` classes add a data buffer of a specified size to the stream path. A buffer can increase efficiency by reducing the number of physical read or write operations that correspond to `read()` or `write()` method calls. You create a buffered stream with an appropriate input or output stream and a buffer size. (You can also wrap another stream around a buffered stream, so that it benefits from the buffering.) Here's a simple buffered input stream called `bis`:

```
BufferedInputStream bis =
  new BufferedInputStream(myInputStream, 4096);
...
bis.read( );
```

In this example, we specify a buffer size of 4096 bytes. If we leave off the size of the buffer in the constructor, a reasonably sized one is chosen for us. On our first call to `read()`, bis tries to fill the entire 4096-byte buffer with data. Thereafter, calls to `read()` retrieve data from the buffer, which is refilled as necessary.

A `BufferedOutputStream` works in a similar way. Calls to `write()` store the data in a buffer; data is actually written only when the buffer fills up. You can also use the `flush()` method to wring out the contents of a `BufferedOutputStream` at any time. The `flush()` method is actually a method of the `OutputStream` class itself. It's important because it allows you to be sure that all data in any underlying streams and filter streams has been sent (before, for example, you wait for a response).

Some input streams such as `BufferedInputStream` support the ability to mark a location in the data and later reset the stream to that position. The `mark()` method sets the return point in the stream. It takes an integer value that specifies the number of bytes that can be read before the stream gives up and forgets about the mark. The `reset()` method returns the stream to the marked point; any data read after the call to `mark()` is read again.

This functionality is especially useful when you are reading the stream in a parser. You may occasionally fail to parse a structure and so must try something else. In this situation, you can have your parser generate an error (a homemade `ParseException`) and then reset the stream to the point before it began parsing the structure:

```
BufferedInputStream input;
...
try {
    input.mark( MAX_DATA_STRUCTURE_SIZE );
    return( parseDataStructure( input ) );
}
catch ( ParseException e ) {
    input.reset( );
    ...
}
```

The BufferedReader and BufferedWriter classes work just like their byte-based counterparts but operate on characters instead of bytes.

PrintWriter

Another useful wrapper stream is java.io.PrintWriter. This class provides a suite of overloaded print() methods that turn their arguments into strings and push them out the stream. A complementary set of println() methods adds a newline to the end of the strings. PrintWriter is an unusual character stream because it can wrap either an OutputStream or another Writer.

PrintWriter is the more capable big brother of the older PrintStream byte stream. The System.out and System.err streams are PrintStream objects; you have already seen such streams strewn throughout this book:

```
System.out.print("Hello world...\n");
System.out.println("Hello world...");
System.out.println( "The answer is: " + 17 );
System.out.println( 3.14 );
```

PrintWriter and PrintStream have a strange, overlapping history. Early versions of Java did not have the Reader and Writer classes and streams such as PrintStream, which must of necessity convert bytes to characters; those versions simply made assumptions about the character encoding. As of Java 1.1, the PrintStream class was enhanced to translate characters to bytes using the system's default encoding scheme. For all new development, however, use a PrintWriter instead of a PrintStream. Because a PrintWriter can wrap an OutputStream, the two classes are more or less interchangeable.

When you create a PrintWriter object, you can pass an additional boolean value to the constructor. If this value is true, the PrintWriter automatically performs a flush() on the underlying OutputStream or Writer each time it sends a newline:

```
boolean autoFlush = true;
PrintWriter p = new PrintWriter( myOutputStream, autoFlush );
```

When this technique is used with a buffered output stream, it corresponds to the behavior of terminals that send data line by line.

Unlike methods in other stream classes, the methods of PrintWriter and PrintStream do not throw IOExceptions. This makes life a lot easier for printing text, which is a very common operation. Instead, if we are interested, we can check for errors with the checkError() method:

```
System.out.println( reallyLongString );
if ( System.out.checkError( ) )              // uh oh
```

Pipes

Normally, our applications are directly involved with one side of a given stream at a time. `PipedInputStream` and `PipedOutputStream` (or `PipedReader` and `PipedWriter`), however, let us create two sides of a stream and connect them together, as shown in Figure 11-4. This can be used to provide a stream of communication between threads, for example, or as a "loopback" for testing.

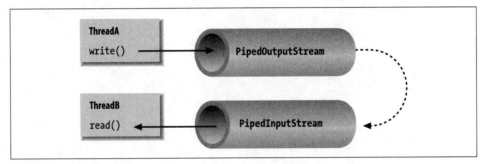

Figure 11-4. Piped streams

To create a byte-stream pipe, we use both a `PipedInputStream` and a `PipedOutputStream`. We can simply choose a side and then construct the other side using the first as an argument:

```
PipedInputStream pin = new PipedInputStream( );
PipedOutputStream pout = new PipedOutputStream( pin );
```

Alternatively:

```
PipedOutputStream pout = new PipedOutputStream( );
PipedInputStream pin = new PipedInputStream( pout );
```

In each of these examples, the effect is to produce an input stream, pin, and an output stream, pout, that are connected. Data written to pout can then be read by pin. It is also possible to create the `PipedInputStream` and the `PipedOutputStream` separately and then connect them with the connect() method.

We can do exactly the same thing in the character-based world, using `PipedReader` and `PipedWriter` in place of `PipedInputStream` and `PipedOutputStream`.

Once the two ends of the pipe are connected, use the two streams as you would other input and output streams. You can use read() to read data from the `PipedInputStream` (or `PipedReader`) and write() to write data to the `PipedOutputStream` (or `PipedWriter`). If the internal buffer of the pipe fills up, the writer blocks and waits until space is available. Conversely, if the pipe is empty, the reader blocks and waits until some data is available.

One advantage to using piped streams is that they provide stream functionality in our code without compelling us to build new, specialized streams. For example, we can use pipes to create a simple logging or "console" facility for our application. We can send messages to the logging facility through an ordinary `PrintWriter`, and then it can do whatever processing or buffering is required before sending the messages off to their ultimate destination. Because we are dealing with string messages, we use the character-based `PipedReader` and `PipedWriter` classes. The following example shows the skeleton of our logging facility:

```java
//file: LoggerDaemon.java
import java.io.*;

class LoggerDaemon extends Thread {
    PipedReader in = new PipedReader( );

    LoggerDaemon( ) {
        start( );
    }

    public void run( ) {
        BufferedReader bin = new BufferedReader( in );
        String s;

        try {
            while ( (s = bin.readLine( )) != null ) {
                // process line of data
            }
        } catch (IOException e ) { }
    }

    PrintWriter getWriter( ) throws IOException {
        return new PrintWriter( new PipedWriter( in ) );
    }
}

class myApplication {
    public static void main ( String [] args ) throws IOException {
        PrintWriter out = new LoggerDaemon( ).getWriter( );

        out.println("Application starting...");
        // ...
        out.println("Warning: does not compute!");
        // ...
    }
}
```

`LoggerDaemon` reads strings from its end of the pipe, the `PipedReader` named in. `LoggerDaemon` also provides a method, getWriter(), which returns a `PipedWriter` that is connected to its input stream. To begin sending messages, we create a new `LoggerDaemon` and fetch the output stream. In order to read strings with the readLine() method, `LoggerDaemon` wraps a `BufferedReader` around its `PipedReader`. For convenience, it also presents its output pipe as a `PrintWriter`, rather than a simple `Writer`.

One advantage of implementing LoggerDaemon with pipes is that we can log messages as easily as we write text to a terminal or any other stream. In other words, we can use all our normal tools and techniques. Another advantage is that the processing happens in another thread, so we can go about our business while the processing takes place.

Streams from Strings and Back

StringReader is another useful stream class; it essentially wraps stream functionality around a String. Here's how to use a StringReader:

```
String data = "There once was a man from Nantucket...";
StringReader sr = new StringReader( data );

char T = (char)sr.read( );
char h = (char)sr.read( );
char e = (char)sr.read( );
```

Note that you will still have to catch IOExceptions thrown by some of the StringReader's methods.

The StringReader class is useful when you want to read data in a String as if it were coming from a stream, such as a file, pipe, or socket. For example, suppose you create a parser that expects to read from a stream, but you want to provide an alternative method that also parses a big string. You can easily add one using StringReader.

Turning things around, the StringWriter class lets us write to a character buffer via an output stream. The internal buffer grows as necessary to accommodate the data. When we are done we can fetch the contents of the buffer as a String. In the following example, we create a StringWriter and wrap it in a PrintWriter for convenience:

```
StringWriter buffer = new StringWriter( );
PrintWriter out = new PrintWriter( buffer );

out.println("A moose once bit my sister.");
out.println("No, really!");

String results = buffer.toString( );
```

First we print a few lines to the output stream, to give it some data, then retrieve the results as a string with the toString() method. Alternately, we could get the results as a StringBuffer object using the getBuffer() method.

The StringWriter class is useful if you want to capture the output of something that normally sends output to a stream, such as a file or the console. A PrintWriter wrapped around a StringWriter is a viable alternative to using a StringBuffer to construct large strings piece by piece.

The ByteArrayInputStream and ByteArrayOutputStream work with bytes in the same way the previous examples worked with characters. You can write byte data to a

ByteArrayOutputStream and retrieve it later with the toByteArray() method. Conversely, you can construct a ByteArrayInputStream from a byte array as StringReader does with a String.

The rot13InputStream Class

Before we leave streams, let's try our hand at making one of our own. We mentioned earlier that specialized stream wrappers are built on top of the FilterInputStream and FilterOutputStream classes. It's quite easy to create our own subclass of FilterInputStream that can be wrapped around other streams to add new functionality.

The following example, rot13InputStream, performs a *rot13* (rotate by 13 letters) operation on the bytes that it reads. *rot13* is a trivial obfuscation algorithm that shifts alphabetic characters to make them not quite human-readable (it simply passes over nonalphabetic characters without modifying them). rot13 *is* cute because it's symmetric; "un-rot13" some text, simply it again. We use the rot13InputStream class in the "Content and Protocol Handlers" section of the expanded material on the CD that comes with this book. So we've put the class in the learningjava.io package to facilitate reuse. Here's our rot13InputStream class:

```
//file: rot13InputStream.java
package learningjava.io;
import java.io.*;

public class rot13InputStream extends FilterInputStream {

    public rot13InputStream ( InputStream i ) {
        super( i );
    }

    public int read( ) throws IOException {
        return rot13( in.read( ) );
    }

    private int rot13 ( int c ) {
        if ( (c >= 'A') && (c <= 'Z') )
            c=(((c-'A')+13)%26)+'A';
        if ( (c >= 'a') && (c <= 'z') )
            c=(((c-'a')+13)%26)+'a';
        return c;
    }
}
```

The FilterInputStream needs to be initialized with an InputStream; this is the stream to be filtered. We provide an appropriate constructor for the rot13InputStream class and invoke the parent constructor with a call to super(). FilterInputStream contains a protected instance variable, in, in which it stores a reference to the specified InputStream, making it available to the rest of our class.

The primary feature of a `FilterInputStream` is that it delegates its input tasks to the underlying `InputStream`. So, for instance, a call to `FilterInputStream`'s `read()` method simply turns around and calls the `read()` method of the underlying `InputStream`, to fetch a byte. The filtering happens when we do our extra work on the data as it passes through. In our example, the `read()` method fetches a byte from the underlying `InputStream`, in, and then performs the rot13 shift on the byte before returning it. Note that the `rot13()` method shifts alphabetic characters while simply passing over all other values, including the end-of-stream value (-1). Our subclass is now a rot13 filter.

`read()` is the only `InputStream` method that `FilterInputStream` overrides. All other normal functionality of an `InputStream`, such as `skip()` and `available()`, is unmodified, so calls to these methods are answered by the underlying `InputStream`.

Strictly speaking, `rot13InputStream` works only on an ASCII byte stream since the underlying algorithm is based on the Roman alphabet. A more generalized character-scrambling algorithm would have to be based on `FilterReader` to handle 16-bit Unicode classes correctly. (Anyone want to try rot32768?) We should also note that we have not fully implemented our filter: we should also override the version of `read()` that takes a byte array and range specifiers, perhaps delegating it to our own read. Unless we do so, a reader using that method would get the raw stream.

Files

Working with files in Java poses some conceptual problems. The host filesystem lies outside of Java's virtual environment, in the real world, and can therefore still suffer from architecture and implementation differences. Java tries to mask some of these differences by providing information to help an application tailor itself to the local environment; we'll mention these areas as they occur.

The java.io.File Class

The `java.io.File` class encapsulates access to information about a file or directory entry in the filesystem. It can be used to get attribute information about a file, list the entries in a directory, and perform basic filesystem operations such as removing a file or making a directory. While the `File` object handles these tasks, it doesn't provide direct access for reading and writing file data; there are specialized streams for that purpose.

File constructors

You can create an instance of `File` from a `String` pathname:

```
File fooFile = new File( "/tmp/foo.txt" );
File barDir = new File( "/tmp/bar" );
```

You can also create a file with a relative path:

```
File f = new File( "foo" );
```

In this case, Java works relative to the current directory of the Java interpreter. You can determine the current working directory by checking the user.dir property in the System Properties list:

```
System.getProperty("user.dir"));
```

An overloaded version of the File constructor lets you specify the directory path and filename as separate String objects:

```
File fooFile = new File( "/tmp", "foo.txt" );
```

With yet another variation, you can specify the directory with a File object and the filename with a String:

```
File tmpDir = new File( "/tmp" );
File fooFile = new File ( tmpDir, "foo.txt" );
```

None of the File constructors throw any exceptions. This means the object is created whether or not the file or directory actually exists; it isn't an error to create a File object for a nonexistent file. You can use the object's exists() instance method to find out whether the file or directory exists. The File object simply exists as a handle for getting information about what is (potentially at least) a file or directory.

Path localization

One of the reasons that working with files in Java is problematic is that pathnames are expected to follow the conventions of the local filesystem. Java's designers intend to provide an abstraction that provides ways to work with some system-dependent filename features, such as the file separator, path separator, device specifier, and root directories.

On some systems, Java can also compensate for differences such as the direction of the file separator slashes in a pathname. For example, in the current implementation on Windows platforms, Java accepts paths with either forward slashes or backslashes. However, under Solaris, Java accepts only paths with forward slashes.

Your best bet is to make sure you follow the filename conventions of the host filesystem. If your application has a GUI that is opening and saving files at the user's request, you should be able to handle that functionality with the Swing JFileDialog class. This class encapsulates a graphical file-selection dialog box. The methods of the JFileDialog take care of system-dependent filename features for you.

If your application needs to deal with files on its own behalf, however, things get a little more complicated. The File class contains a few static variables to make this task possible. File.separator defines a String that specifies the file separator on the local host (e.g., / on Unix and Macintosh systems and \ on Windows systems); File.separatorChar provides the same information as a char.

You can use this system-dependent information in several ways. Probably the simplest way to localize pathnames is to pick a convention you use internally, for instance the forward slash (/), and do a String replace to substitute for the localized separator character:

```
// we'll use forward slash as our standard
String path = "mail/1999/june/merle";
path = path.replace('/', File.separatorChar);
File mailbox = new File( path );
```

Alternately, you could work with the components of a pathname and build the local pathname when you need it:

```
String [] path = { "mail", "1999", "june", "merle" };

    StringBuffer sb = new StringBuffer(path[0]);
for (int i=1; i< path.length; i++)
    sb.append( File.separator + path[i] );
File mailbox = new File( sb.toString( ) );
```

One thing to remember is that Java interprets the backslash character (\) as an escape character when used in a String. To get a backslash in a String, you have to use \\.

Another issue to grapple with is that some operating systems use special identifiers for the roots of filesystems. For example, Windows uses C:\. Should you need it, the File class provides the static method listRoots(), which returns an array of File objects corresponding to the filesystem root directories.

File operations

Once we have a File object, we can use it to ask for information about the file or directory and to perform standard operations on it. A number of methods let us ask certain questions about the File. For example, isFile() returns true if the File represents a file while isDirectory() returns true if it's a directory. isAbsolute() indicates whether the File has an absolute or relative path specification.

Components of the File pathname are available through the following methods: getName(), getPath(), getAbsolutePath(), and getParent(). getName() returns a String for the filename without any directory information; getPath() returns the directory information without the filename. If the File has an absolute path specification, getAbsolutePath() returns that path. Otherwise it returns the relative path appended to the current working directory. getParent() returns the parent directory of the File.

The string returned by getPath() or getAbsolutePath() may not follow the same case conventions as the underlying filesystem. You can retrieve the filesystem's own or "canonical" version of the file's path using the method getCanonicalPath(). In Windows, for example, you can create a File object whose getAbsolutePath() is *C:\Autoexec.bat* but whose getCanonical-Path() is *C:\AUTOEXEC.BAT*. This is useful for comparing filenames that may have been supplied with different case conventions or for showing them to the user.

You can get or set the modification time of a file or directory with `lastModified()` and `setLastModified()` methods. The value is a `long` that is the number of milliseconds since the *epoch* (Jan 1, 1970, 00:00:00 GMT). We can also get the size of the file in bytes with `length()`.

Here's a fragment of code that prints some information about a file:

```
File fooFile = new File( "/tmp/boofa" );

String type = fooFile.isFile( ) ? "File " : "Directory ";
String name = fooFile.getName( );
long len = fooFile.length( );
System.out.println(type + name + ", " + len + " bytes " );
```

If the `File` object corresponds to a directory, we can list the files in the directory with the `list()` method or the `listFiles()` method:

```
String [] fileNames = fooFile.list( );
File [] files = fooFile.listFiles( );
```

`list()` returns an array of `String` objects that contains filenames. `listFiles()` returns an array of `File` objects. Note that in neither case are the files guaranteed to be in any kind of order (alphabetical, for example). You can use the Collections API to sort strings alphabetically like so:

```
List list = Arrays.asList( sa );
Collections.sort(l);
```

If the `File` refers to a nonexistent directory, we can create the directory with `mkdir()` or `mkdirs()`. The `mkdir()` method creates a single directory; `mkdirs()` creates all the intervening directories in a `File` specification. Use `renameTo()` to rename a file or directory and `delete()` to delete a file or directory.

Although we can create a directory using the `File` object, this isn't the most common way to create a file; that's normally done implicitly with a `FileOutputStream` or `FileWriter`, as we'll discuss in a moment. The exception is the `createNewFile()` method, which can be used to attempt to create a new zero-length file at the location pointed to by the `File` object. The useful thing about this method is that the operation is guaranteed to be "atomic" with respect to all other file creation. `createNewFile()` returns a boolean value that tells you whether the file was created.

You can use this to implement simple file locking from Java. (The NIO package supports true file locks, as we'll see later). This is useful in combination with `deleteOnExit()`, which flags the file to be automatically removed when the Java Virtual Machine exits. Another file creation method related to the `File` class itself is the static method `createTempFile()`, which creates a file in a specified location using an automatically generated unique name. This, too, is useful in combination with `deleteOnExit()`.

The toURL() method converts a file path to a file: URL object. We'll talk about URLs in Chapter 13. They are an abstraction that allows you to point to any kind of object anywhere on the Net. Converting a File reference to a URL may be useful for consistency with more general routines that deal with URLs.

Table 11-1 summarizes the methods provided by the File class.

Table 11-1. File methods

Method	Return type	Description
canRead()	Boolean	Is the file (or directory) readable?
canWrite()	Boolean	Is the file (or directory) writable?
createNewFile()	Boolean	Creates a new file
createTempFile (String *pfx*, String *sfx*)	File	Static method to create a new file, with the specified prefix and suffix, in the default temp file directory
delete()	Boolean	Deletes the file (or directory)
deleteOnExit()	Void	When it exits, Java runtime system deletes the file
exists()	boolean	Does the file (or directory) exist?
getAbsolutePath()	String	Returns the absolute path of the file (or directory)
getCanonicalPath()	String	Returns the absolute, case-correct path of the file (or directory)
getName()	String	Returns the name of the file (or directory)
getParent()	String	Returns the name of the parent directory of the file (or directory)
getPath()	String	Returns the path of the file (or directory)
isAbsolute()	boolean	Is the filename (or directory name) absolute?
isDirectory()	boolean	Is the item a directory?
isFile()	boolean	Is the item a file?
lastModified()	long	Returns the last modification time of the file (or directory)
length()	long	Returns the length of the file
list()	String []	Returns a list of files in the directory
listfiles()	File[]	Returns the contents of the directory as an array of File objects
mkdir()	boolean	Creates the directory
Mkdirs()	boolean	Creates all directories in the path
renameTo(File *dest*)	boolean	Renames the file (or directory)
setLastModified()	boolean	Sets the last-modified time of the file (or directory)
setReadOnly()	boolean	Sets the file to read-only status
toURL()	java.net.URL	Generates a URL object for the file (or directory)

File Streams

Java provides two specialized streams for reading from and writing to files in the filesystem: FileInputStream and FileOutputStream. These streams provide the basic

InputStream and OutputStream functionality applied to reading and writing files. They can be combined with the filter streams described earlier to work with files in the same way we do other stream communications.

Because FileInputStream is a subclass of InputStream, it inherits all standard InputStream functionality for reading a file. FileInputStream provides only a low-level interface to reading data, however, so you'll typically wrap it with another stream, such as a DataInputStream.

You can create a FileInputStream from a String pathname or a File object:

```
FileInputStream in = new FileInputStream( "/etc/passwd" );
```

When you create a FileInputStream, the Java runtime system attempts to open the specified file. Thus, the FileInputStream constructors can throw a FileNotFoundException if the specified file doesn't exist, or an IOException if some other I/O error occurs. You must catch these exceptions in your code. When the stream is first created, its available() method and the File object's length() method should return the same value. To save resources, you can call the close() method when you are done with the file.

To read characters from a file, you can wrap an InputStreamReader around a FileInputStream. If you want to use the default character-encoding scheme, you can use the FileReader class instead, which is provided as a convenience. FileReader works just like FileInputStream, except that it reads characters instead of bytes and wraps a Reader instead of an InputStream.

The following class, ListIt, is a small utility that sends the contents of a file or directory to standard output:

```
//file: ListIt.java
import java.io.*;

class ListIt {
    public static void main ( String args[] ) throws Exception {
        File file = new File( args[0] );

        if ( !file.exists() || !file.canRead( ) ) {
            System.out.println( "Can't read " + file );
            return;
        }

        if ( file.isDirectory( ) ) {
            String [] files = file.list( );
            for (int i=0; i< files.length; i++)
                System.out.println( files[i] );
        } else
            try {
                FileReader fr = new FileReader ( file );
                BufferedReader in = new BufferedReader( fr );
                String line;
                while ((line = in.readLine( )) != null)
```

```
            System.out.println(line);
        }
        catch ( FileNotFoundException e ) {
            System.out.println( "File Disappeared" );
        }
    }
}
```

ListIt constructs a File object from its first command-line argument and tests the File to see whether it exists and is readable. If the File is a directory, ListIt outputs the names of the files in the directory. Otherwise, ListIt reads and outputs the file.

FileOutputStream is a subclass of OutputStream, so it inherits all the standard OutputStream functionality for writing to a file. Just like FileInputStream though, FileOutputStream provides only a low-level interface to writing data. You'll typically wrap another stream, such as a DataOutputStream or a PrintWriter, around the FileOutputStream to provide higher-level functionality.

You can create a FileOutputStream from a String pathname or a File object. Unlike FileInputStream, however, the FileOutputStream constructors don't throw a FileNotFoundException. If the specified file doesn't exist, the FileOutputStream creates the file. The FileOutputStream constructors can throw an IOException if some other I/O error occurs, so you still need to handle this exception.

If the specified file does exist, the FileOutputStream opens it for writing. When you subsequently call the write() method, the new data overwrites the current contents of the file. If you need to append data to an existing file, you can use a form of the constructor that accepts an append flag:

```
FileInputStream fooOut = new FileOutputStream( fooFile );
FileInputStream pwdOut = new FileOutputStream( "/etc/passwd", true );
```

Another way to append data to files is with RandomAccessFile, as we'll discuss shortly.

To write characters (instead of bytes) to a file, you can wrap an OutputStreamWriter around a FileOutputStream. If you want to use the default character-encoding scheme, you can use instead the FileWriter class, which is provided as a convenience. FileWriter works just like FileOutputStream, except that it writes characters instead of bytes and wraps a Writer instead of an OutputStream.

The following example reads a line of data from standard input and writes it to the file */tmp/foo.txt*:

```
String s = new BufferedReader(
    new InputStreamReader( System.in ) ).readLine( );
File out = new File( "/tmp/foo.txt" );
FileWriter fw = new FileWriter ( out );
PrintWriter pw = new PrintWriter( fw )
pw.println( s );
fw.close( );
```

Notice how we wrapped a `PrintWriter` around the `FileWriter` to facilitate writing the data. Also, to be a good filesystem citizen, we've called the `close()` method when we're done with the `FileWriter`.

The java.io.RandomAccessFile Class

The `java.io.RandomAccessFile` class provides the ability to read and write data at a specified location in a file. `RandomAccessFile` implements both the `DataInput` and `DataOutput` interfaces, so you can use it to read and write strings and primitive types. In other words, `RandomAccessFile` defines the same methods for reading and writing data as `DataInputStream` and `DataOutputStream`. However, because the class provides random, rather than sequential, access to file data, it's not a subclass of either `InputStream` or `OutputStream`.

You can create a `RandomAccessFile` from a `String` pathname or a `File` object. The constructor also takes a second `String` argument that specifies the mode of the file. Use r for a read-only file or rw for a read-write file. Here's how we would start to create a simple database to keep track of user information:

```
try {
    RandomAccessFile users =
        new RandomAccessFile( "Users", "rw" )
} catch (IOException e) { ... }
```

When you create a `RandomAccessFile` in read-only mode, Java tries to open the specified file. If the file doesn't exist, `RandomAccessFile` throws an `IOException`. If, however, you're creating a `RandomAccessFile` in read-write mode, the object creates the file if it doesn't exist. The constructor can still throw an `IOException` if another I/O error occurs, so you still need to handle this exception.

After you have created a `RandomAccessFile`, call any of the normal reading and writing methods, just as you would with a `DataInputStream` or `DataOutputStream`. If you try to write to a read-only file, the write method throws an `IOException`.

What makes a `RandomAccessFile` special is the `seek()` method. This method takes a long value and uses it to set the location for reading and writing in the file. You can use the `getFilePointer()` method to get the current location. If you need to append data to the end of the file, use `length()` to determine that location, then `seek()` to it. You can write or seek beyond the end of a file, but you can't read beyond the end of a file. The `read()` method throws an `EOFException` if you try to do this.

Here's an example of writing some data to a user database:

```
users.seek( userNum * RECORDSIZE );
users.writeUTF( userName );
users.writeInt( userID );
```

Of course, in this naïve example we assume that the `String` length for userName, along with any data that comes after it, fits within the specified record size.

Applets and Files

Unless otherwise restricted, a Java application can read and write to the host filesystem with the same level of access as the user running the Java interpreter. For security reasons, untrusted applets and applications are not permitted to read from or write to arbitrary places in the filesystem. The ability of untrusted code to read and write files, as with any kind of system resource, is under the control of the system security policy, through a `SecurityManager` object. A security policy is set by the application that is running the untrusted code, such as `appletviewer` or a Java-enabled web browser. All filesystem access must first pass the scrutiny of the `SecurityManager`.

Some web browsers allow untrusted applets to have access to specific files designated by the user. Netscape Navigator and Internet Explorer currently do not allow untrusted applets any access to the filesystem. However, as we'll see in Chapter 22, signed applets can be given arbitrary access to the filesystem, just like a standalone Java application.

It's not unusual to want an applet to maintain some kind of state information on the system on which it's running. But for a Java applet that is restricted from access to the local filesystem, the only option is to store data over the network on its server (or possibly in a client-side cookie). Applets have at their disposal powerful general means for communicating data over networks. The only limitation is that, by convention, an applet's network communication is restricted to the server that launched it. This limits the options for where the data will reside.

Currently, the only way for a Java program to send data to a server is through a network socket or tools such as RMI, which run over sockets. In Chapter 11 we'll take a detailed look at building networked applications with sockets. With the tools described in that chapter, it's possible to build powerful client/server applications. Sun also has a Java extension called WebNFS, which allows applets and applications to work with files on an NFS server in much the same way as the ordinary File API.

Loading Application Resources

We often package data files and other objects with our applications. Java provides many ways to access these resources. In a standalone application, we can simply open files and read the bytes. In both standalone applications and applets, we can construct URLs to well-known locations. The problem with these methods is that we generally have to know where our application lives in order to find our data. This is not always as easy as it seems. What is needed is a universal way to access resources associated with our application and our application's individual classes. The `Class` class's `getResource()` method provides just this.

What does getResource() do for us? To construct a URL to a file, we normally have to figure out a home directory for our code and construct a path relative to that. As we'll see in Chapter 22, in an applet, we could use getCodeBase() or getDocumentBase() to find the base URL and then use that base to create the URL for the resource we want. But these methods don't help a standalone application, and there's no reason that a standalone application and an applet shouldn't be written in the same way anyway. To solve this problem, the getResource() method provides a standard way to get objects relative to a given class file or to the system classpath. getResource() returns a special URL that uses the class's class loader. This means that no matter where the class came from—a web server, the local filesystem, or even a JAR file—we can simply ask for an object, get a URL for the object, and use the URL to access the object.

getResource() takes as an argument a slash-separated pathname for the resource and returns a URL. There are two kinds of paths: absolute and relative. An absolute path begins with a slash, for example, */foo/bar/blah.txt*. In this case, the search for the object begins at the top of the classpath. If there is a directory *foo/bar* in the classpath, getResource() searches that directory for the *blah.txt* file. A relative URL does not begin with a slash. In this case, the search begins at the location of the class file, whether it is local, on a remote server, or in a JAR file (either local or remote). So if we were calling getResource() on a class loader that loaded a class in the foo.bar package, we could refer to the file as *blah.txt*. In this case, the class itself would be loaded from the directory *foo/bar* somewhere on the classpath, and we'd expect to find the file in the same directory.

For example, here's an application that looks up some resources:

```
//file: FindResources.java
package mypackage;
import java.net.URL;
import java.io.IOException;

public class FindResources {
    public static void main( String [] args ) throws IOException {
        // absolute from the classpath
        URL url = FindResources.class.getResource("/mypackage/foo.txt");
        // relative to the class location
        url = FindResources.class.getResource("foo.txt");
        // another relative document
        url = FindResources.class.getResource("docs/bar.txt");
    }
}
```

The FindResources class belongs to the mypackage package, so its class file will live in a *mypackage* directory somewhere on the classpath. FindResources locates the document *foo.txt* using an absolute and then a relative URL. At the end, FindResources uses a relative path to reach a document in the *mypackage/docs* directory. In each case we refer to the FindResources's Class object using the static .class notation.

Alternatively, if we had an instance of the object, we could use its getClass() method to reach the Class object.

For an applet, the search is similar but occurs on the host from which the applet was loaded. getResource() first checks any JAR files loaded with the applet, and then searches the normal remote applet classpath, constructed relative to the applet's codebase URL.

getResource() returns a URL for whatever type of object you reference. This could be a text file or properties file that you want to read as a stream, or it might be an image or sound file or some other object. If you want the data as a stream, the Class class also provides a getResourceAsStream() method. In the case of an image, you'd probably hand the URL over to the getImage() method of a Swing component for loading.

Serialization

Using a DataOutputStream, you could write an application that saves the data content of your objects as simple types. However Java provides an even more powerful mechanism called object serialization that does almost all the work for you. In its simplest form, *object serialization* is an automatic way to save and load the state of an object. However, object serialization has depths that we cannot plumb within the scope of this book, including complete control over the serialization process and interesting conundrums such as class versioning.

Basically, an object of any class that implements the Serializable interface can be saved and restored from a stream. Special stream subclasses, ObjectInputStream and ObjectOutputStream, are used to serialize primitive types and objects. Subclasses of Serializable classes are also serializable. The default serialization mechanism saves the value of an object's nonstatic and nontransient (see the following explanation) member variables.

One of the most important (and tricky) things about serialization is that when an object is serialized, any object references it contains are also serialized. Serialization can capture entire "graphs" of interconnected objects and put them back together on the receiving end (we'll demonstrate this in an upcoming example). The implication is that any object we serialize must contain only references to other Serializable objects. We can take control by marking nonserializable members as transient or overriding the default serialization mechanisms. The transient modifier can be applied to any instance variable to indicate that its contents are not useful outside of the current context and should never be saved.

In the following example, we create a Hashtable and write it to a disk file called *h.ser*. The Hashtable object is serializable because it implements the Serializable interface.

```
//file: Save.java
import java.io.*;
import java.util.*;
```

```
public class Save {
  public static void main(String[] args) {
    Hashtable h = new Hashtable( );
    h.put("string", "Gabriel Garcia Marquez");
    h.put("int", new Integer(26));
    h.put("double", new Double(Math.PI));

    try {
      FileOutputStream fileOut = new FileOutputStream("h.ser");
      ObjectOutputStream out = new ObjectOutputStream(fileOut);
      out.writeObject(h);
    }
    catch (Exception e) {
      System.out.println(e);
    }
  }
}
```

First we construct a Hashtable with a few elements in it. Then, in the three lines of code inside the try block, we write the Hashtable to a file called *h.ser*, using the writeObject() method of ObjectOutputStream. The ObjectOutputStream class is a lot like the DataOutputStream class, except that it includes the powerful writeObject() method.

The Hashtable we created has internal references to the items it contains. Thus, these components are automatically serialized along with the Hashtable. We'll see this in the next example when we deserialize the Hashtable.

```
//file: Load.java
import java.io.*;
import java.util.*;

public class Load {
  public static void main(String[] args) {
    try {
      FileInputStream fileIn = new FileInputStream("h.ser");
      ObjectInputStream in = new ObjectInputStream(fileIn);
      Hashtable h = (Hashtable)in.readObject( );
      System.out.println(h.toString( ));
    }
    catch (Exception e) {
      System.out.println(e);
    }
  }
}
```

In this example, we read the Hashtable from the *h.ser* file, using the readObject() method of ObjectInputStream. The ObjectInputStream class is a lot like DataInputStream, except that it includes the readObject() method. The return type of readObject() is Object, so we need to cast it to a Hashtable. Finally, we print out the contents of the Hashtable using its toString() method.

Initialization with readObject( )

Often simple deserialization alone is not enough to reconstruct the full state of an object. For example, the object may have had transient fields representing state that could not be serialized, such as network connections, event registration, or decoded image data. Objects have an opportunity to do their own setup after deserialization by implementing a special method named readObject().

Not to be confused with the readObject() method of the ObjectInputStream, this method is implemented by the serializable object itself. The readObject() method must have a specific signature, and it must be private. The following snippet is taken from an animated JavaBean that we'll talk about in Chapter 21:

```
private void readObject(ObjectInputStream s)
    throws IOException, ClassNotFoundException
{
    s.defaultReadObject();
    initialize();
    if ( isRunning )
        start();
}
```

When the readObject() method with this signature exists in an object it is called during the deserialization process. The argument to the method is the ObjectInputStream doing the object construction. We delegate to its defaultReadObject() method to do the normal deserialization and then do our custom setup. In this case we call one of our methods, named initialize(), and optionally a method called start().

We'll talk more about serialization in Chapter 21 when we discuss JavaBeans. There we'll see that it is even possible to serialize a graphical GUI component in mid-use and bring it back to life later.

Data Compression

The java.util.zip package contains classes you can use for data compression. In this section, we'll talk about how to use these classes. We'll also present two useful example programs that build on what you have just learned about streams and files. The classes in the java.util.zip package support two widespread compression formats: GZIP and ZIP.

Compressing Data

The java.util.zip class provides two FilterOutputStream subclasses to write compressed data to a stream. To write compressed data in the GZIP format, simply wrap a GZIPOutputStream around an underlying stream and write to it. The following is a complete example that shows how to compress a file using the GZIP format.

```
//file: GZip.java
import java.io.*;
import java.util.zip.*;

public class GZip {
  public static int sChunk = 8192;

  public static void main(String[] args) {
    if (args.length != 1) {
      System.out.println("Usage: GZip source");
      return;
    }
    // create output stream
    String zipname = args[0] + ".gz";
    GZIPOutputStream zipout;
    try {
      FileOutputStream out = new FileOutputStream(zipname);
      zipout = new GZIPOutputStream(out);
    }
    catch (IOException e) {
      System.out.println("Couldn't create " + zipname + ".");
      return;
    }
    byte[] buffer = new byte[sChunk];
    // compress the file
    try {
      FileInputStream in = new FileInputStream(args[0]);
      int length;
      while ((length = in.read(buffer, 0, sChunk)) != -1)
        zipout.write(buffer, 0, length);
      in.close( );
    }
    catch (IOException e) {
      System.out.println("Couldn't compress " + args[0] + ".");
    }
    try { zipout.close( ); }
    catch (IOException e) {}
  }
}
```

First we check to make sure we have a command-line argument representing a file-name. Then we construct a GZIPOutputStream wrapped around a FileOutputStream representing the given filename, with the *.gz* suffix appended. With this in place, we open the source file. We read chunks of data and write them into the GZIPOutputStream. Finally, we clean up by closing our open streams.

Writing data to a ZIP archive file is a little more involved but still quite manageable. While a GZIP file contains only one compressed file, a ZIP file is actually a collection of files, some (or all) of which may be compressed. Each item in the ZIP file is represented by a ZipEntry object. When writing to a ZipOutputStream, you'll need to call putNextEntry() before writing the data for each item. The following example shows how to create a `ZipOutputStream`. You'll notice it's just like creating a `GZIPOutputStream`:

```
ZipOutputStream zipout;
try {
  FileOutputStream out = new FileOutputStream("archive.zip");
  zipout = new ZipOutputStream(out);
}
catch (IOException e) {}
```

Let's say we have two files we want to write into this archive. Before we begin writing, we need to call `putNextEntry()`. We'll create a simple entry with just a name. There are other fields in `ZipEntry` that you can set, but most of the time you won't need to bother with them.

```
try {
  ZipEntry entry = new ZipEntry("First");
  zipout.putNextEntry(entry);
  ZipEntry entry = new ZipEntry("Second");
  zipout.putNextEntry(entry);
  . . .
}
catch (IOException e) {}
```

Decompressing Data

To decompress data, you can use one of the two `FilterInputStream` subclasses provided in `java.util.zip`. To decompress data in the GZIP format, simply wrap a `GZIPInputStream` around an underlying `FileInputStream` and read from it. The following is a complete example that shows how to decompress a GZIP file:

```
//file: GUnzip.java
import java.io.*;
import java.util.zip.*;

public class GUnzip {
  public static int sChunk = 8192;
  public static void main(String[] args) {
    if (args.length != 1) {
      System.out.println("Usage: GUnzip source");
      return;
    }
    // create input stream
    String zipname, source;
    if (args[0].endsWith(".gz")) {
      zipname = args[0];
      source = args[0].substring(0, args[0].length( ) - 3);
    }
    else {
      zipname = args[0] + ".gz";
      source = args[0];
    }
    GZIPInputStream zipin;
```

```
      try {
        FileInputStream in = new FileInputStream(zipname);
        zipin = new GZIPInputStream(in);
      }
      catch (IOException e) {
        System.out.println("Couldn't open " + zipname + ".");
        return;
      }
      byte[] buffer = new byte[sChunk];
      // decompress the file
      try {
        FileOutputStream out = new FileOutputStream(source);
        int length;
        while ((length = zipin.read(buffer, 0, sChunk)) != -1)
          out.write(buffer, 0, length);
        out.close( );
      }
      catch (IOException e) {
        System.out.println("Couldn't decompress " + args[0] + ".");
      }
      try { zipin.close( ); }
      catch (IOException e) {}
    }
  }
```

First we check to make sure we have a command-line argument representing a file-name. If the argument ends with *.gz*, we figure out what the filename for the uncompressed file should be. Otherwise, we use the given argument and assume the compressed file has the *.gz* suffix. Then we construct a GZIPInputStream wrapped around a FileInputStream, representing the compressed file. With this in place, we open the target file. We read chunks of data from the GZIPInputStream and write them into the target file. Finally, we clean up by closing our open streams.

Again, the ZIP archive presents a little more complexity than the GZIP file. When reading from a ZipInputStream, you should call getNextEntry() before reading each item. When getNextEntry() returns null, there are no more items to read. The following example shows how to create a ZipInputStream. You'll notice it's just like creating a GZIPInputStream:

```
ZipInputStream zipin;
try {
  FileInputStream in = new FileInputStream("archive.zip");
  zipin = new ZipInputStream(in);
}
catch (IOException e) {}
```

Suppose we want to read two files from this archive. Before we begin reading, we need to call getNextEntry(). At the least, the entry will give us a name of the item we are reading from the archive:

```
try {
  ZipEntry first = zipin.getNextEntry( );
```

```
        }
        catch (IOException e) {}
```

At this point, you can read the contents of the first item in the archive. When you come to the end of the item, the read() method will return -1. Now you can call getNextEntry() again to read the second item from the archive:

```
    try {
        ZipEntry second = zipin.getNextEntry( );
    }
    catch (IOException e) {}
```

If you call getNextEntry(), and it returns null, there are no more items, and you have reached the end of the archive.

The NIO Package

The java.nio package is a major new addition in Java 1.4. The name NIO stands for "new I/O," which may seem to imply that it is to be a replacement for the java.io package. In fact, much of the NIO functionality does overlap with existing APIs. NIO was added primarily to address specific issues of scalability for large systems, especially in networked applications. That said, NIO also provides several new features Java lacked in basic I/O, so there are some tools here that you'll want to look at even if you aren't planning to write any large or high-performance services. The primary features of NIO are outlined in the following sections.

Asynchronous I/O

Most of the need for the NIO package was driven by the desire to add nonblocking and selectable I/O to Java. Prior to NIO, most read and write operations in Java were bound to threads that were forced to block for unpredictable amounts of time. Although certain APIs such as Sockets (which we'll see in Chapter 12) provided specific means to limit how long an I/O call could take, this was a workaround to compensate for the lack of a more general mechanism. Prior to the introduction of threads, in many languages I/O could still be done efficiently by setting I/O streams to a nonblocking mode and testing them for their readiness to send or receive data. In a nonblocking mode, a read or write does only as much work as can be done immediately—filling or emptying a buffer and then returning. Combined with the ability to test for readiness, this allows a single thread to continuously service many channels efficiently. The main thread "selects" a stream that is ready and works with it until it blocks, then moves to another. On a single processor system, this is fundamentally equivalent to using multiple threads. Even now, this style of processing has advantages when using a pool of threads (rather than just one). We'll discuss this in detail in Chapter 12 when we discuss networking and building servers that can handle many clients simultaneously.

In addition to nonblocking and selectable I/O, the NIO package enables closing and interrupting I/O operations asynchronously. As discussed in Chapter 8, prior to NIO there was no reliable way to stop or wake up a thread blocked in an I/O operation. With NIO, threads blocked in I/O operations always wake up when interrupted or when the channel is closed by anyone. Additionally, if you interrupt a thread while it is blocked in an NIO operation, its channel is automatically closed. (Closing the channel because the thread is interrupted might seem too strong, but usually it's the right thing to do.)

Performance

Channel I/O is designed around the concept of *buffers*, which are a more sophisticated form of array, tailored to working with communications. The NIO package supports the concept of *direct buffers*, buffers that maintain their memory outside the Java virtual machine, in the native host operating system. Since all real I/O operations ultimately have to work with the host OS, by maintaining the buffer space there, some operations can be made much more efficient. Data can be transferred without first copying it into Java and back out.

Mapped and Locked Files

NIO provides two general-purpose file-related features—memory-mapped files and file locking. We'll discuss memory-mapped files later, but suffice it to say that they allow you to work with file data as if it were all magically resident in memory. File locking supports the concept of shared and exclusive locks on regions of files—useful for concurrent access by multiple applications.

Channels

While java.io deals with streams, java.nio works with channels. A *channel* is an endpoint for communication. Although in practice channels are similar to streams, the underlying notion of a channel is a bit more abstract and primitive. Whereas streams in java.io are defined in terms of input or output with methods to read and write bytes, the basic channel interface says nothing about how communications happen. It simply defines whether the channel is open or closed, via the methods isOpen() and close(). Implementations of channels for files, network sockets, or arbitrary devices then add their own methods for operations such as reading, writing, or transferring data. The following channels are provided by NIO:

- FileChannel
- Pipe.SinkChannel, Pipe.SourceChannel
- SocketChannel, ServerSocketChannel, DatagramChannel

We'll cover FileChannel in this chapter. The Pipe channels are simply the channel equivalents of the java.io Pipe facilities. We'll talk about Socket and Datagram channels in Chapter 12.

All these basic channels implement the ByteChannel interface, designed for channels that have read and write methods such as I/O streams. ByteChannels read and write ByteBuffers, however, not byte arrays.

In addition to these native channels, you can bridge to channels from java.io I/O streams and readers and writers for interoperability. Know that, if you mix these features, you may not get the full benefits of performance and asynchronous I/O.

Buffers

Most of the utilities of the java.io and java.net packages operate on byte arrays. The corresponding tools of the NIO package are built around ByteBuffers (with another type of buffer, CharBuffer, serving as a bridge to the text world). Byte arrays are simple, so why are buffers necessary? They serve several purposes.

- They formalize the usage patterns for buffered data and they provide for things like read-only buffers and keep track of read/write positions and limits within a large buffer space. They also provide a mark/reset facility like that of BufferedInputStream.

- They provide additional APIs for working with raw data representing primitive types. You can create buffers that "view" your byte data as a series of larger primitives such as shorts, ints, or floats. The most general type of data buffer, ByteBuffer, includes methods that let you read and write all primitive types like DataOutputStream does for streams.

- They abstract the underlying storage of the data, allowing for special optimizations by Java. Specifically, buffers may be allocated as direct buffers that use native buffers of the host operating system instead of arrays in Java's memory. The NIO Channel facilities that work with buffers can recognize direct buffers automatically and try to optimize I/O to use them. For example, a read from a file channel into a Java byte array normally requires Java to copy the data for the read from the host operating system into Java's memory. But with a direct buffer the data can remain outside Java's normal memory space, in the host operating system.

Buffer operations

Buffer is a subclass of java.nio.Buffer object. The base Buffer is something like an array with state. The base Buffer class does not specify what type of elements it holds (that is for subtypes to decide), but it does define functionality common to all data buffers. A Buffer has a fixed size called its *capacity*. Although all the standard Buffers provide "random access" to their contents, a Buffer expects to be read and written sequentially, so Buffers maintain the notion of a *position* where the next element is read or written. In addition to the position a Buffer can maintain two other pieces of state information: a *limit*, which is a position that is a "soft" limit to the extent of a read or write, and a *mark*, which can be used to remember an earlier position for future recall.

Implementations of Buffer add specific, typed get and put methods that read and write the buffer contents. For example, ByteBuffer is a buffer of bytes and it has get() and put() methods that read and write bytes and arrays of bytes (along with many other useful methods we'll discuss later). Getting from and putting to the Buffer changes the position marker, so the Buffer keeps track of its contents somewhat like a stream. Attempting to read or write past the limit marker generates a BufferUnderflowException or BufferOverflowException, respectively.

The mark, position, limit, and capacity values always obey the formula:

$$\text{mark} \leq \text{position} \leq \text{limit} \leq \text{capacity}$$

The position for reading and writing the Buffer is always greater than the mark, which serves as a lower bound, and the limit, which serves as an upper bound. The capacity represents the physical extent of the buffer space.

You can set the position and limit markers explicitly with the position() and limit() methods. But several convenience methods are provided for the common usage patterns. The reset() method sets the position back to the mark. If no mark has been set, an InvalidMarkException is thrown. The clear() method resets the position to zero and makes the limit the capacity, readying the buffer for new data (the mark is discarded). Note that the clear() method does not actually do anything to the data in the buffer; it simply changes the position markers.

The flip() method is used for the common pattern of writing data into the buffer and then reading it back out. flip makes the current position the limit and then resets the current position to zero (any mark is thrown away). This saves having to keep track of how much data was read. Another method, rewind(), simply resets the position to zero, leaving the limit alone. You might use it to write the same data again. Here is a snippet of code that uses these methods to read data from a channel and writes it to two channels:

```
ByteBuffer buff = ...
while ( inChannel.read( buff ) > 0 ) { // position = ?
    buff.flip();      // limit = position; position = 0;
    outChannel.write( buff );
    buff.rewind();    // position = 0
    outChannel2.write( buff );
    buff.clear();     // position = 0; limit = capacity
}
```

This might be confusing the first time you look at it because here the read from the Channel is actually a write to the Buffer and vice versa. Because this example writes all the available data up to the limit, either `flip()` or `rewind()` have the same effect in this case.

Buffer types

As stated earlier, various buffer types add get and put methods for reading and writing specific data types. There is a buffer type for each of the Java primitive types: `ByteBuffer`, `CharBuffer`, `ShortBuffer`, `IntBuffer`, `LongBuffer`, `FloatBuffer` and `DoubleBuffer`. Each provides get and put methods for reading and writing its type and arrays of its type. Of these, `ByteBuffer` is the most flexible. Because it has the "finest grain" of all the buffers, it has been given a full complement of get and put methods for reading and writing all the other data types, as well as byte. Here are some `ByteBuffer` methods:

```
byte get( )
char getChar( )
short getShort( )
int getInt( )
long getLong( )
float getFloat( )
double getDouble( )

void put(byte b)
void put(ByteBuffer src)
void put(byte[] src, int offset, int length)
void put(byte[] src)
void putChar(char value)
void putShort(short value)
void putInt(int value)
void putLong(long value)
void putFloat(float value)
void putDouble(double value)
```

As we said, all the standard buffers also support random access. So for each of the aforementioned methods of `ByteBuffer`, there is an additional form that takes an index:

```
getLong( int index )
putLong( int index, long value )
```

But that's not all. `ByteBuffer` can also provide "views" of itself as any of the larger grained types. For example, you can fetch a `ShortBuffer` view of a `ByteBuffer` with the `asShortBuffer()` method. The `.ShortBuffer` view is *backed* by the `ByteBuffer`, which means that they work on the same data, and changes to either one affect the other. The view buffer's extent starts at the `ByteBuffer`'s current position, and its capacity is a function of the remaining number of bytes, divided by the new type's size. (For example, shorts and floats consume two bytes each, longs and doubles four.) View buffers are convenient for reading and writing large blocks of a contiguous type within a `ByteBuffer`.

CharBuffers are interesting as well, primarily because of their integration with Strings. Both CharBuffers and Strings implement the java.lang.CharSequence interface. This is the interface that provides the standard charAt() and length() methods. Because of this, newer APIs (such as the java.util.regex package) allow you to use a CharBuffer or a String interchangeably. In this case, the buffer acts like a String with user-configurable start and end positions.

Byte order

Now, since we're talking about reading and writing types larger than a byte here, the question arises: in what order do the bytes of multibyte values (e.g. shorts, ints) get written? There are two camps in this world: "big endian" and "little endian."[*] Big endian means that the most significant bytes come first; little endian is the reverse. If you're writing binary data for consumption by some native application, this is important. Intel-compatible computers use little endian, and many workstations that run Unix use big endian. The ByteOrder class encapsulates the choice. You can specify the byte order to use with the ByteArray order() method, using the identifiers ByteOrder.BIG_ENDIAN and ByteOrder.LITTLE_ENDIAN like so:

```
byteArray.order( ByteOrder.BIG_ENDIAN );
```

You can retrieve the native ordering for your platform using the static ByteOrder. nativeOrder() method.

Allocating buffers

You can create a buffer either by allocating it explicitly using allocate() or by wrapping an existing array type. Each buffer type has a static allocate() method that takes a capacity (size) and also a wrap() method that takes an existing array:

```
CharBuffer cbuf = CharByffer.allocate( 64*1024 );
```

A direct buffer is allocated in the same way, with the allocateDirect() method:

```
ByteBuffer bbuf = ByteByffer.allocateDirect( 64*1024 );
```

As we described earlier, direct buffers can use native host operating-system memory structures that are optimized for use with some kinds of I/O operations. The tradeoff is that allocating a direct buffer is a little slower than a plain buffer, so you should try to use them for longer term buffers. (For example, on a 400-MHz Sparc Ultra 60, it took about 10 milliseconds to allocate a 1-MB direct buffer versus 2 milliseconds for a plain buffer of the same size.)

---

[*] The terms "big endian" and "little endian" come from Jonathan Swift's novel *Gulliver's Travels*, where it denoted two camps of Lilliputians: those who eat their eggs from the big end and those who eat them from the little end.

Character Encoders and Decoders

Character encoders and decoders turn characters into raw bytes and vice versa, mapping from the Unicode standard to particular encoding schemes. Encoders and decoders have always existed in Java for use by Reader and Writer streams and in the methods of the String class that work with byte arrays. However, prior to Java 1.4, there was no API for working with encoding explicitly; you simply referred to encoders and decoders wherever necessary by name as a String. The java.nio.charset package formalizes the idea of a Unicode character set with the Charset class.

The Charset class is a factory for Charset instances, which know how to encode character buffers to byte buffers and decode byte buffers to character buffers. You can look up a character set by name with the static Charset.forName() method and use it in conversions:

```
Charset charset = Charset.forName("US-ASCII");
CharBuffer charBuff = charset.decode( byteBuff );  // to ascii
ByteBuffer byteBuff = charset.encode( charBuff );  // and back
```

You can also test to see if an encoding is available with the static Charset.isSupported() method.

The following character sets are guaranteed to be supplied:

- US-ASCII
- ISO-8859-1
- UTF-8
- UTF-16BE
- UTF-16LE
- UTF-16

You can list all the encoders available on your platform using the static availableCharsets() method:

```
Map map = Charset.availableCharsets();
Iterator it = map.keySet().iterator();
while ( it.hasNext() )
    System.out.println( it.next() );
```

The result of availableCharsets() is a map because character sets may have "aliases" and appear under more than one name.

In addition to the buffer-oriented classes of the java.nio package, the InputStreamReader and OutputStreamWriter bridge classes of the java.io package have been updated to work with Charset as well. You can specify the encoding as a Charset object or by name.

CharsetEncoder and CharsetDecoder

You can get more control over the encoding and decoding process by creating an instance of CharsetEncoder or CharsetDecoder (codec) with the Charset newEncoder() and newDecoder() methods. In our earlier example, we assumed that all the data was available in a single buffer. More often, however, we might have to process data as it arrives in chunks. The encoder/decoder API allows for this by providing more general encode() and decode() methods that take a flag specifying whether more data is expected. The codec needs to know this because it might have been left hanging in the middle of a multibyte character conversion when the data ran out. If it knows that more data is coming, it will not throw an error on this incomplete conversion. In the following snippet, we use a decoder to read from a ByteBuffer bbuff and accumulate character data into a CharBuffer cbuff:

```
CharsetDecoder decoder = Charset.forName("US-ASCII").newDecoder();

boolean done = false;
while ( !done ) {
    bbuff.clear();
    done = ( in.read( bbuff ) == -1 );
    bbuff.flip();
    decoder.decode( bbuff, cbuff, done );
}
cbuff.flip();
// use cbuff. . .
```

Here we look for the end of input condition on the in channel to set the flag done. The encode() and decode() methods also return a special result object, CoderResult, that can determine the progress of encoding. The methods isError(), isUnderflow(), and isOverflow() on the CoderResult specify why encoding stopped: for an error, a lack of bytes on the input buffer, or a full output buffer, respectively.

FileChannel

Now that we've covered the basics of channels and buffers, it's time to look at a real channel type. The FileChannel is the NIO equivalent of the java.io.RandomAccessFile, but it provides several basic new features, in addition to some performance optimizations. You will want to use a FileChannel in place of a plain java.io file stream if you wish to use file locking, memory mapped file access, or perform highly optimized data transfer between files or between file and network channels.

A FileChannel is constructed from a FileInputStream, FileOutputStream, or RandomAccessFile:

```
FileChannel readOnlyFc = new FileInputStream("file.txt").getChannel();
FileChannel readWriteFc =
    new RandomAccessFile("file.txt", "rw").getChannel();
```

FileChannels for file input and output streams are read-only or write-only, respectively. To get a read-write FileChannel you must construct a RandomAccessFile with read-write permissions, as in the previous example.

Using a FileChannel is just like a RandomAccessFile, but it works with ByteBuffer instead of byte arrays:

```
bbuf.clear();
readOnlyFc.position( index );
readOnlyFc.read( bbuf );
bbuf.flip();
readWriteFc.write( bbuf );
```

You can control how much data is read and written either by setting buffer position and limit markers or using another form of read/write that takes a buffer starting position and length. You can also read and write to a random position using:

```
readWriteFc.read( bbuf, index )
readWriteFc.write( bbuf, index2 );
```

In each case, the actual number of bytes read or written depends on several factors. The operation tries to read or write to the limit of the buffer and the vast majority of the time that is what happens with local file access. But the operation is only guaranteed to block until at least one byte has been processed. Whatever happens, the number of bytes processed is returned, and the buffer position is updated accordingly. This is one of the things that is convenient about buffers; they can manage the count for you. Like standard streams, the channel read() method returns -1 upon reaching the end of input.

The size of the file is always available with the size() method. It can change if you write past the end of the file. Conversely, you can truncate the file to a specified length with the truncate() method.

Concurrent access

FileChannels are safe for use by multiple threads and guarantee that data "viewed" by them is consistent across channels in the same VM. However no guarantees are made about how quickly writes are propagated to the storage mechanism. If you need to be sure that data is safe before moving on, you can use the force() method to flush changes to disk. The force() method takes a boolean argument indicating whether or not file metadata, including timestamp and permissions, must be written. Some systems keep track of reads on files as well as writes, so you can save a lot of updates if you set the flag to false, which indicates that you don't care about syncing that data immediately.

As with all Channels, a FileChannel may be closed by any thread. Once closed all its read/write and position-related methods throw a ClosedChannelException.

File locking

FileChannels support exclusive and shared locks on regions of files through the lock() method:

```
FileLock fileLock = fileChannel.lock();
int start = 0, len = fileChannel2.size();
FileLock readLock = fileChannel2.lock( start, len, true );
```

Locks may be either shared or exclusive. An *exclusive* lock prevents others from acquiring a lock of any kind on the specified file or file region. A *shared* lock allows others to acquire overlapping shared locks but not exclusive locks. These are useful as write locks and read locks respectively. When you are writing, you don't want others to be able to write until you're done, but when reading, you need only to block others from writing, not reading concurrently.

The simple lock() method in the previous example attempts to acquire an exclusive lock for the whole file. The second form accepts a starting and length parameter, as well as a flag indicating whether the lock should be shared (or exclusive). The FileLock object returned by the lock() method can be used to release the lock:

```
fileLock.release();
```

Note that file locks are a cooperative API; they do not necessarily prevent anyone from reading or writing to the locked file contents. In general the only way to guarantee that locks are obeyed is for both parties to attempt to acquire the lock and use it. Also, shared locks are not implemented on some systems, in which case all requested locks are exclusive. You can test if a lock is shared with the isShared() method.

Memory mapped files

One of the most interesting new features offered through FileChannel is the ability to map a file into memory. When a file is *memory mapped*, like magic it becomes accessible through a single ByteBuffer—just as if the entire file was read into memory at once. The implementation of this is extremely efficient, generally among the fastest ways to access the data. In fact, for working with large files, memory mapping can save a lot of resources and time.

This may seem counterintuitive; we're getting a conceptually easier way to access our data and it's also faster and more efficient? What's the catch? There really is no catch. The reason for this is that all modern operating systems are based on the idea of virtual memory. In a nutshell, that means the operating system makes disk space act like memory by continually paging (swapping 4K blocks called "pages") between memory and disk, transparent to the applications. Operating systems are very good at this; they efficiently cache the data the application is using and let go of what is not. So memory mapping a file is really just taking advantage of what the OS is doing internally.

A good example of where a memory-mapped file would be useful is in a database. Imagine a 100-MB file containing records indexed at various positions. By mapping the file we can work with a standard ByteBuffer, reading and writing data at arbitrary positions and let the native operating system read and write the underlying data in fine grained pages, as necessary. We could emulate this behavior with RandomAccessFile or FileChannel, but we would have to explicitly read and write data into buffers first, and the implementation would almost certainly not be as efficient.

A mapping is created with the FileChannel map() method. For example:

```
FileChannel fc = new RandomAccessFile("index.db", "rw").getChannel( );
MappedByteBuffer mappedBuff =
    fc.map( FileChannel.MapMode.READ_WRITE, 0, fc.size( ) );
```

The map() method returns a MappedByteBuffer, which is simply the standard ByteBuffer with a few additional methods relating to the mapping. The most important is force(), which ensures that any data written to the buffer is flushed out to permanent storage on the disk. The READ_ONLY and READ_WRITE constant identifiers of the FileChannel.MapMode static inner class specify the type of access. Read-write access is available only when mapping a read-write file channel. Data read through the buffer is always consistent within the same Java VM. It can also be consistent across applications on the same host machine, but this is not guaranteed.

Again, a MappedByteBuffer acts just like a ByteBuffer. Continuing with the previous example, we could decode the buffer with a character decoder and search for a pattern like so:

```
CharBuffer cbuff = Charset.forName("US-ASCII").decode( mappedBuff );
Matcher matcher = Pattern.compile("abc*").matcher( cbuff );
while ( matcher.find( ) )
        print( matcher.start( )+": "+matcher.group(0) );
```

Here we have effectively implemented the Unix *grep* command in about five lines of code (thanks to the fact that the Regular Expression API can work with our CharBuffer as a CharSequence). Of course in this example, the CharBuffer allocated by the decode() method is as large as the mapped file and must be held in memory. More generally, we can use the CharsetDecoder shown earlier to iterate through a large mapped space.

Direct transfer

The final feature of FileChannel that we'll look at is performance optimization. FileChannel supports two highly optimized data transfer methods: transferFrom() and transferTo(), which move data between the file channel and another channel. These methods can take advantage of direct buffers internally to move data between the channels as fast as possible, often without copying the bytes into Java's memory space at all. The following example is currently the fastest way to implement a file copy in Java:

```
import java.io.*;
import java.nio.*;
import java.nio.channels.*;

public class CopyFile {
    public static void main( String [] args ) throws Exception
    {
        String fromFileName = args[0];
        String toFileName = args[1];
        FileChannel in = new FileInputStream( fromFileName ).getChannel();
        FileChannel out = new FileOutputStream( toFileName ).getChannel();
        in.transferTo( 0, (int)in.size(), out );
        in.close();
        out.close();
    }
}
```

Scaleable I/O with NIO

We've laid the groundwork for using the NIO package in this chapter but left out some of the important pieces. In the next chapter, we'll see more of the real motivation for java.nio when we talk about nonblocking and selectable I/O. In addition to the performance optimizations that can be made through direct buffers, these capabilities make possible a design for network servers that uses fewer threads and can scale well to large systems. We'll also look at the other significant Channel types: SocketChannel, ServerSocketChannel, and DatagramChannel.

CHAPTER 12

Network Programming

The network is the soul of Java. Most of what is new and exciting about Java centers around the potential for new kinds of dynamic, networked applications. In this chapter, we'll start our discussion of the java.net package, which contains the fundamental classes for communications and working with networked resources. Then we'll talk about the java.rmi package, which provides Java's powerful, high-level, remote method invocation facilities. Finally, we'll complete our discussion of the java.nio package, which is highly efficient for implementing large servers.

The classes of java.net fall into two categories: the Sockets API and tools for working with uniform resource locators (URLs). Figure 12-1 shows the java.net package.

Java's Sockets API provides access to the standard network protocols used for communications between hosts on the Internet. Sockets are the mechanism underlying all other kinds of portable networked communications. Sockets are your lowest-level tool—you can use sockets for any kind of communications between client and server or peer applications on the Net, but you have to implement your own application-level protocols for handling and interpreting the data. Higher-level networking tools, such as remote method invocation and other distributed object systems, are implemented on top of sockets.

Java remote method invocation (RMI) is a powerful tool that leverages Java object serialization, allowing you to transparently work with objects on remote machines as if they were local. With RMI, it is easy to write distributed applications in which clients and servers work with each other's data as full-fledged Java objects rather than raw streams or packets of data.

In this chapter, we'll provide some simple and practical examples of Java network programming at both levels, using sockets and RMI. In Chapter 13, we'll look at the other half of the java.net package, which lets clients work with web services via URLs. Chapter 14 covers the Servlets API, which allows you to write application components for web servers.

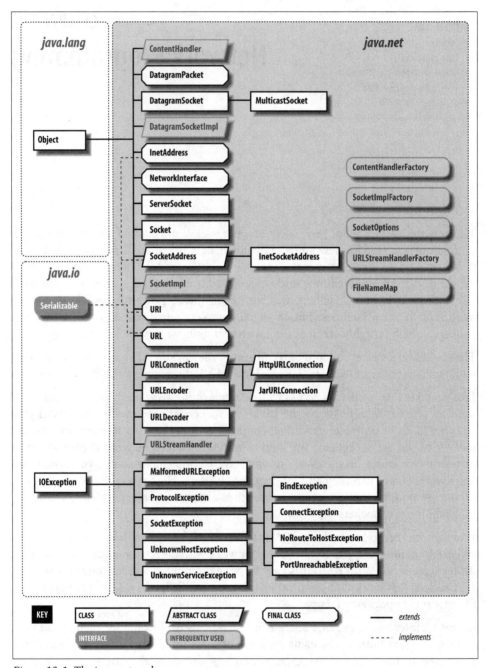

Figure 12-1. The java.net package

Sockets

Sockets are a low-level programming interface for networked communications. They send streams of data between applications that may or may not be on the same host. Sockets originated in BSD Unix and are, in other languages, hairy and complicated things with lots of small parts that can break off and choke little children. The reason for this is that most socket APIs can be used with almost any kind of underlying network protocol. Since the protocols that transport data across the network can have radically different features, the socket interface can be quite complex.*

The java.net package supports a simplified, object-oriented interface to sockets that makes network communications considerably easier. If you have done network programming using sockets in C or another structured language, you should be pleasantly surprised at how simple things can be when objects encapsulate the gory details. If this is the first time you've come across sockets, you'll find that talking to another application over the network can be as simple as reading a file or getting user input from a terminal. Most forms of I/O in Java, including most network I/O, use the stream classes described in Chapter 11. Streams provide a unified I/O interface so that reading or writing across the Internet is similar to reading or writing on the local system.

Java provides sockets to support three distinct classes of underlying protocols: Sockets, DatagramSockets, and MulticastSockets. In this first section, we look at Java's basic Socket class, which uses a *connection-oriented* protocol. A connection-oriented protocol provides the equivalent of a telephone conversation; after establishing a connection, two applications can send streams of data back and forth—the connection stays in place even when no one is talking. The protocol ensures that no data is lost and that whatever you send always arrives in the order that you sent it. In the next section, we look at the DatagramSocket class, which uses a connectionless protocol. A *connectionless protocol* is more like the postal service. Applications can send short messages to each other, but no end-to-end connection is set up in advance, and no attempt is made to keep the messages in order. It is not even guaranteed that the messages will arrive at all. A MulticastSocket is a variation of a DatagramSocket that perform multicasting—sending data to multiple recipients simultaneously. Working with multicast sockets is very much like working with datagram sockets. Because multicasting is not widely supported across the Internet at this time, we do not cover it here.

Again, in theory, just about any protocol family can be used underneath the socket layer: Novell's IPX, Apple's AppleTalk, etc. But in practice, there's only one

---

* For a discussion of sockets in general, see *Unix Network Programming* by Richard Stevens (Prentice-Hall). For a complete discussion of network programming in Java, see *Java Network Programming* by Elliotte Rusty Harold (O'Reilly).

protocol family people care about on the Internet, and only one protocol family that Java supports: the Internet Protocol (IP). The Socket class speaks TCP, the connection-oriented flavor of IP, and the DatagramSocket class speaks UDP, the connectionless kind. These protocols are generally available on any system connected to the Internet.

Clients and Servers

When writing network applications, it's common to talk about clients and servers. The distinction is increasingly vague, but the side that initiates the conversation is usually considered the *client*. The side that accepts the request is usually the *server*. In the case where there are two peer applications using sockets to talk, the distinction is less important, but for simplicity we'll use this definition.

For our purposes, the most important difference between a client and a server is that a client can create a socket to initiate a conversation with a server application at any time, while a server must be prepared to listen for incoming conversations in advance. The java.net.Socket class represents one side of an individual socket connection on both the client and server. In addition, the server uses the java.net. ServerSocketclass to listen for new connections from clients. In most cases, an application acting as a server creates a ServerSocket object and waits, blocked in a call to its accept() method, until a connection arrives. When it does, the accept() method creates a Socket object the server uses to communicate with the client. A server may carry on conversations with multiple clients at once; in this case there is still only a single ServerSocket but the server has multiple Socket objects—one associated with each client, as shown in Figure 12-2.

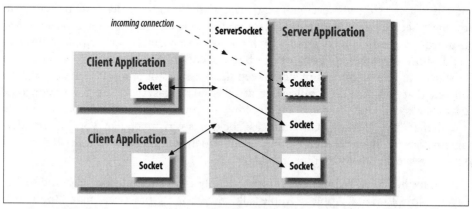

Figure 12-2. Clients and servers, Sockets and ServerSockets

A client needs two pieces of information to locate and connect to a server on the Internet: a *hostname* (used to find the host's network address) and a *port number*. The port number is an identifier that differentiates between multiple clients or servers on the same host. A server application listens on a prearranged port while waiting for connections. Clients select the port number assigned to the service they want to access. If you think of the host computers as hotels and the applications as guests, then the ports are like the guests' room numbers. For one person to call another, he or she must know the other party's hotel name and room number.

Clients

A client application opens a connection to a server by constructing a Socket that specifies the hostname and port number of the desired server:

```
try {
    Socket sock = new Socket("wupost.wustl.edu", 25);
} catch ( UnknownHostException e ) {
    System.out.println("Can't find host.");
} catch ( IOException e ) {
    System.out.println("Error connecting to host.");
}
```

This code fragment attempts to connect a Socket to port 25 (the SMTP mail service) of the host *wupost.wustl.edu*. The client handles the possibility that the hostname can't be resolved (UnknownHostException) and that it might not be able to connect to it (IOException). The constructor also works with a string containing the host's IP address:

```
Socket sock = new Socket("22.66.89.167", 25);
```

Once a connection is made, input and output streams can be retrieved with the Socket getInputStream() and getOutputStream() methods. The following (rather arbitrary) code sends and receives some data with the streams:

```
try {
    Socket server = new Socket("foo.bar.com", 1234);
    InputStream in = server.getInputStream( );
    OutputStream out = server.getOutputStream( );

    // write a byte
    out.write(42);

    // write a newline or carriage return delimited string
    PrintWriter pout = new PrintWriter( out, true );
    pout.println("Hello!");

    // read a byte
    byte back = (byte)in.read( );

    // read a newline or carriage return delimited string
    BufferedReader bin =
      new BufferedReader( new InputStreamReader( in ) );
    String response = bin.readLine( );

    // send a serialized Java object
```

```
        ObjectOutputStream oout = new ObjectOutputStream( out );
        oout.writeObject( new java.util.Date( ) );
        oout.flush( );

        server.close( );
    }
    catch (IOException e ) { ... }
```

In this exchange, the client first creates a Socket for communicating with the server. The Socket constructor specifies the server's hostname (*foo.bar.com*) and a prearranged port number (1234). Once the connection is established, the client writes a single byte to the server using the OutputStream's write() method. It then wraps a PrintWriter around the OutputStream in order to send a string of text more easily. Next, it performs the complementary operations: reading a byte from the server using InputStream's read() and then creating a BufferedReader from which to get a full string of text. Finally, we do something really funky and send a serialized Java object to the server, using an ObjectOutputStream. (We'll talk in depth about sending serialized objects later in this chapter.) The client then terminates the connection with the close() method. All these operations have the potential to generate IOExceptions; the catch clause is where our application would deal with these.

Servers

After a connection is established, a server application uses the same kind of Socket object for its side of the communications. However, to accept a connection from a client, it must first create a ServerSocket, bound to the correct port. Let's recreate the previous conversation from the server's point of view:

```
    // Meanwhile, on foo.bar.com...
    try {
        ServerSocket listener = new ServerSocket( 1234 );

        while ( !finished ) {
            Socket client = listener.accept( );   // wait for connection

            InputStream in = client.getInputStream( );
            OutputStream out = client.getOutputStream( );

            // read a byte
            byte someByte = (byte)in.read( );

            // read a newline or carriage-return-delimited string
            BufferedReader bin =
              new BufferedReader( new InputStreamReader( in ) );
            String someString = bin.readLine( );

            // write a byte
            out.write(43);

            // say goodbye
            PrintWriter pout = new PrintWriter( out, true );
```

```
        pout.println("Goodbye!");

        // read a serialized Java object
        ObjectInputStream oin = new ObjectInputStream( in );
        Date date = (Date)oin.readObject( );

        client.close( );
    }

    listener.close( );
}
catch (IOException e ) { ... }
catch (ClassNotFoundException e2 ) { ... }
```

First, our server creates a ServerSocket attached to port 1234. On some systems, there are rules about what ports an application can use. Port numbers below 1024 are usually reserved for system processes and standard, *well-known* services, so we pick a port number outside of this range. The ServerSocket is created only once; thereafter we can accept as many connections as arrive.

Next we enter a loop, waiting for the accept() method of the ServerSocket to return an active Socket connection from a client. When a connection has been established, we perform the server side of our dialog, then close the connection and return to the top of the loop to wait for another connection. Finally, when the server application wants to stop listening for connections altogether, it calls the close() method of the ServerSocket.

This server is single-threaded; it handles one connection at a time, not calling accept() to listen for a new connection until it's finished with the current connection. A more realistic server would have a loop that accepts connections concurrently and passes them off to their own threads for processing. There is a lot to be said about implementing multithreaded servers. Later in this chapter we'll create a tiny web server that starts a new thread for each connection and also a slightly more complex web server that uses the NIO package to handle many connections with a small number of threads.

Sockets and security

The previous examples presuppose that the client has permission to connect to the server and that the server is allowed to listen on the specified socket. If you're writing a general, standalone application this is normally the case. However, applets and other untrusted applications run under the auspices of a security policy that can impose arbitrary restrictions on what hosts they may or may not talk to, and whether or not they can listen for connections.

The security policy imposed on applets by the SDK appletviewer and most browsers allow untrusted applets to open socket connections only to the host that served them. That is, they can talk back only to the server from which their class files were retrieved. Untrusted applets are not allowed to open server sockets themselves. Now, this doesn't mean that an untrusted applet can't cooperate with its server to communicate with anyone, anywhere. The applet's server could run a proxy that lets the applet communicate indirectly with anyone it likes. What this security policy prevents is malicious applets poking around inside corporate firewalls, making connections to trusted services. It places the burden of security on the originating server, and not the client machine. Restricting access to the originating server limits the usefulness of "Trojan" applications that do annoying things from the client side. (You probably won't let your proxy mail-bomb people, because you'll be blamed.)

While fully trusted code and applications that are run without any security policy can perform any kind of activities, the default security policy that comes with Java 1.2 and later disallows most network access. So, if you are going to run your application under the default security manager (using the -Djava.security.manager option on the command line or by manually installing the security manager within your application), you must modify the policy file to grant the appropriate permissions to your code. (See the section "Policy Files" in Chapter 3.) The following policy file fragment sets the socket permissions to allow connections to or from any host, on any nonprivileged port:

```
grant {
  permission java.net.SocketPermission
    "*:1024-", "listen,accept,connect";
};
```

When starting the Java interpreter, you can install the security manager and use this file (call it *mysecurity.policy*):

```
java -Djava.security.manager
    -Djava.security.policy=mysecurity.policy MyApplication
```

The DateAtHost Client

Many networked workstations run a time service that dispenses their local clock time on a well-known port. This was a precursor of NTP, the more general Network Time Protocol. In the next example, DateAtHost, we'll make a specialized subclass of java.util.Date that fetches the time from a remote host instead of initializing itself from the local clock. (See Chapter 10 for a complete discussion of the Date class.)

DateAtHost connects to the time service (port 37) and reads four bytes representing the time on the remote host. These four bytes have a peculiar specification which we'll decode to get the time. Here's the code:

```
//file: DateAtHost.java
import java.net.Socket;
import java.io.*;

public class DateAtHost extends java.util.Date {
    static int timePort = 37;
```

```
    // seconds from start of 20th century to Jan 1, 1970 00:00 GMT
    static final long offset = 2208988800L;

    public DateAtHost( String host ) throws IOException {
        this( host, timePort );
    }

    public DateAtHost( String host, int port ) throws IOException {
        Socket server = new Socket( host, port );
        DataInputStream din =
          new DataInputStream( server.getInputStream( ) );
        int time = din.readInt( );
        server.close( );

        setTime( (((1L << 32) + time) - offset) * 1000 );
    }
}
```

That's all there is to it. It's not very long, even with a few frills. We have supplied two possible constructors for DateAtHost. Normally we'd expect to use the first, which simply takes the name of the remote host as an argument. The second constructor specifies the hostname and the port number of the remote time service. (If the time service were running on a nonstandard port, we would use the second constructor to specify the alternate port number.) This second constructor does the work of making the connection and setting the time. The first constructor simply invokes the second (using the this() construct) with the default port as an argument. Supplying simplified constructors that invoke their siblings with default arguments is a common and useful technique; that is the only reason we've shown it here.

The second constructor opens a socket to the specified port on the remote host. It creates a DataInputStream to wrap the input stream and then reads a four-byte integer using the readInt() method. It's no coincidence that the bytes are in the right order. Java's DataInputStream and DataOutputStream classes work with the bytes of integer types in *network byte order* (most significant to least significant). The time protocol (and other standard network protocols that deal with binary data) also uses the network byte order, so we don't need to call any conversion routines. Explicit data conversions would probably be necessary if we were using a nonstandard protocol, especially when talking to a non-Java client or server. In that case we'd have to read byte by byte and do some rearranging to get our four-byte value. After reading the data, we're finished with the socket, so we close it, terminating the connection to the server. Finally, the constructor initializes the rest of the object by calling Date's setTime() method with the calculated time value.

The four bytes of the time value are interpreted as an integer representing the number of seconds since the beginning of the 20th century. DateAtHost converts this to Java's variant of the absolute time (milliseconds since January 1, 1970, a date that should be familiar to Unix users). The conversion first creates a long value, which is the unsigned equivalent of the integer time. It subtracts an offset to make the time relative to the epoch (January 1, 1970) rather than the century, and multiplies by 1000 to convert to milliseconds. It then uses the converted time to initialize itself.

The DateAtHost class can work with a time retrieved from a remote host almost as easily as Date is used with the time on the local host. The only additional overhead is that we have to deal with the possible IOException that can be thrown by the DateAtHost constructor:

```
try {
    Date d = new DateAtHost( "sura.net" );
    System.out.println( "The time over there is: " + d );
}
catch ( IOException e ) { ... }
```

This example fetches the time at the host *sura.net* and prints its value.

The TinyHttpd Server

Have you ever wanted to write your very own web server? Well, you're in luck. In this section, we're going to build TinyHttpd, a minimal but functional HTTP daemon. TinyHttpd listens on a specified port and services simple HTTP GET requests. They look something like this:

```
GET /path/filename [ optional stuff ]
```

Your web browser sends one or more of these requests for each document it retrieves from a web server. Upon reading a request, our server attempts to open the specified file and send its contents. If that document contains references to images or other items to be displayed inline, the browser follows up with additional GET requests. For best performance TinyHttpd services each request in its own thread. Therefore, TinyHttpd can service several requests concurrently.

This example works, but it's a bit oversimplified. Remember that file pathnames are still somewhat architecture-dependent in Java. This example should work, as is, on most systems, but could require some enhancement to work everywhere. It's possible to write slightly more elaborate code that uses the environmental information provided by Java to tailor itself to the local system. (Chapter 11 gives some hints about how.)

 Unless you have a firewall or other security in place, the next example serves files from your host without protection. Don't try this at work.

Now, without further ado, here's TinyHttpd:

```
//file: TinyHttpd.java
import java.net.*;
import java.io.*;
```

```
import java.util.regex.*;

public class TinyHttpd {
  public static void main( String argv[] ) throws IOException {
    ServerSocket ss =
        new ServerSocket( Integer.parseInt(argv[0]) );
    while ( true )
      new Thread( new TinyHttpdConnection( ss.accept() ) ).start( );
  }
}

class TinyHttpdConnection implements Runnable {
  Socket client;
  TinyHttpdConnection ( Socket client ) throws SocketException {
    this.client = client;
  }
  public void run( ) {
    try {
      BufferedReader in = new BufferedReader(
        new InputStreamReader(client.getInputStream( ), "8859_1" ) );
      OutputStream out = client.getOutputStream( );
      PrintWriter pout = new PrintWriter(
        new OutputStreamWriter(out, "8859_1"), true );
      String request = in.readLine( );
      System.out.println( "Request: "+request);

      Matcher get = Pattern.compile("GET /?(\\S*).*").matcher( request );
      if ( get.matches( ) ) {
        request = get.group(1);
        if ( request.endsWith("/") || request.equals("") )
          request = request + "index.html";
        try {
          FileInputStream fis = new FileInputStream ( request );
          byte [] data = new byte [ 64*1024 ];
          for(int read; (read = fis.read( data )) > -1; )
              out.write( data, 0, read );
          out.flush( );
        } catch ( FileNotFoundException e ) {
          pout.println( "404 Object Not Found" ); }
      } else
        pout.println( "400 Bad Request" );
      client.close( );
    } catch ( IOException e ) {
      System.out.println( "I/O error " + e ); }
  }
}
```

Compile TinyHttpd and place it in your classpath, as described in Chapter 3. Go to a directory with some interesting documents and start the daemon, specifying an unused port number as an argument. For example:

```
% java TinyHttpd 1234
```

You should now be able to use your web browser to retrieve files from your host. You'll have to specify the port number you chose in the URL. For example, if your hostname is *foo.bar.com*, and you started the server as shown, you could reference a file as in:

```
http://foo.bar.com:1234/welcome.htm
```

Or if you're running both the server and your web browser on the same machine:

```
http://localhost:1234/welcome.html
```

TinyHttpd looks for files relative to its current directory, so the pathnames you provide should be relative to that location. Retrieved some files? (Did you notice that when you retrieved an HTML file, your web browser automatically generated more requests for items like images that were contained within it?) Let's take a closer look.

The TinyHttpd application has two classes. The public TinyHttpd class contains the main() method of our standalone application. It begins by creating a ServerSocket, attached to the specified port. It then loops, waiting for client connections and creating instances of the second class, a TinyHttpdConnection, to service each request. The while loop waits for the ServerSocket accept() method to return a new Socket for each client connection. The Socket is passed as an argument to construct the TinyHttpdConnection thread that handles it.

TinyHttpdConnection is a Runnable object. For each connection we start a thread, which lives long enough to handle the single client connection and then dies. The body of TinyHttpdConnection's run() method is where all the magic happens. First, we fetch an OutputStream for talking back to our client. The second line reads the GET request from the InputStream into the variable request. This request is a single newline-terminated String that looks like the GET request we described earlier. For this we use a BufferedInputStream wrapped around an InputStreamReader. (We'll say more about the InputStreamReader in a moment.)

We then parse the contents of request to extract a filename. Here we are using the Regular Expression API (see Chapter 9 for a full discussion of regular expressions and the Regular Expression API). The pattern simply looks for the "GET " followed by an optional slash and then any string of non-whitespace characters. We add the ". *" at the end to cause the pattern to match the whole input, so that we can use the Matcher match() method to test if the whole request made sense to us or not. The part that matches the filename is in a capture group: "(\\S*)". This allows us to retrieve that text with the Matcher group() method. Finally, we check to see if the requested filename looks like a directory name (i.e., ends in a slash) or is empty. In these cases, we append the familiar default filename *index.html* as a convenience.

Once we have the filename, we try to open the specified file and send its contents using a large byte array. Here we loop, reading a buffer at a time and writing to the client via the OutputStream. If we can't parse the request or the file doesn't exist, we use the PrintStream to send a textual message. Then we return an appropriate HTTP error message. Finally, we close the socket and return from `run()`, removing our Thread.

Do French web servers speak French?

In `TinyHttpd`, we explicitly created the `InputStreamReader` for our `BufferedRead` and the `OutputStreamWriter` for our `PrintWriter`. We do this so that we can specify the character encoding to use when converting to and from the byte representation of the HTTP protocol messages. (Note that we're not talking about the body of the file to be sent—that is simply a stream of raw bytes to us; rather we're talking here about the `GET` and response messages.) If we didn't specify, we'd get the default character encoding for the local system. For many purposes that may be correct, but in this case we are speaking of a well-defined international protocol, and we should be specific. The RFC for HTTP specifies that web clients and servers should use the ISO8859-1 character encoding. We specify this encoding explicitly when we construct the `InputStreamReader` and `OutputStreamWriter`. Now as it turns out, ISO8859-1 is just plain ASCII and conversion to and from Unicode should always leave ASCII values unchanged, so again we would probably not be in any trouble if we did not specify an encoding. But it's important to think about these things at least once—and now you have.

Taming the daemon

An important problem with `TinyHttpd` is that there are no restrictions on the files it serves. With a little trickery, the daemon would happily send any file in your filesystem to the client. It would be nice if we could enforce the restriction that `TinyHttpd` serve only files that are in the current working directory or a subdirectory, as it normally does. An easy way to do this is to activate the Java Security Manager. Normally, a security manager is used to prevent Java code downloaded over the Net from doing anything suspicious. However, we can press the security manager into service to restrict file access in our application as well.

You can use a policy like the simple one that we provided in the previous section "Sockets and security"; it allows the server to accept connections on a specified range of sockets. Fortuitously, the default file-access security policy does just what we want: it allows an application access to files in its current working directory and subdirectories. So simply installing the security manager provides exactly the kind of file protection that we wanted in this case. (It would be easy to add additional permissions if you wish to extend the server's range to other well-defined areas.)

With the security manager in place, the daemon cannot access anything outside the current directory and its subdirectories. If it tries to, the security manager throws an exception and prevents access to the file. In that case, we should have `TinyHttpd` catch the `SecurityException` and return a proper message to the web browser. Add the following catch clause after the `FileNotFoundException`'s catch clause.

```
...
} catch ( Security Exception e ) {
    pout.println("403 Forbidden");
}
```

Room for improvement

TinyHttpd still has quite a bit of room for improvement. Technically it implements only an obsolete subset of the HTTP protocol (Version 0.9) in which the server expects only the GET request and returns just the content. All modern servers speak either HTTP 1.0 or 1.1, which allows for additional metadata in both the HTTP request and response and requires certain data (like version number, content length, etc.). HTTP 1.1 also allows multiple requests to be sent over one socket connection.

And of course real web servers can do all sorts of other things. For example, you might consider adding a few lines of code to read directories and generate linked HTML listings as most web servers do. Have fun with this example, and you can learn quite a bit!

Socket Options

As we've said, the Java sockets API is a somewhat simplified interface to the general socket mechanisms. In other environments, where all the gory details of the network are visible to you, a lot of complex and sometimes esoteric options can be set on sockets to govern the behavior of the underlying protocols. Java gives us access to a few important ones. We'll refer to them by their standard (C language) names so that you can recognize them in other networking books.

SO_TIMEOUT

The SO_TIMEOUT option sets a timer on all I/O methods of a socket that block so that you don't have to wait forever if they don't return. This works for operations such as accept() on server sockets and read() or write() on all sockets. If the timer expires before the operation would complete, an InterruptedIOException is thrown. You can catch the exception and continue to use the socket normally if it is appropriate, or you can take the opportunity to bail out of the operation. Multi-threaded, blocking servers such as TinyHttpd can use this sort of technique for their "shutdown" logic:

```
serverSocket.setSoTimeout( 2000 ); // 2 seconds

while ( !shutdown ) {
    try {
        Socket client = serverSocket.accept( );
        handleClient( client );
    } catch ( InterruptedIOException e ) {
        // ignore the exception
    }
```

```
        // exit
    }
```

You set the timer by calling the setSoTimeout() method of the Socket class with the timeout period, in milliseconds, as an int argument. This works for regular Sockets, ServerSockets (TCP), and DatagramSockets (UDP), discussed in the next section. To find the current timeout value, call getSoTimeout().

This feature is a workaround for the fact that stream-oriented I/O operations in Java are "blocking," and there is no way to test, or poll, them for activity. Later in this chapter we'll complete our discussion of the NIO package, which provides full non-blocking I/O for all types of operations, including sockets.

TCP_NODELAY

This option turns off a feature of TCP called Nagle's algorithm, which tries to prevent certain interactive applications from flooding the network with very tiny packets. You can turn this feature off if you have a fast network, and you want all packets sent as soon as possible. The Socket setTcpNoDelay() method takes a boolean argument specifying whether the delay is on or off. To find out whether the TCP_NODELAY option is enabled, call getTcpNoDelay(), which returns a boolean.

SO_LINGER

This option controls what happens to any unsent data when you perform a close() on an active socket connection. Normally the system blocks on the close and tries to deliver any network buffered data and close the connection gracefully. The setSoLinger() method of the Socket class takes two arguments: a boolean that enables or disables the option and an int that sets the time to wait (the *linger* value), in seconds. If you set the linger value to 0, any unsent data is discarded, and the TCP connection is aborted (terminated with a reset). To find the current linger value, call getSoLinger().

TCP_KEEPALIVE

This option can be enabled with the setKeepAlive() method. It triggers a feature of TCP that polls the other side every two hours if there is no other activity. Normally, when there is no data flowing on a TCP connection, no packets are sent. This can make it difficult to tell whether the other side is simply being quiet or has disappeared. If one side of the connection closes properly, this is detected. But if the other side simply disappears, we don't know unless and until we try to talk to it. For this reason, servers often use TCP_KEEPALIVE to detect lost client connections (where they might otherwise only respond to requests, rather than initiate them). Keepalive is not part of the TCP specification; it's an add-on that's not guaranteed to be implemented everywhere. If you have the option, the best way to detect lost clients is to implement the polling as part of your own protocol.

Half close

In TCP, it is technically possible to close one direction of a stream but not the other. In other words, you can shut down sending but not receiving, or vice versa. A few protocols use this to indicate the end of a client request by closing the client side of the stream, allowing the end of stream to be detected by the server. You can shut down either half of a socket connection with shutdownOutput() or shutdownInput().

Proxies and Firewalls

Many networks are behind firewalls, which prevent applications from opening direct socket connections to the outside network. Instead, they provide a service called SOCKS (named for sockets) that serves as a proxy server for socket connections, giving the administrators more control over what connections are allowed. Alternatively, firewalls can choose to proxy only HTTP level requests at a higher level using an HTTP proxy. Java has built-in support for both SOCKS and HTTP proxies. All you have to do is set some system properties in your application (in an applet, this should be already taken care of for you, because you wouldn't have authority to set those properties). Here's a list of the properties that configure Java to use a socket proxy server:

socksproxyHost
> The SOCKS proxy server name

socksproxyPort
> The SOCKS proxy port number

It's similar for an HTTP proxy:

http.proxySet
> A boolean (true or false) indicating whether to use the proxy

http.proxyHost
> The proxy server name

http.proxyPort
> The proxy port number

You can set these properties on the command line using the Java interpreter's -D option or by calling the System.setProperty() method. The following command runs MyProgram using the HTTP proxy server at *foo.bar.com* on port 1234:

```
% java -Dhttp.proxySet=true -Dhttp.proxyServer=foo.bar.com
    -Dhttp.proxyPort=1234 MyProgram
```

If the firewall does not allow any outside socket connections, your applet or application may still be able to communicate with the outside world by using HTTP to send and receive data in this way. See Chapter 13 for an example of how to perform an HTTP POST operation to send data.

Datagram Sockets

TinyHttpd used a Socket to create a connection to the client using the TCP protocol. In that example, TCP itself took care of data integrity; we didn't have to worry about data arriving out of order or incorrect. Now we take a walk on the wild side, building an applet that uses a java.net.DatagramSocket, which uses the UDP protocol. A datagram is sort of like a letter sent via the postal service: it's a discrete chunk of data transmitted in one packet. Unlike the previous example, where we could get a convenient OutputStream from our Socket and write the data as if writing to a file, with a DatagramSocket we have to work one datagram at a time. (Of course, the TCP protocol was taking our OutputStream and slicing the data into packets, but we didn't have to worry about those details.)

UDP doesn't guarantee that the data is received. If the data packets are received, they may not arrive in the order in which we sent them; it's even possible for duplicate datagrams to arrive (under rare circumstances). Using UDP is something like cutting the pages out of the encyclopedia, putting them into separate envelopes, and mailing them to your friend. If your friend wants to read the encyclopedia, it's his or her job to put the pages in order. If some pages get lost in the mail, your friend has to send you a letter asking for replacements.

Obviously, you wouldn't use UDP to send a huge amount of data without error correction. But it's significantly more efficient than TCP, particularly if you don't care about the order in which messages arrive, or whether 100% of their arrival is guaranteed. For example, in a simple periodic database lookup, the client can send a query; the server's response itself constitutes an acknowledgment. If the response doesn't arrive within a certain time, the client can send another query. It shouldn't be hard for the client to match responses to its original queries. Some important applications that use UDP are the Domain Name System (DNS) and Sun's Network File System (NFS).

The HeartBeat Applet

In this section, we build a simple applet, HeartBeat, that sends a datagram to its server each time it's started and stopped. We also build a simple standalone server application, Pulse, that receives these datagrams and prints them. By tracking the output, you can have a crude measure of who is currently looking at your web page at any given time (assuming that firewalls do not block the UDP packets). This is an ideal application for UDP: we don't want the overhead of a TCP socket, and if the datagrams get lost, it's no big deal.

First, the HeartBeat applet:

```
//file: HeartBeat.java
import java.net.*;
import java.io.*;
```

```
public class HeartBeat extends java.applet.Applet {
    String myHost;
    int myPort;

    public void init( ) {
        myHost = getCodeBase( ).getHost( );
        myPort = Integer.parseInt( getParameter("myPort") );
    }

    private void sendMessage( String message ) {
        try {
            byte [] data = message.getBytes( );
            InetAddress addr = InetAddress.getByName( myHost );
            DatagramPacket pack =
                new DatagramPacket(data, data.length, addr, myPort );
            DatagramSocket ds = new DatagramSocket( );
            ds.send( pack );
            ds.close( );
        } catch ( IOException e ) {
            System.out.println( e );  // Error creating socket
        }
    }

    public void start( ) {
        sendMessage("Arrived");
    }
    public void stop( ) {
        sendMessage("Departed");
    }
}
```

Compile the applet and include it in an HTML document with an `<APPLET>` tag:

```
<APPLET height=10 width=10 code=HeartBeat>
    <PARAM name="myPort" value="1234">
</APPLET>
```

Make sure to place the compiled HeartBeat.class file in the same directory as the HTML document. If you're not familiar with embedding applets in HTML documents, consult Chapter 22.

The myPort parameter should specify the port number on which our server application listens for data.

Next, the server-side application, Pulse:

```
//file: Pulse.java
import java.net.*;
import java.io.*;

public class Pulse {
    public static void main( String [] argv ) throws IOException {
        DatagramSocket s =
            new DatagramSocket( Integer.parseInt(argv[0]) );
```

```
        while ( true ) {
            DatagramPacket packet =
                new DatagramPacket(new byte [1024], 1024);
            s.receive( packet );
            String message = new String( packet.getData( ) );
            System.out.println( "Heartbeat from: "
                + packet.getAddress( ).getHostName( )
                + " - " + message );
        }
    }
}
```

Compile Pulse and run it on your web server, specifying a port number as an argument:

```
% java Pulse 1234
```

The port number should be the same as the one you used in the myPort parameter of the <APPLET> tag for HeartBeat.

Now, pull up the web page in your browser. You won't see anything interesting there (a better application might do something visual as well), but you should get a blip from the Pulse application. Leave the page and return to it a few times. Each time the applet is started or stopped, it sends a message, and Pulse reports it:

```
Heartbeat from: foo.bar.com - Arrived
Heartbeat from: foo.bar.com - Departed
Heartbeat from: foo.bar.com - Arrived
Heartbeat from: foo.bar.com - Departed
...
```

Cool, eh? Just remember the datagrams are not guaranteed to arrive (although it's highly unlikely you'll ever see them fail on a normal network), and it's possible that you could miss an arrival or a departure. Now let's look at the code.

The HeartBeat applet code

HeartBeat overrides the init(), start(), and stop() methods of the Applet class and implements one private method of its own, sendMessage(), which sends a datagram. (Again, we haven't covered applets yet, so if you want more details you'll have to refer to Chapter 22.) HeartBeat begins its life in init(), where it determines the destination for its messages. It uses the Applet getCodeBase() and getHost() methods to find the name of its originating host and fetches the correct port number from the myPort parameter of the <APPLET> tag. After init() has finished, the start() and stop() methods are called whenever the applet is started or stopped. These methods merely call sendMessage() with the appropriate message.

sendMessage() is responsible for sending a String message to the server as a datagram. It takes the text as an argument, constructs a datagram packet containing the message, and then sends the datagram. All the datagram information is packed into a java.net.DatagramPacket object, including the destination and port number. The DatagramPacket is like an addressed envelope, stuffed with our bytes. After the DatagramPacket is created, sendMessage() simply has to open a DatagramSocket and send it.

The first five lines of sendMessage() build the DatagramPacket:

```
try {
    byte [] data = message.getBytes( );
    InetAddress addr = InetAddress.getByName( myHost );
    DatagramPacket pack =
      new DatagramPacket(data, data.length, addr, myPort );
```

First, the contents of message are placed into an array of bytes called data. Next a java.net.InetAddress object is created from the name myHost. An InetAddress holds the network address information for a host in a special format. We get an InetAddress object for our host using the static getByName() method of the InetAddress class. (We can't construct an InetAddress object directly.) Finally, we call the DatagramPacket constructor with four arguments: the byte array containing our data, the length of the data, the destination address object, and the port number.

The remaining lines construct a default client DatagramSocket and call its send() method to transmit the DatagramPacket. After sending the datagram, we close the socket:

```
DatagramSocket ds = new DatagramSocket( );
ds.send( pack );
ds.close( );
```

Two operations throw a type of IOException: the InetAddress.getByName() lookup and the DatagramSocket send() method. InetAddress.getByName() can throw an UnknownHostException, which is a type of IOException that indicates the hostname can't be resolved. If send() throws an IOException, it implies a serious client-side problem in talking to the network. We need to catch these exceptions; our catch block simply prints a message telling us that something went wrong. If we get one of these exceptions, we can assume the datagram never arrived. However, we can't assume the inverse: even if we don't get an exception, we still don't know that the host is actually accessible or that the data actually arrived; with a DatagramSocket, we never find out from the API.

The Pulse server code

The Pulse server corresponds to the HeartBeat applet. First, it creates a DatagramSocket to listen on our prearranged port. This time, we specify a port number in the constructor; we get the port number from the command line as a string (argv[0]) and convert it to an integer with Integer.parseInt(). Note the difference between this call to the constructor and the call in HeartBeat. In the server, we need to listen for incoming datagrams on a prearranged port, so we need to specify the port when creating the DatagramSocket. The client just sends datagrams, so we don't have to specify the port in advance; we build the port number into the `DatagramPacket` itself.

Second, `Pulse` creates an empty `DatagramPacket` of a fixed size to receive an incoming datagram. This alternative constructor for `DatagramPacket` takes a byte array and a length as arguments. As much data as possible is stored in the byte array when it's received. (A practical limit on the size of a UDP datagram that can be sent over the Internet is 8K, although they can be larger for local network use—theoretically up to 64K.) Finally, `Pulse` calls the `DatagramSocket`'s `receive()` method to wait for a packet to arrive. When a packet arrives, its contents are printed by turning them to a string using the default system encoding.

As you can see, `DatagramSockets` are slightly more tedious than regular `Sockets`. With datagrams, it's harder to spackle over the messiness of the socket interface. The Java API rather slavishly follows the Unix interface, and that doesn't help. It's easy to imagine conveniences that would make all this simpler; perhaps we'll have them in a future release.

Simple Serialized Object Protocols

Earlier in this chapter, we showed a hypothetical conversation in which a client and server exchanged some primitive data and a serialized Java object. Passing an object between two programs may not have seemed like a big deal at the time, but in the context of Java as a portable bytecode language, it has profound implications. In this section, we show how a protocol can be built using serialized Java objects.

Before we move on, it's worth considering network protocols. Most programmers would consider working with sockets to be "low-level" and unfriendly. Even though Java makes sockets much easier to use than many other languages, sockets still provide only an unstructured flow of bytes between their endpoints. If you want to do serious communications using sockets, the first thing you have to do is come up with a protocol that defines the data you'll be sending and receiving. The most complex part of that protocol usually involves how to marshal (package) your data for transfer over the Net and unpack it on the other side.

As we've seen, Java's `DataInputStream` and `DataOuputStream` classes solve this problem for simple data types. We can read and write numbers, `Strings`, and Java primitives in a standard format that can be understood on any other Java platform. But to do real work, we need to be able to put simple types together into larger structures. Java object serialization solves this problem elegantly, by allowing us to send our data just as we use it, as the state of Java objects. Serialization can even pack up entire graphs of interconnected objects and put them back together at a later time, in another Java VM.

A Simple Object-Based Server

In the following example, a client sends a serialized object to the server, and the server responds in kind. The object sent by the client represents a request and the object returned by the server represents the response. The conversation ends when the client closes the connection. It's hard to imagine a simpler protocol. All the hairy details are taken care of by object serialization, which allows us to work with standard Java objects as we are used to.

To start, we define a class—Request—to serve as a base class for the various kinds of requests we make to the server. Using a common base class is a convenient way to identify the object as a type of request. In a real application, we might also use it to hold basic information such as client names and passwords, timestamps, serial numbers, etc. In our example, Request can be an empty class that exists so others can extend it:

```
//file: Request.java
public class Request implements java.io.Serializable {}
```

Request implements Serializable, so all its subclasses are serializable by default. Next we create some specific kinds of Requests. The first, DateRequest, is also a trivial class. We use it to ask the server to send us a java.util.Date object as a response:

```
//file: DateRequest.java
public class DateRequest extends Request {}
```

Next, we create a generic WorkRequest object. The client sends a WorkRequest to get the server to perform some computation for it. The server calls the WorkRequest object's execute() method and returns the resulting object as a response:

```
//file: WorkRequest.java
public abstract class WorkRequest extends Request {
    public abstract Object execute( );
}
```

For our application, we subclass WorkRequest to create MyCalculation, which adds code that performs a specific calculation; in this case, we just square a number:

```
//file: MyCalculation.java
public class MyCalculation extends WorkRequest {
    int n;

    public MyCalculation( int n ) {
        this.n = n;
    }
    public Object execute( ) {
        return new Integer( n * n );
    }
}
```

As far as data content is concerned, MyCalculation really doesn't do much; it only transports an integer value for us. But keep in mind that a request object could hold lots of data, including references to many other objects in complex structures such as arrays or linked lists. The only requirement is that all the objects to be sent must be serializable or must be able to be discarded by marking them as transient (see the section "Serialization" in Chapter 11). An important thing to note here is that MyCalculation also contains behavior—the execute() operation. While Java object serialization sends only the data content of a class, in our discussion of RMI below we'll see how Java's ability to dynamically download bytecode for classes can make both the data content and behavior portable over the network.

Now that we have our protocol, we need the server. The following Server class looks a lot like the TinyHttpd server we developed earlier in this chapter:

```java
//file: Server.java
import java.net.*;
import java.io.*;

public class Server {
  public static void main( String argv[] ) throws IOException {
    ServerSocket ss = new ServerSocket( Integer.parseInt(argv[0]) );
    while ( true )
      new ServerConnection( ss.accept( ) ).start( );
  }
} // end of class Server

class ServerConnection extends Thread {
  Socket client;
  ServerConnection ( Socket client ) throws SocketException {
    this.client = client;
  }

  public void run( ) {
    try {
      ObjectInputStream in =
        new ObjectInputStream( client.getInputStream( ) );
      ObjectOutputStream out =
        new ObjectOutputStream( client.getOutputStream( ) );
      while ( true ) {
        out.writeObject( processRequest( in.readObject( ) ) );
        out.flush( );
      }
    } catch ( EOFException e3 ) { // Normal EOF
      try {
        client.close( );
      } catch ( IOException e ) { }
    } catch ( IOException e ) {
      System.out.println( "I/O error " + e ); // I/O error
    } catch ( ClassNotFoundException e2 ) {
      System.out.println( e2 ); // unknown type of request object
    }
  }

  private Object processRequest( Object request ) {
```

```
    if ( request instanceof DateRequest )
      return new java.util.Date( );
    else if ( request instanceof WorkRequest )
      return ((WorkRequest)request).execute( );
    else
      return null;
  }
}
```

The Server handles each request in a separate thread. For each connection, the run()
method creates an ObjectInputStream and an ObjectOutputStream, which the server
uses to receive the request and send the response. The processRequest() method
decides what the request means and comes up with the response. To figure out what
kind of request we have, we use the instanceof operator to look at the object's type.

Finally, we get to our Client, which is even simpler:

```
//file: Client.java
import java.net.*;
import java.io.*;

public class Client {
  public static void main( String argv[] ) {
    try {
      Socket server =
        new Socket( argv[0], Integer.parseInt(argv[1]) );
      ObjectOutputStream out =
        new ObjectOutputStream( server.getOutputStream( ) );
      ObjectInputStream in =
        new ObjectInputStream( server.getInputStream( ) );

      out.writeObject( new DateRequest( ) );
      out.flush( );
      System.out.println( in.readObject( ) );

      out.writeObject( new MyCalculation( 2 ) );
      out.flush( );
      System.out.println( in.readObject( ) );

      server.close( );
    } catch ( IOException e ) {
      System.out.println( "I/O error " + e ); // I/O error
    } catch ( ClassNotFoundException e2 ) {
      System.out.println( e2 ); // unknown type of response object
    }
  }
}
```

Just like the server, Client creates the pair of object streams. It sends a DateRequest
and prints the response; it then sends a MyCalculation object and prints the response.
Finally, it closes the connection. On both the client and the server, we call the
flush() method after each call to writeObject(). This method forces the system to
send any buffered data; it's important because it ensures that the other side sees the

entire request before we wait for a response. When the client closes the connection, our server catches the EOFException that is thrown and ends the session. Alternatively, our client could write a special object, perhaps null, to end the session; the server could watch for this item in its main loop.

The order in which we construct the object streams is important. We create the output streams first because the constructor of an ObjectInputStream tries to read a header from the stream to make sure that the InputStream really is an object stream. If we tried to create both of our input streams first, we would deadlock waiting for the other side to write the headers.

Finally, we run the example, giving it a port number as an argument:

```
% java Server 1234
```

Then we run the Client, telling it the server's hostname and port number:

```
% java Client flatland 1234
```

The result should look something like this:

```
Sun Mar 3 14:25:25 PDT 2002
4
```

All right, the result isn't that impressive, but it's easy to imagine more substantial applications. Imagine that you need to perform some complex computation on many large datasets. Using serialized objects makes maintenance of the data objects natural and sending them over the wire trivial. There is no need to deal with byte-level protocols at all.

Limitations

There is one catch in this scenario: both the client and server need access to the necessary classes. That is, all the Request classes—including MyCalculation, which is really the property of the Client—have to be in the classpath on both the client and the server machines. As we hinted earlier, in the next section we'll see that it's possible to send the Java bytecode along with serialized objects to allow completely new kinds of objects to be transported over the network dynamically. We could create this solution on our own, adding to the earlier example using a network class loader to load the classes for us. But we don't have to: Java's RMI facility handles that for us. The ability to send both serialized data and class definitions over the network is not always needed but it makes Java a powerful tool for developing advanced distributed applications.

Remote Method Invocation

The most fundamental means of interobject communication in Java is method invocation. Mechanisms such as the Java event model are built on simple method invocations between objects in the same virtual machine. Therefore, when we want to communicate between virtual machines on different hosts, it's natural to want a mechanism with similar capabilities and semantics. Java's Remote Method Invocation (RMI) mechanism does just that. It lets us get a reference to an object on a remote host and use it as if it were in our own virtual machine. RMI lets us invoke methods on remote objects, passing real Java objects as arguments and getting real Java objects as returned values.

Remote invocation is nothing new. For many years C programmers have used remote procedure calls (RPC) to execute a C function on a remote host and return the results. The primary difference between RPC and RMI is that RPC, being an off-shoot of the C language, is primarily concerned with data structures. It's relatively easy to pack up data and ship it around, but for Java, that's not enough. In Java we don't just work with data structures; we work with objects that contain both data and methods for operating on the data. Not only do we have to be able to ship the state of an object (the data) over the wire, but the recipient has to be able to interact with the object (use its methods) after receiving it. With Java RMI, you can work with network services in an object-oriented fashion, using real, extensible types.

It should be no surprise that RMI uses object serialization, which allows us to send graphs of objects (objects and all the connected objects that they reference). When necessary, RMI can also use dynamic class loading and the security manager to transport Java classes safely. So, in addition to making remote method calls almost as easy to use as local calls, RMI also makes it possible to ship both data and behavior (code) around the Net.

Remote and Nonremote Objects

Before an object can be used remotely through RMI, it must be serializable. But that's not sufficient. Remote objects in RMI are real distributed objects. As the name suggests, a remote object can be an object on a different machine, or it can be an object on the local host. The term *remote* means that the object is used through a special kind of object interface that can be passed over the network. Like normal Java objects, remote objects are passed by reference. Regardless of where the reference is used, the method invocation occurs at the original object, which still lives on its original host. If a remote host returns a reference to one of its remote objects to you, you can call the object's methods; the actual method invocations happen on the remote host, where the object resides.

Nonremote objects are simpler; they're just normal serializable objects. (You can pass these over the network as we did in the previous section "A Simple Object-Based Server.") The catch is that when you pass a nonremote object over the network, it is simply copied, so references to the object on one host are not the same as those on the remote host. Nonremote objects are passed by copy (as opposed to by reference). This may be acceptable for many kinds of data-oriented objects in your application, such as the client requests and server responses in our previous example.

Stubs and skeletons

No, we're not talking about a gruesome horror movie. Stubs and skeletons are used in the implementation of remote objects. When you invoke a method on a remote object (which could be on a different host), you are actually calling some local code that serves as a proxy for that object. This is the stub. (It is called a *stub* because it is something like a truncated placeholder for the object.) The *skeleton* is another proxy that lives with the real object on its original host. It receives remote method invocations from the stub and passes them to the object.

After you create stubs and skeletons you never have to work with them directly; they are hidden from you (in the closet, so to speak). Stubs and skeletons for your remote objects are created by running the *rmic* (RMI compiler) utility. After compiling your Java source files normally, you run *rmic* on the remote object classes as a second pass. It's easy; we'll show you how in the following examples.

Remote interfaces

Remote objects are objects that implement a special *remote interface* that specifies which of the object's methods can be invoked remotely. The remote interface must be explicitly created, and it must extend the java.rmi.Remote interface. Your remote object then implements its remote interface, as does the stub object that is automatically generated for it. In the rest of your code, you should then refer to the remote object as an instance of the remote interface—not as an instance of its actual class. Because both the real object and stub implement the remote interface, they are equivalent as far as we are concerned (for method invocation); locally, we never have to worry about whether we have a reference to a stub or to an actual object. This "type equivalence" means that we can use normal language features such as casting, with remote objects. Of course public fields (variables) of the remote object are not accessible through an interface, so you must make accessor methods if you want to manipulate the remote object's fields.

All methods in the remote interface must declare that they can throw the exception java.rmi.RemoteException. This exception (or one of its subclasses) is thrown when any kind of networking error happens, for example, a server crash, a network failure, or a request for an unavailable object.

Here's a simple example of the remote interface that defines the behavior of RemoteObject; we give it two methods that can be invoked remotely, both of which return some kind of Widget object:

```
import java.rmi.*;

public interface RemoteObject extends Remote {
    public Widget doSomething( ) throws RemoteException;
    public Widget doSomethingElse( ) throws RemoteException;
}
```

The UnicastRemoteObject class

The actual implementation of a remote object (not the interface we discussed previously) usually extends java.rmi.server.UnicastRemoteObject. This is the RMI equivalent to the familiar Object class. When a subclass of UnicastRemoteObject is constructed, the RMI runtime system automatically "exports" it to start listening for network connections from remote interfaces (stubs) for the object. Like java.lang.Object, this superclass also provides implementations of equals(), hashcode(), and toString() that make sense for a remote object.

Here's a remote object class that implements the RemoteObject interface; we haven't shown implementations for the two methods or the constructor:

```
public class MyRemoteObject implements RemoteObject
        extends java.rmi.UnicastRemoteObject
{
    public RemoteObjectImpl( ) throws RemoteException {...}
    public Widget doSomething( ) throws RemoteException {...}
    public Widget doSomethingElse( ) throws RemoteException {...}
    // other non-public methods
    ...
}
```

This class can have as many additional methods as it needs; presumably, most of them will be private, but that isn't strictly necessary. We have to supply a constructor explicitly, even if the constructor does nothing, because the constructor (like any method) can throw a RemoteException; we therefore can't use the default constructor.

What if we can't or don't want to make our remote object implementation a subclass of UnicastRemoteObject? Suppose, for example, that it has to be a subclass of BankAccount or some other special base type for our system. Well, we can simply take over the job of exporting the object ourselves, using the static method exportObject() of UnicastRemoteObject. The exportObject() method takes as an argument a Remote interface and accomplishes what the UnicastRemoteObject constructor normally does for us. It returns as a value the remote object's client stub. However, you will normally not do anything with this directly. In the next section, we'll discuss how to get stubs to your client through the RMI registry (a lookup service).

Normally, exported objects listen on individual ephemeral (randomly assigned) port numbers by default. (This is implementation-dependent.) You can control the port number allocation explicitly by exporting your objects using another form of UnicastRemoteObject.exportObject(), which takes both a Remote interface and a port number as arguments.

Finally, the name UnicastRemoteObject begs the question, "What other kinds of remote objects are there?" Right now, none. It's possible that Sun will develop remote objects using other protocols or multicast techniques in the future.

The RMI registry

The registry is the RMI phone book. You use the registry to look up a reference to a registered remote object on another host. We've already described how remote references can be passed back and forth by remote method calls. But the registry is needed to bootstrap the process: the client needs some way of looking up some initial object.

The registry is implemented by a class called Naming and an application called rmiregistry. This application must be running on the local host before you start a Java program that uses the registry. You can then create instances of remote objects and bind them to particular names in the registry. (Remote objects that bind themselves to the registry sometimes provide a main() method for this purpose.) A registry name can be anything you choose; it takes the form of a slash-separated path. When a client object wants to find your object, it constructs a special URL with the rmi: protocol, the hostname, and the object name. On the client, the RMI Naming class then talks to the registry and returns the remote object reference.

So, which objects need to register themselves with the registry? Well, initially this can be any object the client has no other way of finding. But a call to a remote method can return another remote object without using the registry. Likewise, a call to a remote method can have another remote object as its argument, without requiring the registry. So you could design your system such that only one object registers itself and then serves as a factory for any other remote objects you need. In other words, it wouldn't be hard to build a simple object request "bouncer" (we won't say "broker") that returns references to all the remote objects your application uses. Depending on how you structure your application, this may happen naturally anyway.

The RMI registry is just one implementation of a lookup mechanism for remote objects. It is not very sophisticated, and lookups tend to be slow. It is not intended to be a general-purpose directory service but simply to bootstrap RMI communications. More generally, the Java Naming and Directory service (JNDI) can be used as a frontend to other name services that can provide this service. It is used with RMI as part of the Enterprise Java Beans APIs. The factory registry that we mentioned is also extremely flexible and useful.

An RMI Example

The first example using RMI is a duplication of the simple serialized object protocol from the previous section. We make a remote RMI object called MyServer on which we can invoke methods to get a Date object or execute a WorkRequest object. First, we define our Remote interface:

```
//file: ServerRemote.java
import java.rmi.*;
import java.util.*;
```

```
public interface ServerRemote extends Remote {
    Date getDate( ) throws RemoteException;
    Object execute( WorkRequest work ) throws RemoteException;
}
```

The `ServerRemote` interface extends the `java.rmi.Remote` interface, which identifies objects that implement it as remote objects. We supply two methods that take the place of our old protocol: `getDate()` and `execute()`.

Next, we implement this interface in a class called `MyServer` that defines the bodies of these methods. (Note that a more common convention for naming the implementation of remote interfaces is to append `Impl` to the class name. Using that convention `MyServer` would instead be named something like `ServerImpl`.)

```
//file: MyServer.java
import java.rmi.*;
import java.util.*;

public class MyServer
    extends java.rmi.server.UnicastRemoteObject
    implements ServerRemote {

    public MyServer( ) throws RemoteException { }

    // implement the ServerRemote interface
    public Date getDate( ) throws RemoteException {
        return new Date( );
    }

    public Object execute( WorkRequest work )
      throws RemoteException {
        return work.execute( );
    }

    public static void main(String args[]) {
        try {
            ServerRemote server = new MyServer( );
            Naming.rebind("NiftyServer", server);
        } catch (java.io.IOException e) {
            // problem registering server
        }
    }
}
```

`MyServer` extends `java.rmi.UnicastRemoteObject`, so when we create an instance of `MyServer`, it is automatically exported and starts listening to the network. We start by providing a constructor, which must throw `RemoteException`, accommodating errors that might occur in exporting an instance. Next, `MyServer` implements the methods of the remote interface `ServerRemote`. These methods are straightforward.

The last method in this class is `main()`. This method lets the object set itself up as a server. `main()` creates an instance of the `MyServer` object and then calls the static method `Naming.rebind()` to place the object in the registry. The arguments to `rebind()` include the name of the remote object in the registry (`NiftyServer`)—which clients use to look up the object—and a reference to the server object itself. We could have called `bind()` instead, but `rebind()` is less prone to problems: if there's already a `NiftyServer` registered, `rebind()` replaces it.

We wouldn't need the `main()` method or this `Naming` business if we weren't expecting clients to use the registry to find the server. That is, we could omit `main()` and still use this object as a remote object. We would be limited to passing the object in method invocations or returning it from method invocations—but that could be part of a factory registry, as we discussed before.

Now we need our client:

```java
//file: MyClient.java
import java.rmi.*;
import java.util.*;

public class MyClient {

    public static void main(String [] args)
        throws RemoteException {
        new MyClient( args[0] );
    }

    public MyClient(String host) {
        try {
            ServerRemote server = (ServerRemote)
                Naming.lookup("rmi://"+host+"/NiftyServer");
            System.out.println( server.getDate( ) );
            System.out.println(
                server.execute( new MyCalculation(2) ) );
        } catch (java.io.IOException e) {
            // I/O Error or bad URL
        } catch (NotBoundException e) {
            // NiftyServer isn't registered
        }
    }
}
```

When we run `MyClient`, we pass it the hostname of the server on which the registry is running. The `main()` method creates an instance of the `MyClient` object, passing the hostname from the command line as an argument to the constructor.

The constructor for `MyClient` uses the hostname to construct a URL for the object. The URL looks something like this: *rmi://hostname/NiftyServer*. (Remember, `NiftyServer` is the name under which we registered our `ServerRemote`.) We pass the URL to the static `Naming.lookup()` method. If all goes well, we get back a reference to a `ServerRemote` (the remote interface). The registry has no idea what kind of object it will return; `lookup()` therefore returns an `Object`, which we must cast to `ServerRemote`.

Compile all the code. Then run *rmic* to make the stub and skeleton files for `MyServer`:

```
% rmic MyServer
```

Let's run the code. For the first pass, we assume you have all the class files, including the stubs and skeletons generated by *rmic*, available in the classpath on both the client and server machines. (You can run this example on a single host to test it if you want.) Make sure your classpath is correct, start the registry, and then start the server:

```
% rmiregistry &     (on Windows: start rmiregistry)
% java MyServer
```

In each case, make sure the registry application has the classpath including your server classes so that it can load the stub class. (Be warned: we're going to tell you to do the opposite later as part of setting up the dynamic class loading!)

Finally, on the client machine, run `MyClient`, passing the hostname of the server:

```
% java MyClient myhost
```

The client should print the date and the number 4, which the server graciously calculated. Hooray! With just a few lines of code, you have created a powerful client/server application.

Dynamic class loading

Before running the example, we told you to distribute all the class files to both the client and server machines. However, RMI was designed to ship classes, in addition to data, around the network; you shouldn't have to distribute all the classes in advance. Let's go a step further and have RMI load classes for us, as needed. This involves several steps.

First, we need to tell RMI where to find any other classes it needs. We can use the system property `java.rmi.server.codebase` to specify a URL on a web server (or FTP server) when we run our client or server. This URL specifies the location of a JAR file or a base directory where RMI begins its search for classes. When RMI sends a serialized object (i.e., an object's data) to some client, it also sends this URL. If the recipient needs the class file in addition to the data, it fetches the file at the specified URL. In addition to stub classes, other classes referenced by remote objects in the application can be loaded dynamically. Therefore, we don't have to distribute many class files to the client; we can let the client download them as necessary. In Figure 12-3, we see an example as `MyClient` is going to the registry to get a reference to the `ServerRemote` object. Then `MyClient` dynamically downloads the stub class for `MyServer` from a web server running on the server object's host.

We can now split our class files between the server and client machines. For example, we could withhold the `MyCalculation` class from the server since it really belongs

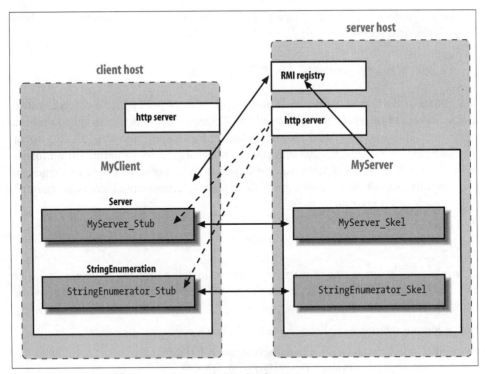

Figure 12-3. RMI applications and dynamic class loading

to the client. Instead, we can make the `MyCalculation` class available via a web server on some machine (probably our client's) and specify the URL when we run `MyClient`:

```
% java -Djava.rmi.server.codebase='http://myserver/foo/' ...
```

Note that the trailing slash in the codebase URL is important: it says that the location is a base directory that contains the class files. In this case, we would expect that `MyCalculation` would be accessible at the URL *http://myserver/foo/MyCalculation. class*.

Next we have to set up security. Since we are loading class files over the network and executing their methods, we must have a security manager in place to restrict the kinds of things those classes may do, at least in the case where they are not coming from a trusted code source. RMI will not load any classes dynamically unless a security manager is installed. One easy way to meet this condition is to install the `RMISecurityManager` as the system security manager for your application. It is an example security manager that works with the default system policy and imposes some basic restrictions on what downloaded classes can do. To install the `RMISecurityManager`, simply add the following line to the beginning of the `main()`

method of both the client and server applications (yes, we'll be sending code both ways in the next section):

```
main( ) {
    System.setSecurityManager( new RMISecurityManager( ) );
    ...
```

The RMISecurityManager works with the system security policy file to enforce restrictions. So you have to provide a policy file that allows the client and server to do basic operations like make network connections. Unfortunately allowing all the operations needed to load classes dynamically requires listing a lot of permission information and we don't want to get into that here. So we're going to resort to suggesting that for this example you simply grant the code all permissions. Here is an example policy file—call it *mysecurity.policy*:

```
grant {
    permission java.security.AllPermission ;
};
```

(It's exceedingly lame, not to mention risky, to install a security manager and then tell it to enforce no real security, but we're more interested in looking at the networking code at the moment.)

So, to run our MyServer application we would run a command like this:

```
% java -Djava.rmi.server.codebase='http://myserver/foo/'
    -Djava.security.policy=mysecurity.policy MyServer
```

Finally, there is one last magic incantation required to enable dynamic class loading. As of the current implementation, the rmiregistry must be run without the classes that are to be loaded being in its classpath. If the classes are in the classpath of rmiregistry, it does not annotate the serialized objects with the URLs of their class files, and no classes are dynamically loaded. This limitation is really annoying; all we can say is to heed the warning for now.

If you meet these conditions, you should be able to get the client started with only the MyClient class and the ServerRemote remote interface. All the other classes are loaded dynamically from a remote location.

Passing remote object references

So far, we haven't done anything that we couldn't have done with the simple object protocol. We used only one remote object, MyServer, and we got its reference from the RMI registry. Now we extend our example to pass some remote references between the client and server, allowing additional remote calls in both directions. We'll add two methods to our remote ServerRemote interface:

```
public interface ServerRemote extends Remote {

    ...
    StringIterator getList( ) throws RemoteException;
```

```
    void asyncExecute( WorkRequest work, WorkListener listener )
        throws RemoteException;
}
```

getList() retrieves a new kind of object from the server: a StringIterator. The
StringIterator is a simple list of strings, with some methods for accessing the strings
in order. We make it a remote object, so that implementations of StringIterator
stay on the server.

Next we spice up our work request feature by adding an asyncExecute() method.
asyncExecute() lets us hand off a WorkRequest object as before, but it does the calculation on its own time. The return type for asyncExecute() is void because it doesn't
actually return a value; we get the result later. Along with the request, our client
passes a reference to a WorkListener object that is to be notified when the
WorkRequest is done. We'll have our client implement WorkListener itself.

Because this is to be a remote object, our interface must extend Remote, and its methods must throw RemoteExceptions:

```
//file: StringIterator.java
import java.rmi.*;

public interface StringIterator extends Remote {
    public boolean hasNext( ) throws RemoteException;
    public String next( ) throws RemoteException;
}
```

Next, we provide a simple implementation of StringIterator, called
MyStringIterator:

```
//file: MyStringIterator.java
import java.rmi.*;

public class MyStringIterator
  extends java.rmi.server.UnicastRemoteObject
  implements StringIterator {

    String [] list;
    int index = 0;

    public MyStringIterator( String [] list )
      throws RemoteException {
        this.list = list;
    }
    public boolean hasNext( ) throws RemoteException {
        return index < list.length;
    }
    public String next( ) throws RemoteException {
        return list[index++];
    }
}
```

MyStringIterator extends UnicastRemoteObject. Its methods are simple: it can give you the next string in the list, and it can tell you if there are any strings you haven't seen yet.

Next, we define the WorkListener remote interface. This is the interface that defines how an object should listen for a completed WorkRequest. It has one method, workCompleted(), which the server executing a WorkRequest calls when the job is done:

```
//file: WorkListener.java
import java.rmi.*;

public interface WorkListener extends Remote {
    public void workCompleted(WorkRequest request, Object result )
        throws RemoteException;
}
```

Next, let's add the new features to MyServer. We need to add implementations of the getList() and asyncExecute() methods, which we just added to the ServerRemote interface:

```
public class MyServer extends java.rmi.server.UnicastRemoteObject
                    implements ServerRemote {
  ...
  public StringIterator getList( ) throws RemoteException {
    return new MyStringIterator(
        new String [] { "Foo", "Bar", "Gee" } );
  }

  public void asyncExecute(
      WorkRequest request , WorkListener listener )
      throws java.rmi.RemoteException {

      // should really do this in another thread
      Object result = request.execute( );
      listener.workCompleted( request, result );
  }
}
```

getList() just returns a StringIterator with some stuff in it. asyncExecute() calls a WorkRequest's execute() method and notifies the listener when it's done.

Note that our implementation of asyncExecute() is a little cheesy. If we were forming a more complex calculation we would want to start a thread to do the calculation and return immediately from asyncExecute(), so the client won't block. The thread would call workCompleted() at a later time, when the computation was done. In this simple example, it would probably take longer to start the thread than to perform the calculation.

We have to modify MyClient to implement the remote WorkListener interface. This turns MyClient into a remote object, so we must make it a UnicastRemoteObject. We also add the workCompleted() method the WorkListener interface requires.

```
public class MyClient
  extends java.rmi.server.UnicastRemoteObject
  implements WorkListener {
    ...
    public void workCompleted( WorkRequest request, Object result)
      throws RemoteException {
        System.out.println("Async work result = " + result);
    }
}
```

Finally, we want MyClient to exercise the new features. Add these lines after the calls to getDate() and execute():

```
// MyClient constructor
    ...
StringIterator se = server.getList( );
while ( se.hasNext( ) )
    System.out.println( se.next( ) );

server.asyncExecute( new MyCalculation(100), this );
```

We use getList() to get the iterator from the server, then loop, printing the strings. We also call asyncExecute() to perform another calculation; this time, we square the number 100. The second argument to asyncExecute() is the WorkListener to notify when the data is ready; we pass a reference to ourselves (this).

Now all we have to do is compile everything and run *rmic* to make the stubs for all our remote objects:

% rmic MyClient MyServer MyStringIterator

Restart the RMI registry and MyServer on your server, and run the client somewhere. You should get the following:

```
Sun Mar 3 23:57:19 PDT 2002
4
Foo
Bar
Gee
Async work result = 10000
```

If you are experimenting with dynamic class loading, you should be able to have the client download all the server's auxiliary classes (the stubs and the StringIterator) from a web server. And, conversely, you should be able to have the MyServer download the Client stub and WorkRequest related classes when it needs them.

We hope that this introduction has given you a feel for the tremendous power that RMI offers through object serialization and dynamic class loading. Java is one of the first programming languages to offer this kind of powerful framework for distributed applications.

RMI Object Activation

One of the newer features of RMI is the ability to create remote objects that are persistent. They can save their state for arbitrary periods of inactivity and be reactivated when a request from a client arrives. This is an important feature for large systems with remote objects that must remain accessible across long periods of time. RMI activation effectively allows a remote object to be stored away—in a database, for example—and automatically reincarnated when it is needed. RMI activation is not particularly easy to use and would not have benefited us in any of our simple examples; we won't delve into it here. Much of the functionality of activatable objects can be achieved by using factories of shorter-lived objects that know how to retrieve some state from a database (or other location). The primary users of RMI activation may be systems such as Enterprise JavaBeans, which need a generalized mechanism to save remotely accessible objects and revive them at later times.

RMI and CORBA

Java supports an important alternative to RMI, called CORBA (Common Object Request Broker Architecture). We won't say much about CORBA here, but you should know that it exists. CORBA is a distributed object standard developed by the Object Management Group (OMG), of which Sun Microsystems is one of the founding members. Its major advantage is that it works across languages: a Java program can use CORBA to talk to objects written in other languages, like C or C++. This is may be a considerable advantage if you want to build a Java frontend for an older program that you can't afford to reimplement. CORBA also provides other services similar to those in the Java Enterprise APIs. CORBA's major disadvantages are that it's complex, inelegant, and somewhat arcane.

Sun and OMG have been making efforts to bridge RMI and CORBA. There is an implementation of RMI that can use IIOP (the Internet Inter-Object Protocol) to allow some RMI-to-CORBA interoperability. However, CORBA currently does not have many of the semantics necessary to support true RMI-style distributed objects. So this solution is somewhat limited at this writing.

Scaleable I/O with NIO

We'll now wrap up the discussion of the NIO package we began in Chapter 10 by talking about nonblocking and selectable network communications. All our server examples in this chapter have used a thread-bound pattern (one thread per I/O operation). In Java this is very natural because of the ease with which we can create threads. It's also very efficient, within limits. Problems arise when you try to build very large scale servers using this style of client handling. While on a large machine it's certainly possible to have hundreds or even thousands of threads (especially if they're mostly idle, waiting for I/O), this is a resource-hungry solution. Every thread you start in Java consumes memory for its internal stack, and the performance of managing this number of threads is highly system-dependent.

An alternative approach is to take a lesson from the old, dark days before threading was available and to use nonblocking I/O operations to manage a lot of communications from a single thread. Better yet, our server will use a configurable pool of threads, taking advantage of machines with many processors.

At the heart of this process is the concept of selectable I/O. It's not good enough to simply have nonblocking I/O operations if you have no way to efficiently poll for work to be done. The NIO package provides for efficient polling using selectable channels. A selectable channel allows for the registration of a special kind of listener called a *selector* that can check the readiness of the channel for operations such as reading and writing or accepting or creating network connections.

The selector and the selection process are not typical Java listeners of the kind we'll see elsewhere in this book, but instead rather slavishly follow the conventions of C language systems. This is mainly for performance reasons; since this API is primarily intended for high-volume servers it is bound very tightly to the traditional, underlying operating system facilities with less regard for ease of use. This, combined with the other details of using the NIO package, mean that this section is somewhat dense and the server we create here is one of the longer and more complex examples in the book. Don't be discouraged if you are a bit put off by this section. You can use the general techniques earlier in this chapter for most applications and reserve this knowledge for creating services that handle very high volumes of simultaneous client requests.

Selectable Channels

A selectable channel implements the SelectableChannel interface, which specifies that the channel can be set to a nonblocking mode and that it provides support for the select process that makes efficient polling possible. In Java 1.4, the primary selectable channels are those for working with the network: SocketChannel, ServerSocketChannel, and DatagramChannel. The only other selectable channel is the Pipe (which can be used in an analogous way for intra-VM communication).

At the heart of the process is the Selector object, which knows about a particular set of selectable channels and provides a select() method for determining their readiness for I/O operations. Conceptually the process is simple; you register one or more channels with a selector and then poll it, asking it to tell you which set of channels is ready to go. In actuality, there are a few additional pieces involved.

First, the Selector does not work directly with channels but instead operates on SelectionKey objects. A SelectionKey object is created implicitly when the channel is registered with the Selector. It encapsulates the selectable channel as well as information about what types of operations (e.g., read, write) we are interested in waiting for. That information is held in the SelectionKey in a set of flags called the *interest set*, which can be changed by the application at any time. SelectionKeys are also used to return the results of a select operation. Each call to select() returns the set of SelectionKeys that are ready for some type of I/O. Each key also has a set of flags called the *ready set* that indicates which operation of interest is actually ready (possibly more than one). For example, a SelectionKey interest set might indicate that we want to know when its channel is ready for reading or writing. After a select operation, if that key is in the set returned by the selector, we know that it is ready for one or more of those operations, and we can check the key's ready set to see which.

Before we go on we should say that although we have been saying that channels are registered with selectors, the API is (confusingly) the other way around. Selectors are actually registered with the channels they manage, but it's better to mentally spackle over this and think of them the other way around.

Using Select

A Selector object is created using the Selector.open() method (Selector uses a factory pattern).

```
Selector selector = Selector.open();
```

To register one or more channels with the selector, set them to nonblocking mode:

```
SelectableChannel channelA = // ...
channelA.configureBlocking( false );
```

Now register the channels:

```
int interestOps = SelectionKey.OP_READ | SelectionKey.OP_WRITE;
SelectionKey key = channelA.register( selector, interestOps );
```

When we register the channel we have an opportunity to set the initial interest operations (or "interest ops"). These are defined by constant fields in the SelectionKey class:

OP_READ	Ready to read
OP_WRITE	Ready to write
OP_CONNECT	Client socket connection ready
OP_ACCEPT	Server socket connection ready

These fields are bit flags; you can OR them together as in the above example to express interest in more than one type of operation.

The result of the register() method is a SelectionKey object. We can use the key to change the interest ops at any time with the SelectionKey interestOps() method or to deregister the channel from the Selector with the key's cancel() method.

This same key is also returned as the result of selection operations when its channel is ready. When the SelectionKey is returned, its ready set holds flags for the operations that do not block if called. We can retrieve the value of the flags with the readySet() method. There are also convenience methods to test for each operation in the ready set: isReadable(), isWritable(), isConnectable() and isAcceptable().

Depending on how you structure your application, it may not be necessary to save the SelectionKey at registration time. In our example, we let the Selector keep track of the keys for us, simply using them when they are ready. In fact, we go even further and put the SelectionKey to work by asking it to hold a reference for us! The SelectionKey attach() method is a convenience that can attach an arbitrary object to the key for use by our application. We'll show you how this can be useful in a bit.

Once one or more channels are registered with the Selector we can perform a select operation using one of its select() methods.

```
int readyCount = selector.select( );
```

Without arguments, the method blocks until at least one channel is ready for some operation or until the Selector's wakeup() method is called. Alternately you can use the form of select() that takes a timeout (in milliseconds) to wait for a ready channel before returning. There is also selectNow(), which always returns immediately. Each of these returns the count of the number of ready channels.

You can use the blocking select() and wakeup() somewhat like wait() and notify(). The wakeup is necessary because once a selection is started, it will not see any changes to its key's interest ops until the next invocation. The Selector is also heavily synchronized; for example, calls to register new channels block until the select is finished. So often it's much easier to simply use select with a short timeout and a loop, like this:

```
while ( selector.select( 50 ) == 0 );
```

Next we can get the set of ready channels from the Selector with the selectedKeys() method and iterate through them, doing whatever our application dictates:

```
Set readySet = selector.selectedKeys( );
for( Iterator it = readySet.iterator( ); it.hasNext( ); ) {
    SelectionKey key = (SelectionKey)it.next( );
    it.remove( );  // remove the key from the ready set
  // use the key
}
```

The ready set is returned to us as a java.util.Set, which we walk through with an Iterator (see the "Collections" section in Chapter 10). One important thing to note is that we've used the Iterator's remove() method to remove the key from the ready set. The select() methods add keys only to the ready set or add flags to keys already in the set; they never remove them. So we must clear the keys when we handle them. You can get the full set of keys a Selector is managing with the keys() method, but you should not attempt to remove keys from that set; use the cancel() method on individual keys instead. Or you can close the entire Selector with its close() method, de-registering all its keys.

LargerHttpd

Now let's put this information to use. In this section we create the big brother of
TinyHttpd (our minimalist web server) called LargerHttpd. The LargerHttpd server is a
nonblocking web server that uses SocketChannels and a pool of threads to service
requests. In this example, a single thread executes a main loop that accepts new connections and checks the readiness of existing client connections for reading or writing. Whenever a client needs attention, it places the job in a queue where a thread
from our thread pool waits to service it. As we said, this example is a bit longer than
we would like, but is really the minimum necessary to show a realistic usage of the
APIs. Here we go:

```
import java.io.*;
import java.util.*;
import java.net.*;
import java.nio.*;
import java.nio.channels.*;
import java.nio.charset.*;
import java.util.regex.*;

public class LargerHttpd {
    Selector clientSelector;
    ClientQueue readyClients = new ClientQueue( );

    public void run( int port, int threads ) throws IOException {
        clientSelector = Selector.open( );
        ServerSocketChannel ssc = ServerSocketChannel.open( );
        ssc.configureBlocking(false);
        InetSocketAddress sa =
            new InetSocketAddress( InetAddress.getLocalHost( ), port );
        ssc.socket( ).bind( sa );
        ssc.register( clientSelector, SelectionKey.OP_ACCEPT );

        for(int i=0; i<threads; i++)   // create thread pool
            new Thread() { public void run() {
                while (true) try { handleClient(); } catch (IOException e) { }
            } }.start();

        while ( true ) try {     // main select loop
            while ( clientSelector.select(50) == 0 );
            Set readySet = clientSelector.selectedKeys( );
            for( Iterator it = readySet.iterator( ); it.hasNext( ); ) {
                SelectionKey key = (SelectionKey)it.next( );
                it.remove( );
                if ( key.isAcceptable( ) )
                    acceptClient( ssc );
                else {
                    key.interestOps( 0 );
                    readyClients.add( key );
                }
            }
        }
```

```
            } catch ( IOException e ) { System.out.println(e); }
        }

        void acceptClient( ServerSocketChannel ssc ) throws IOException {
            SocketChannel clientSocket = ssc.accept();
            clientSocket.configureBlocking(false);
            SelectionKey key =
                clientSocket.register( clientSelector, SelectionKey.OP_READ );
            HttpdConnection client = new HttpdConnection( clientSocket );
            key.attach( client );
        }

        void handleClient() throws IOException {
            SelectionKey key = (SelectionKey)readyClients.next();
            HttpdConnection client = (HttpdConnection)key.attachment();
            if ( key.isReadable() )
                client.read( key );
            else
                client.write( key );
        }

        public static void main( String argv[] ) throws IOException {
            new LargerHttpd().run( Integer.parseInt(argv[0]) );
        }
    }

    class HttpdConnection {
        static Charset charset = Charset.forName("8859_1");
        static Pattern httpGetPattern = Pattern.compile("(?s)GET /?(\\S*).*");
        SocketChannel clientSocket;
        ByteBuffer buff = ByteBuffer.allocateDirect( 64*1024 );
        String request;
        String response;
        FileChannel file;
        int filePosition;

        HttpdConnection ( SocketChannel clientSocket ) {
            this.clientSocket = clientSocket;
        }

        void read( SelectionKey key ) throws IOException {
            if ( request == null && (clientSocket.read( buff ) == -1
                  || buff.get( buff.position()-1 ) == '\n' ) )
                processRequest( key );
            else
                key.interestOps( SelectionKey.OP_READ );
        }

        void processRequest( SelectionKey key ) {
            buff.flip();
            request = charset.decode( buff ).toString();
            Matcher get = httpGetPattern.matcher( request );
            if ( get.matches() ) {
                request = get.group(1);
```

```
            if ( request.endsWith("/") || request.equals("") )
                request = request + "index.html";
            //System.out.println( "Request: "+request);
            try {
                file = new FileInputStream ( request ).getChannel( );
            } catch ( FileNotFoundException e ) {
                response = "404 Object Not Found";
            }
        } else
            response = "400 Bad Request" ;

        if ( response != null ) {
            buff.clear( );
            charset.newEncoder( ).encode(
                CharBuffer.wrap( response ), buff, true );
            buff.flip( );
        }
        key.interestOps( SelectionKey.OP_WRITE );
    }


    void write( SelectionKey key ) throws IOException {
        if ( response != null ) {
            clientSocket.write( buff );
            if ( buff.remaining( ) == 0 )
                response = null;
        } else if ( file != null ) {
            int remaining = (int)file.size( )-filePosition;
            int got = file.transferTo( filePosition, remaining, clientSocket );
            if ( got == -1 || remaining <= 0 ) {
                file.close( );
                file = null;
            } else
                filePosition += got;
        }
        if ( response == null && file == null ) {
            clientSocket.close( );
            key.cancel( );
        } else
            key.interestOps( SelectionKey.OP_WRITE );
    }
}

class ClientQueue extends ArrayList {
    synchronized void add( SelectionKey key ) {
        super.add(key);
        notify( );
    }
    synchronized SelectionKey next( ) {
        while ( isEmpty( ) )
            try { wait( ); } catch ( InterruptedException e ) { }
        return (SelectionKey)remove(0);
    }
}
```

From a bird's eye view, the structure of LargerHttpd is the same as TinyHttpd. There is the main class, LargerHttpd, which accepts connections, and a connection class, HttpdConnection, which encapsulates a socket and handles the conversation with the client. However this time, instead of each connection object being a Runnable serviced in its own thread, its functionality is broken into two primary methods called read() and write(). The job of our LargerHttpd is to accept new client socket connections, wrap them in an instance of HttpdConnection, and then watch the client's status with a Selector. Whenever we detect that a client is ready for some operation, we place its key into a queue (for which we've created the class ClientQueue). A set of threads waits in the queue, pulling out the keys and calling read() or write() on the corresponding client, based on which operation is ready.

The HttpConnection object encapsulates the state of the conversation with the client. Since its interface is rather coarse, it must keep track of whether it is waiting to read more input, when it's time to generate a response, and when to write output. The HttpdConnection also manages the interest set of its key, so that it can effectively schedule itself to be woken up when it's ready for reading or for writing. The association between the HttpdConnection and the key is made using the key's attach() and attachment() methods. LargerHttpd's acceptClient() method does several things. First, it accepts the new socket connection. Next, it configures and registers it with the selector with an initial interest set for reading. Finally it creates the HttpdConnection object, wrapping the socket, and attaches that object to the key for later retrieval.

The main loop of LargerHttpd is fairly straightforward. First we set up the ServerSocketChannel. This is similar to setting up a plain ServerSocket, except that we must first create an InetSocketAddress object to hold the local address and port combination of our server socket and then explicitly bind or socket to that address with the ServerSocketChannel bind() method. We also configure the server socket to nonblocking mode and register it with our main Selector, so that we can select for client connections in the same loop that we use to select for client read and write readiness.

In the main select loop, we check whether the key is ready for an accept operation and if so we call acceptClient(); if not we set the key's interest set to zero with the interestOps() method and dispatch the key to our queue for work to be done. It's important that we set the interest set to zero to clear it before the next loop; otherwise we'd be in a race to see whether the thread pool performed its maximum work before we detected another ready condition. Setting the interest ops to 0, and resetting it in the HttpdConnection object, combined with synchronization in our ClientQueue object, ensures that only one thread is handling a client at a time.

Prior to entering the main select loop, we start one or more threads, each entering the handleClient() method, which blocks until a key is ready on the queue. (The queue itself simply uses wait() and notify() to block until new keys arrive. See the

Producer/Consumer example in the "Passing Messages" section in Chapter 8.) For each ready key, we retrieve the associated HttpdConnection object and call the appropriate service method based on whether the key is ready for reading or writing. After that, it's up to the connection object to do its job. Each call to the read() method simply does what would be one iteration of a read loop in a thread-bound application. Each read gets as much data as available and checks to see if we've reached the end of a line (a \n newline character). Upon reaching the end of line we dispatch the call to the processRequest() method, which turns the byte buffer into text and uses the same techniques as our TinyHttpd to parse the request into a file pathname. On each incomplete call to read(), we set the interest ops of our key back to OP_READ. Upon completing the read and processing the request, we switch to using OP_WRITE, because we are now ready for sending a response.

The write() method keeps track of whether it's sending a text response (error message) or a file, using the response and file instance variables. When sending a file, we use the FileChannel's transferTo() method to transfer bytes from the file directly to the network socket, without copying them into Java's memory space. (This is indeed an efficient little web server.) And that's about it. When we're done, we close the client socket and cancel our key, which causes it to be removed from the Selector's key set during the next select operation (discarding our HttpdConnection object with it).

Nonblocking Client-Side Operations

Our example showed SocketChannel used for nonblocking, selectable I/O in a typical server application. It's less common to need nonblocking I/O from a client, but there is certainly no reason you can't do it. Perhaps you're writing a peer-to-peer (P2P) application that manages many connections from both sides.

For the client side of communications, there is one additional tool provided: a nonblocking socket-connect operation. The process of creating a TCP connection from the client side involves contacting the remote host in a two-phase acknowledgement. This process normally blocks until the connection is established. However the NIO package provides an alternative that allows you to initiate the connection and then poll for its status. When set to nonblocking mode, a call to a SocketChannel's connect() method returns immediately. The connection is then attempted (and possibly succeeds or fails) in the background. Later, a Selector can be used, checking for the OP_CONNECT flag to see when the socket is ready to "finish connecting." The connection is finished by invoking the SocketChannel's finishConnect() method, which either returns or throws an IOException indicating the failure. The process of finishing the connection is really more about collecting the results of the asynchronous connection—acknowledging its success or failure—than about doing work.

CHAPTER 13

Programming for the Web

When you think about the Web, you probably think of applications—web browsers, web servers—and the many kinds of content that those applications move around the network. But it's important to note that standards and protocols, not the applications themselves, have enabled the Web's growth. Since the earliest days of the Internet, there have been ways to move files from here to there, and document formats that were just as powerful as HTML, but there was not a unifying model for how to identify, retrieve, and display information nor was there a universal way for applications to interact with that data over the network. Since the web explosion began, HTML has reigned supreme as a common format for documents, and most developers have at least some familiarity with it. In this chapter, we're going to talk a bit about its cousin, HTTP, the protocol that handles communications between web clients and servers, and URLs, which provide a standard for naming and addressing objects on the Web. Java provides a very simple API for working with URLs to address objects on the Web. We'll discuss how to write web clients that can interact with the servers using the HTTP GET and POST methods. In Chapter 14, we'll take a look at servlets, simple Java programs that run on web servers and implement the other side of these conversations.

Uniform Resource Locators (URLs)

A URL points to an object on the Internet.* It's a text string that identifies an item, tells you where to find it, and specifies a method for communicating with it or retrieving it from its source. A URL can refer to any kind of information source. It might point to static data, such as a file on a local filesystem, a web server, or an FTP archive; or it can point to a more dynamic object such as a news article on a news

---

* The term URL was coined by the Uniform Resource Identifier (URI) working group of the IETF to distinguish URLs from the more general notion of Uniform Resource Names or URNs (see RFC-2396). Look for the "URLs, URNs, and URIs" section later in this chapter.

spool or a record in a database. URLs can even refer to less tangible resources such as Telnet sessions and mailing addresses.

A URL is usually presented as a string of text, like an address. Since there are many different ways to locate an item on the Net, and different mediums and transports require different kinds of information, there are different formats for different kinds of URLs. The most common form has three components: a network host or server, the name of the item, its location on that host, and a protocol by which the host should communicate:

```
protocol://hostname/path/item-name
```

protocol (also called the "scheme") is an identifier such as http, ftp, or gopher; *hostname* is an Internet hostname; and the *path* and *item* components form a unique path that identifies the object on that host. Variants of this form allow extra information to be packed into the URL, specifying for example, port numbers for the communications protocol and fragment identifiers that reference parts inside the object.

We sometimes speak of a URL that is relative to another URL, called a *base URL*. In that case we are using the base URL as a starting point and supplying additional information. For example, the base URL might point to a directory on a web server; a relative URL might name a particular file in that directory.

The URL Class

Bringing this down to a more concrete level is the Java URL class. The URL class represents a URL address and provides a simple API for accessing web resources, such as documents and applications on servers. It uses an extensible set of protocol and content handlers to perform the necessary communication and even data conversion. With the URL class, an application can open a connection to a server on the network and retrieve content with just a few lines of code. As new types of servers and new formats for content evolve, additional URL handlers can be supplied to retrieve and interpret the data without modifying your applications.

A URL is represented by an instance of the java.net.URL class. A URL object manages all the component information within a URL string and provides methods for retrieving the object it identifies. We can construct a URL object from a URL specification string or from its component parts:

```
try {
    URL aDoc =
        new URL( "http://foo.bar.com/documents/homepage.html" );
    URL sameDoc =
        new URL("http","foo.bar.com","documents/homepage.html");
}
catch ( MalformedURLException e ) { }
```

These two URL objects point to the same network resource, the *homepage.html* document on the server *foo.bar.com*. Whether the resource actually exists and is available isn't known until we try to access it. When initially constructed, the URL object contains only data about the object's location and how to access it. No connection to the server has been made. We can examine the URL's components with the getProtocol(), getHost(), and getFile() methods. We can also compare it to another URL with the sameFile() method (which has an unfortunate name for something which may not point to a file). sameFile() determines whether two URLs point to the same resource. It can be fooled, but sameFile() does more than compare the URLs for equality; it takes into account the possibility that one server may have several names, and other factors. (It doesn't go as far as to fetch the resources and compare them, however.)

When a URL is created, its specification is parsed to identify just the protocol component. If the protocol doesn't make sense, or if Java can't find a protocol handler for it, the URL constructor throws a MalformedURLException. A *protocol handler* is a Java class that implements the communications protocol for accessing the URL resource. For example, given an http URL, Java prepares to use the HTTP protocol handler to retrieve documents from the specified server.

Stream Data

The lowest level and most general way to get data back from a URL is to ask for an InputStream from the URL by calling openStream(). Getting the data as a stream may also be useful if you want to receive continuous updates from a dynamic information source. The drawback is that you have to parse the contents of the byte stream yourself. Not all types of URLs support the openStream() method because not all types of URLs refer to concrete data; you'll get an UnknownServiceException if the URL doesn't.

The following code prints the contents of an HTML file:

```
try {
    URL url = new URL("http://server/index.html");

    BufferedReader bin = new BufferedReader (
        new InputStreamReader( url.openStream( ) ));

    String line;
    while ( (line = bin.readLine( )) != null )
        System.out.println( line );
} catch (Exception e) { }
```

We ask for an InputStream with openStream() and wrap it in a BufferedReader to read the lines of text. Because we specify the http protocol in the URL, we enlist the services of an HTTP protocol handler. As we'll discuss later, that raises some questions about what kinds of handlers are available. This example partially works around those issues because no content handler (only the protocol handler) is involved; we read the data and interpret the content ourselves, by simply printing it.

One note about applets. In the applet environment, you typically have additional security restrictions that limit the URLs to which you may communicate. To be sure that you can access the specified URL and use the correct protocol handler, you should construct URLs relative to the base URL that identifies the applet's *codebase*— the location of the applet code. This insures that any data you load comes via the same protocol and from the same server as your applet itself. For example:

```
new URL( getCodeBase( ), "foo/bar.gif" );
```

Alternately, if you are just trying to get data files or media associated with an applet, there is a more general way; see the discussion of getResource( ) in Chapter 11.

Getting the Content as an Object

As we said previously, reading content from a stream is the most general mechanism for accessing data over the Web. openStream( ) leaves the parsing of data up to you. The URL class supports a more sophisticated, pluggable, content-handling mechanism that we'll discuss now, but be aware that this is not widely used because of lack of standardization and limitations in how you can deploy new handlers. Consider this section to be mainly for educational purposes.

When Java knows the type of content being retrieved from a URL, and a proper content handler is available (installed), you can retrieve the item the URL addresses as a native Java object by calling the URL's getContent( ) method. In this mode of operation, getContent( ) initiates a connection to the host, fetches the data for you, determines the Multipurpose Internet Mail Extensions (MIME) type of the contents, and invokes a content handler to turn the bytes into a Java object. (It acts just as if you had read a serialized Java object, as in Chapter 12). MIME is the standard developed to facilitate multimedia email, but it has become widely used as a general way to specify how to treat data. Java uses MIME to help it pick the right content handler. This sounds good, but generally requires that you supply the correct handlers with your application or install them in the Java runtime environment. Unfortunately, there is not a standard way to do this. (The HotJava web browser provides a mechanism for adding new handlers, but it is not a widely deployed browser, so that doesn't help us much in practical terms.)

For example, given the URL *http://foo.bar.com/index.html*, a call to getContent( )uses the HTTP protocol handler to retrieve data and an HTML content handler to turn the data into an appropriate document object. A URL that points to a plain-text file might use a text-content handler that returns a String object. Similarly, a GIF file might be turned into an ImageProducer object using a GIF content handler. If we access the GIF file using an FTP URL, Java uses the same content handler but uses the FTP protocol handler to receive the data.

getContent( ) returns the output of the content handler but leaves us wondering what kind of object we got. Since the content handler has to be able to return anything, the return type of getContent( ) is Object. In a moment, we'll describe how we could ask the protocol handler about the object's MIME type, which it discovered. Based on this, and whatever other knowledge we have about the kind of object we are expecting, we can cast the Object to its appropriate, more specific type. For example, if we expect a String, we'll cast the result of getContent( ) to a String:

```
try {
    String content = (String)myURL.getContent( );
} catch ( ClassCastException e ) { ... }
```

Various kinds of errors can occur when trying to retrieve the data. For example, getContent( ) can throw an IOException if there is a communications error. Other kinds of errors can occur at the application level: some knowledge of how the application-specific content and protocol handlers deal with errors is necessary. One problem that could arise is that a content handler for the data's MIME type wouldn't be available. In this case, getContent( ) invokes a special "unknown type" handler that returns the data as a raw InputStream. A sophisticated application might interpret this behavior and try to decide what to do with the data on its own.

In some situations, we may also need knowledge of the protocol handler. For example, consider a URL that refers to a nonexistent file on an HTTP server. When requested, the server returns the familiar "404 Not Found" message. To deal with protocol-specific operations like this, we may need to talk to the protocol handler, which we'll discuss next.

The openStream( ) and getContent( ) methods both implicitly create the connection to the remote URL object. When the connection is set up, the protocol handler is consulted to create a URLConnection object. The URLConnection manages the protocol-specific communications. We can get a URLConnection for our URL with the openConnection( ) method. One of the things we can do with the URLConnection is ask for the object's content type. For example:

```
URLConnection connection = myURL.openConnection( );
String mimeType = connection.getContentType( );
...
Object contents = myURL.getContents( );
```

We can also get protocol-specific information. Different protocols provide different types of URLConnection objects. The HttpURLConnection object, for instance, can interpret the "404 Not Found" message and tell us about the problem. We'll talk more about the HttpURLConnection later in this chapter.

Handlers in Practice

The content- and protocol-handler mechanisms we've described are very flexible; to handle new types of URLs, you need only add the appropriate handler classes. One interesting application of this would be Java-based web browsers that could handle new and specialized kinds of URLs by downloading them over the Net. The idea for this was touted since the earliest days of Java. Unfortunately, it has never come to fruition. There is no API for dynamically downloading new content and protocol handlers. In fact, there is no standard API for determining what content and protocol handlers exist on a given platform. Although content and protocol handlers are part of the Java API and an intrinsic part of the mechanism for working with URLs, specific content and protocol handlers aren't defined. The standard Java classes don't, for example, include content handlers for HTML, GIF, MPEG, or other common data types. Sun's SDK and all of the other Java environments do come with these kinds of handlers, but these are installed on an application-level basis and not documented.

There are two real issues here:

- There isn't a standard that says that certain types of handlers have to be provided in each environment along with the core Java API. Instead we have to rely on the application to decide what kinds of data types it needs. This may make sense but is frustrating when it should be reasonable to expect certain basic types to be handled in all environments.

- There isn't any standard that tells you what kind of object the content handler should return. Maybe GIF data should be returned as an ImageProducer object, but at the moment, that's an application-level decision. If you're writing your own application and your own content handlers, that isn't an issue: you can make any decision you want. (In practical terms, few developers take this approach.) But if you're writing content handlers that are to be used by arbitrary applications you need to know what they expect.

The HotJava web browser supports the content and protocol handler mechanism, and you can install handlers locally (as for all Java applications), but other web browsers such as Netscape and Internet Explorer do not directly support handlers at all. You can install them for use in your own (perhaps intranet-based) applets but you cannot use them to extend the capabilities of the browser. Netscape and Internet Explorer are currently classic monolithic applications: knowledge about certain kinds of objects, like HTML and GIF files, is built in. These browsers can be extended via a plug-in mechanism, which is a much less fine-grained and powerful approach than Java's handler mechanism. If you're writing applets for use in Netscape or Internet Explorer now, about all you can do is use the openStream() method to get a raw input stream from which to read data.

Other Handler Frameworks

The idea of dynamically downloadable handlers could also be applied to other kinds of handler-like components. For example, the Java XML community is fond of referring to XML as a way to apply semantics to documents and to Java as a portable way to supply the behavior that goes along with those semantics. It's possible that an XML viewer could be built with downloadable handlers for displaying XML tags.

The JavaBeans APIs also touch upon this subject with the Java Activation Framework. The JAF provides a way to detect the type of a stream of data and "encapsulate access to it" in a JavaBean. If this sounds suspiciously like the content handler's job, it is. Unfortunately, it looks like these APIs will not be merged and, outside of the Java Mail API, the JAF has not been widely used.

Writing Content and Protocol Handlers

Although content and protocol handlers are used fairly extensively in Java, they have not been leveraged very much by developers for their own applications. We discussed some of the reasons for this earlier. But, if you're adventurous and want to try leveraging content and protocol handlers in your own applications, you can find all the information you'll need in Appendix A, which covers creating and installing your own handlers.

Talking to Web Applications

Web browsers are the universal clients for web applications. They retrieve documents for display and serve as a user interface, primarily through the use of HTML forms and links. In the remainder of this chapter, we will show how to write client-side Java code that uses HTTP through the URL class to work with web applications directly. There are many reasons an application (or applet) might want to communicate in this way. For example, compatibility with another browser-based application might be important, or you might need to gain access to a server through a firewall where direct socket connections (and hence RMI) are not available. HTTP has become the lingua franca of the Net and despite its limitations (or more likely because of its simplicity), it has rapidly become one of the most widely supported protocols in the world. As for using Java on the client side, all the other reasons you would write a client GUI application (as opposed to a pure Web/HTML-based application) also present themselves. A client-side GUI can do sophisticated presentation and validation while, with the techniques presented here, still use web-enabled services over the network.

The primary task we discuss here is sending data to the server, specifically HTML form-encoded data. In a web browser, the name/value pairs of HTML form fields are encoded in a special format and sent to the server using one of two methods. The first method, using the HTTP command GET, encodes the user's input into the URL and requests the corresponding document. The server recognizes that the first part of the URL refers to a program and invokes it, passing along the information encoded in the URL as a parameter. The second method uses the HTTP command POST to ask the server to accept the encoded data and pass it to a web application as a stream. In

Java, we can create a URL that refers to a server-side program and send it data using either the GET or POST methods. (In Chapter 14 we'll see how to build web applications that implement the other side of this conversation.)

Using the GET Method

Using the GET method of encoding data in a URL is pretty easy. All we have to do is create a URL pointing to a server program and use a simple convention to tack on the encoded name/value pairs that make up our data. For example, the following code snippet opens a URL to a CGI program called *login.cgi* on the server *myhost* and passes it two name/value pairs. It then prints whatever text the CGI sends back:

```
URL url = new URL(
    // this string should be URL-encoded as well
    "http://myhost/cgi-bin/login.cgi?Name=Pat&Password=foobar");

BufferedReader bin = new BufferedReader (
  new InputStreamReader( url.openStream( ) ));

String line;
while ( (line = bin.readLine( )) != null )
    System.out.println( line );
```

To form the new URL, we start with the URL of *login.cgi*; we add a question mark (?), which marks the beginning of the form data, followed by the first name/value pair. We can add as many pairs as we want, separated by ampersand (&) characters. The rest of our code simply opens the stream and reads back the response from the server. Remember that creating a URL doesn't actually open the connection. In this case, the URL connection was made implicitly when we called openStream(). Although we are assuming here that our server sends back text, it could send anything. (In theory of course we could use the getContentType() method of the URL to check the MIME type of any returned data and try to retrieve the data as an object using getContent() as well).

It's important to point out that we have skipped a step here. This example works because our name/value pairs happen to be simple text. If any "non-printable" or special characters (including ? or &) are in the pairs, they have to be encoded first. The java.net.URLEncoder class provides a utility for encoding the data. We'll show how to use it in the next example.

Another important thing to note is that although this example sends a password field, you should never do so using this simplistic approach. All of the data we're sending goes in clear text across the network (it is not encrypted). And in this case, the password field would appear anywhere the URL is printed as well (e.g., server logs and bookmarks). We'll talk about secure web communications later in this chapter and when we discuss writing web applications using servlets in Chapter 14.

Using the POST Method

Next we'll create a small application that acts like an HTML form. It gathers data from two text fields—name and password—and posts the data to a specified URL using the HTTP POST method. Here we are writing a Swing-based client application that works with a server-side web-based application, just like a web browser.

Here's the code:

```
//file: Post.java
import java.net.*;
import java.io.*;
import java.awt.*;
import java.awt.event.*;
import javax.swing.*;

public class Post extends JPanel implements ActionListener {
  JTextField nameField, passwordField;
  String postURL;

  GridBagConstraints constraints = new GridBagConstraints( );
  void addGB( Component component, int x, int y ) {
    constraints.gridx = x;  constraints.gridy = y;
    add ( component, constraints );
  }

  public Post( String postURL ) {
    this.postURL = postURL;
    JButton postButton = new JButton("Post");
    postButton.addActionListener( this );
    setLayout( new GridBagLayout( ) );
    addGB( new JLabel("Name:"), 0,0 );
    addGB( nameField = new JTextField(20), 1,0 );
    addGB( new JLabel("Password:"), 0,1 );
    addGB( passwordField = new JPasswordField(20),1,1 );
    constraints.gridwidth = 2;
    addGB( postButton, 0,2 );
  }

  public void actionPerformed(ActionEvent e) {
    postData( );
  }

  protected void postData( ) {
    StringBuffer sb = new StringBuffer( );
    sb.append( URLEncoder.encode("Name") + "=" );
    sb.append( URLEncoder.encode(nameField.getText( )) );
    sb.append( "&" + URLEncoder.encode("Password") + "=" );
    sb.append( URLEncoder.encode(passwordField.getText( )) );
    String formData = sb.toString( );

    try {
      URL url = new URL( postURL );
```

```
        HttpURLConnection urlcon =
            (HttpURLConnection) url.openConnection( );
        urlcon.setRequestMethod("POST");
        urlcon.setRequestProperty("Content-type",
            "application/x-www-form-urlencoded");
        urlcon.setDoOutput(true);
        urlcon.setDoInput(true);
        PrintWriter pout = new PrintWriter( new OutputStreamWriter(
            urlcon.getOutputStream( ), "8859_1"), true );
        pout.print( formData );
        pout.flush( );

        // read results...
        if ( urlcon.getResponseCode( ) != HttpURLConnection.HTTP_OK )
          System.out.println("Posted ok!");
        else {
          System.out.println("Bad post...");
          return;
        }
        //InputStream in = urlcon.getInputStream( );
        // ...

      } catch (MalformedURLException e) {
        System.out.println(e);      // bad postURL
      } catch (IOException e2) {
        System.out.println(e2);     // I/O error
      }
    }

    public static void main( String [] args ) {
      JFrame frame = new JFrame("SimplePost");
      frame.getContentPane( ).add( new Post( args[0] ), "Center" );
      frame.pack( );
      frame.setVisible(true);
    }
  }
```

When you run this application, you must specify the URL of the server program on the command line. For example:

```
% java Post http://www.myserver.example/cgi-bin/login.cgi
```

The beginning of the application creates the form; there's nothing here that won't be obvious after you've read Chapters 15–17. All the magic happens in the protected postData() method. First we create a StringBuffer and load it with name/value pairs, separated by ampersands. (We don't need the initial question mark when we're using the POST method because we're not appending to a URL string.) Each pair is first encoded using the static URLEncoder.encode() method. We run the name fields through the encoder as well as the value fields, even though we know that they contain no special characters.

Next we set up the connection to the server program. In our previous example, we didn't have to do anything special to send the data because the request was made by the web browser for us. Here, we have to carry some of the weight of talking to the remote web server. Fortunately, the HttpURLConnection object does most of the work for us; we just have to tell it that we want to do a POST to the URL and the type of data we are sending. We ask for the URLConnection object using the URL's openConnection() method. We know that we are using the HTTP protocol, so we should be able to cast it safely to an HttpURLConnection type, which has the support we need.

Next we use setRequestMethod() to tell the connection we want to do a POST operation. We also use setRequestProperty() to set the "Content-Type" field of our HTTP request to the appropriate type—in this case, the proper MIME type for encoded form data. (This is necessary to tell the server what kind of data we're sending.) Finally, we use the setDoOutput() and setDoInput() methods to tell the connection that we want to both send and receive stream data. The URL connection infers from this combination that we are going to do a POST operation and expects a response. Next we get an output stream from the connection with getOutputStream() and create a PrintWriter so we can easily write our encoded data.

After we post the data, our application calls getResponseCode() to see whether the HTTP response code from the server indicates the POST was successful. Other response codes (defined as constants in HttpURLConnection) indicate various failures. At the end of our example, we indicate where we could have read back the text of the response. For this application, we'll assume that simply knowing the post was successful is sufficient.

Although form-encoded data (as indicated by the MIME type we specified for the Content-Type field) is the most common, other types of communications are possible. We could have used the input and output streams to exchange arbitrary data types with the server program. The POST operation accepts nonform data as well; the server application simply has to know how to handle it. One final note: if you are writing an application that needs to decode form data, you can use the java.net. URLDecoder to undo the operation of the URLEncoder. If you use the Servlet API, this happens automatically, as you'll see in Chapter 14.

The HttpURLConnection

Other information from the request is available from the HttpURLConnection as well. We could use getContentType() and getContentEncoding() to determine the MIME type and encoding of the response. We could also interrogate the HTTP response headers using getHeaderField(). (HTTP response headers are metadata name/value pairs carried with the response.) There are also convenience methods to fetch integer- and date-formatted header fields: getHeaderFieldInt() and getHeaderFieldDate(), which return an int and a long type, respectively. The content length and last modification date are also provided through getContentLength() and getLastModified().

SSL and Secure Web Communications

The previous examples sent a field called Password to the server. However, standard HTTP doesn't provide encryption to hide our data. Fortunately, adding security for GET and POST operations like this is easy (trivial in fact, for the developer). Where available you simply have to use a secure form of the HTTP protocol—HTTPS:

```
https://www.myserver.example/cgi-bin/login.cgi
```

HTTPS is a version of the standard HTTP protocol run over SSL (Secure Sockets Layer), which uses public-key encryption techniques to encrypt the data sent. Most web browsers and servers currently come with built-in support for HTTPS (or raw SSL sockets). Therefore, if your web server supports HTTPS, you can use a browser to send and receive secure data simply by specifying the https protocol in your URLs. There is a lot more to know in general about SSL and related aspects of security such as authenticating whom you are actually talking to. But as far as basic data encryption goes, this is all you have to do. It is not something your code has to deal with directly. As of Java 1.4, the standard distribution from Sun is shipped with SSL and HTTPS support. Applets written using the Java Plug-in also have access to the HTTPS protocol handler. We'll discuss writing secure web applications in more detail in Chapter 14.

URLs, URNs, and URIs

Earlier we talked about URLs and distinguished them from the concept of URNs or Uniform Resource Names. Whereas a URL points to a specific location on the Net and specifies a protocol or *scheme* for accessing its contents, a URN is simply a globally unique name. A URL is analogous to giving someone your phone number. But a URN is more like giving them your social security number. Your phone number may change, but your social security number uniquely identifies you forever.

While it's possible that some mechanism might be able to look at a given URN and resolve it to a location (a URL), it is not necessarily so. URNs are intended only to be permanent, unique, abstract identifiers for an item whereas a URL is a mechanism you can use to get in touch with a resource right now. You can use a phone number to contact me today, but you can use my social security number to uniquely identify me anytime.

An example of a URN is *http://www.w3.org/1999/XSL/Transform*, which is the identifier for a version of the Extensible Stylesheet Language, standardized by the W3C. Now, it happens that this is also a URL (you can go to that address and find information about the standard), but that is for convenience only. This URNs primary mission is to uniquely label the version of the programming language in a way that never changes.

Collectively, URLs and URNs are called Uniform Resource Identifiers or URIs. A URI is simply a URL or URN. So, we can talk about URLs and URNs as kinds of

URIs. The reason for this abstraction is that URLs and URNs, by definition, have some things in common. All URIs are supposed to be human-readable and "transcribable" (it should be possible to write them on the back of a napkin). They always have a hierarchical structure, and they are always unique. Both URLs and URNs also share some common syntax, which is described by the URI RFC-2396.

Java 1.4 introduced the java.net.URI class to formalize these distinctions. Prior to that, there was only the URL class in Java. The difference between the URI and URL classes is that the URI class does not try to parse the contents of the identifier and apply any "meaning." The URL class immediately attempts to parse the scheme portion of the URL and locate a protocol handler, whereas the URI class doesn't interpret its content. It serves only to allow us to work with the identifier as structured text, according to the general rules of URI syntax. With the URI class, you can construct the string, resolve relative paths, and perform equality or comparison operations, but no hostname or protocol resolution is done.

CHAPTER 14

Servlets and Web Applications

Now we're going to take a leap from the client side to the server side to learn how to write Java applications for web servers. The Java Servlet API is a framework for writing *servlets*, application components for web services, just as *applets* are application components for a web browser. The Servlet API provides a simple yet powerful architecture for web-based applications. The Servlet API lives in the `javax.servlet` package, a standard Java API extension, so technically it isn't part of the core Java APIs. In this book, we haven't talked about many standard extension packages, but this one is particularly important. This chapter covers the Java Servlet API 2.3.

Most web servers support the Servlet API either directly or indirectly through add-on modules. Servers that support the full set of Java Enterprise APIs (including servlets, JSPs, and Enterprise JavaBeans) are called *application servers*. JBoss is a free, open source Java application server available from *http://www.jboss.org*, and BEA's WebLogic is a popular commercial application server. Components that handle just the servlets are more precisely called *servlet containers* or *servlet runners*.

We try to avoid talking about details of particular servlet environments, but we will use the Apache Project's Tomcat server for the examples in this book. Tomcat is a popular, free servlet engine that can be used by itself or in conjunction with popular web servers. It is easy to configure and is a pure Java application, so you can use it on any platform that has a Java VM. You can download it from *http://jakarta.apache.org/tomcat/*. Tomcat has been adopted by Sun as part of the J2EE reference implementation, so it always has an up-to-date implementation of the specifications available in both source and binary form. The Servlet APIs and Java documentation can be downloaded directly from *http://java.sun.com/products/servlet/*. You might consider taking a look at the Java servlet specification white paper, also available at that location. It is unusually readable for a reference document.

Servlets: Powerful Tools

Many different ways of writing server-side software for web applications have evolved over the years. Early on, the standard was CGI, usually in combination with a scripting language such as Perl. Various web servers also offered native-language APIs for pluggable software modules. Java, however—and in particular the Java Servlet API—is rapidly becoming the most popular architecture for building web-based applications. Java servlet containers (engines) are available for virtually every web server.

So, why has Java become so popular on the server side? Servlets let you write web applications in Java and derive all the benefits of Java and the virtual machine environment (along with the same limitations, of course). Java is generally faster than scripting languages, especially in a server-side environment where long-running applications can be highly optimized by the virtual machine. Servlets have an additional speed advantage over traditional CGI programs, because servlets execute in a multithreaded way within one instance of a virtual machine. Older CGI applications required the server to start a separate process, pipe data to it, and receive the response as a stream. The unique runtime safety of Java also beats most native APIs in a production web-server environment, where it would be very bad to have an errant transaction bring down the server.

So, speed and safety are factors, but perhaps the most important reason for using Java is that it makes writing large and complex applications much more manageable. Java servlets may not be as easy to write as scripts, but they are easier to update with new features, and servlets are far better at scaling for complex, high-volume applications. From servlet code, you can access all the standard Java APIs within the virtual machine while your servlets are handling requests. This means that your Java servlet code can work well in a multitiered architecture, accessing "live" database connections with JDBC or communicating with other network services that have already been established. This kind of behavior has been hacked into CGI environments, but for Java, it is both robust and natural.

Before we move on, we should also mention servlets' relationships to two other technologies: Java Server Pages (JSPs) and XML/XSL. JSPs are another way to write server-side applications. They consist primarily of HTML content with Java-like syntax embedded within the documents. JSPs are compiled dynamically by the web server into Java servlets and can work with Java APIs directly and indirectly to generate dynamic content for the pages. XML is a powerful set of standards for working with structured information in text form. The Extensible Stylesheet Language (XSL) is a language for transforming XML documents into other kinds of documents, including HTML. The combination of servlets that can generate XML content and XSL stylesheets that can transform content for presentation is a very exciting direction, covered in detail in Chapter 23.

Web Applications

So far we've used the term "web application" generically. Now we are going to have to be more precise with that term. In the context of the Java Servlet API, a web application is a collection of servlets, supporting Java classes, and content such as HTML or JSP pages and images. For deployment (installation into a web server), a web application is bundled into a Web Application Resources (WAR) file. We'll discuss WAR files in detail later, but suffice it to say that they are essentially JAR archives containing the application files along with some deployment information. The important thing is that the standardization of WAR files means not only that the Java code is portable, but also that the process of deploying all the application's parts is standardized.

At the heart of the WAR archive is the *web.xml* file. This file describes which servlets and JSPs are to be run, their names and URL paths, their initialization parameters and a host of other information, including security and authentication requirements.

Web applications, or WebApps, also have a very well-defined runtime environment. Each WebApp has its own "root" path on the web server, meaning that all the URLs addressing its servlets and files start with a common unique prefix (e.g., *www.oreilly. com/someapplication/*). The WebApp's servlets are also isolated from those of other web applications. WebApps cannot directly access each other's files (although they may be allowed to do so through the web server, of course). Each WebApp also has its own servlet context. We'll discuss the servlet context in more detail, but in brief, it is a common area for servlets to share information and get resources from the environment. The high degree of isolation between web applications is intended to support the dynamic deployment and updating of applications required by modern business systems.

The Servlet Life Cycle

Let's jump ahead now to the Servlet API itself so that we can get started building servlets right away. We'll fill in the gaps later when we discuss various parts of the APIs and WAR file structure in more detail. The Servlet API is very simple, almost exactly paralleling the Applet API. There are three life-cycle methods—init(), service(), and destroy()—along with some methods for getting configuration parameters and servlet resources. Before a servlet is used the first time, it's initialized by the server through its init() method. Thereafter the servlet spends its time handling service() requests and doing its job until (presumably) the server is shut down, and the servlet's destroy() method is called, giving it an opportunity to clean up.

Generally only one instance of each deployed servlet class is instantiated per server. To be more precise, it is one instance per entry in the *web.xml* file, but we'll talk more about servlet deployment later. And there is an exception to that rule when using the special SingleThreadModel, described below.

The service() method of a servlet accepts two parameters: a servlet "request" object and a servlet "response" object. These provide tools for reading the client request and generating output; we'll talk about them in detail in the examples.

By default, servlets are expected to handle multithreaded requests; that is, the servlet's service methods may be invoked by many threads at the same time. This means that you cannot store client-related data in instance variables of your servlet object. (Of course, you can store general data related to the servlet's operation, as long as it does not change on a per-request basis.) Per-client state information can be stored in a client session object (such as a cookie), which persists across client requests. We'll talk about that later as well.

If for some reason you have developed a servlet that cannot support multithreaded access, you can indicate this to the servlet container by implementing the flag interface SingleThreadModel. This interface has no methods, serving only to indicate that the servlet should be invoked in a single-threaded manner. When implementing the SingleThreadModel, the container may create more than one instance of your servlet per VM in order to pool requests.

Web Servlets

There are actually two packages of interest in the Servlet API. The first is the javax.servlet package, which contains the most general Servlet APIs. The second important package is javax.servlet.http, which contains APIs specific to servlets that handle HTTP requests for web servers. In the rest of this section, we are going to discuss servlets pretty much as if all servlets were HTTP-related. You can write servlets for other protocols, but that's not what we're currently interested in.

The primary tool provided by the javax.servlet.http package is the HttpServlet base class. This is an abstract servlet that provides some basic implementation related to handling an HTTP request. In particular, it overrides the generic servlet service() request and breaks it out into several HTTP-related methods, including doGet(), doPost(), doPut(), and doDelete(). The default service() method examines the request to determine what kind it is and dispatches it to one of these methods, so you can override one or more of them to implement the specific web server behavior you need.

doGet() and doPost() correspond to the standard HTTP GET and POST operations. GET is the standard request for retrieving a file or document at a specified URL. POST is the method by which a client sends an arbitrary amount of data to the server. HTML forms are the most common use for POST.

To round these out, HttpServlet provides the doPut() and doDelete() methods. These methods correspond to a poorly supported part of the HTTP protocol, meant to provide a way to upload and remove files. doPut() is supposed to be like POST but with different semantics; doDelete() would be its opposite. These aren't widely used.

HttpServlet also implements three other HTTP-related methods for you: doHead(), doTrace(), and doOptions(). You don't normally need to override these methods. doHead() implements the HTTP HEAD request, which asks for the headers of a GET request without the body. HttpServlet implements this by default by performing the GET method and then sending only the headers. You may wish to override doHead() with a more efficient implementation if you can provide one as an optimization. doTrace() and doOptions() implement other features of HTTP that allow for debugging and simple client/server capabilities negotiation. You generally shouldn't need to override these.

Along with HttpServlet, javax.servlet.http also includes subclasses of the ServletRequest and ServletResponse objects, HttpServletRequest and HttpServletResponse. These subclasses provide, respectively, the input and output streams needed to read and write client data. They also provide the APIs for getting or setting HTTP header information and, as we'll see, client session information. Rather than document these dryly, we'll show them in the context of some examples. As usual, we'll start with the simplest possible example.

The HelloClient Servlet

Here's our servlet version of "Hello World"— HelloClient:

```
//file: HelloClient.java
import java.io.*;
import javax.servlet.ServletException;
import javax.servlet.http.*;

public class HelloClient extends HttpServlet {

    public void doGet(HttpServletRequest request,
                      HttpServletResponse response)
        throws ServletException, IOException {

        // must come first
        response.setContentType("text/html");
        PrintWriter out = response.getWriter( );

        out.println(
            "<html><head><title>Hello Client</title></head><body>"
            + "<h1> Hello Client </h1>"
            + "</body></html>" );
        out.close( );
    }
}
```

If you want to try out this servlet right away, skip ahead to the sections "WAR Files and Deployment" and "Deploying HelloClient," where we walk through the process of running this servlet. It's simply a matter of packaging up the servlet class file along with a simple *web.xml* file that describes it and placing it on your server. But for now we're going to discuss just the servlet example code itself.

Let's have a look at the example. HelloClient extends the base HttpServlet class and overrides the doGet() method to handle simple requests. In this case, we want to respond to any GET request by sending back a one-line HTML document that says "Hello Client." First we tell the container what kind of response we are going to generate, using the setContentType()method of the HttpServletResponse object. Then we get the output stream using the getWriter() method and print the message to it. Finally, we close the stream to indicate we're done generating output. (It shouldn't strictly be necessary to close the output stream, but we show it for completeness.)

Servlet Exceptions

The doGet() method of our example servlet declares that it can throw a ServletException. All of the service methods of the Servlet API may throw a ServletException to indicate that a request has failed. A ServletException can be constructed with a string message and an optional Throwable parameter that can carry any corresponding exception representing the root cause of the problem:

```
throw new ServletException("utter failure", someException );
```

By default, the web server determines exactly what is shown to the user when a ServletException is thrown, but often the exception and its stack trace are displayed. Through the *web.xml* file, you can designate custom error pages; see "Error and Index Pages" later in this chapter for details.

Alternatively, a servlet may throw an UnavailableException, a subclass of ServletException, to indicate that it cannot handle requests. This exception can be constructed to indicate that the condition is permanent or that it should last for a specified period of seconds.

Content Type

Before fetching the output stream and writing to it, we must specify the kind of output we are sending by calling the response parameter's setContentType() method. In this case, we set the content type to text/html, which is the proper MIME type for an HTML document. In general, though, it's possible for a servlet to generate any kind of data, including sound, video, or some other kind of text. If we were writing a generic FileServlet to serve files like a regular web server, we might inspect the filename extension and determine the MIME type from that or from direct inspection of the data. For writing binary data, you can use the getOutputStream() method to get an OutputStream as opposed to a Writer.

The content type is used in the Content-Type: header of the server's HTTP response, which tells the client what to expect even before it starts reading the result. This allows your web browser to prompt you with the "Save File" dialog when you click on a ZIP archive or executable program. When the content-type string is used in its full form to specify the character encoding (for example, text/html; charset=ISO-8859-1), the information is also used by the servlet engine to set the character encoding of the PrintWriter output stream. As a result, you should always call the setContentType() method before fetching the writer with the getWriter() method.

The Servlet Response

In addition to providing the output stream for writing content to the client, the HttpServletResponse object provides methods for controlling other aspects of the HTTP response, including headers, error result codes, redirects, and servlet container buffering.

HTTP headers are metadata name/value pairs sent with the response. You can add headers (standard or custom) to the response with the setHeader() and addHeader() methods (headers may have multiple values). There are also convenience methods for setting headers with integer and date values:

```
response.setIntHeader("MagicNumber", 42);
response.setDateHeader("CurrentTime", System.currentTimeMillis() );
```

When you write data to the client, the servlet container automatically sets the HTTP response code to a value of 200, which means OK. Using the sendError() method, you can generate other HTTP response codes. HttpServletResponse contains predefined constants for all of the standard codes. Here are a few common ones:

```
HttpServletResponse.SC_OK
HttpServletResponse.SC_BAD_REQUEST
HttpServletResponse.SC_FORBIDDEN
HttpServletResponse.SC_NOT_FOUND
HttpServletResponse.SC_INTERNAL_SERVER_ERROR
HttpServletResponse.SC_NOT_IMPLEMENTED
HttpServletResponse.SC_SERVICE_UNAVAILABLE
```

When you generate an error with sendError(), the response is over, and you can't write any content to the client. You can specify a short error message, however, which may be shown to the client. (See the section"A Simple Filter," for an example.)

An HTTP redirect is a special kind of response that tells the client web browser to go to a different URL. Normally this happens quickly and without any interaction from the user. You can send a redirect with the sendRedirect() method:

```
response.sendRedirect(http://www.oreilly.com/);
```

We should say a few words about buffering. Most responses are buffered internally by the servlet container until the servlet service method has exited. This allows the container to set the HTTP content-length header automatically, telling the client how much data to expect. You can control the size of this buffer with the setBufferSize() method, specifying a size in bytes. You can even clear it and start over if no data has been written to the client. To clear the buffer, use isCommitted() to test whether any data has been set, then use resetBuffer() to dump the data if none has been sent. If you are sending a lot of data, you may wish to set the content length explicitly with the setContentLength() method.

Servlet Parameters

Our first example shows how to accept a basic request. A more sophisticated servlet might do arbitrary processing or handle database queries, for example. Of course, to do anything really useful we'll need to get some information from the user. Fortunately, the servlet engine handles this for us, interpreting both GET- and POST-encoded form data from the client and providing it to us through the simple getParameter() method of the servlet request.

GET, POST, and the "Extra Path"

There are essentially two ways to pass information from your web browser to a servlet or CGI program. The most general is to "post" it, which means that your client encodes the information and sends it as a stream to the program, which decodes it. Posting can be used to upload large amounts of form data or other data, including files. The other way to pass information is to somehow encode the information in the URL of your client's request. The primary way to do this is to use GET-style encoding of parameters in the URL string. In this case, the web browser encodes the parameters and appends them to the end of the URL string. The server decodes them and passes them to the application.

As we described in Chapter 13, GET-style encoding takes the parameters and appends them to the URL in a name/value fashion, with the first parameter preceded by a question mark (?) and the rest separated by ampersands (&). The entire string is expected to be *URL-encoded*: any special characters (such as spaces, ?, and & in the string) are specially encoded.

A less sophisticated form of encoding data in the URL is called *extra path*. This simply means that when the server has located your servlet or CGI program as the target of a URL, it takes any remaining path components of the URL string and simply hands it over as an extra part of the URL. For example, consider these URLs:

```
http://www.myserver.example/servlets/MyServlet
http://www.myserver.example/servlets/MyServlet/foo/bar
```

Suppose the server maps the first URL to the servlet called MyServlet. When subsequently given the second URL, the server still invokes MyServlet, but considers /foo/bar to be an "extra path" that can be retrieved through the servlet request getExtraPath() method.

Both GET and POST encoding can be used with HTML forms on the client by specifying get or post in the action attribute of the form tag. The browser handles the encoding; on the server side, the servlet engine handles the decoding.

The content type used by a client to post form data to a servlet is the same as that for any CGI: "application/x-www-form-urlencoded." The Servlet API automatically parses this kind of data and makes it available through the getParameter() method. However, if you do not use the getParameter() method, the data remains available in the input stream and can be read by the servlet directly.

GET or POST: Which One to Use?

To users, the primary difference between GET and POST is that they can see the GET information in the encoded URL shown in their web browser. This can be useful because the user can cut and paste that URL (the result of a search, for example) and mail it to a friend or bookmark it for future reference. POST information is not visible to the user and ceases to exist after it's sent to the server. This behavior goes along with the protocol's perspective that GET and POST are intended to have different semantics. By definition, the result of a GET operation is not supposed to have any side effects. That is, it's not supposed to cause the server to perform any subsequent operations (such as making an e-commerce purchase). In theory, that's the job of POST. That's why your web browser warns you about reposting form data again if you hit reload on a page that was the result of a form posting.

The extra path method is not useful for form data but would be useful for a servlet that retrieves files or handles a range of URLs in a human-readable way not driven by forms.

The ShowParameters Servlet

Our first example didn't do anything interesting. This example prints the values of any parameters that were received. We'll start by handling GET requests and then make some trivial modifications to handle POST as well. Here's the code:

```
//file: ShowParameters.java
import java.io.*;
import javax.servlet.ServletException;
import javax.servlet.http.*;
import java.util.Enumeration;

public class ShowParameters extends HttpServlet {
```

```
public void doGet(HttpServletRequest request,
                  HttpServletResponse response)
  throws ServletException, IOException {
    showRequestParameters( request, response );
}

void showRequestParameters(HttpServletRequest request,
                           HttpServletResponse response)
  throws IOException {
    response.setContentType("text/html");
    PrintWriter out = response.getWriter( );

    out.println(
      "<html><head><title>Show Parameters</title></head><body>"
      + "<h1>Parameters</h1><ul>");

    for ( Enumeration e=request.getParameterNames( );
         e.hasMoreElements( ); ) {
        String name = (String)e.nextElement( );
        String value = request.getParameter( name );
        if (! value.equals("") )
            out.println("<li>"+ name +" = "+ value );
    }

    out.close( );
  }
}
```

There's not much new here. As in the first example, we override the doGet() method. Here, we delegate the request to a helper method that we've created, called showRequestParameters(). This method just enumerates the parameters using the request object's getParameterNames() method and prints the names and values. (To make it pretty, we listed them in an HTML list by prefixing each with an <li> tag.)

As it stands, our servlet would respond to any URL that contains a GET request. Let's round it out by adding our own form to the output and also accommodating POST method requests. To accept posts, we override the doPost() method. The implementation of doPost() could simply call our showRequestParameters() method, but we can make it simpler still. The API lets us treat GET and POST requests interchangeably because the servlet engine handles the decoding of request parameters. So we simply delegate the doPost() operation to doGet().

Add the following method to the example:

```
public void doPost( HttpServletRequest request,
                    HttpServletResponse response)
  throws ServletException, IOException {
    doGet( request, response );
}
```

Now let's add an HTML form to the output. The form lets the user fill in some parameters and submit them to the servlet. Add this line to the showRequestParameters() method before the call to out.close():

```
out.println(
    "</ul><p><form method=\"POST\" action=\""
    + request.getRequestURI( ) + "\">"
    + "Field 1 <input name=\"Field 1\" size=20><br>"
    + "Field 2 <input name=\"Field 2\" size=20><br>"
    + "<br><input type=\"submit\" value=\"Submit\"></form>"
);
```

The form's action attribute is the URL of our servlet so that the servlet will get the data. We use the getRequestURI() method to ask for the location of our servlet. For the method attribute, we've specified a POST operation, but you can try changing the operation to GET to see both styles.

So far, we haven't done anything that you couldn't do easily with your average CGI script. In the following section, we'll show something more interesting: how to manage a user session. But before we go on, we should mention a useful standard servlet that is a kin of our example above, SnoopServlet.

SnoopServlet

Most servlet containers come with some useful servlets that serve as examples or debugging aids. One of the most basic tools you have for debugging servlets is the "SnoopServlet." We place that name in quotes because you will find many different implementations of this with various names. But the original SnoopServlet came with the Java servlet development kit and is currently supplied with the Tomcat server distribution. This very simple debugging servlet displays everything about its environment, including all of its request parameters, just as our ShowParameters example did. There is a lot of useful information there. In the default Tomcat 4.0 distribution, you can access this servlet at *http://myserver:8080/examples/snoop*.

User Session Management

One of the nicest features of the Servlet API is its simple mechanism for managing a user session. By a session, we mean that the servlet can maintain information over multiple pages and through multiple transactions as navigated by the user; this is also called maintaining state. Providing continuity through a series of web pages is important in many kinds of applications, such as handling a login process or tracking purchases in a shopping cart. In a sense, session data takes the place of instance data in your servlet object. It lets you store data between invocations of your service methods.

Session tracking is supported by the servlet engine; you don't have to worry about the details of how it's accomplished. It's done in one of two ways: using client-side cookies or URL rewriting. *Client-side cookies* are a standard HTTP mechanism for getting the client web browser to cooperate in storing state information for you. A cookie is basically just a name/value attribute that is issued by the server, stored on the client, and returned by the client whenever it is accessing a certain group of URLs on a specified server. Cookies can track a single session or multiple user visits.

URL rewriting appends session-tracking information to the URL, using GET-style encoding or extra path information. The term "rewriting" applies because the server rewrites the URL before it is seen by the client and absorbs the extra information before it is passed back to the servlet. In order to support URL rewriting, a servlet must take the extra step to encode any URLs it generates in content (e.g., HTML links that may return to the page) using a special method of the HttpServletResponse object. We'll describe this later.

To the servlet programmer, state information is made available through an HttpSession object, which acts like a hashtable for storing whatever objects you would like to carry through the session. The objects stay on the server side; a special identifier is sent to the client through a cookie or URL rewriting. On the way back, the identifier is mapped to a session, and the session is associated with the servlet again.

The ShowSession Servlet

Here's a simple servlet that shows how to store some string information to track a session:

```
//file: ShowSession.java
import java.io.*;
import javax.servlet.ServletException;
import javax.servlet.http.*;
import java.util.Enumeration;

public class ShowSession extends HttpServlet {

    public void doPost(
        HttpServletRequest request, HttpServletResponse response)
        throws ServletException, IOException
    {
        doGet( request, response );
    }

    public void doGet(
        HttpServletRequest request, HttpServletResponse response)
        throws ServletException, IOException
    {
        HttpSession session = request.getSession(  );
        boolean clear = request.getParameter("clear") != null;
        if ( clear )
            session.invalidate();
        else {
```

```java
        String name = request.getParameter("Name");
        String value = request.getParameter("Value");
        if ( name != null && value != null )
            session.setAttribute( name, value );
    }

    response.setContentType("text/html");
    PrintWriter out = response.getWriter( );
    out.println(
      "<html><head><title>Show Session</title></head><body>");

    if ( clear )
        out.println("<h1>Session Cleared:</h1>");
    else {
        out.println("<h1>In this session:</h1><ul>");
        Enumeration names = session.getAttributeNames( );
        while ( names.hasMoreElements( ) ) {
            String name = (String)names.nextElement( );
            out.println( "<li>"+name+" = " +session.getAttribute( name ) );
        }
    }

    out.println(
      "</ul><p><hr><h1>Add String</h1>"
      + "<form method=\"POST\" action=\""
      + request.getRequestURI( ) +"\">"
      + "Name: <input name=\"Name\" size=20><br>"
      + "Value: <input name=\"Value\" size=20><br>"
      + "<br><input type=\"submit\" value=\"Submit\">"
      + "<input type=\"submit\" name=\"clear\" value=\"Clear\"></form>"
    );
  }
}
```

When you invoke the servlet, you are presented with a form that prompts you to enter a name and a value. The value string is stored in a session object under the name provided. Each time the servlet is called, it outputs the list of all data items associated with the session. You will see the session grow as each item is added (in this case, until you restart your web browser or the server).

The basic mechanics are much like our ShowParameters servlet. Our doGet() method generates the form, which refers back to our servlet via a POST method. We override doPost() to delegate back to our doGet() method, allowing it to handle everything. Once in doGet(), we attempt to fetch the user session object from the request parameter using getSession(). The HttpSession object supplied by the request functions like a hashtable. There is a setAttribute() method, which takes a string name and an Object argument, and a corresponding getAttribute() method. In our example, we use the getAttributeNames() method to enumerate the values currently stored in the session and to print them.

By default, getSession() creates a session if one does not exist. If you want to test for a session or explicitly control when one is created, you can call the overloaded version getSession(false), which does not automatically create a new session and returns null if there is no session. To clear a session immediately, we can use the invalidate() method. After calling invalidate() on a session, we are not allowed to access it again, so we set a flag in our example and show the "Session Cleared" message. Sessions may also become invalid on their own by timing out. You can control session timeout in the application server or through the *web.xml* file (via the "session-timeout" value of the "session config" section). User sessions are private to each web application and are not shared across applications.

We mentioned earlier that an extra step is required to support URL rewriting for web browsers that don't support cookies. To do this, we must make sure that any URLs we generate in content are first passed through the HttpServletResponse encodeURL() method. This method takes a string URL and returns a modified string only if URL rewriting is necessary. Normally, when cookies are available, it returns the same string. In our previous example, we should have encoded the server form URL retrieved from getRequestURI() before passing it to the client.

The ShoppingCart Servlet

Now we build on the previous example to make a servlet that could be used as part of an online store. ShoppingCart lets users choose items and add them to their basket until checkout time:

```java
//file: ShoppingCart.java
import java.io.*;
import javax.servlet.ServletException;
import javax.servlet.http.*;
import java.util.Enumeration;

public class ShoppingCart extends HttpServlet {
    String [] items = new String [] {
        "Chocolate Covered Crickets", "Raspberry Roaches",
        "Buttery Butterflies", "Chicken Flavored Chicklets(tm)" };

    public void doPost(
        HttpServletRequest request, HttpServletResponse response)
        throws IOException, ServletException
    {
        doGet( request, response );
    }

    public void doGet(
        HttpServletRequest request, HttpServletResponse response)
        throws ServletException, IOException
    {
        response.setContentType("text/html");
        PrintWriter out = response.getWriter(  );
```

```
// get or create the session information
HttpSession session = request.getSession(  );
int [] purchases = (int [])session.getAttribute("purchases");
if ( purchases == null ) {
    purchases = new int [ items.length ];
    session.setAttribute( "purchases", purchases );
}

out.println( "<html><head><title>Shopping Cart</title>"
             + "</title></head><body><p>" );

if ( request.getParameter("checkout") != null )
    out.println("<h1>Thanks for ordering!</h1>");
else  {
    if ( request.getParameter("add") != null ) {
        addPurchases( request, purchases );
        out.println(
            "<h1>Purchase added.  Please continue</h1>");
    } else {
        if ( request.getParameter("clear") != null )
            for (int i=0; i<purchases.length; i++)
                purchases[i] = 0;
        out.println("<h1>Please Select Your Items!</h1>");
    }
    doForm( out, request.getRequestURI(  ) );
}
showPurchases( out, purchases );
out.close(  );
}

void addPurchases( HttpServletRequest request, int [] purchases ) {
    for (int i=0; i<items.length; i++) {
        String added = request.getParameter( items[i] );
        if ( added !=null && !added.equals("") )
            purchases[i] += Integer.parseInt( added );
    }
}

void doForm( PrintWriter out, String requestURI ) {
    out.println( "<form method=POST action="+ requestURI +">" );

    for(int i=0; i< items.length; i++)
        out.println( "Quantity <input name=\"" + items[i]
            + "\" value=0 size=3> of: " + items[i] + "<br>");
    out.println(
        "<p><input type=submit name=add value=\"Add To Cart\">"
        + "<input type=submit name=checkout value=\"Check Out\">"
        + "<input type=submit name=clear value=\"Clear Cart\">"
        + "</form>" );
}

void showPurchases( PrintWriter out, int [] purchases )
    throws IOException {
```

```
            out.println("<hr><h2>Your Shopping Basket</h2>");
            for (int i=0; i<items.length; i++)
                if ( purchases[i] != 0 )
                    out.println( purchases[i] +"  "+ items[i] +"<br>" );
    }
}
```

ShoppingCart has some instance data: a String array that holds a list of products. We're making the assumption that the product selection is the same for all customers. If it's not, we'd have to generate the product list on the fly or put it in the session for the user.

We see the same basic pattern as in our previous servlets, with doPost() delegating to doGet(), and doGet() generating the body of the output and a form for gathering new data. Here we've broken down the work using a few helper methods: doForm(), addPurchases(), and showPurchases(). Our shopping cart form has three submit buttons: one for adding items to the cart, one for checkout, and one for clearing the cart. In each case, we display the contents of the cart. Depending on the button pressed, we add new purchases, clear the list, or simply show the results as a checkout window.

The form is generated by our doForm() method, using the list of items for sale. As in the other examples, we supply our servlet's address as the target of the form. Next, we have placed an integer array called purchases into the user session. Each element in purchases holds a count of the number of each item the user wants to buy. We create the array after retrieving the session simply by asking the session for it. If this is a new session, and the array hasn't been created, getValue() gives us a null array to populate. Since we generate the form using the names from the items array, it's easy for addPurchases() to check for each name using getParameter() and increment the purchases array for the number of items requested. We also test for the value being equal to the empty string, because some broken web browsers send empty strings for unused field values. Finally, showPurchases() simply loops over the purchases array and prints the name and quantity for each item that the user has purchased.

Cookies

In our previous examples, a session lived only until you shut down your web browser or the server. You can do more long-term user tracking or identification by managing cookies explicitly. You can send a cookie to the client by creating a javax.servlet.http.Cookie object and adding it to the servlet response using the addCookie() method. Later you can retrieve the cookie information from the servlet request and use it to look up persistent information in a database. The following servlet sends a "Learning Java" cookie to your web browser and displays it when you return to the page:

```
//file: CookieCutter.java
import java.io.*;
```

```
import java.text.*;
import java.util.*;
import javax.servlet.*;
import javax.servlet.http.*;

public class CookieCutter extends HttpServlet {

    public void doGet(HttpServletRequest request,
                        HttpServletResponse response)
        throws IOException, ServletException {
        response.setContentType("text/html");
        PrintWriter out = response.getWriter( );

        if ( request.getParameter("setcookie") != null ) {
            Cookie cookie = new Cookie("Learningjava", "Cookies!");
            cookie.setMaxAge(3600);
            response.addCookie(cookie);
            out.println("<html><body><h1>Cookie Set...</h1>");
        } else {
            out.println("<html><body>");
            Cookie[] cookies = request.getCookies( );
            if ( cookies.length == 0 )
                out.println("<h1>No cookies found...</h1>");
            else
                for (int i = 0; i < cookies.length; i++)
                    out.print("<h1>Name: "+ cookies[i].getName( )
                        + "<br>"
                        + "Value: " + cookies[i].getValue( )
                        + "</h1>" );
            out.println("<p><a href=\""+ request.getRequestURI( )
                +"?setcookie=true\">"
                +"Reset the Learning Java cookie.</a>");
        }
        out.println("</body></html>");
        out.close( );
    }
}
```

This example simply enumerates the cookies supplied by the request object using the
getCookies() method and prints their names and values. We provide a GET-style link
that points back to our servlet with a parameter setcookie, indicating that we should
set the cookie. In that case, we create a Cookie object using the specified name and
value and add it to the response with the addCookie() method. We set the maximum
age of the cookie to 3600 seconds, so it remains in the browser for an hour before
being discarded (we'll talk about tracking a cookie across multiple sessions later).
You can specify an arbitrary time period here or a negative time period to indicate
that the cookie should not be stored persistently on the client. Indicating a negative
time period is a good way to erase an existing cookie of the same name.

Two other Cookie methods are of interest: setDomain() and setPath(). These methods allow you to specify the domain name and path component that limits the

servers to which the client will send the cookie. If you're writing some kind of purchase applet for L.L. Bean, you don't want clients sending your cookies over to Eddie Bauer. In practice, however, this cannot happen. The default domain is the domain of the server sending the cookie. (You may not be able to specify other domains for security reasons.) The path parameter defaults to the base URL of the servlet, but you can specify a wider (or narrower) range of URLs on the server by setting this parameter manually.

The ServletContext API

Web applications have access to the server environment through the ServletContext API. A reference to the ServletContext can be obtained from the HttpServlet getServletContext() method.

```
ServetContext context = getServletContext( );
```

Each WebApp has its own ServletContext. The context provides a shared space in which a WebApp's servlets may rendezvous and post objects. Objects may be placed into the context with the setAttribute() method and retrieved by name with the getAttribute() method.

```
context.setAttribute("myapp.statistics", myObject);
Object stats = context.getAttribute("myapp.statistics");
```

Attribute names beginning with "java." and "javax." are reserved for use by Java. Use the standard package-naming conventions for your attributes in order to avoid conflicts. One standard attribute that can be accessed through the servlet context is a reference to a private working directory java.io.File object. This temp directory is guaranteed unique to the WebApp. No guarantees are made about it being cleared upon exit, however, so you should use the temporary file API to create files here (unless you wish to try to keep them beyond the server exit). For example:

```
File tmpDir = (File)context.getAttribute("javax.servlet.context.tempdir");
File tmpFile = File.createTempFile( "appprefix", "appsuffix", tmpDir );
```

The servlet context also provides direct access to the WebApp's files from its root directory. The getResource() method is similar to the Class getResource() method (see Chapter 11). It takes a pathname and returns a special local URL for accessing that resource. In this case, it takes a path rooted in the servlet base directory (WAR file). The servlet may obtain references to files, including those in the *WEB-INF* directory, using this method. For example, a servlet may fetch an input stream for its own *web.xml* file:

```
InputStream in = context.getResourceAsStream("/WEB-INF/web.xml");
```

It could also use a URL reference to get one of its images:

```
URL bunnyURL = context.getResource("/images/happybunny.gif");
```

The method getResourcePaths() may be used to fetch a directory-style listing of all the resource files available matching a specified path. The return value is a java.util.Set collection of strings naming the resources available under the specified path. For example, the path / lists all files in the WAR file; the path /WEB-INF/ lists at least the *web.xml* file and *classes* directory.

The ServletContext is also a factory for RequestDispatcher objects.

WAR Files and Deployment

As we described in the introduction to this chapter, a WAR file is an archive that contains all the parts of a web application: Java class files for servlets, JSPs, HTML pages, images, and other resources. The WAR file is simply a JAR file with specified directories for the Java code and one very important file: the *web.xml* file, which tells the application server what to run and how to run it. WAR files always have the extension *.war*, but they can be created and read with the standard *jar* tool.

The contents of a typical WAR file might look like this, as revealed by the *jar* tool:

```
$ jar tvf shoppingcart.war

        index.html
        purchase.html
        receipt.html
        images/happybunny.gif
        WEB-INF/web.xml
        WEB-INF/classes/com/mycompany/PurchaseServlet.class
        WEB-INF/classes/com/mycompany/ReturnServlet.class
        WEB-INF/lib/thirdparty.jar
```

When deployed, the name of the WAR file becomes, by default, the root path of the web application, in this case *shoppingcart*. Thus the base URL for this WebApp, if deployed on *www.oreilly.com*, is *http://www.oreilly.com/shoppingcart/*, and all references to its documents, images, and servlets start with that path. The top level of the WAR file becomes the document root (base directory) for serving files. Our *index.html* file appears at the base URL we just mentioned, and our *happybunny.gif* image is referenced as *http://www.oreilly.com/shoppingcart/images/happybunny.gif*.

The *WEB-INF* directory (all caps, hyphenated) is a special directory that contains all deployment information and application code. This directory is protected by the web server, and its contents are not visible, even if you add *WEB-INF* to the base URL. Your application classes can load additional files from this area directly using getResource(), however, so it is a safe place to store application resources. The *WEB-INF* directory contains the all-important *web.xml* file, which we'll talk about more in a moment.

The *WEB-INF/classes* and *WEB-INF/lib* directories contain Java class files and JAR libraries, respectively. The *WEB-INF/classes* directory is automatically added to the classpath of the web application, so any class files placed here (using the normal Java package conventions) are available to the application. After that, any JAR files located in *WEB-INF/lib* are appended to the WebApp's classpath (the order in which they are appended is, unfortunately, not specified). You can place your classes in either location. During development, it is often easier to work with the "loose" *classes* directory and use the *lib* directory for supporting classes and third-party tools. Usually it's also possible to install classes and JAR files in the main system classpath of the servlet container to make them available to all WebApps running on that server. The procedure for doing this, however, is not standard and any classes that are deployed in this way cannot be automatically reloaded if changed—a feature of WAR files that we'll discuss later.

The web.xml File

The *web.xml* file is an XML file that lists the servlets to be run, the relative names (URL paths) under which to run them, their initialization parameters, and their deployment details, including security and authorization. We will assume that you have at least a passing familiarity with XML or that you can simply imitate the examples in a cut-and-paste fashion. (For details about working with Java and XML, see Chapter 23.) Let's start with a simple *web.xml* file for our HelloClient servlet example. It looks like this:

```
<web-app>
    <servlet>
        <servlet-name>helloclient1</servlet-name>
        <servlet-class>HelloClient</servlet-class>
    </servlet>
    <servlet-mapping>
        <servlet-name>helloclient1</servlet-name>
        <url-pattern>/hello</url-pattern>
    </servlet-mapping>
</web-app>
```

The top-level element of the document is called <web-app>. Many types of entries may appear inside the <web-app>, but the most basic are <servlet> declarations and <servlet-mapping> deployment mappings. The <servlet> declaration tag is used to declare an instance of a servlet and, optionally, to give it initialization and other parameters. One instance of the servlet class is instantiated for each <servlet> tag appearing in the *web.xml* file.

At minimum, the <servlet> declaration requires two pieces of information: a <servlet-name>, which is used as a handle to reference the servlet elsewhere in the *web.xml* file, and the <servlet-class> tag, which specifies the Java class name of the servlet. Here, we named the servlet helloclient1. We named it like this to emphasize that we could declare other instances of the same servlet if we wanted to, possibly giving them different initialization parameters, etc. The class name for our servlet is of course `HelloClient`. In a real application, the servlet class would likely have a full package name such as `com.oreilly.servlets.HelloClient`.

A servlet declaration may also include one or more initialization parameters, which are made available to the servlet through the `ServletConfig` object's `getInitParameter()` method:

```
<servlet>
    <servlet-name>helloclient1</servlet-name>
    <servlet-class>HelloClient</servlet-class>
    <init-param>
        <param-name>foo</param-name>
        <param-value>bar</param-value>
    </init-param>
</servlet>
```

Next, we have our `<servlet-mapping>`, which associates the servlet instance with a path on the web server. Servlet mapping entries appear in the *web.xml* file after all the servlet declaration entries:

```
<servlet-mapping>
    <servlet-name>helloclient1</servlet-name>
    <url-pattern>/hello</url-pattern>
</servlet-mapping>
```

Here we mapped our servlet to the path */hello*. If we later name our WAR file *learningjava.war* and deploy it on *www.oreilly.com*, the full path to this servlet would be *http://www.oreilly.com/learningjava/hello*. Just as we could declare more than one servlet instance with the `<servlet>` tag, we could declare more than one `<servlet-mapping>` for a given servlet instance. We could, for example, redundantly map the same helloclient1 instance to the paths */hello* and */hola*. The `<url-pattern>` tag provides some very flexible ways to specify the URLs that should match a servlet. We'll talk about this in detail in the next section.

Finally, we should mention that although the *web.xml* example listed earlier will probably work on most application servers, it is technically incomplete because it is missing a formal header that specifies the version of XML it is using and the version of the *web.xml* file standard with which it complies.

```
<?xml version="1.0" encoding="ISO-8859-1"?>
<!DOCTYPE web-app
    PUBLIC "-//Sun Microsystems, Inc.//DTD Web Application 2.3//EN"
    "http://java.sun.com/dtd/web-app_2_3.dtd">
```

You can paste these four lines onto the beginning of each *web.xml* file we use in this book. You should do so, in fact, because with this information, if you make a mistake in the *web.xml* file, the web server can give you much better error messages.

URL Pattern Mappings

The `<url-pattern>` specified in the previous example was a simple string, "/hello". For this pattern, only an exact match ending in "/hello" would invoke our servlet. The `<url-pattern>` tag is capable of more powerful patterns, however, including wildcards. For example, specifying a `<url-pattern>` of "/hello*" allows our servlet to be invoked by URLs such as *www.oreilly.com/learningjava/helloworld* or "…/hellobaby". You can even specify wildcards with extensions, e.g., "*.html" or "*.foo", meaning that the servlet is invoked for any path that ends with those characters.

Using wildcards can result in more than one match. Consider, for example, the mappings "/scooby*" and "/scoobydoo*". Which should be matched for the URL ending with "…/scooby"? What if we have a third possible match because of a wildcard suffix extension mapping? The rules for resolving these are as follows.

First, any exact match is taken. For example, "/hello" matches the "/hello" URL pattern in our example regardless of any additional "/hello*". Failing that, the container looks for the longest prefix match. So "/scoobydoobiedoo" matches the second pattern, "/scoobydoo*", because it is longer and presumably more specific. Failing any matches there, the container looks at wildcard suffix mappings. A request ending in "*.foo" matches a "*.foo" mapping at this point in the process. Finally, failing any matches there, the container looks for a default, catchall mapping named "/*". A servlet mapped to "/*" picks up anything unmatched by this point. If there is no default servlet mapping, the request fails with a "404 not found" message.

Deploying HelloClient

Now let's deploy our `HelloClient` servlet. Once you've deployed the servlet, it should be easy to add examples to the WAR file as you work with them in this chapter. In this section, we'll show you how to build a WAR file by hand. In the later section "Building WAR Files with Ant," we'll show a more realistic way to manage your applications using the wonderful tool, Ant. You can also grab the full set of examples, along with their source code, in the *learningjava.war* file on the CD-ROM that comes with this book.

To create the WAR file by hand, we first create the *WEB/INF* and *WEB-INF/classes* directories. Place *web.xml* into *WEB-INF* and *HelloClient.class* into *WEB-INF/classes*. Use the *jar* command to create *learningjava.war*:

```
$ jar cvf learningjava.war WEB-INF
```

You can also include some documents in the top level of this WAR file by adding their names after the *WEB-INF* directory above. This command produces the file *learningjava.war*. You can verify the contents using the *jar* command:

```
$ jar tvf learningjava.war
```

Now all that is necessary is to drop the WAR file into the correct location for your server. We assume you have downloaded and installed Tomcat. With Version 4.0 of Tomcat, the location for WAR files is the path for Tomcat, followed by */webapps*. Place your WAR file here, and start the server. If Tomcat is configured with the default port number, you should be able to point to the HelloClient servlet with the following URLs: *http://localhost:8080/learningjava/hello* or *http://<yourserver>:8080/learningjava/hello*, where <yourserver> is the name or IP address of your server.

Reloading WebApps

All servers should provide a facility for automatically reloading WAR files and possibly individual servlet classes after they have been modified. This is part of the servlet specification and is especially useful during development. Unfortunately, support for this feature varies. BEA's WebLogic application server, when configured in development mode, allows you simply to replace the WAR file, and it handles redeployment. At the time of this writing, Tomcat is not quite so friendly. It supports reloading of servlet classes but does not handle reloading WAR files very well. Some servers, including the current version of Tomcat, "explode" WAR files by unpacking them into the *webapps* directory, or they allow you explicitly to configure a root directory for your WebApp. In this mode, they may allow you to replace individual files. After changing servlets or other classes, you can prompt Tomcat to reload the WebApp using a special URL with the format *http://<yourserver>:8080/manager/reload?path=/learningjava*. Even so, Tomcat does not currently reload the *web.xml* file. Until this situation improves, your safest bet is to remove this exploded directory, drop in your new WAR file, and restart the server (our apologies).

Error and Index Pages

One of the finer points of writing a professional-looking web application is taking care to handle errors well. Nothing annoys a user more than getting a funny-looking page with some technical mumbo-jumbo error information on it when they expected the receipt for their Christmas present. Through the *web.xml* file, it is possible to specify documents or servlets to handle error pages shown for various conditions, as well as the special case of index files (welcome files) for directories. Let's start with error handling.

You can designate a page or servlet that can handle various HTTP error status codes, such as "404 not found", "403 forbidden", etc., using one or more <error-page> declarations:

```
<web-app>
...
    <error-page>
        <error-code>404</error-code>
        <location>/notfound.html</location>
```

```
        </error-page>
        <error-page>
            <error-code>403</error-code>
            <location>/secret.html</location>
        </error-page>
```

Additionally, you can designate error pages based on Java exception types that may be thrown from the servlet. For example:

```
<error-page>
    <exception-type>java.lang.IOException</exception-type>
    <location>/ioexception.html</location>
</error-page>
```

This declaration catches any IOExceptions generated from servlets in the WebApp and displays the *ioexception.html* page. If no matching exceptions are found in the <error-page> declarations, and the exception is of type ServletException (or a subclass), the container makes a second try to find the correct handler. It looks for a wrapped exception (instigating exception) contained in the ServletException and attempts to match it to an error page declaration.

As we've mentioned, you can use a servlet to handle your error pages, just as you can use a static document. In fact, the container supplies several helpful pieces of information to an error-handling servlet, which the servlet can use in generating a response. The information is made available in the form of servlet request attributes through the method getAttribute():

```
    Object attribute = servletRequest.getAttribute("name");
```

Attributes are like servlet parameters, except that they can be arbitrary objects. We have seen attributes of the ServletContext in a previous section. In this case, we are talking about attributes of the request. When a servlet (or JSP or filter) is invoked to handle an error condition, the following string attributes are set in the request:

```
    javax.servlet.error.servlet_name
    javax.servlet.error.request_uri
    javax.servlet.error.message
```

Depending on whether the <error-page> declaration was based on an <error-code> or <exception-type> condition, the request also contains one of the following two attributes:

```
    // status code Integer or Exception object
    javax.servlet.error.status_code
    javax.servlet.error.exception
```

In the case of a status code, the attribute is an Integer representing the code. In the case of the exception type, the object is the actual instigating exception.

Index files can be designated in a similar way. Normally, when a user specifies a directory URL path, the web server searches for a default file in that directory to be displayed. The most common example of this is the ubiquitous *index.html* file. You can designate your own ordered list of files to look for by adding a `<welcome-file-list>` entry to your *web.xml* file. For example:

```
<welcome-file-list>
    <welcome-file>index.html</welcome-file>
    <welcome-file>index.htm</welcome-file>
</welcome-file-list>
```

`<welcome-file-list>` specifies that when a partial request (directory path) is received, the server should search first for a file named *index.html* and, if that is not found, a file called *index.htm*. If none of the specified welcome files is found, it is left up to the server to decide what kind of page to display. Servers are generally configured to display a directory-like listing or to produce an error message.

Security and Authentication

One of the most powerful features of WebApp deployment with the 2.3 Servlet API is the ability to define *declarative security* constraints. Declarative security means that you can simply spell out in the *web.xml* file exactly which areas of your WebApp (URL paths to documents, directories, servlets, etc.) are login-protected, the types of users allowed access to them, and the class of security protocol required for communications. It is not necessary to write code in your servlets to implement these basic security procedures.

There are two types of entries in the *web.xml* file that control security and authentication. First are the `<security-constraint>` entries, which provide authorization based on user roles and secure transport of data, if desired. Second is the `<login-config>` entry, which determines the kind of authentication used for the web application.

Assigning Roles to Users

Let's take a look at a simple example. The following *web.xml* excerpt defines an area called "My secret documents" with a URL pattern of */secure/** and designates that only users with the role "secretagent" may access them. It specifies the simplest form of login process: the BASIC authentication model, which causes the browser to prompt the user with a simple pop-up username and password dialog box.

```
<web-app>
    ...
    <security-constraint>
        <web-resource-collection>
            <web-resource-name>Secret documents</web-resource-name>
            <url-pattern>/secret/*</url-pattern>
        </web-resource-collection>
        <auth-constraint>
            <role-name>secretagent</role-name>
```

```
        </auth-constraint>
    </security-constraint>

    <login-config>
        <auth-method>BASIC</auth-method>
    </login-config>
```

The security constraint entry comes after all servlet and filter-related entries in the *web.xml* file. Each `<security-constraint>` block has one `<web-resource-collection>` section that designates a named list of URL patterns for areas of the WebApp, followed by an `<auth-constraint>` section listing user roles that are allowed to access those areas. You can add the example setup to the *web.xml* file for the *learningjava.war* file and prepare to try it out. However, there is one additional step you'll have to take to get this working: create the user role "secretagent" and an actual user with this role in your application server.

Access to protected areas is granted to user roles, not individual users. A user role is effectively just a group of users; instead of granting access to individual users by name, access is granted to roles, and users are assigned one or more roles. A user role is an abstraction from users. Actual user information (name and password, etc.) is handled outside the scope of the WebApp, in the application server environment (possibly integrated with the host platform operating system). Generally, application servers have their own tools for creating users and assigning individuals (or actual groups of users) their roles. A given username may have many roles associated with it.

When attempting to access a login-protected area, the user's valid login will be assessed to see if she has the correct role for access. For the Tomcat server, adding users and assigning them roles is easy; simply edit the file *conf/tomcat-users.xml*. To add a user named "bond" with the "secretagent" role, you'd add an entry like this:

```
    <user name="bond" password="007" roles="secretagent"/>
```

For other servers, you'll have to refer to the documentation to determine how to add users and assign security roles.

Secure Data Transport

Before we move on, there is one more piece of the security constraint to discuss: the transport guarantee. Each `<security-constraint>` block may end with a `<user-data-constraint>` entry, which designates one of three levels of transport security for the protocol used to transfer data to and from the protected area. For example:

```
    <security-constraint>
    ...
        <user-data-constraint>
            <transport-guarantee>CONFIDENTIAL</transport-guarantee>
        </user-data-constraint>
    </security-constraint>
```

The three levels are NONE, INTEGRAL, and CONFIDENTIAL. NONE is equivalent to leaving out the section, indicating no special transport is required. This is the standard for normal web traffic, which is generally sent in plain text over the network. The INTEGRAL level of security specifies that any transport protocol used must guarantee the data sent is not modified in transit. This implies the use of digital signatures or some other method of validating the data at the receiving end but it does not require that the data be encrypted and hidden while it is transported. Finally, CONFIDENTIAL implies both INTEGRAL and encrypted. In practice, the only widely used secure transport used in web browsers is SSL. Requiring a transport guarantee other than NONE typically forces the use of SSL by the client browser.

Authenticating Users

The `<login-conf>` section determines exactly how a user authenticates (identifies) himself or herself to the protected area. The `<auth-method>` tag allows four types of login authentication to be specified: BASIC, DIGEST, FORM, and CLIENT-CERT. In our example, we showed the BASIC method, which uses the standard web browser login and password pop-up dialog. BASIC authentication sends the user's name and password in plain text over the Internet unless a transport guarantee has been used separately to start SSL and encrypt the data stream. DIGEST is a variation on BASIC that hides the text of the password but adds little real security; it is not widely used. FORM is equivalent to BASIC, but instead of using the browser's dialog, we are allowed to use our own HTML form or servlet to post the username and password data. Again, form data is sent in plain text unless otherwise protected by a transport guarantee (SSL). CLIENT-CERT is an interesting option. It specifies that the client must be identified using a client-side public key certificate. This implies the use of a protocol like SSL, which allows for secure exchange and mutual authentication using digital certificates.

The FORM method is most useful because it allows us to customize the look of the login page (we recommend using SSL to secure the data stream). We can also specify an error page to use if the authentication fails. Here is a sample `<login-config>` using the form method:

```
<login-config>
    <auth-method>FORM</auth-method>
    <form-login-config>
        <form-login-page>/login.html</form-login-page>
        <form-error-page>/login_error.html</form-error-page>
    </form-login-config>
</login-config>
```

The login page must contain an HTML form with a specially named pair of fields for the name and password. Here is a simple *login.html* file:

```
<html>
<head><title>Login</title></head>
<body>
    <form method="POST" action="j_security_check">
        Username: <input type="text" name="j_username"><br>
        Password: <input type="password" name="j_password"><br>
        <input type="submit" value="submit">
    </form>
</body>
</html>
```

The username field is called j_username, the password is called j_password, and the URL used for the form action attribute is j_security_check. There are no special requirements for the error page, but normally you will want to provide a "try again" message and repeat the login form.

Procedural Security

We should mention that in addition to the declarative security offered by the *web. xml* file, servlets may perform their own active procedural (or programmatic) security using all the authentication information available to the container. We won't cover this in detail, but here are the basics.

The name of the authenticated user is available through the HttpServletRequest getRemoteUser() method, and the type of authentication provided can be determined with the getAuthType() method. Servlets can work with security roles using the isUserInRole() method. (To do this requires adding some additional mappings in the *web.xml* file allowing the servlet to refer to the security roles by reference names). For advanced applications, a java.security.Principal object for the user can be retrieved with the getUserPrincipal() method. In the case where a secure transport like SSL was used, the method isSecure() returns true, and detailed information about the cipher type, key size, and certificate chain is made available through request attributes.

Servlet Filters

The servlet Filter API generalizes the Java Servlet API to allow modular component "filters" to operate on the server request and responses in a sort of pipeline. Filters are said to be *chained*, meaning that when more than one filter is applied, the servlet request is passed through each filter in succession, with each having an opportunity to act upon or modify the request before passing it to the next filter. Similarly, upon completion, the servlet result is effectively passed back through the chain on its return trip to the browser. Servlet filters may operate on any requests to a web application, not just those handled by the servlets; they may filter static content, as well.

Filters are declared and mapped to servlets in the *web.xml* file. There are two ways to map a filter: using a URL pattern like those used for servlets or by specifying a servlet by its instance name (`<servlet-name>`). Filters obey the same basic rules as servlets when it comes to URL matching, but when multiple filters match a path, they are all invoked.

The order of the chain is determined by the order in which matching filter mappings appear in the *web.xml* file, with `<url-pattern>` matches taking precedence over `<servlet-name>` matches. This is contrary to the way servlet URL matching is done, with specific matches taking the highest priority. Filter chains are constructed as follows. First, each filter with a matching URL pattern is called in the order in which it appears in the *web.xml* file; next, each filter with a matching servlet name is called, also in order of appearance. URL patterns take a higher priority than filters specifically associated with a servlet, so in this case, patterns such as /* have first crack at an incoming request.

The Filter API is very simple and mimics the Servlet API. A servlet filter implements the `javax.servlet.Filter` interface and implements three methods: `init()`, `doFilter()`, and `destroy()`. The `doFilter()` method is where the work is performed. For each incoming request, the `ServletRequest` and `ServletResponse` objects are passed to `doFilter()`. Here we have a chance to examine and modify these objects— or even substitute our own objects for them—before passing them to the next filter and ultimately the servlet (or user) on the other side. Our link to the rest of the filter chain is another parameter of `doFilter()`, the `FilterChain` object. With `FilterChain`, we can invoke the next element in the pipeline. The following section presents an example.

A Simple Filter

For our first filter, we'll do something easy but practical: create a filter that limits the number of connections to its URLs. We'll simply have our filter keep a counter of the active connections passing through it and turn away new requests when they exceed a specified limit.

```java
import java.io.*;
import javax.servlet.*;
import javax.servlet.http.*;

public class ConLimitFilter implements Filter
{
    int limit;
    int count;

    public void init( FilterConfig filterConfig )
        throws ServletException
    {
        String s = filterConfig.getInitParameter("limit");
        if ( s == null )
```

```
            throw new ServletException("Missing init parameter: "+limit);
        limit = Integer.parseInt( s );
    }

    public void doFilter (
        ServletRequest req, ServletResponse res, FilterChain chain )
            throws IOException, ServletException
    {
        if ( count > limit ) {
            HttpServletResponse httpRes = (HttpServletResponse)res;
            httpRes.sendError(
                httpRes.SC_SERVICE_UNAVAILABLE, "Too Busy.");
        } else {
            ++count;
            chain.doFilter( req, res );
            --count;
        }
    }

    public void destroy( ) { }
}
```

ConLimitFilter implements the three life-cycle methods of the Filter interface:
init(), doFilter(), and destroy(). In our init() method, we use the FilterConfig
object to look for an initialization parameter named "limit" and turn it into an integer. Users can set this value in the section of the *web.xml* file where the instance of
our filter is declared. The doFilter() method implements all our logic. First, it
receives ServletRequest and ServletResponse object pairs for incoming requests.
Depending on the counter, it then either passes them down the chain by invoking the
next doFilter() method on the FilterChain object, or rejects them by generating its
own response. We use the standard HTTP message "504 Service Unavailable" when
we deny new connections.

Calling doFilter() on the FilterChain object continues processing by invoking the
next filter in the chain or by invoking the servlet if ours is the last filter. Alternatively, when we choose to reject the call, we use the ServletResponse to generate our
own response and then simply allow doFilter() to exit. This stops the processing
chain at our filter, although any filters called before us still have an opportunity to
intervene as the request effectively traverses back to the client.

Notice that ConLimitFilter increments the count before calling doFilter() and dec-
rements it after. Prior to calling doFilter() is our time to work on the request before
it reaches the rest of the chain and the servlet. After the call to doFilter(), the servlet has completed, and the request is, in effect, on the way back to the client. This is
our opportunity to do any post-processing of the response. We'll discuss this a bit
later.

Finally, we should mention that although we've been talking about the servlet
request and response as if they were HttpServletRequest and HttpServletResponse,

the doFilter() method actually takes the more generic ServletRequest and ServletResponse objects as parameters. As filter implementers, we are expected to determine when it is safe to treat them as HTTP traffic and perform the cast as necessary (which we do here in order to use the sendError() HTTP response method).

A Test Servlet

Before we go on, here is a simple test servlet you can use to try out this filter and the other filters we'll develop in this section. It's called WaitServlet, and as its name implies, it simply waits. You can specify how long it waits as a number of seconds with the servlet parameter time.

```java
import java.io.*;
import javax.servlet.*;
import javax.servlet.http.*;

public class WaitServlet extends HttpServlet
{
    public void doGet( HttpServletRequest request, HttpServletResponse response)
        throws ServletException, IOException
    {
        String waitStr = request.getParameter("time");
        if ( waitStr == null )
            throw new ServletException("Missing parameter: time");
        int wait = Integer.parseInt(waitStr);

        try {
            Thread.sleep( wait * 1000 );
        } catch( InterruptedException e ) {
            throw new ServletException(e);
        }

        response.setContentType("text/html");
        PrintWriter out = response.getWriter( );
        out.println(
            "<html><body><h1>WaitServlet Response</h1></body></html>");
        out.close( );
    }
}
```

By making multiple simultaneous requests to the WaitServlet, you can try out the ConLimitFilter. Be careful, though, because some web browsers (namely Opera) won't open multiple requests to the same URL. You may have to add extraneous parameters to trick the web browser. See the *learningjava.war* application on the CD-ROM that accompanies this book.

Declaring and Mapping Filters

Filters are declared and mapped in the *web.xml* file much as servlets are. Like servlets, one instance of a filter class is created for each filter declaration in the *web.xml* file. A filter declaration looks like this:

```
<filter>
    <filter-name>defaultsfilter1</filter-name>
    <filter-class>RequestDefaultsFilter</filter-class>
</filter>
```

It specifies a filter handle name to be used for reference within the *web.xml* file and the filter's Java class name. Filter declarations may also contain <init-param> parameter sections, just like servlet declarations.

Filters are mapped to resources with <filter-mapping> declarations that specify the filter handle name and either the specific servlet handle name or a URL pattern, as we discussed earlier.

```
<filter-mapping>
    <filter-name>conlimitfilter1</filter-name>
    <servlet-name>waitservlet1</servlet-name>
</filter-mapping>

<filter-mapping>
    <filter-name>conlimitfilter1</filter-name>
    <url-pattern>/*</url-pattern>
</filter-mapping>
```

Filter mappings appear after all filter declarations in the *web.xml* file.

Filtering the Servlet Request

Our first filter example was not very exciting because it did not actually modify any information going to or coming from the servlet. Next, let's do some actual "filtering" by modifying the incoming request before it reaches a servlet. In this example, we'll create a request "defaulting" filter that automatically supplies default values for specified servlet parameters when they are not provided in the incoming request. Despite its simplicity, this example might be very useful. Here is the RequestDefaultsFilter:

```
import java.io.*;
import javax.servlet.*;
import javax.servlet.http.*;

public class RequestDefaultsFilter implements Filter
{
    FilterConfig filterConfig;

    public void init( FilterConfig filterConfig ) throws ServletException
    {
```

```
        this.filterConfig = filterConfig;
    }

    public void doFilter (
        ServletRequest req, ServletResponse res, FilterChain chain )
            throws IOException, ServletException
    {
        WrappedRequest wrappedRequest =
            new WrappedRequest( (HttpServletRequest)req );
        chain.doFilter( wrappedRequest, res );
    }

    public void destroy() { }

    class WrappedRequest extends HttpServletRequestWrapper
    {
        WrappedRequest( HttpServletRequest req ) {
            super( req );
        }

        public String getParameter( String name ) {
            String value = super.getParameter( name );
            if ( value == null )
                value = filterConfig.getInitParameter( name );
            return value;
        }
    }
}
```

To interpose ourselves in the data flow, we must do something drastic. We kidnap the incoming HttpServletRequest object and replace it with an evil twin that does our bidding. The technique, which we'll use here for modifying the request object and later for modifying the response, is to wrap the real request with an adapter, allowing us to override some of its methods. Here we will take control of the HttpServletRequest's getParameter() method, modifying it to look for default values where it would otherwise return null.

Again, we implement the three life-cycle methods of Filter, but this time, before invoking doFilter() on the filter chain to continue processing, we wrap the incoming HttpServletRequest in our own class, WrappedRequest. WrappedRequest extends a special adapter called HttpServletRequestWrapper. This wrapper class is a convenience utility that extends HttpServletRequest. It accepts a reference to a target HttpServletRequest object and, by default, delegates all of its methods to that target. This makes it very convenient for us to simply override one or more methods of interest to us. All we have to do is override getParameter() in our WrappedRequest class and add our functionality. Here we simply call our parent's getParameter(), and in the case where the value is null, we try to substitute a filter initialization parameter of the same name.

Try this example out using the `WaitServlet` with a filter declaration and mapping as follows:

```
<filter>
    <filter-name>defaultsfilter1</filter-name>
    <filter-class>RequestDefaultsFilter</filter-class>
    <init-param>
        <param-name>time</param-name>
        <param-value>3</param-value>
    </init-param>
</filter>
...
<filter-mapping>
    <filter-name>defaultsfilter1</filter-name>
    <servlet-name>waitservlet1</servlet-name>
</filter-mapping>
```

Now the `WaitServlet` receives a default time value of three seconds even when you don't specify one.

Filtering the Servlet Response

Filtering the request was fairly easy, and we can do something similar with the response object using exactly the same technique. There is a corresponding `HttpServletResponseWrapper` that we can use to wrap the response before the servlet uses it to communicate back to the client. By wrapping the response, we can intercept methods that the servlet uses to write the response, just as we intercepted the `getParameter()` method that the servlet used in reading the incoming data. For example, we could override the `sendError()` method of the `HttpServletResponse` object and modify it to redirect to a specified page. In this way, we could create a servlet filter that emulates the programmable error page control offered in the *web.xml* file. But the most interesting technique available to us, and the one we'll show here, involves actually modifying the data written by the servlet before it reaches the client. To do this we have to pull a double "switcheroo." We wrap the servlet response to override the `getWriter()` method and then create our own wrapper for the client's `PrintWriter` object supplied by this method, one that buffers the data written and allows us to modify it. This is a useful and powerful technique, but it can be tricky.

Our example is called `LinkResponseFilter`. It is an automatic hyperlink-generating filter that reads HTML responses and searches them for patterns supplied as regular expressions. When it matches a pattern, it turns it into an HTML link. The pattern and links are specified in the filter initialization parameters. You could extend this example with access to a database or XML file and add additional rules to make it into a very powerful site management helper. Here it is:

```
import java.io.*;
import java.util.*;
import javax.servlet.*;
import javax.servlet.http.*;
```

```java
public class LinkResponseFilter implements Filter
{
    FilterConfig filterConfig;

    public void init( FilterConfig filterConfig )
        throws ServletException
    {
        this.filterConfig = filterConfig;
    }

    public void doFilter (
        ServletRequest req, ServletResponse res, FilterChain chain )
            throws IOException, ServletException
    {
        WrappedResponse wrappedResponse =
            new WrappedResponse( (HttpServletResponse)res );
        chain.doFilter( req, wrappedResponse );
        wrappedResponse.close();
    }

    public void destroy() { }

    class WrappedResponse extends HttpServletResponseWrapper
    {
        boolean linkText;
        PrintWriter client;

        WrappedResponse( HttpServletResponse res ) {
            super( res );
        }

        public void setContentType( String mime ) {
            super.setContentType( mime );
            if ( mime.startsWith("text/html") )
                linkText = true;
        }

        public PrintWriter getWriter() throws IOException {
            if ( client == null )
                if ( linkText )
                    client = new LinkWriter(
                        super.getWriter(), new ByteArrayOutputStream() );
                else
                    client = super.getWriter();
            return client;
        }

        void close() {
            if ( client != null )
                client.close();
        }
    }
}
```

```
class LinkWriter extends PrintWriter
{
    ByteArrayOutputStream buffer;
    Writer client;

    LinkWriter( Writer client, ByteArrayOutputStream buffer ) {
        super( buffer );
        this.buffer = buffer;
        this.client = client;
    }

    public void close() {
        try {
            flush();
            client.write( linkText( buffer.toString() ) );
            client.close();
        } catch ( IOException e ) {
            setError();
        }
    }

    String linkText( String text ) {
        Enumeration en = filterConfig.getInitParameterNames();
        while ( en.hasMoreElements() ) {
            String pattern = (String)en.nextElement();
            String value = filterConfig.getInitParameter( pattern );
            text = text.replaceAll(
                pattern, "<a href="+value+">$0</a>" );
        }
        return text;
    }
}
```

That was a bit longer than our previous examples, but the basics are the same. We have wrapped the HttpServletResponse object with our own WrappedResponse class using the HttpServletResponseWrapper helper class. Our WrappedResponse overrides two methods: getWriter() and setContentType(). We override setContentType() in order to set a flag indicating whether the output is of type "text/html" (an HTML document). We don't want to be performing regular-expression replacements on binary data such as images, for example, should they happen to match our filter. We also override getWriter() to provide our substitute writer stream, LinkWriter. Our LinkWriter class is a PrintStream that takes as arguments the client PrintWriter and a ByteArrayOutputStream that serves as a buffer for storing output data before it is written. We are careful to substitute our LinkWriter only if the linkText boolean set by setContent() is true. When we do use our LinkWriter, we cache the stream so that any subsequent calls to getWriter() return the same object. Finally, we have added one method to the response object: close(). A normal HttpServletResponse does not have a close() method. We use ours on the return trip to the client to indicate that the LinkWriter should complete its processing and write the actual data to the client.

We do this in case the client does not explicitly close the output stream before exiting the servlet service methods.

This explains the important parts of our filter-writing example. Let's wrap up by looking at the `LinkWriter`, which does the magic in this example. `LinkWriter` is a `PrintStream` that holds references to two other `Writer`s: the true client `PrintWriter` and a `ByteArrayOutputStream`. The `LinkWriter` calls its superclass constructor, passing the `ByteArrayOutputStream` as the target stream, so all of its default functionality (its `print()` methods) writes to the byte array. Our only real job is to intercept the `close()` method of the `PrintStream` and add our text linking before sending the data. When `LinkWriter` is closed, it flushes itself to force any data buffered in its superclass out to the `ByteArrayOutputStream`. It then retrieves the buffered data (with the `ByteArrayOutputStream toString()` method) and invokes its `linkText()` method to create the hyperlinks before writing the linked data to the client. The `linkText()` method simply loops over all the filter initialization parameters, treating them as patterns, and uses the String `replaceAll()` method to turn them into hyperlinks. (See Chapter 9 for more about `replaceAll()`).

This example works, but it has limitations. First, we cannot buffer an infinite amount of data. A better implementation would have to make a decision about when to start writing data to the client, potentially based on the client-specified buffer size of the HttpServletResponse API. Next, our implementation of `linkText()` could probably be speeded up by constructing one large regular expression using alternation. You will no doubt find other ways it can be improved.

Building WAR Files with Ant

Thus far in this book, we have not become too preoccupied with special tools to help you construct Java applications. Partly, this is because it's outside the scope of this text, and partly it reflects a small bias of the authors against getting too entangled with particular development environments. There is, however, one universal tool that should be in the arsenal of every Java developer: the Jakarta Project's Ant. Ant is a project builder for Java, a pure Java application that fills the role that *make* does for C applications. Ant has many advantages over *make* when building Java code, not the least of which is that it comes with a wealth of special "targets" (declarative commands) to perform common Java-related operations such as building WAR files. Ant is fast, portable, and easy to install and use. Make it your friend.

We won't cover the usage of Ant in any detail here. You can learn more and download it from its home page, *http://jakarta.apache.org/ant/* or grab it from the CD-ROM accompanying this book. We give you a sample build file here to get you started.

A Development-Oriented Directory Layout

At the beginning of this chapter, we described the layout of a WAR file, including the standard files and directories that must appear inside the archive. While this file organization is necessary for deployment inside the archive, it may not be the best way to organize your project during development. Maintaining *web.xml* and libraries inside a directory named *WEB-INF* under all of your content may be convenient for running the *jar* command, but it doesn't line up well with how those areas are created or maintained from a development perspective. Fortunately, with a simple Ant build file, we can create our WAR from an arbitrary project layout.

Let's choose a directory structure that is a little more oriented towards project development. For example:

```
myapplication
|
|-- src
|-- lib
|-- docs
|-- web.xml
```

We place our source-code tree under *src*, required library JAR files under *lib*, and our content under *docs*. We leave *web.xml* at the top where it's easy to tweak parameters, etc.

Here is a simple Ant *build.xml* file for constructing a WAR file from the new directory structure:

```
<project name="myapplication" default="compile" basedir=".">

    <property name="war-file" value="${ant.project.name}.war"/>
    <property name="src-dir" value="src" />
    <property name="build-dir" value="classes" />
    <property name="docs-dir" value="docs" />
    <property name="webxml-file" value="web.xml" />
    <property name="lib-dir" value="lib" />

    <target name="compile" depends="">
        <mkdir dir="${build-dir}"/>
        <javac srcdir="${src-dir}" destdir="${build-dir}"/>
    </target>

    <target name="war" depends="compile">
        <war warfile="${war-file}" webxml="${webxml-file}">
            <classes dir="${build-dir}"/>
            <fileset dir="${docs-dir}"/>
            <lib dir="${lib-dir}"/>
        </war>
    </target>

    <target name="clean">
        <delete dir="${build-dir}"/>
```

```
        <delete file="${war-file}"/>
    </target>

</project>
```

Place the *build.xml* file in the *myapplication* directory. You can now compile your code simply by running ant, or you can compile and build the WAR file with the command ant war. Ant automatically finds all the Java files under the *src* tree that need building and compiles them into a "build" directory named *classes*. Running ant war creates the file *myapplication.war*. You can remove the build directory and WAR file with the *ant clean* command.

There is nothing really project-specific in this sample build file except the project name attribute in the first line, which you replace with your application's name. And we reference that only to specify the name of the WAR file to generate. Feel free to customize the names of any of the files or directories by changing the property declarations at the top. The *learningjava.war* file example supplied on the accompanying CD-ROM comes with a version of this Ant *build.xml* file.

Swing

Swing is Java's user interface toolkit. It was developed during the life of Java 1.1 and became part of the core APIs with 1.2. Swing provides classes representing interface items such as windows, buttons, combo boxes, trees, tables, and menus—everything you need to build a user interface for your Java application. The javax.swing package (and its numerous subpackages) contain the Swing user interface classes.[*]

Swing is part of a larger collection of software called the Java Foundation Classes (JFC). JFC includes the following APIs:

- The Abstract Window Toolkit (AWT), the original user interface toolkit

- Swing, the pure Java user interface toolkit

- Accessibility, which provides tools for integrating nonstandard input and output devices into your user interfaces

- The 2D API, a comprehensive set of classes for high-quality drawing

- Drag and Drop, an API that supports the drag-and-drop metaphor

JFC is the largest and most complicated part of the standard Java platform, so it shouldn't be any surprise that we'll take several chapters to discuss it. In fact, we won't even get to talk about all of it, just the most important parts—Swing and the 2D API. Here's the lay of the land:

- This chapter covers the basic concepts you need to understand how to build user interfaces with Swing.

- Chapter 16 discusses the basic components from which user interfaces are built: buttons, lists, text fields, checkboxes, and so on.

- Chapter 17 dives further into the Swing toolkit, describing text components, trees, tables, and other neat stuff.

---

[*] Don't be fooled by the javax prefix, which usually denotes a standard extension API. Swing is an integral part of the core APIs in Java 2 Standard Edition.

- Chapter 18 discusses layout managers, which are responsible for arranging components within a window.

- Chapter 19 discusses the fundamentals of drawing, including simple image displays.

- Chapter 20 covers the image generation and processing tools that are in the `java.awt.image` package. We'll throw in audio and video for good measure.

We can't cover the full functionality of Swing in this book; if you want the whole story, see *Java Swing* by Marc Loy, Robert Eckstein, Dave Wood, Brian Cole, and James Elliott (O'Reilly). Instead, we'll cover the basic tools you are most likely to use and show some examples of what can be done with some of the more advanced features. Figure 15-1 shows the user interface component classes of the `javax.swing` package.

To understand Swing, it helps to understand its predecessor, the Abstract Window Toolkit (AWT). As its name suggests, AWT is an abstraction. Like the rest of Java it was designed to be portable; its functionality is the same for all Java implementations. However, people generally expect their applications to have a consistent look and feel and that is usually different on different platforms. So AWT was designed to work in the same way on all platforms, yet have the appearance of a native application. You could choose to write your code under Windows, then run it on an X Window System or a Macintosh. To achieve platform independence, AWT uses interchangeable *toolkits* that interact with the host windowing system to display user interface components. This shields your application from the details of the environment it's running in. Let's say you ask AWT to create a button. When your application or applet runs, a toolkit appropriate to the host environment renders the button appropriately: on Windows, you can get a button that looks like other Windows buttons; on a Macintosh, you can get a Mac button; and so on.

AWT had some serious shortcomings. The worst was that the use of platform-specific toolkits meant that AWT applications might be subtly incompatible on different platforms. Furthermore, AWT lacked advanced user interface components, like trees and grids, that were not common to all environments.

Swing takes a fundamentally different approach. Instead of using native toolkits to supply interface items such as buttons and combo boxes, components in Swing are implemented in Java itself. This means that, whatever platform you're using, by default a Swing button (for example) looks the same. However, Swing also provides a powerful, pluggable look-and-feel API that allows native operating system appearance to be substituted at the Java level. Working purely in Java makes Swing much less prone to platform-specific bugs, which were a problem for AWT. It also means that Swing components are much more flexible and can be extended and modified in your applications.

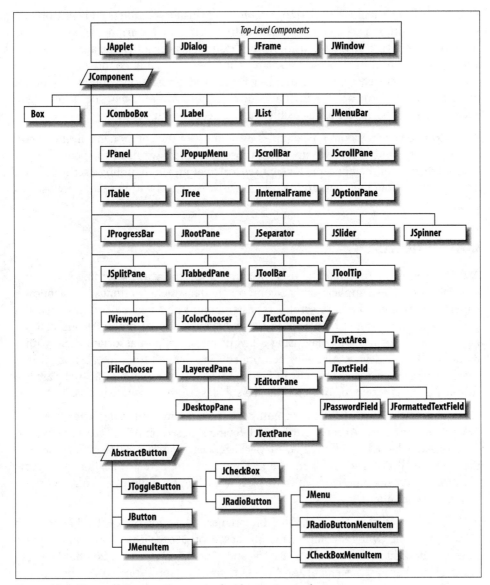

Figure 15-1. User interface components in the javax.swing package

Working with user interface components in Swing is meant to be easy. When building a user interface for your application, you'll be working with prefabricated components. It's easy to assemble a collection of user interface components (buttons, text areas, etc.) and arrange them inside containers to build complex layouts. You can also use simple components as building blocks for making entirely new kinds of interface gadgets that are completely portable and reusable.

Swing uses *layout managers* to arrange *components* inside *containers* and control their sizing and positioning. Layout managers define a strategy for arranging components instead of specifying absolute positions. For example, you can define a user interface with a collection of buttons and text areas and be reasonably confident that it will always display correctly, even if the user resizes the application window. It doesn't matter what platform or user interface look-and-feel you're using; the layout manager should still position them sensibly with respect to each other.

The next two chapters contain examples using most of the components in the javax. swing package. But before we dive into those examples, we need to spend a bit of time talking about the concepts Swing uses for creating and handling user interfaces. This material should get you up to speed on GUI concepts and how they are used in Java.

Components

A *component* is the fundamental user interface object in Java. Everything you see on the display in a Java application is a component. This includes things like windows, panels, buttons, checkboxes, scrollbars, lists, menus, and text fields. To be used, a component usually must be placed in a *container*. Container objects group components, arrange them for display using a layout manager, and associate them with a particular display device. All Swing components are derived from the abstract javax. swing.JComponent class, as you saw in Figure 15-1. For example, the JButton class is a subclass of AbstractButton, which is itself a subclass of the JComponent class.

JComponent is the root of the Swing component hierarchy, but it descends from the AWT Container class. At this bottom level, Swing is based on AWT, so our conversation occasionally delves into the AWT package. Container's superclass is Component, the root of all AWT components, and Component's superclass is, finally, Object. Because JComponent inherits from Container, it has the capabilities of both a component and a container.

AWT and Swing, then, have parallel hierarchies. The root of AWT's hierarchy is Component, while Swing's components are based on JComponent. You'll find similar classes in both hierarchies, such as Button and JButton, List and JList. But Swing is much more than a replacement for AWT—it contains sophisticated components as well as a real implementation of the Model-View-Controller (MVC) paradigm, which we'll discuss later.

For the sake of simplicity, we can split the functionality of the JComponent class into two categories: appearance and behavior. The JComponent class contains methods and variables that control an object's general appearance. This includes basic attributes such as its visibility, its current size and location, and certain common graphical defaults, such as font and color. The JComponent class also contains methods implemented by specific subclasses to produce graphical displays.

When a component is first displayed, it's associated with a particular display device. The JComponent class encapsulates access to its display area on that device. It includes tools for accessing graphics, for working with off-screen resources, and for receiving user input.

When we talk about a component's behavior, we mean the way it responds to user-driven events. When the user performs an action (such as pressing the mouse button) within a component's display area, a Swing thread delivers an event object that describes what happened. The event is delivered to objects that have registered themselves as listeners for that type of event from that component. For example, when the user clicks on a button, the button delivers an ActionEvent object. To receive those events, an object registers with the button as an ActionListener.

Events are delivered by invoking designated event-handler methods within the receiving object (the "listener"). A listener object prepares itself to receive events by implementing methods (e.g., actionPerformed()) for the types of events in which it is interested. Specific types of events cover different categories of component user interaction. For example, MouseEvents describe activities of the mouse within a component's area, KeyEvents describe key presses, and higher-level events (such as ActionEvents) indicate that a user interface component has done its job.

We will describe events thoroughly in this chapter because they are so fundamental to the way in which user interfaces function in Java. But they aren't limited to building user interfaces; they are an important interobject communications mechanism, which may be used by completely nongraphical parts of an application, as well. They are particularly important in the context of JavaBeans, which uses events as an extremely general notification mechanism.

Swing's event architecture is very flexible. Instead of requiring every component to listen for and handle events for its own bit of the user interface, an application may register event "handler" objects to receive the events for one or more components and "glue" those events to the correct application logic. A container might, for example, process the events relating to its child components.

One responsibility a container always has is laying out the components it contains. A component informs its container when it does something that might affect other components in the container, such as changing its size or visibility. The container then tells its layout manager that it is time to rearrange the child components.

As mentioned, Swing components are also containers. Containers can manage and arrange JComponent objects without knowing what they are or what they are doing. Components can be swapped and replaced with new versions easily and combined into composite user interface objects that can be, themselves, treated as individual components. This lends itself well to building larger, reusable user interface items.

Peers

Swing components are peerless, or lightweight. To understand these terms, you'll have to understand the peer system that AWT used (or still uses). Getting data out to a display medium and receiving events from input devices involve crossing the line from Java to the real world. The real world can be a nasty place full of architecture dependence, local peculiarities, and strange physical devices such as mice, trackballs, and '69 Buicks.

At some level, our components have to talk to objects that contain native methods to interact with the host operating environment. To keep this interaction as clean and well-defined as possible, AWT used a set of peer interfaces. The peer interface made it possible for a pure Java-language graphic component to use a corresponding real component—the peer object—in the native environment. You didn't generally deal directly with peer interfaces or the objects behind them; peer handling was encapsulated within the Component class.

AWT relied heavily on peers. For example, if you created a window and added eight buttons to it, AWT would create nine peers for you—one for the window and one for each of the buttons. As an application programmer, you wouldn't ever have to worry about the peers, but they would always be lurking under the surface, doing the real work of interacting with your operating system's windowing toolkit.

In Swing, by contrast, most components are *peerless*, or *lightweight*. This means that Swing components don't have any direct interaction with the underlying windowing system. They draw themselves in their parent container and respond to user events, all without the aid of a peer. All the components in Swing are written in pure Java, with no native code involved. In Swing, only the top-level (lowest API level) windows interact with the windowing system. These Swing containers descend from AWT counterparts, and thus still have peers. In Swing, if you create a window and add eight buttons to it, only one peer is created—for the window. Because it has fewer interactions with the underlying windowing system than AWT, Swing is more reliable.

With lightweight components, it is easy to change their appearance. Since each component draws itself, instead of relying on a peer, it can decide at runtime how to render itself. Accordingly, Swing supports different *look-and-feel* schemes, which can be changed at runtime. (A look-and-feel is the collected appearance of components in an application.) Look-and-feels based on Windows, Macintosh, and Motif are available (though licensing issues may encumber their use on various platforms), as well as an entirely original one called Metal or the "Java Look and Feel," which is the default scheme.

The Model-View-Controller Framework

Before continuing our discussion of GUI concepts, we want to make a brief aside and talk about the Model-View-Controller (MVC) framework. MVC is a method of building reusable components that logically separates the structure, presentation, and behavior of a component into separate pieces. MVC is primarily concerned with building user interface components, but the basic ideas can be applied to many design issues; its principles can be seen throughout Java.

The fundamental idea behind MVC is the separation of the data model for an item from its presentation. For example, we can draw different representations (e.g., bar graphs, pie charts) of the data in a spreadsheet. The data is the *model*; the particular representation is the *view*. A single model can have many views that present the data differently. A user interface component's *controller* defines and governs its behavior. Typically, this includes changes to the model, which, in turn, cause the view(s) to change, also. For a checkbox component, the data model could be a single boolean variable, indicating whether it's checked or not. The behavior for handling mouse-click events would alter the model, and the view would examine that data when it draws the on-screen representation.

The way in which Swing objects communicate, by passing events from sources to listeners, is part of this MVC concept of separation. Event listeners are "observers" (controllers) and event sources are "observables" (models).* When an observable changes or performs a function, it notifies all its observers of the activity.

Swing components explicitly support MVC. Each component is actually composed of two pieces. One piece, called the UI-delegate, is responsible for the "view" and "controller" roles. It takes care of drawing the component and responding to user events. The second piece is the data model itself. This separation makes it possible for multiple Swing components to share a single data model. For example, a read-only text box and a drop-down list box could use the same list of strings as a data model.

Painting

In an event-driven environment such as Swing, components can be asked to draw themselves at any time. In a more procedural programming environment, you might expect a component to be involved in drawing only when first created or when it changes its appearance. In Java, components act in a way that is closely tied to the underlying behavior of the display environment. For example, when you obscure a

---

* In Chapter 10 we described the Observer class and Observable interface of the java.util package. Swing doesn't use these classes directly, but it does use exactly the same design pattern for handling event sources and listeners.

component with another window and then reexpose it, a Swing thread may ask the component to redraw itself.

Swing asks a component to draw itself by calling its paint() method. paint() may be called at any time, but in practice, it's called when the object is first made visible, whenever it changes its appearance, or whenever some tragedy in the display system messes up its area. Because paint() can't make any assumptions about why it was called, it must redraw the component's entire display. The system may limit the drawing if only part of the component needs to be redrawn, but you don't have to worry about this.

A component never calls its paint() method directly. Instead, if a component requires redrawing, it schedules a call to paint() by invoking repaint(). The repaint() method asks Swing to schedule the component for repainting. At some point in the future, a call to paint() occurs. Swing is allowed to manage these requests in whatever way is most efficient. If there are too many requests to handle, or if there are multiple requests for the same component, the thread can reschedule a number of repaint requests into a single call to paint(). This means that you can't predict exactly when paint() is called in response to a repaint(); all you can expect is that it happens at least once, after you request it.

Calling repaint() is normally an implicit request to be updated as soon as possible. Another form of repaint() allows you to specify a time period within which you would like an update, giving the system more flexibility in scheduling the request. The system tries to repaint the component within the time you specify, but if you happen to make more than one repaint request within that time period, the system may simply condense them to carry out a single update within the time you specified. An application performing animation could use this method to govern its refresh rate (by specifying a period that is the inverse of the desired frame rate).

Swing components can act as containers, holding other components. Because every Swing component does its own drawing, Swing components are responsible for telling contained components to draw themselves. Fortunately, this is all taken care of for you by a component's default paint() method. If you override this method, however, you have to make sure to call the superclass's implementation like this:

```
public void paint(Graphics g) {
    super.paint(g);
    ...
}
```

There's a cleaner way around this problem. All Swing components have a method called paintComponent(). While paint() is responsible for drawing the component as well as its contained components, paintComponent()'s sole responsibility is drawing the component itself. If you override paintComponent() instead of paint(), you won't have to worry about drawing contained components.

Both paint() and paintComponent() receive a single argument: a Graphics object. The Graphics object represents the component's graphics context. It corresponds to the area of the screen on which the component can draw and provides the methods for performing primitive drawing and image manipulation. (We'll look at the Graphics class in detail in Chapter 17.)

Enabling and Disabling Components

Standard Swing components can be turned on and off by calling the setEnabled() method. When a component such as a JButton or JTextField is disabled, it becomes "ghosted" or "greyed-out" and doesn't respond to user input.

For example, let's see how to create a component that can be used only once. This requires getting ahead of the story; we won't explain some aspects of this example until later. Earlier, we said that a JButton generates an ActionEvent when it is pressed. This event is delivered to the listeners' actionPerformed() method. The following code disables whatever component generated the event:

```
public boolean void actionPerformed(ActionEvent e ) {
    ((JComponent)e.getSource( )).setEnabled(false);
}
```

This code calls getSource() to find out which component generated the event. We cast the result to JComponent because we don't necessarily know what kind of component we're dealing with; it might not be a button, because other kinds of components can generate action events. Once we know which component generated the event, we disable it.

You can also disable an entire container. Disabling a JPanel, for instance, disables all the components it contains.

Focus, Please

In order to receive keyboard events, a component has to have keyboard *focus*. The component with the focus is the currently selected component on the screen and is usually highlighted visually. It receives all keyboard event information until the focus changes to a new component. Typically a component receives focus when the user clicks on it with the mouse or navigates to it using the keyboard. A component can ask for focus with the JComponent's requestFocus() method. You can configure whether a given component is eligible to receive focus with the setFocusable() method. By default most components, including things such as buttons and checkboxes, are "focusable." To make an entire window and its components nonfocusable, use the Window setFocusableWindowState() method.

The control of focus is at the heart of the user's experience with an application. Especially with text entry fields and forms, users are accustomed to a smooth transfer of focus with the use of keyboard navigation cues (e.g., Tab and Shift-Tab for forward and backward field navigation). The management of focus in a large GUI with many components could be complex. Fortunately, as of Java 1.4, Swing handles almost all this behavior for you, so in general you don't have to implement code to specify how focus is transferred. The 1.4 release introduced an entirely new focus subsystem. The flexible KeyboardFocusManager API provides the expected common behavior by default and allows customization via FocusTraversalPolicy objects. We'll discuss focus-related events later in this chapter and focus navigation more in Chapter 17.

Other Component Methods

The JComponentclass is very large; it has to provide the base-level functionality for all the various kinds of Java GUI objects. It inherits a lot of functionality from its parent Container and Component classes. We don't have room to document every method of the JComponent class here, but we'll flesh out our discussion by covering some more of the important ones:

Container getParent()
> Return the container that holds this component.

String getName()
void setName(String *name*)
> Get or assign the String name of this component. Naming a component is useful for debugging. The name is returned by toString().

void setVisible(boolean *visible*)
> Make the component visible or invisible, within its container. If you change the component's visibility, the container's layout manager automatically lays out its visible components.

Color getForeground()
void setForeground(Color *c*)
Color getBackground()
void setBackground(Color *c*)
> Get and set the foreground and background colors for this component. The foreground color of any component is the default color used for drawing. For example, it is the color used for text in a text field as well as the default drawing color for the Graphics object passed to the component's paint() and paintComponent() methods. The background color is used to fill the component's area when it is cleared by the default implementation of update().

Dimension getSize()
void setSize(int *width,* int *height*)
> Get and set the current size of the component. Note that a layout manager may change the size of a component even after you've set its size yourself. To change the size a component "wants" to be, use setPreferredSize(). There are other methods in JComponent to set its location, but normally this is the job of a layout manager.

```
Dimension getPreferredSize()
void setPreferredSize(Dimension preferredSize)
```
Use these methods to examine or sets the preferred size of a component. Layout managers attempt to set components to their preferred sizes. If you change a component's preferred size, you must call the method revalidate() on the component to get it laid out again.

```
Cursor getCursor()
void setCursor(Cursor cursor)
```
Get or set the type of cursor (mouse pointer) used when the mouse is over this component's area. For example:

```
JComponent myComponent = ...;
Cursor crossHairs =
    Cursor.getPredefinedCursor( Cursor.CROSSHAIR_CURSOR );
myComponent.setCursor( crossHairs );
```

Containers

A container is a kind of component that holds and manages other components. JComponent objects can be containers because the JComponent class descends from the Container class. However, you wouldn't normally add components directly to specialized components such as buttons or lists.

Three of the most useful general container types are JFrame, JPanel, and JApplet. A JFrame is a top-level window on your display. JFrame is derived from JWindow, which is pretty much the same but lacks a border. A JPanel is a generic container element that groups components inside JFrames and other JPanels. The JApplet class is a kind of container that provides the foundation for applets that run inside web browsers. Like other JComponents, a JApplet can contain other user-interface components. You can also use the JComponent class directly, like a JPanel, to hold components inside another container. With the exception of JFrame and JWindow, all the components and containers in Swing are lightweight.

A container maintains the list of "child" components it manages and has methods for dealing with those components. Note that this child relationship refers to a visual hierarchy, not a subclass/superclass hierarchy. By themselves, most components aren't very useful until they are added to a container and displayed. The add() method of the Container class adds a component to the container. Thereafter, this component can be displayed in the container's display area and positioned by its layout manager. You can remove a component from a container with the remove() method.

Layout Managers

A *layout manager* is an object that controls the placement and sizing of components within the display area of a container. A layout manager is like a window manager in a display system; it controls where the components go and how big they are. Every container has a default layout manager, but you can install a new one by calling the container's setLayout() method.

Swing comes with a few layout managers that implement common layout schemes. The default layout manager for a JPanel is a FlowLayout, which tries to place objects at their preferred size from left to right and top to bottom in the container. The default for a JFrame is a BorderLayout, which places objects at specific locations within the window, such as NORTH, SOUTH, and CENTER. Another layout manager, GridLayout, arranges components in a rectangular grid. The most general (and difficult to use) layout manager is GridBagLayout, which lets you do the kinds of things you can do with HTML tables. (We'll get into the details of all these layout managers in Chapter 16.)

When you add a component to a container using a simple layout manager, you'll often use the version of add() that takes a single Component as an argument. However, if you're using a layout manager that uses "constraints," such as BorderLayout or GridBagLayout, you must specify additional information about where to put the new component. For that you can use the version that takes a constraint object. Here's how to place a component at the top edge of a container that uses a BorderLayout manager:

```
myContainer.add(myComponent, BorderLayout.NORTH);
```

In this case, the constraint object is the static member variable NORTH. GridBagLayout uses a much more complex constraint object to specify positioning.

Insets

Insets specify a container's margins; the space specified by the container's insets won't be used by a layout manager. Insets are described by an Insets object, which has four public int fields: top, bottom, left, and right. You normally don't need to worry about the insets; the container sets them automatically, taking into account extras like the menu bar that may appear at the top of a frame. To find the insets, call the component's getInsets() method, which returns an Insets object.

Z-Ordering (Stacking Components)

With the standard layout managers, components are not allowed to overlap. However, if you use custom-built layout managers or absolute positioning, components within a container may overlap. If they do, the order in which components were added to a container matters. When components overlap, they are "stacked" in the order in which they were added: the first component added to the container is on top, and the last is on the bottom. To give you more control over stacking, two additional forms of the add() method take an additional integer argument that lets you specify the component's exact position in the container's stacking order.

The revalidate( ) and doLayout( ) Methods

A layout manager arranges the components in a container only when asked to. Several things can mess up a container after it's initially laid out:

- Changing its size
- Resizing or moving one of its child components
- Adding, showing, removing, or hiding a child component

Any of these actions cause the container to be marked *invalid*. This means that it needs to have its child components readjusted by its layout manager. In most cases, Swing readjusts the layout automatically. All components, not just containers, maintain a notion of when they are valid or invalid. If the size, location, or internal layout of a Swing component changes, its revalidate() method is automatically called. Internally, the revalidate() method first calls the method invalidate() to mark the component and all its enclosing containers as invalid. It then validates the tree. Validation descends the hierarchy, starting at the nearest *validation root* container, recursively validating each child. Validating a child Container means invoking its doLayout() method, which asks the layout manager to do its job and then notes that the Container has been reorganized by setting its state to valid again. A validation root is a container that can accommodate children of any size such as JScrollPane.

There are a few cases in which you may need to tell Swing to fix things manually. One example is when you change the preferred size of a component (as opposed to its actual onscreen size). To clean up the layout, call the revalidate() method. So, for example, if you have a small JPanel—say a keypad holding some buttons—and you change the preferred size of the JPanel by calling its setPreferredSize() method, you should also call revalidate() on the panel or its immediate container. The layout manager of the panel then rearranges its buttons to fit inside its new area.

Managing Components

There are a few additional tools of the Container class we should mention:

Component[] getComponents()
> Returns the container's components in an array.

void list(PrintWriter out, int indent)
> Generates a list of the components in this container and writes them to the specified PrintWriter.

```
Component getComponentAt(int x, int y)
```
Tells you what component is at the specified coordinates in the container's coordinate system.

Listening for Components

You can use the `ContainerListener` interface to automate setting up a container's new components. A container that implements this interface can receive an event whenever it gains or loses a component. This facility makes it easy for a container to micro-manage its components.

Windows and Frames

Windows and frames are the top-level containers for Java components. A `JWindow` is simply a plain, graphical screen that displays in your windowing system. Windows have no frills; they are mainly suitable for making "splash" screens and pop-up windows. `JFrame`, on the other hand, is a subclass of `JWindow` that has a border and can hold a menu bar. You can drag a frame around on the screen and resize it, using the ordinary controls for your windowing environment. Figure 15-2 shows a `JFrame` on the left and a `JWindow` on the right.

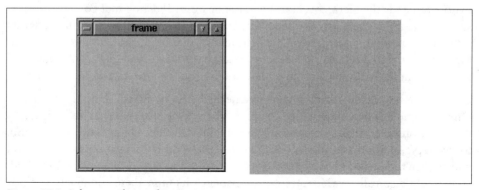

Figure 15-2. A frame and a window

All other Swing components and containers must be held, at some level, inside a `JWindow` or `JFrame`. Applets are a kind of `Container`. Even applets must be housed in a frame or window, though normally you don't see an applet's parent frame because it is part of (or simply is) the browser or `appletviewer` displaying the applet.

`JFrame`s and `JWindow`s are the only components that can be displayed without being added or attached to another `Container`. After creating a `JFrame` or `JWindow`, you can call the `setVisible()` method to display it. The following short application creates a `JFrame` and a `JWindow` and displays them side by side, just like in Figure 15-2.

```
//file: TopLevelWindows.java
import javax.swing.*;

public class TopLevelWindows {
  public static void main(String[] args) {
    JFrame frame = new JFrame("The Frame");
    frame.setSize(300, 300);
    frame.setLocation(100, 100);

    JWindow window = new JWindow( );
    window.setSize(300, 300);
    window.setLocation(500, 100);

    frame.setVisible(true);
    window.setVisible(true);
  }
}
```

The JFrame constructor can take a String argument that supplies a title, displayed in the JFrame's titlebar. (Or you can create the JFrame with no title and call setTitle() to supply the title later.) The JFrame's size and location on your desktop is determined by the calls to setSize() and setLocation(). After creating the JFrame, we create a JWindow in almost exactly the same way. The JWindow doesn't have a titlebar, so there are no arguments to the JWindow constructor.

Once the JFrame and JWindow are set up, we call setVisible(true) to get them on the screen. The setVisible() method returns immediately, without blocking. Fortunately, our application does not exit, even though we've reached the end of the main() method, because the windows are still visible. You can close the JFrame by clicking on the close button in the titlebar. JFrame's default behavior is to hide itself when you click on the box by calling setVisible(false). You can alter this behavior by calling the setDefaultCloseOperation() method or by adding an event listener, which we'll cover later. Since we haven't arranged any other means here, you will have to hit Ctrl-C or whatever keystroke kills a process on your machine to stop execution of the TopLevelWindows application.

Other Methods for Controlling Frames

The setLocation() method of the Component class can be used on a JFrame or JWindow to set its position on the screen. The x and y coordinates are relative to the screen's origin (the top left corner).

You can use the toFront() and toBack() methods to place a JFrame or JWindow in front of, or behind, other windows. By default, a user is allowed to resize a JFrame, but you can prevent resizing by calling setResizable(false) before showing the JFrame.

On most systems, frames can be "iconified"; that is, they can be shrunk down and represented by a little icon image. You can get and set a frame's icon image by calling getIconImage() and setIconImage(). As you can with all components, you can set the cursor by calling the setCursor() method.

Using Content Panes

Windows and frames don't behave exactly like regular containers. With other containers, you can add child components with the add() method. JFrame and JWindow have some extra stuff in them (mostly to support Swing's peerless components), so you can't just add() components directly. Instead, you need to add the components to the associated *content pane*. The content pane is just a Container that covers the visible area of the JFrame or JWindow. Whenever you create a new JFrame or JWindow, a content pane is automatically created for you. You can retrieve it with getContentPane(). Here's another example that creates a JFrame and adds some components to its content pane:

```
//file: MangoMango1.java
import java.awt.*;
import javax.swing.*;

public class MangoMango1 {
  public static void main(String[] args) {
    JFrame frame = new JFrame("The Frame");
    frame.setLocation(100, 100);

    Container content = frame.getContentPane( );
    content.setLayout(new FlowLayout( ));
    content.add(new JLabel("Mango"));
    content.add(new JButton("Mango"));

    frame.pack( );
    frame.setVisible(true);
  }
}
```

The call to JFrame's pack() method tells the frame window to resize itself to the minimum size required to hold all its components. Instead of having to determine the size of the JFrame, pack tells it to be "just big enough." If you do want to set the absolute size of the JFrame yourself, call setSize() instead.

If you create your own Container, you can make it the content pane of a JFrame or JWindow by passing it to setContentPane(). Using this strategy, you could rewrite the previous example as follows:

```
//file: MangoMango2.java
import java.awt.*;
import javax.swing.*;

public class MangoMango2 {
  public static void main(String[] args) {
    JFrame f = new JFrame("The Frame");
    f.setLocation(100, 100);
```

```
    Container content = new JPanel( );
    content.add(new JLabel("Mango"));
    content.add(new JButton("Mango"));
    f.setContentPane(content);

    f.pack( );
    f.setVisible(true);
  }
}
```

We'll cover labels and buttons in Chapter 16 and layouts in Chapter 18. The important thing to remember is that you can't add components directly to a JFrame or JWindow. Instead, add them to the automatically created content pane or create an entirely new content pane. If you try to add components directly to one of these containers you will get an informative runtime exception directing you to do otherwise.

Events

We've spent a lot of time discussing the different kinds of objects in Swing—components, containers, and special containers such as frames and windows. Now it's time to discuss interobject communication in detail.

Swing objects communicate by sending events. The way we talk about events— "firing" them and "handling" them—makes it sound as if they are part of some special Java language feature. But they aren't. An event is simply an ordinary Java object that is delivered to its receiver by invoking an ordinary Java method. Everything else, however interesting, is purely convention. The entire Java event mechanism is really just a set of conventions for the kinds of descriptive objects that should be delivered; these conventions prescribe when, how, and to whom events should be delivered.

Events are sent from a single source object to one or more listeners (or receivers). A listener implements prescribed event-handling methods that enable it to receive a type of event. It then registers itself with a source of that kind of event. Sometimes an adapter object may be interposed between the event source and the listener, but in any case, registration of a listener is always established before any events are delivered.

An event object is an instance of a subclass of java.util.EventObject; it holds information about something that's happened to its source. The EventObject class itself serves mainly to identify event objects; the only information it contains is a reference to the event source (the object that sent the event). Components don't normally send or receive EventObjects as such; they work with subclasses that provide more specific information.

AWTEvent is a subclass of java.awt.EventObject; further subclasses of AWTEvent provide information about specific event types. Swing has events of its own that descend directly from EventObject. For the most part, you'll just be working with specific event subclasses from the AWT or Swing packages.

ActionEvents correspond to a decisive "action" a user has taken with the component—like pressing a button or pressing Enter. An ActionEvent thus carries the name of an action to be performed (the *action command*) by the program. MouseEvents are generated when a user uses the mouse within a component's area. They describe the state of the mouse and therefore carry such information as the x and y coordinates and the state of your mouse buttons at the time the MouseEvent was created.

ActionEvent operates at a higher semantic level than MouseEvent: an ActionEvent lets us know that a component has performed its job; a MouseEvent simply confers a lot of information about the mouse at a given time. You could figure out that somebody clicked on a JButton by examining mouse events, but it is simpler to work with action events. The precise meaning of an event, however, can depend on the context in which it is received.

Event Receivers and Listener Interfaces

An event is delivered by passing it as an argument to the receiving object's event-handler method. ActionEvents, for example, are always delivered to a method called actionPerformed() in the receiver:

```
public void actionPerformed( ActionEvent e ) {
    ...
}
```

For each type of event, there is a corresponding listener interface that prescribes the method(s) it must provide to receive those events. In this case, any object that receives ActionEvents must implement the ActionListener interface:

```
public interface ActionListener extends java.util.EventListener {
    public void actionPerformed( ActionEvent e );
}
```

All listener interfaces are subinterfaces of java.util.EventListener, which is an empty interface. It exists only to help Java-based tools such as IDEs identify listener interfaces.

Listener interfaces are required for a number of reasons. First, they help to identify objects that can receive a given type of event. This way we can give the event-handler methods friendly, descriptive names and still make it easy for documentation, tools, and humans to recognize them in a class. Next, listener interfaces are useful because several methods can be specified for an event receiver. For example, the FocusListener interface contains two methods:

```
abstract void focusGained( FocusEvent e );
abstract void focusLost( FocusEvent e );
```

Although these methods each take a FocusEvent as an argument, they correspond to different reasons for firing the event; in this case, whether the FocusEvent means that focus was received or lost. In this case you could also figure out what happened by inspecting the event; all AWTEvents contain a constant specifying the event's type. But by using two methods, the FocusListener interface saves you the effort: if focusGained() is called, you know the event type was FOCUS_GAINED.

Similarly, the MouseListener interface defines five methods for receiving mouse events (and MouseMotionListener defines two more), each of which gives you some additional information about why the event occurred. In general, the listener interfaces group sets of related event-handler methods; the method called in any given situation provides a context for the information in the event object.

There can be more than one listener interface for dealing with a particular kind of event. For example, the MouseListener interface describes methods for receiving MouseEvents when the mouse enters or exits an area or a mouse button is pressed or released. MouseMotionListener is an entirely separate interface that describes methods to get mouse events when the mouse is moved (no buttons pressed) or dragged (buttons pressed). By separating mouse events into these two categories, Java lets you be a little more selective about the circumstances under which you want to receive MouseEvents. You can register as a listener for mouse events without receiving mouse motion events; because mouse motion events are extremely common, you don't want to handle them if you don't need to.

Two simple patterns govern the naming of Swing event listener interfaces and handler methods:

- Event-handler methods are public methods that return type void and take a single event object (a subclass of java.util.EventObject) as an argument.[*]
- Listener interfaces are subclasses of java.util.EventListener that are named with the suffix "Listener"—for example, MouseListener and ActionListener.

These may seem pretty obvious, but they are important because they are our first hint of a design pattern governing how to build components that work with events.

Event Sources

The previous section described the machinery an event receiver uses to listen for events. In this section, we'll describe how a receiver tells an event source to send it events, as they occur.

To receive events, an eligible listener must register itself with an event source. It does this by calling an "add listener" method in the event source and passing a reference

---

[*] This rule is not complete. The JavaBeans conventions (see Chapter 19) allows event-handler methods to take additional arguments when absolutely necessary and also to throw checked exceptions.

to itself. (Thus, this scheme implements a *callback* facility.) For example, the Swing JButton class is a source of ActionEvents. Here's how a TheReceiver object might register to receive these events:

```
// receiver of ActionEvents
class TheReceiver implements ActionListener
{
    // source of ActionEvents
    JButton theButton = new JButton("Belly");

    TheReceiver( ) {
        ...
        theButton.addActionListener( this );
    }

    public void actionPerformed( ActionEvent e ) {
        // Belly Button pushed...
    }
```

The receiver makes a call to addActionListener() to become eligible to receive ActionEvents from the button when they occur. It passes the reference this to register itself as an ActionListener.

To manage its listeners, an ActionEvent source (like the JButton) always implements two methods:

```
// ActionEvent source
public void addActionListener(ActionListener listener) {
    ...
}
public void removeActionListener(ActionListener listener) {
    ...
}
```

The removeActionListener() method removes the listener from the list so that it will not receive future events of that kind. Swing components supply implementations of both methods; normally, you won't need to implement them yourself. It's important to pay attention to how your application uses event sources and listeners. It's okay to throw away an event source without removing its listeners, but it isn't okay to throw away listeners without removing them from the source first because the event source maintains references to them, preventing them from being garbage-collected.

Now, you may be expecting an EventSource interface listing these two methods, but there isn't one. There are no event source interfaces in the current conventions. If you are analyzing a class and trying to determine what events it generates, you have to look for the add and remove methods. For example, the presence of the addActionListener() and removeActionListener() methods define the object as a source of ActionEvents. If you happen to be a human being, you can simply look at the documentation, but if the documentation isn't available, or if you're writing a program that needs to analyze a class (a process called *reflection*), you can look for this design pattern.(There is a utility, the java.beans.Introspector, which can do this for you).

A source of FooEvent events for the FooListener interface must implement a pair of add/remove methods:

```
addFooListener(FooListener listener)
removeFooListener(FooListener listener)
```

If an event source can support only one event listener (unicast delivery), the add listener method can throw the java.util.TooManyListenersException.

So what do all the naming patterns up to this point accomplish? Well, for one thing, they make it possible for automated tools and integrated development environments to divine sources of particular events. Tools that work with JavaBeans will use the Java reflection and introspection APIs to search for these kinds of design patterns and identify the events that can be fired by a component.

At a more concrete level, it also means that event hookups are strongly typed, just like the rest of Java. So it's impossible to accidentally hook up the wrong kind of components; for example, you can't register to receive ItemEvents from a JButton because a button doesn't have an addItemListener() method. Java knows at compile time what types of events can be delivered to whom.

Event Delivery

Swing and AWT events are multicast; every event is associated with a single source but can be delivered to any number of receivers. When an event is fired, it is delivered individually to each listener on the list (Figure 15-3).

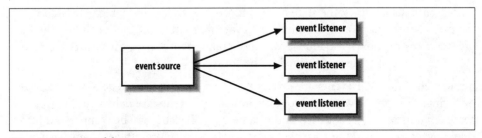

Figure 15-3. Event delivery

There are no guarantees about the order in which events are delivered. Nor are there any guarantees about what happens if you register yourself more than once with an event source; you may or may not get the event more than once. Similarly, you should assume that every listener receives the same event data. In general, events are immutable; they can't be changed by their listeners.

To be complete, we could say that event delivery is synchronous with respect to the event source, but that follows from the fact that the event delivery is really just the invocation of a normal Java method. The source of the event calls the handler method of each listener. However, listeners shouldn't assume all the events will be sent in the same thread, unless they are AWT/Swing events, which are always sent serially by a global event dispatcher thread.

Event Types

All the events used by Swing GUI components are subclasses of java.util. EventObject. You can use or subclass any of the EventObject types for use in your own components. We describe the important event types here.

The events and listeners that are used by Swing fall into two packages: java.awt. event and javax.swing.event. As we've discussed, the structure of components has changed significantly between AWT and Swing. The event mechanism, however, is fundamentally the same, so the events and listeners in java.awt.event are used by Swing components. In addition, Swing has added event types and listeners in the javax.swing.event package.

java.awt.event.ComponentEvent is the base class for events that can be fired by any component. This includes events that provide notification when a component changes its dimensions or visibility as well as the other event types for mouse operations and key presses. ContainerEvents are fired by containers when components are added or removed.

The java.awt.event.InputEvent Class

MouseEvents, which track the state of the mouse, and KeyEvents, which are fired when the user uses the keyboard, are kinds of java.awt.event.InputEvents. When the user presses a key or moves the mouse within a component's area, the events are generated with that component identified as the source.

Input events and GUI events are processed in a special event queue that is managed by Swing. This gives Swing control over how all its events are delivered. First, under some circumstances, a sequence of the same type of event may be compressed into a single event. This is done to make some event types more efficient—in particular, mouse events and some special internal events used to control repainting. Perhaps more important to us, input events are delivered with extra information that lets listeners decide if the component itself should act on the event.

Mouse and Key Modifiers on InputEvents

InputEvents come with a set of flags for special modifiers. These let you detect whether the Shift, Control, or Alt keys were held down during a mouse button or key press, and, in the case of a mouse button press, distinguish which mouse button was involved. The following are the flag values contained in java.awt.event.InputEvent:

```
SHIFT_MASK
CTRL_MASK
META_MASK
ALT_MASK
BUTTON1_MASK
BUTTON2_MASK
BUTTON3_MASK
```

To check for one or more flags, evaluate the bitwise AND of the complete set of modifiers and the flag or flags you're interested in. The complete set of modifiers involved in the event is returned by the InputEvent's getModifiers() method:

```
public void mousePressed (MouseEvent e) {
    int mods = e.getModifiers( );
    if ((mods & InputEvent.SHIFT_MASK) != 0) {
        // shifted Mouse Button press
    }
}
```

The three BUTTON flags can determine which mouse button was pressed on a two- or three-button mouse. If you use these, you run the risk that your program won't work on platforms without multibutton mice. Currently, BUTTON2_MASK is equivalent to ALT_MASK, and BUTTON3_MASK is equivalent to META_MASK. This means that pushing the second mouse button is equivalent to pressing the first (or only) button with the Alt key depressed, and the third button is equivalent to the first with the Meta key depressed. These provide some minimal portability even for systems that don't provide multibutton mice. However, for the most common uses of these buttons—pop-up menus—you don't have to write explicit code; Swing provides special support that automatically maps to the correct gesture in each environment (see the PopupMenu class in Chapter 16).

Mouse-wheel events

Java 1.4 added support for the mouse wheel. (A mouse wheel is a scrolling device in place of a middle mouse button.) By default, Swing handles mouse-wheel movement for scrollable components, so you should not have to write explicit code to handle this. Mouse wheel events are handled a little differently from other events because the conventions for using the mouse wheel don't always require the mouse to be over a scrolling component. If the immediate target component of a mouse-wheel event is not registered to receive it, a search is made for the first enclosing container that wants to consume the event. This allows components enclosed in ScrollPanes to operate as expected.

If you wish to explicitly handle mouse-wheel events, you can register to receive them using the MouseWheelListener interface shown in Table 15-1 in the next section.

Mouse-wheel events encapsulate information about the amount of scrolling and the type of scroll unit, which on most systems may be configured externally to be fine-grained scroll units or large blocks. If you want a physical measure of how far the wheel was turned, you can get that with the getWheelRotation() method, which returns a number of clicks.

Focus Events

As we mentioned earlier, focus handling is largely done automatically in Swing applications and we'll discuss it more in Chapter 17. However, understanding how focus events are handled will help you understand and customize components.

As we described, a component can make itself eligible to receive focus using the JComponent setFocusable() method (windows may use setFocusableWindowState()). A component normally receives focus when the user clicks on it with the mouse. It can also programmatically request focus using the requestFocus() or requestFocusInWindow() methods. The requestFocusInWindow() method acts just like requestFocus() except that it does not ask for transfer across windows. (There are currently limitations on some platforms that prevent focus transfer from native applications to Java applications, so using requestFocusInWindow() guarantees portability by adding this restriction.)

Although a component can request focus explicitly, the only way to verify when a component has received or lost focus is by using the FocusListener interface (see Tables 15-1 and 15-2 later in this chapter). You can use this interface to customize the behavior of your component when it is ready for input (e.g., the TextField's blinking cursor). Also, input components often respond to the loss of focus by committing their changes. For example, JTextFields and other components can be arranged to validate themselves when the user attempts to move to a new field and to prevent the focus change until the field is valid (as we'll see in Chapter 17).

Assuming that there is currently no focus, the following sequence of events happens when a component receives focus:

```
WINDOW_ACTIVATED
WINDOW_GAINED_FOCUS
FOCUS_GAINED
```

The first two are WindowEvents delivered to the component's containing Window, and the third is a FocusEvent, sent to the component itself. If a component in another window subsequently receives focus, the following complementary sequence will occur:

```
FOCUS_LOST
WINDOW_FOCUS_LOST
WINDOW_DEACTIVATED
```

These events carry a certain amount of context with them. The receiving component can determine from what component the focus is being transferred and from what `Window`. The yielding component and window are called "opposites" and are available with the `FocusEvent` `getOppositeComponent()` and `WindowEvent` `getOppositeWindow()` methods. If the opposite is part of a native non-Java application, then these values may be `null`.

Focus gained and lost events may also be marked as "temporary," as determined by the `FocusEvent` `isTemporary()` method. The concept of a temporary focus change is used for components such as pop-up menus, scrollbars, and window manipulation where control is expected to return to the primary component later. The distinction is made for components to "commit" or validate data upon losing focus. No commit should happen on a temporary loss of focus.

Event Summary

Tables 15-1 and 15-2 summarize commonly used Swing events, which Swing components fire them, and the methods of the listener interfaces that receive them. The events and listeners are divided between the `java.awt.event` and `javax.swing.event` packages.

Table 15-1. Swing component and container events

Event	Fired by	Listener interface	Handler method
java.awt.event. ComponentEvent	All components	ComponentListener	componentResized( ) componentMoved( ) componentShown( ) componentHidden( )
java.awt.event. FocusEvent	All components	FocusListener	focusGained( ) focusLost( )
java.awt.event. KeyEvent	All components	KeyListener	keyTyped( ) keyPressed( ) keyReleased( )
java.awt.event. MouseEvent	All components	MouseListener	mouseClicked( ) mousePressed( ) mouseReleased( ) mouseEntered( ) mouseExited( )
		MouseMotionListener	mouseDragged( ) mouseMoved( )
java.awt.event. ContainerEvent	All containers	ContainerListener	componentAdded( ) componentRemoved()

Table 15-2. Component-specific swing events

Event	Fired by	Listener interface	Handler method
java.awt.event. ActionEvent	JButton JCheckBoxMenuItem JComboBox JFileChooser JList JRadioButton- MenuItem JTextField JToggleButton	ActionListener	actionPerformed( )
java.awt.event. AdjustmentEvent	JScrollBar	Adjustment- Listener	adjustmentValue- Changed( )
javax.swing.event. CaretEvent	JTextComponent	CaretListener	caretUpdate( )
javax.swing.event. HyperlinkEvent	JEditorPane, JTextPane	HyperlinkListener	hyperlinkUpdate( )
java.awt.event. InternalFrameEvent	JInternalFrame	InternalFrame- Listener	internalFrame- Activated( ) internalFrameClosed( ) internalFrame- Closing( ) internalFrame- Deactivated( ) internalFrame- Deiconified( ) internalFrame- Iconified( ) internalFrameOpened( )
java.awt.event. ItemEvent	JCheckBoxMenuItem JComboBox JRadioButton- MenuItem JToggleButton	ItemListener	itemStateChanged( )
javax.swing.event. ListDataEvent	ListModel	ListDataListener	contentsChanged( ) intervalAdded( ) intervalRemoved( )
javax.swing.event. ListSelectionEvent	JList ListSelectionModel	ListSelection- Listener	valueChanged( )
javax.swing.event. MenuEvent	JMenu	MenuListener	menuCanceled( ) menuDeselected( ) menuSelected( )
javax.swing.event. PopupMenuEvent	JPopupMenu	PopupMenuListener	popupMenuCanceled( ) popupMenuWill- BecomeInvisible( ) popupMenuWill- BecomeVisible( )
javax.swing.event. MenuKeyEvent	JMenuItem	MenuKeyListener	menuKeyPressed( ) menuKeyReleased( ) menuKeyTyped( )

Table 15-2. Component-specific swing events (continued)

Event	Fired by	Listener interface	Handler method
javax.swing.event. MenuDragMouseEvent	JMenuItem	MenuDragMouse- Listener	menuDragMouse- Dragged( ) menuDragMouse- Entered( ) menuDragMouse- Exited( ) menuDragMouse- Released( )
javax.swing.event. TableColumnModel- Event	TableColumnModel[a]	TableColumn- ModelListener	columnAdded( ) columnMarginChanged( ) columnMoved( ) columnRemoved( ) columnSelection- Changed( )
javax.swing.event. TableModelEvent	TableModel	TableModel- Listener	tableChanged( )
javax.swing.event. TreeExpansionEvent	JTree	TreeExpansion- Listener	treeCollapsed( ) treeExpanded( )
javax.swing.event. TreeModelEvent	TreeModel	TreeModelListener	treeNodesChanged( ) treeNodesInserted( ) treeNodesRemoved( ) treeStructure- Changed( )
javax.swing.event. TreeSelectionEvent	JTree TreeSelectionModel	TreeSelection- Listener	valueChanged( )
javax.swing.event. UndoableEditEvent	javax.swing.text. Document	UndoableEdit- Listener	undoableEdit- Happened( )
java.awt.event. WindowEvent	JDialog JFrame JWindow	WindowListener	windowOpened( ) windowClosing( ) windowClosed( ) windowIconified( ) windowDeiconified( ) windowActivated( ) windowDeactivated( )

[a] The TableColumnModel class breaks with convention in the names of the methods that add listeners. They are addColumnModelListener( ) and removeColumnModelListener( ).

In Swing, a component's model and view are distinct. Strictly speaking, components don't fire events; models do. When you press a JButton, for example, it's actually the button's data model that fires an ActionEvent, not the button itself. But JButton has a convenience method for registering ActionListeners; this method passes its argument through to register the listener with the button model. In many cases (as with JButtons), you don't have to deal with the data model separately from the view, so we can speak loosely of the component itself firing the events. InputEvents are, of course, generated by the native input system and fired for the appropriate component, although the listener responds as though they're generated by the component.

Adapter Classes

It's not ideal to have your application components implement a bunch of listener interfaces and receive events directly. Sometimes it's not even possible. Being an event receiver forces you to modify or subclass your objects to implement the appropriate event listener interfaces and add the code necessary to handle the events. And since we are talking about Swing events here, a more subtle issue is that you would be, of necessity, building GUI logic into parts of your application that shouldn't have to know anything about the GUI. Let's look at an example.

In Figure 15-4, we have drawn the plans for our Vegomatic food processor. Here we have made our Vegomatic object implement the ActionListener interface so that it can receive events directly from the three JButton components: Chop, Puree, and Frappe. The problem is that our Vegomatic object now has to know more than how to mangle food. It also has to be aware that it is driven by three controls—specifically, buttons that send action commands—and be aware of which methods it should invoke for those commands. Our boxes labeling the GUI and application code overlap in an unwholesome way. If the marketing people should later want to add or remove buttons or perhaps just change the names, we have to be careful. We may have to modify the logic in our Vegomatic object. All is not well.

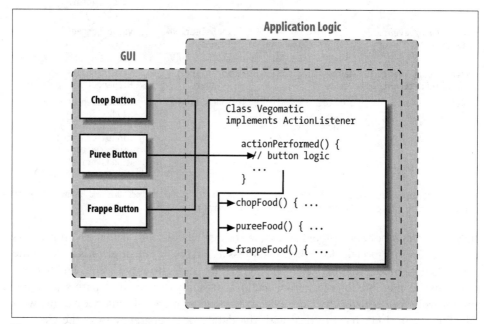

Figure 15-4. Implementing the ActionListener interface directly

An alternative is to place an adapter class between our event source and receiver. An *adapter* is a simple object whose sole purpose is to map an incoming event to an outgoing method.

Figure 15-5 shows a better design that uses three adapter classes, one for each button. The implementation of the first adapter might look like:

```
class VegomaticAdapter1 implements ActionListener {
    Vegomatic vegomatic;
    VegomaticAdapter1 ( Vegotmatic vegomatic ) {
        this.vegomatic = vegomatic;
    }
    public void actionPerformed( ActionEvent e ) {
        vegomatic.chopFood( );
    }
}
```

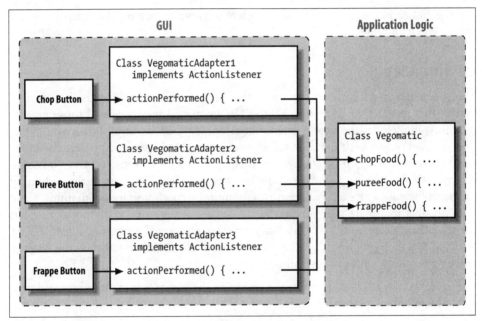

Figure 15-5. Implementing the ActionListener interface using adapter classes

So somewhere in the code where we build our GUI, we could register our listener like this:

```
Vegomatic theVegomatic = ...;
Button chopButton = ...;

// make the hookup
chopButton.addActionListener( new VegomaticAdapter1(theVegomatic) );
```

Instead of registering itself (this) as the Button's listener, the adapter registers the Vegomatic object (theVegomatic). In this way, the adapter acts as an intermediary, hooking up an event source (the button) with an event receiver (the virtual chopper).

We have completely separated the messiness of our GUI from the application code. However, we have added three new classes to our application, none of which does very much. Is that good? It depends on your vantage point.

Under different circumstances, our buttons may have been able to share a common adapter class that was simply instantiated with different parameters. Various trade-offs can be made between size, efficiency, and elegance of code. Adapter classes will often be generated automatically by development tools. The way we have named our adapter classes VegomaticAdapter1, VegomaticAdapter2, and VegomaticAdapter3 hints at this. More often, when hand-coding, you'll use an anonymous inner class, as we'll see in the next section. At the other extreme, we can forsake Java's strong typing and use the Reflection API to create a completely dynamic hookup between an event source and its listener.

Dummy Adapters

Many listener interfaces contain more than one event-handler method. Unfortunately, this means that to register yourself as interested in any one of those events, you must implement the whole listener interface. And to accomplish this you might find yourself typing in dummy "stubbed-out" methods, simply to complete the interface. There is really nothing wrong with this, but it is a bit tedious. To save you some trouble, AWT and Swing provide some helper classes that implement these dummy methods for you. For each of the most common listener interfaces containing more than one method, there is an adapter class containing the stubbed methods. You can use the adapter class as a base class for your own adapters. So when you need a class to patch together your event source and listener, you can simply subclass the adapter and override only the methods you want.

For example, the MouseAdapter class implements the MouseListener interface and provides the following implementation:

```
public void mouseClicked(MouseEvent e) {};
public void mousePressed(MouseEvent e) {};
public void mouseReleased(MouseEvent e) {};
public void mouseEntered(MouseEvent e) {};
public void mouseExited(MouseEvent e) {};
```

This isn't a tremendous time saver; it's simply a bit of sugar. The primary advantage comes into play when we use the MouseAdapter as the base for our own adapter in an anonymous inner class. For example, suppose we want to catch a mousePressed() event in some component and blow up a building. We can use the following to make the hookup:

```
someComponent.addMouseListener( new MouseAdapter( ) {
    public void MousePressed(MouseEvent e) {
        building.blowUp( );
    }
} );
```

We've taken artistic liberties with the formatting, but it's very readable. Moreover, we've avoided creating stub methods for the four unused event-handler methods. Writing adapters is common enough that it's nice to avoid typing those extra few lines and perhaps stave off the onset of carpal tunnel syndrome for a few more hours. Remember that any time you use an inner class, the compiler is generating a class for you, so the messiness you've saved in your source still exists in the output classes.

The AWT Robot!

This topic may not be of immediate use to everyone, but sometimes an API is just interesting enough that it deserves mentioning. In Java 1.3 a class with the intriguing name java.awt.Robot was added. The AWT robot provides an API for generating input events such as keystrokes and mouse gestures programmatically. It can be used to build automated GUI testing tools and the like. The following example uses the Robot class to move the mouse to the upper left area of the screen and perform a series of events corresponding to a double click. On most Windows systems, this opens up the *My Computer* folder that lives in that region of the screen.

```
public class RobotExample
{
    public static void main( String [] args ) throws Exception
    {
        Robot r = new Robot( );
        r.mouseMove(35,35);
        r.mousePress( InputEvent.BUTTON1_MASK );
        r.mouseRelease( InputEvent.BUTTON1_MASK );
        Thread.sleep(50);
        r.mousePress( InputEvent.BUTTON1_MASK );
        r.mouseRelease( InputEvent.BUTTON1_MASK );
    }
}
```

Multithreading in Swing

An important compromise was made early in the design of Swing relating to speed, GUI consistency, and thread safety. To provide maximum performance and simplicity in the common case, Swing does not explicitly synchronize access to most Swing component methods. This means that most Swing components are, technically, not thread-safe for multithreaded applications. Now don't panic: it's not as bad as it sounds because there is a plan. All event processing in AWT/Swing is handled by a single, system thread using a single system event queue. The queue serves two purposes. First, it eliminates thread-safety issues by making all GUI modifications happen in a single thread. Second, the queue imposes a strict ordering of all activity in Swing. Because painting is handled in Swing using events, all screen updating is also ordered with respect to all event handling.

What this means for you is that multithreading programs need to be careful about how they update Swing components after they are *realized* (added to a visible container). If you make arbitrary modifications to Swing components from your own threads, you run the risk of malformed rendering on the screen and inconsistent behavior.

There are several conditions under which it is always safe to modify a Swing component. First, Swing components can be modified before they are realized. The term *realized* originates from the days when the component would have created its peer object. It is the point when it is added to a visible container or when it is made visible in the case of a window. Most of our examples in this book set up GUI components in their main() method, add them to a JFrame, and then, as their final action cause the JFrame to be displayed using setVisible(). This style of setup is safe because components are not realized until the container is made visible. Actually, that last sentence is not entirely true. Technically, components can also be realized by the JFrame() pack() method. However since no GUI is shown until the container is made visible, it is unlikely that any GUI activity can be mishandled.

Second, it's safe to modify Swing components from code that is already running from the system event handler's thread. Because all events are processed by the event queue, the methods of all Swing event listeners are normally invoked by the system event handling thread. This means that event handler methods and, transitively, any methods called from those methods during the lifetime of that call can freely modify Swing GUI components because they are already running in the system event-dispatching thread. If you are unsure of whether some bit of code will ever be called outside the normal event thread, you can use the static method SwingUtilities. isEventDispatchThread() to test the identity of the current thread. You can then perform your activity using the alternate mechanism we'll talk about later.

Finally, Swing components can be safely modified when the API documentation explicitly says that the method is thread-safe. Many important methods of Swing components are explicitly documented as thread-safe. These include the JComponent repaint() and revalidate() methods, many methods of Swing text components, and all listener add and remove methods.

If you can't meet any of the requirements for thread safety listed previously, you can use a simple API to get the system event queue to perform arbitrary activities for you on the event handling thread. This is accomplished using the invokeAndWait() or invokeLater() static methods of the javax.swing.SwingUtilities class.

```
public static void invokeLater(Runnable doRun)
```
 Use this method to ask Swing to execute the run() method of the specified
 Runnable.

```
public static void invokeAndWait(Runnable doRun)throws
InterruptedException,InvocationTargetException
```
 This method is just like invokeLater() except that it waits until the run()
 method has completed before returning.

You can put whatever activities you want inside a Runnable object and cause the
event dispatcher to perform them using these methods. Often you'll use an inner
class, for example:

```
SwingUtilities.invokeLater( new Runnable() {
    public void run() {
        MyComponent.setVisible(false);
    }
} );
```

You may find that you won't have to use the event dispatcher in simple GUI applications because most activity happens in response to user interface events where it is
safe to modify components. However, consider these caveats when you create
threads to perform long-running tasks such as loading data or communicating over
the network.

## CHAPTER 16

Using Swing Components

In the previous chapter, we discussed a number of concepts, including how Java's user interface facility is put together and how the larger pieces work. You should understand what components and containers are, how you use them to create a display, what events are, how components use them to communicate with the rest of your application, and what layout managers are.

Now that we're through with the general concepts and background, we'll get to the fun stuff: how to do things with Swing. We will cover most of the components that the Swing package supplies, how to use these components in applets and applications, and how to build your own components. We will have lots of code and lots of pretty examples to look at.

There's more material than fits in a single chapter. In this chapter, we'll cover all the basic user interface components. In the next chapter, we'll cover some of the more involved topics: text components, trees, tables, and creating your own components.

Buttons and Labels

We'll start with the simplest components: buttons and labels. Frankly, there isn't much to say about them. If you've seen one button, you've seen them all, and you've already seen buttons in the applications in Chapter 2 (HelloJava3 and HelloJava4). A button generates an ActionEvent when the user presses it. To receive these events, your program registers an ActionListener, which must implement the actionPerformed() method. The argument passed to actionPerformed() is the event itself.

There's one more thing worth saying about buttons, which applies to any component that generates an action event. Java lets us specify an "action command" string for buttons (and other components, like menu items, that can generate action events). The action command is less interesting than it sounds. It is just a String that serves to identify the component that sent the event. By default, the action command of a `JButton` is the same as its label; it is included in action events, so you can use it to figure out which button an event came from.

To get the action command from an action event, call the event's `getAction-Command()` method. The following code checks whether the user pressed the button labeled *Yes*:

```
public void actionPerformed(ActionEvent e){
    if (e.getActionCommand( ).equals("Yes") {
        //the user pressed "Yes"; do something
        ...
    }
}
```

Yes is a string, not a command per se. You can change the action command by calling the button's `setActionCommand()` method. The following code changes button `myButton`'s action command to "confirm":

```
myButton.setActionCommand("confirm");
```

It's a good idea to get used to setting action commands explicitly; this helps to prevent your code from breaking when you or some other developer "internationalizes" it or otherwise changes the button's label. If you rely on the button's label, your code stops working as soon as that label changes; a French user might see the label `Oui` rather than `Yes`. By setting the action command, you eliminate one source of bugs; for example, the button `myButton` in the previous example always generates the action command `confirm`, regardless of what its label says.

Swing buttons can have an image in addition to a label. The `JButton` class includes constructors that accept an `Icon` object, which knows how to draw itself. You can create buttons with captions, images, or both. A handy class called `ImageIcon` takes care of loading an image for you and can be used to add an image to a button. The following example shows how this works:

```
//file: PictureButton.java
import java.awt.*;
import java.awt.event.*;
import javax.swing.*;

public class PictureButton {
  public static void main(String[] args)
  {
    JFrame frame = new JFrame();
    Icon icon = new ImageIcon("rhino.gif");
    JButton button = new JButton(icon);

    button.addActionListener( new ActionListener() {
      public void actionPerformed(ActionEvent ae) {
        System.out.println("Urp!");
      }
    });
```

```
    frame.getContentPane( ).add( button );
    frame.pack( );
    frame.setDefaultCloseOperation( JFrame.EXIT_ON_CLOSE );
    frame.setVisible(true);
  }
}
```

The example creates an ImageIcon from the *rhino.gif* file. Then a JButton is created from the ImageIcon. The whole thing is displayed in a JFrame. This example also shows the idiom of using an anonymous inner class as an ActionListener.

There's even less to be said about JLabel components. They're just text strings or images housed in a component. There aren't any special events associated with labels; about all you can do is specify the text's alignment, which controls the position of the text within the label's display area. As with buttons, JLabels can be created with Icons if you want to create a picture label. The following code creates some labels with different options:

```
// default alignment (CENTER)
JLabel label1 = new JLabel("Lions");

// left aligned
JLabel label2 = new JLabel("Tigers", SwingConstants.LEFT);

//label with no text, default alignment
JLabel label3 = new JLabel( );

// create image icon
Icon icon = new ImageIcon("rhino.gif");

// create image label
JLabel label4 = new JLabel(icon);

// assigning text to label3
label3.setText("and Bears");

// set alignment
label3.setHorizontalAlignment(SwingConstants.RIGHT);
```

The alignment constants are defined in the SwingConstants interface.

Now we've built several labels, using a variety of constructors and several of the class's methods. To display the labels, just add them to a container by calling the container's add( ) method.

You can set other label characteristics, such as changing their font or color, using the methods of the Component class, JLabel's distant ancestor. For example, you can call setFont( ) and setColor( ) on a label, as with any other component.

Given that labels are so simple, why do we need them at all? Why not just draw a text string directly on the container object? Remember that a JLabel is a JComponent. That's important; it means that labels have the normal complement of methods for

---

setting fonts and colors that we mentioned earlier as well as the ability to be persistently and sensibly managed by a layout manager. Therefore, they're much more flexible than a text string drawn at an absolute location within a container. Speaking of layouts—if you use the setText() method to change the text of your label, the label's preferred size may change. But the label's container automatically lays out its components when this happens, so you don't have to worry about it.

HTML Text in Buttons and Labels

Swing can interpret HTML-formatted text in JLabel and JButton labels. The following example shows how to create a button with some HTML-formatted text:

```
JButton button = new JButton(
  "<html>"
  + "S<font size=-1>MALL<font size=+0> "
  + "C<font size=-1>APITALS");
```

Older versions of Java may not render complex HTML very well. But as of 1.4, most basic HTML features are supported, including crazy things such as images and tables.

Figure 16-1 uses an HTML table to arrange its text.

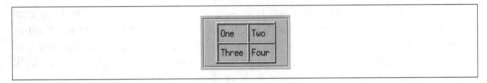

Figure 16-1. Button using HTML table

Figure 16-2 uses an HTML image tag to display an image.

Figure 16-2. Button using HTML img tag

The code for the two figures looks like this:

```
String html=
    "<html><table border=1>"
    +"<tr><td>One</td><td>Two</td></tr>"
    +"<tr><td>Three</td><td>Four</td></tr>"
    +"</table>";
JButton button = new JButton(html);

String html2=
    "<html><h3>Learning Java</h3>"
    +"<img src=\"http://www.ora.com/catalog/covers/learnjava2.gif\">";
Jbutton button2 = new JButton(html2);
```

Checkboxes and Radio Buttons

A checkbox is a labeled toggle switch. Each time the user clicks it, its state toggles between checked and unchecked. Swing implements the checkbox as a special kind of button. Radio buttons are similar to checkboxes, but they are normally used in groups. Clicking on one radio button in the group automatically turns the others off. They are named for the mechanical preset buttons on old car radios (like some of us had in high school).

Checkboxes and radio buttons are represented by instances of JCheckBox and JRadioButton, respectively. Radio buttons can be tethered together using an instance of another class called ButtonGroup. By now you're probably well into the swing of things (no pun intended) and could easily master these classes on your own. We'll use an example to illustrate a different way of dealing with the state of components and to show off a few more things about containers.

A JCheckBox sends ItemEvents when it's pushed. Because a checkbox is a kind of button, it also fires ActionEvents when checked. For something like a checkbox, we might want to be lazy and check on the state of the buttons only at some later time, such as when the user commits an action. For example, when filling out a form you may only care about the user's choices when the submit button is pressed.

The next application, DriveThrough, lets us check off selections on a fast food menu, as shown in Figure 16-3.

DriveThrough prints the results when we press the *Place Order* button. Therefore, we can ignore all the events generated by our checkboxes and radio buttons and listen only for the action events generated by the regular button.

```
//file: DriveThrough.java
import java.awt.*;
import java.awt.event.*;
import javax.swing.*;

public class DriveThrough
{
```

Figure 16-3. The DriveThrough application

```java
public static void main(String[] args) {
  JFrame frame = new JFrame("Lister v1.0");

  JPanel entreePanel = new JPanel( );
  final ButtonGroup entreeGroup = new ButtonGroup( );
  JRadioButton radioButton;
  entreePanel.add(radioButton = new JRadioButton("Beef"));
  radioButton.setActionCommand("Beef");
  entreeGroup.add(radioButton);
  entreePanel.add(radioButton = new JRadioButton("Chicken"));
  radioButton.setActionCommand("Chicken");
  entreeGroup.add(radioButton);
  entreePanel.add(radioButton = new JRadioButton("Veggie", true));
  radioButton.setActionCommand("Veggie");
  entreeGroup.add(radioButton);

  final JPanel condimentsPanel = new JPanel( );
  condimentsPanel.add(new JCheckBox("Ketchup"));
  condimentsPanel.add(new JCheckBox("Mustard"));
  condimentsPanel.add(new JCheckBox("Pickles"));

  JPanel orderPanel = new JPanel( );
  JButton orderButton = new JButton("Place Order");
  orderPanel.add(orderButton);

  Container content = frame.getContentPane( );
  content.setLayout(new GridLayout(3, 1));
  content.add(entreePanel);
  content.add(condimentsPanel);
  content.add(orderPanel);

  orderButton.addActionListener(new ActionListener( ) {
    public void actionPerformed(ActionEvent ae) {
      String entree =
        entreeGroup.getSelection( ).getActionCommand( );
      System.out.println(entree + " sandwich");
      Component[] components = condimentsPanel.getComponents( );
      for (int i = 0; i < components.length; i++) {
        JCheckBox cb = (JCheckBox)components[i];
        if (cb.isSelected( ))
          System.out.println("With " + cb.getText( ));
```

```
                }
            }
        });

        frame.setDefaultCloseOperation( JFrame.EXIT_ON_CLOSE );
        frame.setSize(300, 150);
        frame.setVisible(true);
    }
}
```

DriveThrough lays out three panels. The radio buttons in the entreePanel are tied together through a ButtonGroup object. We add() the buttons to a ButtonGroup to make them mutually exclusive. The ButtonGroup object is an odd animal. One might expect it to be a container or a component, but it isn't; it's simply a helper object that allows only one RadioButton to be selected at a time.

In this example, the button group forces you to choose a beef, chicken, or veggie entree, but not more than one. The condiment choices, which are JCheckBoxes, aren't in a button group, so you can request any combination of ketchup, mustard, and pickles on your sandwich.

When the *Place Order* button is pushed, we receive an ActionEvent in the actionPerformed() method of our inner ActionListener. At this point, we gather the information in the radio buttons and checkboxes and print it. actionPerformed() simply reads the state of the various buttons. We could have saved references to the buttons in a number of ways; this example demonstrates two. First, we find out which entree was selected. To do so, we call the ButtonGroup's getSelection() method. This returns a ButtonModel, upon which we immediately call getActionCommand(). This returns the action command as we set it when we created the radio buttons. The action commands for the buttons are the entrée names, which is exactly what we need.

To find which condiments were selected, we use a more complicated procedure. The problem is that condiments aren't mutually exclusive, so we don't have the convenience of a ButtonGroup. Instead, we ask the condiments JPanel for a list of its components. The getComponents() method returns an array of references to the container's child components. We'll use this to loop over the components and print the results. We cast each element of the array back to JCheckBox and call its isSelected() method to see if the checkbox is on or off. If we were dealing with different types of components in the array, we could determine each component's type with the instanceof operator. Or, more generally, we could maintain references to the elements of our form in some explicit way (a map by name, perhaps).

Lists and Combo Boxes

JLists and JComboBoxes are a step up on the evolutionary chain from JButtons and JLabels. Lists let the user choose from a group of alternatives. They can be

---

configured to force a single selection or allow multiple choices. Usually, only a small group of choices is displayed at a time; a scrollbar lets the user move to the choices that aren't visible. The user can select an item by clicking on it. She can expand the selection to a range of items by holding down Shift and clicking on another item. To make discontinuous selections, the user can hold down the Control key instead of the Shift key (on a Mac, this is the Command key).

A combo box is a cross-breed between a text field and a list. It displays a single line of text (possibly with an image) and a downward pointing arrow on one side. If you click on the arrow, the combo box opens up and displays a list of choices. You can select a single choice by clicking on it. After a selection is made, the combo box closes up; the list disappears, and the new selection is shown in the text field.

Like other components in Swing, lists and combo boxes have data models that are distinct from visual components. The list also has a selection model that controls how selections may be made on the list data.

Lists and combo boxes are similar because they have similar data models. Each is simply an array of acceptable choices. This similarity is reflected in Swing, of course: the type of a JComboBox's data model is a subclass of the type used for a JList's data model. The next example demonstrates this relationship.

The following example creates a window with a combo box, a list, and a button. The combo box and the list use the same data model. When you press the button, the program writes out the current set of selected items in the list (see Figure 16-4).

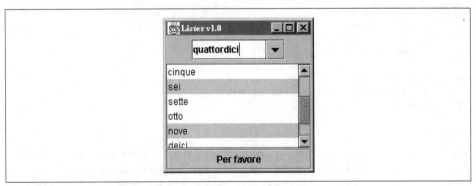

Figure 16-4. A combo box and a list using the same data model

Here's the code for the example:

```
//file: Lister.java
import java.awt.*;
import java.awt.event.*;
import javax.swing.*;
```

```java
public class Lister {
  public static void main(String[] args) {
    JFrame frame = new JFrame("Lister v1.0");

    // create a combo box
    String [] items = { "uno", "due", "tre", "quattro", "cinque",
                        "sei", "sette", "otto", "nove", "deici",
                        "undici", "dodici" };
    JComboBox comboBox = new JComboBox(items);
    comboBox.setEditable(true);

    // create a list with the same data model
    final JList list = new JList(comboBox.getModel( ));

    // create a button; when it's pressed, print out
    // the selection in the list
    JButton button = new JButton("Per favore");
    button.addActionListener(new ActionListener( ) {
      public void actionPerformed(ActionEvent ae) {
        Object[] selection = list.getSelectedValues( );
        System.out.println("-----");
        for (int i = 0; i < selection.length; i++)
          System.out.println(selection[i]);
      }
    });

    // put the controls the content pane
    Container c = frame.getContentPane( );
    JPanel comboPanel = new JPanel( );
    comboPanel.add(comboBox);
    c.add(comboPanel, BorderLayout.NORTH);
    c.add(new JScrollPane(list), BorderLayout.CENTER);
    c.add(button, BorderLayout.SOUTH);

    frame.setSize(200, 200);
    frame.setDefaultCloseOperation( JFrame.EXIT_ON_CLOSE );
    frame.setVisible(true);
  }
}
```

The combo box is created from an array of strings. This is a convenience—behind the scenes, the JComboBox constructor creates a data model from the strings you supply and sets the JComboBox to use that data model. The list is created using the data model of the combo box. This works because JList expects to use a ListModel for its data model, and the ComboBoxModel used by the JComboBox is a subclass of ListModel.

The button's action event handler simply prints out the selected items in the list, which are retrieved with a call to getSelectedValues(). This method actually returns an object array, not a string array. List and combo box items, like many other things in Swing, are not limited to text. You can use images, drawings, or some combination of text and images.

You might expect that selecting one item in the combo box would select the same item in the list. In Swing components, selection is controlled by a selection model. The combo box and the list have distinct selection models; after all, you can select only one item from the combo box while it's possible to select multiple items from the list. Thus, while the two components share a data model, they have separate selection models.

We've made the combo box editable. By default, it would not be editable: the user could choose only one item in the drop-down list. With an editable combo box, the user can type in a selection, as if it were a text field. Noneditable combo boxes are useful if you just want to offer a limited set of choices; editable combo boxes are handy when you want to accept any input but offer some common choices.

There's a great class tucked away in the last example that deserves some recognition. It's JScrollPane. In Lister, you'll notice we created one when we added the List to the main window. JScrollPane simply wraps itself around another Component and provides scrollbars as necessary. The scrollbars show up if the contained Component's preferred size (as returned by getPreferredSize()) is greater than the size of the JScrollPane itself. In the previous example, the scrollbars show up whenever the size of the List exceeds the available space.

You can use JScrollPane to wrap any Component, including components with drawings or images or complex user interface panels. We'll discuss JScrollPane in more detail later in this chapter, and we'll use it frequently with the text components in Chapter 17.

The Spinner

Jlist and JComboBox are two ways to let the user choose from a set of values. A JComboBox has added flexibility when it is made editable, but in general both of these components are limited in that they can only prompt the user from a fixed set of choices. In Java 1.4, Swing added a new component, JSpinner, which is useful for large or open-ended sequences of values such as numbers or dates. The JSpinner is a cousin of the JComboBox; it displays a value in a field, but instead of providing a drop-down list of choices, it gives the user a small pair of up and down arrows for moving over a range of values (see Figure 16-5). Like the combo box, a JSpinner can also be made editable, allowing the user to type a valid value directly into the field.

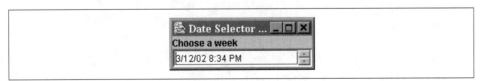

Figure 16-5. Image of DateSelector application

Swing provides three basic types of Spinners, represented by three different data models for the JSpinner component: SpinnerListModel, SpinnerNumberModel, and SpinnerDateModel.

The SpinnerListModel acts like a combo box, specifying a fixed set of objects:

```
String [] options = new String [] { "small", "medium", "large", "huge" };
SpinnerListModel model = new SpinnerListModel( options );
JSpinner spinner = new JSpinner( model );
```

You can retrieve the current value from the model at any time:

```
String value = (String)model.getValue( );
```

Alternatively, you can register a ChangeListener to receive updates as the user changes values. With a SpinnerListModel, if the spinner is editable and the user enters a value directly, it is validated against the set of choices before being accepted. This behavior is a little different from the other types of SpinnerModels, which when editable accept any valid value of the correct type (e.g., a number or date).

The SpinnerNumberModel displays numeric values. It can be configured with initial, minimum, and maximum values:

```
double initial=5.0, min=0.0, max=10.0, increment=0.1;
SpinnerNumberModel model =
    new SpinnerNumberModel( initial, min, max, increment );
JSpinner spinner = new JSpinner(model);
```

Here we have constructed a spinner with an initial value of 5.0 that allows the user to change the value to between 0 and 10.0 in increments of 0.1. The SpinnerNumberModel getNumber() method retrieves the current value.

Perhaps the most interesting feature of the JSpinner is the SpinnerDateModel, which allows the user to choose calendar dates by moving in specified increments of time. The SpinnerDateModel accepts a range, such as the SpinnerNumberModel, but the values are Date objects, and the increment is a java.util.Calendar constant field such as Calendar.DAY, Calendar.WEEK, and so on. The following example, DateSelector, creates a JSpinner showing the current date and time. It allows the user to change the date in increments of one week, over a range of one year (six months forward or back). A ChangeListener is registered with the model to display the values as they are modified:

```
import java.awt.*;
import java.awt.event.*;
import javax.swing.*;
import javax.swing.event.*;
import java.util.*;

public class DateSelector {
  public static void main(String[] args)
  {
    JFrame frame = new JFrame("DateSelector v1.0");
```

```
        Calendar now = Calendar.getInstance( );
        Calendar earliest = (Calendar)now.clone( );
        earliest.add( Calendar.MONTH, -6 );
        Calendar latest = (Calendar)now.clone( );
        latest.add( Calendar.MONTH, 6 );
        SpinnerModel model = new SpinnerDateModel(
            now.getTime( ), earliest.getTime( ), latest.getTime( ),
            Calendar.WEEK_OF_YEAR);
        final JSpinner spinner = new JSpinner(model);

        model.addChangeListener( new ChangeListener( ) {
            public void stateChanged(ChangeEvent e) {
                System.out.println( ((SpinnerDateModel)e.getSource( )).getDate( ) );
            }
        } );

        frame.getContentPane( ).add( "North", new JLabel("Choose a week") );
        frame.getContentPane( ).add( "Center", spinner );
        frame.pack( );
        frame.setDefaultCloseOperation( JFrame.EXIT_ON_CLOSE );
        frame.setVisible(true);
    }
}
```

As we said, the SpinnerCalendarModel acts just like the SpinnerNumberModel, except that it works with Date objects and uses the special Calendar constants as increments. To create dates, we construct a Calendar object for the correct time and use its getTime( ) method. In this example, we used the Calendar's add( ) method to set the minimum and maximum values six months in each direction. Table 16-1 shows values for increments in the Calendar.

Table 16-1. Calendar field values

Field value	Increment
Calendar.MILLISECOND	One millisecond
Calendar.SECOND	One second
Calendar.MINUTE	One minute
Calendar.HOUR, Calendar.HOUR_OF_DAY	One hour
Calendar.AM_PM	A.M. or P.M.
Calendar.DAY_OF_WEEK, Calendar.DAY_OF_MONTH, Calendar.DAY_OF_YEAR	One day
Calendar.MONTH	One month
Calendar.YEAR	One year
Calendar.ERA	B.C. or A.D. in the Gregorian Calendar

The SpinnerDateModel uses the Calendar add( ) method with a value of 1 or -1 and the corresponding constant value to increment or decrement the value. Increments of 1 have the same effect on several of the constants, as indicated in Table 16-1.

Borders

Any Swing component can have a decorative border. JComponent includes a method called setBorder(); all you have to do is call setBorder(), passing it an appropriate implementation of the Border interface.

Swing provides many useful Border implementations in the javax.swing.border package. You could create an instance of one of these classes and pass it to a component's setBorder() method, but there's an even simpler technique.

The BorderFactory class creates any kind of border for you using static "factory" methods. Creating and setting a component's border, then, is simple:

```
JLabel labelTwo = new JLabel("I have an etched border.");
labelTwo.setBorder(BorderFactory.createEtchedBorder( ));
```

Every component has a setBorder() method, from simple labels and buttons right up to the fancy text and table components we cover in Chapter 17.

BorderFactory is convenient, but it does not offer every option of every border type. For example, if you want to create a raised EtchedBorder instead of the default lowered border, you'll need to use EtchedBorder's constructor, like this:

```
JLabel labelTwo = new JLabel("I have a raised etched border.");
labelTwo.setBorder( new EtchedBorder(EtchedBorder.RAISED) );
```

The Border implementation classes are listed and briefly described here:

BevelBorder
: This border draws raised or lowered beveled edges, giving an illusion of depth.

SoftBevelBorder
: This border is similar to BevelBorder, but thinner.

EmptyBorder
: Doesn't do any drawing, but does take up space. You can use it to give a component a little breathing room in a crowded user interface.

EtchedBorder
: A lowered etched border gives the appearance of a rectangle that has been chiseled into a piece of stone. A raised etched border looks like it is standing out from the surface of the screen.

LineBorder
: Draws a simple rectangle around a component. You can specify the color and width of the line in LineBorder's constructor.

MatteBorder
: A souped-up version of LineBorder. You can create a MatteBorder with a certain color and specify the size of the border on the left, top, right, and bottom of the component. MatteBorder also allows you to pass in an Icon that will be used to

draw the border. This could be an image (ImageIcon) or any other implementation of the Icon interface.

TitledBorder

A regular border with a title. TitledBorder doesn't actually draw a border; it just draws a title in conjunction with another border object. You can specify the locations of the title, its justification, and its font. This border type is particularly useful for grouping different sets of controls in a complicated interface.

CompoundBorder

A border that contains two other borders. This is especially handy if you want to enclose a component in an EmptyBorder and then put something decorative around it, such as an EtchedBorder or a MatteBorder.

The following example shows off some different border types. It's only a sampler, though; many more border types are available. Furthermore, the example only encloses labels with borders. You can put a border around any component in Swing. The example is shown in Figure 16-6; the source code follows.

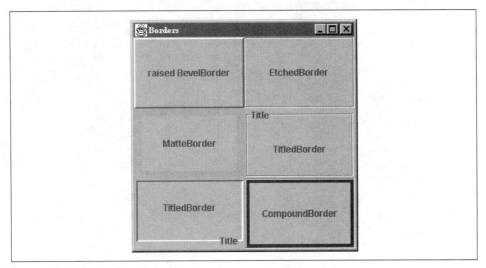

Figure 16-6. A bevy of borders

```
//file: Borders.java
import java.awt.*;
import java.awt.event.*;
import javax.swing.*;
import javax.swing.border.*;

public class Borders {
  public static void main(String[] args) {
    // create a JFrame to hold everything
    JFrame frame = new JFrame("Borders");
```

```
    // Create labels with borders.
    int center = SwingConstants.CENTER;
    JLabel labelOne = new JLabel("raised BevelBorder", center);
    labelOne.setBorder(
        BorderFactory.createBevelBorder(BevelBorder.RAISED));
    JLabel labelTwo = new JLabel("EtchedBorder", center);
    labelTwo.setBorder(BorderFactory.createEtchedBorder( ));
    JLabel labelThree = new JLabel("MatteBorder", center);
    labelThree.setBorder(
        BorderFactory.createMatteBorder(10, 10, 10, 10, Color.pink));
    JLabel labelFour = new JLabel("TitledBorder", center);
    Border etch = BorderFactory.createEtchedBorder( );
    labelFour.setBorder(
        BorderFactory.createTitledBorder(etch, "Title"));
    JLabel labelFive = new JLabel("TitledBorder", center);
    Border low = BorderFactory.createLoweredBevelBorder( );
    labelFive.setBorder(
        BorderFactory.createTitledBorder(low, "Title",
        TitledBorder.RIGHT, TitledBorder.BOTTOM));
    JLabel labelSix = new JLabel("CompoundBorder", center);
    Border one = BorderFactory.createEtchedBorder( );
    Border two =
        BorderFactory.createMatteBorder(4, 4, 4, 4, Color.blue);
    labelSix.setBorder(BorderFactory.createCompoundBorder(one, two));

    // add components to the content pane
    Container c = f.getContentPane( );
    c.setLayout(new GridLayout(3, 2));
    c.add(labelOne);
    c.add(labelTwo);
    c.add(labelThree);
    c.add(labelFour);
    c.add(labelFive);
    c.add(labelSix);

    frame.setDefaultCloseOperation( JFrame.EXIT_ON_CLOSE );
    frame.pack( );
    frame.setVisible(true);
  }
}
```

Menus

A JMenu is a standard pull-down menu with a fixed name. Menus can hold other menus as submenu items, enabling you to implement complex menu structures. In Swing, menus are first-class components, just like everything else. You can place them wherever a component would go. Another class, JMenuBar, holds menus in a horizontal bar. Menu bars are real components, too, so you can place them wherever you want in a container: top, bottom, or middle. But in the middle of a container, it usually makes more sense to use a JComboBox rather than some kind of menu.

Menu items may have associated images and shortcut keys; there are even menu items that look like checkboxes and radio buttons. Menu items are really a kind of button. Like buttons, menu items fire action events when they are selected. You can respond to menu items by registering action listeners with them.

There are two ways to use the keyboard with menus. The first is called *mnemonics*. A mnemonic is one character in the menu name. If you hold down the Alt key and type a menu's mnemonic, the menu drops down, just as if you had clicked on it with the mouse. Menu items may also have mnemonics. Once a menu is dropped down, you can select individual items in the same way.

Menu items may also have accelerators. An *accelerator* is a key combination that selects the menu item, whether or not the menu that contains it is showing. A common example is the accelerator Ctrl-C, which is frequently used as a shortcut for the *Copy* item in the *Edit* menu.

The next example demonstrates several different features of menus. It creates a menu bar with three different menus. The first, *Utensils*, contains several menu items, a submenu, a separator, and a *Quit* item that includes both a mnemonic and an accelerator. The second menu, *Spices*, contains menu items that look and act like checkboxes. Finally, the *Cheese* menu demonstrates radio button menu items.

The application is shown in Figure 16-7 with one of its menus dropped down. Choosing *Quit* from the *Utensils* menu (or pressing Ctrl-Q) removes the window.

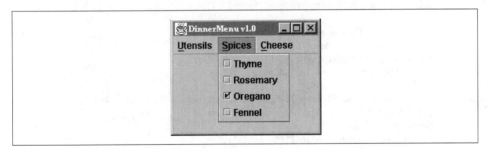

Figure 16-7. The DinnerMenu application

```
//file: DinnerMenu.java
import java.awt.*;
import java.awt.event.*;
import javax.swing.*;

public class DinnerMenu
{
  public static void main(String[] args) {
    JFrame frame = new JFrame("Dinner Menu");

    // create the Utensils menu
    JMenu utensils = new JMenu("Utensils");
```

```java
utensils.setMnemonic(KeyEvent.VK_U);
utensils.add(new JMenuItem("Fork"));
utensils.add(new JMenuItem("Knife"));
utensils.add(new JMenuItem("Spoon"));
JMenu hybrid = new JMenu("Hybrid");
hybrid.add(new JMenuItem("Spork"));
hybrid.add(new JMenuItem("Spife"));
hybrid.add(new JMenuItem("Knork"));
utensils.add(hybrid);
utensils.addSeparator( );

// do some fancy stuff with the Quit item
JMenuItem quitItem = new JMenuItem("Quit");
quitItem.setMnemonic(KeyEvent.VK_Q);
quitItem.setAccelerator(
    KeyStroke.getKeyStroke(KeyEvent.VK_Q, Event.CTRL_MASK));
quitItem.addActionListener(new ActionListener( ) {
  public void actionPerformed(ActionEvent e) { System.exit(0); }
});
utensils.add(quitItem);

// create the Spices menu
JMenu spices = new JMenu("Spices");
spices.setMnemonic(KeyEvent.VK_S);
spices.add(new JCheckBoxMenuItem("Thyme"));
spices.add(new JCheckBoxMenuItem("Rosemary"));
spices.add(new JCheckBoxMenuItem("Oregano", true));
spices.add(new JCheckBoxMenuItem("Fennel"));

// create the Cheese menu
JMenu cheese = new JMenu("Cheese");
cheese.setMnemonic(KeyEvent.VK_C);
ButtonGroup group = new ButtonGroup( );
JRadioButtonMenuItem rbmi;
rbmi = new JRadioButtonMenuItem("Regular", true);
group.add(rbmi);
cheese.add(rbmi);
rbmi = new JRadioButtonMenuItem("Extra");
group.add(rbmi);
cheese.add(rbmi);
rbmi = new JRadioButtonMenuItem("Blue");
group.add(rbmi);
cheese.add(rbmi);

// create a menu bar and use it in this JFrame
JMenuBar menuBar = new JMenuBar( );
menuBar.add(utensils);
menuBar.add(spices);
menuBar.add(cheese);
frame.setJMenuBar(menuBar);

frame.setDefaultCloseOperation( JFrame.EXIT_ON_CLOSE );
frame.setSize(200,200);
```

```
        frame.setVisible(true);
    }
}
```

Yes, we know. *Quit* doesn't belong in the *Utensils* menu. If it's driving you crazy, you can go back and add a *File* menu as an exercise when we're through.

Creating menus is pretty simple work. You create a JMenu object, specifying the menu's title. Like the text of JButtons and JLabels, menu labels can contain simple HTML. Then you just add JMenuItems to the JMenu. You can also add JMenus to a JMenu; they show up as submenus. This is shown in the creation of the *Utensils* menu:

```
JMenu utensils = new JMenu("Utensils");
utensils.setMnemonic(KeyEvent.VK_U);
utensils.add(new JMenuItem("Fork"));
utensils.add(new JMenuItem("Knife"));
utensils.add(new JMenuItem("Spoon"));
JMenu hybrid = new JMenu("Hybrid");
hybrid.add(new JMenuItem("Spork"));
hybrid.add(new JMenuItem("Spife"));
hybrid.add(new JMenuItem("Knork"));
utensils.add(hybrid);
```

In the second line, we set the mnemonic for this menu using a constant defined in the KeyEvent class.

You can add those pretty separator lines with a single call:

```
utensils.addSeparator( );
```

The *Quit* menu item has some bells and whistles we should explain. First, we create the menu item and set its mnemonic, just as we did before for the *Utensils* menu:

```
JMenuItem quitItem = new JMenuItem("Quit");
quitItem.setMnemonic(KeyEvent.VK_Q);
```

Now we want to create an accelerator for the menu item. We do this with the help of a class called KeyStroke:

```
quitItem.setAccelerator(
    KeyStroke.getKeyStroke(KeyEvent.VK_Q, Event.CTRL_MASK));
```

Finally, to actually do something in response to the menu item, we register an action listener:

```
quitItem.addActionListener(new ActionListener( ) {
    public void actionPerformed(ActionEvent e) { System.exit(0); }
});
```

Our action listener exits the application when the *Quit* item is selected.

Creating the *Spices* menu is just as easy, except that we use JCheckBoxMenuItems instead of regular JMenuItems. The result is a menu full of items that behave like checkboxes.

The next menu, *Cheese*, is a little more tricky. We want the items to be radio buttons, but we need to place them in a `ButtonGroup` to ensure they are mutually exclusive. Each item, then, is created, added to the button group, and added to the menu itself.

The final step is to place the menus we've just created in a `JMenuBar`. This is simply a component that lays out menus in a horizontal bar. We have two options for adding it to our `JFrame`. Since the `JMenuBar` is a real component, we could add it to the content pane of the `JFrame`. Instead, we use a convenience method called `setJMenuBar()`, which automatically places the `JMenuBar` at the top of the frame's content pane. This saves us the trouble of altering the layout or size of the content pane; it is adjusted to coexist peacefully with the menu bar.

The PopupMenu Class

One of Swing's nifty components is `JPopupMenu`, a menu that automatically appears when you press the appropriate mouse button inside a component. (On a Windows system, for example, clicking the right mouse button invokes a pop-up menu.) Which button you press depends on the platform you're using; fortunately, you don't have to care—Swing figures it out for you.

The care and feeding of `JPopupMenu` is basically the same as any other menu. You use a different constructor (`JPopupMenu()`) to create it, but otherwise, you build a menu and add elements to it the same way. The big difference is you don't need to attach it to a `JMenuBar`. Instead, just pop up the menu whenever you need it.

The following example, `PopupColorMenu`, contains three buttons. You can use a `JPopupMenu` to set the color of each button or the frame itself, depending on where you press the mouse.

```
//file: PopUpColorMenu.java
import java.awt.*;
import java.awt.event.*;
import javax.swing.*;

public class PopUpColorMenu implements ActionListener
{
  Component selectedComponent;

  public PopUpColorMenu( ) {
    JFrame frame = new JFrame("PopUpColorMenu v1.0");

    final JPopupMenu colorMenu = new JPopupMenu("Color");
    colorMenu.add(makeMenuItem("Red"));
    colorMenu.add(makeMenuItem("Green"));
    colorMenu.add(makeMenuItem("Blue"));

    MouseListener mouseListener = new MouseAdapter() {
      public void mousePressed(MouseEvent e) { checkPopup(e); }
```

```java
      public void mouseClicked(MouseEvent e) { checkPopup(e); }
      public void mouseReleased(MouseEvent e) { checkPopup(e); }
      private void checkPopup(MouseEvent e) {
        if (e.isPopupTrigger(  )) {
          selectedComponent = e.getComponent(  );
          colorMenu.show(e.getComponent(), e.getX(), e.getY(  ));
        }
      }
    };

    Container content = frame.getContentPane( );
    content.setLayout(new FlowLayout(  ));
    JButton button = new JButton("Uno");
    button.addMouseListener(mouseListener);
    content.add(button);
    button = new JButton("Due");
    button.addMouseListener(mouseListener);
    content.add(button);
    button = new JButton("Tre");
    button.addMouseListener(mouseListener);
    content.add(button);

    frame.getContentPane( ).addMouseListener(mouseListener);

    frame.setSize(200,50);
    frame.setDefaultCloseOperation( JFrame.EXIT_ON_CLOSE );
    frame.setVisible(true);
  }

  public void actionPerformed(ActionEvent e) {
    String color = e.getActionCommand(  );
    if (color.equals("Red"))
      selectedComponent.setBackground(Color.red);
    else if (color.equals("Green"))
      selectedComponent.setBackground(Color.green);
    else if (color.equals("Blue"))
      selectedComponent.setBackground(Color.blue);
  }

  private JMenuItem makeMenuItem(String label) {
    JMenuItem item = new JMenuItem(label);
    item.addActionListener( this );
    return item;
  }

  public static void main(String[] args) {
    new PopUpColorMenu( );
  }
}
```

Figure 16-8 shows the example in action; the user is preparing to change the color of the bottom button.

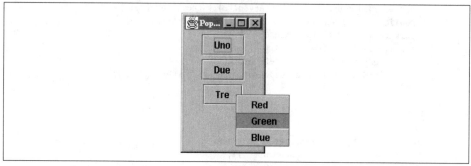

Figure 16-8. The PopupColorMenu application

Because the pop-up menu is triggered by mouse events, we need to register a MouseListener for any of the components to which it applies. In this example, all three buttons and the content pane of the frame are eligible for the color pop-up menu. Therefore, we add a mouse event listener for all these components explicitly. The same instance of an anonymous inner MouseAdapter subclass is used in each case. In this class, we override the mousePressed(), mouse-Released(), and mouseClicked() methods to display the pop-up menu when we get an appropriate event. How do we know what an "appropriate event" is? Fortunately, we don't need to worry about the specifics of our user's platform; we just need to call the event's isPopupTrigger() method. If this method returns true, we know the user has done whatever normally displays a pop-up menu on his system.

Once we know that the user wants to raise a pop-up menu, we display the pop-up menu by calling its show() method with the mouse event coordinates as arguments.

If we want to provide different menus for different types of components or the background, we create different mouse listeners for each different kind of component. The mouse listeners invoke different kinds of pop-up menus as appropriate.

The only thing left is to handle the action events from the pop-up menu items. We use a helper method called makeMenuItem() to register the PopUpColorMenu window as an action listener for every item we add. The example implements ActionListener and has the required actionPerformed() method. This method reads the action command from the event, which is equal to the selected menu item's label by default. It then sets the background color of the selected component appropriately.

The JScrollPane Class

We used JScrollPane earlier in this chapter without explaining much about it. In this section we'll remedy the situation.

A JScrollPane is a container that can hold one component. Said another way, a JScrollPane *wraps* another component. By default, if the wrapped component is larger than the JScrollPane itself, the JScrollPane supplies scrollbars. JScrollPane handles the events from the scrollbars and displays the appropriate portion of the contained component.

Technically, JScrollPane is a Container, but it's a funny one. It has its own layout manager, which can't be changed. It can accommodate only one component at a time. This seems like a big limitation, but it isn't. If you want to put a lot of stuff in a JScrollPane, just put your components into a JPanel, with whatever layout manager you like, and put that panel into the JScrollPane.

When you create a JScrollPane, you specify the conditions under which its scrollbars are displayed. This is called the *scrollbar display policy*; a separate policy is used for the horizontal and vertical scrollbars. The following constants can be used to specify the policy for each of the scrollbars:

HORIZONTAL_SCROLLBAR_AS_NEEDED
VERTICAL_SCROLLBAR_AS_NEEDED
  Displays a scrollbar only if the wrapped component doesn't fit.

HORIZONTAL_SCROLLBAR_ALWAYS
VERTICAL_SCROLLBAR_ALWAYS
  Always shows a scrollbar, regardless of the contained component's size.

HORIZONTAL_SCROLLBAR_NEVER
VERTICAL_SCROLLBAR_NEVER
  Never shows a scrollbar, even if the contained component won't fit. If you use this policy, you should provide some other way to manipulate the JScrollPane.

By default, the policies are HORIZONTAL_SCROLLBAR_AS_NEEDED and VERTICAL_SCROLLBAR_AS_NEEDED.

Support for scrolling with mouse wheels is automatic as of JDK 1.4. You do not have to do anything explicit in your application to get this to work.

The following example uses a JScrollPane to display a large image (see Figure 16-9). The application itself is very simple; all we do is place the image in a JLabel, wrap a JScrollPane around it, and put the JScrollPane in a JFrame's content pane.

Here's the code:

```
//file: ScrollPaneFrame.java
import java.awt.*;
import java.awt.event.*;
import javax.swing.*;

public class ScrollPaneFrame
{
  public static void main(String[] args) {
    String filename = "Piazza di Spagna.jpg";
    if (args.length > 0)
      filename = args[0];
```

Figure 16-9. The ScrollPaneFrame application

```
        JFrame frame = new JFrame("ScrollPaneFrame v1.0");
        JLabel image = new JLabel( new ImageIcon(filename) );
        frame.getContentPane( ).add( new JScrollPane(image) );

        frame.setSize(300, 300);
        frame.setDefaultCloseOperation( JFrame.EXIT_ON_CLOSE );
        frame.setVisible(true);
    }
}
```

To hold the image we have used a JLabel and ImageIcon. The ImageIcon class preloads the image using a MediaTracker and determines its dimensions. It's also possible to have the ImageIcon show the image as it loads or to ask it for information on the status of loading the image. We'll discuss image observers in Chapter 20.

The JSplitPane Class

A *split pane* is a special container that holds two components, each in its own subpane. A *splitter bar* adjusts the sizes of the two subpanes. In a document viewer, you could use a split pane to show a table of contents next to a full document.

The following example uses two JLabels containing ImageIcons, like the previous example. It displays the two labels, wrapped in JScrollPanes, on either side of a JSplitPane (see Figure 16-10). You can drag the splitter bar back and forth to adjust the sizes of the two contained components.

```
    //file: SplitPaneFrame.java
    import java.awt.*;
    import java.awt.event.*;
    import javax.swing.*;
```

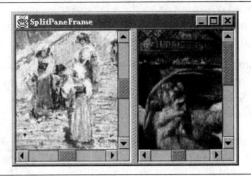

Figure 16-10. Using a split pane

```
import javax.swing.border.*;

public class SplitPaneFrame {
  public static void main(String[] args) {
    String fileOne = "Piazza di Spagna.jpg";
    String fileTwo = "L1-Light.jpg";
    if (args.length > 0) fileOne = args[0];
    if (args.length > 1) fileTwo = args[1];

    JFrame frame = new JFrame("SplitPaneFrame");

    JLabel leftImage = new JLabel( new ImageIcon( fileOne ) );
    Component left = new JScrollPane(leftImage);
    JLabel rightImage = new JLabel( new ImageIcon( fileTwo ) );
    Component right = new JScrollPane(rightImage);

    JSplitPane split =
      new JSplitPane(JSplitPane.HORIZONTAL_SPLIT, left, right);
    split.setDividerLocation(100);
    frame.getContentPane( ).add(split);

    frame.setDefaultCloseOperation( JFrame.EXIT_ON_CLOSE );
    frame.setSize(300, 200);
    frame.setVisible(true);
  }
}
```

The JTabbedPane Class

If you've ever dealt with the Control Panel in Windows, you already know what a JTabbedPane is. It's a container with labeled tabs. When you click on a tab, a new set of controls is shown in the body of the JTabbedPane. In Swing, JTabbedPane is simply a specialized container.

Each tab has a name. To add a tab to the JTabbedPane, simply call addTab(). You'll need to specify the name of the tab as well as a component that supplies the tab's contents. Typically, it's a container holding other components.

Even though the JTabbedPane only shows one set of components at a time, be aware that all the components on all the pages are in memory at one time. If you have components that hog processor time or memory, try to put them into some "sleep" state when they are not showing.

The following example shows how to create a JTabbedPane. It adds standard Swing components to a tab named *Controls*. The second tab is filled with a scrollable image, which was presented in the previous examples.

```java
//file: TabbedPaneFrame.java
import java.awt.*;
import java.awt.event.*;
import javax.swing.*;
import javax.swing.border.*;

public class TabbedPaneFrame {
  public static void main(String[] args)
  {
    JFrame frame = new JFrame("TabbedPaneFrame");
    JTabbedPane tabby = new JTabbedPane( );

    // create the controls pane
    JPanel controls = new JPanel( );
    controls.add(new JLabel("Service:"));
    JList list = new JList(
        new String[] { "Web server", "FTP server" });
    list.setBorder(BorderFactory.createEtchedBorder( ));
    controls.add(list);
    controls.add(new JButton("Start"));

    // create an image pane
    String filename = "Piazza di Spagna.jpg";
    JLabel image = new JLabel( new ImageIcon(filename) );
    JComponent picture = new JScrollPane(image);
    tabby.addTab("Controls", controls);
    tabby.addTab("Picture", picture);

    frame.getContentPane( ).add(tabby);

    frame.setSize(200, 200);
    frame.setDefaultCloseOperation( JFrame.EXIT_ON_CLOSE );
    frame.setVisible(true);
  }
}
```

The code isn't especially fancy, but the result is an impressive-looking user interface. The first tab is a JPanel that contains some other components, including a JList with an etched border. The second tab simply contains the JLabel with ImageIcon wrapped in a JScrollPane. The running example is shown in Figure 16-11.

Figure 16-11. Using a tabbed pane

Our example has only two tabs, and they fit quite easily, but in a realistic application it is easy to run out of room. By default, when there are too many tabs to display in a single row, JTabbedPane automatically wraps them into additional rows. This behavior fits with the tab notion quite well, giving the appearance of a filing cabinet, but it also necessitates that when you select a tab from the back row, the tabs must be rearranged to bring the selected tab to the foreground. Many users find this confusing, and it violates a principal of user interface design that says that controls should remain in the same location. Alternatively the tabbed pane can be configured to use a single, scrolling row of tabs by specifying a scrolling tab layout policy like this:

```
setTabLayoutPolicy( JTabbedPane.SCROLL_TAB_LAYOUT );
```

Scrollbars and Sliders

JScrollPane is such a handy component that you may not ever need to use scrollbars by themselves. In fact, if you ever do find yourself using a scrollbar by itself, chances are you really want to use another component called a *slider*.

There's not much point in describing the appearance and functionality of scrollbars and sliders. Instead, let's jump right in with an example that includes both components. Figure 16-12 shows a simple example with both a scrollbar and a slider.

Here is the source code for this example:

```
//file: Slippery.java
import java.awt.*;
import java.awt.event.*;
import javax.swing.*;
import javax.swing.event.*;

public class Slippery {
  public static void main(String[] args)
  {
```

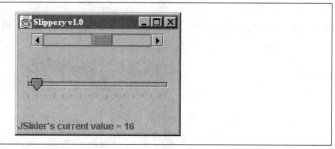

Figure 16-12. Using a scrollbar and a slider

```java
JFrame frame = new JFrame("Slippery v1.0");
Container content = frame.getContentPane( );

JPanel main = new JPanel(new GridLayout(2, 1));
JPanel scrollBarPanel = new JPanel( );
final JScrollBar scrollBar =
    new JScrollBar(JScrollBar.HORIZONTAL, 0, 48, 0, 255);
int height = scrollBar.getPreferredSize( ).height;
scrollBar.setPreferredSize(new Dimension(175, height));
scrollBarPanel.add(scrollBar);
main.add(scrollBarPanel);

JPanel sliderPanel = new JPanel( );
final JSlider slider =
    new JSlider(JSlider.HORIZONTAL, 0, 255, 128);
slider.setMajorTickSpacing(48);
slider.setMinorTickSpacing(16);
slider.setPaintTicks(true);
sliderPanel.add(slider);
main.add(sliderPanel);

content.add(main, BorderLayout.CENTER);

final JLabel statusLabel =
    new JLabel("Welcome to Slippery v1.0");
content.add(statusLabel, BorderLayout.SOUTH);

// wire up the event handlers
scrollBar.addAdjustmentListener(new AdjustmentListener( ) {
  public void adjustmentValueChanged(AdjustmentEvent e) {
    statusLabel.setText("JScrollBar's current value = "
                      + scrollBar.getValue( ));
  }
});

slider.addChangeListener(new ChangeListener( ) {
  public void stateChanged(ChangeEvent e) {
    statusLabel.setText("JSlider's current value = "
                      + slider.getValue( ));
  }
});
```

```
        frame.pack( );
        frame.setDefaultCloseOperation( JFrame.EXIT_ON_CLOSE );
        frame.setVisible(true);
    }
}
```

All we've really done here is added a `JScrollBar` and a `JSlider` to our main window. If the user adjusts either of these components, the current value of the component is displayed in a `JLabel` at the bottom of the window.

The `JScrollBar` and `JSlider` are both created by specifying an orientation, either `HORIZONTAL` or `VERTICAL`. You can also specify the minimum and maximum values for the components, as well as the initial value. The `JScrollBar` supports one additional parameter, the *extent*. The extent simply refers to what range of values is represented by the slider within the scroll bar. For example, in a scrollbar that runs from 0 to 255, an extent of 128 means that the slider will be half the width of the scrollable area of the scrollbar.

`JSlider` supports the idea of *tick marks*, lines drawn at certain values along the slider's length. *Major* tick marks are slightly larger than *minor* tick marks. To draw tick marks, just specify an interval for major and minor tick marks, and then paint the tick marks:

```
slider.setMajorTickSpacing(48);
    slider.setMinorTickSpacing(16);
    slider.setPaintTicks(true);
```

`JSlider` also supports labeling the ticks with text strings, using the `setLabelTable()` method.

Responding to events from the two components is straightforward. The `JScrollBar` sends out `AdjustmentEvents` every time something happens; the `JSlider` fires off `ChangeEvents` when its value changes. In our simple example, we display the new value of the changed component in the `JLabel` at the bottom of the window.

Dialogs

A dialog is another standard feature of user interfaces. Dialogs are frequently used to present information to the user ("Your fruit salad is ready.") or to ask a question ("Shall I bring the car around?"). Dialogs are used so commonly in GUI applications that Swing includes a handy set of prebuilt dialogs. These are accessible from static methods in the `JOptionPane` class. Many variations are possible; `JOptionPane` groups them into four basic types:

Message dialog
    Displays a message to the user, usually accompanied by an *OK* button.

Confirmation dialog
    Ask a question and displays answer buttons, usually *Yes*, *No*, and *Cancel*.

Input dialog

Asks the user to type in a string.

Option dialogs

The most general type; you pass it your own components, which are displayed in the dialog.

A confirmation dialog is shown in Figure 16-13.

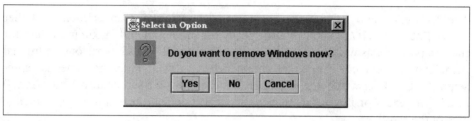

Figure 16-13. Using a confirmation dialog

Let's look at examples of each kind of dialog. The following code produces a message dialog:

```
JOptionPane.showMessageDialog(f, "You have mail.");
```

The first parameter to showMessageDialog() is the parent component (in this case f, an existing JFrame). The dialog will be centered on the parent component. If you pass null for the parent component, the dialog is centered in your screen. The dialogs that JOptionPane displays are *modal*, which means they block other input to your application while they are showing.

Here's a slightly fancier message dialog. We've specified a title for the dialog and a message type, which affects the icon that is displayed:

```
JOptionPane.showMessageDialog(f, "You are low on memory.",
        "Apocalyptic message", JOptionPane.WARNING_MESSAGE);
```

Here's how to display the confirmation dialog shown in Figure 16-13:

```
int result = JOptionPane.showConfirmDialog(null,
        "Do you want to remove Windows now?");
```

In this case, we've passed null for the parent component. Special values are returned from showConfirmDialog() to indicate which button was pressed. There's a full example below that shows how to use this return value.

Sometimes you need to ask the user to type some input. The following code puts up a dialog requesting the user's name:

```
String name = JOptionPane.showInputDialog(null,
        "Please enter your name.");
```

Whatever the user types is returned as a String or null if the user presses the *Cancel* button.

The most general type of dialog is the option dialog. You supply an array of objects you wish to be displayed; JOptionPane takes care of formatting them and displaying the dialog. The following example displays a text label, a JTextField, and a JPasswordField. (Text components are described in the next chapter.)

```
JTextField userField = new JTextField( );
JPasswordField passField = new JPasswordField( );
String message = "Please enter your user name and password.";
result = JOptionPane.showOptionDialog(f,
    new Object[] { message, userField, passField },
    "Login", JOptionPane.OK_CANCEL_OPTION,
    JOptionPane.QUESTION_MESSAGE,
    null, null, null);
```

We've also specified a dialog title ("Login") in the call to showOptionDialog(). We want *OK* and *Cancel* buttons, so we pass OK_CANCEL_OPTION as the dialog type. The QUESTION_MESSAGE argument indicates we'd like to see the question-mark icon. The last three items are optional: an Icon, an array of different choices, and a current selection. Since the icon parameter is null, a default is used. If the array of choices and the current selection parameters were not null, JOptionPane might try to display the choices in a list or combo box.

The following application includes all the examples we've covered:

```
import javax.swing.*;

public class ExerciseOptions {
  public static void main(String[] args) {
    JFrame frame = new JFrame("ExerciseOptions v1.0");
    frame.setSize(200, 200);
    frame.setVisible(true);

    JOptionPane.showMessageDialog(frame, "You have mail.");
    JOptionPane.showMessageDialog(frame, "You are low on memory.",
        "Apocalyptic message", JOptionPane.WARNING_MESSAGE);

    int result = JOptionPane.showConfirmDialog(null,
        "Do you want to remove Windows now?");
    switch (result) {
      case JOptionPane.YES_OPTION:
        System.out.println("Yes"); break;
      case JOptionPane.NO_OPTION:
        System.out.println("No"); break;
      case JOptionPane.CANCEL_OPTION:
        System.out.println("Cancel"); break;
      case JOptionPane.CLOSED_OPTION:
        System.out.println("Closed"); break;
    }

    String name = JOptionPane.showInputDialog(null,
        "Please enter your name.");
    System.out.println(name);
```

```
JTextField userField = new JTextField( );
JPasswordField passField = new JPasswordField( );
String message = "Please enter your user name and password.";
result = JOptionPane.showOptionDialog(frame,
    new Object[] { message, userField, passField },
    "Login", JOptionPane.OK_CANCEL_OPTION,
    JOptionPane.QUESTION_MESSAGE,
    null, null, null);
if (result == JOptionPane.OK_OPTION)
  System.out.println(userField.getText( ) +
      " " + new String(passField.getPassword( )));

System.exit(0);
  }
}
```

File Selection Dialog

A JFileChooser is a standard file-selection box. As with other Swing components, JFileChooser is implemented in pure Java, so it looks and acts the same on different platforms.

Selecting files all day can be pretty boring without a greater purpose, so we'll exercise the JFileChooser in a minieditor application. Editor provides a text area in which we can load and work with files. (The JFileChooser created by Editor is shown in Figure 16-14.) We'll stop just shy of the capability to save and let you fill in the blanks (with a few caveats).

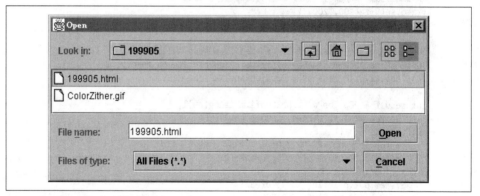

Figure 16-14. Using a JFileChooser

Here's the code:

```
import java.awt.*;
import java.awt.event.*;
import java.io.*;
import javax.swing.*;
```

```java
public class Editor extends JFrame implements ActionListener
{
  private JEditorPane textPane = new JEditorPane( );

  public Editor( ) {
    super("Editor v1.0");
    Container content = getContentPane( );
    content.add(new JScrollPane(textPane), BorderLayout.CENTER);
    JMenu menu = new JMenu("File");
    menu.add(makeMenuItem("Open"));
    menu.add(makeMenuItem("Save"));
    menu.add(makeMenuItem("Quit"));
    JMenuBar menuBar = new JMenuBar( );
    menuBar.add(menu);
    setJMenuBar(menuBar);
    setSize(300, 300);
    setDefaultCloseOperation( JFrame.EXIT_ON_CLOSE );
  }

  public void actionPerformed(ActionEvent e) {
    String command = e.getActionCommand( );
    if (command.equals("Quit")) System.exit(0);
    else if (command.equals("Open")) loadFile( );
    else if (command.equals("Save")) saveFile( );
  }

  private void loadFile ( ) {
    JFileChooser chooser = new JFileChooser( );
    int result = chooser.showOpenDialog(this);
    if (result == JFileChooser.CANCEL_OPTION) return;
    try {
      File file = chooser.getSelectedFile( );
      java.net.URL url = file.toURL( );
      textPane.setPage(url);
    }
    catch (Exception e) {
      textPane.setText("Could not load file: " + e);
    }
  }

  private void saveFile( ) {
    JFileChooser chooser = new JFileChooser( );
    chooser.showSaveDialog(this);
    // Save file data...
  }

  private JMenuItem makeMenuItem( String name ) {
    JMenuItem m = new JMenuItem( name );
    m.addActionListener( this );
    return m;
  }
```

```
    public static void main(String[] s) {
new Editor( ).setVisible(true);
    }
}
```

Editor is a JFrame that lays itself out with a JEditorPane (which is covered in Chapter 17) and a pull-down menu. From the pull-down *File* menu, we can *Open*, *Save*, or *Quit*. The actionPerformed() method catches the events associated with these menu selections and takes the appropriate action.

The interesting parts of Editor are the private methods loadFile() and saveFile(). The loadFile() method creates a new JFileChooser and calls its showOpenDialog() method.

A JFileChooser does its work when the showOpenDialog() method is called. This method blocks the caller until the dialog completes its job, at which time the file chooser disappears. After that, we can retrieve the designated file with the getFile() method. In loadFile(), we convert the selected File to a URL and pass it to the JEditorPane, which displays the selected file. As you'll learn in the next chapter, JEditorPane can display HTML and RTF files.

You can fill out the unfinished saveFile() method if you wish, but it would be prudent to add the standard safety precautions. For example, you could use one of the confirmation dialogs we just looked at to prompt the user before overwriting an existing file.

The Color Chooser

Swing is chock full of goodies. JColorChooser is yet another ready-made dialog supplied with Swing; it allows your users to choose colors. The following very brief example shows how easy it is to use JColorChooser:

```java
import java.awt.*;
import java.awt.event.*;
import javax.swing.*;

public class LocalColor {
  public static void main(String[] args) {
    final JFrame frame = new JFrame("LocalColor v1.0");
    final Container content = frame.getContentPane( );
    content.setLayout(new GridBagLayout( ));
    JButton button = new JButton("Change color...");
    content.add(button);

    button.addActionListener(new ActionListener( ) {
      public void actionPerformed(ActionEvent e) {
        Color c = JColorChooser.showDialog(frame,
            "Choose a color", content.getBackground( ));
        if (c != null) content.setBackground(c);
      }
    });
```

```
        frame.setSize(200, 200);
        frame.setDefaultCloseOperation( JFrame.EXIT_ON_CLOSE );
        frame.setVisible(true);
    }
}
```

This example shows a frame window with a single button. When you click on the button, a color chooser pops up. After you select a color, it becomes the background color of the frame window.

Basically all we have to do is call JColorChooser's static method showDialog(). In this example, we specified a parent component, a dialog title, and an initial color value. But you can get away with just specifying a parent component. Whatever color the user chooses is returned; if the user presses the *Cancel* button, null is returned.

## CHAPTER 17

More Swing Components

In the previous chapter, we described most of the components that Swing offers for building user interfaces. In this chapter, you'll find out about the rest. These include Swing's text components, trees, and tables. These types of components have considerable depth but are quite easy to use if you accept their default options. We'll show you the easy way to use these components and start to describe the more advanced features of each. Later in this chapter we'll also give an example of how to implement your own, custom components in Swing.

Text Components

Swing offers sophisticated text components, from plain-text entry boxes to HTML interpreters. For full coverage of Swing's text capabilities, see O'Reilly's *Java Swing*. In that encyclopedic book, several meaty chapters are devoted to text. It's a huge subject; we'll just scratch the surface here.

Let's begin by examining the simpler text components. JTextArea is a multiline text editor, and JTextField is a simple, single-line text editor. Both JTextField and JTextArea derive from the JTextComponent class, which provides the functionality they have in common. This includes methods for setting and retrieving the displayed text, specifying whether the text is "editable" or read-only, manipulating the cursor position within the text, and manipulating text selections.

Observing changes in text components requires an understanding of how the components implement the Model-View-Controller (MVC) architecture. You may recall from the last chapter that Swing components implement a true MVC architecture. It's in the text components that you first get an inkling of a clear separation between the M and VC parts of the MVC architecture. The model for text components is an object called a Document. When you add or remove text from a JTextField or a JTextArea, the corresponding Document is changed. It's the document itself, not the visual components, that generates text-related events when something changes. To receive notification of JTextArea changes, therefore, you register with the underlying Document, not with the JTextArea component itself:

```
JTextArea textArea = new JTextArea( );
Document d = textArea.getDocument( );
d.addDocumentListener(someListener);
```

As you'll see in an upcoming example, you can easily have more than one visual text component use the same underlying data model, or Document.

In addition, JTextField components generate ActionEvents whenever the user presses the Return key within the field. To get these events, implement the ActionListener interface and register your listener using the addActionListener() method.

The next sections contain a couple of simple applications that show you how to work with text areas and fields.

The TextEntryBox Application

Our first example, TextEntryBox, creates a JTextArea and ties it to a JTextField, as you can see in Figure 17-1.

Figure 17-1. The TextEntryBox application

When the user hits Return in the JTextField, we receive an ActionEvent and add the line to the JTextArea's display. Try it out. You may have to click your mouse in the JTextField to give it focus before typing in it. If you fill up the display with lines, you can test-drive the scrollbar:

```
//file: TextEntryBox.java
import java.awt.*;
import java.awt.event.*;
import javax.swing.*;

public class TextEntryBox {

  public static void main(String[] args) {
    JFrame frame = new JFrame("Text Entry Box");
```

```
        final JTextArea area = new JTextArea( );
        area.setFont(new Font("Serif", Font.BOLD, 18));
        area.setText("Howdy!\n");
        final JTextField field = new JTextField( );

        Container content = frame.getContentPane( );
        content.add(new JScrollPane(area), BorderLayout.CENTER);
        content.add(field, BorderLayout.SOUTH);
        field.requestFocus( );

        field.addActionListener(new ActionListener( ) {
          public void actionPerformed(ActionEvent ae) {
            area.append(field.getText( ) + '\n');
            field.setText("");
          }
        });

        frame.setDefaultCloseOperation( JFrame.EXIT_ON_CLOSE );
        frame.setSize(200, 300);
        frame.setVisible(true);
      }
    }
```

TextEntryBox is exceedingly simple; we've done a few things to make it more interesting. We give the text area a bigger font using Component's setFont( ) method; fonts are discussed in Chapter 19. Finally, we want to be notified whenever the user presses Return in the text field, so we register an anonymous inner class as a listener for action events.

Pressing Return in the JTextField generates an action event, and that's where the fun begins. We handle the event in the actionPerformed( ) method of our inner ActionListener implementation. Then we use the getText( ) and setText( ) methods to manipulate the text the user has typed. These methods can be used for JTextField and JTextArea since these components are both derived from the JTextComponent class and therefore have some common functionality.

The event handler, actionPerformed( ), calls field.getText( ) to read the text that the user typed into our JTextField. It then adds this text to the JTextArea by calling area.append( ). Finally, we clear the text field by calling the method field.setText(""), preparing it for more input.

Remember, the text components really are distinct from the text data model, the Document. When you call setText( ), getText( ), or append( ), these methods are shorthand for operations on an underlying Document.

By default, JTextField and JTextArea are editable; you can type and edit in both text components. They can be changed to output-only areas by calling setEditable(false). Both text components also support *selections*. A selection is a range of text that is highlighted for copying, cutting, or pasting in your windowing system. You select text by dragging the mouse over it; you can then cut, copy and paste it into other text windows using the default keyboard gestures. On most systems these are Ctrl-C for copy, Ctrl-V for paste, and Ctrl-X for cut. You can also programmatically manage these operations using the JTextComponent's cut(), copy(), and paste() methods. You could, for example, create a pop-up menu with the standard cut, copy, and paste options using these methods. The current text selection is returned by getSelectedText(), and you can set the selection using selectText(), which takes an index range or selectAll().

Notice how JTextArea fits neatly inside a JScrollPane. The scroll pane gives us the expected scrollbars and scrolling behavior if the text in the JTextArea becomes too large for the available space.

Formatted Text

Java 1.4 introduced JFormattedTextField. This component provides explicit support for editing complex formatted values such as numbers and dates. JFormattedTextField acts somewhat like a JTextField, except that it accepts a format-specifying object in its constructor and manages a complex object type (such as Date or Integer) through its setValue() and getValue() methods. The following example shows the construction of a simple form with different types of formatted fields:

```java
import java.text.*;
import javax.swing.*;
import javax.swing.text.*;
import java.util.Date;

public class FormattedFields
{
    public static void main( String[] args ) throws Exception {
        Box form = Box.createVerticalBox();
        form.add( new JLabel("Name:") );
        form.add( new JTextField("Joe User") );

        form.add( new JLabel("Birthday:") );
        JFormattedTextField birthdayField =
            new JFormattedTextField(new SimpleDateFormat("MM/dd/yy"));
        birthdayField.setValue( new Date() );
        form.add( birthdayField );

        form.add( new JLabel("Age:") );
        form.add(new JFormattedTextField(new Integer(32)));

        form.add( new JLabel("Hairs on Body:") );
        JFormattedTextField hairsField
            = new JFormattedTextField( new DecimalFormat("###,###") );
        hairsField.setValue(new Integer(100000));
        form.add( hairsField );
```

```
        form.add( new JLabel("Phone Number:") );
        JFormattedTextField phoneField =
            new JFormattedTextField( new MaskFormatter("(###)###-####") );
        phoneField.setValue("(314)555-1212");
        form.add( phoneField );

        JFrame frame = new JFrame("User Information");
        frame.getContentPane( ).add(form);
        frame.pack( );
        frame.setDefaultCloseOperation( JFrame.EXIT_ON_CLOSE );
        frame.setVisible(true);
    }
}
```

The JFormattedTextField can be constructed with a variety of format-specifying objects including java.lang.Number (e.g., Integer and Float), java.text. NumberFormat, java.text.DateFormat, and the more arbitrary java.text. MaskFormatter. The NumberFormat and DateFormat classes of the java.text package are discussed in Chapters 9 and 10. MaskFormatter allows you to construct arbitrary physical layout conventions. In a moment we'll discuss input filtering and component validation, which also allow you to restrict the kinds of characters that could fill the fields or perform arbitrary checks on the data. Finally we should mention that in this example we've used a Box container. A Box is just a Swing container that uses a BoxLayout, which we'll discuss more in Chapter 18.

After construction you can set a valid value using setValue() and retrieve the last valid value with getValue(). To do this, you'll have to cast the value back to the correct type based on the format you are using. For example, this statement retrieves the date from our birthday field:

```
    Date bday = (Date)birthdayField.getValue( );
```

JFormattedTextField validates its text when the user attempts to shift focus to a new field (either by clicking with the mouse outside of the field or using keyboard navigation). By default, JFormattedTextField handles invalid input by simply reverting to the last valid value. If you wish to allow invalid input to remain in the field, you can set the setFocusLostBehavior() method with the value JFormattedTextField.COMMIT (the default is COMMIT_OR_REVERT).

Filtering Input

JFormattedTextField does not know about all format types itself and uses AbstractFormatter objects that know about particular format types. The AbstractFormatters in turn provide implementations of two interfaces: DocumentFilter and NavigationFilter. A DocumentFilter attaches to implementations of Document and allows you to intercept editing commands, modifying them as you wish. A NavigationFilter can be attached to JTextComponents to control the movement of the cursor (as in a mask-formatted field). You can implement your own

AbstractFormatters for use with JFormattedTextField, and, more generally, you can use the DocumentFilter interface to control how documents are edited in any type of text component. For example, you could create a DocumentFilter that maps characters to uppercase or strange symbols. DocumentFilter provides a low-level, edit-by-edit means of controlling or mapping user input. In the next section we discuss high-level field validation to ensure the correctness of data once it is entered.

DocumentFilter

The following example, DocFilter, applies a document filter to a JTextField. Our DocumentFilter simply maps any input to uppercase. Here is the code:

```
import java.text.*;
import javax.swing.*;
import javax.swing.text.*;

public class DocFilter
{
    public static void main( String[] args ) throws Exception
    {
        JTextField field = new JTextField(30);

        ((AbstractDocument)(field.getDocument( ))).setDocumentFilter(
            new DocumentFilter( )
        {
            public void insertString(
                FilterBypass fb, int offset, String string, AttributeSet attr)
                    throws BadLocationException
            {
                fb.insertString( offset, string.toUpperCase( ), attr );
            }

            public void replace(
                FilterBypass fb, int offset, int length, String string,
                AttributeSet attr) throws BadLocationException
            {
                fb.replace( offset, length, string.toUpperCase( ), attr );
            }
        } );

        JFrame frame = new JFrame("User Information");
        frame.getContentPane( ).add( field );
        frame.pack( );
        frame.setDefaultCloseOperation( JFrame.EXIT_ON_CLOSE );
        frame.setVisible(true);
    }
}
```

The methods insertString() and replace() of the DocumentFilter are called when text is added to the document or modified. Within them we have an opportunity to filter the text before passing it on. When we are ready to apply the text, we use the FilterBypass reference. FilterBypass has the same methods, which apply the changes directly to the document. The `DocumentFilter` `remove()` method can also be used to intercept edits to the document that remove characters. One thing to note in our example is that not all `Documents` have a `setDocumentFilter()` method. Instead, we have to cast our document to an `AbstractDocument`. Only document implementations that extend `AbstractDocument` accept filters (unless you implement your own). This is because the Document Filter API was added in Java 1.4, and it was decided that changes could not be made to the original `Document` interface.

Validating Data

Low-level input filtering prevents you from doing such things as entering a number where a character should be. In this section we're going to talk about high-level validation, which accounts for things like February having only 28 days or a credit-card number being for a Visa or MasterCard. Whereas character filtering prevents you from entering incorrect data, field validation happens after data has been entered. Normally validation occurs when the user tries to change focus and leave the field, either by clicking the mouse or through keyboard navigation. Java 1.4 added the `InputVerifier` API, which allows you to validate the contents of a component before focus is transferred. Although we are going to talk about this in the context of text fields, an `InputVerifier` can actually be attached to any `JComponent` to validate its state in this way.

The following example creates a pair of text fields. The first allows any value to be entered, while the second rejects any value that is not a number between 0 and 100. When both fields are happy, you can freely move between them. However, when you enter an invalid value in the second field and try to leave, the program just beeps and selects the text. The focus remains trapped until you correct the problem.

```
import javax.swing.*;

public class Validator
{
    public static void main( String[] args ) throws Exception {
        Box form = Box.createVerticalBox( );
        form.add( new JLabel("Any Value") );
        form.add( new JTextField("5000") );

        form.add( new JLabel("Only 0-100") );
        JTextField rangeField = new JTextField("50");
        rangeField.setInputVerifier( new InputVerifier() {
            public boolean verify( JComponent comp ) {
                JTextField field = (JTextField)comp;
                boolean passed = false;
                try {
                    int n = Integer.parseInt(field.getText( ));
                    passed = ( 0 <= n && n <= 100 );
                } catch (NumberFormatException e) { }
                if ( !passed ) {
```

```
                comp.getToolkit().beep();
                field.selectAll();
            }
            return passed;
        }
    } );
    form.add( rangeField );

    JFrame frame = new JFrame("User Information");
    frame.getContentPane().add(form);
    frame.setDefaultCloseOperation( JFrame.EXIT_ON_CLOSE );
    frame.pack();
    frame.setVisible(true);
    }
}
```

Here we have created an anonymous inner class extending `InputVerifier`. The API is very simple; at validation time our `verify()` method is called, and we are passed a reference to the component needing checking. Here we cast to the correct type (we know what we are verifying of course) and parse the number. If it is out of range, we beep and select the text. We then return `true` or `false` indicating whether the value passes validation.

You can use an `InputVerifier` in combination with a `JFormattedTextField` to both guide user input into the correct format and validate the semantics of what the user entered.

Say the Magic Word

Before we move on from our discussion of formatted text, we should mention that Swing includes a class just for typing passwords, called `JPasswordField`. A `JPasswordField` behaves just like a `JTextField` (it's a subclass), except every character typed is echoed as a single character, typically an asterisk. Figure 17-2 shows the option dialog example that was presented in Chapter 16. The example includes a `JTextField` and a `JPasswordField`.

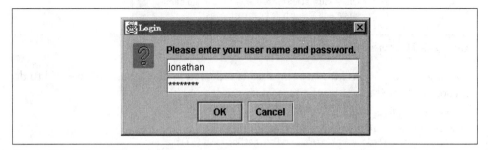

Figure 17-2. Using a JPasswordField in a dialog

The creation and use of JPasswordField is basically the same as for JTextField. If you find asterisks distasteful, you can tell the JPasswordField to use a different character using the setEchoChar() method.

Normally, you would use getText() to retrieve the text typed into the JPasswordField. This method, however, is deprecated; you should use getPassword() instead. The getPassword() method returns a character array rather than a String object. This is done because character arrays are less vulnerable than Strings to discovery by memory-snooping password sniffer programs. If you're not that concerned, you can simply create a new String from the character array. Note that methods in the Java cryptographic classes accept passwords as character arrays, not strings, so you can pass the results of a getPassword() call directly to methods in the cryptographic classes without ever creating a String.

Sharing a Data Model

Our next example shows how easy it is to make two or more text components share the same Document; Figure 17-3 shows what the application looks like.

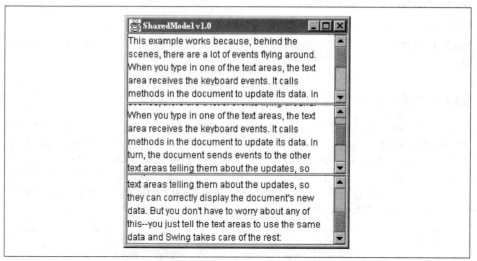

Figure 17-3. Three views of the same data model

Anything the user types into any text area is reflected in all of them. All we had to do is make all the text areas use the same data model, like this:

```
JTextArea areaFiftyOne = new JTextArea( );
JTextArea areaFiftyTwo = new JTextArea( );
areaFiftyTwo.setDocument(areaFiftyOne.getDocument( ));
JTextArea areaFiftyThree = new JTextArea( );
areaFiftyThree.setDocument(areaFiftyOne.getDocument( ));
```

We could just as easily make seven text areas sharing the same document or seventy. While this example may not look very useful, keep in mind that you can scroll different text areas to different places in the same document. That's one of the beauties of putting multiple views on the same data; you get to examine different parts of it. Another useful technique is viewing the same data in different ways. You could, for example, view some tabular numerical data as both a spreadsheet and a pie chart. The MVC architecture that Swing uses means that it's possible to do this in an intelligent way so that if numbers in a spreadsheet are updated, a pie chart that uses the same data is automatically updated also.

This example works because, behind the scenes, there are a lot of events flying around. When you type in one of the text areas, the text area receives the keyboard events. It calls methods in the document to update its data. In turn, the document sends events to the other text areas telling them about the updates so that they can correctly display the document's new data. But don't worry about any of this; you just tell the text areas to use the same data, and Swing takes care of the rest:

```java
//file: SharedModel.java
import java.awt.*;
import java.awt.event.*;
import javax.swing.*;

public class SharedModel {
    public static void main(String[] args) {
    JFrame frame = new JFrame("Shared Model");

    JTextArea areaFiftyOne = new JTextArea( );
    JTextArea areaFiftyTwo = new JTextArea( );
    areaFiftyTwo.setDocument(areaFiftyOne.getDocument( ));
    JTextArea areaFiftyThree = new JTextArea( );
    areaFiftyThree.setDocument(areaFiftyOne.getDocument( ));

    Container content = frame.getContentPane( );
    content.setLayout(new GridLayout(3, 1));
    content.add(new JScrollPane(areaFiftyOne));
    content.add(new JScrollPane(areaFiftyTwo));
    content.add(new JScrollPane(areaFiftyThree));

    frame.setDefaultCloseOperation( JFrame.EXIT_ON_CLOSE );
    frame.setSize(300, 300);
    frame.setVisible(true);
    }
}
```

Setting up the display is simple. We use a GridLayout (discussed in the next chapter) and add three text areas to the layout. Then all we have to do is tell the text areas to use the same Document.

HTML and RTF for Free

Most user interfaces will use only two subclasses of JTextComponent. These are the simple JTextField and JTextArea classes that we just covered. That's just the tip of the iceberg, however. Swing offers sophisticated text capabilities through two other subclasses ofJTextComponent: JEditorPane and JTextPane.

The first of these, JEditorPane, can display HTML and RTF documents. It also fires one more type of event, a HyperlinkEvent. Subtypes of this event are fired off when the mouse enters, exits, or clicks on a hyperlink. Combined with JEditorPane's HTML display capabilities, it's easy to build a simple browser. The following browser, as shown in Figure 17-4, has only about 70 lines of code.

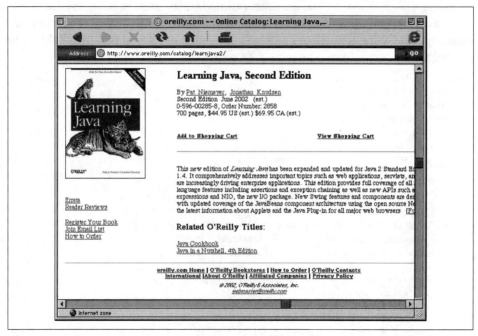

Figure 17-4. The CanisMinor application, a simple web browser

```
//file: CanisMinor.java
import java.awt.*;
import java.awt.event.*;
import java.net.*;
import javax.swing.*;
import javax.swing.event.*;

public class CanisMinor extends JFrame {
  protected JEditorPane mEditorPane;
  protected JTextField mURLField;
```

```
public CanisMinor(String urlString) {
  super("CanisMinor v1.0");
  createGUI(urlString);
}

protected void createGUI( String urlString ) {
  Container content = getContentPane( );
  content.setLayout(new BorderLayout( ));

  JToolBar urlToolBar = new JToolBar( );
  mURLField = new JTextField(urlString, 40);
  urlToolBar.add(new JLabel("Location:"));
  urlToolBar.add(mURLField);
  content.add(urlToolBar, BorderLayout.NORTH);

  mEditorPane = new JEditorPane( );
  mEditorPane.setEditable(false);
  content.add(new JScrollPane(mEditorPane), BorderLayout.CENTER);

  openURL(urlString);

  mURLField.addActionListener(new ActionListener( ) {
    public void actionPerformed(ActionEvent ae) {
      openURL(ae.getActionCommand( ));
    }
  });

  mEditorPane.addHyperlinkListener(new LinkActivator( ));

  setSize(500, 600);
  setDefaultCloseOperation( JFrame.EXIT_ON_CLOSE );
}

protected void openURL(String urlString) {
  try {
    URL url = new URL(urlString);
    mEditorPane.setPage(url);
    mURLField.setText(url.toExternalForm( ));
  }
  catch (Exception e) {
    System.out.println("Couldn't open " + urlString + ":" + e);
  }
}

class LinkActivator implements HyperlinkListener {
  public void hyperlinkUpdate(HyperlinkEvent he) {
    HyperlinkEvent.EventType type = he.getEventType( );
    if (type == HyperlinkEvent.EventType.ACTIVATED)
      openURL(he.getURL( ).toExternalForm( ));
  }
}

public static void main(String[] args) {
  String urlString = "http://www.oreilly.com/catalog/learnjava2/";
```

```
        if (args.length > 0)
          urlString = args[0];
        new CanisMinor( urlString ).setVisible( true );
      }
    }
```

JEditorPane is the center of this little application. Passing a URL to setPage() causes the JEditorPane to load a new page, either from a local file or from somewhere across the Internet. To go to a new page, enter it in the text field at the top of the window and press Return. This fires an ActionEvent that sets the new page location of the JEditorPane. It can display RTF files, too (Rich Text Format is the text or nonbinary storage format for Microsoft Word documents).

Responding to hyperlinks correctly is simply a matter of responding to the HyperlinkEvents thrown by the JEditorPane. This behavior is encapsulated in the LinkActivator inner class. In this case the only activity we are interested in is when the user "activates" the hyperlink by clicking on it. We respond by setting the location of the JEditorPane to the location given under the hyperlink. Surf away!

Behind the scenes, something called an EditorKit handles displaying documents for the JEditorPane. Different kinds of EditorKits can display different kinds of documents. For HTML, the HTMLEditorKit class (in the javax.swing.text.html package) handles the display. Currently, this class supports HTML 3.2. Subsequent releases of the SDK will contain enhancements to the capabilities of HTMLEditorKit; eventually, it will support HTML 4.0.

There's another component here that we haven't covered before—the JToolBar. This nifty container houses our URL text field. Initially, the JToolBar starts out at the top of the window. But you can pick it up by clicking on the little dotted box near its left edge, then drag it around to different parts of the window. You can place this toolbar at the top, left, right, or bottom of the window, or you can drag it outside the window entirely. It will then inhabit a window of its own. All this behavior comes for free from the JToolBar class. All we had to do was create a JToolBar and add some components to it. The JToolBar is just a container, so we add it to the content pane of our window to give it an initial location.

Managing Text Yourself

Swing offers one last subclass of JTextComponent that can do just about anything you want: JTextPane. The basic text components, JTextField and JTextArea, are limited to a single font in a single style. But JTextPane, a subclass of JEditorPane, can display multiple fonts and multiple styles in the same component. It also includes support for a cursor (caret), highlighting, image embedding, and other advanced features.

We'll just take a peek at JTextPane here by creating a text pane with some styled text. Remember, the text itself is stored in an underlying data model, the Document. To create styled text, we simply associate a set of text attributes with different parts of the

---

document's text. Swing includes classes and methods for manipulating sets of attributes, like specifying a bold font or a different color for the text. Attributes themselves are contained in a class called SimpleAttributeSet; these attribute sets are manipulated with static methods in the StyleConstants class. For example, to create a set of attributes that specifies the color red, you could do this:

```
SimpleAttributeSet redstyle = new SimpleAttributeSet( );
StyleConstants.setForeground(redstyle, Color.red);
```

To add some red text to a document, you would just pass the text and the attributes to the document's insertString() method, like this:

```
document.insertString(6, "Some red text", redstyle);
```

The first argument to insertString() is an offset into the text. An exception is thrown if you pass in an offset that's greater than the current length of the document. If you pass null for the attribute set, the text is added in the JTextPane's default font and style.

Our simple example creates several attribute sets and uses them to add plain and styled text to a JTextPane, as shown in Figure 17-5.

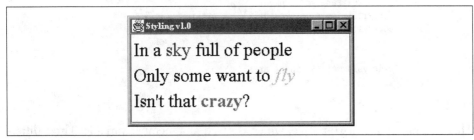

Figure 17-5. Using styled text in a JTextPane

```
//file: Styling.java
import java.awt.*;
import java.awt.event.*;
import javax.swing.*;
import javax.swing.text.*;

public class Styling extends JFrame {
  private JTextPane textPane;

  public Styling( ) {
    super("Stylin' v1.0");
    setSize(300, 200);

    textPane = new JTextPane( );
    textPane.setFont(new Font("Serif", Font.PLAIN, 24));

    // create some handy attribute sets
    SimpleAttributeSet red = new SimpleAttributeSet( );
    StyleConstants.setForeground(red, Color.red);
```

```
        StyleConstants.setBold(red, true);
        SimpleAttributeSet blue = new SimpleAttributeSet(  );
        StyleConstants.setForeground(blue, Color.blue);
        SimpleAttributeSet italic = new SimpleAttributeSet(  );
        StyleConstants.setItalic(italic, true);
        StyleConstants.setForeground(italic, Color.orange);

        // add the text
        append("In a ", null);
        append("sky", blue);
        append(" full of people\nOnly some want to ", null);
        append("fly", italic);
        append("\nIsn't that ", null);
        append("crazy", red);
        append("?", null);

        Container content = getContentPane(  );
        content.add(new JScrollPane(textPane), BorderLayout.CENTER);
        setDefaultCloseOperation( JFrame.EXIT_ON_CLOSE );
    }

    protected void append(String s, AttributeSet attributes) {
        Document d = textPane.getDocument(  );
        try { d.insertString(d.getLength(  ), s, attributes); }
        catch (BadLocationException ble) {}
    }

    public static void main(String[] args) {
        new Styling( ).setVisible(true);
    }
}
```

This example creates a JTextPane, which is saved in a member variable. Three different attribute sets are created using combinations of text styles and foreground colors. Then, using a helper method called append(), text is added to the JTextPane.

The append() method tacks a text String on the end of the JTextPane's document, using the supplied attributes. Remember that if the attributes are null, the text is displayed with the JTextPane's default font and style.

You can go ahead and add your own text if you wish. If you place the caret inside one of the differently styled words and type, the new text comes out in the appropriate style. Pretty cool, eh? You'll also notice that JTextPane gives us word-wrapping behavior for free. And since we've wrapped the JTextPane in a JScrollPane, we get scrolling for free, too. Swing allows you to do some really cool stuff without breaking a sweat. Just wait—there's plenty more to come.

This simple example should give you some idea of what JTextPane can do. It's reasonably easy to build a simple word processor with JTextPane, and complex commercial-grade word processors are definitely possible.

If JTextPane still isn't good enough for you, or you need some finer control over character, word, and paragraph layout, you can actually draw text, carets, and highlight shapes yourself. A class in the 2D API called TextLayout simplifies much of this work, but it's outside the scope of this book. For coverage of TextLayout and other advanced text drawing topics, see *Java 2D Graphics* by Jonathan Knudsen (O'Reilly).

Focus Navigation

We've brought up the topic of focus many times in our discussion so far, and we've told you that the handling and user navigation of focus is mostly done automatically. This is largely due to a new focus system introduced in Java 1.4. The new focus system is very powerful and can be heavily customized through the use of "focus traversal policy" objects that control keyboard navigation. In general, for typical application behavior, you won't have to deal with this directly. But we'll explain a few features you should know about.

Swing handles keyboard focus navigation through the KeyboardFocusManager class. This class uses FocusTraversalPolicy "strategy" objects that implement the actual schemes for locating the next component to receive focus. There are two primary FocusTraversalPolicy types supplied with Java. The first, DefaultFocusTraversalPolicy, is part of the AWT package. It emulates the old AWT-style focus management by navigating components in the order in which they were added to their container. The next, LayoutFocusTraversalPolicy, is the default for all Swing applications. It examines the layout and attempts to provide the expected navigation from left to right, top to bottom, based on component position and size.

The focus traversal policy is inherited from containers and oriented around groups of components known as "root cycles." By default every window and JInternalFrame is a root cycle. That means that focus traverses all of its child components repeatedly (jumping from the last component back to the first), and won't, by default, leave the container through keyboard navigation.

The default Swing policy uses the following keys for keyboard navigation:

Forward
> Tab or Ctrl-Tab (Ctrl-Tab also works inside text areas)

Back
> Shift-Tab or Ctrl-Shift-Tab (Ctrl-Shift-Tab also works inside text areas)

You can define your own focus traversal keys for forward and back navigation, as well as for navigation across root cycles using the setFocusTraversalKeys() method of a container. Here is an example that adds the keystroke Ctrl-N to the list of forward key navigation for components in a Frame:

```
frame.getFocusTraversalKeys(
    KeyboardFocusManager.FORWARD_TRAVERSAL_KEYS );
AWTKeyStroke ks = AWTKeyStroke.getAWTKeyStroke(
```

```
    KeyEvent.VK_N, InputEvent.CTRL_DOWN_MASK );
Set new = new HashSet( old );
set.add( ks );
frame.setFocusTraversalKeys(
    KeyboardFocusManager.FORWARD_TRAVERSAL_KEYS,set);
```

Keys are defined by the AWTKeyStroke class, which encapsulates the key and input modifiers, in this case the Control key. Constants in the KeyboardFocusManager specify forward, back, and up or down root cycle transfer across windows.

Finally, you can also move focus programmatically using the following methods of KeyboardFocusManager:

```
focusNextComponent( )
focusPreviousComponent( )
upFocusCycle( )
downFocusCycle( )
```

Trees

One of Swing's advanced components is JTree. Trees are good for representing hierarchical information, like the contents of a disk drive or a company's organizational chart. As with all Swing components, the data model is distinct from the visual representation. This means you can do things such as update the data model and trust that the visual component will be updated properly.

JTree is powerful and complex. It's so complicated, in fact, that like the text tools, the classes that support JTree have their own package, javax.swing.tree. However, if you accept the default options for almost everything, JTree is very easy to use. Figure 17-6 shows a JTree running in a Swing application that we'll describe later.

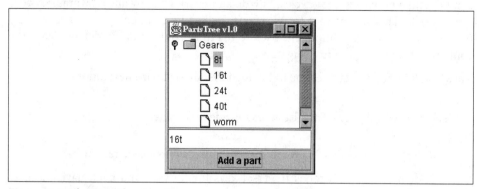

Figure 17-6. The JTree class in action

Nodes and Models

A tree's data model is made up of interconnected nodes. A node has a name, typically, a parent, and some number of children (possibly 0). In Swing, a node is represented by the TreeNode interface. Nodes that can be modified are represented by MutableTreeNode. A concrete implementation of this interface is DefaultMutableTreeNode. One node, called the *root* node, usually resides at the top of the hierarchy.

A tree's data model is represented by the TreeModel interface. Swing provides an implementation of this interface called DefaultTreeModel. You can create a DefaultTreeModel by passing a root TreeNode to its constructor.

You could create a TreeModel with just one node like this:

```
TreeNode root = new DefaultMutableTreeNode("Root node");
TreeModel model = new DefaultTreeModel(root);
```

Here's another example with a real hierarchy. The root node contains two nodes, Node 1 and Group. The Group node contains Node 2 and Node 3 as subnodes.

```
MutableTreeNode root = new DefaultMutableTreeNode("Root node");
MutableTreeNode group = new DefaultMutableTreeNode("Group");
root.insert(group, 0);
root.insert(new DefaultMutableTreeNode("Node 1"), 1);
group.insert(new DefaultMutableTreeNode("Node 2"), 0);
group.insert(new DefaultMutableTreeNode("Node 3"), 1);
```

The second parameter to the insert() method is the index of the node in the parent. Once you've got your nodes organized, you can create a TreeModel in the same way as before:

```
TreeModel model = new DefaultTreeModel(root);
```

Save a Tree

Once you have a tree model, creating a JTree is simple:

```
JTree tree = new JTree(model);
```

The JTree behaves like a souped-up JList. As Figure 17-6 shows, the JTree automatically shows nodes with no children as a sheet of paper, while nodes that contain other nodes are shown as folders. You can expand and collapse nodes by clicking on the little knobs to the left of the folder icons. You can also expand and collapse nodes by double-clicking on them. You can select nodes; multiple selections are possible using the Shift and Control keys. And, like a JList, you should put a JTree in a JScrollPane if you want it to scroll.

Tree Events

A tree fires off several flavors of events. You can find out when nodes have been expanded and collapsed, when nodes are about to be expanded or collapsed (because the user has clicked on them), and when selections occur. Three distinct event listener interfaces handle this information.

```
TreeExpansionListener
TreeWillExpandListener
TreeSelectionListener
```

Tree selections are a tricky business. You can select any combination of nodes by using the Control key and clicking on nodes. Tree selections are described by a TreePath, which describes how to get from the root node to the selected nodes.

The following example registers an event listener that prints out the last selected node:

```
tree.addTreeSelectionListener(new TreeSelectionListener( ) {
  public void valueChanged(TreeSelectionEvent e) {
    TreePath tp = e.getNewLeadSelectionPath( );
    System.out.println(tp.getLastPathComponent( ));
  }
});
```

A Complete Example

This section contains an example that showcases the following tree techniques:

- Construction of a tree model, using DefaultMutableTreeNode
- Creation and display of a JTree
- Listening for tree selection events
- Modifying the tree's data model while the JTree is showing

Here's the source code for the example:

```
//file: PartsTree.java
import java.awt.*;
import java.awt.event.*;
import javax.swing.*;
import javax.swing.event.*;
import javax.swing.tree.*;

public class PartsTree {
  public static void main(String[] args) {
    // create a hierarchy of nodes
    MutableTreeNode root = new DefaultMutableTreeNode("Parts");
    MutableTreeNode beams = new DefaultMutableTreeNode("Beams");
    MutableTreeNode gears = new DefaultMutableTreeNode("Gears");
    root.insert(beams, 0);
    root.insert(gears, 1);
    beams.insert(new DefaultMutableTreeNode("1x4 black"), 0);
    beams.insert(new DefaultMutableTreeNode("1x6 black"), 1);
    beams.insert(new DefaultMutableTreeNode("1x8 black"), 2);
    beams.insert(new DefaultMutableTreeNode("1x12 black"), 3);
    gears.insert(new DefaultMutableTreeNode("8t"), 0);
    gears.insert(new DefaultMutableTreeNode("24t"), 1);
    gears.insert(new DefaultMutableTreeNode("40t"), 2);
```

```java
    gears.insert(new DefaultMutableTreeNode("worm"), 3);
    gears.insert(new DefaultMutableTreeNode("crown"), 4);

    // create the JTree
    final DefaultTreeModel model = new DefaultTreeModel(root);
    final JTree tree = new JTree(model);

    // create a text field and button to modify the data model
    final JTextField nameField = new JTextField("16t");
    final JButton button = new JButton("Add a part");
    button.setEnabled(false);
    button.addActionListener(new ActionListener( ) {
      public void actionPerformed(ActionEvent e) {
        TreePath tp = tree.getSelectionPath( );
        MutableTreeNode insertNode =
            (MutableTreeNode)tp.getLastPathComponent( );
        int insertIndex = 0;
        if (insertNode.getParent( ) != null) {
          MutableTreeNode parent =
              (MutableTreeNode)insertNode.getParent( );
          insertIndex = parent.getIndex(insertNode) + 1;
          insertNode = parent;
        }
        MutableTreeNode node =
            new DefaultMutableTreeNode(nameField.getText( ));
        model.insertNodeInto(node, insertNode, insertIndex);
      }
    });
    JPanel addPanel = new JPanel(new GridLayout(2, 1));
    addPanel.add(nameField);
    addPanel.add(button);

    // listen for selections
    tree.addTreeSelectionListener(new TreeSelectionListener( ) {
      public void valueChanged(TreeSelectionEvent e) {
        TreePath tp = e.getNewLeadSelectionPath( );
        button.setEnabled(tp != null);
      }
    });

    // create a JFrame to hold the tree
    JFrame frame = new JFrame("PartsTree v1.0");

    frame.setDefaultCloseOperation( JFrame.EXIT_ON_CLOSE );
    frame.setSize(200, 200);
    frame.getContentPane( ).add(new JScrollPane(tree));
    frame.getContentPane( ).add(addPanel, BorderLayout.SOUTH);
    frame.setVisible(true);
  }
}
```

The example begins by creating a node hierarchy. The root node is called `Parts`. It contains two subnodes, `Beams` and `Gears`, as shown:

```
MutableTreeNode root = new DefaultMutableTreeNode("Parts");
MutableTreeNode beams = new DefaultMutableTreeNode("Beams");
MutableTreeNode gears = new DefaultMutableTreeNode("Gears");
root.insert(beams, 0);
root.insert(gears, 1);
```

The `Beams` and `Gears` nodes contain a handful of items each.

The *Add a part* button inserts a new item into the tree at the level of the current node, and just after it. You can specify the name of the new node by typing it in the text field above the button. To determine where the node should be added, the current selection is first obtained in the anonymous inner class `ActionListener`:

```
TreePath tp = tree.getSelectionPath( );
MutableTreeNode insertNode =
  (MutableTreeNode)tp.getLastPathComponent( );
```

The new node should be added to the parent node of the current node, so it ends up being a sibling of the current node. The only hitch here is that if the current node is the root node, it won't have a parent. If a parent does exist, we determine the index of the currently selected node, and then add the new node at the next index:

```
int insertIndex = 0;
if (insertNode.getParent( ) != null) {
  MutableTreeNode parent =
      (MutableTreeNode)insertNode.getParent( );
  insertIndex = parent.getIndex(insertNode) + 1;
  insertNode = parent;
}
MutableTreeNode node =
    new DefaultMutableTreeNode(nameField.getText( ));
model.insertNodeInto(node, insertNode, insertIndex);
```

You must add the new node to the tree's data model, using `insertNodeInto()`, not to the `MutableTableNode` itself. The model notifies the `JTree` that it needs to update itself.

We have another event handler in this example, one that listens for tree selection events. Basically, we want to enable our *Add a part* button only if a current selection exists:

```
tree.addTreeSelectionListener(new TreeSelectionListener( ) {
  public void valueChanged(TreeSelectionEvent e) {
    TreePath tp = e.getNewLeadSelectionPath( );
    button.setEnabled(tp != null);
  }
});
```

When you first start this application, the button is disabled. As soon as you select something, it is enabled, and you can add nodes to the tree with abandon. If you want to see the button disabled again, you can unselect everything by holding the Control key and clicking on the current selection.

Tables

Tables present information in orderly rows and columns. This is useful for presenting financial figures or representing data from a relational database. Like trees, tables in Swing are incredibly powerful and customizable. If you go with the default options, they're also pretty easy to use.

The JTable class represents a visual table component. A JTable is based on a TableModel, one of a dozen or so supporting interfaces and classes in the javax.swing.table package.

A First Stab: Freeloading

JTable has one constructor that creates a default table model for you from arrays of data. You just need to supply it with the names of your column headers and a 2D array of Objects representing the table's data. The first index selects the table's row; the second index selects the column. The following example shows how easy it is to get going with tables using this constructor:

```
//file: DullShipTable.java
import java.awt.*;
import java.awt.event.*;
import javax.swing.*;
import javax.swing.table.*;

public class DullShipTable {
  public static void main(String[] args) {
    // create some tabular data
    String[] headings =
      new String[] {"Number", "Hot?", "Origin",
                    "Destination", "Ship Date", "Weight" };
    Object[][] data = new Object[][] {
      { "100420", Boolean.FALSE, "Des Moines IA", "Spokane WA",
          "02/06/2000", new Float(450) },
      { "202174", Boolean.TRUE, "Basking Ridge NJ", "Princeton NJ",
          "05/20/2000", new Float(1250) },
      { "450877", Boolean.TRUE, "St. Paul MN", "Austin TX",
          "03/20/2000", new Float(1745) },
      { "101891", Boolean.FALSE, "Boston MA", "Albany NY",
          "04/04/2000", new Float(88) }
    };

    // create the data model and the JTable
    JTable table = new JTable(data, headings);

    JFrame frame = new JFrame("DullShipTable v1.0");
    frame.getContentPane( ).add(new JScrollPane(table));
```

```
        frame.setDefaultCloseOperation( JFrame.EXIT_ON_CLOSE );
        frame.setSize(500, 200);
        frame.setVisible(true);
    }
}
```

This small application produces the display shown in Figure 17-7.

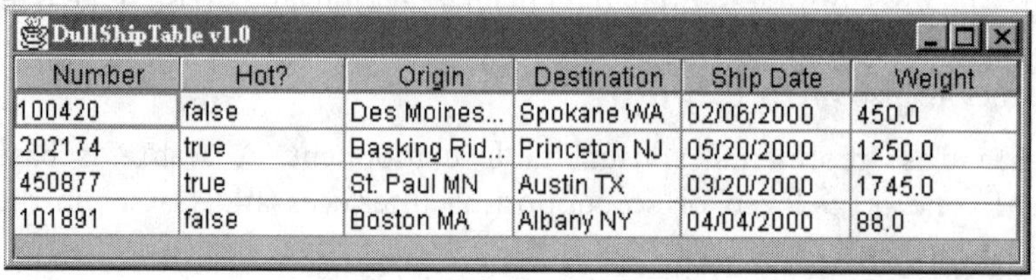

Figure 17-7. A rudimentary JTable

For very little typing, we've gotten some pretty impressive stuff. Here are a few things that come for free:

Column headings

> The JTable has automatically formatted the column headings differently than the table cells. It's clear that they are not part of the table's data area.

Cell overflow

> If a cell's data is too long to fit in the cell, it is automatically truncated and shown with an ellipses (...). This is shown in the *Origin* cell in the first two rows in Figure 17-7.

Row selection

> You can click on any cell in the table to select its entire row. This behavior is controllable; you can select single cells, entire rows, entire columns, or some combination of these. To configure the JTable's selection behavior, use the setCellSelectionEnabled(), setColumnSelectionAllowed(), and set-RowSelectionAllowed() methods.

Cell editing

> Double-clicking on a cell opens it for editing; you'll get a little cursor in the cell. You can type directly into the cell to change the cell's data.

Column sizing

> If you position the mouse cursor between two column headings, you'll get a little left-right arrow cursor. Click and drag to change the size of the column to the left. Depending on how the JTable is configured, the other columns may also change size. The resizing behavior is controlled with the setAutoResizeMode() method.

Column reordering

If you click and drag on a column heading, you can move the entire column to another part of the table.

Play with this for a while; it's fun.

Round Two: Creating a Table Model

JTable is a very powerful component. You get a lot of very nice behavior for free. However, the default settings are not quite what we wanted for this simple example. In particular, we intended the table entries to be read-only; they should not be editable. Also, we'd like entries in the *Hot?* column to be checkboxes instead of words. Finally, it would be nice if the *Weight* column were formatted appropriately for numbers rather than for text.

To achieve more flexibility with JTable, we'll write our own data model by implementing the TableModel interface. Fortunately, Swing makes this easy by supplying a class that does most of the work, AbstractTableModel. To create a table model, we'll just subclass AbstractTableModel and override whatever behavior we want to change.

At a minimum, all AbstractTableModel subclasses have to define the following three methods:

```
public int getRowCount()
public int getColumnCount()
```
Returns the number of rows and columns in this data model.

```
public Object getValueAt(int row, int column)
```
Returns the value for the given cell.

When the JTable needs data values, it calls the getValueAt() method in the table model. To get an idea of the total size of the table, JTable calls the getRowCount() and getColumnCount() methods in the table model.

A very simple table model looks like this:

```
public static class ShipTableModel extends AbstractTableModel {
    private Object[][] data = new Object[][] {
        { "100420", Boolean.FALSE, "Des Moines IA", "Spokane WA",
            "02/06/2000", new Float(450) },
        { "202174", Boolean.TRUE, "Basking Ridge NJ", "Princeton NJ",
            "05/20/2000", new Float(1250) },
        { "450877", Boolean.TRUE, "St. Paul MN", "Austin TX",
            "03/20/2000", new Float(1745) },
        { "101891", Boolean.FALSE, "Boston MA", "Albany NY",
            "04/04/2000", new Float(88) }
    };

    public int getRowCount( ) { return data.length; }
    public int getColumnCount( ) { return data[0].length; }
```

```
    public Object getValueAt(int row, int column) {
      return data[row][column];
    }
  }
```

We'd like to use the same column headings we used in the previous example. The table model supplies these through a method called getColumnName(). We could add column headings to our simple table model like this:

```
  private String[] headings = new String[] {
    "Number", "Hot?", "Origin", "Destination", "Ship Date", "Weight"
  };

  public String getColumnName(int column) {
    return headings[column];
  }
```

By default, AbstractTableModel makes all its cells noneditable, which is what we wanted. No changes need to be made for this.

The final modification is to have the *Hot?* column and the *Weight* column formatted specially. To do this, we give our table model some knowledge about the column types. JTable automatically generates checkbox cells for Boolean column types and specially formatted number cells for Number types. To give the table model some intelligence about its column types, we override the getColumnClass() method. The JTable calls this method to determine the data type of each column. It may then represent the data in a special way. This table model returns the class of the item in the first row of its data:

```
  public Class getColumnClass(int column) {
    return data[0][column].getClass( );
  }
```

That's really all there is to do. The following complete example illustrates how you can use your own table model to create a JTable using the techniques just described:

```
//file: ShipTable.java
import java.awt.*;
import java.awt.event.*;
import javax.swing.*;
import javax.swing.table.*;

public class ShipTable {
  public static class ShipTableModel extends AbstractTableModel {
    private String[] headings = new String[] {
      "Number", "Hot?", "Origin", "Destination", "Ship Date", "Weight"
    };
    private Object[][] data = new Object[][] {
      { "100420", Boolean.FALSE, "Des Moines IA", "Spokane WA",
          "02/06/2000", new Float(450) },
      { "202174", Boolean.TRUE, "Basking Ridge NJ", "Princeton NJ",
          "05/20/2000", new Float(1250) },
      { "450877", Boolean.TRUE, "St. Paul MN", "Austin TX",
```

```
        "03/20/2000", new Float(1745) },
      { "101891", Boolean.FALSE, "Boston MA", "Albany NY",
        "04/04/2000", new Float(88) }
  };

  public int getRowCount( ) { return data.length; }
  public int getColumnCount( ) { return data[0].length; }

  public Object getValueAt(int row, int column) {
    return data[row][column];
  }

  public String getColumnName(int column) {
    return headings[column];
  }

  public Class getColumnClass(int column) {
    return data[0][column].getClass( );
  }
}

public static void main(String[] args)
{
  // create the data model and the JTable
  TableModel model = new ShipTableModel( );
  JTable table = new JTable(model);

  table.setAutoResizeMode(JTable.AUTO_RESIZE_OFF);

  JFrame frame = new JFrame("ShipTable v1.0");
  frame.getContentPane( ).add(new JScrollPane(table));
  frame.setDefaultCloseOperation( JFrame.EXIT_ON_CLOSE );
  frame.setSize(500, 200);
  frame.setVisible(true);
}
}
```

The running application is shown in Figure 17-8.

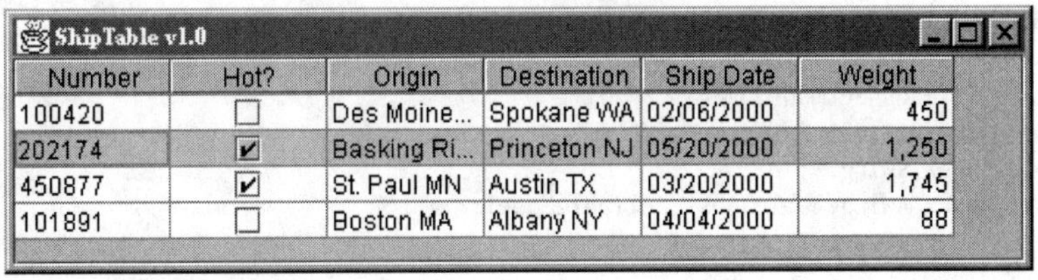

Number	Hot?	Origin	Destination	Ship Date	Weight
100420	☐	Des Moine...	Spokane WA	02/06/2000	450
202174	☑	Basking Ri...	Princeton NJ	05/20/2000	1,250
450877	☑	St. Paul MN	Austin TX	03/20/2000	1,745
101891	☐	Boston MA	Albany NY	04/04/2000	88

Figure 17-8. Customizing a table

Round Three: A Simple Spreadsheet

To illustrate just how powerful and flexible the separation of the data model from the GUI can be, we'll show a more complex model. In the following example, we'll implement a very slim but functional spreadsheet (see Figure 17-9) using almost no customization of the JTable. All of the data processing is in a TableModel called SpreadSheetModel.

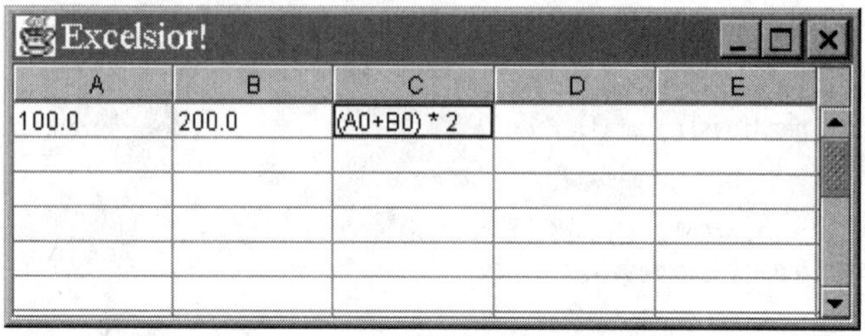

Figure 17-9. A simple spreadsheet

Our spreadsheet does the expected stuff—allowing you to enter numbers or mathematical expressions such as (A1*B2)+C3 into each cell.[*] All cell editing and updating is driven by the standard JTable. We implement the methods necessary to set and retrieve cell data. Of course we don't do any real validation here, so it's easy to break our table. (For example, there is no check for circular dependencies, which may be undesirable.)

As you will see, the bulk of the code in this example is in the inner class used to parse the value of the equations in the cells. If you don't find this part interesting you might want to skip ahead. But if you have never seen an example of this kind of parsing before, we think you will find it to be very cool. Through the magic of recursion and Java's powerful String manipulation, it takes us only about 50 lines of code to implement a parser capable of handling basic arithmetic with arbitrarily nested parentheses.

Here's the code:

```
//file: SpreadsheetModel.java
import java.util.StringTokenizer;
import javax.swing.*;
import javax.swing.table.AbstractTableModel;
import java.awt.event.*;

public class SpreadsheetModel extends AbstractTableModel {
    Expression [][] data;
```

---

[*] You may need to double-click on a cell to edit it.

```
public SpreadsheetModel( int rows, int cols ) {
  data = new Expression [rows][cols];
}

public void setValueAt(Object value, int row, int col) {
  data[row][col] = new Expression( (String)value );
  fireTableDataChanged(  );
}

public Object getValueAt( int row, int col ) {
  if ( data[row][col] != null )
    try { return data[row][col].eval(  ) + ""; }
    catch ( BadExpression e ) { return "Error"; }
  return "";
}
public int getRowCount(  ) { return data.length; }
public int getColumnCount(  ) { return data[0].length; }
public boolean isCellEditable(int row, int col) { return true; }

class Expression {
  String text;
  StringTokenizer tokens;
  String token;

  Expression( String text ) { this.text = text.trim(  ); }

  float eval(  ) throws BadExpression {
    tokens = new StringTokenizer( text, " */+-( )", true );
    try { return sum(  ); }
    catch ( Exception e ) { throw new BadExpression(  ); }
  }

  private float sum(  ) {
    float value = term(  );
    while( more(  ) && match("+-") )
      if ( match("+") ) { consume(); value = value + term(  ); }
      else { consume(); value = value - term(  ); }
    return value;
  }
  private float term(  ) {
    float value = element(  );
    while( more(  ) && match( "*/") )
      if ( match("*") ) { consume(); value = value * element(  ); }
      else { consume(); value = value / element(  ); }
    return value;
  }
  private float element(  ) {
    float value;
    if ( match( "(") ) { consume(); value = sum(  ); }
    else {
      String svalue;
      if ( Character.isLetter( token(  ).charAt(0) ) ) {
      int col = findColumn( token(  ).charAt(0) + "" );
      int row = Character.digit( token(  ).charAt(1), 10 );
```

```
              svalue = (String)getValueAt( row, col );
            } else
              svalue = token(  );
            value = Float.parseFloat( svalue );
          }
          consume(  ); // ")" or value token
          return value;
        }
        private String token(  ) {
          if ( token == null )
            while ( (token=tokens.nextToken(  )).equals(" ") );
          return token;
        }
        private void consume(  ) { token = null; }
        private boolean match( String s ) { return s.indexOf( token(  ) )!=-1; }
        private boolean more() { return tokens.hasMoreTokens(  ); }
      }

      class BadExpression extends Exception { }

      public static void main( String [] args ) {
        JFrame frame = new JFrame("Excelsior!");
        JTable table = new JTable( new SpreadsheetModel(15, 5) );
        table.setPreferredScrollableViewportSize( table.getPreferredSize() );
        table.setCellSelectionEnabled(true);
        frame.getContentPane( ).add( new JScrollPane( table ) );
        frame.setDefaultCloseOperation( JFrame.EXIT_ON_CLOSE );
        frame.pack( );
        frame.show( );
      }
    }
```

Our model extends AbstractTableModel and overrides just a few methods. As you can see, our data is stored in a 2D array of Expression objects. The setValueAt() method of our model creates Expression objects from the strings typed by the user and stores them in the array. The getValueAt() method returns a value for a cell by calling the expression's eval() method. If the user enters some invalid text in a cell, a BadExpression exception is thrown, and the word "error" is placed in the cell as a value. The only other methods of TableModel we must override are getRowCount(), getColumnCount(), and isCellEditable() to determine the dimensions of the spreadsheet and to allow the user to edit the fields. That's it! The helper method findColumn() is inherited from the AbstractTableModel.

Now on to the good stuff. We'll employ our old friend StringTokenizer to read the expression string as separate values and the mathematical symbols (+-*/()) one by one. These tokens are then processed by the three parser methods: sum(), term(), and element(). The methods call one another generally from the top down, but it might be easier to read them in reverse to see what's happening.

At the bottom level, element() reads individual numeric values or cell names, e.g., 5.0 or B2. Above that, the term() method operates on the values supplied by element() and applies any multiplication or division operations. And at the top, sum() operates on the values that are returned by term() and applies addition or subtraction to them. If the element() method encounters parentheses, it makes a call to sum() to handle the nested expression. Eventually the nested sum returns (possibly after further recursion), and the parenthesized expression is reduced to a single value, which is returned by element(). The magic of recursion has untangled the nesting for us. The other small piece of magic here is in the ordering of the three parser methods. Having sum() call term() and term() call element() imposes the precedence of operators; i.e., "atomic" values are parsed first (at the bottom), then multiplication, and finally addition or subtraction.

The grammar parsing relies on four simple helper methods that make the code more manageable: token(), consume(), match(), and more(). token() calls the string tokenizer to get the next value, and match() compares it with a specified value. consume() is used to move to the next token, and more() indicates when the final token has been processed.

Desktops

At this point, you might be thinking that there's nothing more that Swing could possibly do. But it just keeps getting better. If you've ever wished that you could have windows within windows in Java, Swing now makes it possible with JDesktopPane and JInternalFrame. Figure 17-10 shows how this works.

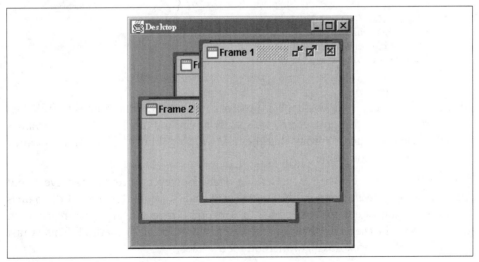

Figure 17-10. Using internal frames on a JDesktopPane

You get a lot of behavior for free from JInternalFrame. Internal frames can be moved by clicking and dragging the titlebar. They can be resized by clicking and dragging on the window's borders. Internal frames can be iconified, which means reducing them to a small icon representation on the desktop. Internal frames may also be made to fit the entire size of the desktop (maximized). To you, the programmer, the internal frame is just a kind of special container. You can put your application's data inside an internal frame.

The following brief example shows how to create the windows shown in Figure 17-10:

```
//file: Desktop.java
import java.awt.*;
import java.awt.event.*;
import javax.swing.*;
import javax.swing.border.*;

public class Desktop {
  public static void main(String[] args) {
    JFrame frame = new JFrame("Desktop");

    JDesktopPane desktop = new JDesktopPane(  );
    for (int i = 0; i < 5; i++) {
      JInternalFrame internal =
          new JInternalFrame("Frame " + i, true, true, true, true);
      internal.setSize(180, 180);
      internal.setLocation(i * 20, i * 20);
      internal.setVisible(true);
      desktop.add(internal);
    }

    frame.setSize(300, 300);
    frame.setDefaultCloseOperation( JFrame.EXIT_ON_CLOSE );
    frame.setContentPane(desktop);
    frame.setVisible(true);
  }
}
```

All we've done here is to create a JDesktopPane and add internal frames to it. When each JInternalFrame is constructed, we specify a window title. The four true values passed in the constructor specify that the new window should be resizable, closable, maximizable, and iconifiable.

JInternalFrames fire off their own set of events. However, InternalFrameEvent and InternalFrameListener are just like WindowEvent and WindowListener with the names changed. If you want to hear about a JInternalFrame closing, just register an InternalFrameListener and define the internalFrameClosing() method. This is just like defining the windowClosing() method for a JFrame.

Pluggable Look-and-Feel

We mentioned before that Swing components can easily change their appearance, like master spies or thespians. Generally, different kinds of components have appearances that are similar in some way. For example, they probably use the same font and the same basic color scheme. The collection of appearances for GUI components is called a look-and-feel (L&F).

Part of the job of designing a GUI for an operating system is designing the L&F. MacOS, therefore, has its own distinctive L&F, as does Windows. Java's standard edition offers several different L&F schemes for Swing components. If you're adept at graphic design, you can write your own L&F schemes and easily convince Swing to use them. This chameleon-like ability to change appearance is called *pluggable look-and-feel*, sometimes abbreviated PLAF (don't pronounce that out loud if others are eating).

Seeing is believing. Here's an example that creates a handful of Swing components. Menu items allow you to change the L&F dynamically, as the application is running:

```java
//file: QuickChange.java
import java.awt.*;
import java.awt.event.*;
import javax.swing.*;

public class QuickChange extends JFrame {

  public QuickChange() {
    super("QuickChange v1.0");
    createGUI();
  }

  protected void createGUI(  ) {
    setSize(300, 200);

    // create a simple File menu
    JMenu file = new JMenu("File", true);
    JMenuItem quit = new JMenuItem("Quit");
    file.add(quit);
    quit.addActionListener(new ActionListener(  ) {
      public void actionPerformed(ActionEvent e) { System.exit(0); }
    });

    // create the Look & Feel menu
    JMenu lnf = new JMenu("Look & Feel", true);
    ButtonGroup buttonGroup = new ButtonGroup(  );
    final UIManager.LookAndFeelInfo[] info =
        UIManager.getInstalledLookAndFeels(  );
    for (int i = 0; i < info.length; i++) {
      JRadioButtonMenuItem item = new
          JRadioButtonMenuItem(info[i].getName(  ), i == 0);
      final String className = info[i].getClassName(  );
```

```
        item.addActionListener(new ActionListener( ) {
          public void actionPerformed(ActionEvent ae) {
            try { UIManager.setLookAndFeel(className); }
            catch (Exception e) { System.out.println(e); }
            SwingUtilities.updateComponentTreeUI(QuickChange.this);
          }
        });
        buttonGroup.add(item);
        lnf.add(item);
      }

      // add the menu bar
      JMenuBar mb = new JMenuBar( );
      mb.add(file);
      mb.add(lnf);
      setJMenuBar(mb);

      // add some components
      JPanel jp = new JPanel( );
      jp.add(new JCheckBox("JCheckBox"));
      String[] names =
        new String[] { "Tosca", "Cavaradossi", "Scarpia",
                       "Angelotti", "Spoletta", "Sciarrone",
                       "Carceriere", "Il sagrestano", "Un pastore" };
      jp.add(new JComboBox(names));
      jp.add(new JButton("JButton"));
      jp.add(new JLabel("JLabel"));
      jp.add(new JTextField("JTextField"));
      JPanel main = new JPanel(new GridLayout(1, 2));
      main.add(jp);
      main.add(new JScrollPane(new JList(names)));
      setContentPane(main);
      setDefaultCloseOperation( JFrame.EXIT_ON_CLOSE );
    }

    public static void main(String[] args) {
      new QuickChange( ).setVisible(true);
    }
  }
```

The interesting part of this application is creating a menu of the available L&Fs.
First, we ask a class called UIManager to tell us all about the available L&Fs on our
computer:

```
final UIManager.LookAndFeelInfo[] info =
      UIManager.getInstalledLookAndFeels( );
```

Information about L&Fs is returned as instances of UIManager.LookAndFeelInfo.
Despite the long name, there's not much to this class; it just associates a name, such
as Metal, and the name of the class that implements the L&F, such as javax.swing.
plaf.metal.MetalLookAndFeel. In the QuickChange example, we create a menu item
from each L&F name. If the menu item is selected, we tell the UIManager to use the
selected L&F class. Then, to make sure all the components are redrawn with the new

L&F, we call a static method in the SwingUtilities class called
updateComponentTreeUI().

The regular SDK includes several L&Fs: one that resembles Windows, one that
resembles Motif, and a L&F called Metal. Metal is used by default on most platforms; you've been staring at it through all the examples in this chapter and the last
chapter.

If you're running Swing on MacOS, there's a MacOS L&F you can install and use. It
does not, however, run on any other platforms because of licensing issues (the Windows L&F has similar restrictions).

Creating Custom Components

In this chapter and the previous, we've worked with different user interface objects.
We've used Swing's impressive repertoire of components as building blocks and
extended their functionality, but we haven't actually created any new components.
In this section, we create an entirely new component from scratch, a *dial*.

Up until now, our examples have been fairly self-contained; they generally know
everything about what to do and don't rely on additional parts to do processing. Our
menu example created a DinnerFrame class that had a menu of dinner options, but it
included all the processing needed to handle the user's selections. If we wanted to
process the selections differently, we'd have to modify the class. A true component
separates the detection of user input from the handling of those choices. It lets the
user take some action and then informs other interested parties by emitting events.

Generating Events

Since we want our new classes to be components, they should communicate the way
components communicate: by generating event objects and sending those events to
listeners. So far, we've written a lot of code that listened for events but haven't seen
an example that generated its own custom events.

Generating events sounds like it might be difficult, but it isn't. You can either create
new kinds of events by subclassing java.util.EventObject, or use one of the standard event types. In either case, you just need to allow registration of listeners for
your events and provide a means to deliver events to those listeners. Swing's
JComponent class provides a protected member variable, listenerList, you can use to
keep track of event listeners. It's an instance of EventListenerList; basically it acts
like the maître d' at a restaurant, keeping track of all event listeners, sorted by type.

Often, you won't need to worry about creating a custom event type. JComponent has
methods that support firing of generic PropertyChangeEvents whenever one of a component's properties changes. The example we'll look at next uses this infrastructure
to fire PropertyChangeEvents whenever a value changes.

A Dial Component

The standard Swing classes don't have a component that's similar to an old fashioned dial—for example, the volume control on your radio. (The JSlider fills this role, of course.) In this section, we implement a Dial class. The dial has a value that can be adjusted by clicking and dragging to "twist" the dial (see Figure 17-11). As the value of the dial changes, DialEvents are fired off by the component. The dial can be used just like any other Java component. We even have a custom DialListener interface that matches the DialEvent class.

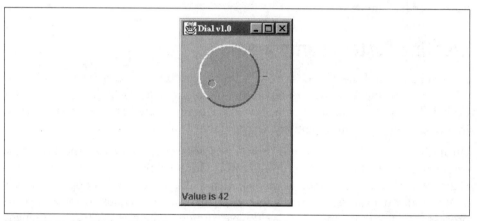

Figure 17-11. The Dial component

Here's the Dial code:

```
//file: Dial.java
import java.awt.*;
import java.awt.event.*;
import java.util.*;
import javax.swing.*;

public class Dial extends JComponent {
  int minValue, nvalue, maxValue, radius;

  public Dial( ) { this(0, 100, 0); }

  public Dial(int minValue, int maxValue, int value) {
    setMinimum( minValue );
    setMaximum( maxValue );
    setValue( value );
    setForeground( Color.lightGray );

    addMouseListener(new MouseAdapter( ) {
      public void mousePressed(MouseEvent e) { spin(e); }
    });
    addMouseMotionListener(new MouseMotionAdapter( ) {
```

```
      public void mouseDragged(MouseEvent e) { spin(e); }
  });
}

protected void spin( MouseEvent e ) {
  int y = e.getY( );
  int x = e.getX( );
  double th = Math.atan((1.0 * y - radius) / (x - radius));
  int value=(int)(th / (2 * Math.PI) * (maxValue - minValue));
  if (x < radius)
    setValue( value + (maxValue-minValue) / 2 + minValue);
  else if (y < radius)
    setValue( value + maxValue );
  else
    setValue( value + minValue);
}

public void paintComponent(Graphics g) {
  Graphics2D g2 = (Graphics2D)g;
  int tick = 10;
  radius = Math.min( getSize().width,getSize( ).height )/2 - tick;
  g2.setPaint( getForeground().darker( ) );
  g2.drawLine( radius * 2 + tick / 2, radius,
      radius * 2 + tick, radius);
  g2.setStroke( new BasicStroke(2) );
  draw3DCircle( g2, 0, 0, radius, true );
  int knobRadius = radius / 7;
  double th = nvalue * (2 * Math.PI) / (maxValue - minValue);
  int x = (int)(Math.cos(th) * (radius - knobRadius * 3)),
  y = (int)(Math.sin(th) * (radius - knobRadius * 3));
  g2.setStroke(new BasicStroke(1));
  draw3DCircle(g2, x + radius - knobRadius,
      y + radius - knobRadius, knobRadius, false );
}

private void draw3DCircle(
    Graphics g, int x, int y, int radius, boolean raised)
{
  Color foreground = getForeground( );
  Color light = foreground.brighter( );
  Color dark = foreground.darker( );
  g.setColor(foreground);
  g.fillOval(x, y, radius * 2, radius * 2);
  g.setColor(raised ? light : dark);
  g.drawArc(x, y, radius * 2, radius * 2, 45, 180);
  g.setColor(raised ? dark : light);
  g.drawArc(x, y, radius * 2, radius * 2, 225, 180);
}

public Dimension getPreferredSize( ) {
  return new Dimension(100, 100);
}
```

```java
  public void setValue( int value ) {
    this.nvalue = value - minValue;
    repaint( );
    fireEvent( );
  }
  public int getValue( )  { return nvalue+minValue; }
  public void setMinimum(int minValue)  { this.minValue = minValue; }
  public int getMinimum( )  { return minValue; }
  public void setMaximum(int maxValue)  { this.maxValue = maxValue; }
  public int getMaximum( )  { return maxValue; }

  public void addDialListener(DialListener listener) {
    listenerList.add( DialListener.class, listener );
  }
  public void removeDialListener(DialListener listener) {
    listenerList.remove( DialListener.class, listener );
  }

  void fireEvent( ) {
    Object[] listeners = listenerList.getListenerList( );
    for ( int i = 0; i < listeners.length; i += 2 )
      if ( listeners[i] == DialListener.class )
        ((DialListener)listeners[i + 1]).dialAdjusted(
          new DialEvent(this, getValue( )) );
  }

  public static void main(String[] args) {
    JFrame frame = new JFrame("Dial v1.0");
    final JLabel statusLabel = new JLabel("Welcome to Dial v1.0");
    final Dial dial = new Dial( );
    frame.getContentPane( ).add(dial, BorderLayout.CENTER);
    frame.getContentPane( ).add(statusLabel, BorderLayout.SOUTH);

    dial.addDialListener(new DialListener( ) {
      public void dialAdjusted(DialEvent e) {
        statusLabel.setText("Value is " + e.getValue( ));
      }
    });

    frame.setDefaultCloseOperation( JFrame.EXIT_ON_CLOSE );
    frame.setSize( 150, 150 );
    frame.setVisible( true );
  }
}
```

Here's DialEvent, a simple subclass of java.util.EventObject:

```java
//file: DialEvent.java
import java.awt.*;

public class DialEvent extends java.util.EventObject {
    int value;
```

```
    DialEvent( Dial source, int value ) {
        super( source );
        this.value = value;
    }

    public int getValue( ) {
        return value;
    }
}
```

Finally, here's the code for DialListener:

```
//file: DialListener.java
public interface DialListener extends java.util.EventListener {
    void dialAdjusted( DialEvent e );
}
```

Let's start from the top of the Dial class. We'll focus on the structure and leave you to figure out the trigonometry on your own.

Dial's main() method demonstrates how to use the dial to build a user interface. It creates a Dial and adds it to a JFrame. Then main() registers a dial listener on the dial. Whenever a DialEvent is received, the value of the dial is examined and displayed in a JLabel at the bottom of the frame window.

The constructor for the Dial class stores the dial's minimum, maximum, and current values; a default constructor provides a minimum of 0, a maximum of 100, and a current value of 0. The constructor sets the foreground color of the dial and registers listeners for mouse events. If the mouse is pressed or dragged, Dial's spin() method is called to update the dial's value. spin() performs some basic trigonometry to figure out what the new value of the dial should be.

paintComponent() and draw3DCircle() do a lot of trigonometry to figure out how to display the dial. draw3DCircle() is a private helper method that draws a circle that appears either raised or depressed; we use this to make the dial look three-dimensional.

The next group of methods provides ways to retrieve or change the dial's current setting and the minimum and maximum values. The important thing to notice here is the pattern of get and set methods for all of the important values used by the Dial. We will talk more about this in Chapter 21. Also, notice that the setValue() method does two important things: it repaints the component to reflect the new value and fires the DialEvent signifying the change.

The final group of methods in the Dial class provides the plumbing necessary for our event firing. addDialListener() and removeDialListener() take care of maintaining the listener list. Using the listenerList member variable we inherited from JComponent makes this an easy task. The fireEvent() method retrieves the registered listeners for this component. It sends a DialEvent to any registered DialListeners.

Model and View Separation

The Dial example is overly simplified. All Swing components, as we've discussed, keep their data model and view separate. In the Dial component, we've combined these elements in a single class, which limits its reusability. To have Dial implement the MVC paradigm, we would have developed a dial data model and something called a UI-delegate that handled displaying the component and responding to user events. For a full treatment of this subject, see the JogShuttle example in O'Reilly's *Java Swing*.

In Chapter 18, we'll take what we know about components and containers and put them together using layout managers to create complex GUIs.

CHAPTER 18

Layout Managers

A *layout manager* arranges the child components of a container, as shown in Figure 18-1. It positions and sets the size of components within the container's display area according to a particular layout scheme. The layout manager's job is to fit the components into the available area while maintaining some spatial relationships among them. AWT and Swing come with several standard layout managers that will collectively handle most situations; you can make your own layout managers if you have special requirements.

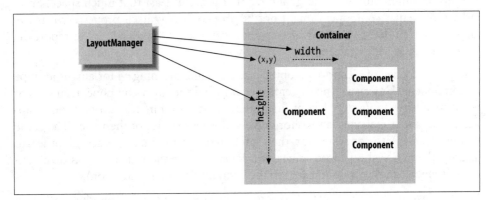

Figure 18-1. A layout manager at work

Every container has a default layout manager; therefore, when you make a new container, it comes with a LayoutManager object of the appropriate type. You can install a new layout manager at any time with the setLayout() method. For example, we can set the layout manager of a Swing container's content pane to a BorderLayout like so:

```
mycontainer.getContentPane().setLayout (new BorderLayout( ));
```

Notice that we have called the BorderLayout constructor, but we haven't bothered to save a reference to the layout manager. This is typical; once you have installed a layout manager, it does its work behind the scenes, interacting with the container. You rarely call the layout manager's methods directly, so you don't usually need a reference (a notable exception is `CardLayout`). However, you do need to know what the layout manager is going to do with your components as you work with them.

The `LayoutManager` is consulted whenever a container's `doLayout()`method is called to reorganize the contents. It does its job by calling the `setLocation()` or `setBounds()` methods of the individual child components to arrange them in the container's display area. A container is laid out the first time it is displayed and thereafter whenever the container's `revalidate()` method is called. Containers that are a subclass of the `Window` class (`Frame`, `JFrame`, and `JWindow`) are automatically validated whenever they are packed or resized. Calling `pack()` sets the window's size as small as possible while granting all its components their preferred sizes.

Every component determines three important pieces of information used by the layout manager in placing and sizing it: a minimum size, a maximum size, and a preferred size. These sizes are reported by the `getMinimumSize()`, `getMaximum-Size()`, and `getPreferredSize()` methods of `Component`, respectively. For example, a plain `JButton` object can normally be changed to any size. However, the button's designer can provide a preferred size for a good-looking button. The layout manager might use this size when there are no other constraints, or it might ignore it, depending on its scheme. Now if we give the button a label, the button may need a new minimum size in order to display itself properly. The layout manager might show more respect for the button's minimum size and guarantee that it has at least that much space. Similarly, a particular component might not be able to display itself properly if it is too large (perhaps it has to scale up an image); it can use `getMaximumSize()` to report the largest size it considers acceptable.

The preferred size of a `Container` object has the same meaning as for any other type of component. However, since a `Container` may hold its own components and want to arrange them in its own layout, its preferred size is a function of its layout manager. The layout manager is therefore involved in both sides of the issue. It asks the components in its container for their preferred (or minimum) sizes in order to arrange them. Based on those values, it calculates the preferred size of its own container (which can be communicated to the container's parent and so on).

When a layout manager is called to arrange its components, it is working within a fixed area. It usually begins by looking at its container's dimensions and the preferred or minimum sizes of the child components. It then doles out screen area and sets the sizes of components according to its scheme and specific constraints. You can override the `getMinimumSize()`, `getMaximumSize()`, and `getPreferredSize()` methods of a component, but you should do this only if you are actually specializing the component, and it has new needs. If you find yourself fighting with a layout manager because it's changing the size of one of your components, you are probably using the wrong kind of layout manager or not composing your user interface properly. Often it's easier to use a number of `JPanel` objects in a given display, each one with its own `LayoutManager`. Try breaking down the problem: place related components in their own JPanel and then arrange the panels in the container. When that becomes unwieldy, you can choose to use a constraint-based layout manager such as GridBagLayout, which we'll discuss later in this chapter.

FlowLayout

FlowLayout is a simple layout manager that tries to arrange components at their preferred sizes, from left to right and top to bottom in the container. A FlowLayout can have a specified row justification of LEFT, CENTER, or RIGHT and a fixed horizontal and vertical padding. By default, a flow layout uses CENTER justification, meaning that all components are centered within the area allotted to them. FlowLayout is the default for JPanels.

The following example adds five buttons to the content pane of a JFrame using the default FlowLayout:

```java
//file: Flow.java
import java.awt.*;
import java.awt.event.*;
import javax.swing.*;

public class Flow extends JPanel {

    public Flow( ) {
        // FlowLayout is default layout manager for a JPanel
        add(new JButton("One"));
        add(new JButton("Two"));
        add(new JButton("Three"));
        add(new JButton("Four"));
        add(new JButton("Five"));
    }

    public static void main(String[] args) {
        JFrame frame = new JFrame("Flow");
        frame.setDefaultCloseOperation( JFrame.EXIT_ON_CLOSE );

        frame.setSize(400, 75);
        frame.setLocation(200, 200);
        Flow flow = new Flow( );
        frame.setContentPane(flow);
        frame.setVisible(true);
    }
}
```

The result is shown in Figure 18-2.

Try resizing the window. If it is made narrow enough, some of the buttons will spill over to a second or third row.

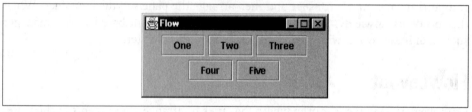

Figure 18-2. A flow layout

GridLayout

GridLayout arranges components into regularly spaced rows and columns. The components are arbitrarily resized to fit the grid; their minimum and preferred sizes are consequently ignored. GridLayout is most useful for arranging identically sized objects—perhaps a set of JPanels, each using a different layout manager.

GridLayout takes the number of rows and columns in its constructor. If you subsequently give it too many objects to manage, it adds extra columns to make the objects fit. You can also set the number of rows or columns to zero, which means that you don't care how many elements the layout manager packs in that dimension. For example, GridLayout(2,0) requests a layout with two rows and an unlimited number of columns; if you put ten components into this layout, you'll get two rows of five columns each.*

The following example sets a GridLayout with three rows and two columns as its layout manager:

```
//file: Grid.java
import java.awt.*;
import java.awt.event.*;
import javax.swing.*;

public class Grid extends JPanel {

  public Grid( ) {
    setLayout(new GridLayout(3, 2));
    add(new JButton("One"));
    add(new JButton("Two"));
    add(new JButton("Three"));
    add(new JButton("Four"));
    add(new JButton("Five"));
  }

  public static void main(String[] args) {
    JFrame frame = new JFrame("Grid");
```

---

* Calling new GridLayout(0, 0) causes a runtime exception; either the rows or columns parameter must be greater than zero.

```
        frame.setDefaultCloseOperation( JFrame.EXIT_ON_CLOSE );
        frame.setSize(200, 200);
        frame.setLocation(200, 200);
        frame.setContentPane(new Grid( ));
        frame.setVisible(true);
    }
}
```

The results are shown in Figure 18-3.

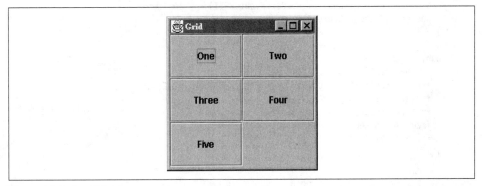

Figure 18-3. A grid layout

The five buttons are laid out, in order, from left to right, top to bottom, with one empty spot.

BorderLayout

BorderLayout is a little more interesting. It tries to arrange objects in one of five geo-graphical locations, represented by constants in the BorderLayout class: NORTH, SOUTH, EAST, WEST, and CENTER, possibly with some padding between. BorderLayout is the default layout for the content panes of JWindow and JFrame objects. Because each component is associated with a direction, BorderLayout can manage at most five components; it squashes or stretches those components to fit its constraints. As we'll see in the second example, this means that you often want to have BorderLayout manage sets of components in their own panels.

When we add a component to a border layout, we need to specify both the compo-nent and the position at which to add it. To do so, we use an overloaded version of the add() method that takes an additional argument as a constraint. This specifies the name of a position within the BorderLayout.

The following application sets a BorderLayout and adds our five buttons again, named for their locations:

```
//file: Border1.java
import java.awt.*;
import java.awt.event.*;
```

```
import javax.swing.*;

public class Border1 extends JPanel {

  public Border1( ) {
    setLayout(new BorderLayout( ));
    add(new JButton("North"), BorderLayout.NORTH);
    add(new JButton("South"), BorderLayout.SOUTH);
    add(new JButton("East"), BorderLayout.EAST);
    add(new JButton("West"), BorderLayout.WEST);
    add(new JButton("Center"), BorderLayout.CENTER);
  }

  public static void main(String[] args) {
    JFrame frame = new JFrame("Border1");
    frame.setDefaultCloseOperation( JFrame.EXIT_ON_CLOSE );
    frame.setSize(300, 300);
    frame.setLocation(200, 200);
    frame.setContentPane(new Border1( ));
    frame.setVisible(true);
  }
}
```

The result is shown in Figure 18-4.

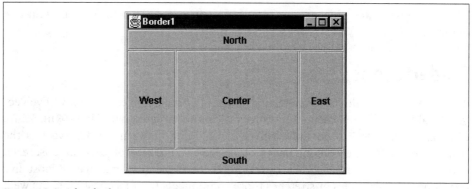

Figure 18-4. A border layout

So, how exactly is the area divided up? Well, the objects at NORTH and SOUTH get their
preferred height and fill the display area horizontally. EAST and WEST components, on
the other hand, get their preferred width, and fill the remaining area between NORTH
and SOUTH vertically. Finally, the CENTER object takes all the rest of the space. As you
can see in Figure 18-4, our buttons get distorted into interesting shapes.

What if we don't want BorderLayout messing with the sizes of our components? One
option would be to put each button in its own JPanel. The default layout for a JPanel
is FlowLayout, which respects the preferred size of components. The preferred sizes of
the panels are effectively the preferred sizes of the buttons, but if the panels are

stretched, they won't pull their buttons with them. The following application illustrates this approach:

```java
//file: Border2.java
import java.awt.*;
import java.awt.event.*;
import javax.swing.*;

public class Border2 extends JPanel {

  public Border2( ) {
    setLayout(new BorderLayout( ));
    JPanel p = new JPanel( );
    p.add(new JButton("North"));
    add(p, BorderLayout.NORTH);
    p = new JPanel( );
    p.add(new JButton("South"));
    add(p, BorderLayout.SOUTH);
    p = new JPanel( );
    p.add(new JButton("East"));
    add(p, BorderLayout.EAST);
    p = new JPanel( );
    p.add(new JButton("West"));
    add(p, BorderLayout.WEST);
    p = new JPanel( );
    p.add(new JButton("Center"));
    add(p, BorderLayout.CENTER);
  }

  public static void main(String[] args) {
    JFrame frame = new JFrame("Border2");
    frame.setDefaultCloseOperation( JFrame.EXIT_ON_CLOSE );
    frame.setSize(225, 150);
    frame.setLocation(200, 200);
    frame.setContentPane(new Border2( ));
    frame.setVisible(true);
  }
}
```

The result is shown in Figure 18-5.

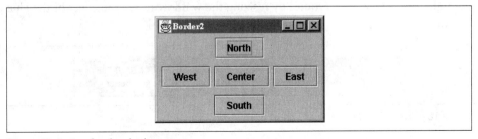

Figure 18-5. Another border layout

In the example, we create a number of panels, put our buttons inside the panels, and put the panels into the frame window, which has the BorderLayout manager. Now, the JPanel for the CENTER button soaks up the extra space that comes from the BorderLayout. Each JPanel's FlowLayout centers the button in the panel and uses the button's preferred size. In this case, it's all a bit awkward. We'll see how we could accomplish this more directly using GridBagLayout shortly.

BoxLayout

Most layout managers were defined back when Java 1.0 was first released. Swing adds a couple of new general-purpose layout managers in the javax.swing package; one is BoxLayout. This layout manager is useful for creating toolbars or vertical button bars. It lays out components in a single row or column. It is similar to FlowLayout but does not wrap components into new rows.

Although you can use BoxLayout directly, Swing includes a handy container called Box that takes care of the details for you. Every Box uses BoxLayout, but you don't really have to worry about it; the Box class includes some very useful methods for laying out components.

You can create a horizontal or vertical box using Box's static methods.

```
Container horizontalBox = Box.createHorizontalBox( );
Container verticalBox = Box.createVerticalBox( );
```

Once the Box is created, you can just add() components as usual:

```
Container box = Box.createHorizontalBox( );
box.add(new JButton("In the"));
```

Box includes several other static methods that create special invisible components that are handy for BoxLayout. The first of these is *glue*; glue is really space between components in the Box. When the Box is resized, glue expands or contracts as more or less space is available. The other special invisible component type is a *strut*. Like glue, a strut represents space between components, but it doesn't resize.

The following example creates a horizontal Box (shown in Figure 18-6) that includes both glue and struts. Play around by resizing the window to see the effect of the glue and the struts.

Figure 18-6. Using the Box class

```
//file: Boxer.java
import java.awt.*;
import java.awt.event.*;
```

```java
import javax.swing.*;

public class Boxer extends JPanel {
    public static void main(String[] args) {
        JFrame frame = new JFrame("Boxer");
        frame.setDefaultCloseOperation( JFrame.EXIT_ON_CLOSE );
        frame.setSize(250, 250);
        frame.setLocation(200, 200);
        Container box = Box.createHorizontalBox( );
        box.add(Box.createHorizontalGlue( ));
        box.add(new JButton("In the"));
        box.add(Box.createHorizontalGlue( ));
        box.add(new JButton("clearing"));
        box.add(Box.createHorizontalStrut(10));
        box.add(new JButton("stands"));
        box.add(Box.createHorizontalStrut(10));
        box.add(new JButton("a"));
        box.add(Box.createHorizontalGlue( ));
        box.add(new JButton("boxer"));
        box.add(Box.createHorizontalGlue( ));
        frame.getContentPane( ).add(box, BorderLayout.CENTER);
        frame.pack( );
        frame.setVisible(true);
    }
}
```

Components are added sequentially for display from left to right or top to bottom with optional "glue" or "strut" constraints placed between them. By default, components simply line up one after another with no space between them. "Glue" acts like a spring, allowing its adjacent components to move to occupy the space evenly. A "strut" imposes a fixed space between adjacent components.

CardLayout

CardLayout is a special layout manager for creating the effect of a stack of cards. Instead of arranging all of the container's components, it displays only one at a time. You might use this kind of layout to implement something like a hypercard stack or a Windows-style set of configuration screens. If CardLayout sounds interesting, you might also want to investigate the JTabbedPane component, described in Chapter 16.

To add a component to a CardLayout, use a two-argument version of the container's add() method; the extra argument is an arbitrary string that serves as the card's name:

```java
add("netconfigscreen", myComponent);
```

To bring a particular card to the top of the stack, call the CardLayout's show() method with two arguments: the parent Container and the name of the card you want to show. There are also methods—first(), last(), next(), and previous() for working with the stack of cards. These are all CardLayout instance methods. To invoke them, you need a reference to the CardLayout object itself, not to the container it manages. Each method takes a single argument: the parent Container. Here's an example:

```java
//file: Card.java
import java.awt.*;
import java.awt.event.*;
import javax.swing.*;

public class Card extends JPanel {
  CardLayout cards = new CardLayout( );

  public Card( ) {
    setLayout(cards);
    ActionListener listener = new ActionListener( ) {
      public void actionPerformed(ActionEvent e) {
        cards.next(Card.this);
      }
    };
    JButton button;
    button = new JButton("one");
    button.addActionListener(listener);
    add(button, "one");
    button = new JButton("two");
    button.addActionListener(listener);
    add(button, "two");
    button = new JButton("three");
    button.addActionListener(listener);
    add(button, "three");
  }

  public static void main(String[] args) {
    JFrame frame = new JFrame("Card");
    frame.setDefaultCloseOperation( JFrame.EXIT_ON_CLOSE );
    frame.setSize(200, 200);
    frame.setLocation(200, 200);
    frame.setContentPane(new Card( ));
    frame.setVisible(true);
  }
}
```

We add three buttons to the layout and cycle through them as they are pressed. An anonymous inner class serves as an action listener for each button; it simply calls CardLayout's next( ) method whenever a button is pressed. The reference to Card. this refers to the Card object, which is the container in this case. In a more realistic example, we would build a group of panels, each of which might implement some part of a complex user interface and add those panels to the layout. Each panel would have its own layout manager. The panels would be resized to fill the entire area available (i.e., the area of the Container they are in), and their individual layout managers would arrange their internal components.

GridBagLayout

GridBagLayout is a very flexible layout manager that allows you to position components relative to one another using constraints. With GridBagLayout (and a fair amount of effort), you can create almost any imaginable layout. Components are arranged at logical coordinates on an abstract grid. We'll call them "logical" coordinates because they really designate positions in the space of rows and columns formed by the set of components. Rows and columns of the grid stretch to different sizes, based on the sizes and constraints of the components they hold.

A row or column in a GridBagLayout expands to accommodate the dimensions and constraints of the largest component it contains. Individual components may span more than one row or column. Components that aren't as large as their grid cell can be anchored (positioned to one side) within their cell. They can also be set to fill or to expand their size in either dimension. Extra area in the grid rows and columns can be parceled out according to the weight constraints of the components. In this way, you can control how various components will grow and stretch when a window is resized.

GridBagLayout is much easier to use in a graphical WYSIWYG GUI builder environment. That's because working with GridBag is kind of like messing with the "rabbit ears" antennae on your television. It's not particularly difficult to get the results that you want through trial and error, but writing out hard and fast rules for how to go about it is difficult. In short, GridBagLayout is complex and has some quirks. It is also simply a bit ugly both in model and implementation. Remember that you can do a lot with nested panels and by composing simpler layout managers within one another. If you look back through this chapter, you'll see some examples of composite layouts; it's up to you to determine how far you should go before making the break from simpler layout managers to a more complex all-in-one layout manager like GridBagLayout.

The GridBagConstraints Class

Having said that GridBagLayout is complex and a bit ugly, we're going to contradict ourselves a little and say that its API is surprisingly simple. There is only one constructor with no arguments (GridBagLayout()), and there aren't a lot of fancy methods to control how the display works.

The appearance of a grid bag layout is controlled by sets of GridBagConstraints, and that's where things get hairy. Each component managed by a GridBagLayout is associated with a GridBagConstraints object. GridBagConstraints holds the following variables, which we'll describe in detail shortly:

int gridx, gridy
   Controls the position of the component on the layout's grid.

int weightx, weighty
Controls how additional space in the row or column is allotted to the component.

int fill
Controls whether the component expands to fill the allotted space.

int gridheight, gridwidth
Controls the number of rows or columns the component spans.

int anchor
Controls the position of the component if there is extra room within the allotted space.

int ipadx, ipady
Controls padding between the component and the borders of its area.

Insets insets
Controls padding between the component and neighboring components.

To make a set of constraints for a component or components, create a new instance of GridBagConstraints and set these public variables to the appropriate values. (There is also a large constructor that takes all 11 arguments.)

The easiest way to associate a set of constraints with a component is to use the version of add() that takes both a component object and a layout object as arguments. This puts the component in the container and associates the GridBagConstraints object with it:

```
Container content = getContentPane( );
JComponent component = new JLabel("constrain me, please...");
GridBagConstraints constraints = new GridBagConstraints( );
constraints.gridx = x;
constraints.gridy = y;
...
content.add(component, constraints);
```

You can also add a component to a GridBagLayout using the single argument add( ) method and then calling the layout's setConstraints() method directly to pass it the GridBagConstraints object for that component:

```
add(component);
...
myGridBagLayout.setConstraints(component, constraints);
```

In either case, the set of constraints is copied when it is applied to the component. It's the individual constraints that apply to the component, not the GridBagConstraints object. Therefore, you're free to create a single set of GridBagConstraints, modify it as needed, and apply it as needed to different objects. You might want to create a helper method that sets the constraints appropriately, then adds the component, with its constraints, to the layout. That's the approach we'll take in our examples; our helper method is called addGB(), and it takes a component plus a pair of coordinates as arguments. These coordinates become the gridx and gridy values for the constraints. We could expand upon this later and overload addGB( ) to take more parameters for other constraints that we often change from component to component.

Grid Coordinates

One of the biggest surprises in the GridBagLayout is that there's no way to specify the size of the grid. There doesn't have to be. The grid size is determined implicitly by the constraints of all the objects; the layout manager picks dimensions large enough so that everything fits. Thus, if you put one component in a layout and set its gridx and gridy constraints to 25, the layout manager creates a 25 × 25 grid, with rows and columns both numbered from 0 to 24. If you then add a second component with a gridx of 30 and a gridy of 13, the grid's dimensions change to 30 × 25. You don't have to worry about setting up an appropriate number of rows and columns. The layout manager does it automatically as you add components.

With this knowledge, we're ready to create some simple displays. We'll start by arranging a group of components in a cross shape. We maintain explicit x and y local variables, setting them as we add the components to our grid. This is partly for clarity, but it can be a handy technique when you want to add a number of components in a row or column. You can simply increment gridx or gridy before adding each component. This is a simple and problem-free way to achieve relative placement. (Later, we'll describe GridBagConstraints's RELATIVE constant, which does relative placement automatically.) The following code shows the first layout (see Figure 18-7).

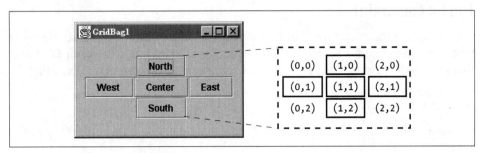

Figure 18-7. A simple GridBagLayout

```
//file: GridBag1.java
import java.awt.*;
import java.awt.event.*;
import javax.swing.*;

public class GridBag1 extends JPanel {
  GridBagConstraints constraints = new GridBagConstraints( );
```

```
    public GridBag1( ) {
      setLayout(new GridBagLayout( ));
      int x, y;  // for clarity
      addGB(new JButton("North"),   x = 1, y = 0);
      addGB(new JButton("West"),    x = 0, y = 1);
      addGB(new JButton("Center"),  x = 1, y = 1);
      addGB(new JButton("East"),    x = 2, y = 1);
      addGB(new JButton("South"),   x = 1, y = 2);
    }

    void addGB(Component component, int x, int y) {
      constraints.gridx = x;
      constraints.gridy = y;
      add(component, constraints);
    }

    public static void main(String[] args) {
      JFrame frame = new JFrame("GridBag1");
      frame.setDefaultCloseOperation( JFrame.EXIT_ON_CLOSE );
      frame.setSize(225, 150);
      frame.setLocation(200, 200);
      frame.setContentPane(new GridBag1( ));
      frame.setVisible(true);
    }
  }
```

The buttons in this example are "clumped" together in the center of their display area. Each button is displayed at its preferred size, without stretching to fill the available space. This is how the layout manager behaves when the "weight" constraints are left unset. We'll talk more about weights in the next two sections.

The fill Constraint

Let's make the buttons expand to fill the entire JFrame window. To do so, we must take two steps: we must set the fill constraint for each button to the value BOTH, and we must set the weightx and weighty to nonzero values, as shown in this example:

```
//file: GridBag2.java
import java.awt.*;
import java.awt.event.*;
import javax.swing.*;

public class GridBag2 extends JPanel {
  GridBagConstraints constraints = new GridBagConstraints( );

  public GridBag2( ) {
    setLayout(new GridBagLayout( ));
    constraints.weightx = 1.0;
    constraints.weighty = 1.0;
    constraints.fill = GridBagConstraints.BOTH;
    int x, y;  // for clarity
    addGB(new JButton("North"),   x = 1, y = 0);
```

```
    addGB(new JButton("West"),   x = 0, y = 1);
    addGB(new JButton("Center"), x = 1, y = 1);
    addGB(new JButton("East"),   x = 2, y = 1);
    addGB(new JButton("South"),  x = 1, y = 2);
  }

  void addGB(Component component, int x, int y) {
    constraints.gridx = x;
    constraints.gridy = y;
    add(component, constraints);
  }

  public static void main(String[] args) {
    JFrame frame = new JFrame("GridBag2");
    frame.setDefaultCloseOperation( JFrame.EXIT_ON_CLOSE );
    frame.setSize(225, 150);
    frame.setLocation(200, 200);
    frame.setContentPane(new GridBag2( ));
    frame.setVisible(true);
  }
}
```

Figure 18-8 shows the resulting layout.

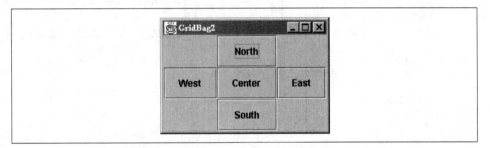

Figure 18-8. Making buttons fill the available space

BOTH is one of the constants of the GridBagConstraints class; it tells the component to fill the available space in both directions. Here are the constants you can use to set the fill field:

HORIZONTAL
> Fill the available horizontal space.

VERTICAL
> Fill the available vertical space.

BOTH
> Fill the available space in both directions.

NONE
> Don't fill the available space; display the component at its preferred size.

We set the weight constraints to 1.0; in this example it doesn't matter what they are, provided each component has the same nonzero weight. Filling doesn't occur if the component weights in the direction you're filling are 0, which is the default value.

Spanning Rows and Columns

One of the most important features of GridBaglayout is that it lets you create arrangements in which components span two or more rows or columns. To do so, set the gridwidth and gridheight variables of the GridBagConstraints. The following example creates such a display; button one spans two columns vertically, and button four spans two horizontally. Figure 18-9 shows the resulting layout.

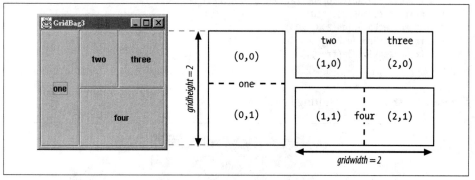

Figure 18-9. Making components span rows and columns

```
//file: GridBag3.java
import java.awt.*;
import java.awt.event.*;
import javax.swing.*;

public class GridBag3 extends JPanel {
  GridBagConstraints constraints = new GridBagConstraints( );

  public GridBag3( ) {
    setLayout(new GridBagLayout( ));
    constraints.weightx = 1.0;
    constraints.weighty = 1.0;
    constraints.fill = GridBagConstraints.BOTH;
    int x, y;  // for clarity
    constraints.gridheight = 2; // span two rows
    addGB(new JButton("one"),   x = 0, y = 0);
    constraints.gridheight = 1; // set it back
    addGB(new JButton("two"),   x = 1, y = 0);
    addGB(new JButton("three"), x = 2, y = 0);
    constraints.gridwidth = 2; // span two columns
    addGB(new JButton("four"),  x = 1, y = 1);
    constraints.gridwidth = 1; // set it back
  }
```

```
    void addGB(Component component, int x, int y) {
      constraints.gridx = x;
      constraints.gridy = y;
      add(component, constraints);
    }

    public static void main(String[] args) {
      JFrame frame = new JFrame("GridBag3");
      frame.setDefaultCloseOperation( JFrame.EXIT_ON_CLOSE );
      frame.setSize(200, 200);
      frame.setLocation(200, 200);
      frame.setContentPane(new GridBag3( ));
      frame.setVisible(true);
    }
  }
```

The size of each element is controlled by the gridwidth and gridheight values of its constraints. For button one, we set gridheight to 2; therefore, it is two cells high. Its gridx and gridy positions are both zero, so it occupies cell (0,0) and the cell directly below it, (0,1). Likewise, button four has a gridwidth of 2 and a gridheight of 1, so it occupies two cells horizontally. We place this button in cell (1,1), so it occupies that cell and its neighbor, (2,1).

In this example, we set the fill to BOTH and weightx and weighty to 1 for all components. By doing so, we tell each button to occupy all the space available. Strictly speaking, this isn't necessary. However, it makes it easier to see exactly how much space each button occupies.

Weighting

The weightx and weighty variables of a GridBagConstraints object determine how "extra" space in the container is distributed among the columns or rows in the layout. As long as you keep things simple, the effect these variables have is fairly intuitive: the larger the weight, the greater the amount of space allocated to the component. Figure 18-10 shows what happens if we vary the weightx constraint from 0.1 to 1.0 as we place three buttons in a row.

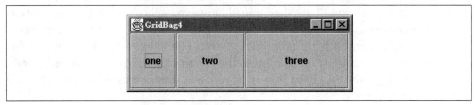

Figure 18-10. Using weight to control component size

Here's the code:

```
//file: GridBag4.java
import java.awt.*;
import java.awt.event.*;
import javax.swing.*;

public class GridBag4 extends JPanel {
  GridBagConstraints constraints = new GridBagConstraints( );

  public GridBag4( ) {
    setLayout(new GridBagLayout( ));
    constraints.fill = GridBagConstraints.BOTH;
    constraints.weighty = 1.0;
    int x, y; // for clarity
    constraints.weightx = 0.1;
    addGB(new JButton("one"),   x = 0, y = 0);
    constraints.weightx = 0.5;
    addGB(new JButton("two"),   ++x,  y);
    constraints.weightx = 1.0;
    addGB(new JButton("three"), ++x,  y);
  }

  void addGB(Component component, int x, int y) {
    constraints.gridx = x;
    constraints.gridy = y;
    add(component, constraints);
  }

  public static void main(String[] args) {
    JFrame frame = new JFrame("GridBag4");
    frame.setDefaultCloseOperation( JFrame.EXIT_ON_CLOSE );
    frame.setSize(300, 100);
    frame.setLocation(200, 200);
    frame.setContentPane(new GridBag4( ));
    frame.setVisible(true);
  }
}
```

The specific values of the weights are not meaningful; it is only their relative proportions that matter. After the preferred sizes of the components (including padding and
insets—see the next section) are determined, any extra space is doled out in propor-
tion to the component's weights. So, for example, if each of our three components
had the same weight, each would receive a third of the extra space. To make this
more obvious, you may prefer to express the weights for a row or column as frac-
tions totaling 1.0—for example: 0.25, 0.25, 0.50. Components with a weight of 0
receive no extra space.

The situation is a bit more complicated when there are multiple rows or columns and
when there is even the possibility of components spanning more than one cell. In the
general case, GridBagLayout calculates an effective overall weight for each row and
column and then distributes the extra space to them proportionally. Note that the

previous single-row example is just a special case where the columns each have one component. The gory details of the calculations follow.

Calculating the weights of rows and columns

For a given row or column ("rank"), GridBagLayout first considers the weights of all the components contained strictly within that rank—ignoring those that span more than one cell. The greatest individual weight becomes the overall weight of the row or column. Intuitively this means that GridBagLayout is trying to accommodate the needs of the weightiest component in that rank.

Next, GridBagLayout considers the components that occupy more than one cell. Here things get a little weird. GridbagLayout wants to evaluate them to see whether they affect the determination of the largest weight in a row or column. However, because these components occupy more than one cell, GridBagLayout divides their weight among the ranks (rows or columns) that they span.

GridBagLayout tries to calculate an effective weight for the portion of the component that occupies each row or column. It does this by trying to divide the weight of the component among the ranks in the same proportions that the length (or height) of the component will be shared by the ranks. But how does it know what the proportions will be before the whole grid is determined? That's what it's trying to calculate after all. It simply guesses based on the row or column weights already determined. GridBagLayout uses the weights determined by the first round of calculations to split up the weight of the component over the ranks that it occupies. For each row or column, it then considers that fraction of the weight to be the component's weight for that rank. That weight then contends for the "heaviest weight" in the row or column, possibly changing the overall weight of that row or column, as we described earlier.

Anchoring

If a component is smaller than the space available for it, it is centered by default. But centering isn't the only possibility. The anchor constraint tells a grid bag layout how to position a component within its cell in the grid. Possible values are GridBagConstraints.CENTER, NORTH, NORTHEAST, EAST, SOUTHEAST, SOUTH, SOUTHWEST, WEST, and NORTHWEST. For example, an anchor of GridBagConstraints.NORTH centers a component at the top of its display area; SOUTHEAST places a component at the bottom-right corner of its area.

Padding and Insets

Another way to control the behavior of a component in a grid bag layout is to use padding and insets. Padding is determined by the ipadx and ipady fields of

GridBagConstraints. They specify horizontal and vertical "growth factors" for the component. In Figure 18-11, the *West* button is larger because we have set the ipadx and ipady values of its constraints to 25. Therefore, the layout manager gets the button's preferred size and adds 25 pixels in each direction to determine the button's actual size. The sizes of the other buttons are unchanged because their padding is set to 0 (the default), but their spacing is different. The *West* button is unnaturally tall, which means that the middle row of the layout must be taller than the others.

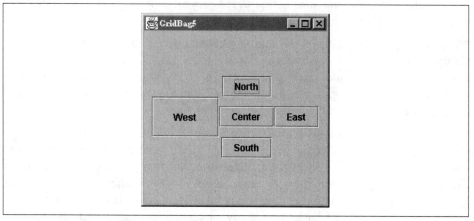

Figure 18-11. Using padding and insets in a layout

```
//file: GridBag5.java
import java.awt.*;
import java.awt.event.*;
import javax.swing.*;

public class GridBag5 extends JPanel {
  GridBagConstraints constraints = new GridBagConstraints( );

  public GridBag5( ) {
    setLayout(new GridBagLayout( ));
    int x, y;  // for clarity
    addGB(new JButton("North"),   x = 1, y = 0);
    constraints.ipadx = 25;  // add padding
    constraints.ipady = 25;
    addGB(new JButton("West"),    x = 0, y = 1);
    constraints.ipadx = 0;   // remove padding
    constraints.ipady = 0;
    addGB(new JButton("Center"), x = 1, y = 1);
    addGB(new JButton("East"),    x = 2, y = 1);
    addGB(new JButton("South"),   x = 1, y = 2);
  }

  void addGB(Component component, int x, int y) {
    constraints.gridx = x;
    constraints.gridy = y;
```

```
      add(component, constraints);
  }

  public static void main(String[] args) {
    JFrame frame = new JFrame("GridBag5");
    frame.setDefaultCloseOperation( JFrame.EXIT_ON_CLOSE );

    frame.setSize(250, 250);
    frame.setLocation(200, 200);
    frame.setContentPane(new GridBag5( ));
    frame.setVisible(true);
  }
}
```

Notice that the horizontal padding, ipadx, is added on both the left and right sides of the button. Therefore, the button grows horizontally by twice the value of ipadx. Likewise, the vertical padding, ipady, is added on both the top and the bottom.

Insets add space between the edges of the component and its cell. They are stored in the insets field of GridBagConstraints, which is an Insets object. An Insets object has four fields to specify the margins on the top, bottom, left, and right of the component. The relationship between insets and padding can be confusing. As shown in Figure 18-12, padding is added to the component itself, increasing its size. Insets are external to the component and represent the margin between the component and its cell.

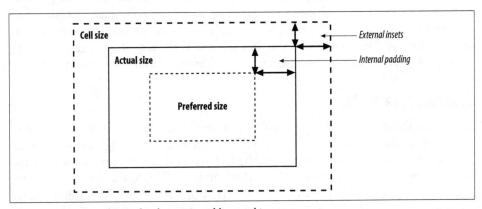

Figure 18-12. The relationship between padding and insets

Padding and weighting have an odd interaction with each other. If you use padding, it's best to use the default weightx and weighty values for each component.

Relative Positioning

In all our grid bag layouts so far, we have specified the gridx and gridy coordinates of each component explicitly using its constraints. Another alternative is relative positioning.

Conceptually, *relative positioning* is simple: we simply say "put this component to the right of (or below) the previous component." To do so you can set gridx or gridy to the constant GridBagConstraints.RELATIVE. Unfortunately, it's not as simple as this. Here are a couple of warnings:

- To place a component to the right of the previous one, set gridx to RELATIVE *and* use the same value for gridy that you used for the previous component.

- Similarly, to place a component below the previous one, set gridy to RELATIVE *and* leave gridx unchanged.

- Setting both gridx and gridy to RELATIVE places all the components in one row, not in a diagonal line, as you might expect. (This is the default.)

In other words, if gridx or gridy is RELATIVE, you had better leave the other value unchanged. RELATIVE makes it easy to arrange a lot of components in a row or a column. That's what it was intended for; if you try to do something else, you're fighting against the layout manager, not working with it.

GridBagLayout allows another kind of relative positioning in which you specify where, in a row or a column, the component should be placed overall. To do so, you use the gridwidth and gridheight fields of GridBagConstraints. Setting either of these to the constant REMAINDER says that the component should be the last item in its row or column and therefore should occupy all the remaining space. Setting either gridwidth or gridheight to RELATIVE says that it should be the second to the last item in its row or column. Unfortunately, you can use these constants to create constraints that can't possibly be met; for example, you can say that two components must be the last component in a row. In these cases, the layout manager tries to do something reasonable, but it will almost certainly do something you don't want.

Composite Layouts

Sometimes things don't fall neatly into little boxes. This is true of layouts as well as life. For example, if you want to use some of GridBagLayout's weighting features for part of your GUI, you could create separate layouts for different parts of the GUI and combine them with yet another layout. That's how we'll build the pocket calculator interface in Figure 18-13. We will use three grid bag layouts: one for the first row of buttons (C, %, +), one for the last (0, ., =) and one for the window itself. The master layout (the window's) manages the text field we use for the display, the panels containing the first and last rows of buttons, and the twelve buttons in the middle.*

Here's the code for the Calculator example. It implements only the user interface (i.e., the keyboard); it collects everything you type in the display field until you

---

* If you're curious, this calculator is based on the ELORG-801, encountered in an online "calculator museum"; see *http://www.taswegian.com/MOSCOW/elorg801.html*.

Figure 18-13. The Calculator application

press C (clear). Figuring out how to connect the GUI to some other code that would perform the operations is up to you. One strategy would be to send an event to the object that does the computation whenever the user presses the equals sign. That object could read the contents of the text field, parse it, do the computation, and display the results.

```java
//file: Calculator.java
import java.awt.*;
import java.awt.event.*;
import javax.swing.*;

public class Calculator extends JPanel implements ActionListener {
  GridBagConstraints gbc = new GridBagConstraints( );
  JTextField theDisplay = new JTextField( );

  public Calculator( ) {
    gbc.weightx = 1.0;  gbc.weighty = 1.0;
    gbc.fill = GridBagConstraints.BOTH;
    ContainerListener listener = new ContainerAdapter( ) {
      public void componentAdded(ContainerEvent e) {
        Component comp = e.getChild( );
        if (comp instanceof JButton)
          ((JButton)comp).addActionListener(Calculator.this);
      }
    };
    addContainerListener(listener);
    gbc.gridwidth = 4;
    addGB(this, theDisplay, 0, 0);
    // make the top row
    JPanel topRow = new JPanel( );
    topRow.addContainerListener(listener);
    gbc.gridwidth = 1;
    gbc.weightx = 1.0;
    addGB(topRow, new JButton("C"), 0, 0);
    gbc.weightx = 0.33;
```

```
    addGB(topRow, new JButton("%"), 1, 0);
    gbc.weightx = 1.0;
    addGB(topRow, new JButton("+"), 2, 0 );
    gbc.gridwidth = 4;
    addGB(this, topRow, 0, 1);
    gbc.weightx = 1.0;   gbc.gridwidth = 1;
    // make the digits
    for(int j=0; j<3; j++)
        for(int i=0; i<3; i++)
            addGB(this, new JButton("" + ((2-j)*3+i+1) ), i, j+2);
    // -, x, and divide
    addGB(this, new JButton("-"), 3, 2);
    addGB(this, new JButton("x"), 3, 3);
    addGB(this, new JButton("\u00F7"), 3, 4);
    // make the bottom row
    JPanel bottomRow = new JPanel( );
    bottomRow.addContainerListener(listener);
    gbc.weightx = 1.0;
    addGB(bottomRow, new JButton("0"), 0, 0);
    gbc.weightx = 0.33;
    addGB(bottomRow, new JButton("."), 1, 0);
    gbc.weightx = 1.0;
    addGB(bottomRow, new JButton("="), 2, 0);
    gbc.gridwidth = 4;
    addGB(this, bottomRow, 0, 5);
  }

  void addGB(Container cont, Component comp, int x, int y) {
    if ((cont.getLayout( ) instanceof GridBagLayout) == false)
      cont.setLayout(new GridBagLayout( ));
    gbc.gridx = x; gbc.gridy = y;
    cont.add(comp, gbc);
  }

  public void actionPerformed(ActionEvent e) {
    if (e.getActionCommand( ).equals("C"))
      theDisplay.setText("");
    else
      theDisplay.setText(theDisplay.getText( )
                      + e.getActionCommand( ));
  }

  public static void main(String[] args) {
    JFrame frame = new JFrame("Calculator");
    frame.setDefaultCloseOperation( JFrame.EXIT_ON_CLOSE );
    frame.setSize(200, 250);
    frame.setLocation(200, 200);
    frame.setContentPane(new Calculator( ));
    frame.setVisible(true);
  }
}
```

Once again, we use an addGB() helper method to add components with their constraints to the layout. Before discussing how to build the layout, let's take a look at addGB( ). We said earlier that three layout managers are in our user interface: one for the application panel itself, one for the panel containing the first row of buttons (topRow), and one for the panel containing the bottom row of buttons (bottomRow). We use addGB() for all three layouts; its first argument specifies the container to add the component to. Thus, when the first argument is this, we're adding an object to the content pane of the JFrame. When the first argument is topRow, we're adding a button to the first row of buttons. addGB() first checks the container's layout manager and sets it to GridBagLayout if it isn't already set properly. It sets the object's position by modifying a set of constraints, gbc, and then uses these constraints to add the object to the container.

We use a single set of constraints throughout the example, modifying fields as we see fit. The constraints are initialized in Calculator's constructor. Before calling addGB( ), we set any fields of gbc for which the defaults are inappropriate. Thus, for the answer display, we set the grid width to 4 and add the answer display directly to the application panel (this). The add() method, which is called by addGB(), makes a copy of the constraints, so we're free to reuse gbc throughout the application.

The first and last rows of buttons motivate the use of multiple GridBagLayout containers, each with its own grid. These buttons appear to straddle grid lines, but you really can't accomplish this using a single grid. Therefore, topRow has its own layout manager, with three horizontal cells, allowing each button in the row to have a grid width of 1. To control the size of the buttons, we set the weightx variables so that the clear and plus buttons take up more space than the percent button. We then add the topRow as a whole to the application, with a grid width of 4. The bottom row is built similarly.

To build the buttons for the digits 1 through 9, we use a doubly nested loop. There's nothing particularly interesting about this loop, except that it's probably a bit too clever for good taste. The minus, multiply, and divide buttons are also simple: we create a button with the appropriate label and use addGB() to place it in the application. It's worth noting that we used a Unicode constant to request a real division sign rather than wimping out and using a slash.

That's it for the user interface; what's left is event handling. Each button generates action events; we need to register listeners for these events. We'll make the application panel, the Calculator, the listener for all the buttons. To register the Calculator as a listener, we'll be clever. Whenever a component is added to a container, the container generates a ContainerEvent. We use an anonymous inner class ContainerListener to register listeners for our buttons. This means that the Calculator must register as a ContainerListener for itself and for the two panels, topRow and bottomRow. The componentAdded() method is very simple. It calls getChild() to find out what component caused the event (i.e., what component was added). If that component is a button, it registers the Calculator as an ActionListener for that button.

`actionPerformed()` is called whenever the user presses any button. It clears the display if the user pressed the C button; otherwise, it appends the button's action command (in this case, its label) to the display.

Combining layout managers is an extremely useful trick. Granted, this example verges on overkill. You won't often need to create a composite layout using multiple grid bags. Composite layouts are most common with `BorderLayout`; you'll frequently use different layout managers for each of a border layout's regions. For example, the `CENTER` region might be a `ScrollPane`, which has its own special-purpose layout manager; the `EAST` and `SOUTH` regions might be panels managed by grid layouts or flow layouts, as appropriate.

Nonstandard Layout Managers

We've covered the basic layout managers; with them, you should be able to create just about any user interface you like.

But that's not all, folks. If you want to experiment with layout managers that are undocumented, may change, and may not be available locally on all platforms, look in the sun.awt classes. You'll find a `HorizBagLayout`, a `VerticalBagLayout`, an `OrientableFlowLayout`, and a `VariableGridLayout`. Furthermore, public domain layout managers of all descriptions are on the Net.

Absolute Positioning

It's possible to set the layout manager to `null`: no layout control. You might do this to position an object on the display at some absolute coordinates. This is usually not the right approach. Components might have different minimum sizes on different platforms, and your interface would not be very portable.

The following example doesn't use a layout manager and works with absolute coordinates instead:

```
//file: MoveButton.java
import java.awt.*;
import java.awt.event.*;
import javax.swing.*;

public class MoveButton extends JPanel {
  JButton button = new JButton("I Move");

  public MoveButton( ) {
    setLayout(null);
    add(button);
    button.setSize(button.getPreferredSize( ));
    button.setLocation(20, 20);
    addMouseListener(new MouseAdapter( ) {
      public void mousePressed(MouseEvent e) {
```

```
        button.setLocation(e.getX( ), e.getY( ));
      }
    });
  }

  public static void main(String[] args) {
    JFrame frame = new JFrame("MoveButton");
    frame.setDefaultCloseOperation( JFrame.EXIT_ON_CLOSE );
    frame.setSize(250, 200);
    frame.setLocation(200, 200);
    frame.setContentPane(new MoveButton( ));
    frame.setVisible(true);
  }
}
```

Click in the window area, outside of the button, to move the button to a new location. Try resizing the window and note that the button stays at a fixed position relative to the window's upper left corner.

SpringLayout

The SpringLayout is a new addition in Java 1.4. It supports a combination of absolute positioning and point-to-point attachments between components (kind of like the "glue" of the BoxLayout). SpringLayout is useful in GUI builder applications because it's easy to translate manual user placement into these kinds of constraints.

SpringLayout uses Spring objects to attach edges of components. Springs have a range of motion and can be anchored at a coordinate or at a component's edge. Any two component edges can also be connected by a Spring. The two edges may belong to two different components, in which case the spring constrains the way the components are placed relative to one another, or they may belong to the same component, in which case the spring constrains the width or height of the component.

We don't cover SpringLayout here, but you can read about it in O'Reilly's *Java Swing*.

## CHAPTER 19

Drawing with
the 2D API

In the last few chapters, you've caught a glimpse of how graphics operations are performed in Java. This chapter goes into more depth about drawing techniques and the tools for working with images in Java. In the next chapter, we'll explore image-processing tools in more detail, and we'll look at the classes that let you generate images, pixel by pixel, on the fly.

The Big Picture

The classes you'll use for drawing come from six packages: java.awt, java.awt.color, java.awt.font, java.awt.geom, java.awt.image, and java.awt.print. Collectively, these classes make up most of the 2D API, a comprehensive API for drawing shapes, text, and images. Figure 19-1 shows a bird's-eye view of these classes. There's much more in the 2D API than we can cover in two chapters. For a full treatment, see Jonathan Knudsen's *Java 2D Graphics* (O'Reilly).

An instance of java.awt.Graphics2D is called a *graphics context*. It represents a drawing surface such as a component's display area, a page on a printer, or an offscreen image buffer. A graphics context provides methods for drawing three kinds of graphics objects: shapes, text, and images. Graphics2D is called a graphics context because it also holds contextual information about the drawing area. This information includes the drawing area's clipping region, painting color, transfer mode, text font, and geometric transformation. If you consider the drawing area to be a painter's canvas, you might think of a graphics context as an easel that holds a set of tools and marks off the work area.

There are four ways to acquire a Graphics2D object. The following list shows them in order, most common to least.

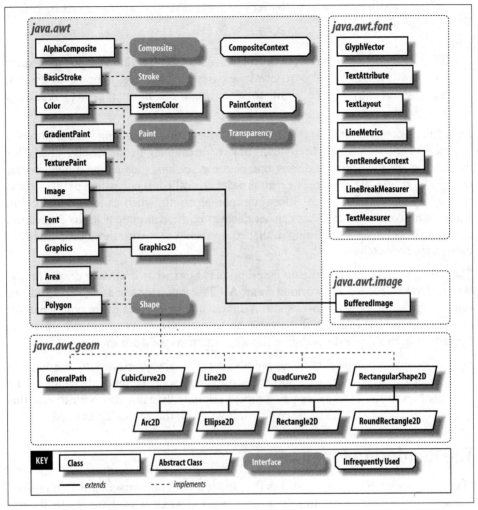

Figure 19-1. Graphics classes of the 2D API

From AWT or Swing as the result of a painting request on a component

In this case, a new graphics context for the appropriate area is created and passed to your component's paint() or update() method. (The update() method really applies only to AWT components, not the newer Swing components.)

Directly from an offscreen image buffer

In this case, we ask the image buffer for a graphics context directly. We'll use this when we discuss techniques such as double buffering.

By copying an existing Graphics2D object

Duplicating a graphics object can be useful for more elaborate drawing operations; different copies of a Graphics2D object can draw on same area, but with different attributes and clipping regions. A Graphics2D can be copied by calling the create() method.

Directly from an onscreen component

It's possible to ask a component to give you a Graphics2D object for its display area. However, this is almost always a mistake; if you feel tempted to do this, think about why you're trying to circumvent the normal paint()/repaint() mechanism.

Each time a component's paint() method is called, the windowing system provides the component with a new Graphics2D object for drawing in the display area. This means that attributes we set during one painting session, such as the drawing color or clipping region, are reset the next time paint()is called. (Each call to paint() starts with a tidy new easel.) For the most common attributes, such as foreground color, background color, and font, we can set defaults in the component itself. Thereafter, the graphics contexts for painting in that component come with those properties initialized appropriately.

The paint() method can make no assumptions about what is already drawn on the screen. However if we are working in an AWT component's update() method, we can assume our onscreen artwork is still intact, and we need to make only whatever changes are needed to bring the display up to date. One way to optimize drawing operations in this case is by setting a clipping region, as we'll see shortly.

For backwards compatibility, a graphics context is always passed to the paint() method as a more primitive Graphics object. If you want to take advantage of the nifty features in the 2D API (as you almost undoubtedly will), you need to cast this reference to a Graphics2D. You'll see how this works in the upcoming examples.

The Rendering Pipeline

One of the strengths of the 2D API is that shapes, text, and images are manipulated in many of the same ways. In this section, we'll describe what happens to shapes, text, and images after you give them to a Graphics2D object. *Rendering* is the process of taking some collection of shapes, text, and images and figuring out how to represent them by coloring pixels on a screen or printer. Graphics2D supports four rendering operations:

- Draw the outline of a shape, with the draw() method.
- Fill the interior of a shape, with the fill() method.
- Draw some text, with the drawString() method.
- Draw an image, with any of the many forms of the drawImage() method.

The graphics context instantiated by a `Graphics2D` object consists of the following properties, whose values are controlled by corresponding accessor methods:

paint

The current *paint* (an object of type `java.awt.Paint`) determines what color or pattern will be used to fill a shape. This affects the drawing of shape outlines and text, as well. You can change the current paint using `Graphics2D`'s `setPaint()` method. Note that the `Color` class implements the `Paint` interface, so you can pass `Color`s to `setPaint()` if you want to use solid colors.

stroke

`Graphics2D` uses the *stroke* to determine how to draw the outline of shapes that are passed to its `draw()` method. In graphics terminology, to "stroke" a shape means to take a path defined by the shape and effectively trace it with a pen or brush of a certain size and characteristics. For example, drawing the shape of a circle using a stroke that acts like a solid line would yield a washer or ring shape. The stroke object in the Graphics2D API is a little more abstract than that. In actuality it accepts the input shape to be stroked and returns an enclosed shape representing the outline, which the `Graphics2D` then fills. You can set the current stroke using `setStroke()`. The 2D API comes with a handy class, `java.awt.BasicStroke`, that implements different line widths, end styles, join styles, and dashing.

font

Text is rendered by creating a shape that represents the characters to be drawn. The current *font* determines what shapes are created for a given set of characters. The resulting text shape is then filled. The current font is set using `setFont()`. The 2D API gives applications access to all the TrueType and PostScript Type 1 fonts that are installed.

transformation

Shapes, text, and images are geometrically *transformed* before they are rendered. This means that they may be moved, rotated, and stretched. `Graphics2D`'s transformation converts coordinates from "user space" to "device space." By default, `Graphics2D` uses a transformation that maps 72 units in user space to one inch on the output device. If you draw a line from point 0, 0 to point 72, 0 using the default transformation, it will be one inch long, regardless of whether it is drawn on your monitor or your printer. The current transformation can be modified using the `translate()`, `rotate()`, `scale()`, and `shear()` methods.

compositing rule

A *compositing rule* determines how the colors of a new drawing operation are combined with existing colors on the `Graphics2D`'s drawing surface. This attribute is set using `setComposite()`, which accepts an instance of `java.awt.AlphaComposite`. Compositing allows you to make parts of a drawing or image completely or partially transparent, or to combine them in other interesting ways.

clipping shape

All rendering operations are limited to the interior of the *clipping shape*. No pixels outside this shape are modified. By default, the clipping shape allows rendering on the entire drawing surface (usually, the rectangular area of a Component). However, you can further limit this using any simple or complex shape, including text shapes.

rendering hints

There are different techniques that can be used to render graphics primitives. Usually these represent a tradeoff between rendering speed and visual quality or vice versa. Rendering hints (constants defined in the RenderingHints class) specify which techniques to use.

Graphics primitives (shapes, text, and images) pass through the rendering engine in a series of operations called the *rendering pipeline*. Let's walk through the pipeline. It can be reduced to four steps; the first step depends on the rendering operation:

1. Transform the shape. For shapes that will be filled, the shape is simply transformed using the Graphics2D's current transformation. For shapes whose outlines are drawn using draw(), the current stroke is used to stroke the shape's outline. Then the stroked outline is transformed, just like any other filled shape. Text is displayed by mapping characters to shapes using the current font. The resulting text shapes are transformed, just like any other filled shape. For images, the outline of the image is transformed using the current transformation.

2. Determine the colors to be used. For a filled shape, the current *paint* object determines what colors should be used to fill the shape. For drawing an image, the colors are taken from the image itself.

3. Combine the colors with the existing drawing surface using the current *compositing rule*.

4. Clip the results using the current *clipping shape*.

The *rendering hints* are used throughout to control the rendering quality.

A Quick Tour of Java 2D

Filling Shapes

The simplest path through the rendering pipeline is for filling shapes. For example, the following code creates an ellipse and fills it with a solid color. (This code would live inside a paint() method somewhere. We'll present a complete, ready-to-run example a little later.)

```
Shape c = new Ellipse2D.Float(50, 25, 150, 150);
g2.setPaint(Color.blue);
g2.fill(c);
```

Here, g2 is our Graphics2D object. The Ellipse2D class is abstract but is implemented by concrete inner subclasses, called Float and Double. The Rectangle2D class, for example, has concrete subclasses Rectangle2D.Float and Rectangle2D.Double.

In the call to setPaint(), we tell the Graphics2D to use a solid color, blue, for all subsequent filling operations. Then, the call to fill() tells Graphics2D to fill the given shape.

All geometric shapes in the 2D API are represented by implementations of the java.awt.geom.Shape interface. This interface defines methods that are common to all shapes, like returning a rectangle bounding box or testing if a point is inside the shape. The java.awt.geompackage is a smorgasbord of useful shape classes, including Rectangle2D, RoundRectangle2D (a rectangle with rounded corners), Arc2D, Ellipse2D, and others. In addition, a few classes in java.awt are Shapes: Rectangle, Polygon, and Area.

Drawing Shape Outlines

Drawing a shape's outline is only a little bit more complicated. Consider the following example:

```
Shape r = new Rectangle2D.Float(100, 75, 100, 100);
g2.setStroke(new BasicStroke(4));
g2.setPaint(Color.yellow);
g2.draw(r);
```

Here, we tell the Graphics2D to use a stroke that is four units wide and a solid color, yellow, for filling the stroke. When we call draw(), Graphics2D uses the stroke to create a new shape, the outline, from the given rectangle. The outline shape is then filled, just as before; this effectively draws the rectangle's outline. The rectangle itself is not filled.

Convenience Methods

Graphics2D includes quite a few convenience methods for drawing and filling common shapes; these methods are actually inherited from the Graphics class. Table 19-1 summarizes these methods. It's a little easier to just call fillRect() rather than instantiating a rectangle shape and passing it to fill().

Table 19-1. Shape-drawing methods in the graphics class

Method	Description
draw3DRect()	Draws a highlighted, 3D rectangle
drawArc()	Draws an arc
drawLine()	Draws a line
drawOval()	Draws an oval

Table 19-1. Shape-drawing methods in the graphics class (continued)

Method	Description
drawPolygon()	Draws a polygon, closing it by connecting the endpoints
drawPolyline()	Draws a line connecting a series of points, without closing it
drawRect()	Draws a rectangle
drawRoundRect()	Draws a rounded-corner rectangle
fill3DRect()	Draws a filled, highlighted, 3D rectangle
fillArc()	Draws a filled arc
fillOval()	Draws a filled oval
fillPolygon()	Draws a filled polygon
fillRect()	Draws a filled rectangle
fillRoundRect()	Draws a filled, rounded-corner rectangle

As you can see, for each of the fill() methods in the table, there is a corresponding draw() method that renders the shape as an unfilled line drawing. With the exception of fillArc() and fillPolygon(), each method takes a simple x, y specification for the top left corner of the shape and a width and height for its size.

The most flexible convenience method draws a polygon, which is specified by two arrays that contain the x and y coordinates of the vertices. Methods in the Graphics class take two such arrays and draw the polygon's outline or fill the polygon.

The methods listed in Table 19-1 are shortcuts for more general methods in Graphics2D. The more general procedure is to first create a java.awt.geom.Shape object and then pass it to the draw() or fill() method of Graphics2D. For example, you could create a Polygon object from coordinate arrays. Since a Polygon implements the Shape interface, you can pass it to Graphics2D's general draw() or fill() method.

The fillArc() method requires six integer arguments. The first four specify the bounding box for an oval—just like the fillOval() method. The final two arguments specify what portion of the oval we want to draw, as a starting angular position and an offset. Both the starting angular position and the offset are specified in degrees. The zero degree mark is at three o'clock; a positive angle is clockwise. For example, to draw the right half of a circle, you might call:

```
g.fillArc(0, 0, radius * 2, radius * 2, -90, 180);
```

draw3DRect() automatically chooses colors by "darkening" the current color. So you should set the color to something other than black, which is the default (maybe gray or white); if you don't, you'll just get a black rectangle with a thick outline.

Drawing Text

Like drawing a shape's outline, drawing text is just a simple variation on filling a shape. When you ask a `Graphics2D` to draw text, it determines the shapes that need to be drawn and fills them. The shapes that represent characters are called *glyphs*. A font is a collection of glyphs. Here's an example of drawing text:

```
g2.setFont(new Font("Times New Roman", Font.PLAIN, 64));
g2.setPaint(Color.red);
g2.drawString("Hello, 2D!", 50, 150);
```

When we call `drawString()`, the `Graphics2D` uses the current font to retrieve the glyphs that correspond to the characters in the string. Then the glyphs (which are really just `Shapes`) are filled using the current `Paint`.

Drawing Images

Images are treated a little differently than shapes. In particular, the current `Paint` is not used to render an image because the image contains its own color information (it *is* the Paint, effectively). The following example loads an image from a file and displays it (you'll have to use your own file here):

```
Image i = Toolkit.getDefaultToolkit().getImage("camel.gif");
g2.drawImage(i, 75, 50, this);
```

In this case, the call to `drawImage()` tells the `Graphics2D` to place the image at the given location.

Transformations and rendering

Four parts of the pipeline affect every graphics operation. In particular, all rendering is transformed, composited, and clipped. Rendering hints are used to affect all of a `Graphics2D`'s rendering.

This example shows how to modify the current transformation with a translation and a rotation:

```
g2.translate(50, 0);
g2.rotate(Math.PI / 6);
```

Every graphics primitive drawn by g2 will now have this transformation applied to it (a shift of 50 units right and a rotation of 30 degrees counterclockwise). We can have a similarly global effect on compositing:

```
AlphaComposite ac = AlphaComposite.getInstance(
    AlphaComposite.SRC_OVER, (float).5);
g2.setComposite(ac);
```

Now every graphics primitive we draw will be half transparent; we'll explain more about this later.

All drawing operations are clipped by the current clipping shape, which is any object implementing the Shape interface. In the following example, the clipping shape is set to an ellipse:

```
Shape e = new Ellipse2D.Float(50, 25, 250, 150);
g2.clip(e);
```

You can obtain the current clipping shape using getClip(); this is handy if you want to restore it later using the setClip() method.

Finally, the rendering hints are used for all drawing operations. In the following example, we tell the Graphics2D to use antialiasing, a technique that smoothes out the rough pixel edges of shapes and text:

```
g2.setRenderingHint(RenderingHints.KEY_ANTIALIASING,
    RenderingHints.VALUE_ANTIALIAS_ON);
```

The RenderingHints class contains other keys and values representing other rendering hints. If you really like to fiddle with knobs and dials, this is a good class to check out.

The Whole Iguana

Let's put everything together now, just to show how graphics primitives travel through the rendering pipeline. The following example demonstrates the use of Graphics2D from the beginning to the end of the rendering pipeline. With very few lines of code, we are able to draw some pretty complicated stuff (see Figure 19-2)

Figure 19-2. Exercising the 2D API

Here's the code:

```java
//file: Iguana.java
import java.awt.*;
import java.awt.event.*;
import java.awt.geom.*;
import javax.swing.*;

public class Iguana extends JComponent {
  private Image image;
  private int theta;

  public Iguana() {
    image = Toolkit.getDefaultToolkit().getImage(
        "Piazza di Spagna.small.jpg");
    theta = 0;
    addMouseListener(new MouseAdapter() {
      public void mousePressed(MouseEvent me) {
        theta = (theta + 15) % 360;
        repaint();
      }
    });
  }

  public void paint(Graphics g) {
    Graphics2D g2 = (Graphics2D)g;

    g2.setRenderingHint(RenderingHints.KEY_ANTIALIASING,
        RenderingHints.VALUE_ANTIALIAS_ON);

    int cx = getSize().width / 2;
    int cy = getSize().height / 2;

    g2.translate(cx, cy);
    g2.rotate(theta * Math.PI / 180);

    Shape oldClip = g2.getClip();
    Shape e = new Ellipse2D.Float(-cx, -cy, cx * 2, cy * 2);
    g2.clip(e);

    Shape c = new Ellipse2D.Float(-cx, -cy, cx * 3 / 4, cy * 2);
    g2.setPaint(new GradientPaint(40, 40, Color.blue,
        60, 50, Color.white, true));
    g2.fill(c);

    g2.setPaint(Color.yellow);
    g2.fillOval(cx / 4, 0, cx, cy);

    g2.setClip(oldClip);

    g2.setFont(new Font("Times New Roman", Font.PLAIN, 64));
    g2.setPaint(new GradientPaint(-cx, 0, Color.red,
        cx, 0, Color.black, false));
    g2.drawString("Hello, 2D!", -cx * 3 / 4, cy / 4);
```

```
AlphaComposite ac = AlphaComposite.getInstance(
    AlphaComposite.SRC_OVER, (float).75);
g2.setComposite(ac);

Shape r = new RoundRectangle2D.Float(0, -cy * 3 / 4,
    cx * 3 / 4, cy * 3 / 4, 20, 20);
g2.setStroke(new BasicStroke(4));
g2.setPaint(Color.magenta);
g2.fill(r);
g2.setPaint(Color.green);
g2.draw(r);

g2.drawImage(image, -cx / 2, -cy / 2, this);
}

public static void main(String[] args) {
    JFrame frame = new JFrame("Iguana");
    Container c = frame.getContentPane();
    c.setLayout(new BorderLayout());
    c.add(new Iguana(), BorderLayout.CENTER);
    frame.setSize(300, 300);
    frame.setDefaultCloseOperation( JFrame.EXIT_ON_CLOSE );
    frame.setVisible(true);
  }
}
```

The Iguana class itself is a subclass of JComponent with a fancy paint() method. The main() method takes care of creating a JFrame that holds the Iguana component.

Iguana's constructor loads a small image (we'll talk more about this later) and sets up a mouse event handler. This handler changes a member variable, theta, and repaints the component. Each time you click, the entire drawing is rotated by 15 degrees.

Iguana's paint() method does some pretty tricky stuff, but none of it is very difficult. First, user space is transformed so that the origin is at the center of the component. The user space is then rotated by theta:

```
g2.translate(cx, cy);
g2.rotate(theta * Math.PI / 180);
```

Iguana saves the current (default) clipping shape before setting it to a large ellipse. Then Iguana draws two filled ellipses. The first is drawn by instantiating an Ellipse2D and filling it; the second is drawn using the fillOval() convenience method. (We'll talk about the color gradient in the first ellipse in the next section.) As you can see in Figure 19-2, both ellipses are clipped by the elliptical clipping shape. After filling the two ellipses, Iguana restores the old clipping shape.

Iguana draws some text next; we'll talk about this in more detail later. The next action is to modify the compositing rule as follows:

```
AlphaComposite ac = AlphaComposite.getInstance(
    AlphaComposite.SRC_OVER, (float).75);
g2.setComposite(ac);
```

All this means is that we want everything to be drawn with transparency. The AlphaComposite class defines constants representing different compositing rules, much the way the Color class contains constants representing different predefined colors. In this case, we're asking for the *source over destination* rule (SRC_OVER), but with an additional alpha multiplier of 0.75. Source over destination means that whatever we're drawing (the source) should be placed on top of whatever's already there (the destination). The alpha multiplier means that everything we draw will be treated at 0.75 or three quarters of its normal opacity, allowing the existing drawing to "show through."

You can see the effect of the new compositing rule in the rounded rectangle and the image, which both allow previously drawn elements to show through.

Filling Shapes

Iguana fills its shapes with a number of colors, using the setPaint() method of Graphics2D. This method sets the current color in the graphics context, so we set it to a different color before each drawing operation. setPaint() accepts any object that implements the Paint interface. The 2D API includes three implementations of this interface, representing solid colors, color gradients, and textures.

Solid Colors

The java.awt.Color class handles color in Java. A Color object describes a single color. You can create an arbitrary Color by specifying the red, green, and blue values, either as integers between 0 and 255 or as floating-point values between 0.0 and 1.0. The (somewhat strange) getColor() method can be used to look up a named color in the system properties table, as described in Chapter 10. getColor() takes a String color property name, retrieves the integer value from the Properties list, and returns the Color object that corresponds to that color.

The Color class also defines a number of static final color values; these are what we used in the Iguana example. These constants, such as Color.black and Color.red, provide a convenient set of basic color objects for your drawings.

Color Gradients

A *color gradient* is a smooth blend from one color to another. The GradientPaint class encapsulates this idea in a handy implementation of the Paint interface. All you need to do is specify two points and the color at each point. The GradientPaint takes care of the details so that the color fades smoothly from one point to the other. For example, in the previous example, the ellipse is filled with a gradient this way:

```
g2.setPaint(new GradientPaint(40, 40, Color.blue,
    60, 50, Color.white, true));
```

The last parameter in GradientPaint's constructor determines whether the gradient is *cyclic*. In a cyclic gradient, the colors keep fluctuating beyond the two points that you've specified. Otherwise, the gradient just draws a single blend from one point to the other. Beyond each endpoint, the color is solid.

Textures

A *texture* is simply an image repeated over and over like a floor tile. This concept is represented in the 2D API with the TexturePaint class. To create a texture, just specify the image to be used and the rectangle that will be used to reproduce it. To do this, you also need to know how to create and use images, which we'll get to a little later.

Desktop Colors

The Color class makes it easy to construct a particular color; however, that's not always what you want to do. Sometimes you want to match a preexisting color scheme. This is particularly important when you are designing a user interface; you might want your components to have the same colors as other components on that platform and to change automatically if the user redefines his or her color scheme.

That's what the SystemColor class is for. A system color represents the color used by the local windowing system in a certain context. The SystemColor class holds lots of predefined system colors, just like the Color class holds some predefined basic colors. For example, the field activeCaption represents the color used for the background of the titlebar of an active window; activeCaptionText represents the color used for the title itself. menu represents the background color of menu selections; menuText represents the color of a menu item's text when it is not selected; textHighlightText is the color used when the menu item is selected; and so on. You could use the window value to set the color of a Window to match the other windows on the user's screen—whether or not they're generated by Java programs.

```
myWindow.setBackground( SystemColor.window );
```

Because the SystemColor class is a subclass of Color, you can use it wherever you would use a Color. However, the SystemColor constants are tricky. They are constant, immutable objects as far as you, the programmer, are concerned (your code is not allowed to modify them), but they can be modified at runtime by the system. If the user changes his color scheme, the system colors are automatically updated to follow suit; as a result, anything displayed with system colors will automatically change color the next time it is redrawn. For example, the window myWindow would automatically change its background color to the new background color.

The SystemColor class has one noticeable shortcoming. You can't compare a system color to a Color directly; the Color.equals() method doesn't return reliable results.

For example, if you want to find out whether the window background color is red, you can't call:

```
Color.red.equals(SystemColor.window);
```

Instead, you should use getRGB() to find the color components of both objects and compare them, rather than comparing the objects themselves.

Stroking Shape Outlines

Just as a Graphics2D object's current paint determines how its shapes are filled, its current stoke determines how its shapes are outlined. The current stroke determines such drawing features as line thickness, line dashing, and end styles. (If you struggled with drawing in earlier versions of Java, you'll be very grateful that there's now a way to change the line thickness.)

To set the current stroke in a Graphics2D, just call setStroke() with any implementation of the Stroke interface. Fortunately, the 2D API includes a BasicStroke class that probably does everything you need. Using BasicStroke, you can create dashed lines, control what decoration is added to line ends, and decide how the corners in an outline should be drawn.

By default, Graphics2D uses a solid stroke with a width of 1. In the previous Iguana example, the line width is changed just before the outline of the rounded rectangle is drawn, like so:

```
g2.setStroke(new BasicStroke(4));
```

Using Fonts

Text fonts in Java are represented by instances of the java.awt.Font class. A Font object is constructed from a name, style identifier, and a point size. We can create a Font object at any time, but it's meaningful only when applied to a particular component on a given display device. Here are a couple of fonts:

```
Font smallFont = new Font("Monospaced", Font.PLAIN, 10);
Font bigFont = new Font("Serif", Font.BOLD, 18);
```

Font names come in three varieties: *family* names, *face* names (also called font names), and *logical* names. Family and font names are closely related. For example, Garamond Italic is a font name for a font whose family name is Garamond.

A *logical name* is a generic name for the font family. The following logical font names should be available on all platforms:

- Serif (generic name for TimesRoman)
- SansSerif (generic name for Helvetica)
- Monospaced (generic name for Courier)

- Dialog

- DialogInput

The logical font name is mapped to an actual font on the local platform. Java's *fonts. properties* files map the font names to the available fonts, covering as much of the Unicode character set as possible. If you request a font that doesn't exist, you get the default font.

One of the big wins in the 2D API is that it can use most of the fonts you have installed on your computer. The following program prints out a full list of the fonts that are available to the 2D API:

```java
//file: ShowFonts.java
import java.awt.*;

public class ShowFonts {
  public static void main(String[] args) {
    Font[] fonts;
    fonts =
    GraphicsEnvironment.getLocalGraphicsEnvironment( ).getAllFonts( );
    for (int i = 0; i < fonts.length; i++) {
      System.out.print(fonts[i].getFontName( ) + " : ");
      System.out.print(fonts[i].getFamily( ) + " : ");
      System.out.print(fonts[i].getName( ));
      System.out.println( );
    }
  }
}
```

Note, however, that the fonts installed on your system may not match the fonts installed on someone else's system. For true portability, you can use one of the logical names (although your application won't look exactly the same on all platforms) or go with the defaults. You can also allow your users to configure the application by choosing fonts themselves.

The static method Font.getFont( )looks up a font name in the system properties list (like Color.getColor( )). getFont( ) takes a String font property name, retrieves the font name from the Properties table, and returns the Font object that corresponds to that font.

The Font class defines three static style identifiers: PLAIN, BOLD, and ITALIC. You can use these values on all fonts. The point size determines the size of the font on a display. If a given point size isn't available, Font substitutes a default size.

You can retrieve information about an existing Font with a number of routines. The getName( ), getSize( ), and getStyle( ) methods retrieve the logical name, point size, and style, respectively. You can use the getFamily( ) method to find out the family name while getFontName( ) returns the face name of the font.

Finally, to actually use a Font object, you can simply specify it as an argument to the setFont( ) method of a Component or Graphics2D object. Subsequent text-drawing commands such as `drawString()` for that component or in that graphics context use the specified font.

Font Metrics

To get detailed size and spacing information for text rendered in a font, we can ask for a `java.awt.font.LineMetrics` object. Different systems have different real fonts available; the available fonts may not match the font you request. Furthermore, the measurements of different characters within a single font may be different, especially in multilingual text. Thus, a `LineMetrics` object presents information about a particular set of text in a particular font on a particular system, not general information about a font. For example, if you ask for the metrics of a nine-point `Monospaced` font, what you get isn't some abstract truth about `Monospaced` fonts; you get the metrics of the font that the particular system uses for nine-point `Monospaced`—which may not be exactly nine points or even fixed width.

Use the `getLineMetrics()` method for a `Font` to retrieve the metrics for text as it would appear for that component. This method also needs to know some information about how you plan to render the text—if you're planning to use antialiasing, for instance, which affects the text measurements. This extra information is encapsulated in the `FontRenderContext` class. Fortunately, you can just ask `Graphics2D` for its current `FontRenderContext` rather than having to create one yourself:

```java
public void paint(Graphics g) {
  Graphics2D g2 = (Graphics2D)g;
  ...
  FontRenderContext frc = g2.getFontRenderContext( );
  LineMetrics metrics = font.getLineMetrics("Monkey", frc);
  ...
}
```

The Font class also has a `getStringBounds()` method that returns the bounding box of a piece of text:

```java
public void paint(Graphics g) {
  Graphics2D g2 = (Graphics2D)g;
  ...
  FontRenderContext frc = g2.getFontRenderContext( );
  float messageWidth =
      (float)font.getStringBounds("Monkey", frc).getWidth( );
  ...
}
```

The following application, `FontShow`, displays a word and draws reference lines showing certain characteristics of its font, as shown in Figure 19-3. Clicking in the application window toggles the point size between a small and a large value.

```java
//file: FontShow.java
import java.awt.*;
import java.awt.event.*;
```

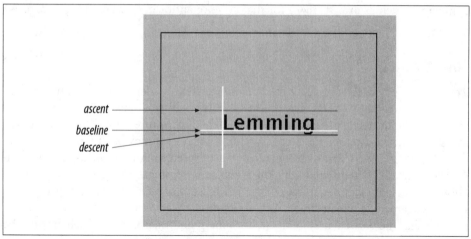

Figure 19-3. The FontShow application

```
import java.awt.font.*;
import javax.swing.*;

public class FontShow extends JComponent
{
  private static final int PAD = 25;    // frilly line padding
  private boolean bigFont = true;
  private String message;

  public FontShow(String message) {
    this.message = message;
    addMouseListener(new MouseAdapter( ) {
      public void mouseClicked(MouseEvent e) {
        bigFont = !bigFont;
        repaint( );
      }
    });
  }

  public void paint(Graphics g)
  {
    Graphics2D g2 = (Graphics2D)g;

    g2.setRenderingHint(RenderingHints.KEY_ANTIALIASING,
        RenderingHints.VALUE_ANTIALIAS_ON);

    int size = bigFont ? 96 : 64;
    Font font = new Font("Dialog", Font.PLAIN, size);
    g2.setFont(font);
    int width = getSize( ).width;
    int height = getSize( ).height;

    FontRenderContext frc = g2.getFontRenderContext( );
    LineMetrics metrics = font.getLineMetrics(message, frc);
```

```
        float messageWidth =
            (float)font.getStringBounds(message, frc).getWidth( );

        // center text
        float ascent = metrics.getAscent( );
        float descent = metrics.getDescent( );
        float x = (width - messageWidth) / 2;
        float y = (height + metrics.getHeight( )) / 2 - descent;

        g2.setPaint(getBackground( ));
        g2.fillRect(0, 0, width, height);

        g2.setPaint(getForeground( ));
        g2.drawString(message, x, y);

        g2.setPaint(Color.white);   // Base lines
        drawLine(g2, x - PAD, y, x + messageWidth + PAD, y);
        drawLine(g2, x, y + PAD, x, y - ascent - PAD);
        g2.setPaint(Color.green);   // Ascent line
        drawLine(g2, x - PAD, y - ascent,
                 x + messageWidth + PAD, y - ascent);
        g2.setPaint(Color.red);     // Descent line
        drawLine(g2, x - PAD, y + descent,
                 x + messageWidth + PAD, y + descent);
    }

    private void drawLine(Graphics2D g2,
        double x0, double y0, double x1, double y1) {
        Shape line = new java.awt.geom.Line2D.Double(x0, y0, x1, y1);
        g2.draw(line);
    }

    public static void main(String args[]) {
        String message = "Lemming";
        if (args.length > 0) message = args[0];

        JFrame frame = new JFrame("FontShow");
        frame.setSize(420, 300);
        frame.setDefaultCloseOperation( JFrame.EXIT_ON_CLOSE );
        frame.getContentPane( ).add(new FontShow(message));
        frame.setVisible(true);
    }
}
```

You can specify the text to be displayed as a command-line argument:

```
% java FontShow "When in the course of human events ..."
```

FontShow may look a bit complicated, but there's really not much to it. The bulk of the code is in paint( ), which sets the font, draws the text, and adds a few lines to illustrate some of the font's characteristics (metrics). For fun, we also catch mouse clicks (using an event handler defined in the constructor) and alternate the font size by setting the bigFont toggle variable and repainting.

By default, text is rendered above and to the right of the coordinates specified in the drawString() method. Think of that starting point as the origin of a coordinate system; the axes are the *baselines* of the font. FontShow draws these lines in white. The greatest height the characters stretch above the baseline is called the *ascent* and is shown by a green line. Some fonts also have parts of letters that fall below the baseline. The farthest distance any character reaches below the baseline is called the *descent*. FontShow illustrates this with a red line.

We ask for the ascent and descent of our font with the LineMetrics class's getAscent() and getDescent() methods. We also ask for the width of our string (when rendered in this font) with Font's getStringBounds() method. This information is used to center the word in the display area. To center the word vertically, we use the height and adjust with the descent to calculate the baseline location. Table 19-2 provides a short list of methods that return useful font metrics.

Table 19-2. LineMetrics methods

Method	Description
getAscent()	Height above baseline
getDescent()	Depth below baseline
getLeading()	Standard vertical spacing between lines
getHeight()	Total line height (ascent + descent + leading)

Leading space is the padding between lines of text. The getHeight() method reports the total height of a line of text, including the leading space.

Displaying Images

So far, we've worked with methods for drawing simple shapes and displaying text. For more complex graphics, we'll be working with images. The 2D API has a powerful set of tools for generating and displaying image data. These tools address the problems of working in a distributed and multithreaded application environment. We'll start with the basics of the java.awt.Image class and see how to get an image into an application and draw it on a display. In general we can let Java handle the details of this for us. In a typical Swing application, the simplest way to get an image onto the screen is to use an ImageIcon with a JLabel. But here we'll be talking about working with image data at a lower level, for painting. In the next chapter, we'll go further to discuss how to manage image loading manually as well as how to create raw image data and feed it efficiently to the rest of an application.

The Image Class

The java.awt.Image class represents a view of an image. The view is created from an image source that produces pixel data. Images can be from a static source, including

GIF, JPEG, or PNG data files, or a dynamic one, such as a video stream or a graphics engine. The Image class in Java 2 also handlesGIF89a animations, so that you can work with simple animations as easily as static images.

Images are created by the getImage() and createImage() methods of the java.awt. Toolkit class. There are two forms of each method, which accept a URL or plain filename, respectively. When packaging images with your application, you should use the Class getResource() method (discussed in Chapter 11) to construct a URL that will references a file from the application classpath. getResource() allows you to bundle images along with your application, inside JAR files or anywhere else in the classpath. The following code fragment shows some examples of loading images with the getImage() method:

```
Toolkit toolkit = Toolkit.getDefaultToolkit( );

// Application resource URL
URL daffyURL = getClass( ).getResource("/cartoons/images/daffy.gif");
Image daffyDuckImage = toolkit.getImage( daffyURL );

// Absolute URL
URL monaURL = new URL( "http://myserver/images/mona_lisa.png");
Image monaImage = toolkit.getImage( monaURL );

// Local file
Image elvisImage = toolkit.getImage("c:/elvis/lateryears/fatelvis1.jpg" );
```

The createImage() method looks just like getImage(); the difference is that getImage() "interns" images and shares them when it receives multiple requests for the same data. The createImage() method does not do this (it creates a new Image object every time) and relies on you to cache and share the image. getImage() is convenient in an application that uses a limited number of images for the life of the application, but it may not ever release the image data. You should use createImage() and cache the Image objects yourself when it's an issue.

Once we have an Image object, we can draw it into a graphics context with the drawImage() method of the Graphics2D class. The simplest form of the drawImage() method takes four parameters: the Image object, the x, y coordinates at which to draw it, and a reference to a special *image observer* object. We'll show an example involving drawImage() soon, but first let's find out about image observers.

Image Observers

Images are processed asynchronously, which means that Java performs image operations such as loading and scaling on its own time (allowing the user code to continue). In a typical client application this might not be important; images may be small, for things like buttons, and are probably bundled with the application for almost instant retrieval. However Java was designed to work with image data over the Web as well as locally, and you will see this expressed in the APIs for working with image data.

For example, the getImage() method always returns immediately, even if the image data has to be retrieved over the network from Mars and isn't available yet. In fact, if it's a new image, Java won't even begin to fetch it until we try to try to display or manipulate it. The advantage of this technique is that Java can do the work of a powerful, multithreaded image-processing environment for us. However, it also introduces several problems. If Java is loading an image for us, how do we know when it's completely loaded? What if we want to work with the image as it arrives? What if we need to know properties of the image (like its dimensions) before we can start working with it? What if there's an error in loading the image?

These problems are handled by *image observers*—designated objects that implement the ImageObserver interface. All operations that draw or examine Image objects return immediately, but they take an image observer object as a parameter. The ImageObserver monitors the image's status and can make that information available to the rest of the application. When image data is loaded from its source by the graphics system, your image observer is notified of its progress, including when new pixels are available, when a complete frame of the image is ready, and if there is an error during loading. The image observer also receives attribute information about the image, such as its dimensions and properties, as soon as they are known.

The drawImage() method, like other image operations, takes a reference to an ImageObserver object as a parameter. drawImage() returns a boolean value specifying whether or not the image was painted in its entirety. If the image data has not yet been loaded or is only partially available, drawImage() paints whatever fraction of the image it can and returns. In the background, the graphics system starts (or continues) loading the image data. The image observer object is registered as interested in information about the image. It's then called repeatedly as more pixel information is available and again when the entire image is complete. The image observer can do whatever it wants with this information. Most often it calls repaint() to prompt the applet to draw the image again with the updated data; a call to repaint() initiates a call to paint() to be scheduled. In this way, an application or applet can redraw the image as it arrives for a progressive loading effect. Alternatively, it could wait until the entire image is loaded before displaying it.

Image observers are covered in Chapter 20. For now, let's avoid the issue by using a prefabricated image observer. The Component class implements the ImageObserver interface and provides some simple repainting behavior, which means every component can serve as its own default image observer. We simply pass a reference to our applet (or other component) as the image observer parameter of a drawImage() call:

```
public void paint( Graphics g ) {
    g.drawImage( monaImage, x, y, this );
    ...
```

Our component serves as the image observer and calls `repaint()` for us to redraw the image as necessary. If the image arrives slowly, our component is notified repeatedly as new chunks become available. As a result, the image appears gradually, as it's loaded. The `awt.image.incrementaldraw` and `awt.image.redrawrate` system properties control this behavior. `redrawrate` limits how often `repaint()` is called; the default value is every 100 milliseconds. `incrementaldraw`'s default value, `true`, enables this behavior. Setting it to `false` delays drawing until the entire image has arrived.

Scaling and Size

Another version of `drawImage()` renders a scaled version of the image:

```
g.drawImage( monaImage, x, y, x2, y2, this );
```

This draws the entire image within the rectangle formed by the points x, y and x2, y2, scaling as necessary. `drawImage()` behaves the same as before; the image is processed by the component as it arrives, and the image observer is notified as more pixel data and the completed image are available. Several other overloaded versions of `drawImage()` provide more complex options: you can scale, crop, and perform some simple transpositions.

Normally, however, for scaling you want to make a scaled copy of an image (as opposed to simply painting one at draw-time), and you can use `getScaledInstance()` for this purpose. Here's how:

```
Image scaledDaffy =
    daffyImage.getScaledInstance(100,200,SCALE_AREA_AVERAGING);
```

This method scales the original image to the given size; in this case, 100 by 200 pixels. It returns a new `Image` that you can draw like any other image. `SCALE_ AREA_ AVERAGING` is a constant that tells `getScaledImage()` what scaling algorithm to use. The algorithm used here tries to do a decent job of scaling at the expense of time. Some alternatives that take less time are `SCALE_REPLICATE`, which scales by replicating scan lines and columns (which is fast but probably not pretty). You can also specify either `SCALE_FAST` or `SCALE_SMOOTH` and let the implementation choose an appropriate algorithm that optimizes for time or quality. If you don't have specific requirements, you should use `SCALE_DEFAULT`, which, ideally, would be set by a preference in the user's environment.

Scaling an image before calling `drawImage()` can improve performance dramatically because the image loading and scaling takes place only once. Otherwise, repeated calls to `drawImage()` with scaling requirements cause the image to be scaled every time, wasting processing time.

The `Image` `getHeight()` and `getWidth()` methods retrieve the dimensions of an image. Since this information may not be available until the image data is completely loaded, both methods also take an `ImageObserver` object as a parameter. If the dimensions aren't yet available, they return values of -1 and notify the observer when the actual value is known. We'll see how to deal with these and other problems a bit later. For now, we'll continue to use our Component as the image observer and move on to some general painting techniques.

Drawing Techniques

Now that we've learned about the basic tools, let's put a few of them together. In this section, we'll look at some techniques for doing fast and flicker-free drawing and painting. If you're interested in animation, this is for you. Drawing operations take time, and time spent drawing leads to delays and imperfect results. Our goals are to minimize the amount of drawing work we do and, as much as possible, to do that work away from the eyes of the user. To do this, we use two techniques: clipping and double buffering. Fortunately, Swing now handles double buffering by default. You won't have to implement this logic on your own, but it's important to understand it.

Our first example, DragImage illustrates some of the issues in updating a display. Like many animations, it has two parts: a constant background and a changing object in the foreground. In this case, the background is a checkerboard pattern, and the object is a small, scaled image we can drag around on top of it, as shown in Figure 19-4.

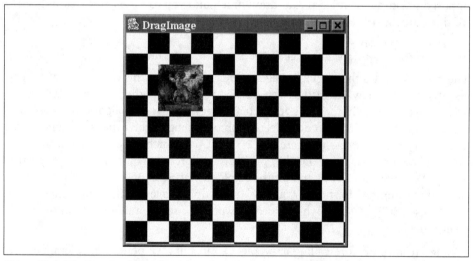

Figure 19-4. The DragImage application

```
import java.awt.*;
import java.awt.event.*;
import javax.swing.*;

public class DragImage extends JComponent
    implements MouseMotionListener
{
```

```java
  static int imageWidth=60, imageHeight=60;
  int grid = 10;
  int imageX, imageY;
  Image image;

  public DragImage(Image i) {
    image = i;
    addMouseMotionListener(this);
  }

  public void mouseDragged(MouseEvent e) {
    imageX = e.getX();
    imageY = e.getY();
    repaint();
  }
  public void mouseMoved(MouseEvent e) {}

  public void paint(Graphics g) {
    Graphics2D g2 = (Graphics2D)g;

    int w = getSize().width / grid;
    int h = getSize().height / grid;
    boolean black = false;
    for (int y = 0; y <= grid; y++)
      for (int x = 0; x <= grid; x++) {
        g2.setPaint(black ? Color.black : Color.white);
        black = !black;
        g2.fillRect(x * w, y * h, w, h);
      }
    g2.drawImage(image, imageX, imageY, this);
  }

  public static void main(String[] args) {
    String imageFile = "L1-Light.jpg";
    if (args.length > 0)
      imageFile = args[0];

    // Turn off double buffering
    //RepaintManager.currentManager(null).setDoubleBufferingEnabled(false);

    Image image = Toolkit.getDefaultToolkit().getImage(
        DragImage.class.getResource(imageFile));
    image = image.getScaledInstance(
        imageWidth,imageHeight,Image.SCALE_DEFAULT);
    JFrame frame = new JFrame("DragImage");
    frame.getContentPane().add( new DragImage(image) );
    frame.setSize(300, 300);
    frame.setDefaultCloseOperation( JFrame.EXIT_ON_CLOSE );
    frame.setVisible(true);
  }
}
```

Run the application by specifying an image file as a command-line argument. Try dragging the image.

DragImage is a custom component that overrides the JComponent paint() method to do its drawing. In the main() method we load the image and prescale it to improve performance. We then create the DragImage component and place it in the content pane. As the mouse is dragged, DragImage keeps track of its position in two instance variables, imageX and imageY. On each call to mouseDragged(), the coordinates are updated, and repaint() is called to ask that the display be updated. When paint() is called, it looks at some parameters, draws the checkerboard pattern to fill the applet's area and finally paints the small version of the image at the latest coordinates.

This example brings up two important differences between using a JComponent and a plain AWT Component. First, the default JComponent update() method simply calls our paint() method. However, prior to Java 1.4, the AWT Component class's default update() method first cleared the screen area using a clearRect() call before calling paint. Recall that the difference between paint() and update() is that paint() draws the entire area; update() assumes the screen region is intact from the last draw. In AWT, update() was overly conservative; in Swing it's more optimistic. This is important to know if you are working with an older AWT-based application. In that case, you can simply override update() to call paint(). The next difference is that Swing by default performs *double buffering*.

Double Buffering

Double buffering means that instead of drawing directly on the screen, Swing first performs drawing operations in an offscreen buffer and then copies the completed work to the display in a single painting operation, as shown in Figure 19-5. It takes the same amount of time to draw a frame, but double buffering instantaneously updates our display when it's ready, so the user does not perceive any flickering or progressively rendered output.

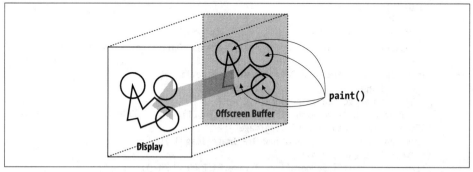

Figure 19-5. Double buffering

We'll show you how you could implement this technique yourself when we use an offscreen buffer later in this chapter. However Swing does this kind of double

---

buffeing for you whenever you use a Swing component in a Swing container. AWT components do not have automatic double-buffering capability.

It is interesting and instructive to take our example and turn off double buffering to see the effect. Each Swing `JComponent` has a method called `setDoubleBuffered()` that can be set to `false` to disable the technique. Or you can disable it for all components using a call to the Swing `RepaintManager`, as we've indicated in comments in the example. Try uncommenting that line of `DragImage` and observe the difference in appearance.

The difference is most dramatic when you are using a slow system or doing complex drawing operations. Double buffering eliminates all of the flickering. However on a slow system, it can decrease performance noticeably, especially on older Unix or X-Windows systems. In some cases it may be beneficial to provide an option to disable double buffering in that environment.

Our example is pretty fast, but we're still doing some wasted drawing. Most of the background stays the same each time it's painted. You might think of trying to make `paint()` smarter, so that it wouldn't redraw these areas but remember that `paint()` has to be able to draw the entire scene because it might be called in situations when the display isn't intact. The solution is to draw only part of the picture whenever the mouse moves. Next we'll talk about clipping.

Limiting Drawing with Clipping

Whenever the mouse is dragged, `DragImage` responds by updating its coordinates and calling `repaint()`. But `repaint()` by default causes the entire component to be redrawn. Most of this drawing is unnecessary. It turns out that there's another version of `repaint()` that lets you specify a rectangular area that should be drawn—in essence, a clipping region.

Why does it help to restrict the drawing area? Well, foremost, drawing operations that fall outside the clipping region are not displayed. If a drawing operation overlaps the clipping region, we see only the part that's inside. A second effect is that, in a good implementation, the graphics context can recognize drawing operations that fall completely outside the clipping region and ignore them altogether. Eliminating unnecessary operations can save time if we're doing something complex, such as filling a bunch of polygons. This doesn't save the time our application spends calling the drawing methods, but the overhead of calling these kinds of drawing methods is usually negligible compared to the time it takes to execute them. (If we were generating an image pixel by pixel, this would not be the case, as the calculations would be the major time sink, not the drawing.)

So we can save some time in our application by redrawing only the affected portion of the display. We can pick the smallest rectangular area that includes both the old image position and the new image position, as shown in Figure 19-6. This is the only portion of the display that really needs to change; everything else stays the same.

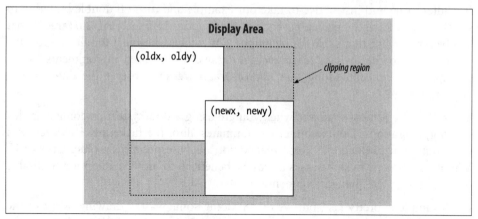

Figure 19-6. Determining the clipping region

A smarter algorithm could save even more time by redrawing only those regions that have changed. However, the simple clipping strategy we've implemented here can be applied to many kinds of drawing and gives good performance, particularly if the area being changed is small.

One important thing to note is that, in addition to looking at the new position, our updating operation now has to remember the last position at which the image was drawn. Let's fix our application so it will use a specified clipping region. To keep this short and emphasize the changes, we'll take some liberties with design and make our next example a subclass of DragImage. Let's call it ClippedDragImage.

```
import java.awt.*;
import java.awt.event.*;
import javax.swing.*;

public class ClippedDragImage extends DragImage {
  int oldX, oldY;

  public ClippedDragImage( Image i ) { super(i); }

  public void mouseDragged(MouseEvent e) {
    imageX = e.getX( );
    imageY = e.getY( );
    Rectangle r = getAffectedArea(
        oldX, oldY, imageX, imageY, imageWidth, imageHeight);
    repaint(r);  // repaint just the affected part of the component
    oldX = imageX;
    oldY = imageY;
  }
```

```
    private Rectangle getAffectedArea(
      int oldx, int oldy, int newx, int newy, int width, int height)
    {
      int x = Math.min(oldx, newx);
      int y = Math.min(oldy, newy);
      int w = (Math.max(oldx, newx) + width) - x;
      int h = (Math.max(oldy, newy) + height) - y;
      return new Rectangle(x, y, w, h);
    }

    public static void main(String[] args) {
      String imageFile = "L1-Light.jpg";
      if (args.length > 0)
        imageFile = args[0];

      // Turn off double buffering
      //RepaintManager.currentManager(null).setDoubleBufferingEnabled(false);

      Image image = Toolkit.getDefaultToolkit( ).getImage(
          ClippedDragImage.class.getResource(imageFile));
      image = image.getScaledInstance(
          imageWidth,imageHeight,Image.SCALE_DEFAULT);
      JFrame frame = new JFrame("ClippedDragImage");
      frame.getContentPane( ).add( new ClippedDragImage(image) );
      frame.setSize(300, 300);
      frame.setDefaultCloseOperation( JFrame.EXIT_ON_CLOSE );
      frame.setVisible(true);
    }
}
```

You may or may not find that ClippedDragImage is significantly faster. Modern desktop computers are so fast that this kind of operation is child's play for them. However the fundamental technique is important and applicable to more sophisticated applications.

So what have we changed? First, we've overridden mouseDragged() so that instead of setting the current coordinates of the image, it figures out the area that has changed. A new, private method helps it do this. getAffectedArea() takes as arguments the new and old coordinates and the width and height of the image. It determines the bounding rectangle as shown in Figure 19-6, then calls repaint() to draw only the affected area of the screen. mouseDragged() also saves the current position by setting the oldX and oldY variables.

Try turning off double buffering on this example and compare it to the unbuffered previous example to see how much less work is being done.

Offscreen Drawing

In addition to serving as buffers for double buffering, offscreen images are useful for saving complex, hard-to-produce, background information. We'll look at a simple example, the doodle pad. DoodlePad is a simple drawing tool that lets us scribble by dragging the mouse, as shown in Figure 19-7. It draws into an offscreen image; its paint() method simply copies the image to the display area.

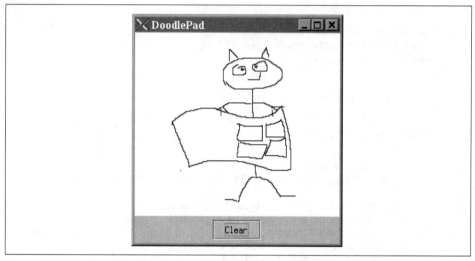

Figure 19-7. The DoodlePad application

```
//file: DoodlePad.java
import java.awt.*;
import java.awt.event.*;
import javax.swing.*;

public class DoodlePad
{
  public static void main(String[] args)
  {
    JFrame frame = new JFrame("DoodlePad");
    Container content = frame.getContentPane( );
    content.setLayout(new BorderLayout( ));
    final DrawPad drawPad = new DrawPad(  );
    content.add(drawPad, BorderLayout.CENTER);
    JPanel panel = new JPanel( );
    JButton clearButton = new JButton("Clear");
    clearButton.addActionListener(new ActionListener(  ) {
      public void actionPerformed(ActionEvent e) {
        drawPad.clear( );
      }
    });
    panel.add(clearButton);
    content.add(panel, BorderLayout.SOUTH);
    frame.setSize(280, 300);
    frame.setDefaultCloseOperation( JFrame.EXIT_ON_CLOSE );
    frame.setVisible(true);
  }
```

```
} // end of class DoodlePad

class DrawPad extends JComponent
{
  Image image;
  Graphics2D graphics2D;
  int currentX, currentY, oldX, oldY;

  public DrawPad( ) {
    setDoubleBuffered(false);
    addMouseListener(new MouseAdapter(  ) {
      public void mousePressed(MouseEvent e) {
        oldX = e.getX( );
        oldY = e.getY( );
      }
    });
    addMouseMotionListener(new MouseMotionListener() {
      public void mouseDragged(MouseEvent e) {
        currentX = e.getX( );
        currentY = e.getY( );
        if (graphics2D != null)
          graphics2D.drawLine(oldX, oldY, currentX, currentY);
        repaint( );
        oldX = currentX;
        oldY = currentY;
      }
    });
  }

  public void paintComponent(Graphics g) {
    if (image == null) {
      image = createImage(getSize( ).width, getSize(  ).height);
      graphics2D = (Graphics2D)image.getGraphics( );
      graphics2D.setRenderingHint(RenderingHints.KEY_ANTIALIASING,
          RenderingHints.VALUE_ANTIALIAS_ON);
      clear( );
    }
    g.drawImage(image, 0, 0, null);
  }

  public void clear(  ) {
    graphics2D.setPaint(Color.white);
    graphics2D.fillRect(0, 0, getSize( ).width, getSize(  ).height);
    graphics2D.setPaint(Color.black);
    repaint( );
  }
}
```

Give it a try. Draw a nice moose or a sunset. We just drew a lovely cartoon of Bill
Gates. If you make a mistake, hit the *Clear* button and start over.

The parts should be familiar by now. We have made a type of JComponent called
DrawPad. The new DrawPad component uses inner classes to supply handlers for the

`MouseListener` and `MouseMotionListener` interfaces. Mouse dragging is handled by drawing lines into an offscreen image and calling `repaint()` to update the display. `DrawPad`'s `paint()` method simply does a `drawImage()` to copy the offscreen drawing area to the display. In this way, `DrawPad` saves our sketch information.

What is unusual about `DrawPad` is that it does some drawing outside of `paint()`. In this example, we want to let the user scribble with the mouse, so we should respond to every mouse movement. Therefore, we do our work, drawing to the offscreen buffer in `mouseDragged()` itself. As a rule, we should be careful about doing heavy work in event-handling methods because we don't want to interfere with other tasks the windowing system's painting thread is performing. In this case, our line-drawing option should not be a burden, and our primary concern is getting as close a coupling as possible between the mouse movement events and the sketch on the screen.

In addition to drawing a line as the user drags the mouse, the `mouseDragged()` handler maintains a set of old coordinates to be used as a starting point for the next line segment. The `mousePressed()` handler resets the old coordinates to the current mouse position whenever the user moves the mouse. Finally, `DrawPad` provides a `clear()` method that clears the offscreen buffer and calls `repaint()` to update the display. The `DoodlePad` application ties the `clear()` method to an appropriately labeled button through another anonymous inner class.

What if we wanted to do something with the image after the user has finished scribbling on it? As we'll see in the next chapter, we could get the pixel data for the image and work with that. It wouldn't be hard to create a save facility that stores the pixel data and reproduces it later. Think about how you might go about creating a networked "bathroom wall," where people could scribble on your web pages.

Printing

Earlier in this chapter, we hinted at the possibility that you could draw the same stuff on the screen and the printer. It's true; all you really need to do is get a `Graphics2D` that represents a printer rather than an area of the screen. Java 2's Printing API provides the necessary plumbing. There isn't room here to describe the whole Printing API, but we will provide you with a short example that will let you get your feet wet (and your paper blackened).

The printing classes are tucked away in the `java.awt.print` package. You can print anything that implements the `Printable` interface. This interface has only one method—you guessed it, `print()`. This method, like the `paint()` methods we've already worked with, accepts a `Graphics` object that represents the drawing surface of the printer's page. It also accepts a `PageFormat` object that encapsulates information about the paper on which you're printing. Finally, `print()` is passed the number of the page that is being rendered.

Your print() implementation should either render the requested page or state that it doesn't exist. You can do this by returning special values from print(), either Printable.PAGE_EXISTS or Printable.NO_SUCH_PAGE.

You can control a print job, including showing print and page setup dialogs, using the PrinterJob class. The following class enables you to get something on paper:

```java
//file: UnbelievablySimplePrint.java
import java.awt.*;
import java.awt.print.*;

public class UnbelievablySimplePrint implements Printable
{
  private static Font sFont = new Font("Serif", Font.PLAIN , 64);

  public int print(Graphics g, PageFormat Pf, int pageIndex)
      throws PrinterException
  {
    if (pageIndex > 0) return NO_SUCH_PAGE;
    Graphics2D g2 = (Graphics2D)g;
    g2.setFont(sFont);
    g2.setPaint(Color.black);
    g2.drawString("Save a tree!", 96, 144);
    return PAGE_EXISTS;
  }

  public static void main(String[] args) {
    PrinterJob job = PrinterJob.getPrinterJob( );
    job.setPrintable(new UnbelievablySimplePrint( ));
    if (job.printDialog( )) {
      try {
        job.print( );
      }
      catch (PrinterException e) {}
    }
    System.exit(0);
  }
}
```

There's not much to this example. We've created an implementation of Printable, called UnbelievablySimplePrint. It has a very simple print() method that draws some text.

The rest of the work, in the main() method, has to do with setting up the print job. First, we create a new PrinterJob and tell it what we want to print:

```java
PrinterJob job = PrinterJob.getPrinterJob( );
job.setPrintable(new UnbelievablySimplePrint( ));
```

Then we use the printDialog() method to show the standard print dialog. If the user presses the *OK* button, printDialog() returns true, and main() goes ahead with the printing.

Notice, in the print() method, how we perform the familiar cast from Graphics to Graphics2D. The full power of the 2D API is available for printing. In a real application, you'd probably have some subclass of Component that was also a Printable. The print() method could simply call the component's paint() method to create a component that performs the same rendering to both the screen and the printer.

Working with Images and Other Media

Up to this point, we've confined ourselves to working with the high-level drawing commands of the Graphics2D class, using images in a hands-off mode. In this section, we'll clear up some of the mystery surrounding images and see how they are created and used. The classes in the java.awt.image package handle images and their internals; Figure 20-1 shows the important classes in this package.

First, we'll return to our discussion of image loading and see how we can get more control over image data using an ImageObserver to watch as it's processed asynchronously by GUI components. Then we'll open the hood and have a look at the inside of a BufferedImage. If you're interested in creating sophisticated graphics, such as rendered images or video streams, this will teach you about the foundations of image construction in Java.

One note before we move on: In early versions of Java (prior to 1.2), creating and modifying images was handled through the use of ImageProducer and ImageConsumer interfaces, which operated on low-level, stream-oriented views of the image data. We won't be covering these topics in this chapter; instead, we'll stick to the new APIs, which are more capable and easier to use in most cases.

ImageObserver

One of the challenges in building software for networked applications is that data is not always instantly available. Since some of Java's roots are in Internet applications such as web browsers, its image-handling APIs were designed specifically to accommodate the fact that images might take some time to load over a slow network, providing for detailed information about image-loading progress. While many typical client applications do not require handling of image data in this way, it's still useful to understand this mechanism if for no other reason than it appears in the most basic image-related APIs. In practice, you'll normally use one of the techniques presented in the next section to handle image loading for you.

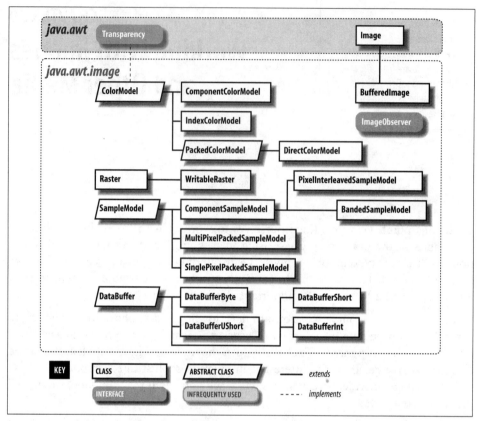

Figure 20-1. The java.awt.image package

In the previous chapter we mentioned that all operations on image data (e.g., loading, drawing, scaling) allow you to specify an "image observer" object as a participant. An image observer implements the ImageObserver interface, allowing it to receive notification as information about the image becomes available. The image observer is essentially a callback that is notified progressively as the image is loaded. For a static image, such as a GIF or JPEG data file, the observer is notified as chunks of image data arrive and also when the entire image is complete. For a video source or animation (e.g., GIF89), the image observer is notified at the end of each frame as the continuous stream of pixel data is generated.

The image observer can do whatever it wants with this information. For example, in the last chapter we used the image observer built into the base Component class. Although you probably didn't see it happen in our examples, the Component image observer invoked repaint() for us each time a new section of the image became available so that the picture, if it had taken a long time to load, would have displayed progressively. A different kind of image observer might have waited for the entire image before telling the application to display it; yet another use for an observer might be to update a loading meter showing how far the image loading had progressed.

To be an image observer, you have to implement the single method, imageUpdate(), defined by the java.awt.image.ImageObserver interface:

```
public boolean imageUpdate(Image image, int flags, int x, int y,
                           int width, int height)
```

imageUpdate() is called by the graphics system, as needed, to pass the observer information about the construction of its view of the image. The image parameter holds a reference to the Image object in question. flags is an integer whose bits specify what information about the image is now available. The flag values are defined as static variables in the ImageObserver interface, as illustrated in this example:

```
//file: ObserveImageLoad.java
import java.awt.*;
import java.awt.image.*;

public class ObserveImageLoad {

  public static void main( String [] args)
  {
   ImageObserver myObserver = new ImageObserver() {
     public boolean imageUpdate(
         Image image, int flags, int x, int y, int width, int height)
       {
         if ( (flags & HEIGHT) !=0 )
           System.out.println("Image height = " + height );
         if ( (flags & WIDTH ) !=0 )
           System.out.println("Image width = " + width );
         if ( (flags & FRAMEBITS) != 0 )
           System.out.println("Another frame finished.");
         if ( (flags & SOMEBITS) != 0 )
            System.out.println("Image section :"
                   + new Rectangle( x, y, width, height ) );
         if ( (flags & ALLBITS) != 0 )
           System.out.println("Image finished!");
         if ( (flags & ABORT) != 0 )
           System.out.println("Image load aborted...");
         return true;
     }
   };

     Toolkit toolkit = Toolkit.getDefaultToolkit( );
     Image img = toolkit.getImage( args[0] );
     toolkit.prepareImage( img, -1, -1, myObserver );
   }
 }
```

Supply an image as the command-line argument and observe the output. You'll see a number of incremental messages about loading the image.

The flags integer determines which of the other parameters, x, y, width, and height, hold valid data and what that data means. To test whether a particular flag in the flags integer is set, we have to resort to some binary shenanigans (using the & (AND) operator). The width and height parameters play a dual role. If SOMEBITS is set, they represent the size of the chunk of the image that has just been delivered. If HEIGHT or WIDTH is set, however, they represent the overall image dimensions. Finally, imageUpdate() returns a boolean value indicating whether or not it's interested in future updates.

In this example, after requesting the Image object with getImage(), we kick-start the loading process with the Toolkit's prepareImage() method, which takes our image observer as an argument. Using an Image API method such as drawImage(), scaleImage(), or asking for image dimensions with getWidth() or getHeight() will suffice to start the operation. Remember that although the getImage() method created the image object, it doesn't begin loading the data until one of the image operations requires it.

The example shows the lowest-level general mechanism for starting and monitoring the process of loading image data. You should be able to see how we could implement all sorts of sophisticated image loading and tracking schemes with this. The two most important strategies (to draw an image progressively, as it's constructed, or to wait until it's complete and draw it in its entirety) are handled for us. We have already seen that the Component class implements the first scheme. Another class, java.awt.MediaTracker, is a general utility that tracks the loading of a number of images or other media types for us. We'll look at it next.

MediaTracker

java.awt.MediaTracker is a utility class simplifies life if we have to wait for one or more images to be loaded completely before they're displayed. A MediaTracker monitors the loading of an image or a group of images and lets us check on them periodically or wait until they are finished. MediaTracker implements the ImageObserver interface that we just discussed, allowing it to receive image updates.

The following code snippet illustrates using a MediaTracker to wait while an image is prepared:

```
//file: StatusImage.java
import java.awt.*;
import javax.swing.*;

public class StatusImage extends JComponent
{
  boolean loaded = false;
  String message = "Loading...";
  Image image;
```

```
public StatusImage( Image image ) { this.image = image; }

public void paint(Graphics g) {
  if (loaded)
      g.drawImage(image, 0, 0, this);
  else {
    g.drawRect(0, 0, getSize().width - 1, getSize(  ).height - 1);
    g.drawString(message, 20, 20);
  }
}
public void loaded( ) {
  loaded = true;
  repaint( );
}
public void setMessage( String msg ) {
  message = msg;
  repaint( );
}

public static void main( String [] args ) {
  JFrame frame = new JFrame("TrackImage");
  Image image = Toolkit.getDefaultToolkit( ).getImage( args[0] );
  StatusImage statusImage = new StatusImage( image );
  frame.getContentPane( ).add( statusImage );
  frame.setSize(300,300);
  frame.setVisible(true);

  MediaTracker tracker = new MediaTracker( statusImage );
  int MAIN_IMAGE = 0;
  tracker.addImage(image, MAIN_IMAGE);
  try {
      tracker.waitForID(MAIN_IMAGE); }
  catch (InterruptedException e) {}
  if ( tracker.isErrorID(MAIN_IMAGE) )
      statusImage.setMessage("Error");
  else
      statusImage.loaded( );
  }
}
```

In this example we have created a trivial component called StatusImage that accepts
an image and draws a text status message until it is told that the image is loaded. It
then displays the image. The only interesting part here is that we use a MediaTracker
to load the image data for us, simplifying our logic.

First, we create a MediaTracker to manage the image. The MediaTracker constructor
takes a Component as an argument; this is supposed to be the component onto which
the image is later drawn. This argument is somewhat of a hold-over from earlier Java
days with AWT. If you don't have the component reference handy, you can simply
substitute a generic component reference like so:

```
Component comp = new Component( );
```

After creating the MediaTracker, we assign it images to manage. Each image is associated with an integer identifier we can use later for checking on its status or to wait for its completion. Multiple images can be associated with the same identifier, letting us manage them as a group. The value of the identifier is also used to prioritize loading when waiting on multiple sets of images; lower IDs have higher priority. In this case, we want to manage only a single image, so we created one identifier called MAIN_IMAGE and passed it as the ID for our image in the call to addImage().

Next, we call the MediaTracker waitforID() routine, which blocks on the image, waiting for it to finish loading. If successful, we tell our example component to use the image and repaint. Another MediaTracker method, waitForAll(), waits for all images to complete, not just a single ID. It is possible to be interrupted here by an InterruptedException. We should also test for errors during image preparation with isErrorID(). In our example, we change the status message if we find one.

The MediaTracker checkID() and checkAll() methods may be used to poll the status of images loading periodically, returning true or false indicating whether loading is finished. The checkAll() method does this for the union of all images being loaded. Additionally, the statusID() and statusAll() methods return a constant indicating the status or final condition of an image load. The value is one of the MediaTracker constant values: LOADING, ABORTED, ERROR, or COMPLETE. For statusAll(), the value is the bitwise OR value of all of the various statuses.

This may seem like a lot of work to go through just to put up a status message while loading a single image. MediaTracker is more valuable when you are working with many raw images that have to be available before you can begin parts of an application. It saves implementing a custom ImageObserver for every application. For general Swing application work, you can use yet another simplification by employing the ImageIcon component to use a MediaTracker; this is covered next.

ImageIcon

In Chapter 16, we discussed Swing components that can work with images using the Icon interface. In particular, the ImageIcon class accepts an image filename or URL and can render it into a component. Internally ImageIcon uses a MediaTracker to fully load the image in the call to its constructor. It can also provide the Image reference back. So, a shortcut to what we did in the last few sections—getting an image loaded fully before using it—would be:

```
ImageIcon icon = new ImageIcon("myimage.jpg");
Image image = icon.getImage();
```

This quirky but useful approach saves a few lines of typing but uses a component in an odd way and is not very clear. ImageIcon also gives you direct access to the MediaTracker it is using through the getMediaTracker() method or tells you the

MediaTracker load status through the `getImageLoadStatus()` method. This returns one of the MediaTracker constants: ABORTED, ERROR, or COMPLETE.

Producing Image Data

There are two approaches to generating image data. The easiest is to treat the image as a drawing surface and use the methods of Graphics2D to render things into the image. The second way is to twiddle the bits that represent the pixels of the image data yourself. This is harder, but it can be useful in specific cases such as loading and saving images in specific formats or mathematically analyzing or creating image data.

Drawing Animations

Let's begin with the simpler approach, rendering on an image through drawing. We'll throw in a twist to make things interesting: we'll build an animation. Each frame will be rendered as we go along. This is very similar to the double buffering we examined in the last chapter, but this time we'll use a timer, instead of mouse events, as the signal to generate new frames.

Swing performs double buffering automatically, so we don't even have to worry about the animation flickering. Although it looks like we're drawing directly to the screen, we're really drawing into an image that Swing uses for double buffering. All we need to do is draw the right thing at the right time.

Let's look at an example, Hypnosis, that illustrates the technique. This example shows a constantly shifting shape that bounces around the inside of a component. When screen savers first came of age, this kind of thing was pretty hot stuff. Hypnosis is shown in Figure 20-2.

Here is its source code:

```
//file: Hypnosis.java
import java.awt.*;
import java.awt.event.*;
import java.awt.geom.GeneralPath;
import javax.swing.*;

public class Hypnosis extends JComponent implements Runnable {
  private int[] coordinates;
  private int[] deltas;
  private Paint paint;

  public Hypnosis(int numberOfSegments) {
    int numberOfCoordinates = numberOfSegments * 4 + 2;
    coordinates = new int[numberOfCoordinates];
    deltas = new int[numberOfCoordinates];
    for (int i = 0 ; i < numberOfCoordinates; i++) {
      coordinates[i] = (int)(Math.random(  ) * 300);
      deltas[i] = (int)(Math.random(  ) * 4 + 3);
```

Figure 20-2. A simple animation

```
      if (deltas[i] > 4) deltas[i] = -(deltas[i] - 3);
    }
    paint = new GradientPaint(0, 0, Color.blue,
        20, 10, Color.red, true);

    Thread t = new Thread(this);
    t.start( );
  }

  public void run( ) {
    try {
      while (true) {
        timeStep( );
        repaint( );
        Thread.sleep(1000 / 24);
      }
    }
    catch (InterruptedException ie) {}
  }

  public void paint(Graphics g) {
    Graphics2D g2 = (Graphics2D)g;
    g2.setRenderingHint(RenderingHints.KEY_ANTIALIASING,
        RenderingHints.VALUE_ANTIALIAS_ON);
    Shape s = createShape( );
    g2.setPaint(paint);
    g2.fill(s);
    g2.setPaint(Color.white);
    g2.draw(s);
  }

  private void timeStep( ) {
```

```
      Dimension d = getSize( );
      if (d.width == 0 || d.height == 0) return;
      for (int i = 0; i < coordinates.length; i++) {
        coordinates[i] += deltas[i];
        int limit = (i % 2 == 0) ? d.width : d.height;
        if (coordinates[i] < 0) {
          coordinates[i] = 0;
          deltas[i] = -deltas[i];
        }
        else if (coordinates[i] > limit) {
          coordinates[i] = limit - 1;
          deltas[i] = -deltas[i];
        }
      }
    }

    private Shape createShape( ) {
      GeneralPath path = new GeneralPath( );
      path.moveTo(coordinates[0], coordinates[1]);
      for (int i = 2; i < coordinates.length; i += 4)
        path.quadTo(coordinates[i], coordinates[i + 1],
            coordinates[i + 2], coordinates[i + 3]);
      path.closePath( );
      return path;
    }

    public static void main(String[] args) {
      JFrame frame = new JFrame("Hypnosis");
      frame.getContentPane( ).add( new Hypnosis(4) );
      frame.setSize(300, 300);
      frame.setDefaultCloseOperation( JFrame.EXIT_ON_CLOSE );
      frame.setVisible(true);
    }
  }
```

The main() method does the usual grunt work of setting up the JFrame that holds our animation component.

The Hypnosis component has a very basic strategy for animation. It holds some number of coordinate pairs in its coordinates member variable. A corresponding array, deltas, holds "delta" amounts that are added to the coordinates each time the figure is supposed to change. To render the complex shape you see in Figure 20-2, Hypnosis creates a special Shape object from the coordinate array each time the component is drawn.

Hypnosis's constructor has two important tasks. First, it fills up the coordinates and deltas arrays with random values. The number of array elements is determined by an argument to the constructor. The constructor's second task is to start up a new thread that drives the animation.

The animation is done in the run() method. This method calls timeStep(), which repaints the component and waits for a short time (details to follow). Each time timeStep() is called, the coordinates array is updated. Then repaint() is called. This results in a call to paint(), which creates a shape from the coordinate array and draws it.

The paint() method is relatively simple. It uses a helper method, called createShape(), to create a shape from the coordinate array. The shape is then filled, using a Paint stored as a member variable. The shape's outline is also drawn in white.

The timeStep() method updates all the elements of the coordinate array by adding the corresponding element of deltas. If any coordinates are now out of the component's bounds, they are adjusted, and the corresponding delta is negated. This produces the effect of bouncing off the sides of the component.

createShape() creates a shape from the coordinate array. It uses the GeneralPathclass, a useful Shape implementation that allows you to build shapes using straight and curved line segments. In this case, we create a shape from a series of quadratic curves, close it to create an area, and fill it.

BufferedImage Anatomy

So far, we've talked about java.awt.Images and how they can be loaded and drawn. What if you really want to get inside the image to examine and update its data? Image doesn't give you access to its data. You'll need to use a more sophisticated kind of image, java.awt.image.BufferedImage. These classes are closely related—BufferedImage, in fact, is a subclass of Image. But BufferedImage gives you all sorts of control over the actual data that makes up the image. BufferedImage provides many capabilities beyond the basic Image class, but because it's a subclass of Image, you can pass still a BufferedImage to any of Graphics2D's methods that accept an Image.

To create an image from raw data arrays, you need to understand exactly how a BufferedImage is put together. The full details can get quite complex—the BufferedImage class was designed to support images in nearly any storage format you could imagine. But for common operations it's not that difficult to use. Figure 20-3 shows the elements of a BufferedImage.

An image is simply a rectangle of colored pixels, which is a simple enough concept. There's a lot of complexity underneath the BufferedImage class, because there are a lot of different ways to represent the colors of pixels. You might have, for instance, an image with RGB data in which each pixel's red, green, and blue values were stored as the elements of byte arrays. Or you might have an RGB image where each pixel was represented by an integer that contained red, green, and blue component values. Or you could have a 16-level grayscale image with 8 pixels stored in each element of an integer array. You get the idea; there are many different ways to store image data, and BufferedImage is designed to support all of them.

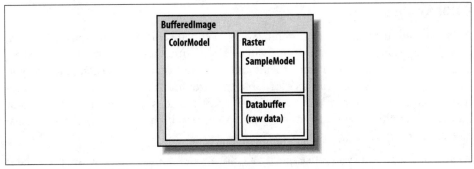

Figure 20-3. Inside a BufferedImage

A `BufferedImage` consists of two pieces, a `Raster` and a `ColorModel`. The `Raster` contains the actual image data. You can think of it as an array of pixel values. It can answer the question, "What are the color data values for the pixel at 51, 17?" The `Raster` for an RGB image would return three values, while a `Raster` for a grayscale image would return a single value. `WritableRaster`, a subclass of `Raster`, also supports modifying pixel data values.

The `ColorModel`'s job is to interpret the image data as colors. The `ColorModel` can translate the data values that come from the `Raster` into `Color` objects. An RGB color model, for example, would know how to interpret three data values as red, green, and blue. A grayscale color model could interpret a single data value as a gray level. Conceptually, at least, this is how an image is displayed on the screen. The graphics system retrieves the data for each pixel of the image from the `Raster`. Then the `ColorModel` tells what color each pixel should be, and the graphics system is able to set the color of each pixel.

The `Raster` itself is made up of two pieces: a `DataBuffer` and a `SampleModel`. A `DataBuffer` is a wrapper for the raw data arrays, which are byte, short, or int arrays. `DataBuffer` has handy subclasses, `DataBufferByte`, `DataBufferShort`, and `DataBufferInt`, that allow you to create a `DataBuffer` from raw data arrays. You'll see an example of this technique later in the `StaticGenerator` example.

The `SampleModel` knows how to extract the data values for a particular pixel from the `DataBuffer`. It knows the layout of the arrays in the `DataBuffer` and is ultimately responsible for answering the question "What are the data values for pixel x, y?" `SampleModels` are a little tricky to work with, but fortunately you'll probably never need to create or use one directly. As we'll see, the `Raster` class has many static ("factory") methods that create preconfigured `Rasters` for you, including their `DataBuffers` and `SampleModels`.

As Figure 20-1 shows, the 2D API comes with various flavors of `ColorModels`, `SampleModels`, and `DataBuffers`. These serve as handy building blocks that cover most common image storage formats. You'll rarely need to subclass any of these classes to create a `BufferedImage`.

Color Models

As we've said, there are many different ways to encode color information: red, green, blue (RGB) values; hue, saturation, value (HSV); hue, lightness, saturation (HLS); and more. In addition, you can provide full-color information for each pixel, or you can just specify an index into a color table (palette) for each pixel. The way you represent a color is called a *color model*. The 2D API provides tools to support any color model you could imagine. Here, we'll just cover two broad groups of color models: *direct* and *indexed*.

As you might expect, you must specify a color model in order to generate pixel data; the abstract class java.awt.image.ColorModel represents a color model. By default, Java 2D uses a direct color model called ARGB. The A stands for "alpha," which is the historical name for transparency. RGB refers to the red, green, and blue color components that are combined to produce a single, composite color. In the default ARGB model, each pixel is represented by a 32-bit integer that is interpreted as four 8-bit fields; in order, the fields represent the alpha (transparency), red, green, and blue components of the color, as shown in Figure 20-4.

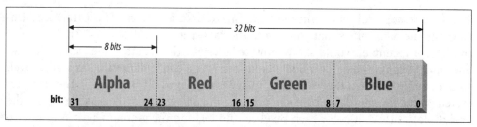

Figure 20-4. ARGB color encoding

To create an instance of the default ARGB model, call the static getRGBdefault() method in ColorModel. This method returns a DirectColorModel object; DirectColorModel is a subclass of ColorModel. You can also create other direct color models by calling a DirectColorModel constructor, but you shouldn't need to unless you have a fairly exotic application.

In an indexed color model, each pixel is represented by a smaller piece of information: an index into a table of real color values. For some applications, generating data with an indexed model may be more convenient. If you have an 8-bit display or smaller, using an indexed model may be more efficient, because your hardware is internally using an indexed color model of some form.

Creating an Image

Let's take a look at producing some image data. A picture is worth a thousand words, and, fortunately, we can generate a picture in significantly fewer than a thousand words of Java. If we just want to render image frames byte by byte, you can put together a BufferedImage pretty easily.

The following application, ColorPan, creates an image from an array of integers holding RGB pixel values:

```java
//file: ColorPan.java
import java.awt.*;
import java.awt.image.*;
import javax.swing.*;

public class ColorPan extends JComponent {
  BufferedImage image;

  public void initialize( ) {
    int width = getSize( ).width;
    int height = getSize( ).height;
    int[] data = new int [width * height];
    int i = 0;
    for (int y = 0; y < height; y++) {
      int red = (y * 255) / (height - 1);
      for (int x = 0; x < width; x++) {
        int green = (x * 255) / (width - 1);
        int blue = 128;
        data[i++] = (red << 16) | (green << 8 ) | blue;
      }
    }
    image = new BufferedImage(width, height,
        BufferedImage.TYPE_INT_RGB);
    image.setRGB(0, 0, width, height, data, 0, width);
  }

  public void paint(Graphics g) {
    if (image == null)
        initialize( );
    g.drawImage(image, 0, 0, this);
  }

  public void setBounds(int x, int y, int width, int height) {
    super.setBounds(x,y,width,height);
    initialize( );
  }

  public static void main(String[] args) {
    JFrame frame = new JFrame("ColorPan");
    frame.getContentPane( ).add(new ColorPan( ));
    frame.setSize(300, 300);
    frame.setDefaultCloseOperation( JFrame.EXIT_ON_CLOSE );
    frame.setVisible(true);
  }
}
```

Give it a try. The size of the image is determined by the size of the application window. You should get a very colorful box that pans from deep blue at the upper-left corner to bright yellow at the bottom right, with green and red at the other extremes.

We create a BufferedImage in the initialize() method and then display the image in paint(). The variable data is a 1D array of integers that holds 32-bit RGB pixel values. In initialize(), we loop over every pixel in the image and assign it an RGB value. The blue component is always 128, half its maximum intensity. The red component varies from 0 to 255 along the y-axis; likewise, the green component varies from 0 to 255 along the x-axis. This statement combines these components into an RGB value:

```
data[i++] = (red << 16) | (green << 8 ) | blue;
```

The bitwise left-shift operator (<<) should be familiar to C programmers. It simply shoves the bits over by the specified number of positions in our 32-bit value.

When we create the BufferedImage, all its data is zeroed out. All we specify in the constructor is the width and height of the image and its type. BufferedImage includes quite a few constants representing image storage types. We've chosen TYPE_INT_RGB here, which indicates we want to store the image as RGB data packed into integers. The constructor takes care of creating an appropriate ColorModel, Raster, SampleModel, and DataBuffer for us. Then we simply use a convenient method, setRGB(), to assign our data to the image. In this way, we've side-stepped the messy innards of BufferedImage. In the next example, we'll take a closer look at the details.

Once we have the image, we can draw it on the display with the familiar drawImage() method. We also override the Component setBounds() method in order to determine when the frame is resized and reinitialize the drawing image to the new size.

Updating a BufferedImage

BufferedImage can also be used to update an image dynamically. Because the image's data arrays are directly accessible, you can simply change the data and redraw the picture whenever you want. This is probably the easiest way to build your own low-level animation software. The following example simulates the static on an old black-and-white television screen. It generates successive frames of random black and white pixels and displays each frame when it is complete. Figure 20-5 shows one frame of random static.

Here's the code:

```
//file: StaticGenerator.java
import java.awt.*;
import java.awt.event.*;
import java.awt.image.*;
import java.util.Random;
import javax.swing.*;
```

Figure 20-5. A frame of random static

```java
public class StaticGenerator extends JComponent implements Runnable {
  byte[] data;
  BufferedImage image;
  Random random;

  public void initialize( ) {
    int w = getSize( ).width, h = getSize( ).height;
    int length = ((w + 7) * h) / 8;
    data = new byte[length];
    DataBuffer db = new DataBufferByte(data, length);
    WritableRaster wr = Raster.createPackedRaster(db, w, h, 1, null);
    ColorModel cm = new IndexColorModel(1, 2,
        new byte[] { (byte)0, (byte)255 },
        new byte[] { (byte)0, (byte)255 },
        new byte[] { (byte)0, (byte)255 });
    image = new BufferedImage(cm, wr, false, null);
    random = new Random( );
  }

  public void run( ) {
    if ( random == null )
        initialize( );
    while (true) {
      random.nextBytes(data);
      repaint( );
      try { Thread.sleep(1000 / 24); }
      catch( InterruptedException e ) { /* die */ }
    }
  }

  public void paint(Graphics g) {
    if (image == null) initialize( );
```

```
        g.drawImage(image, 0, 0, this);
    }

    public void setBounds(int x, int y, int width, int height) {
        super.setBounds(x,y,width,height);
        initialize();
    }

    public static void main(String[] args) {
        //RepaintManager.currentManager(null).setDoubleBufferingEnabled(false);
        JFrame frame = new JFrame("StaticGenerator");
        StaticGenerator staticGen = new StaticGenerator();
        frame.getContentPane().add( staticGen );
        frame.setSize(300, 300);
        frame.setDefaultCloseOperation( JFrame.EXIT_ON_CLOSE );
        frame.setVisible(true);
        new Thread( staticGen ).start();
    }
}
```

The initialize() method sets up the BufferedImage that produces the sequence of images. We build this image from the bottom up, starting with the raw data array. Since we're only displaying two colors here, black and white, we need only one bit per pixel. We want a 0 bit to represent black and a 1 bit to represent white. This calls for an indexed color model, which we'll create a little later.

We'll store our image data as a byte array, where each array element holds eight pixels from our black-and-white image. The array length, then, is calculated by multiplying the width and height of the image and dividing by eight. To keep things simple, we'll arrange for each image row to start on a byte boundary. For example, an image 13 pixels wide actually uses 2 bytes (16 bits) for each row:

```
int length = ((w + 7) * h) / 8;
```

Next, the actual byte array is created. The member variable data holds a reference to this array. Later, we'll use data to change the image data dynamically. Once we have the image data array, it's easy to create a DataBufferfrom it:

```
data = new byte[length];
DataBuffer db = new DataBufferByte(data, length);
```

DataBuffer has several subclasses, such as DataBufferByte, that make it easy to create a data buffer from raw arrays.

The next step, logically, is to create a SampleModel. We could then create a Raster from the SampleModel and the DataBuffer. Lucky for us, though, the Raster class contains a bevy of useful static methods that create common types of Rasters. One of these methods creates a Raster from data that contains multiple pixels packed into array elements. We simply use this method, supplying the data buffer, the width and height, and indicating that each pixel uses one bit:

```
WritableRaster wr = Raster.createPackedRaster(db, w, h, 1, null);
```

The last argument to this method is a java.awt.Point that indicates where the upper-left corner of the Raster should be. By passing null, we use the default of 0, 0.

The last piece of the puzzle is the ColorModel. Each pixel is either 0 or 1, but how should that be interpreted as color? In this case, we use an IndexColorModelwith a very small palette. The palette has only two entries, one each for black and white:

```
ColorModel cm = new IndexColorModel(1, 2,
        new byte[] { (byte)0, (byte)255 },
        new byte[] { (byte)0, (byte)255 },
        new byte[] { (byte)0, (byte)255 });
```

The IndexColorModel constructor that we've used here accepts the number of bits per pixel (one), the number of entries in the palette (two), and three byte arrays that are the red, green, and blue components of the palette colors. Our palette consists of two colors: black (0, 0, 0) and white (255, 255, 255).

Now that we've got all the pieces, we just need to create a BufferedImage. This image is also stored in a member variable so we can draw it later. To create the BufferedImage, we pass the color model and writable raster we just created:

```
image = new BufferedImage(cm, wr, false, null);
```

All the hard work is done now. Our paint() method just draws the image, using drawImage().

The init() method starts a thread that generates the pixel data. The run() method takes care of generating the pixel data. It uses a java.util.Random object to fill the data image byte array with random values. Since the data array is the actual image data for our image, changing the data values changes the appearance of the image. Once we fill the array with random data, a call to repaint() shows the new image on the screen.

To run, try turning off double buffering by uncommenting the line involving the RepaintManager. Now it will look even more like an old TV with flickering and all!

That's about all there is. It's worth noting how simple it is to create this animation. Once we have the BufferedImage, we treat it like any other image. The code that generates the image sequence can be arbitrarily complex. But that complexity never infects the simple task of getting the image on the screen and updating it.

Filtering Image Data

An *image filter* is an object that performs transformations on image data. The Java 2D API supports image filtering through the BufferedImageOp interface. An image filter takes a BufferedImage as input (the *source image*) and performs some processing on the image data, producing another BufferedImage (the *destination image*).

The 2D API comes with a handy toolbox of BufferedImageOp implementations, as summarized in Table 20-1.

Table 20-1. Image operators in the 2D API

Name	Description
AffineTransformOp	Transforms an image geometrically
ColorConvertOp	Converts from one color space to another
ConvolveOp	Performs a convolution, a mathematical operation that can be used to blur, sharpen, or otherwise process an image
LookupOp	Uses one or more lookup tables to process image values
RescaleOp	Uses multiplication to process image values

Let's take a look at two of the simpler image operators. First, try the following application. It loads an image (the first command-line argument is the filename) and processes it in different ways as you select items from the combo box. The application is shown in Figure 20-6.

Figure 20-6. The ImageProcessor application

Here's the source code:

```
//file: ImageProcessor.java
import java.awt.*;
import java.awt.event.*;
import java.awt.geom.*;
import java.awt.image.*;
import javax.swing.*;

public class ImageProcessor extends JComponent {
  private BufferedImage source, destination;
  private JComboBox options;
```

```java
public ImageProcessor( BufferedImage image ) {
    source = destination = image;
    setBackground(Color.white);
    setLayout(new BorderLayout( ));
    // create a panel to hold the combo box
    JPanel controls = new JPanel( );
    // create the combo box with the names of the area operators
    options = new JComboBox(
        new String[] { "[source]", "brighten", "darken", "rotate", "scale" }
    );
    // perform some processing when the selection changes
    options.addItemListener(new ItemListener( ) {
        public void itemStateChanged(ItemEvent ie) {
            // retrieve the selection option from the combo box
            String option = (String)options.getSelectedItem( );
            // process the image according to the selected option
            BufferedImageOp op = null;
            if (option.equals("[source]"))
                destination = source;
            else if (option.equals("brighten"))
                op = new RescaleOp(1.5f, 0, null);
            else if (option.equals("darken"))
                op = new RescaleOp(.5f, 0, null);
            else if (option.equals("rotate"))
                op = new AffineTransformOp(
                    AffineTransform.getRotateInstance(Math.PI / 6), null);
            else if (option.equals("scale"))
                op = new AffineTransformOp(
                    AffineTransform.getScaleInstance(.5, .5), null);
            if (op != null) destination = op.filter(source, null);
            repaint( );
        }
    });
    controls.add(options);
    add(controls, BorderLayout.SOUTH);
}

public void paintComponent(Graphics g) {
    int imageWidth = destination.getWidth( );
    int imageHeight = destination.getHeight( );
    int width = getSize( ).width;
    int height = getSize( ).height;
    g.drawImage(destination,
        (width - imageWidth) / 2, (height - imageHeight) / 2, null);
}

public static void main(String[] args) {
    String filename = args[0];

    ImageIcon icon = new ImageIcon(filename);
    Image i = icon.getImage( );

    // draw the Image into a BufferedImage
    int w = i.getWidth(null), h = i.getHeight(null);
```

```
BufferedImage buffImage = new BufferedImage(w, h,
    BufferedImage.TYPE_INT_RGB);
Graphics2D imageGraphics = buffImage.createGraphics();
imageGraphics.drawImage(i, 0, 0, null);

JFrame frame = new JFrame("ImageProcessor");
frame.getContentPane().add(new ImageProcessor(buffImage));
frame.setSize(buffImage.getWidth(), buffImage.getHeight());
frame.setDefaultCloseOperation( JFrame.EXIT_ON_CLOSE );
frame.setVisible(true);
  }
}
```

There's quite a bit packed into the ImageProcessor application. After you've played around with it, come back and read about the details.

How ImageProcessor Works

The basic operation of ImageProcessor is very straightforward. It loads a source image, specified with a command-line argument, in its main() method. The image is displayed along with a combo box. When you select different items from the combo box, ImageProcessor performs some image-processing operation on the source image and displays the result (the destination image). Most of this work occurs in the ItemListener event handler that is created in ImageProcessor's constructor. Depending on what option is selected, a BufferedImageOp (called op) is instantiated and used to process the source image, like this:

```
destination = op.filter(source, null);
```

The destination image is returned from the filter() method. If we already had a destination image of the right size, we could have passed it as the second argument to filter(), which would improve the performance of the application a bit. If you just pass null, as we have here, an appropriate destination image is created and returned to you. Once the destination image is created, paint()'s job is very simple; it just draws the destination image, centered on the component.

Converting an Image to a BufferedImage

Image processing is performed on BufferedImages, not Images. This example demonstrates an important technique: how to convert an Image to a BufferedImage. The main() method loads an Image from a file using Toolkit's getImage() method:

```
Image i = Toolkit.getDefaultToolkit( ).getImage(filename);
```

Next, main() uses a MediaTracker to make sure the image data is fully loaded.

The trick of converting an Image to a BufferedImage is to draw the Image into the drawing surface of the BufferedImage. Because we know the Image is fully loaded, we just need to create a BufferedImage, get its graphics context, and draw the Image into it:

```
BufferedImage bi = new BufferedImage(w, h,
        BufferedImage.TYPE_INT_RGB);
Graphics2D imageGraphics = bi.createGraphics( );
imageGraphics.drawImage(i, 0, 0, null);
```

Using the RescaleOp Class

Rescaling is an image operation that multiplies all the pixel values in the image by some constant. It doesn't affect the size of the image in any way (in case you thought *rescaling* meant *scaling*), but it does affect the colors of its pixels. In an RGB image, for example, each of the red, green, and blue values for each pixel would be multiplied by the rescaling multiplier. If you want, you can also adjust the results by adding an offset. In the 2D API, rescaling is performed by the java.awt.image.RescaleOp class. To create such an operator, specify the multiplier, offset, and a set of hints that control the quality of the conversion. In this case, we'll use a zero offset and not bother with the hints (by passing null):

```
op = new RescaleOp(1.5f, 0, null);
```

Here we've specified a multiplier of 1.5 and an offset of 0. All values in the destination image will be 1.5 times the values in the source image, which has the net result of making the image brighter. To perform the operation, we call the filter() method from the BufferedImageOp interface.

Using the AffineTransformOp Class

An Affine Transformation is a kind of 2D transformation that preserves parallel lines; this includes operations like scaling, rotating, and shearing. The java.awt.image. AffineTransformOp image operator geometrically transforms a source image to produce the destination image. To create an AffineTransformOp, specify the transformation you want, in the form of an java.awt.geom.AffineTransform. The ImageProcessor application includes two examples of this operator, one for rotation and one for scaling. As before, the AffineTransformOp constructor accepts a set of hints; we'll just pass null to keep things simple:

```
else if (option.equals("rotate"))
  op = new AffineTransformOp(
      AffineTransform.getRotateInstance(Math.PI / 6), null);
else if (option.equals("scale"))
  op = new AffineTransformOp(
      AffineTransform.getScaleInstance(.5, .5), null);
```

In both cases, we obtain an AffineTransform by calling one of its static methods. In the first case, we get a rotational transformation by supplying an angle. This transformation is wrapped in an AffineTransformOp. This operator has the effect of rotating the source image around its origin to create the destination image. In the second case, a scaling transformation is wrapped in an `AffineTransformOp`. The two scaling values, .5 and .5, specify that the image should be reduced to half its original size in both the x and y axes.

One interesting aspect of `AffineTransformOp` is that you may "lose" part of your image when it's transformed. For example, when using the rotate image operator in the `ImageProcessor` application, the destination image will have clipped some of the original image out. Both the source and destination images have the same origin, so if any part of the image gets transformed into negative x or y space, it is lost. To work around this problem, you can structure your transformations such that the entire destination image would be in positive coordinate space.

Simple Audio

Now we'll turn from images and open our ears to audio. The Java Sound API became a core API in Java 1.3. It provides fine-grained support for the creation and manipulation of both sampled audio and MIDI music. There's space here only to scratch the surface by examining how to play simple sampled sound and MIDI music files. With the standard JavaSound support bundled with Java you can play a wide range of file formats including AIFF, AU, Windows WAV, standard MIDI files, and Rich Music Format (RMF) files. We'll discuss other formats (such as MP3) along with video media in the next section.

`java.applet.AudioClip` defines the simplest interface for objects that can play sound. An object that implements `AudioClip` can be told to `play()` its sound data, `stop()` playing the sound, or `loop()` continuously.

The `Applet` class provides a handy static method, `newAudioClip()`, that retrieves sounds from files or over the network. (And there is no reason we can't use it in a nonapplet application.) The method takes an absolute or relative URL to specify where the audio file is located and returns an `AudioClip`. The following application, `NoisyButton`, gives a simple example:

```
//file: NoisyButton.java
import java.applet.*;
import java.awt.*;
import java.awt.event.*;
import javax.swing.*;

public class NoisyButton {

    public static void main(String[] args) throws Exception {
        JFrame frame = new JFrame("NoisyButton");
        java.io.File file = new java.io.File( args[0] );
        final AudioClip sound = Applet.newAudioClip(file.toURL(  ));
```

```
    JButton button = new JButton("Woof!");
    button.addActionListener(new ActionListener(  ) {
      public void actionPerformed(ActionEvent e) { sound.play(  ); }
    });

    Container content = frame.getContentPane( );
    content.setBackground(Color.pink);
    content.setLayout(new GridBagLayout( ));
    content.add(button);
    frame.setVisible(true);
    frame.setSize(200, 200);
    frame.setDefaultCloseOperation( JFrame.EXIT_ON_CLOSE );
    frame.setVisible(true);
  }
}
```

Run NoisyButton, passing the name of the audio file you wish to use as the argument. (We've supplied one called *bark.aiff*.)

NoisyButton retrieves the AudioClip using a File and the toURL()method to reference it as a URL. When the button is pushed, we call the play() method of the AudioClip to start things. After that, it plays to completion unless we call the stop() method to interrupt it.

This interface is simple, but there is a lot of machinery behind the scenes. Next we'll look at the Java Media Framework, which supports wider ranging types of media.

Java Media Framework

Get some popcorn—Java can play movies! To do this though we'll need one of Java's standard extension APIs, the Java Media Framework (JMF). The JMF defines a set of interfaces and classes in the javax.media and javax.media.protocol packages. You can download the latest JMF from *http://java.sun.com/products/java-media/jmf/*. To use the JMF, add *jmf.jar* to your classpath. Or, depending on what version of the JMF you download, a friendly installation program may do this for you.

We'll only scratch the surface of JMF here, by working with an important interface called Player. Specific implementations of Player deal with different media types, like Apple QuickTime (*.mov*) and Windows Video (*.avi*). There are also players for audio types including MP3. Players are handed out by a high-level class in the JMF called Manager. One way to obtain a Player is to specify the URL of a movie:

```
Player player = Manager.createPlayer(url);
```

Because video files are so large and playing them requires significant system resources, Players have a multistep life cycle from the time they're created to the time they actually play something. We'll just look at one step, *realizing*. In this step, the `Player` finds out (by looking at the media file) what system resources it needs to play the media file.

```
player.realize( );
```

The `realize()` method returns right away; it kicks off the realizing process in a separate thread. When the player is finished realizing, it sends out an event. Once you receive this event, you can obtain one of two `Components` from the Player. The first is a visual component that, for visual media types, shows the media. The second is a control component that provides a prefab user interface for controlling the media presentation. The control normally includes start, stop, and pause buttons, along with volume controls and attendant goodies.

The `Player` has to be realized before you ask for these components so that it has important information, like how big the component should be. After that, getting the component is easy. Here's an example:

```
Component c = player.getVisualComponent( );
```

Now we just need to add the component to the screen somewhere. We can play the media right away (although this actually moves the `Player` through several other internal states):

```
player.start( );
```

The following example, `MediaPlayer`, uses the JMF to load and display a movie or audio file from a specified URL:

```java
//file: MediaPlayer.java
import java.awt.*;
import java.net.URL;
import javax.swing.*;
import javax.media.*;

public class MediaPlayer
{
    public static void main( String[] args ) throws Exception {
        final JFrame frame = new JFrame("MediaPlayer");
        frame.setDefaultCloseOperation( JFrame.EXIT_ON_CLOSE );
        URL url = new URL( args[0] );
        final Player player = Manager.createPlayer( url );

        player.addControllerListener( new ControllerListener() {
            public void controllerUpdate( ControllerEvent ce ) {
                if ( ce instanceof RealizeCompleteEvent )
                {
                    Component visual = player.getVisualComponent();
                    Component control = player.getControlPanelComponent( );
                    if ( visual != null )
                        frame.getContentPane().add( visual, "Center" );
                    frame.getContentPane().add( control, "South" );
                    frame.pack( );
                    frame.setVisible( true );
```

```
                player.start( );
            }
        }
    });

    player.realize( );
    }
}
```

This class creates a JFrame that holds the media. Then it creates a Player from the URL specified on the command line and tells the Player to realize(). There's nothing else we can do until the Player is realized, so the rest of the code operates inside a ControllerListener after the RealizeCompleteEvent is received.

In the event handler, we get the Player's visual and controller components and add them to the JFrame. We then display the JFrame and, finally, we play the movie. It's very simple!

To use the MediaPlayer, pass it the URL of a movie or audio file on the command line. Here are a couple of examples:

```
% java MediaPlayer file:dancing_baby.avi
% java MediaPlayer http://myserver/mp3s/TheCure/KissMe/catch.mp3
```

Figure 20-7 shows the "dancing baby" AVI running in the MediaPlayer. Feel free to dance along, if you want.

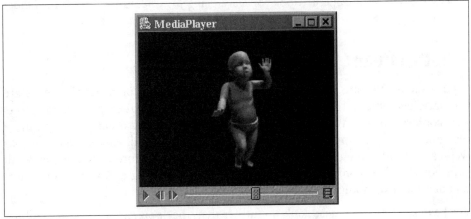

Figure 20-7. Image of the dancing baby AVI

CHAPTER 21

JavaBeans

JavaBeans is a component architecture for Java. It is a set of rules for writing highly reusable software elements that can be linked together in a plug-and-play fashion to build applications. Writing objects to the JavaBeans specification means you won't have to write as much custom code to glue them together. It also allows you to leverage JavaBean-aware development tools. With some integrated development environments (IDEs), it is even possible to build large parts of applications just by connecting prefabricated JavaBeans.

JavaBeans is a rich topic, but we can't give it more than a brief overview here. If this overview whets your appetite, look for *Developing Java Beans* by Robert Englander (O'Reilly).

What's a Bean?

What exactly is or are JavaBeans? JavaBeans defines a set of rules; JavaBeans are ordinary Java objects that play by these rules. That is, JavaBeans are Java objects that conform to the JavaBeans API and design patterns. By doing so, they can be recognized and manipulated within visual application builder environments, as well as by hand coding. Beans live and work in the Java runtime system, as do all Java objects. They communicate with their neighbors using events and other normal method invocations.

For Bean examples, we need look no further than the javax.swing packages. All the familiar components, such as JButton, JTextArea, JScrollpane, etc., are not only suitable for Beans, but are also, in fact, Beans! Much of what you learned in Chapter 15 about the Swing components has prepared you for understanding Beans. Although most of the Swing components aren't very useful in isolation, in general Beans can also be large and complex application components, such as spreadsheets or document editors. The HotJavaBrowser Bean, for example, is a complete web browser cast in the form of a JavaBean. We'll talk more about exactly what makes a Bean a Bean in a moment. For now, we want to give you a better sense of how they are used.

JavaBeans are intended to be manipulated visually within a graphical application builder. They are generally chosen from a palette of tools and manipulated graphically in an application builder's workspace. In this sense, Beans resemble widgets used in a traditional GUI builder: user interface components that can be assembled to make application "screens." In traditional GUI builders, the result is usually just some automatically generated code that provides a skeleton on which you hang the meat of your application. GUI builders generally build GUIs, not entire applications.

In contrast, JavaBeans can be not only simple UI components such as buttons and sliders, but also more complex and abstract components. It is easy to get the impression that Beans are, themselves, always graphical objects (like the Swing components that we mentioned), but JavaBeans can implement any part of an application, including "invisible" parts that perform calculations, storage, and communications. Ideally, we would like to snap together a substantial application using prefabricated Beans, without ever writing a line of code! Three characteristics of the JavaBeans architecture make it possible to work with application components at this level:

Design patterns

The most important characteristic of a JavaBean is simply a layer of standardization. Design patterns (i.e., coding conventions) let tools and humans recognize the basic features of a Bean and manipulate it without knowing how it is implemented. We might say that Beans are "self-documenting." By examining a Bean, we can tell what events it can fire and receive; we can also learn about its properties (the equivalent of its public variables) and methods. Beans can also provide explicit information about their features tailored specifically for IDEs.

Reflection

Reflection is an important feature of the Java language. (It's discussed in Chapter 7.) Reflection makes it possible for Java code to inspect and manipulate new Java objects at runtime. In the context of JavaBeans, reflection lets a development tool analyze a Bean's capabilities, examine the values of its fields, and invoke its methods. Essentially, reflection allows Java objects that meet at runtime to do all the things that could be done if the objects had been put together at compile time. Even if a Bean doesn't come bundled with any "built-in" documentation, we can still gather information about its capabilities and properties by directly inspecting the class using reflection.

Object serialization

Finally, the Java Serialization API allows us to "freeze-dry" (some prefer the word "pickle") a live application or application component and revive it later. This is a very important step; it makes it possible to piece together applications without extensive code generation. Rather than customizing and compiling large amounts of Java code to build our application on startup, we can simply paste together Beans, configure them, tweak their appearance, and then save them. Later, the Beans can be restored with all their state and interconnections intact. This makes possible a fundamentally different way of thinking about the design process. It is easy to use serialized objects from handwritten Java code, as well, so we can freely mix "freeze-dried" Beans with plain old Bean classes and other Java code. In Java 1.4, a new "long-term" object serialization mechanism was added that saves JavaBeans in an XML format that is very resilient to changes in classes.

How Big Is a Bean?

Our Bean examples have ranged from simple buttons to spreadsheets. Obviously, a button Bean would be much less complex than a spreadsheet and would be used at a different level of the application's design. At what level are Beans intended to be used? The JavaBeans architecture is supposed to scale well from small to large; simple Beans can be used to build larger Beans. A small Bean may consist of a single class; a large Bean may have many. Beans can also work together through their container to provide services to other Beans.

Simple Beans are little more than ordinary Java objects. In fact, any Java class that has a default (empty) constructor could be considered a Bean. A Bean should also be serializable, although the JavaBeans specification doesn't strictly require that. These two criteria ensure that we can create an instance of the Bean dynamically and that we can later save the Bean, as part of a group or composition of Beans. There are no other requirements. Beans are not required to inherit from a base Bean class, and they don't have to implement any special interface.

A useful Bean would want to send and receive events and expose its properties to the world. To do so, it follows the appropriate design patterns for naming the relevant methods so that these features can be automatically discovered. Most nontrivial Beans intended for use in an IDE also provide information about themselves in the form of a `BeanInfo` class. A `BeanInfo` class implements the `BeanInfo` interface, which holds methods that describe a Bean's features in more detail, along with extra packaging, such as icons for display to the user. Normally, this "Bean info" is supplied by a separate class that is named for and supplied with the Bean.

The NetBeans IDE

We can't have a meaningful discussion of Beans without spending a little time talking about the builder environments in which they are used. In this book, we use the NetBeans IDE to demonstrate our Beans. NetBeans is a popular, pure Java development environment for Java. In this case, the "integrated" in "integrated development environment" means that NetBeans offers powerful source-editor capabilities, templates that aid in the creation of various types of Java classes; and the ability to compile, run, and debug applications, all in one tool.

NetBeans is an open source project* with a modular architecture that allows it to be easily extended with new capabilities. For example, there are XML modules that assist you in creating and editing XML documents, as well as web modules that allow the IDE to edit documents and even act as a web server for testing. NetBeans even comes with a version of BeanShell, the Java scripting language created by one of the authors of this book! (See Appendix B.)

Because NetBeans is a full-blown production development environment, it has many features we don't use in these examples. For that reason, we can't really provide a full introduction to NetBeans in this book. We will provide only bare-bones directions here for demonstrating the JavaBeans in this chapter. But we hope that once you get into the tool and start looking around, you will want to learn more.

Some examples of other Java development environments that support JavaBeans are:

- IBM's Visual Age for Java (*http://www7.software.ibm.com/vad.nsf/Data/Document4600*)
- Borland/Inprise's JBuilder (*http://www.inprise.com/jbuilder*)
- Metrowerks's CodeWarrior (*http://www.metrowerks.com*)

Installing and Running NetBeans

You have to install the Java 1.4 SDK before you can install NetBeans. Both the SDK (Version 1.4.0) and NetBeans itself (Version 3.3.1) are included on the CD-ROM that accompanies this book. They can also be downloaded from *http://java.sun.com/j2se/* and *http://www.netbeans.org*, respectively. Follow the simple installation instructions for those packages (you may have to reboot if you installed Java) and then launch NetBeans.

The first time it runs, NetBeans asks you to specify a default directory for your project files and whether you prefer multiple smaller windows or the single-window (full-screen) mode. We chose full-screen mode, as you will see in the examples, starting with Figure 21-1. NetBeans also asks if you want to associate Java files with it. If you answer yes, you can launch NetBeans by double-clicking on a Java file (at least in Windows).

When you first start NetBeans, a welcome screen appears. Close it. Figure 21-1 shows the NetBeans application. The tab selected at the top is *GUI Editing*. This is where we'll be doing most of our work. The left side of the workspace is a file browser called Explorer, and the center is the GUI editor, showing one of our examples. Key parts of the GUI editor are the top "palettes" of Beans, the central layout

---

* Sun has its own, commercial version of NetBeans called Forte for Java. Forte is largely the same as NetBeans but includes additional tools for enterprise development.

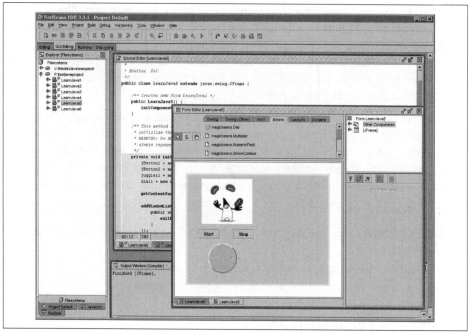

Figure 21-1. NetBeans

area, and the properties editor or "customizer" on the right side. The properties editor changes its contents based on the current Bean selected in the work area.

NetBeans includes all the standard Swing components and provides a few more Beans of its own. Before we get started, we'll have to add the example Beans used in this chapter to the NetBeans palette as well. To do this, grab our demo Beans JAR file, *magicbeans.jar,* from the accompanying CD-ROM or from *http://www.oreilly. com/catalog/learnjava2/.* Save the file locally and then select *Install New JavaBean* from the *Tools* menu to add the beans. The wizard asks you to locate the JAR file and then shows you a list of Beans that it contains. Select all of them (shift-click on the first and last), then click *ok.* NetBeans prompts you for the *Palette Category* under which you wish to file these; select *Beans.* We'll see these Beans soon, when we start editing an application.

Now we must open a new Java class file to begin editing. First, select in the Explorer the folder where you'd like the new class file to be stored so that NetBeans will store it there for you. Now click on the "new file" icon on the far left of the toolbar or select *New...* from the *File* menu. NetBeans prompts you with a wizard for setting up the type of file you wish to create. Expand the folder labeled *GUI Forms,* and select *JFrame.* This gives us a Java class file extending JFrame with the basic structure of a GUI application already set up for us. Click *Next,* then give the file a name, such as *LearnJava1,* and choose a location for the file. You may leave the package set to the default package if you wish. Now click *Finish.*

NetBeans should now open two windows, as in Figure 21-2: the *Source Editor*, showing the LearnJava1 class it has started for us, and the *Form Editor* window. Select the *Swing* tab at the top of the *Form Editor* to see some of the Swing components available as Beans (they are shown as icons at the top of the window). Now select the *Beans* tab to see the Beans we imported earlier. You should see the friendly *Dial* component Bean from Chapter 17, along with a waving Duke (the Java mascot) and a small clock icon. The rest of our Beans have no pretty icons and can't easily be distinguished. That's because these simple example Beans aren't packaged as completely as the others. (We'll talk about packaging later in the chapter.) For now, right-click on one of the Beans, and select the *Show Names* option to display the class names of all the Beans in the palette. (You'll want to resize the border so you can see all the Beans).

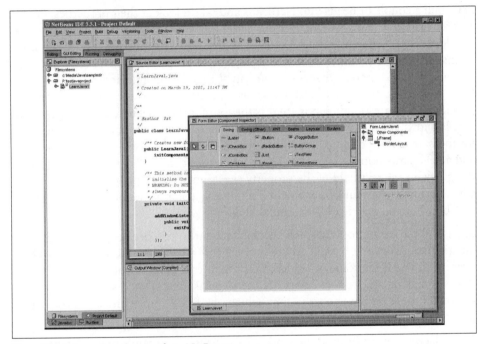

Figure 21-2. LearnJava1 example in NetBeans

To place a Bean into the workspace, simply click on it and then click in the workspace. The top right of the *Form Editor* holds a tree that shows all the components (visible and invisible) in the project. By right-clicking on the JFrame (our top-level container) in either the workspace or the tree, you can select the *Set Layout* option to specify the layout manager for the frame. For now, try using the *AbsoluteLayout*, provided by NetBeans. This allows you to arbitrarily place and move Beans within the container.

Properties and Customizers

Properties represent the "state" or "data" content of a Bean. They are features that can be manipulated externally to configure the Bean. For a Bean that's a GUI component, you might expect its properties to include its size, color, and other features of its basic appearance. Properties are similar in concept to an object's public variables. Like a variable, a property can be a primitive type (such as a number or boolean), or it can be a complex object type (such as a String or a collection of spreadsheet data). Unlike variables, properties are always manipulated using methods; this enables a Bean to take action whenever a property changes. By sending an event when a property changes, a Bean can notify other interested Beans of the change (see "Binding Properties," later in this chapter).

Let's pull a couple of Beans into NetBeans and take a look at their properties. Grab a JButton from the Swing palette, and place it in the workspace. When the JButton was first loaded by NetBeans, it was inspected to discover its properties. When we select an instance of the button, NetBeans displays these properties in the properties sheet and allows us to modify them. As you can see in the figure, the button has seven basic properties. foreground and background are colors; their current values are displayed in the corresponding box. font is the font for the label text; an example of the font is shown. text is the text of the button's label. You can also set an image icon for the button, the "tool tip" text that appears when the mouse hovers over the item, and a keyboard-shortcut identifier, called a *mnemonic* in NetBeans. Try typing something new in the text field of the property sheet, and watch the button label change. Click on the background color to enter a numeric color value, or, better yet, hit the "..." button to pop up a color-chooser dialog.

Most of these basic properties will become familiar to you because many GUI Beans inherit them from the base JComponent class. If you click on the tab labeled *Other Properties*, you'll see some 40 additional properties inherited from JComponent. NetBeans is making an effort to categorize these for us. But as we'll see when we create our own Beans, we can choose to limit which of a Bean's properties are shown in the properties editor.

Now place a Juggler Bean in the workspace (this is one of Sun's original demonstration JavaBeans that we have updated). The animation starts, and Duke begins juggling his coffee Beans, as shown in Figure 21-3. If he gets annoying, don't worry, we'll have him under our control soon enough.

You can see that this Bean has a different set of properties. The most interesting is the one called animationRate. It is an integer property that controls the interval in milliseconds between displays of the juggler's frames. Try changing its value. The juggler changes speed as you type each value. Good Beans give you immediate feedback on changes to their properties. Set the juggling property to *False* to stop the show.

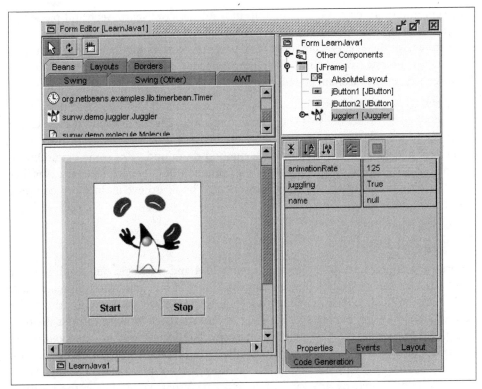

Figure 21-3. Juggling Beans

Notice that the property sheet provides a way to display and edit each of the different property types. For the foreground and background properties of the JButton, the sheet displays the color; if you click on them, a color selection dialog pops up. Similarly, if you click on the font property, you get a font dialog. For integer and string values, you can type a new value into the field. NetBeans understands and can edit the most useful basic Java types.

Since the property types are open-ended, NetBeans can't possibly anticipate them all. Beans with more complex property types can supply a *property editor*. The Molecule Bean that we'll play with in the next section, for example, uses a custom property editor that lets us choose the type of molecule. If it needs even more control over how its properties are displayed, a Bean can provide a *customizer*. A customizer allows a Bean to provide its own GUI for editing its properties.

Event Hookups and Adapters

Beans use events to communicate. As we mentioned in Chapter 15, events are not limited to GUI components but can be used for signaling and passing information in more general applications. An event is simply a notification; information describing the event and other data are wrapped up in a subclass of EventObject and passed to the receiving object by a method invocation. Event sources register listeners who want to receive the events when they occur. Event receivers implement the appropriate listener interface containing the method needed to receive the events. This is Java's general event mechanism in a nutshell.

It's useful to place an adapter between an event source and a listener. An adapter can be used when an object doesn't know how to receive a particular event; it enables the object to handle the event anyway. The adapter can translate the event into some other action, such as a call to a different method or an update of some data. One of the jobs of NetBeans is to help us hook up event sources to event listeners. Another job is to produce adapter code that allows us to hook up events in more complex ways.

Taming the Juggler

Before we get into details, let's look at Figure 21-4 and try to get our Juggler under control. Using the properties sheet, change the label of our first button to read *Start*. Now click the small *Connection Wizard* icon at the top of the GUI builder (this is the second icon, showing two arrows pointing at one another). Now select first the button and then the Juggler by clicking on them. NetBeans pops up the *Connection Wizard*, indicating the source component (the button) and prompting you to choose from a large list of events (see Figure 21-4). Most of these are standard Swing events that can be generated by any kind of JComponent. What we're after is the button's action event. Expand the folder named *action*, and select *actionPerformed* as the target method. Choose *Next* to go to the target component screen for the Juggler. The wizard prompts us to choose a property to set on the Juggler as in Figure 21-5. The display shows three of the Juggler's properties. Choose *juggling* as the target and click *Next*. Now enter **true** in the *value* box and click *Finish*. We have completed a hookup between the button and the Juggler. When the button fires an action event, the "juggling" property of the Juggler is set to true.

If you take a look at the *Source Editor* window, you can see that NetBeans has generated some code to make this connection for us. Specifically, in the initComponents() method of our template class, it has created an anonymous inner class to serve as the ActionListener for ActionEvents from our button (which it has named jButton1):

```
jButton1.addActionListener(new java.awt.event.ActionListener() {
    public void actionPerformed(java.awt.event.ActionEvent evt) {
        jButton1ActionPerformed(evt);
    }
});
```

The adapter calls a private method that sets the property on our Juggler:

```
private void jButton1ActionPerformed(java.awt.event.ActionEvent evt) {
    juggler1.setJuggling(true);
}
```

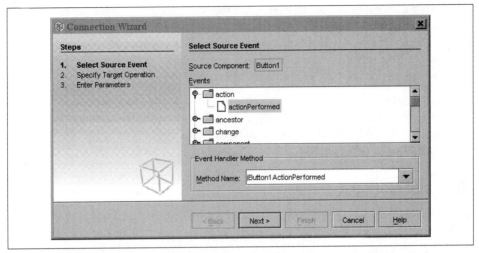

Figure 21-4. Selecting a source event in the Connection Wizard

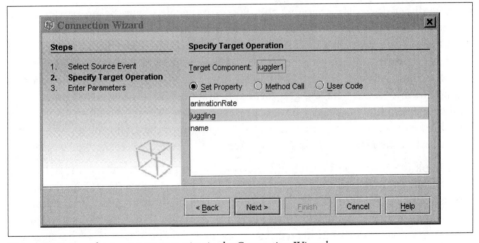

Figure 21-5. Specifying a target operation in the Connection Wizard

You'll notice that most of the text that was written for us is shaded light blue. This is to indicate that it is autogenerated and can't be directly modified. The body of the private method is open, however, and we could modify it to perform arbitrary activities when the button is pushed. In NetBeans the hookup is just a starting point.

This may all seem a little obtuse. After all, if we had made the Juggler an ActionListener in the first place, we would expect to hook it directly to the button. The use of adapters provides a great deal of flexibility, however, as we'll see next.

To complete our example, repeat the process and add a second JButton labeled *Stop*. Click the *Connection Wizard* icon; select the *Stop* button and the Juggler as its target. Again, choose the actionPerformed method as the source, but this time, instead of selecting a property on the Juggler, click the *Method call* radio button to see a list of available methods on the Juggler Bean. Scroll all the way down and select the stopJuggling() method. Click *Finish* to complete the hookup, and look at the generated code if you wish. Now we have seen an example of hooking up a source of action events to produce an arbitrary method call on a Bean.

Now the Juggler will do our bidding. Hit the green arrow "run" icon and watch as NetBeans compiles and runs our example. You should be able to start and stop Duke with the buttons! When you are done, close the window, and return to the GUI editor. Save and close this example, and let's move on.

Molecular Motion

Let's look at one more interesting example, shown in Figure 21-6. Create a new project class as before, choosing the JFrame template. Call this one LearnJava2.

Grab a Molecule Bean and place it in the workspace. If you run the example now, you will see that by dragging the mouse within the image, you can rotate the model in three dimensions. Try changing the type of molecule using the properties sheet: ethane is fun.* Now let's see what we can do with our molecule. Grab a Timer Bean from the palette. Timer is a clock. Every so many seconds, Timer fires an event. The timer is controlled by an integer property called delay, which determines the number of seconds between events. Timer is an "invisible" Bean; it is not derived from a JComponent and doesn't have a graphical appearance, just as an internal timer in an application wouldn't normally have a presence on the screen. NetBeans represents invisible Beans in the component tree at the top right of the GUI builder. When you wish to select the Timer, click on it in the tree.

Let's hook the Timer to our Molecule. Activate the connection wizard and select the Timer (from the tree) and then the Molecule. Choose the Timer onTime() method from the list. Click *Next* and select the *Method call* radio button. Find and select the rotateOnX() method and click *Finish*. Run the example. Now the Molecule should turn on its own every time it receives an event from the timer. Try changing the timer's interval. You can also hook the Timer to the Molecule's rotateOnY() method, Use a different instance of TickTock and, by setting different intervals, make it turn at different rates in each dimension. There's no end to the fun.

---

* As of this writing, Sun's Molecule example has some problems when used in NetBeans. Selecting a molecule type other than the default causes a compile-time error. You can use the *Test Form* button on the NetBeans form editor to try the other molecule types.

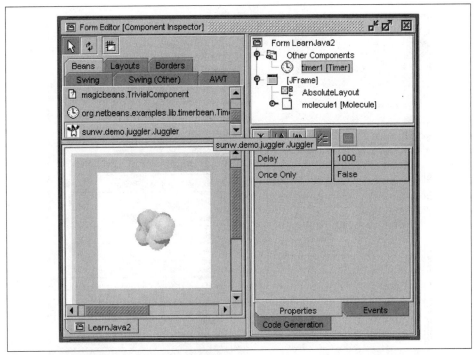

Figure 21-6. The Molecule Bean and the Timer

Binding Properties

By using a combination of events and adapters, we can connect Beans in many interesting ways. We can even "bind" two Beans together so that if a property changes in the first Bean, the corresponding property is automatically changed in the second Bean. In this scenario, the Beans don't necessarily have to be of the same type, but to make sense, the properties do.

Close the Molecule project and start a new one. Grab two NumericField Beans from the palette, drop them in NetBeans, and select one of them, as shown in Figure 21-7. You'll notice that a NumericField has many of the standard properties of a Swing component. If you select the *Other Properties* tab, you can also find an integer property called value. This is the value of the field. You can set it or enter a number directly into the field. NumericField rejects nonnumeric text.

Now let's bind the value property of the fields. Activate the connection wizard and choose the propertyChange() method. This is the listener method for PropertyChangeEvent, a generic event sent by Beans when one of their properties changes. When a Bean fires property-change events in response to changes in a particular property, that property is said to be "bound." This means that it is possible to

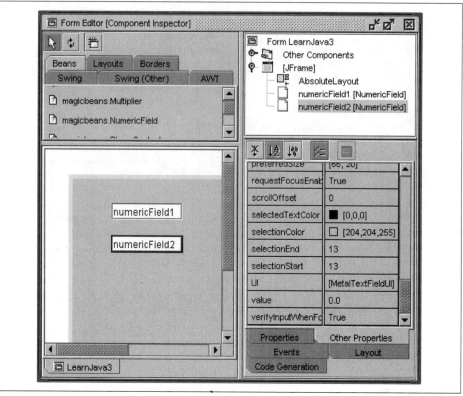

Figure 21-7. Binding properties

bind the property to another Bean through the generic mechanism. In this case, the value of our NumericField Beans is a bound property.

Choose *Next*, and select the value property as the target on the other NumericField. Click *Next* again, and select *Property* on the *Parameters* screen. Click the "..." editor button to pop up a *Select Property* dialog. Select the source numeric field (probably named numericField1) from the pulldown menu, and then choose the value property. Click *Ok* and *Finish* to complete the hookup.

Run the application, and try entering values in the first field. The second field should change each time. The second Bean's value property has been bound to the first.

Try binding the value property in the other direction as well so that you can change the value in either Bean, and the changes are propagated in both directions. (Some simple logic in the Beans prevents infinite loops from happening here.)

NetBeans has again generated an adapter for us. This time the adapter listens for PropertyChangeEvents and invokes the setValue() method of our target field. Note that we haven't done anything earth-shaking. The PropertyChangeEvent does carry some extra information—the old and new values of the property—but we're not using them here. And with the connection wizard, you can use any event source as the impetus to set a property on your target Bean. Finally, as we've seen, the property can derive its value from any other Bean in the layout. The flexibility of the connection wizard is, to some extent, masking the purpose of the events, but that's okay. If we are interested in the specific property that changed, or if we want to apply logic about the value, we can fill in the generated method with our own code.

Constraining properties

In the previous section, we discussed how Beans fire `PropertyChangeEvents` to notify other Beans (and adapters) that a property has changed. In that scenario, the object that receives the event is simply a passive listener, as far as the event's source is concerned. JavaBeans also supports *constrained properties*, in which the event listener gets to say whether it will allow a Bean to change the property's value. If the new value is rejected, the change is cancelled; the event source keeps its old value.

The concept of constrained properties has not been heavily used in the normal operation of Swing, so we won't cover it in detail here. But it goes something like this. Normally, `PropertyChangeEvents` are delivered to a `propertyChange()` method in the listener. Constrained properties are implemented by delivering `PropertyChangeEvents` to a separate listener method called `vetoableChange()`. The `vetoableChange()` method throws a `PropertyVetoException` if it doesn't like a proposed change. In this way, components can govern the acceptable values of other components.

Building Beans

Now that you have a feel for how Beans look from the user's perspective, let's build some. In this section, we will become the Magic Beans Company. We will create some Beans, package them for distribution, and use them in NetBeans to build a very simple application. (The complete JAR file, along with all the example code for this chapter, is on the CD-ROM that accompanies this book, and at *http://www.oreilly. com/catalog/learnjava2.*)

The first thing we'll remind you of is that absolutely anything can be a Bean. Even the following class is a Bean, albeit an invisible one:

```
public class Trivial implements java.io.Serializable {}
```

Of course, this Bean isn't very useful: it doesn't have any properties, and it doesn't do anything. But it's a Bean nonetheless, and we can drag it into NetBeans as long as we package it correctly. If we modify this class to extend JComponent, we suddenly have a graphical Bean that be seen in the layout, with lots of standard Swing properties, such as size and color information:

```
public class TrivialComponent extends JComponent {}
```

Next let's look at a Bean that's a bit more useful.

The Dial Bean

We created a nifty Dial component in Chapter 17. What would it take to turn it into a Bean? Well, surprise: it is already a Bean! The Dial has a number of properties that it exposes in the way prescribed by JavaBeans. A get method retrieves the value of a property; for example, getValue() retrieves the dial's current value. Likewise, a set method (setValue()) modifies the dial's value. The dial has two other properties, which also have get and set methods: minimum and maximum. This is all the Dial needs to inform a tool such as NetBeans what properties it has and how to work with them. Because Dial is a JComponent, it also has all the standard Swing properties, such as color and size. The JComponent provides the set and get methods for all its properties.

In order to use our Dial, we'll put it in a Java package named magicBeans and store it in a JAR file that can be loaded by NetBeans. The source code, which can be found on the accompanying CD-ROM, includes an Ant build file (see "Building WAR Files with Ant" in Chapter 14) that compiles the code and creates the final JAR file.

First, create a directory called *magicBeans* to hold our Beans, add a package statement to the source files *Dial.java*, *DialEvent.java*, and *DialListener.java*, put the source files into the *magicBeans* directory, and compile them (javac magicBeans/Dial.java) to create class files. Next, we need to create a manifest file that tells Net-Beans which of the classes in the JAR file are Beans and which are support files or unrelated. At this point, we have only one Bean, *Dial.class*, so create the following file, called *magicBeans.manifest*:

```
Name: magicbeans/Dial.class
Java-Bean: True
```

The Name: label identifies the class file as it will appear in the JAR: magicbeans/Dial.class. Specifications appearing after an item's Name: line and before an empty line apply to that item. (See "Java Archive (JAR) Files" in Chapter 3 for more details.) We have added the attribute Java-Bean: True, which flags this class as a Bean to tools that read the manifest. We will add an entry like this for each Bean in our package. We don't need to flag support classes (such as DialEvent and DialListener) as Beans, because we won't want to manipulate them directly with NetBeans; in fact, we don't need to mention them in the manifest at all.

To create the JAR file, including our manifest information, enter this command:

```
% jar cvmf magicbeans.manifest magicbeans.jar magicbeans/*.class
```

If you loaded the precompiled examples as instructed earlier, then you already have the Dial Bean loaded into NetBeans. The version supplied in the precompiled *magicbeans.jar* file has additional packaging that allows it to appear with a spiffy icon in the palette, as we'll discuss a bit later. If you haven't loaded the example JAR, you can import the one we just created using the *Import JavaBean* wizard on the Net-Beans *Tools* menu, as we described earlier. If you want to replace the Dial Bean on your palette, you can remove it by right-clicking on the icon and selecting the *Delete* option before importing the new JAR. Note that you may have to restart NetBeans in order for it to recognize that a Bean has changed.

You should now have an entry for Dial in the Bean palette. Drop an instance of the Dial Bean into NetBeans.

As Figure 21-8 shows, the Dial's properties—*value, minimum,* and *maximum*—are on the properties sheet and can be modified by NetBeans. If you created the previous Dial JAR, you'll see these properties along with all the Swing properties inherited from the JComponent class. The figure shows the Dial Bean as it appears later in this chapter, after we've learned about the BeanInfo class. We're almost there.

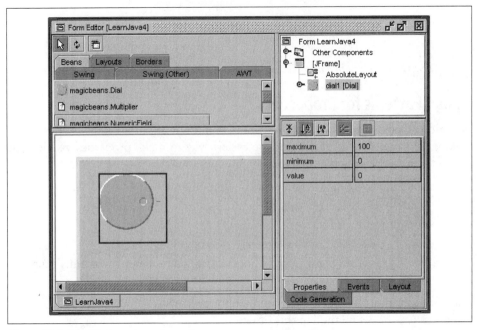

Figure 21-8. The Dial component as a Bean

Now we're ready to put the Dial to use. Reopen the Juggler example that we asked you to save in the first section of this chapter. (Did you save it?) Add an instance of our new magic Dial Bean to the scenario, as shown in Figure 21-9.

Bind the value property of the Dial to the animationRate of the Juggler. Use the connection wizard, as before, selecting the *Dial* and then the *Juggler*. Select the *DialEvent* source and bind the *animationRate* property, selecting the Dial's value as the property source. When you complete the hookup, you should be able to vary the speed of the juggler by turning the dial. Try changing the *maximum* and *minimum* values of the dial to change the range.

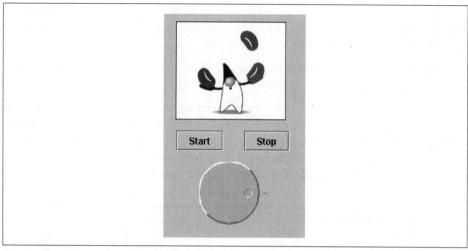

Figure 21-9. The Juggler with a dialable animation rate

Design Patterns for Properties

We said earlier that tools such as NetBeans found out about a Bean's properties by looking at its get and set methods. The easiest way to make properties visible is to follow these simple design patterns:

- Method for getting the current value of a property:

  ```
  public PropertyType getPropertyName( )
  ```
- Method for setting the value of a property:

  ```
  public void setPropertyName( PropertyType arg )
  ```
- Method for determining whether a boolean-valued property is currently true:

  ```
  public boolean isPropertyName( )
  ```

The last method is optional and is used only for properties with boolean values. (You could just use the get method in this situation.)

The appropriate set and get methods for these features of our Bean are already in the Dial class, either methods that we added or methods inherited from the java.awt. Component and javax.swing.JComponent classes:

```
// inherited from Component
public Color getForeground( )
public void setForeground(Color c)

public Color getBackground( )
public void setBackground(Color c)

public Font getFont( )
public void setFont(Font f)
```

```
// many others from Component and JComponent

// part of the Dial itself
public int getValue( )
public void setValue(int v)

public int getMinimum( )
public void setMinimum(int m)

public int getMaximum( )
public void setMaximum(int m)
```

JavaBeans allows read-only and write-only properties, which are implemented simply by leaving out the get or set method.

NetBeans uses the Reflection API to find out about the Dial Bean's methods; it then uses these naming conventions to figure out what properties are available. When we use the properties editor to change a value, NetBeans dynamically invokes the correct set method to change the value.

If you look further at the JComponent class, you'll notice that other methods match the design pattern. For example, what about the setCursor() and getCursor() pair? NetBeans doesn't know how to display or edit a cursor, and we didn't supply an editor, so it ignores those properties in the properties sheet.

NetBeans automatically pulls the property's name from the name of its accessor methods; it then lowercases the name for display on the properties sheet. For example, the font property is not listed as Font. Later, we'll show how to provide a BeanInfo class that overrides the way these properties are displayed, letting you provide your own friendly property names.

Bean patterns in NetBeans

NetBeans automatically recognizes JavaBeans get and set method patterns in classes. In the Explorer, expand the link for the class, and you'll see a *Bean Patterns* folder. You can add properties automatically by right-clicking on the *Bean Patterns* folder and selecting *Add*, then *Property*. After you supply the name and type of the property, NetBeans automatically creates the necessary get and set methods. You can add instance variable and bound property support as well.

A (Slightly) More Realistic Example

We now have one nifty Bean for the Magic Beans products list. Let's round out the set before we start advertising. Our goal is to build the Beans we need to make a very simple form. The application performs a simple calculation after data is entered on the form.

A Bean for validating numeric data

One component we're sure to need in a form is a text field that accepts numeric data. Let's build a text-entry Bean that accepts and validates numbers and makes the values available as a property. You should recognize all the parts of the `NumericField` Bean:

```java
//file: NumericField.java
package magicbeans;

import javax.swing.*;
import java.awt.event.*;

public class NumericField extends JTextField
{
    private double value;

    public NumericField( ) {
        super(6);
        setInputVerifier( new InputVerifier( ) {
            public boolean verify( JComponent comp ) {
                JTextField field = (JTextField)comp;
                boolean passed = false;
                try {
                    setValue( Double.parseDouble( field.getText( ) ) );
                } catch ( NumberFormatException e ) {
                    comp.getToolkit( ).beep( );
                    field.selectAll( );
                    return false;
                }
                return true;
            }
        } );

        addActionListener( new ActionListener( ) {
            public void actionPerformed( ActionEvent e ) {
                getInputVerifier( ).verify( NumericField.this );
            }
        } );
    }

    public double getValue( ) {
        return value;
    }
    public void setValue( double newValue ) {
        double oldValue = value;
        value = newValue;
        setText( "" + newValue );
        firePropertyChange( "value", oldValue, newValue );
    }
}
```

NumericField extends the Swing JTextField component. The constructor defaults the text field to a width of six columns, but you can change its size in NetBeans through the "columns" property.

The heart of NumericField is the InputVerifier, which we have implemented as an anonymous inner class (see "Validating Data" in Chapter 17). Our verifier is called to parse the user's entry as a number, giving it a Double value. We have also added an ActionListener that validates when the user hits *Enter* in the field.

If parsing succeeds, we update the value property using our setValue() method. setValue() then fires a PropertyChangeEvent to notify any interested Beans. If the text doesn't parse properly as a number, we give feedback to the user by selecting (highlighting) the text.

Using NetBeans, verify the operation of this Bean by placing two NumericFields in the workspace and binding the value property of one to the other. You should be able to enter a new floating point value and see the change reflected in the other.

An invisible multiplier

Now, let's make an invisible Bean that performs a calculation rather than forming part of a user interface. Multiplier is a simple invisible Bean that multiplies the values of two of its properties (A and B) to produce the value of a third read-only property (C). Here's the code:

```java
//file: Multiplier.java
package magicbeans;

import java.beans.*;

public class Multiplier implements java.io.Serializable {
   private double a, b, c;

   synchronized public void setA( double val ) {
      a = val;
      multiply( );
   }

   synchronized public double getA( ) {
      return a;
   }

   synchronized public void setB( double val ) {
      b = val;
      multiply( );
   }

   synchronized public double getB( ) {
      return b;
   }
```

```
    synchronized public double getC( ) {
       return c;
    }

    synchronized public void setC( double val ) {
       multiply( );
    }

    private void multiply( ) {
       double oldC = c;
       c = a * b;
       propChanges.firePropertyChange(
          "c", new Double(oldC) , new Double(c) );
    }

    private PropertyChangeSupport propChanges =
  new PropertyChangeSupport(this);

    public void addPropertyChangeListener(
    PropertyChangeListener listener)
    {
        propChanges.addPropertyChangeListener(listener);
    }
    public void removePropertyChangeListener(
    PropertyChangeListener listener)
    {
        propChanges.removePropertyChangeListener(listener);
    }
  }
```

To make a Multiplier a source of PropertyChangeEvents, we enlist the help of a PropertyChangeSupport object. To implement Multiplier's methods for registering property-change listeners, we simply call the corresponding methods in the PropertyChangeSupport object. Similarly, a Multiplier fires a property change event by calling the PropertyChangeSupport object's firePropertyChange() method. This is the easiest way to get an arbitrary class to be a source of PropertyChangeEvents.

The code is straightforward. Whenever the value of property a or b changes, we call multiply(), which multiplies their values and fires a PropertyChangeEvent. So we can say that Multiplier supports binding of its c property.

Putting them together

Finally, let's demonstrate that we can put our Beans together in a useful way. Arrange three JLabels, three NumericFields, and a Multiplier as shown in Figure 21-10.

Bind the values of the first two NumericFields to the a and b properties of the Multiplier; bind the c value to the third NumericField. Now we have a simple calculator. Try some other arrangements. Can you build a calculator that squares a

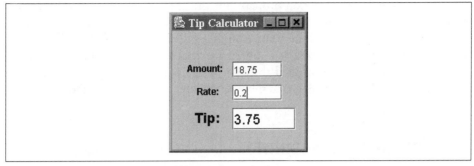

Figure 21-10. TextLabels, NumericFields, and a Multiplier

number? Can you see how you might build a simple spreadsheet? Well, perhaps not. We'll address some of the limitations in the next section.

Limitations of Visual Design

The last example proved that we can create at least a trivial application by hooking Beans together in a mostly visual way. In other development environments, this kind of Bean hookup would have been even more streamlined. For example, Sun's "Bean-Box" reference JavaBean container takes a different approach from NetBeans. It allows the developer to work with "live" JavaBean instances, dynamically generating adapter code at runtime and relying solely on object serialization to save the resulting work. This kind of design is, in a sense, the real goal of the JavaBeans architecture. It is true "what you see is what you get" (WYSIWYG) programming. However, pure visual design without the ability to integrate handwritten code, as we can do in NetBeans, has not yet proven to scale beyond these kinds of simple applications, and pure visual programming environments have thus far failed to catch on.

Sun is currently working on a replacement for the BeanBox called BeanBuilder. You can find out more about it at *http://java.sun.com/products/javabeans/beanbuilder/*.

Serialization Versus Code Generation

If you've been keeping an eye on the NetBeans source window while we've been working, you may have noticed the code that is being generated when you modify properties of Beans. By default, NetBeans generates method calls to the appropriate set methods after creating the Bean. But if you click on the *Code Generation* tab in the *Property Editor* window, you'll see that we have another option. By changing the *Code Generation* property from *Generate Code* to *Serialize,* you change NetBeans' behavior. Instead of generating method calls in the source code, it saves your fully configured Bean as a serialized object and then generates the appropriate code to load the freeze-dried Bean into the application from a file.

Try changing the code generation property for the Juggler Bean to *Serialize*. In the initComponents() area, you'll now see a line for that Bean that uses the static Beans. instantiate() method to load the Bean. Run the application. In the file browser window, you'll now see a serialized Java object file called something like *LearnJava1_ juggler1.ser* (the name is controlled through the Serialize To property). We'll discuss working with serialized Beans in more detail later in this chapter and ask you to refer to this stored Bean file.

Customizing with BeanInfo

So far, everything NetBeans has known about our Beans has been determined by low-level reflection—that is, by looking at the methods of our classes. The java. Beans.Introspector class gathers information on a Bean using reflection, then analyzes and describes a Bean to any tool that wants to know about it. The introspection process works only if the class follows the JavaBeans naming conventions for its methods; furthermore, it gives us little control over exactly what properties and events appear in NetBeans menus. For example, we've seen that NetBeans by default shows all the stuff we inherit from the base Swing component. We can change that by creating BeanInfo classes for our Beans. A BeanInfo class provides the JavaBeans introspector with explicit information about the properties, methods, and events of a Bean; we can even use it to customize the text that appears in menus in NetBeans (and in other IDEs).

A BeanInfo class implements the BeanInfo interface. That's a complicated proposition; in most situations, the introspector's default behavior is reasonable. So instead of implementing the BeanInfo interface, we extend the SimpleBeanInfo class, which implements all BeanInfo's methods. We can override specific methods to provide the information we want; when we don't override a method, we'll get the introspector's default behavior.

In the next few sections, we'll develop a DialBeanInfo class that provides explicit information about our Dial Bean.

Getting Properties Information

We'll start out by describing the Dial's properties. To do so, we must implement the getPropertyDescriptors() method. This method simply returns an array of PropertyDescriptor objects—one for each property we want to publicize.

To create a PropertyDescriptor, call its constructor with two arguments: the property's name and the class. In the following code, we create descriptors for the Dial's value, minimum, and maximum properties. We then call a few methods of the PropertyDescriptor class to provide additional information about each property. If our methods were bound (generated PropertyChangeEvents when modified), we'd call the setBound() method of their PropertyDescriptors. Our code is prepared to catch an IntrospectionException, which can occur if something goes wrong while creating the property descriptors, such as encountering a nonexistent method:

```java
//file: DialBeanInfo.java
package magicbeans;
import java.beans.*;

public class DialBeanInfo extends SimpleBeanInfo {

  public PropertyDescriptor[] getPropertyDescriptors( ) {
    try {
      PropertyDescriptor value =
        new PropertyDescriptor("value", Dial.class);
      PropertyDescriptor minimum =
        new PropertyDescriptor("minimum", Dial.class);
      PropertyDescriptor maximum =
        new PropertyDescriptor("maximum", Dial.class);

      return new PropertyDescriptor [] { value, minimum, maximum };
    }
    catch (IntrospectionException e) {
      return null;
    }
  }
}
```

Perhaps the most useful thing about DialBeanInfo is that by providing explicit information for our properties, we automatically hide other properties introspection might find. After compiling DialBeanInfo and packaging it with the Dial, you'll see that its JComponent properties no longer appear in the NetBeans properties editor. (This has been the case all along if you started with the precompiled example JAR.)

A PropertyDescriptor can provide a lot of other information about a property: the names of the accessor methods (if you decide not to use the standard naming convention), information on whether the property is constrained, and a class to use as a property editor (if the standard property editors aren't sufficient).

Getting events information

The Dial Bean defines its own event: the DialEvent. We'd like to tell development tools about this event so that we can build applications using it. The process for telling the world about our event is similar to what we did previously: we add a method to the DialBeanInfo class called getEventSetDescriptors(), which returns an array of EventSetDescriptors.

Events are described in terms of their listener interfaces, not in terms of the event classes themselves, so our getEventSetDescriptors() method creates a descriptor for the DialListener interface. Here's the code to add to the DialBeanInfo class:

```java
public EventSetDescriptor[] getEventSetDescriptors( ) {
  try {
```

```
      EventSetDescriptor dial = new EventSetDescriptor(
        Dial.class, "dialAdjusted",
        DialListener.class, "dialAdjusted");
      dial.setDisplayName("Dial Adjusted");

      return new EventSetDescriptor [] { dial };
    }
    catch (IntrospectionException e) {
      return null;
    }
  }
```

In this method, we create an `EventSetDescriptor` object: `dial`. The constructor for an `EventSetDescriptor` takes four arguments: the class that generates the event, the name of the event (the name that is displayed, by default, by a development tool), the listener class, and the name of the method to which the event can be delivered. (Other constructors let you deal with listener interfaces that have several methods). After creating the descriptor, we call the `setDisplayName()` method to provide a more friendly name to be displayed by development tools such as NetBeans. (This overrides the default name specified in the constructor.)

Just as the property descriptors we supply hide the properties that were discovered by reflection, the `EventSetDescriptors` can hide the other events that are inherited from the base component classes. In theory, when you recompile `DialBeanInfo`, package it in a JAR, and load it into NetBeans, you should see only the two events that we have explicitly described: our own `DialEvent` and `PropertyChangeEvent` (displayed as "Dial Adjusted" and "Bound property change"). Unfortunately, the current version of NetBeans ignores this information.

Once we have an `EventSetDescriptor`, we can provide other kinds of information about the event. For example, we can state that the event is *unicast*, which means that it can have only one listener.

Supplying icons

Some of the Beans that come with NetBeans are displayed on the palette with a cute icon. This makes life more pleasant for everyone. To supply an icon for the `BeanInfo` object we have been developing, we have it implement the `getIcon()` method. You may supply up to four icons, with sizes of 16 × 16 or 32 × 32, in either color or monochrome. Here's the `getIcon()` method for `DialBeanInfo`:

```
public class DialBeanInfo extends SimpleBeanInfo {
  ...
  public java.awt.Image getIcon(int iconKind) {

    if (iconKind == BeanInfo.ICON_COLOR_16x16) {
      return loadImage("DialIconColor16.gif");
    } else
    if (iconKind == BeanInfo.ICON_COLOR_32x32) {
      return loadImage("DialIconColor32.gif");
```

```
    } else
    if (iconKind == BeanInfo.ICON_MONO_16x16) {
      return loadImage("DialIconMono16.gif");
    } else
    if (iconKind == BeanInfo.ICON_MONO_32x32) {
      return loadImage("DialIconMono32.gif");
    }
    return null;
}
```

This method is called with a constant indicating what kind of icon is being requested; for example, BeanInfo.ICON_COLOR_16x16 requests a 16 × 16 color image. If an appropriate icon is available, it loads the image and returns an Image object. If the icon isn't available, it returns null. For convenience, you can package the images in the same JAR file as the Bean and its BeanInfo class.

Though we haven't used them here, you can also use a BeanInfo object to provide information about other public methods of your Bean (for example, array-valued properties) and other features.

Creating customizers and property editors

JavaBeans also lets you provide a customizer for your Beans. Customizers are objects that do advanced customization for a Bean as a whole; they let you provide your own GUI for tweaking your Bean. (For example, the Select Bean uses a customizer rather than the standard properties sheet.) We won't show you how to write a customizer; it's not too difficult, but it's beyond the scope of this chapter. Suffice it to say that a customizer must implement the java.beans.Customizer interface and should extend Component (or JComponent) so that it can be displayed.

A property editor isn't quite as fancy as a customizer. Property editors are a way of giving the properties sheet additional capabilities. For example, you would supply a property editor to let you edit a property type that is specific to your Bean. You could provide a property editor that would let you edit an object's price in dollars and cents. We've already seen a couple of property editors: the editor used for Color-valued properties is fundamentally no different from a property editor you might write yourself. In addition, the Molecule Bean uses a property editor to specify its moleculeName property.

Again, describing how to write a property editor is beyond the scope of this chapter. Briefly, a property editor must implement the PropertyEditor interface; it usually does so by extending the PropertyEditorSupport class, which provides default implementations for most of the methods.

Hand-Coding with Beans

So far, we've seen how to create and use Beans within a Bean application builder environment. That is the primary role of a JavaBean in development. But Beans are not limited to being used by automated tools. There's no reason we can't use Beans in handwritten code. You might use a builder to assemble Beans for the user interface of your application and then load that serialized Bean or a collection of Beans in your own code, just as NetBeans does when told to use object serialization. We'll give an example of that in a moment.

Bean Instantiation and Type Management

Beans are an abstraction over simple Java classes. They add, by convention, features that are not part of the Java language. To enable certain additional capabilities of JavaBeans, we have to use some special tools that take the place of basic language operations. Specifically, when working with Beans, we are provided with replacements for three basic Java operations: creating an object with new, checking the type of an object with the instanceof operator, and casting a type with a cast expression. In place of these, use the corresponding static methods of the java.beans.Beans class, shown in Table 21-1.

Table 21-1. Methods of the java.beans.Beans class

Operator	Equivalent
New	Beans.instantiate(classloader, name)
Instanceof	Beans.isInstanceOf(object, class)
Explicit cast	Beans.getInstanceOf(object, class)

Beans.instantiate() is the new operation for Beans. It takes a class loader and the name of a Bean class or serialized Bean as arguments. Its advantage over the plain new operator is that it can also load Beans from a serialized form. If you use instantiate(), you don't have to specify in advance whether you will provide the Bean as a class or as a serialized object. The instantiate() method first tries to load a resource file based on the name Bean, by turning package-style names (with dots) into a path-style name with slashes and then appending the suffix *.ser*. For example, magicbeans.NumericField becomes *magicbeans/NumericField.ser*. If the serialized form of the Bean is not found, the instantiate() method attempts to create an instance of the class by name. This feature will probably become more important in the future as other forms of Bean serialization are added. In Java 1.4, a new XMLEncoder was added to the java.beans package, allowing Beans to be serialized to an XML file format.

Beans.isInstanceOf() and Beans.getInstanceOf() do the jobs of checking a Bean's type and casting it to a new type. These methods are intended to allow one or more

Beans to work together to implement "virtual" or dynamic types. In the future, these methods may be used to let Beans take control of this behavior, providing different "views" of themselves. However, they currently don't add any functionality.

Working with Serialized Beans

Remember the Juggler we serialized a while back? Well, it's time to revive him, just like Han Solo from his "Carbonite" tomb in Star Wars. We'll assume that you saved the Juggler by flipping on the *Serialization* property while working with the LearnJava1 class and that NetBeans therefore saved him in the file *LearnJava1_juggler1.ser*. If you didn't do this, you can use the following snippet of code to serialize the Bean to a file of your choice:

```
import sunw.demo.juggler.Juggler;
import java.io.ObjectOutpuStream;

Juggler duke = new Juggler();
ObjectOutputStream oout = new ObjectOutputStream(
    new FileOutputStream("duke.ser") );
oout.writeObject( duke );
oout.close();
```

Once you have the frozen Duke, compile the following small application:

```
//file: BackFromTheDead.java
import java.awt.Component;
import javax.swing.*;
import java.beans.*;

public class BackFromTheDead extends JFrame {

  public BackFromTheDead( String name ) {
    super("Revived Beans!");
    try {
      Object bean = Beans.instantiate(
        getClass().getClassLoader( ), name );

      if ( Beans.isInstanceOf(bean, Component.class) ) {
        Component comp = (Component)
          Beans.getInstanceOf(bean, Component.class);
        getContentPane( ).add("Center", comp);
      } else {
          System.out.println("Bean is not a Component...");
      }
    } catch ( java.io.IOException e1 ) {
      System.out.println("Error loading the serialized object");
    } catch ( ClassNotFoundException e2 ) {
      System.out.println(
        "Can't find the class that goes with the object");
    }
  }
```

```
    public static void main(String [] args) {
      JFrame frame = new BackFromTheDead( args[0] );
      frame.pack( );
      frame.setVisible(true);
    }
  }
```

Run this program, passing the name of your serialized object file as an argument and making sure that our *magicbeans.jar* file is in your classpath. Duke should spring back to life, juggling once again as shown in Figure 21-11.

Figure 21-11. The restored Juggler

In BackFromTheDead, we use Beans.instantiate() to load our serialized Bean by name. Then we check to see whether it is a GUI component using Beans.isInstanceOf(). (It is, because the Juggler is a subclass of java.awt.Component.) Finally, we cast the instantiated object to a Component with Beans.getInstanceOf() and add it to our application's JFrame. Notice that we still need a static Java cast to turn the Object returned by getInstanceOf() into a Component. This cast may seem gratuitous, but it is the bridge between the dynamic Beans lookup of the type and the static, compile-time view of the type.

Note that everything we've done above could be done using the plain java.io. ObjectInputStream discussed in Chapter 11. But these Bean management methods are intended to shield the user from details of how the Beans are implemented and stored.

One more thing before we move on. We blithely noted the fact that when the Juggler was restored, the Bean began juggling again. This implies that threads were started when the Bean was deserialized. Serialization doesn't automatically manage transient resources such as threads or even loaded images. But it's easy to take control of the process to finish reconstructing the Bean's state when it is deserialized. Have a look at the Juggler source code (provided with the examples) and refer to Chapter 11 for a discussion of object deserialization using the readObject() method.

Runtime Event Hookups with Reflection

We've discussed reflection largely in terms of how design tools use it to analyze classes. But more and more reflection is finding its way into applications to perform dynamic activities that wouldn't be possible otherwise. In this section, we'll look at a dynamic event adapter that can be configured at runtime.

In Chapter 15, we saw how adapter classes could be built to connect event firings to arbitrary methods in our code, allowing us to cleanly separate GUI and logic in our applications. In this chapter, we have seen how NetBeans interposes this adapter code between Beans to do this for us.

The AWT/Swing event model reduces the need to subclass components to perform simple hookups. But if we start relying heavily on special adapter classes, we can quickly end up with as many adapters as objects. Anonymous inner classes let us hide these classes, but they're still there. A potential solution for large or specialized applications is to create *generic* event adapters that serve a number of event sources and targets simultaneously.

In Java 1.4, a new tool was added to the java.beans package; the EventHandler is a dynamic event dispatcher that simply calls methods in response to events.[*] What makes the EventHandler unique in Java (so far) is that it is the first standard utility to use reflection to allow us to specify the method by *name*. In other words, you ask the EventHandler to direct events to a handler by specifying the handler object and the string name of the method to invoke on that object. This is a big change from the normal style of coding in Java and comes with some associated risks. We'll talk more about those later.

We can use the create() method of EventHandler to get an adapter for a specified type of event listener, specifying a target object and method name to call when that event occurs. The target object doesn't have to be a listener for the particular event type or any other particular kind of object. The following application, DynamicHookup, uses the EventHandler to connect a button to a launchTheMissiles() method in our class:

```
//file: DynamicHookup.java
import javax.swing.*;
import java.awt.event.*;
import java.beans.EventHandler;

public class DynamicHookup extends JFrame {
  JLabel label = new JLabel( "Ready...", JLabel.CENTER );
  int count;
```

---

[*] Prior to Java 1.3, we developed our own dynamic event adapter in this chapter. That example is still instructive if you want to work with Beans using reflection. You can find it in the file *DynamicActionAdapter.java* in the examples on the accompanying CD-ROM or the web site for this book.

```
    public DynamicHookup( ) {
      JButton launchButton = new JButton("Launch!");
      getContentPane( ).add( launchButton, "South" );
      getContentPane( ).add( label, "Center" );
        launchButton.addActionListener(
            (ActionListener)EventHandler.create(
                ActionListener.class, this, "launchTheMissiles"));
    }
    public void launchTheMissiles( ) {
      label.setText("Launched: "+ count++ );
    }

    public static void main(String[] args) {
      JFrame frame = new DynamicHookup( );
        frame.setDefaultCloseOperation( JFrame.EXIT_ON_CLOSE );
      frame.setSize(150, 150);
      frame.setVisible( true );
    }
  }
```

Here we call the EventHandler's create() method, passing it the ActionListener class,
the target object (this), and a string with the name of the method to invoke on the
target when the event arrives. EventHandler internally creates a listener of the appropriate type and registers our target information. Not only do we eliminate an inner
class, but the implementation of EventHandler may allow it to share adapters internally, producing very few objects.

The above example shows how we would call a method that takes no arguments. But
the EventHandler can actually do more, setting JavaBeans properties in response to
events. The following form of create() tells EventHandler to call the
launchTheMissiles() method, passing the "source" property of the ActionEvent as an
the argument:

```
    EventHandler.create(ActionListener.class, target, "launchTheMissiles", "source")
```

All events have a source property (via the getSource()) method. But we can go further, specifying a chain of property "gets" separated by dots, which are applied
before the value is passed to the method. For example:

```
    EventHandler.create(ActionListener.class, target, "launchTheMissiles", "source.text")
```

The source.text parameter causes the value getSource().getText() to be passed as
an argument to launchTheMissiles(). In our case, that would be the label of our button. Other forms of create() allow more flexibility in selecting which methods of a
multimethod listener interface are used and other options. We won't cover every
detail of the tool here.

Safety implications

The EventHandler is a powerful tool, but it was, in actuality, primarily intended for
use by IDEs, not developers. Reflection allows you to do things at runtime that you

couldn't do otherwise. Therein lies the problem with this technique: by using reflection to locate and invoke methods, we abandon Java's strong typing and head off in the direction of scripting languages. We add power at the expense of safety. If the method name specified to EventHandler doesn't exist, or if it exists but wants the wrong type of arguments, you may receive a runtime exception, or worse, it may be silently ignored.

How it works

The EventHandler uses a powerful new reflection feature introduced in Java 1.3. The java.lang.reflect.Proxy class is a factory that can generate adapters implementing any type of interface at runtime. By specifying one or more event listener interfaces (e.g., ActionListener), we get an adapter that implements those listener interfaces generated for us on the fly. The adapter is a specially created class that delegates all the method calls on its interfaces to a designated InvocationHandler object. See Chapter 7 for more information about the reflection interface proxy.

BeanContext and BeanContextServices

So far we've talked about some sophisticated mechanisms for connecting JavaBeans together at design time and runtime. However, we haven't talked at all about the environment in which JavaBeans live. To build advanced, extensible applications, we'd like a way for JavaBeans to find each other or "rendezvous" at runtime. The java.beans.beancontext package provides this kind of container environment. It also provides a generic "services" lookup mechanism for Beans that wish to advertise their capabilities. These mechanisms have existed for some time, but they haven't found much use in the standard Java packages. Still, they are interesting and important facilities that you can use in your own applications.

You can find a full explanation and example of how to use the Bean context to find Beans and listen for services in the expanded material on the CD-ROM that comes with the book.

The Java Activation Framework

The Java Activation Framework (JAF) is a standard extension that can be used by Beans that work with many external data types, such as media retrieved from files and streams. It is essentially a generalized content/protocol handler mechanism for JavaBeans. The JAF is an extensible set of classes that wrap arbitrary, raw data sources to provide access to their data as streams or objects, identify the MIME type of the data, and enumerate a registered set of "commands" for operating on the data.

The JAF provides two primary interfaces: DataSource and DataHandler. The DataSource acts like the protocol handlers we discussed in Chapter 13. It wraps the data source and determines a MIME type for the data stream. The `DataHandler` acts like a content handler except it provides a great deal more than access to the data. A `DataHandler` is constructed to wrap a `DataSource` and interpret the data in different forms. It also provides a list of command operations that can be used to access the data. `DataHandler` also implements the `java.awt.datatransfer.Transferable` interface, allowing data to be passed among application components in a well-defined way.

The JAF hasn't been used much outside the Java Mail API, but you can find out more about JAF from Sun at *http://java.sun.com/beans/glasgow/jaf.html*.

Enterprise JavaBeans

Enterprise JavaBeans is a very big topic, and we can't do more than provide a few paragraphs to whet your appetite. If you want more information, see *Enterprise Java-Beans* by Richard Monson-Haefel (O'Reilly). The thrust of EJB is to take the Java-Beans philosophy of portable, pluggable components and extend it to the server side to accommodate the sorts of things that multitiered networked and database-centric applications require. Although EJB pays homage to the basic JavaBeans concepts, it is much larger and more special purpose. It doesn't have a lot in common with the kinds of things we've been talking about in this chapter. EJBs are server-side components for networked applications. What EJBs have in common with plain JavaBeans are the concepts of reusable, portable components that can be deployed and config-ured for specific environments. But in this case, the components encapsulate access to business logic and database tables instead of GUI and program elements.

EJB ties together a number of other Java enterprise-oriented APIs, including data-base access, transactions, and name services, into a single component model for server applications. EJB imposes a lot more structure on how you write code than plain old JavaBeans. But it does so in order to allow the server-side EJB container to take on a lot of responsibility and optimize your application's activities without you having to write a lot of code. Here are a few things Enterprise JavaBeans tackles:

- Object life cycle and remote access
- Container-managed persistence
- Transaction management
- Server resource pooling and management
- Deployment configuration

EJB divides the world into two camps: *Entity Beans*, which represent data in a data-base, and *Session Beans*, which implement services and operations over entity Beans. These correspond well to the second and third tiers in a three-tiered business appli-cation. "Business logic" is represented by Session Bean services, and database access is made transparent through automated object mapping by Entity Beans.

Many aspects of EJB behavior can be controlled through "deployment descriptors" that customize Bean behavior for the target environment. The result is a high level of abstraction over ordinary business-specific code. It allows powerful, networked business application components to be packaged and reused in the sort of way that ordinary Beans are reused to build client-side applications.

Sun has created a reference EJB platform as part of Java 2 Enterprise Edition (J2EE); currently, the most robust EJB implementations are provided by third parties. Usually, the EJB container is packaged as part of a more general application server that performs other duties, such as running web services, servlets, and JSPs. There are many vendors of commercial EJB servers. Two popular alternatives are BEA's WebLogic, an application server with many high-end features, and JBoss, an open source application server and implementation of the J2EE APIs. JBoss can be downloaded from *http://www.jboss.org*.

Applets

One of the original tenets of Java was that applications could be delivered over the network to your computer as needed. Instead of buying a shrink-wrapped box containing a word processor, installing it, and upgrading it every few years, it should be possible to use the software directly from the Internet, safely and on any platform. This new model of software distribution would be a boon for both free software and for commercial products that could offer a new pay-per-use sales model. Unfortunately, this revolutionary idea has been hampered by the realities of a slow Internet and the uneven progress of Java on browsers (for reasons both technical and political). Even so, Java has maintained a toehold in this arena through small downloadable applications called applets.

An *applet* is part of a web page, just like an image or hyperlink. It "owns" some rectangular area of the user's screen. It can draw whatever it wants and respond to keyboard and mouse events in that area. When the web browser loads a page that contains a Java applet, it knows how to load the classes of the applet and run them.

This chapter describes how applets work and how to put them in web pages. We'll also describe how to use Sun's Java Plug-In to take advantage of the latest Java features. Finally, we'll cover the details of creating signed applets, which can step outside the typical applet security restrictions to do client-side things, such as reading and writing files.

The Politics of Applets

The potential for applets to add dynamic content to web pages was one of the driving forces behind the spread of the Java programming language. Prior to Java's introduction in 1994, there was really no standard way to do this; even the now ubiquitous animated GIF images were not yet widely supported. Sun's HotJava Java-based web browser was the first to support applets. It was Java's original "killer application." Later, in 1995, Netscape announced that it would support the Applet API in its browsers, and soon after that Microsoft jumped on the bandwagon. For a while it seemed that Java would flourish on the Web. But there have been some bumps along the road.

Many problems, both technical and political, plagued the early years of Java's use in client-side applications. Performance issues were to be expected in such a young language. But what really crippled Java early on was the nonportable and buggy AWT, Java's original GUI toolkit. Many people overlook the fact that Java's success as a portable language is in large part a result of just how much of the Java API is implemented *in* Java. You might be surprised to learn just how many Java internals involve no native code—everything from cryptography to DNS has been done in Java—requiring no porting for new platforms. The renaissance of Java GUI applications seen in recent years (since Java 1.2) is due almost entirely to the introduction of the pure Java Swing GUI toolkit. In contrast, the original AWT system was based on native code, which had to be ported to each new system, taking into account subtle and tricky platform dependencies. AWT was effectively a large, graphical C program that Java talked to through a set of interfaces and Java was, to some extent, unfairly painted as nonportable and buggy by association.

Java faced other, less technical obstacles as well. Netscape forced the original AWT upon the world when it insisted that Java be released with "native look and feel" in lieu of a less capable, but portable initial toolkit. Later, Microsoft effectively stuck us with this by freezing the level of the Applet API in its browsers at Java 1.1 for many years. Applets have thus been stuck with AWT while lawsuits between Sun and Microsoft have dragged on. The result is that support for Applets in web browsers is a mess. There are a lot of applets on the Web today, but they only hint at Java's original promise. There is, however, some light on the horizon.

Sun has made an attempt to insulate Java from the browser battles with the introduction of the Java Plug-in. The Plug-in allows applets to run in an up-to-date Java VM, identically, in all major browsers. But for most browsers it requires installation by the user, which is less than desirable. More recently, Netscape 6 supports versions of Java using the Plug-in directly. If Netscape 6 sees wide distribution, we may finally have an up-to-date platform for applets. Newer APIs such as Java Web Start also offer the alternative of simple, zero administration, local installation of Java applications. It will be interesting to see if these catch on.

The JApplet Class

A JApplet is something like a JPanel with a mission. It is a GUI container that has some extra structure to allow it to be used in an "alien" environment, such as a browser. Applets also have a life cycle that lets them act more like an application than a static component, such as a paragraph of text or an image. Although applets tend to be relatively simple, there's no inherent restriction on their complexity, other than download speed. There's no reason you couldn't write a big application like a word processor as an applet.

The java.applet.Applet class defines the core functionality of an applet. It was used early on with AWT. The javax.swing.JApplet class is a simple extension of Applet that adds the plumbing necessary for Swing.

Structurally, an applet is a sort of wrapper for your Java code. In contrast to a standalone graphical Java application, which starts up from a main() method and creates a GUI, an applet is itself a component that expects to be dropped into some-one else's GUI. Thus, an applet can't run by itself; it runs in the context of a web browser or a special applet-viewer program (which we'll talk about later). Instead of having your application create a JFrame to hold your GUI, you stuff your application inside a JApplet (which is itself a Container) and let someone else add your applet to their GUI.

Applets are placed on web pages with the <APPLET> HTML tag, which we'll cover later in this chapter. At its simplest, you just specify the name of the applet class and a size for the applet:

```
<APPLET code="AnalogClock" width="100" height="100"></APPLET>
```

Pragmatically, an applet is an intruder into someone else's environment and there-fore has to be treated with suspicion. The web browsers that run applets impose restrictions on what the applet is allowed to do. The restrictions are enforced by an applet security manager. The browser provides everything the applet needs through an applet context—the API the applet uses to interact with its environment.

A JApplet expects to be embedded in a GUI (perhaps a document) and used in a viewing environment that provides it with resources. In all other respects, however, applets are just ordinary Panel objects. As Figure 22-1 shows, an applet is a kind of Panel. Like any other Panel, a JApplet can contain user-interface components and use all the basic drawing and event-handling capabilities of the Component class. You can draw on a JApplet by overriding its paint() method and respond to events in the JApplet's display area by providing the appropriate event listeners. Applets have additional structure that helps them interact with the viewer environment.

Aside from the top-level structure and the security restrictions, there is no difference between an applet and an application. If your application can live within the limits imposed by a browser's security manager, you can easily structure it to function as an applet and a standalone application. Normally you'll use the your applet class only as a handle to manage the life cycle and appearance of your application—create the GUI, start, and stop. So the bulk of your code should be easily adaptable to either a standalone or applet deployment.

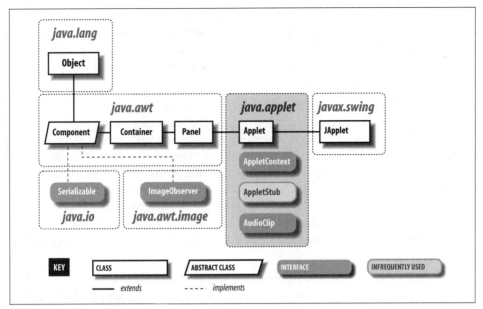

Figure 22-1. The java.applet package

Applet Life Cycle

The Applet class contains four methods that can be overridden to guide it through its life cycle. The init(), start(), stop(), and destroy() methods are called by the appletviewer or web browser to direct the applet's behavior. init() is called once, after the applet is created. The init() method is where you perform basic setup such as parsing parameters, building a user interface, and loading resources.

By convention applets don't provide an explicit constructor to do any setup. The reason for this is that the constructor is meant to be called by the applet's environment, for simple creation of the applet. This might happen before the applet has access to certain resources, such as information about its environment. Therefore, an applet doesn't normally do any work there; instead it relies on the default constructor for the JApplet class and does its initialization in the init() method.

The start() method is called whenever the applet becomes visible; it shouldn't be a surprise then that the stop() method is called whenever the applet becomes invisible. init() is called only once in the life of an applet, but start() and stop() can be called any number of times (although always in the logical sequence). The start() method is called when the applet is displayed, such as when it scrolls onto the screen; stop() is called if the applet scrolls off the screen, or the viewer leaves the document. start() tells the applet it should be active. The applet may want to create threads, animate, or otherwise perform useful (or annoying) activity. stop() is called to let the applet know it should go dormant. Applets should cease CPU-intensive or wasteful activity when they are stopped and resume it when (and if) they are restarted. However, there's no requirement that an invisible applet stop computing; in some applications, it may be useful for the applet to continue running in the background. Just be considerate of your user, who doesn't want an invisible applet dragging down system performance.

Finally, the destroy() method gives the applet a last chance to clean up before it's removed—some time after the last call to stop(). For example, an applet might want to close down suspended communications channels or remove graphics frames. Exactly when destroy() is called depends on the browser; Netscape calls destroy() just prior to deleting the applet from its cache. This means that although an applet can cling to life after being told to stop(), how long it can go on is unpredictable. If you want to maintain your applet as the user progresses through other pages of activities, you may have to put it in an HTML frame, so that it remains visible and won't be told to stop(). See the "Applet persistence and navigation" section later in this chapter.

If you've been through the rest of this book you've already seen a couple of applets that snuck in among other topics. In Chapter 8, we created a simple clock applet, and in Chapter 12, we used an applet to send packets of information from a web browser. Now let's try a simple Swing-based example using JApplet. The following example, shown in Figure 22-2, ShowApplet, does nothing special, but you can use it to test the version of Java that's running in your browser (and see if the Plug-in is installed) and to see when the applet is started and stopped. It's a good reference.

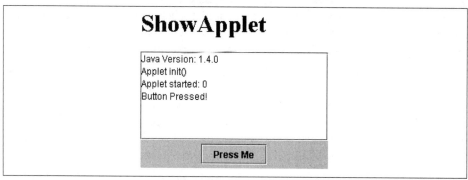

Figure 22-2. ShowApplet

```
import javax.swing.*;
import java.awt.event.*;

public class ShowApplet extends JApplet {
    JTextArea text = new JTextArea( );
    int startCount;

    public void init( ) {
        JButton button = new JButton("Press Me");
```

```
        button.addActionListener( new ActionListener() {
            public void actionPerformed( ActionEvent e ) {
                text.append("Button Pressed!\n");
            }
        } );
        getContentPane( ).add( "Center", new JScrollPane( text ) );
        JPanel panel = new JPanel( );
        panel.add( button );
        getContentPane( ).add( "South", panel );
        text.append( "Java Version: "
            +System.getProperty("java.version")+"\n" );
        text.append( "Applet init( )\n" );
    }
    public void start( ) {
        text.append( "Applet started: "+ startCount++ +"\n" );
    }
    public void stop( ) {
        text.append( "Applet stopped.\n" );
    }
}
```

After compiling the applet, we have to create an HTML page in which to embed it. The following will do:

```
<html><head><title>ShowApplet</title></head>
<body>
<applet code="ShowApplet" WIDTH="300" HEIGHT="300">
    Your browser does not understand Java.</applet>
</body>
</html>
```

We'll discuss the APPLET tag and other issues related to embedding applets in documents in detail later in this chapter. For now, just save this in a file called *showapplet. html*. Now load the file with your favorite web browser (we suggest Netscape 6.2 or later, which comes with a recent version of Java) and see what happens. If you have access to a web server you can use it. Otherwise you may have to use a URL like the following to point to your file:

```
file://localhost/c:/somedirectory/showapplet.html
```

The applet shows the version of Java running it and prints messages when its button is pressed. It also prints messages when its start() and stop() methods are called, along with a count. You can use this to experiment with different browsers and page-layout configurations to see when your applet is reloaded or restarted. If your browser fails to display the applet, don't despair. Later in this chapter we'll talk about how to convert the HTML to force the browser to use the Java Plug-in.

The Applet Security Sandbox

Applets are quarantined within the browser by an applet SecurityManager. The SecurityManager is part of the web browser or appletviewer. It is installed before the browser loads any applets and implements the basic restrictions that let the user run untrusted applets (loaded over the Internet) safely. Remember, there are no inherent security restrictions on a standalone Java application. It is the browser that limits what applets are allowed to do using a security policy.

Most browsers impose the following restrictions on untrusted applets:

- Untrusted applets can't read or write files on the local host.
- Untrusted applets can open network connections (sockets) only to the server from which they originated.
- Untrusted applets can't start other processes on the local host.
- Untrusted applets can't have native methods.

The motivation for these restrictions should be fairly obvious: you clearly wouldn't want a program coming from some random Internet site to access your files or run arbitrary programs. Although untrusted applets can't directly read and write files on the client side or talk to arbitrary hosts on the network, applets can work with servers to store data and communicate. For example, an applet can use Java's RMI facility to do processing on its server. An applet can communicate with other applets on the Net by proxy through its server.

Trusted applets

We've been using the term *untrusted applet*, so it should come as no surprise that it is also possible to have such a thing as a *trusted applet*. Applets become trusted through the use of digital signatures, by *signing* the JAR file containing your applet code. Because a signature identifies the applet's origin unambiguously, we can now distinguish between trusted applets (i.e., applets that come from a site or person you trust not to do anything harmful) and run-of-the-mill untrusted applets. In browser environments that support signing, trusted applets can be granted permission to "go outside" of the applet security sandbox. Trusted applets can be allowed to do most of the things that standalone Java applications can do: read and write files, open network connections to arbitrary machines, and interact with the local operating system by starting processes. Trusted applets still can't have native methods, but including native methods in an applet would destroy its portability anyway.

Chapter 3 discussed how to package your applet's class files and resources into a JAR file. Later in this chapter we'll show you how to sign an applet with your digital signature.

Getting Applet Resources

An applet must communicate with its browser or applet viewer. For example, it may need configuration parameters from the HTML document in which it appears. An applet may also need to load images, audio clips, and other items. It may also want to ask the viewer about other applets on the same HTML page in order to communicate with them. To get resources from the environment, applets use the `AppletStub` and `AppletContext` interfaces, provided by the browser.

Applet parameters

An applet gets its parameters from <PARAM> tags placed inside the <APPLET> tag in the HTML document, as we'll describe later. You can retrieve these parameters using Applet's getParameter() method. For example, the following code reads parameters called imageName and sheep from its HTML page:

```
String imageName = getParameter( "imageName" );
try {
    int numberOfSheep = Integer.parseInt(getParameter( "sheep" ));
} catch ( NumberFormatException e ) { /* use default */ }
```

There is an API that allows an applet to provide information (help) about the parameters it accepts. The applet's getParameterInfo() can return an array of string arrays, listing and describing the applet's parameters. For each parameter, three strings are provided: the parameter name, its possible values or value types, and a verbose description. For example:

```
public String [][] getParameterInfo( ) {
  String [][] appletInfo = {
      {"logo",  "url", "Main logo image"},
      {"timer", "int",  "Time to wait before becoming annoying"},
      {"flashing", "constant|intermittant", "Flag for how to flash"}
  };
  return appletInfo;
}
```

However it's unclear who, if anyone, uses this API.

Applet resources

An applet can find out where it lives using the getDocumentBase() and getCodeBase() methods. getDocumentBase() returns the base URL of the document in which the applet appears; getCodeBase() returns the base URL of the Applet's class files (these two are often the same). An applet can use these methods to construct relative URLs from which to load other resources from its server like images, sounds, and other data. The getImage() method takes a URL and asks for an image from the viewer environment. The image may be pulled from a cache or loaded asynchronously when later used. The getAudioClip() method, similarly, retrieves sound clips.

The following example uses getCodeBase() to construct a URL and load a properties configuration file, located in the same remote directory as the applet's class file:

```
Properties props = new Properties( );
try {
  URL url = new URL(getCodeBase( ), "appletConfig.props");
```

```
        props.load( url.openStream( ) );
    } catch ( IOException e ) { /* failed */ }
```

A much better way to load resources is by calling the getResource() and getResourceAsStream() methods of the Class class, which search the applet's JAR files (if any) as well as its codebase. The following code loads the same properties file in a more portable way:

```
Properties props = new Properties( );
try {
    props.load( getClass( ).getResourceAsStream("appletConfig.props") );
} catch ( IOException e ) { /* failed */ }
```

An applet can ask its viewer to retrieve an image by calling the getImage() method. The location of the image to be retrieved is given as a URL, either absolute or fetched from an applet's resources:

```
public class MyApplet extends javax.swing.JApplet {
    public void init( ) {
        try {
            // absolute URL
            URL monaURL =
                new URL( "http://myserver/images/mona_lisa.gif");
            Image monaImage = getImage( monaURL );
            // applet resource URL
            URL daffyURL =
                getClass( ).getResource("cartoons/images/daffy.gif");
            Image daffyDuckImage = getImage( daffyURL );
        }
        catch ( MalformedURLException e ) {
            // unintelligable url
        }
    }
    // ...
}
```

Again, using getResource() is preferred; it looks for the image in the applet's JAR file (if there is one), before looking elsewhere in the server's filesystem.

Driving the browser

The *status line* is a blurb of text that usually appears somewhere in the web browser's display, indicating a current activity. An applet can request that some text be placed in the status line with the showStatus() method. (The browser isn't required to do anything in response to this call, but most browsers will oblige you.)

An applet can also ask the browser to show a new document. To do this, the applet makes a call to the showDocument(url) method of the AppletContext. You can get a reference to the AppletContext with the applet's getAppletContext() method. Calling showDocument(url) replaces the currently showing document, which means that your currently running applet will be stopped.

Another version of showDocument() takes an additional String argument to tell the browser where to display the new URL:

```
getAppletContext( ).showDocument( url, name );
```

The name argument can be the name of an existing labeled HTML frame; the document referenced by the URL is displayed in that frame. You can use this method to create an applet that "drives" the browser to new locations dynamically but keeps itself active on the screen in a separate frame. If the named frame doesn't exist, the browser creates a new top-level window to hold it. Alternatively, name can have one of the following special values:

self
> Show in the current frame

_parent
> Show in the parent of our frame

_top
> Show in outermost (top-level) frame

_blank
> Show in a new top-level browser window

Both showStatus() and showDocument() requests may be ignored by a cold-hearted viewer or web browser.

Inter-applet communication

Applets that are embedded in documents loaded from the same location on a web site can use a simple mechanism to locate one another (rendezvous). Once an applet has a reference to another applet, it can communicate with it, just as with any other object, by invoking methods and sending events. The getApplet() method of the applet context looks for an applet by name:

```
Applet clock = getAppletContext( ).getApplet("theClock");
```

Give an applet a name within your HTML document using the name attribute of the <APPLET> tag. Alternatively, you can use the getApplets() method to enumerate all the available applets in the pages.

The tricky thing with applet communications is that applets run inside the security sandbox. An untrusted applet can "see" and communicate only with objects that were loaded by the same class loader. Currently, the only reliable criterion for when applets share a class loader is when they share a common base URL. For example, all the applets contained in web pages loaded from the base URL of *http://foo.bar.com/mypages/* should share a class loader and should be able to see each other. This includes documents such as *mypages/foo.html* and *mypages/bar.html*, but not *mypages/morestuff/foo.html*.

When applets do share a class loader, other techniques are possible too. As with any other class, you can call static methods in applets by name. So you could use static methods in one of your applets as a "registry" to coordinate your activities.

Applet persistence and navigation

One of the biggest shortcomings of the Applet API is the lack of a real context for coordinating their activities during navigation across a multi-page document or web application. The Applet API simply wasn't designed for this. Although an applet's life cycle is well-defined in terms of its API, it is not well-defined in terms of management by the browser or scope of visibility. As we described in the previous section, applets loaded from the same code base can rendezvous at runtime using their name attributes. But there are no guarantees about how long an applet will live—or whether it will be stopped as opposed to being destroyed—once it is out of view. If you experiment with our ShowApplet in various browsers and in the Java Plug-in (which we'll discuss later), you'll see that in some cases the applet is stopped and restarted when the user leaves the page, but more often the applet is reinitialized from scratch. This makes designing multipage applications difficult.

One solution has been to use static methods as a shared "registry," as mentioned earlier. However the details governing how classes loaded by applets are managed are even less well-defined than the management of the applet's themselves. In Java 1.4, a new pair of methods was added to the AppletContext to support short-term applet persistence: setStream() and getStream(). With these methods, an applet can ask the context to save a stream of byte data by a key value and return it later. The notion of providing the state to the context as a stream is a little odd but easy enough to accommodate. Here is an example:

```
getAppletContext.setStream("myStream",
    new ByteArrayInputStream( "This is some test data...".getBytes() ) );
```

Later, the stream data can be retrieved:

```
InputStream in = getAppletContext.getStream( "myStream" );
```

Currently the data is retained only as long as the browser is running. But it's possible that a longer term persistence API will come about in the future. If you need more complex state and navigation capabilities, you might consider using a signed applet to write to a file or taking advantage of the new Java Web Start API to install your application locally.

Applets versus standalone applications

The following lists summarize the methods of the Applet API. The first is from the AppletStub interface:

```
boolean isActive( );
URL getDocumentBase( );
URL getCodeBase( );
```

```
String getParameter(String name);
AppletContext getAppletContext( );
void appletResize(int width, int height);
```

The second is from the AppletContext interface:

```
AudioClip getAudioClip(URL url);
Image getImage(URL url);
Applet getApplet(String name);
Enumeration getApplets( );
void showDocument(URL url);
public void showDocument(URL url, String target);
void showStatus(String status);
```

These are the methods provided by the applet-viewer environment. If your applet doesn't happen to use any of them, or if you can provide alternatives to handle common cases (such as loading images), your applet can function as a standalone application as well as an applet. The basic idea is to add a main() method that provides a window (JFrame) in which the applet can run. Here's an outline of the strategy:

```
//file: MySuperApplet.java
import java.applet.Applet;
import java.awt.*;
import javax.swing.*;

public class MySuperApplet extends JApplet {

    // applet's own code, including constructor
    // and init( ) and start( ) methods

    public static void main( String [] args ) {
        // instantiate the applet
        JApplet theApplet = new MySuperApplet( );

        // create a window for the applet to run in
        JFrame theFrame = new JFrame( );
        theFrame.setSize(200,200);

        // place the applet in the window
        theFrame.getContentPane( ).add("Center", theApplet);

        // start the applet
        theApplet.init( );
        theApplet.start( );

        // display the window
        theFrame.setVisible(true);
    }
}
```

Here we get to play "applet viewer" for a change. We have created an instance of the class, MySuperApplet, using its constructor—something we don't normally do—and added it to our own JFrame. We call its init() method to give the applet a chance to wake up and then call its start() method. In this example, MySuperApplet doesn't implement `init()` and `start()`, so we're calling methods inherited from the `Applet` class. This is the procedure an applet viewer would use to run an applet. (If we wanted to go further, we could implement our own `AppletContext` and `AppletStub` and set them in the `JApplet` before startup.)

Trying to make your applets into applications as well often doesn't make sense and is not always trivial. We show this example only to get you thinking about the real differences between applets and applications.

The \<APPLET\> Tag

Applets are embedded in HTML documents with the `<APPLET>` tag. The `<APPLET>` tag resembles the HTML `<IMG>` image tag. It contains attributes that identify the applet to be displayed and, optionally, give the web browser hints about how it should be shown.*

The standard image tag sizing and alignment attributes, such as height and width, can be used inside the applet tag. However, unlike images, applets have both an opening `<APPLET>` and a closing `</APPLET>` tag. Sandwiched between these can be any number of `<PARAM>` tags that contain data to be passed to the applet:

```
<APPLET attribute attribute ... >
    <PARAM parameter >
    <PARAM parameter >
    ...
</APPLET>
```

Attributes

Attributes are name/value pairs that are interpreted by a web browser or applet viewer. Attributes of the `<APPLET>` tag specify general features that apply to any applet, such as size and alignment.† The definition of the `<APPLET>` tag lists a fixed set of recognized attributes; specifying an incorrect or nonexistent attribute should be considered an HTML error.

Three attributes are required in the `<APPLET>` tag. Two of these attributes, `width` and `height`, specify the space the applet occupies on the screen. The third required attribute must be either `code` or `object`; you must supply one of these attributes, and you can't specify both. The `code` attribute specifies the class file from which the applet is loaded; the `object` attribute specifies a serialized representation of an

---

* If you aren't familiar with HTML or other markup languages, you may want to refer to *HTML and XHTML: The Definitive Guide* by Chuck Musciano and Bill Kennedy (O'Reilly) for a complete reference on HTML and structured web documents.

† Many HTML tags besides `<APPLET>` have attributes.

applet. Most often, you'll use the code attribute; the tools for creating serialized applets aren't quite there yet.

The following is an HTML fragment for a hypothetical simple clock applet that takes no parameters and requires no special HTML layout:

```
<APPLET code="AnalogClock" width="100" height="100"></APPLET>
```

The HTML file that contains this `<APPLET>` tag must be stored in the same directory as the `AnalogClock.class` class file. The applet tag is not sensitive to spacing, so the previous code is therefore equivalent to:

```
<APPLET
    code="AnalogClock"
    width="100"
    height="100">
</APPLET>
```

Which is a bit more readable.

Parameters

Parameters are analogous to command-line arguments; they provide a way to pass information to an applet. Each `<PARAM>` tag contains a name and a value that are passed as strings to the applet:

```
<PARAM name = "parameter_name" value = "parameter_value">
```

Parameters provide a means of embedding application-specific data and configuration information within an HTML document. Our `AnalogClock` applet, for example, might accept a parameter that selects between local and universal time:

```
<APPLET code="AnalogClock" width="100" height="100">
    <PARAM name="zone" value="GMT">
</APPLET>
```

Presumably, this `AnalogClock` applet is designed to look for a parameter named zone with a possible value of GMT.

Parameter names and values should be quoted and can contain spaces and other whitespace characters.

The parameters a given applet expects are, of course, determined by the developer of that applet. There is no standard set of parameter names or values; it's up to the applet to interpret the parameter name/value pairs that are passed to it. Any number of parameters can be specified, and the applet may choose to use or ignore them as it sees fit.

¿Habla Applet?

Web browsers are supposed to ignore tags they don't understand; if the web browser doesn't know about the `<APPLET>` or `<PARAM>` tags, we would expect them to disappear, and any HTML between the <APPLET> and </APPLET> tags to appear normally. By convention, Java-enabled web browsers ignore any extra HTML between the <APPLET> and </APPLET> tags. Combined, this means we can place some alternative HTML inside the <APPLET> tag, which is displayed only by web browsers that can't run the applet.

For our AnalogClock example, we could display a small text explanation and an image of the clock applet as a teaser:

```
<APPLET code="AnalogClock" width="100" height="100">
    <PARAM name="zone" value="GMT">
    <strong>If you see this you don't have a Java-enabled Web
    browser. Here's a picture of what you are missing.</strong>
    <img src="clockface.gif">
</APPLET>
```

The Complete <APPLET> Tag

We can now spell out the syntax for the full-blown <APPLET> tag:

```
<APPLET
    code = class_name
or:
    object = serialized_applet_name

    width = pixels_high
    height = pixels_wide

    [ codebase = location_URL ]
    [ archive = comma_separated_list_of_archive_files ]
    [ name = applet_instance_name ]
    [ alt = alternate_text ]
    [ align = style ]
    [ vspace = vertical_pad_pixels ]
    [ hspace = horizontal_pad_pixels ]
>
    [ <PARAM name = parameter_name value = parameter_value> ]
    [ <PARAM ...   ]

    [ HTML code for non-Java-aware browsers ]
</APPLET>
```

Either the code attribute or the object attribute must be present to specify the applet to run. The code attribute specifies the applet's class file; you'll see this most frequently. The object attribute specifies a serialized (pickled) representation of an applet. When you use the object attribute to load an applet, the applet's init() method is not called. However, the serialized applet's start() method is called.

The width, height, align, vspace, and hspace attributes determine the preferred size, alignment, and padding, respectively. The width and height attributes are required.

The codebase attribute specifies the base URL to be searched for the applet's class files. If this attribute isn't present, the browser looks in the same location as the HTML file. The archive attribute specifies a list of JAR or ZIP files in which the applet's class files are located. To put two or more files in the list, separate the filenames with commas; for example, the following attribute tells the browser to search three archives for the applet:

```
archive="Part1.jar,Part2.jar,Utilities.jar"
```

The archive files listed by the archive tag are loaded from the codebase URL. When searching for classes, a browser checks the archives before searching any other locations on the server.

The alt attribute specifies alternate text that is displayed by browsers that understand the <APPLET> tag and its attributes but can't actually run applets. This attribute can also describe the applet because, in this case, any alternate HTML between <APPLET> and </APPLET> is, by convention, ignored by Java-enabled browsers.

The name attribute specifies an instance name for the executing applet. This is a name specified as a unique label for each copy of an applet on a particular HTML page. For example, if we include our clock twice on the same page (using two applet tags), we should give each instance a unique name to differentiate them:

```
<APPLET code="AnalogClock" name="bigClock" width="300" height="300">
</APPLET>
<APPLET code="AnalogClock" name="smallClock" width="50" height="50">
</APPLET>
```

Applets can use instance names to recognize and communicate with other applets on the same page. We could, for instance, create a "clock setter" applet that knows how to set the time on an AnalogClock applet and pass it the instance name of a particular target clock on this page as a parameter. This might look something like:

```
<APPLET code="ClockSetter">
    <PARAM name="clockToSet" value="bigClock">
</APPLET>
```

Loading Class Files

The code attribute of the <APPLET> tag should specify the name of an applet. This is either a simple class name or a package path and class name. For now, let's look at simple class names; we'll discuss packages in a moment. By default, the Java runtime system looks for the class file in the same location as the HTML document that contains it. This location is known as the *base URL* for the document.

Consider an HTML document, *clock.html*, that contains our clock applet example:

```
<APPLET code="AnalogClock" width="100" height="100"></APPLET>
```

Let's say we retrieve the document at the following URL:

```
http://www.time.ch/documents/clock.html
```

Java tries to retrieve the applet class file from the same base location:

```
http://www.time.ch/documents/AnalogClock.class
```

The codebase attribute of the <APPLET> tag specifies an alternative base URL for the class file search. Let's say our HTML document now specifies codebase, as in the following example:

```
<APPLET
    codebase="http://www.joes.ch/stuff/"
    code="AnalogClock"
    width="100"
    height="100">
</APPLET>
```

Java now looks for the applet class file at:

```
http://www.joes.ch/stuff/AnalogClock.class
```

Packages

For "loose" applet class files that are not packaged into archives, Java uses the standard package name to directory path mapping to locate files on the server. The only difference is that the requests are not local file lookups but requests to the web server at the applet's codebase URL. Before a class file is retrieved from a server, its package-name component is translated by the client into a relative path name under the applet's codebase.

Let's suppose that our AnalogClock has been placed into a package called time.clock (a subordinate package for clock-related classes, within a package for time-related classes). The fully qualified name of our class is time.clock.AnalogClock. Our simple <APPLET> tag would now look like:

```
<APPLET code="time.clock.AnalogClock" width="100" height="100"></APPLET>
```

Let's say the *clock.html* document is once again retrieved from:

```
http://www.time.ch/documents/clock.html
```

Java now looks for the class file in the following location:

```
http://www.time.ch/documents/time/clock/AnalogClock.class
```

The same is true when specifying an alternative codebase:

```
<APPLET
    codebase="http://www.joes.ch/stuff/"
    code="time.clock.AnalogClock"
    width="100"
    height="100">
</APPLET>
```

Java now tries to find the class in the corresponding path under this base URL:

```
http://www.joes.ch/stuff/time/clock/AnalogClock.class
```

Viewing Applets

Sun's SDK comes with an applet-viewer program, aptly called `appletviewer`. To use `appletviewer`, specify the URL of the document on the command line. For example, to view our (still only theoretical) `AnalogClock` at the URL shown earlier, use the following command:

```
% appletviewer http://www.time.ch/documents/clock.html
```

`appletviewer` retrieves all applets in the specified document and displays each one in a separate window. `appletviewer` isn'tt a web browser; it doesn't attempt to display HTML. It's primarily a convenience for testing and debugging applets. If the document doesn't contain `<APPLET>` tags, `appletviewer` complains and does nothing.

Using the Java Plug-in

The disadvantage of the `<APPLET>` tag is that you have to rely on the browser's Java interpreter. This is bad for two reasons:

- The version of Java that is included in popular browsers lags the current version of Java by years. It was a painfully long time, for instance, between the release of Java 1.1 and the time that version was supported in Netscape and Internet Explorer. As a matter of fact, it hasn't ever been fully supported in Internet Explorer. Only Netscape 6.x now supports an up-to-date version of Java out of the box (using the Plug-in that we'll talk about in this section).

- Historically Microsoft's version of Java has had its own bugs and idiosyncrasies, which were different from the bugs and idiosyncrasies of Sun's version. This effectively meant that testing had to be done on each platform, contrary to Java's write-once, run-anywhere proposition.

At the time of this writing, most popular versions of Netscape and Internet Explorer are moderately stable for Java 1.1 development. As a developer, though, you will want to use modern features of Java including Swing, Collections, and so on. So what can we do?

What Is the Java Plug-in?

We might take the state of Java in the browser to indicate that applets are dead. But wait! A clever technology called the Java Plug-in saves the day. A *plug-in* is simply a loadable application module that is used to support new content types in a web browser. Both Navigator and Internet Explorer have a *plug-in* mechanism that allows the browser to be extended in this way.

Microsoft calls this technique ActiveX custom controls. But it's exactly the same concept: the browser gives control for a part of a web page to another piece of code. For example, you can view movies in your browser using Apple's QuickTime plug-in.

You can view interactive multimedia with Macromedia's Shockwave plug-in. The idea is very similar to applets; basically the browser hands-off responsibility for some rectangular area on the screen to someone else's code. The Java Plug-in is simply a Java runtime environment implemented as a browser plug-in.

Applets that use the Java Plug-in can take advantage of the very latest Java platform features. With the Plug-in, Java developers can specify the version of Java they require, and their applets should run in exactly the same way in any browser using it. The browser isn't even really running the applet anymore; the Plug-in takes care of it.

This is nifty technology, but it does come at a price. Users who want to use the Java Plug-in to run applets have to download and install it first. While this is not a huge burden, it is a barrier to universal acceptance. Netscape 6.x comes with the Java Plug-in installed and uses it automatically. Netscape also supports the automated download of new Plug-in versions as they become available. But with the wide installed base of browser versions by both Microsoft and Netscape, installation will be an issue for some time to come.

Messy Tags

The HTML for web pages that contain Plug-in applets is much messier than the <APPLET> tag you've already seen. Part of the problem is that you have to use specialized tags for Internet Explorer and Navigator. Navigator uses the <EMBED> tag for plug-ins, while Internet Explorer uses the <OBJECT> tag. However if you are clever about fitting the <EMBED> tag inside the <OBJECT> tag, you'll end up with some HTML that both browsers recognize and run correctly.

These tags have their own little syntax, but basically you're still providing the same information to the browser. You specify the size of the applet, the class name to use, the location of additional classes, and parameters that should be passed to the applet itself. Fortunately, you don't have to worry too much about the details. Sun provides a handy utility, the HTML Converter, which converts <APPLET> tags to the appropriate <EMBED> and <OBJECT> tags. Assuming you've set up your <APPLET> tag correctly, you should have no trouble converting your HTML page to use the Java Plug-in. This utility is available for download at *http://java.sun.com/products/plugin/index-1.4.html*

Suppose, for example, that you create a web page called *ShowOff.html*. Once you have the <APPLET> tag set up the way you want (you can test it with appletviewer), you can use the HTML Converter to set up your web page to use the Plug-in. The HTML Converter runs as a Swing application. To run it, navigate to the directory where you installed the HTML Converter and type the following:

```
C:\> java HTMLConverter
```

The window is pretty self-explanatory. You can convert all HTML files in a directory or just convert a single HTML file. The conversion is done "in-place," which means that your original HTML is overwritten with the new stuff. The Converter automatically backs up your old files unless you tell it otherwise.

You can perform different kinds of conversions, represented by different templates. By default, the HTML Converter uses the "standard" template that produces a page that works with Navigator and Internet Explorer on Windows and Solaris. If you choose "extended," it tries to produce a more elaborate version that should work on a wider set of browsers. In addition to adding the <EMBED> and <OBJECT> tags, the "extended" template preserves the original <APPLET> tag. This has the added benefit that you'll still be able to test your applet with appletviewer.

We should also note that in version 1.4, the Java Plug-in has a new feature: once installed, the Plug-in takes over control of the regular <APPLET> tag (at least for Internet Explorer) so that, by default, all applets begin to use the Plug-in. Once the Plug-in installation is boot-strapped, all applets benefit from it, regardless of whether the page uses the special tags. This is a major coup for Sun, and it will be interesting to see if it is supported in the future.

Viewing Plug-in Applets

What actually happens when users browse to a page with a Plug-in applet? It depends, of course, on which browser you're using and what has been installed. If you are on a "virgin" system, Internet Explorer asks the user for permission to download and run the Java Plug-in to display the applet. Older versions of Netscape Navigator direct the user to the Java Runtime Environment (JRE) download page. (The Java Plug-in is distributed as part of the JRE.) In either case, the download and installation times vary, depending on network speed and user comfort level. You can expect that most Internet users will have to spend five to ten minutes downloading and installing the JRE.

The good news is that the installation needs to be done only once. When JRE is installed and running, you can view Plug-in applets immediately (at least as soon as the browser loads the Plug-in). The only time the user needs to install a new Plug-in is when a new version of Java comes out.

Despite the price of installation and HTML tag messiness, the Plug-in is powerful medicine indeed. No longer do you have to wait for browser vendors to implement the latest Java platform features; the Plug-in makes the latest Java releases available to applets immediately, and it provides a more hospitable environment for applets, regardless of what browser displays them.

Java Web Start

The Java Web Start API is an interesting alternative to using applets. Java Web Start uses the Java Network Launching Protocol (JNLP) to transparently download and install Java applications locally. All the user has to do is to click on the install link on a web page. The installed applications can then be launched just like any installed application, by clicking on an icon on the desktop or through the Start menu, but they continue to be managed by the Java security policy and to be checked for automatic upgrades. Java Web Start is a form of *zero administration* client installation, which implies that the client doesn't have to do any work to install or maintain the application. JNLP applications may be signed, allowing the user to grant them fine-grained privileges, or unsigned. But even unsigned JNLP applications can take advantage of standard APIs that prompt the user for permission to perform basic operations such as opening files and printing.

Packaging your application to use JNLP is relatively easy, but we won't get into it here. The process mainly involves creating a JNLP deployment file that lists your JARs and specifies any special permission they require. You must then include an appropriate link in your web page that uses Web Start. The first time a user tries to install a JNLP application, they will have to install the Web Start plug-in (just like the Java Plug-in is installed). Thereafter, the plug-in manages all JNLP installs. See *http://java.sun.com/products/javawebstart/* for more information.

Using Digital Signatures

Digital signatures provide a way to authenticate documents and other data. They solve one of the Internet's biggest problems: given that you've received a message from Ms. X, how do you know that the message really came from Ms. X and not an imposter? Just as important for Java, let's say that you've downloaded a great new applet written by your favorite author, Pat Niemeyer, and you'd like to grant it some additional privileges, so that it can do something cool for you. You trust that this particular author wouldn't intentionally distribute something harmful. But how do you know that this person really is who he says he is? And what if you downloaded the applet from a third-party location, like an archive? How can you be sure that someone hasn't modified the applet since the author wrote it? With Java's default security policies for web browsers, such an applet can't do anything serious, but when we're talking about configuring your browser to grant additional privileges to applets coming from trusted sites, you would be in for trouble—if it weren't for digital signatures.

Like their inky analogs, digital signatures associate a name with an item in a way that is difficult to forge. In reality, a digital signature is much more difficult to forge than a traditional signature. Furthermore, digital signatures provide another benefit: they allow you to authenticate a document, proving that it hasn't been altered in transit. In other words, you know who the sender is, and that the data you received is exactly what the sender sent. Some malicious person can't clip out a digital signature, modify the original document (or applet), and attach the old signature to the result. And he can't generate a new signature; at least, he can't generate a signature claiming that the document came from its original sender. (He could, of course, attach his own signature, but that would be like signing the stick-up note you hand to the bank teller.)

Digital signatures are based on public-key cryptography, which is beyond the scope of this book. However, the basics are important and interesting.* In a public-key system, there are two pieces of information: a public key and a private one. The keys have a special, asymmetric relationship, such that a message encrypted with one key can only be decrypted with the other key. Furthermore, if you know only one key, it is very difficult to compute the other. Therefore, if I give you my public key, you can use it to create an encrypted message that only I can read. No one else, including you, has enough information to go through the process of decrypting the encoded message, so it's safe to send it over untrusted networks. Furthermore, I can (and probably will) give my public key to anyone in the world, since the public key only lets people send me messages; it doesn't let them read my messages.

Digital signatures are based on the reverse process. If I encrypt something with my private key, anyone can use my public key to read the message. That may not sound very useful, since I already said that I'd give my public key away to anyone who wants it. But in this case, we're not trying to keep the message secret, we're trying to prove that I'm the only one who could have sent the message. And that's exactly what we've done. No one else has my private key, so no one else can send a message that can be decrypted with my public key. Therefore, only the real me could have sent the message.

We've simplified the process in one crucial way. Encrypting a large message with complex algorithms takes a long time, even with fast computers. And some public-key algorithms just aren't suitable for encrypting large amounts of data for other reasons, as well. For digital signatures, then, we don't usually encrypt the entire message. First, we use a standard algorithm to create a "hash" or "message digest." To produce the signature, we then encrypt the (relatively small) message digest with the private key. The recipient can then decrypt the signature with the public key and check whether the resulting message digest matches the message he received. If it does, the recipient knows the message hasn't been altered, and the sender is who he claims to be.

Digital signatures can be used to authenticate Java class files and other types of data sent over the network. The author of an object signs the data with his or her digital signature, and we use the author's public key to authenticate that signature after we retrieve it. We don't have to communicate with anyone in order to verify the authenticity of the data. We don't even have to make sure that the communications by which we received the data are secure. We simply check the signature after the data

---

* See Bruce Schneier's encyclopedic *Applied Cryptography* (John Wiley & Sons) or Jonathan Knudsen's *Java Cryptography* (O'Reilly).

arrives. If it is valid, we know that we have the authentic data and that it hasn't been tampered with. Or do we?

Well, there is a larger problem digital signatures alone don't solve: verifying identity. If the signature checks out, we know that only the person (or entity) that published the public key could have sent the data. But how do we know that the public key really belongs to whomever we think it does? How do we associate an identity with that public key in the first place? We've made it more difficult to counterfeit a message, but it's not impossible. A forger could conceivably create a counterfeit Java class, sign it with his own private key, and try to trick you into believing that his public key is that of the real author or the trusted web site. In this case, you'll download the bad applet, then use the wrong public key to verify the applet, and be tricked into thinking that there's nothing wrong. This is where *certificates* and *certificate authorities* come into play.

Certificates

A certificate is a document that lists a name and a public key. By a name, we mean some real-world information describing a person or entity. For example, a certificate might contain your full name and address or the name of a company and the location of its headquarters. We'll consider the combination of a name and a public key in this way to make up an *identity*. If we have valid information for a particular identity, we can verify data that the identity has signed.

A certificate is signed with the digital signature of a certificate authority (CA)—the entity that issued the certificate. The certificate is, in effect, a proclamation by the CA that the identity listed is valid—in other words, that the listed public key really does belong to the entity named. If we decide to trust the CA, we can then believe the identities contained in the certificates it issues are valid. The certificate acts as a sort of electronic ID card, backed up by the credentials of the CA. Of course, we no longer issue certificates on fancy vellum scrolls, as shown in Figure 22-3; the digital format for modern certificates is described by a standard called X.509.

Certificate authority certificates

This is all well and good, but the original problem remains: in order to verify the authenticity of a certificate, we need to verify its signature. Now, to do that, we need to know the CA's public key; rather than solving the problem, we simply seem to have shifted the problem to a new front. If a counterfeiter could substitute her public key for the public key of one entity, she might be able to do the same for the CA. But shifting the problem helps quite a bit. We have reduced the number of public keys we need to know from an unlimited number (all the identities we might ever encounter) to a very small number: one for each CA. We have chained our trust of the identity to the trust of the CA's identity. Chaining can be allowed to extend further, to an arbitrary depth, allowing CAs to back up lower CAs, and so on. At some

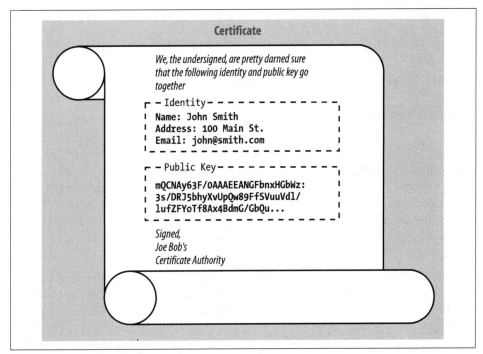

Figure 22-3. An old-fashioned certificate

point, of course, the chain has to stop, and that usually happens with a "self-signed" or *certificate authority certificate*; that is, a certificate that is issued by the CA for itself, containing its own public key. "What good is that?" you might ask.

As for the authenticity of the top-level CAs themselves, we have to rely on strong, well-known certificates that we have acquired by very secure or perhaps very tangible means. Web browsers, such as Netscape Navigator and Microsoft Internet Explorer, come with CA certificates for several popular CAs. Netscape Navigator and MSIE are, for example, shipped with a CA certificate for Verisign (*http://www.verisign.com*), so that you can safely verify any certificates signed by Verisign, wherever you encounter them. So, if all is working, we've reduced the problem to just that of your getting your copy of the web-browser software securely the first time. As far as maintenance goes, browsers like Netscape let you download new CA certificates dynamically, using a secure connection.

Site certificates

Certificates are presented to your web browser for verification when you encounter signed objects (signed JAR files). They are also issued by web servers when you make a secure connection using the HTTPS (HTTP Secure Sockets Layer) protocol. Browsers like Netscape and Internet Explorer may save these certificates encountered from third-party locations so that you can assign privileges or attributes to those identities and so that they can be recognized again. We'll call these certificates *site certificates*—though they may belong to any third party, like a person or an organization. For example, you might declare that objects signed by a certain site are allowed to write local files. The browser then saves that site's certificate, marking it with the privileges (writing local files) that it should grant.

User (signer) certificates

Finally, you, the user, can have your own identity and your own certificates to validate your identity. Browsers such as Netscape Navigator store *user certificates* that can identify you to third parties. A user certificate is associated with a private key—the private key that goes with the public key in the certificate. When you use a private key to sign an object, the corresponding certificate is shipped as part of the signature. Remember, the recipient needs the public key in your certificate to validate your signature. The certificate says on whose authority the recipient should trust that public key.

So, where do you get private keys, public keys, and certificates validating your public keys? Well, as for the keys, you generate those yourself. No other party should ever have access to your private key, much less generate it for you. After you generate a public and private key pair, you send your public key to the CA to request that they certify you. The CA can make you jump through whatever hoops are necessary; when they are satisfied that you are who you say you are, they grant you a certificate.

In Netscape Navigator, this entire process can be accomplished by the user, within the browser, using the KEYGEN extension to HTML. You can then use Netscape tools to sign JAR files, send secure email, etc. The general Java tools are not quite as slick. The Java SDK supplies the *keytool* utility to manage keys and certificates.

The keytool Utility

keytool is the standard Java utility for managing a database of identities. With it, you can generate or import key pairs and certificates. You can then use these keys and certificates to sign JAR files.

The packages that implement cryptography in Java are part of the Java Cryptography Extension (JCE). As of Java 1.4, the JCE is bundled with the standard edition of Java. Prior to that it was an optional package (and subject to export restrictions). The JCE provides both framework and implementations of algorithms. The implementations are called "provider" packages; Sun's security provider package comes with the SDK by default. Other packages can be installed to provide additional or alternate implementations of the cryptographic algorithms. By default, *keytool* uses the implementations found in Sun's provider package, though it can use other packages if any are available.

The user interface to *keytool* is awkward. It's a good bet that someone will implement a key management utility with a friendlier GUI; maybe it will be supplied with a future version of Java. In any event, we won't spend a great deal of time discussing the details of *keytool*; it's more important to understand the concepts.

What about Netscape and Internet Explorer?

Before the debut of the Java Plug-in, Netscape and Microsoft both invented their own code-signing schemes. As a result, signed applets in the Java 1.1 world were a disaster. There were three different ways to sign and deploy code, one each for Netscape Navigator, Sun's HotJava, and Microsoft's Internet Explorer. Unless you knew in advance that you had only one kind of browser worry about, you were pretty much out of luck.

The Java Plug-in levels the field for signed applets, because the packaging and deployment strategy is the same for all browsers.

The TestWrite example

Before we dive into the details, let's take a look at an example, just to show that the process really works with the Java Plug-in. Use your browser to navigate to *http://examples.oreilly.com/learnjava2/TestWrite/Unsigned.html*. You'll see the applet shown in Figure 22-4. When you push the button, this applet attempts to write a harmless file on the local host. Give it a try. The applet should fail with a security exception and display a message.

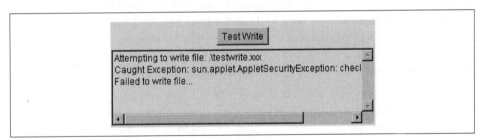

Figure 22-4. An unsigned applet violating security policy

Now try a web page that displays the same applet: *http://examples.oreilly.com/learnjava2/TestWrite/Signed.html*. The only difference is that we've signed the JAR file containing the applet, with a key and certificate generated using *keytool*.

When the Java Plug-in loads the applet's JAR file, it examines the signature. What happens next depends on whether you're using the latest Java Plug-in. With Java 1.4, the Plug-in prompts the user to decide whether or not to trust the code. In that case you get a dialog like Figure 22-5.

The dialog informs you that the applet is signed, in this case by Pat Niemeyer, and asks if you want to grant access to it. You can get information about the certificate

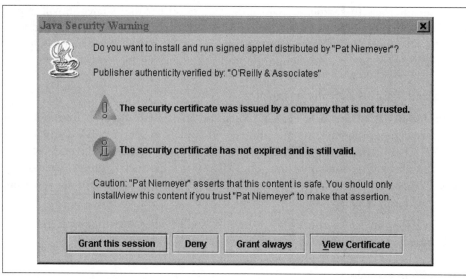

Figure 22-5. Signed applet prompt

used to sign the JAR by clicking on *View Certificate*. The two fields of interest are Issuer and Subject. In this case, we have signed the JAR file with our own *self-issued* certificate; the issuer and subject (or signer) are both identified as "Pat Niemeyer." After pondering our trustworthiness, you can grant the TestWrite applet permissions or deny them. You can also specify whether the permissions last for one session or are remembered until the certificate expires. If you deny permissions, the applet may still run; it depends on what it tries to do and how it handles being denied access. In this case, the applet prints the security exception when it tries to write the file. If you granted the applet permissions, hitting the button should show a successful write. In the next section, we'll look at how we created our certificate and signed this JAR.

If you have an older version of the Plug-in (Java 1.3 or lower) Java informs you it can't verify the signature. This is because Java doesn't know about our certificate, and older versions didn't prompt the user to accept unknown signers. We could manually install our certificate in the local Java environment, but this procedure is complicated. Fortunately with the Plug-in, we can specify the version required if we want to. (If you are interested in learning how to install keys manually for older versions of Java, you can find out all about it in the expanded material included on the accompanying CD-ROM.)

Keystores, Keys, and Certificates

The SDK supports *keystores* that hold identities along with their public keys, private keys, and certificates. It includes the utility we covered earlier, *keytool*. We'll use this database as a repository while we create and work with our identity locally.

An identity can be a person, an organization, or perhaps a logical part of an organization. Before it can be used, an identity must have a public key and at least one certificate validating its public key. *keytool* refers to entities in the local database by IDs or aliases. These names are arbitrary and are not used outside the keystore (and possibly local Java security policy files that reference the keystore). Identities that have a private key stored locally in the keystore, as well as a public key, are called *signers*. These identities can be used to sign JAR files.

The default location for a keystore is the file *.keystore* in the user's home directory. On a single user system, the Java installation directory is used instead of the user's home directory. The default keystore location is used by *keytool* unless you specify another keystore with the -keystore option.

If you are going to maintain any private keys in a keystore (if you will have any signers), you must take special care to keep the keystore file safe (and not publicly readable). Private keys must be kept private.

Public and private keys

We can create a new entry in the default keystore, complete with a key pair, with the following *keytool* command:

```
C:\> keytool -genkey -alias Pat -keyalg DSA -keysize 1024 -dname "CN=Pat Niemeyer,
OU=Technical Publications, O=O'Reilly & Associates, C=US" -keypass secure -storepass
boofa
```

There are a lot of options to explain. The most important one is -genkey, which tells *keytool* to create a new key pair for this entry. A key pair enables this entry to sign code. The -alias option supplies an alias for this entry, Pat. The -keyalg argument, DSA, is the algorithm for which we are going to generate the keys. The current release of Java supports only DSA, the Digital Signature Algorithm, which is a U.S. government standard for signing. The -keysize argument is the key length in bits. For most algorithms, larger key sizes provide stronger encryption. DSA supports keys of either 512 or 1024 bits. You should use the latter, unless you have a specific reason to do otherwise.

keytool generates the keys and places them in the default keystore. Private keys are specially protected using the -keypass option. To retrieve Pat's private key, you need the correct key password. The integrity of the keystore as a whole is protected by the -storepass option. You need to supply the same keystore password to retrieve data from this keystore later.

Once we've created a keystore entry, we can display it with the command:

```
C:\> keytool -list -alias Pat -storepass boofa
```

To see more detail, add the -v option (for "verbose"):

```
C:\> keytool -list -alias Pat -v -storepass boofa
```

We can also list the entire contents of the database:

```
C:\> keytool -list -storepass boofa
```

Certificates

Now that we have keys, we want a certificate in which to wrap our public key for distribution. Ideally, at this point, we'd send a public key to a trusted CA and receive a certificate in return. *keytool* can generate such a request in a standard format called a Certificate Signing Request (CSR). To generate a signing request for the entry we just created, you would do this:

```
C:\> keytool -csr -alias Pat -file Pat.csr -keypass secure -storepass boofa
```

You need to specify the alias for the entry you want, a filename where the CSR will be written, and the password for the private key. The output file will contain the public key, along with the name and organizational information you provided. Once you've generated the CSR file, you can send it off to your favorite Certificate Authority. After they've performed some identity checks on you, and once you pay them, they will send a certificate back to you. Suppose they send it back in a file called *Pat. x509*. You can then use *keytool* to import this certificate as follows:

```
C:\> keytool -import -alias Pat -file Pat.x509 -keypass secure -storepass boofa
```

To demonstrate the features of *keytool*, we can serve as our own authority (as we did in the example) and use our own self-signed certificate. It turns out that *keytool* already did this for us when we created keys! A self-signed certificate already exists in the keystore; all we have to do is export it as follows:

```
C:\> keytool -export -alias Pat -file Pat.cer -storepass boofa
```

The jarsigner Utility

If we have a signer keystore entry, initialized with its private and public keys, we are ready to sign JAR files. This is accomplished using another command-line utility, *jarsigner*. All we need to do is specify which keystore entry should do the signing, which JAR needs to be signed, and the keystore password:

```
C:\> jarsigner -storepass boofa testwrite.jar Pat
```

If we now list the archive, we see that *jarsigner* has added two files to the *META-INF* directory: *PAT.SF* and *PAT.DSA*. *PAT.SF* is the signature file; it's like the manifest file for this particular signature. The signature file lists the objects that were signed and the signature algorithms. *PAT.DSA* is the actual binary signature.

In this chapter, we covered the events that led to the current, fractured applet world and set the scene for what's to come. The Java Plug-in is currently our best hope for Java in the browser to succeed, but newer technologies such as Java Web Start are making inroads. It's an exciting time for Java as it begins to bloom on the client side just as it has on the server side for a number of years.

Every now and then, an idea comes along that in retrospect seems just so simple and obvious that everyone wonders why it hadn't been seen all along. Often when that happens, it turns out that the idea isn't really all that new after all. The Java revolution began by drawing on ideas from all the programming languages that came before it. Now, XML—the Extensible Markup Language—is doing for content what Java did for programming: providing a portable language for describing data.

XML is a simple, common format for representing structured information as text. The concept of XML follows the success of HTML as a universal document presentation format and generalizes it to handle any kind of data. In the process, XML has not only recast HTML but is transforming the way that businesses think about their information. In the context of a world driven more and more by documents and data exchange, XML's time has come.

A Bit of Background

XML and HTML are called markup languages because of the way they add structure to plain-text documents—by surrounding parts of the text with tags that indicate structure or meaning, much as someone with a pen might highlight a sentence and add a note. While HTML predefines a set of tags and their structure, XML is a blank slate in which the author gets to define the tags, the rules, and their meanings.

Both XML and HTML owe their lineage to Standard Generalized Markup Language (SGML)—the mother of all markup languages. SGML has been used in the publishing industry for many years (including at O'Reilly). But it wasn't until the Web captured the world that it came into the mainstream through HTML. HTML started as a very small application of SGML, and if HTML has done anything at all, it has proven that simplicity reigns.

HTML flourished but eventually showed its limitations. Documents using HTML have an unhealthy mix of structural information (such as <head> and <body>) and presentation information (for an egregious example, `<blink>`). Mixing the model and the user interface in this way limits the usefulness of HTML as a format for data exchange; it's hard for a machine to understand. XML documents consist purely of structure, and it is up to the reader of the document to apply meaning. As we'll see in this chapter, several related languages exist to help interpret and transform XML for presentation or further processing.

Text Versus Binary

When Tim Berners-Lee began postulating the Web back at CERN in the late 1980s, he wanted to organize project information using hypertext.* When the Web needed a protocol, HTTP—a simple, text-based client-server protocol—was invented. So what exactly is so enchanting about the idea of plain text? Why, for example, didn't Tim turn to the Microsoft Word format as the basis for Web documents? Surely a binary, non-human-readable format and protocol would be more efficient? Since the Web's inception, there have now been trillions of HTTP transactions. Was it really a good idea for them to use (English) words like "GET" and "POST"?

The answer, as we've all seen, is yes! What humans can read, human developers can work with more easily. There is a time and place for a high level of optimization (and obscurity), but when the goal is universal acceptance and cross-platform portability, simplicity and transparency are paramount. This is the first, fundamental proposition of XML.

A Universal Parser

Using text to exchange data is not exactly a new idea, either, but historically, for every new document format that came along, a new *parser* would have to be written. A parser is an application that reads a document and understands its formatting conventions, usually enforcing some rules about the content. For example, the Java `Properties` class has a parser for the standard properties file format (Chapter 10). In our simple spreadsheet in Chapter 17, we wrote a parser capable of understanding basic mathematical expressions. As we've seen, depending on complexity, parsing can be quite tricky.

With XML, we can represent data without having to write this kind of custom parser. This isn't to say that it's reasonable to use XML for everything (e.g., typing math expressions into our spreadsheet), but for the common types of information that we exchange on the Net, we should no longer have to write parsers that deal with basic syntax and string manipulation. In conjunction with document-verifying

---

* To read Berners-Lee's original proposal to CERN, go to *http://www.w3.org/History/1989/proposal.html*.

components (DTDs or XML Schema), much of the complex error checking is also done automatically. This is the second fundamental proposition of XML.

The State of XML

The APIs we'll discuss in this chapter are powerful and well tested. They are being used around the world to build enterprise-scale systems today. Unfortunately, the current slate of XML tools bundled with Java only partially remove the burden of parsing from the developer. Although we have taken a step up from low-level string manipulation to a common, structured document format, the standard tools still generally require the developer to write low-level code to traverse the content and interpret the string data manually. The resulting program remains somewhat fragile, and much of the work can be tedious. The next step, as we'll discuss briefly later in this chapter, is to begin to use generating tools that read a description of an XML document (an XML DTD or Schema) and generate Java classes or bind existing classes to XML data automatically.

The XML APIs

As of Java 1.4, all the basic APIs for working with XML are bundled with Java. This includes the javax.xml standard extension packages for working with Simple API for XML (SAX), Document Object Model (DOM), and Extensible Stylesheet Language (XSL) transforms. If you are using an older version of Java, you can still use all these tools, but you will have to download the packages separately from *http://java.sun.com/xml/*.

XML and Web Browsers

Microsoft's Internet Explorer web browser was the first to support XML explicitly. If you load an XML document in IE 5.0 or greater, it is displayed as a tree using a special stylesheet. The stylesheet uses dynamic HTML to allow you to collapse and expand nodes while viewing the document. IE also supports basic XSL transformation directly in the browser. We'll talk about XSL later in this chapter.

Netscape 6.x and the latest Mozilla browsers also understand XML content and support the rendering of documents using XSL. At the time of this writing, however, they don't offer a friendly viewer by default. You can use the "view source" option to display an XML document in a nicely formatted way. But in general, if you load an XML document into either of these browsers, or any browser that doesn't explicitly transform it, it simply displays the text of the document with all the tags (structural information) stripped off. This is the prescribed behavior for working with XML.

XML Basics

The basic syntax of XML is extremely simple. If you've worked with HTML, you're already halfway there. As with HTML, XML represents information as text using *tags* to add structure. A tag begins with a name sandwiched between less-than (<) and greater-than (>) characters. Unlike HTML, XML tags must always be *balanced*; in other words, an opening tag must always be followed by a closing tag. A closing tag looks just like the opening tag but starts with a less-than sign and a slash (</). An opening tag, closing tag, and any content in between are collectively referred to as an *element* of the XML document. Elements can contain other elements, but they must be properly nested (all tags started within an element must be closed before the element itself is closed). Elements can also contain plain text or a mixture of elements and text. Comments are enclosed between <!-- and --> markers. Here are a few examples:

```
<!-- Simple -->
<Sentence>This is text.</Sentence>

<!-- Element -->
<Paragraph><Sentence>This is text.</Sentence></Paragraph>

<!-- Mixed -->
<Paragraph>
        <Sentence>This <verb>is</verb> text.</Sentence>
</Paragraph>

<!-- Empty -->
<PageBreak></PageBreak>
```

An empty tag can be written more compactly with a single tag ending with a slash and a greater-than sign (/>):

```
<PageBreak/>
```

Attributes

An XML element can contain *attributes*, which are simple name-value pairs supplied inside the start tag.

```
<Document type="LEGAL" ID="42">...</Document>
<Image name="truffle.jpg"/>
```

The attribute value must always be enclosed in quotes. You can use double (") or single (') quotes. Single quotes are useful if the value contains double quotes.

Attributes are intended to be used for simple, unstructured properties or identifiers associated with the element data. It is always possible to make an attribute into a child element, so there is no real need for attributes. But they often make the XML easier to read and more logical. In the case of the Document element in our snippet above, the attributes type and ID represent metadata about the document. We might expect that a Java class representing the `Document` would have static identifiers for document types such as `LEGAL`. In the case of the `Image` element, the attribute is simply a more compact way of including the filename. As a rule, attributes should be atomic, with no significant internal structure; by contrast, child elements can have arbitrary complexity.

XML Documents

An XML document begins with the following header and has one *root element*:

```
<?xml version="1.0" encoding="UTF-8"?>
<MyDocument>
</MyDocument>
```

The header identifies the version of XML and the character encoding used. The root element is simply the top of the element hierarchy, which can be considered a tree. If you omit this header or have XML text without a single root element, technically what you have is called an XML *fragment*.

Encoding

The default encoding for an XML document is UTF-8, the ASCII-friendly 8-bit Unicode encoding. But an XML document may specify an encoding using the encoding attribute of the XML header.

Within an XML document, certain characters are necessarily sacrosanct: for example, the "<" and ">" characters that indicate element tags. When you need to include these in your text, you must encode them. XML provides an escape mechanism called "entities" that allows for encoding special structures. There are five predefined entities in XML, as shown in Table 23-1.

Table 23-1. XML entities

Entity	Encodes
&amp;	& (ampersand)
&lt;	< (less than)
&gt;	> (greater than)
&quot;	" (quotation mark)
&apos;	' (apostrophe)

An alternative to encoding text in this way is to use a special "unparsed" section of text called a character data (CDATA) section. A CDATA section starts with `<![CDATA[` and ends with `]]>`, like this:

```
<![CDATA[ Learning Java, O'Reilly & Associates ]]>
```

The CDATA section looks a little like a comment, but the data is really part of the document, just opaque to the parser.

Namespaces

You've probably seen that HTML has a `<body>` tag that is used to structure web pages. Suppose for a moment that we are writing XML for a funeral home that also uses the tag `<body>` for some other, more macabre, purpose. This could be a problem if we want to mix HTML with our mortuary information.

If you consider HTML and the funeral home tags to be a language in this case, the elements (tag names) used in a document are really the vocabulary of those languages. An XML *namespace* is a way of saying whose dictionary you are using for a given element, allowing us to mix them freely. (Later we'll talk about XML Schema, which enforce the grammar and syntax of the language.)

A namespace is specified with the `xmlns` attribute, whose value is a Universal Resource Identifier (URI) that uniquely defines the set (and usually the meaning) of tags from that namespace:

```
<element xmlns="namespaceURI">
```

Recall from Chapter 13 that a URI is not necessarily a URL. URIs are more general than URLs. In practical terms, a URI is simply to be treated as a unique string. Often, the URI is, in fact, also a URL for a document describing the namespace, but that is only by convention.

An `xmlns` namespace attribute can be applied to an element and all its children; this is called a default namespace for the element:

```
<body xmlns="http://funeral-procedures.org/">
```

But more often it is desirable to specify namespaces on a tag-by-tag basis. To do this, we can use the `xmlns` attribute to define a special identifier for the namespace and then use that identifier as a prefix on the tags in question. For example:

```
<funeral xmlns:fun="http://funeral-procedures.org/">
    <html><head></head><body>
    <fun:body>Corpse #42</fun:body>
</funeral>
```

In the above snippet of XML, we've qualified the body tag with the prefix "fun:" that we defined in the `<funeral>` tag. In this case, we should also qualify the root tag as well, reflexively:

```
<fun:funeral xmlns:fun="http://funeral-procedures.org/">
```

In the history of XML, support for namespaces is relatively new. Not all parsers support them. To accommodate this, the XML parser factories that we discuss later have a switch to specify whether you want a parser that understands namespaces.

```
factory.setNamespaceAware(true);
```

We'll talk more about parsing in the sections on SAX and DOM later in this chapter.

Validation

A document that conforms to the basic rules of XML, with proper encoding and balanced tags, is called a *well-formed* document. Just because a document is syntactically correct doesn't mean that it makes sense, however. Two related specifications, Document Type Definitions (DTDs) and XML Schema, define ways to provide a grammar for your XML elements. This allows you to create syntactic rules, such as "a City element can appear only once inside an Address element." XML Schema goes further to provide a flexible language for describing the validity of data content of the tags, including both simple and compound data types made of numbers and strings. Although XML Schema is the ultimate solution (it includes data validation and not just rules about elements), it is more theory than practice at present, at least in terms of its integration with Java. (We hope that will change soon.)

A document that is checked against a DTD or XML Schema description and follows the rules is called a *valid* document. A document can be well-formed without being valid, but not vice versa.

HTML to XHTML

To speak very loosely, we could say that the most popular and widely used form of XML in the world today is HTML. The terminology is loose because HTML is not even well-formed XML. HTML tags violate XML's rule forbidding empty elements; the common <p> tag is typically used without a closing tag, for example. HTML attributes also don't require quotes. XML tags are case-sensitive; <P> and <p> are two different tags in XML. We could generously say that HTML is "forgiving" with respect to details like this, but as a developer, you know that sloppy syntax results in ambiguity. XHTML is a version of HTML that is clear and unambiguous. Fortunately, you don't have to manually clean up all your HTML documents; Tidy (*http://tidy.sourceforge.net*) is an open source program that automatically converts HTML to XHTML, validates it, and corrects common mistakes.

SAX

SAX is a low-level, event-style mechanism for parsing XML documents. SAX originated in Java but has been implemented in many languages.

The SAX API

To use SAX, we'll be using classes from the org.xml.sax package, available from the W3C (World Wide Web Consortium). To perform the actual parsing, we'll need the javax.xml.parsers package, which is the standard Java package for accessing XML parsers. The java.xml.parsers package is part of the Java API for XML Processing (JAXP), which allows different parser implementations to be used with Java.

To read an XML document with SAX, we first register an `org.xml.sax.`
`ContentHandler` class with the parser. The `ContentHandler` has methods that are called
in response to parts of the document. For example, the `ContentHandler`'s
`startElement()` method is called when an opening tag is encountered, and the
`endElement()` method is called when the tag is closed. Attributes are provided with
the `startElement()` call. Text content of elements is passed through a separate
method called `characters()`. The `characters()` method can be invoked repeatedly to
supply more text as it is read, but it often gets the whole string in one bite. The following are the method signatures of these methods of the `ContentHandler` class.

```
public void startElement(
    String namespace, String localname, String qname, Attributes atts );
public void characters(
    char[] ch, int start, int len );
public void endElement(
    String namespace, String localname, String qname );
```

The qname parameter is the qualified name of the element. This is the element name,
prefixed with namespace if it has one. When working with namespaces, the
namespace and localname parameters are also supplied, providing the namespace and
unqualified name.

The `ContentHandler` interface also contains methods called in response to the start
and end of the document, `startDocument()` and `endDocument()`, as well as those for
handling namespace mapping, special XML instructions, and whitespace that can be
ignored. We'll confine ourselves to the three methods above for our examples. As
with many other Java interfaces, a simple implementation, `org.xml.sax.helpers.`
`DefaultHandler`, is provided for us that allows us to override just the methods we're
interested in.

JAXP

To perform the parsing, we'll need to get a parser from the javax.xml.parsers package. The process of getting a parser is abstracted through a *factory pattern*, allowing
different parser implementations to be plugged into the Java platform. The following snippet constructs a SAXParser object and an XMLReader used to parse a file:

```
import javax.xml.parsers.*;

SAXParserFactory factory = SAXParserFactory.newInstance( );
SAXParser saxParser = factory.newSAXParser( );
XMLReader parser = saxParser.getXMLReader( );

parser.setContentHandler( myContentHandler );
parser.parse( myfile.xml" );
```

You might expect the SAXParser to have the parse method. The XMLReader intermediary was added to support changes in the SAX API between 1.0 and 2.0. Later we'll
discuss some options that can be set to govern how XML parsers operate. These

options are normally set through methods on the parser factory (e.g., SAXParserFactory) and not the parser itself. This is because the factory may wish to use different implementations to support different required features.

SAX's strengths and weaknesses

The primary motivation for using SAX instead of the higher-level APIs that we'll discuss later is that it is lightweight and event-driven. SAX doesn't require maintaining the entire document in memory. If, for example, you need to grab the text of just a few elements from a document, or if you need to extract elements from a large stream of XML, you can do so efficiently with SAX. The event-driven nature of SAX also allows you to take actions as the beginning and end tags are parsed. This can be useful for directly manipulating your own models without first going through another representation. The primary weakness of SAX is that you are operating on a tag-by-tag level with no help from the parser to maintain context.

Building a Model Using SAX

The ContentHandler mechanism for receiving SAX events is very simple. It should be easy to see how one could use it to capture the value or attributes of a single element in a document. What may be harder to see is how one could use SAX to build a real Java object model from an XML document. The following example, SAXModelBuilder, does just that. This example is a bit unusual in that we resort to using reflection to do a job that would otherwise be a burden on the developer. Later, we'll discuss more powerful tools for automatically generating and building models for use with XML documents.

In this section, we'll start by creating some XML along with corresponding Java classes that serve as the model for this XML. We'll see later that it's possible to work with XML more dynamically, without first constructing Java classes that hold all the content, but we want to start out in the most concrete and general way possible. The final step in this example is to create the generic model builder that reads the XML and populates the model classes with their data. The idea here is that the developer is creating only XML and model classes—no custom code—to do the basic parsing.

Building the XML file

The first thing we'll need is a nice XML document to parse. Luckily, it's inventory time at the zoo! The following document, zooinventory.xml, describes two of the zoo's residents, including some vital information about their diets:

```
<?xml version="1.0" encoding="UTF-8"?>
<!- file zooinventory.xml -->
<Inventory>
    <Animal class="mammal">
        <Name>Song Fang</Name>
        <Species>Giant Panda</Species>
```

```
        <Habitat>China</Habitat>
        <Food>Bamboo</Food>
        <Temperament>Friendly</Temperament>
    </Animal>
    <Animal class="mammal">
        <Name>Cocoa</Name>
        <Species>Gorilla</Species>
        <Habitat>Central Africa</Habitat>
        <FoodRecipe>
            <Name>Gorilla Chow</Name>
            <Ingredient>Fruit</Ingredient>
            <Ingredient>Shoots</Ingredient>
            <Ingredient>Leaves</Ingredient>
        </FoodRecipe>
        <Temperament>Know-it-all</Temperament>
    </Animal>
</Inventory>
```

The document is fairly simple. The root element, <Inventory>, contains two <Animal> elements as children. <Animal> contains several simple text elements for things like name, species, and habitat. It also contains either a simple <Food> element or a compound <FoodRecipe> element. Finally, note that the <Animal> element has one attribute (class) that describes the zoological classification of the creature.

The model

Now let's make a Java object model for our zoo inventory. This part is very mechanical—easy, but tedious to do by hand. We simply create objects for each of the complex element types in our XML, using the standard JavaBeans property design patterns ("setters" and "getters") so that our builder can automatically use them later. (We'll prove the usefulness of these patterns later when we see that these same model objects can be understood by the Java XMLEncoder tool.) For convenience, we'll have our model objects extend a base SimpleElement class that handles text content for any element.

```
public class SimpleElement {
    StringBuffer text = new StringBuffer();
    public void addText( String s ) { text.append( s ); }
    public String getText() { return text.toString(); }
    public void setAttributeValue( String name, String value ) {
        throw new Error( getClass()+": No attributes allowed");
    }
}
public class Inventory extends SimpleElement {
    List animals = new ArrayList();
    public void addAnimal( Animal animal ) { animals.add( animal ); }
    public List getAnimals() { return animals; }
    public void setAnimals( List animals ) { this.animals = animals; }
}
```

```
public class Animal extends SimpleElement {
    public final static int MAMMAL = 1;
    int animalClass;
    String name, species, habitat, food, temperament;
    FoodRecipe foodRecipe;

    public void setName( String name ) { this.name = name ; }
    public String getName() { return name; }
    public void setSpecies( String species ) { this.species = species ; }
    public String getSpecies() { return species; }
    public void setHabitat( String habitat ) { this.habitat = habitat ; }
    public String getHabitat() { return habitat; }
    public void setFood( String food ) { this.food = food ; }
    public String getFood() { return food; }
    public void setFoodRecipe( FoodRecipe recipe ) {
        this.foodRecipe = recipe; }
    public FoodRecipe getFoodRecipe() { return foodRecipe; }
    public void setTemperament( String temperament ) {
        this.temperament = temperament ; }
    public String getTemperament() { return temperament; }

    public void setAnimalClass( int animalClass ) {
        this.animalClass = animalClass; }
    public int getAnimalClass() { return animalClass; }
    public void setAttributeValue( String name, String value ) {
        if ( name.equals("class") && value.equals("mammal") )
            setAnimalClass( MAMMAL );
        else
            throw new Error("Invalid attribute: "+name);
    }
    public String toString() { return name +"("+species+")"; }
}

public class FoodRecipe extends SimpleElement {
    String name;
    List ingredients = new ArrayList();
    public void setName( String name ) { this.name = name ; }
    public String getName() { return name; }
    public void addIngredient( String ingredient ) {
        ingredients.add( ingredient ); }
    public void setIngredients( List ingredients ) {
        this.ingredients = ingredients; }
    public List getIngredients() { return ingredients; }
    public String toString() { return name + ": "+ ingredients.toString(); }
}
```

If you are working in the NetBeans IDE, you can use the *Bean Patterns* wizard for your class to help you create all those get and set methods (see the "Bean patterns in NetBeans" section in Chapter 21 for details).

SAX model builder

Now let's get down to business and write our builder tool. The SAXModelBuilder we create in this section receives SAX events from parsing an XML file and constructs classes corresponding to the names of the tags. Our model builder is simple, but it handles the most common structures: elements with text or simple element data. We handle attributes by passing them to the model class, allowing it to map them to fixed identifiers (e.g., Animal.MAMMAL). Here is the code:

```java
import org.xml.sax.*;
import org.xml.sax.helpers.*;
import java.util.*;
import java.lang.reflect.*;

public class SAXModelBuilder extends DefaultHandler
{
    Stack stack = new Stack( );
    SimpleElement element;

    public void startElement(
        String namespace, String localname, String qname, Attributes atts )
      throws SAXException
    {
      SimpleElement element = null;
        try {
            element = (SimpleElement)Class.forName(qname).newInstance( );
        } catch ( Exception e ) {/*No class for element*/}
        if ( element == null )
            element = new SimpleElement( );
        for(int i=0; i<atts.getLength( ); i++)
            element.setAttributeValue( atts.getQName(i), atts.getValue(i) );
        stack.push( element );
     }
    public void endElement( String namespace, String localname, String qname)
        throws SAXException
    {
      element = (SimpleElement)stack.pop( );
      if ( !stack.empty( ) )
          try {
              setProperty( qname, stack.peek( ), element );
          } catch ( Exception e ) { throw new SAXException( "Error: "+e ); }
    }
    public void characters(char[] ch, int start, int len ) {
        String text = new String( ch, start, len );
        ((SimpleElement)(stack.peek( ))).addText( text );
    }

    void setProperty( String name, Object target, Object value )
        throws SAXException
    {
      Method method = null;
        try {
          method = target.getClass( ).getMethod(
```

```
           "add"+name, new Class[] { value.getClass( ) } );
      } catch ( NoSuchMethodException e ) { }
      if ( method == null ) try {
         method = target.getClass( ).getMethod(
            "set"+name, new Class[] { value.getClass( ) } );
      } catch ( NoSuchMethodException e ) { }
      if ( method == null ) try {
         value = ((SimpleElement)value).getText( );
         method = target.getClass( ).getMethod(
            "add"+name, new Class[] { String.class } );
      } catch ( NoSuchMethodException e ) { }
      try {
         if ( method == null )
            method = target.getClass( ).getMethod(
               "set"+name, new Class[] { String.class } );
         method.invoke( target, new Object [] { value } );
      } catch ( Exception e ) { throw new SAXException( e.toString( ) ); }
   }
   public SimpleElement getModel( ) { return element; }
}
```

The `SAXModelBuilder` extends `DefaultHandler` to help us implement the `ContentHandler` interface. We use the `startElement()`, `endElement()`, and `characters()` methods to receive information from the document.

Because SAX events follow the structure of the XML document, we use a simple stack to keep track of which object we are currently parsing. At the start of each element, the model builder attempts to create an instance of a class with the same name and push it onto the top of the stack. Each nested opening tag creates a new object on the stack until we encounter a closing tag. Upon reaching an end of the element, we pop the current object off the stack and attempt to apply its value to its parent (the enclosing element), which is the new top of the stack. The final closing tag leaves the stack empty, but we save the last value in the result variable.

Our `setProperty()` method uses reflection and the standard JavaBeans naming conventions to look for the appropriate property "setter" method to apply a value to its parent object. First we check for a method named add<Property> or set<Property>, accepting an argument of the child element type (for example, the addAnimal(Animal animal) method of our Inventory object). Failing that, we look for an "add" or "set" method accepting a `String` argument and use it to apply any text content of the child object. This convenience saves us from having to create trivial classes for properties containing only text.

The common base class `SimpleElement` helps us in two ways. First, it provides a method allowing us to pass attributes to the model class. Next, we use `SimpleElement` as a placeholder when no class exists for an element, allowing us to store the text of the tag.

Test drive

Finally, we can test-drive the model builder with the following class, TestModelBuilder, which calls the SAX parser, setting an instance of our SAXModelBuilder as the content handler. The test class then prints some of the information parsed from the *zooinventory.xml* file:

```
import org.xml.sax.*;
import org.xml.sax.helpers.*;
import javax.xml.parsers.*;

public class TestModelBuilder
{
    public static void main( String [] args ) throws Exception
    {
        SAXParserFactory factory = SAXParserFactory.newInstance( );
        SAXParser saxParser = factory.newSAXParser( );
        XMLReader parser = saxParser.getXMLReader( );
        SAXModelBuilder mb = new SAXModelBuilder( );
        parser.setContentHandler( mb );
        parser.parse( "zooinventory.xml" );

        Inventory inventory = (Inventory)mb.getModel( );
        System.out.println("Animals = "+inventory.getAnimals( ));
        Animal cocoa = (Animal)(inventory.getAnimals( ).get(1));
        FoodRecipe recipe = cocoa.getFoodRecipe( );
        System.out.println( "Recipe = "+recipe );
    }
}
```

The output should look like this:

```
Animals = [Song Fang(Giant Panda), Cocoa(Gorilla)]
Recipe = Gorilla Chow: [Fruit, Shoots, Leaves]
```

In the following sections we'll generate the equivalent output using different tools.

Limitations and possibilities

To make our model builder more complete, we could use more robust naming conventions for our tags and model classes (taking into account packages and mixed capitalization, etc.). But more generally, we might not want to name our model classes strictly based on tag names. And, of course, there is the problem of taking our model and going the other way, using it to generate an XML document. Furthermore, as we've said, writing the model classes is tedious and error-prone. All this is a good indication that this area is ripe for autogeneration of classes. We'll discuss tools that do that a bit later in the chapter.

XMLencoder/decoder

Java 1.4 introduced a tool for serializing JavaBeans classes to XML. The java.beans package XMLEncoder and XMLDecoder classes are analogous to java.io

`ObjectInputStream` and `ObjectOutputStream`. Instead of using the native Java serialization format, they store the object state in a high-level XML format. We say that they are analogous, but the XML encoder is not a general replacement for Java object serialization. Instead, it is specialized to work with objects that follow the JavaBeans design patterns, and it can only store and recover state of the object that is expressed through a bean's public properties in this way (using getters and setters).

In memory, the `XMLEncoder` attempts to construct a copy of the graph of beans that you are serializing, using only public constructors and JavaBean properties. As it works, it writes out these steps as "instructions" in an XML format. Later, the `XMLDecoder` executes these instructions and produces the result. The primary advantage of this process is that it is highly resilient to changes in the class implementation. While standard Java object serialization can accommodate many kinds of "compatible changes" in classes, it requires some help from the developer to get it right. Because the `XMLEncoder` uses only public APIs and writes instructions in simple XML, it is expected that this form of serialization will be the most robust way to store the state of JavaBeans. The process is referred to as "long-term persistence" for JavaBeans.

Give it a whirl. You can use the model-builder example to create the beans and compare the output to our original XML. You can add this bit to our `TestModelBuilder` class, which will populate the beans for you to write:

```
import java.beans.XMLEncoder;

XMLEncoder xmle = new XMLEncoder( System.out );
xmle.writeObject(inventory);
xmle.close( );
```

Fun!

Further thoughts

It might seem at first like this would obviate the need for our `SAXModelBuilder` example. Why not simply write our XML in the format that `XMLDecoder` understands and use it to build our model? Well, although `XMLEncoder` is very efficient at eliminating redundancy, you can see that its output is still very verbose (about four times as large as our original XML) and not very human-friendly. Although it's possible to write it by hand, this XML format wasn't really designed for that. Finally, although `XMLEncoder` can be customized for how it handles specific object types, it suffers from the same problem that our model builder does in that "binding" (the namespace of tags) is determined strictly by our Java class names. As we've said before, what is really needed is a more general tool to generate classes or to map our own classes to XML and back.

DOM

In the last section, we used SAX to parse an XML document and build a Java object model representing it. In that case, we created specific Java types for each of our complex elements. If we were planning to use our model extensively in an application, this technique would give us a great deal of flexibility. But often it is sufficient (and much easier) to use a "generic" model that simply represents the content of the XML in a neutral form. The Document Object Model (DOM) is just that. The DOM API parses an XML document into a full, memory-resident representation consisting of classes such as `Element` and `Attributes` with text values.

As we saw in our zoo example, once you have an object model, using the data is a breeze. So a generic DOM would seem like an appealing solution, especially when working mainly with text. The only catch in this case is that DOM didn't evolve first as a Java API, and it doesn't map well to Java. DOM is very complete and provides access to every facet of the original XML document, but it's so generic (and language-neutral), it's cumbersome to use in Java. In our example, we'll start by making a couple of helper methods to smooth things over. Later, we'll also mention a native Java alternative to DOM called JDOM that is more pleasant to use.

The DOM API

The core DOM classes belong to the `org.w3c.dom` package. The result of parsing an XML document with DOM is a `Document` object from this package (see Figure 23-1). The `Document` is a factory and a container for a hierarchical collection of `Node` objects, representing the document structure. A node has a parent and may have children, which can be traversed using its `getChildNodes()`, `getFirstChild()`, or `getLastChild()` methods. A node may also have "attributes" associated with it, which consist of a named map of nodes.

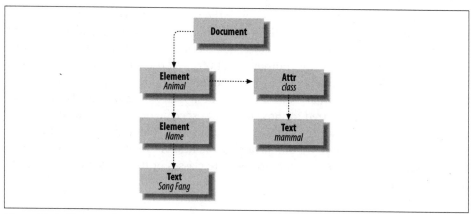

Figure 23-1. The parsed DOM

Subtypes of Node—Element, Text, and Attr—represent elements, text, and attributes in XML. Some types of nodes (including these) have a text "value." For example, the value of a Text node is the text of the element it represents. The same is true of an attribute, cdata, or comment node. The value of a node can be accessed by the getNodeValue() and setNodeValue() methods.

The Element node provides "random" access to its child elements through its getElementsByTagName() method, which returns a NodeList (a simple collection type). You can also fetch an attribute by name from the Element using the getAttribute() method.

The javax.xml.parsers package contains a factory for DOM parsers, just as it does for SAX parsers. An instance of DocumentBuilderFactory can be used to create a DocumentBuilder object to parse the file and produce a Document result.

Test-Driving DOM

Let's use DOM to parse our zoo inventory and print the same information as our model-builder example. Using DOM saves us from having to create all those model classes and makes our example much shorter. But before we even begin, we're going to make a couple of utility methods to save us a great deal of pain. The following class, DOMUtil, covers two very common operations on an element: retrieving a simple (singular) child element by name and retrieving the text of a simple child element by name. Here is the code:

```
import org.w3c.dom.*;

public class DOMUtil
{
    public static Element getFirstElement( Element element, String name ) {
        NodeList nl = element.getElementsByTagName( name );
        if ( nl.getLength() < 1 )
            throw new RuntimeException(
                "Element: "+element+" does not contain: "+name);
        return (Element)nl.item(0);
    }

    public static String getSimpleElementText( Element node, String name )
    {
        Element namedElement = getFirstElement( node, name );
        return getSimpleElementText( namedElement );
    }

    public static String getSimpleElementText( Element node )
    {
        StringBuffer sb = new StringBuffer();
        NodeList children = node.getChildNodes();
```

```
            for(int i=0; i<children.getLength(); i++) {
                Node child = children.item(i);
                if ( child instanceof Text )
                    sb.append( child.getNodeValue() );
            }
            return sb.toString();
        }
    }
```

With that out of the way we can present our TestDOM class:

```
mport javax.xml.parsers.*;
import org.w3c.dom.*;

public class TestDOM
{
    public static void main( String [] args ) throws Exception
    {
        DocumentBuilderFactory factory = DocumentBuilderFactory.newInstance();
        DocumentBuilder parser = factory.newDocumentBuilder();
        Document document = parser.parse( "zooinventory.xml" );
        Element inventory = document.getDocumentElement();
        NodeList animals = inventory.getElementsByTagName("Animal");

        System.out.println("Animals = ");
        for( int i=0; i<animals.getLength(); i++ ) {
            String name = DOMUtil.getSimpleElementText(
                (Element)animals.item(i),"Name" );
            String species = DOMUtil.getSimpleElementText(
                (Element)animals.item(i), "Species" );
            System.out.println( "  "+ name +" ("+species+")" );
        }

        Element foodRecipe = DOMUtil.getFirstElement(
            (Element)animals.item(1), "FoodRecipe" );
        String name = DOMUtil.getSimpleElementText( foodRecipe, "Name" );
        System.out.println("Recipe = " + name );
        NodeList ingredients = foodRecipe.getElementsByTagName("Ingredient");
        for(int i=0; i<ingredients.getLength(); i++)
            System.out.println( "  " + DOMUtil.getSimpleElementText(
                (Element)ingredients.item(i) ) );
    }
}
```

TestDOM creates an instance of a DocumentBuilder and uses it to parse our *zooinventory.xml* file. We use the Document getDocumentElement() method to get the root element of the document, from which we will begin our traversal. From there, we ask for all the Animal child nodes. The getElementbyTagName() method returns a NodeList object, which we then use to iterate through our creatures. For each animal, we use our DOMUtil.getSimpleElementText() method to retrieve the basic name and species information. Next, we use the DOMUtil.getFirstElement() method to retrieve the element called FoodRecipe from the second animal. We use it to fetch a NodeList for the tags matching Ingredient and print them as before. The output should contain the same information as our SAX-based example.

Generating XML with DOM

Thus far, we've used the SAX and DOM APIs to parse XML. But what about generating XML? Sure, it's easy to generate trivial XML documents simply by emitting the appropriate strings. But if we plan to create a complex document on the fly, we might want some help with all those quotes and closing tags. What we can do is to build a DOM representation of our object in memory and then transform it to text. This is also useful if we want to read a document and then make some alterations to it. To do this, we'll use of the java.xml.transform package. This package does a lot more than just printing XML. As its name implies, it's part of a general transformation facility. It includes the XSL/XSLT languages for generating one XML document from another. (We'll talk about XSL later in this chapter.)

We won't discuss the details of constructing a DOM in memory here, but it follows fairly naturally from what you've learned about traversing the tree in our previous example. The following example, PrintDOM, simply parses our *zooinventory.xml* file to a DOM and then prints it back to the screen:

```
import javax.xml.parsers.*;
import org.w3c.dom.*;
import javax.xml.transform.*;
import javax.xml.transform.dom.DOMSource;
import javax.xml.transform.stream.StreamResult;

public class PrintDOM {
    public static void main( String [] args ) throws Exception
    {
        DocumentBuilder parser =
            DocumentBuilderFactory.newInstance().newDocumentBuilder();
        Document document=parser.parse( "zooinventory.xml" );
        Transformer transformer =
            TransformerFactory.newInstance().newTransformer();
        Source source = new DOMSource( document );
        Result output = new StreamResult( System.out );
        transformer.transform( source, output );
    }
}
```

Note that the imports are almost as long as the entire program! Here we are using an instance of a Transformer object in its simplest capacity to copy from a source to an output. We'll return to the Transformer later when we discuss XSL.

JDOM

As we promised earlier, we'll now describe an easier DOM API: JDOM, created by Jason Hunter and Brett McLaughlin, two fellow O'Reilly authors (*Java Servlet*

Programming and *Java and XML*, respectively). It is a more natural Java DOM that uses real Java collection types such as List for its hierarchy and provides more streamlined methods for building documents. You can get the latest JDOM from *http://www.jdom.org/*. Here's the JDOM version of our standard "test" program:

```java
import org.jdom.*;
import org.jdom.input.*;
import org.jdom.output.*;
import java.util.*;

public class TestJDOM {
    public static void main( String[] args ) throws Exception {
        Document doc = new SAXBuilder( ).build("zooinventory.xml");
        List animals = doc.getRootElement( ).getChildren("Animal");
        System.out.println("Animals = ");
        for( int i=0; i<animals.size(); i++ ) {
            String name = ((Element)animals.get(i)).getChildText("Name");
            String species = ((Element)animals.get(i)).getChildText("Species");
            System.out.println( "   "+ name +" ("+species+")" );
        }
        Element foodRecipe = ((Element)animals.get(1)).getChild("FoodRecipe");
        String name = foodRecipe.getChildText("Name");
        System.out.println("Recipe = " + name );
        List ingredients = foodRecipe.getChildren("Ingredient");
        for(int i=0; i<ingredients.size(); i++)
            System.out.println( "   "+((Element)ingredients.get(i)).getText() );
    }
}
```

JDOM has convenience methods that take the place of our homemade DOM helper methods. Namely, the JDOM element has getChild() and getChildren() methods as well as a getChildText() method for retrieving node text.

Validating Documents

> *"Words, words, mere words, no matter from the heart."*
> William Shakespeare, *Troilus and Cressida*

In this section, we talk about DTDs and XML Schema, two ways to enforce rules an XML document must follow. A DTD is a grammar for an XML document, defining which tags may appear where and in what order, with what attributes, etc. XML Schema is the next generation of DTD. With XML Schema, you can describe the data content of the document in terms of primitives such as numbers, dates, and simple regular expressions. The word *schema* means a blueprint or plan for structure, so we'll refer to DTDs and XML Schema collectively as schema where either applies

Now for a reality check. Unfortunately, Java support for XML Schema isn't entirely mature at the time of this writing. XML support in Java 1.4.0 is based on the Apache

Project's Crimson parser (which in turn is based on Sun's "Project X" parser). The Crimson engine doesn't support XML Schema. However, a future release of Java will migrate the XML implementation to the Apache Xerces2 engine, and at that time, XML Schema should begin to be supported.

Using Document Validation

XML's validation of documents is a key piece of what makes it useful as a data format. Using a schema is somewhat analogous to the way Java classes enforce type checking in the language. Schema define document types. Documents conforming to a given schema are often referred to as *instance documents*.

This type safety provides a layer of protection that eliminates having to write complex error-checking code. However, validation may not be necessary in every environment. For example, when the same tool generates XML and reads it back, validation should not be necessary in normal operation. It is invaluable, though, during development. Often, document validation is used during development and turned off in production environments.

DTDs

The Document Type Definition language is fairly simple. A DTD is primarily a set of special tags that define each element in the document and, for complex types, provide a list of the elements it may contain. The DTD <!ELEMENT> tag consists of the name of the tag and either a special keyword for the data type or a parenthesized list of elements.

```
<!ELEMENT Name ( #PCDATA )>
<!ELEMENT Document ( Head, Body )>
```

The special identifier #PCDATA indicates character data (a string). When a list is provided, the elements are expected to appear in that order. The list may contain sublists, and items may be made optional using a vertical bar (|) as an OR operator. Special notation can also be used to indicate how many of each item may appear; a few examples of this notation are shown in Table 23-2.

Table 23-2. DTD notation defining occurrences

Character	Meaning
*	Zero or more occurrences
?	Zero or one occurrences
+	One or more occurrences

Attributes of an element are defined with the `<!ATTLIST>` tag. This tag enables the DTD to enforce rules about attributes. It accepts a list of identifiers and a default value:

```
<!ATTLIST Animal class (unknown | mammal | reptile) "unknown">
```

This ATTLIST says that the Animal element has a class attribute that can have one of three values: unknown, mammal, or reptile. The default is unknown.

We won't cover everything you can do with DTDs here. But the following example will guarantee *zooinventory.xml* follows the format we've described. Place the following in a file called *zooinventory.dtd* (or grab this file from the CD-ROM or web site for the book):

```
<!ELEMENT Inventory ( Animal* )>
<!ELEMENT Animal (Name, Species, Habitat, (Food | FoodRecipe), Temperament)>
<!ATTLIST Animal class (unknown | mammal | reptile) "unknown">
<!ELEMENT Name ( #PCDATA )>
<!ELEMENT Species ( #PCDATA )>
<!ELEMENT Habitat ( #PCDATA )>
<!ELEMENT Food ( #PCDATA )>
<!ELEMENT FoodRecipe ( Name, Ingredient+ )>
<!ELEMENT Ingredient ( #PCDATA )>
<!ELEMENT Temperament ( #PCDATA )>
```

The DTD says that an Inventory consists of any number of Animal elements. An Animal has a Name, Species, and Habitat tag followed by either a Food or FoodRecipe. FoodRecipe's structure is further defined later.

To use our DTD, we must associate it with the XML document. We do this by placing a DOCTYPE declaration in the XML itself. When a validating parser encounters the DOCTYPE, it attempts to load the DTD and validate the document. There are several forms the DOCTYPE can have, but the one we'll use is:

```
<!DOCTYPE Inventory SYSTEM "zooinventory.dtd">
```

Both SAX and DOM parsers can automatically validate documents that contain a DOCTYPE declaration. However, you have to explicitly ask the parser factory to provide a parser that is capable of validation. To do this, set the validating property of the parser factory to true before you ask it for an instance of the parser. For example:

```
SAXParserFactory factory = SAXParserFactory.newInstance();
factory.setValidating( true );
```

Try inserting the setValidating() line in our model builder example at the location indicated above. Now abuse the *zooinventory.xml* file by adding or removing an element or attribute and see what happens when you run the example.

To really use the validation, we would have to register an org.xml.sax.ErrorHandler object with the parser, but by default Java installs one that simply prints the errors for us.

XML Schema

Although DTDs can define the basic structure of an XML document, they can't adequately describe data and validate it programmatically. The evolving XML Schema standard is the next logical step and should replace DTDs in the near future. For more information about XML Schema, see *http://www.w3.org/XML/Schema*. As mentioned earlier, we expect an upcoming Java release to support XML Schema.

JAXB and Code Generation

The ultimate goal of XML will be reached by automated binding of XML to Java classes. There are several tools today that provide this, but they are hampered by the slow adoption of XML Schema.

The standard Java solution is the forthcoming Java XML Binding (JAXB) project. Unfortunately, at the time of this writing, JAXB is not mature. It is difficult to use and doesn't support XML Schema (necessary to fully describe document content). JAXB also requires its own "binding" language to be used, even for simple cases. We hope that the final release of JAXB will provide a good solution for XML binding. You can find information about JAXB at *http://java.sun.com/xml/jaxb*.

Unlike JAXB, Castor, an open source XML binding framework for Java, works with XML Schema and is relatively easy to use. Unfortunately, at the time of this writing, Castor doesn't support DTDs, and most industry- or task-specific XML standards are still written in terms of DTDs. You can find out more about Castor at *http://www.castor.org/*.

XSL/XSLT

Earlier in this chapter, we used a Transformer object to copy a DOM representation of an example back to XML text. We mentioned then that we were not really tapping the potential of the Transformer. Now we'll give you the full story.

The javax.xml.transform package is the API for using the XSL/XSLT transformation language. XSL stands for Extensible Stylesheet Language. Like Cascading Stylesheets for HTML, XSL allows us to "mark up" XML documents by adding tags that provide presentation information. XSL Transformation (XSLT) takes this further by adding the ability to completely restructure the XML and produce arbitrary output. XSL and XSLT together comprise their own programming language for processing an XML document as input and producing another (usually XML) document as output. (From here on in we'll refer to them collectively as XSL.)

XSL is extremely powerful, and new applications for its use arise every day. For example, consider a web portal that is frequently updated and which must provide access to a variety of mobile devices, from PDAs to cell phones to traditional browsers. Rather than recreating the site for these and additional platforms, XSL can transform the content to an appropriate format for each platform. Multilingual sites also benefit from XSL.

You can probably guess the caveat that we're going to issue next: XSL is a big topic worthy of its own books (see, for example, O'Reilly's *Java and XSLT* by Eric Burke, a fellow St. Louis author), and we can only give you a taste of it here. Furthermore, some people find XSL difficult to understand at first glance because it requires thinking in terms of recursively processing document tags. Don't be put off if you have trouble following this example; just file it away and return to it when you need it. At some point, you will be interested in the power transformation can offer you.

XSL Basics

XSL is an XML-based standard, so it should come as no surprise that the language is based on XML. An XSL *stylesheet* is an XML document using special tags defined by the XSL namespace to describe the transformation. The most basic XSL operations include matching parts of the input XML document and generating output based on their contents. One or more XSL *templates* live within the stylesheet and are called in response to tags appearing in the input. XSL is often used in a purely input-driven way, where input XML tags trigger output in the order that they appear, using only the information they contain. But more generally, the output can be constructed from arbitrary parts of the input, drawing from it like a database, composing elements and attributes. The XSLT transformation part of XSL adds things like conditionals and for loops to this mix, enabling arbitrary output to be generated based on the input.

An XSL stylesheet contains as its root element a stylesheet tag. By convention, the stylesheet defines a namespace prefix xsl for the XSL namespace. Within the stylesheet are one or more template tags containing a match attribute describing the element upon which they operate.

```
<xsl:stylesheet
    xmlns:xsl="http://www.w3.org/1999/XSL/Transform" version="1.0">

    <xsl:template match="/">
      I found the root of the document!
    </xsl:template>

</xsl:stylesheet>
```

When a template matches an element, it has an opportunity to handle all the children of the element. The simple stylesheet above has one template that matches the root of the input document and simply outputs some plain text. By default, input not matched is simply copied to the output with its tags stripped (HTML convention). But here we match the root so we consume the entire input.

The match attribute can refer to elements in a hierarchical path fashion starting with the root. For example, `match="/Inventory/Animal"` would match only the `Animal` elements from our *zooinventory.xml* file. The path may be absolute (starting with "/") or relative, in which case the template detects whenever that element appears in any context. The match attribute actually uses an expression format called XPath that allows you to describe element names using a syntax somewhat similar to a regular expression. XPath is a powerful syntax for describing sets of nodes in XML, and it includes notation for describing sets of child nodes based on path and even attributes.

Within the template, we can put whatever we want, as long as it is well-formed XML (if not, we can use a CDATA section). But the real power comes when we use parts of the input to generate output. The XSL `value-of` tag is used to output the content of an element or a child of the element. For example, the following template would match an `Animal` element and output the value of its `Name` child:

```
<xsl:template match="Animal">
   Name: <xsl:value-of select="Name"/>
</xsl:template>
```

The select attribute uses a similar expression format to match. Here we tell it to print the value of the `Name` element within `Animal`. We could have used a relative path to a more deeply nested element within `Animal` or even an absolute path to another part of the document. To refer to its own element, we can simply use "." as the path. The select expression can also retrieve attributes from the elements it refers to.

Now if we try to add the `Animal` template to our simple example, it won't generate any output. What's the problem? Well, if you recall, we said that a template matching an element has the opportunity to process all its children. We already have a template matching the root ("/"), so it is consuming all the input. The answer to our dilemma—and this is where things get a little tricky—is to delegate the matching to other templates using the `apply-templates` tag. The following example correctly prints the names of all the animals in our document:

```
<xsl:stylesheet
   xmlns:xsl="http://www.w3.org/1999/XSL/Transform" version="1.0">

   <xsl:template match="/">
      Found the root!
      <xsl:apply-templates/>
   </xsl:template>

   <xsl:template match="Animal">
      Name: <xsl:value-of select="Name"/>
   </xsl:template>

</xsl:stylesheet>
```

Note that we still have the opportunity to add output before and after the apply-templates tag. But upon invoking it, the template matching continues from the current node. Next we'll use what we have so far and add a few bells and whistles.

Transforming the Zoo Inventory

Your boss just called, and it's now imperative that your zoo clients have access to the zoo inventory through the Web, today! Well, after reading Chapter 14, you should be thoroughly prepared to build a nice "zoo portal." Let's get you started by creating an XSL stylesheet to turn our *zooinventory.xml* into HTML:

```
<xsl:stylesheet
    xmlns:xsl="http://www.w3.org/1999/XSL/Transform" version="1.0">

    <xsl:template match="/Inventory">
        <html><head><title>Zoo Inventory</title></head>
        <body><h1>Zoo Inventory</h1>
        <table border="1">
        <tr><td><b>Name</b></td><td><b>Species</b></td>
        <td><b>Habitat</b></td><td><b>Temperament</b></td>
        <td><b>Diet</b></td></tr>
           <xsl:apply-templates/>
             <!-- Process Inventory -->
        </table>
        </body>
        </html>
    </xsl:template>
    <xsl:template match="Inventory/Animal">
        <tr><td><xsl:value-of select="Name"/></td>
           <td><xsl:value-of select="Species"/></td>
          <td><xsl:value-of select="Habitat"/></td>
          <td><xsl:value-of select="Temperament"/></td>
          <td><xsl:apply-templates select="Food|FoodRecipe"/>
             <!-- Process Food,FoodRecipe--></td></tr>
    </xsl:template>

    <xsl:template match="FoodRecipe">
        <table>
        <tr><td><em><xsl:value-of select="Name"/></em></td></tr>
        <xsl:for-each select="Ingredient">
           <tr><td><xsl:value-of select="."/></td></tr>
        </xsl:for-each>
        </table>
    </xsl:template>

</xsl:stylesheet>
```

The stylesheet contains three templates. The first matches /Inventory and outputs the beginning of our HTML document (the header) along with the start of a table for the animals. It then delegates using apply-templates before closing the table and adding the HTML footer. The next template matches Inventory/Animal, printing one row of an HTML table for each animal. Although there are no other Animal elements in the document, it still doesn't hurt to specify that we will match an Animal only in the context of an Inventory, because in this case we are relying on Animal to start and end our table. (This template makes sense only in the context of an Inventory.) Finally, we provide a template that matches FoodRecipe and prints a small (nested) table for that information. FoodRecipe makes use of the for-each operation to loop over child nodes with a select specifying that we are only interested in Ingredient children. For each Ingredient, we output its value in a row.

There is one more thing to note in the Animal template. Our apply-templates element has a select attribute that limits the elements affected. In this case, we are using the "|" regular expression–like syntax to say that we want to apply templates for only the Food *or* FoodRecipe child elements. Why do we do this? Because we didn't match the root of the document (only Inventory), we still have the default stylesheet behavior of outputting the plain text of nodes that aren't matched. We want this behavior for the Food element in the event that a FoodRecipe isn't there. But we don't want it for all the other elements of Animal that we've handled explicitly. Alternatively, we could have been more verbose, adding a template matching the root and another template just for the Food element. That would also mean that new tags added to our XML would be ignored and not change the output. This may or may not be the behavior you want, and there are other options as well. As with all powerful tools, there is usually more than one way to do something.

XSLTransform

Now that we have a stylesheet, let's apply it! The following simple program, XSLTransform, uses the javax.xml.transform package to apply the stylesheet to an XML document and print the result. You can use it to experiment with XSL and our example code.

```
import javax.xml.transform.*;
import javax.xml.transform.stream.*;

public class XSLTransform
{
    public static void main( String [] args ) throws Exception
    {
        if ( args.length < 2 || !args[0].endsWith(".xsl") ) {
            System.err.println("usage: XSLTransform file.xsl file.xml");
            System.exit(1);
        }
        TransformerFactory factory = TransformerFactory.newInstance( );
        Transformer transformer =
            factory.newTransformer( new StreamSource( args[0] ) );
        StreamSource xmlsource = new StreamSource( args[1] );
```

```
        StreamResult output = new StreamResult( System.out );
        transformer.transform( xmlsource, output );
    }
}
```

Run XSLTransform, passing the XSL stylesheet and XML input, as in the following command:

```
% java XSLTransform zooinventory.xsl zooinventory.xml > zooinventory.html
```

The output should look like Figure 23-2.

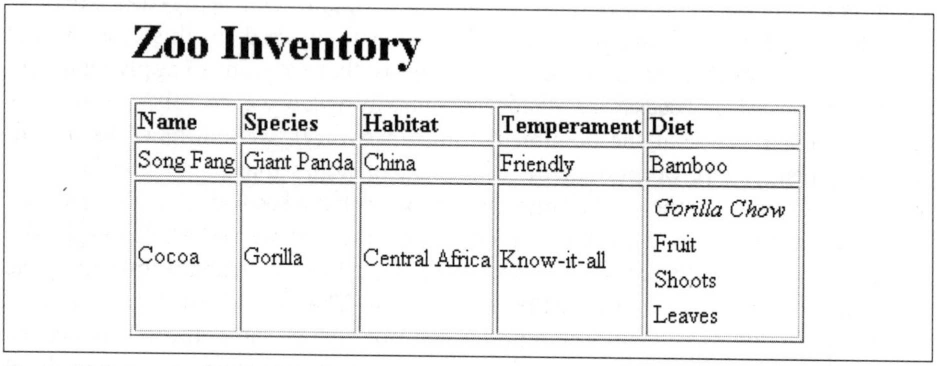

Zoo Inventory

Name	Species	Habitat	Temperament	Diet
Song Fang	Giant Panda	China	Friendly	Bamboo
Cocoa	Gorilla	Central Africa	Know-it-all	*Gorilla Chow* Fruit Shoots Leaves

Figure 23-2. Image of the zoo inventory table

Constructing the transform is a similar process to that of getting a SAX or DOM parser. The difference from our earlier use of the TransformerFactory is that this time we construct the transformer, passing it the XSL stylesheet source. The resulting Transformer object is then a dedicated machine that knows how to take input XML and generate output according to its rules.

One important thing to note about XSLTransform is that it is not guaranteed thread-safe. If you must make concurrent transformations in many threads, they must either coordinate their use of the transformer or have their own instances.

XSL in the Browser

With our XSLTransform example, you can see how you'd go about rendering XML to an HTML document on the server side. But as mentioned in the introduction, modern web browsers support XSL on the client side as well. Internet Explorer 5.x and above, Netscape 6.x, and Mozilla can automatically download an XSL stylesheet and use it to transform an XML document. To make this happen, just add a standard XSL stylesheet reference in your XML. You can put the stylesheet directive next to your DOCTYPE declaration in the *zooinventory.xml* file:

```
<?xml-stylesheet type="text/xsl" href="zooinventory.xsl"?>
```

Now, as long as the *zooinventory.xsl* file is available at the same location (base URL) as the *zooinventory.xml* file, the browser will use it to render HTML on the client side.

Web Services

One of the most interesting directions for XML is web services. A web service is simply an application service supplied over the network, making use of XML to describe the request and response. Normally, web services run over HTTP and use an XML-based protocol called SOAP. SOAP stands for Simple Object Access Protocol and is an evolving W3C standard. The combination of XML and HTTP provides a universally accessible interface for services.

SOAP and other XML-based remote procedure call mechanisms can be used in place of Java RMI for cross-platform communications and as an alternative to CORBA. There is a lot of excitement surrounding web services, and it is likely that they will grow in importance in coming years. To learn more about SOAP, see *http://www.w3. org/TR/SOAP/.* To learn more about Java APIs related to web services, keep an eye on *http://java.sun.com/webservices/*.

Well, that's it for our brief introduction to XML. There is a lot more to learn about this exciting new area, and many of the APIs are evolving rapidly. We hope we've given you a good start.

With this chapter we also wrap up the main part of our book. We hope that you've enjoyed *Learning Java*. We welcome your feedback to help us keep making this book better in the future.

Content and Protocol Handlers

Content and protocol handlers represent one of the most interesting ideas from the original Java vision. Unfortunately, as far as we can tell, no one has taken up the challenge of using this intriguing facility. We considered dropping them from the book entirely, but that decision just felt bad. Instead, we banished the discussion of how to write content and protocol handlers to an appendix. If you let us know that this material is important to you, we'll keep it in the next edition. If you feel "yes, this is interesting, but why do I care?" we'll drop them from the book. (You can send comments via the book's web page at *http://www.oreilly.com/catalog/learnjava2.*)

This appendix picks up where we left our discussion of content and protocol handlers in Chapter 13. We'll show you how to write your own handlers, which can be used in any Java application, including the HotJava web browser. In this section, we'll write a content handler that reads Unix tar files and a protocol handler that implements a pluggable encryption scheme. You should be able to drop both into your class path and start using them in the HotJava web browser right away.

Writing a Content Handler

The URL class's getContent( ) method invokes a content handler whenever it's called to retrieve an object at some URL. The content handler must read the flat stream of data produced by the URL's protocol handler (the data read from the remote source), and construct a well-defined Java object from it. By "flat," we mean that the data stream the content handler receives has no artifacts left from retrieving the data and processing the protocol. It's the protocol handler's job to fetch and decode the data before passing it along. The protocol handler's output is your data, pure and simple.

The roles of content and protocol handlers do not overlap. The content handler doesn't care how the data arrives or what form it takes. It's concerned only with what kind of object it's supposed to create. For example, if a particular protocol involves sending an object over the network in a compressed format, the protocol handler should do whatever is necessary to unpack it before passing the data on to the content handler. The same content handler can then be used again with a completely different protocol handler to construct the *same* type of object received via a *different* transport mechanism.

Let's look at an example. The following lines construct a URL that points to a GIF file on an FTP archive and attempt to retrieve its contents:

```
try {
  URL url =
      new URL ("ftp://ftp.wustl.edu/graphics/gif/a/apple.gif");
  ImageProducer imgsrc = (ImageProducer)url.getContent();
  ...
```

When we construct the URL object, Java looks at the first part of the URL string (everything prior to the colon) to determine the protocol and locate a protocol handler. In this case, it locates the FTP protocol handler, which is used to open a connection to the host and transfer data for the specified file.

After making the connection, the URL object asks the protocol handler to identify the resource's MIME type. The handler can try to resolve the MIME type through a variety of means, but in this case, it might just look at the filename extension (*.gif*) and determine that the MIME type of the data is image/gif. Here, image/gif is a string that denotes that the content falls into the category of images and is, more specifically, a GIF image. The protocol handler then looks for the content handler responsible for the image/gif type and uses it to construct the right kind of object from the data. The content handler returns an ImageProducer object, which getContent() returns to us as an Object. As we've seen before, we cast this Object back to its real type so we can work with it.

In an upcoming section, we'll build a simple content handler. To keep things simple, our example produces text as output; the URL's get-Content() method returns this as a String object.

Locating Content Handlers

When Java searches for a class, it translates package names into filesystem pathnames. (The classes may also be in a JAR file in the class path, but we refer to them as files and directories anyway.) This applies to locating content-handler classes as well as other kinds of classes. For example, a class in a package named foo.bar.handlers would live in a directory with *foo/bar/handlers/* as part of its pathname. To allow Java to find handler classes for arbitrary new MIME types, content handlers are organized into packages corresponding to the basic MIME type categories. The handler classes themselves are named after the specific MIME type, which allows Java to map MIME types directly to class names. The only remaining information Java needs is a list of packages in which the handlers might reside. To supply this information, you should use the system properties java.content.handler.pkgs and java.protocol.handler.pkgs. In these properties, you can use a vertical bar (|) to separate different packages in a list.

We'll put our content handlers in the learningjava.contenthandlers package. According to the scheme for naming content handlers, a handler for the image/gif MIME type is called gif and placed in a package that is called learningjava. contenthandlers.image. The fully qualified name of the class would then be learningjava.contenthandlers.image.gif, and it would be located in the file *learningjava/contenthandlers/image/gif.class*, somewhere in the local class path, or, perhaps someday, on a server. Likewise, a content handler for the video/mpeg MIME type would be called mpeg, and an *mpeg.class* file would be located in a *learningjava/ contenthandlers/video/* directory somewhere in the class path.

Many MIME type names include a dash (-), which is illegal in a class name. You should convert dashes and other illegal characters into underscores (_) when building Java class and package names. Also note that there are no capital letters in the class names. This violates the coding convention used in most Java source files, in which class names start with capital letters. However, capitalization is not significant in MIME type names, so it is simpler to name the handler classes accordingly.

The application/x-tar Handler

In this section, we'll build a simple content handler that reads and interprets tar (tape archive) files. tar is an archival format widely used in the Unix-world to hold collections of files, along with their basic type and attribute information.[*] A tar file is similar to a JAR file, except that it's not compressed. Files in the archive are stored sequentially, in flat text or binary with no special encoding. In practice, tar files are usually compressed for storage using an application like Unix *compress* or GNU *gzip* and then named with a filename extension like *.tar.gz* or *.tgz*.

Most web browsers, upon retrieving a tar file, prompt the user with a File Save dialog. The assumption is that if you are retrieving an archive, you probably want to save it for later unpacking and use. We would like to implement a *tar* content handler that allows an application to read the contents of the archive and give us a listing of the files that it contains. In itself, this would not be the most useful thing in the world, because we would be left with the dilemma of how to get at the archive's contents. However, a more complete implementation of our content handler, used in conjunction with an application like a web browser, could generate HTML output or pop up a dialog that lets us select and save individual files within the archive.

---

[*] There are several slightly different versions of the tar format. This content handler understands the most widely used variant.

Some code that fetches a tar file and lists its contents might look like this:

```
try {
    URL listing =
        new URL("http://somewhere.an.edu/lynx/lynx2html.tar");
    String s = (String)listing.getContents();
    System.out.println( s );
    ...
```

Our handler produces a listing similar to the Unix *tar* application's output:

```
Tape Archive Listing:

0      Tue Sep 28 18:12:47 CDT 1993 lynx2html/
14773  Tue Sep 28 18:01:55 CDT 1993 lynx2html/lynx2html.c
470    Tue Sep 28 18:13:24 CDT 1993 lynx2html/Makefile
172    Thu Apr 01 15:05:43 CST 1993 lynx2html/lynxgate
3656   Wed Mar 03 15:40:20 CST 1993 lynx2html/install.csh
490    Thu Apr 01 14:55:04 CST 1993 lynx2html/new_globals.c
...
```

Our handler will dissect the file to read the contents and generate the listing. The URL's getContent( ) method will return that information to an application as a String object.

First we must decide what to call our content handler and where to put it. The MIME-type hierarchy classifies the tar format as an *application type extension*. Its proper MIME type is then application/x-tar. Therefore, our handler belongs in the learningjava.contenthandlers.application package and goes into the class file *learningjava/contenthandlers/application/x_tar.class*. Note that the name of our class is x_tar, rather than x-tar; you'll remember the dash is illegal in a class name so, by convention, we convert it to an underscore.

Here's the code for the content handler; compile it and put it in *learningjava/contenthandlers/application/*, somewhere in your class path:

```
//file: x_tar.java
package learningjava.contenthandlers.application;

import java.net.*;
import java.io.*;
import java.util.Date;

public class x_tar extends ContentHandler {
    static int
        RECORDLEN = 512,
        NAMEOFF = 0, NAMELEN = 100,
        SIZEOFF = 124, SIZELEN = 12,
        MTIMEOFF = 136, MTIMELEN = 12;

    public Object getContent(URLConnection uc) throws IOException {
        InputStream is = uc.getInputStream( );
        StringBuffer output =
            new StringBuffer( "Tape Archive Listing:\n\n" );
```

```
byte [] header = new byte[RECORDLEN];
int count = 0;

while ( (is.read(header) == RECORDLEN)
        && (header[NAMEOFF] != 0) ) {
  String name =
      new String(header, NAMEOFF, NAMELEN, "8859_1"). trim( );
  String s =
      new String(header, SIZEOFF, SIZELEN, "8859_1").trim( );
  int size = Integer.parseInt(s, 8);
  s = new String(header, MTIMEOFF, MTIMELEN, "8859_1").trim( );
  long l = Integer.parseInt(s, 8);
  Date mtime = new Date( l*1000 );

  output.append( size + " " + mtime + " " + name + "\n" );

  count += is.skip( size ) + RECORDLEN;
  if ( count % RECORDLEN != 0 )
    count += is.skip ( RECORDLEN - count % RECORDLEN);
}

if ( count == 0 )
  output.append("Not a valid TAR file\n");

return( output.toString( ) );
  }
}
```

The ContentHandler class

Our x_tar handler is a subclass of the abstract class java.net.ContentHandler. Its job is to implement one method: getContent( ), which takes as an argument a special "protocol connection" object and returns a constructed Java Object. The getContent( ) method of the URL class ultimately uses this getContent( ) method when we ask for the contents of the URL. The code looks formidable, but most of it's involved with processing the details of the tar format. If we remove these details, there isn't much left:

```
public class x_tar extends ContentHandler {

  public Object getContent( URLConnection uc ) throws IOException {
    // get input stream
    InputStream is = uc.getInputStream( );

    // read stream and construct object
    // ...

    // return the constructed object
    return( output.toString( ) );
  }
}
```

That's really all there is to a content handler; it's relatively simple.

The URLConnection

The java.net.URLConnection object that getContent( ) receives represents the protocol handler's connection to the remote resource. It provides a number of methods for examining information about the URL resource, such as header and type fields, and for determining the kinds of operations the protocol supports. However, its most important method is getInputStream( ), which returns an InputStream from the protocol handler. Reading this InputStream gives you the raw data for the object the URL addresses. In our case, reading the InputStream feeds x_tar the bytes of the tar file it's to process.

Constructing the object

The majority of our getContent( ) method is devoted to interpreting the stream of bytes of the tar file and building our output object: the String that lists the contents of the tar file. Again, this means that this example involves the particulars of reading tar files, so you shouldn't fret too much about the details.

After requesting an InputStream from the URLConnection, x_tar loops, gathering information about each file. Each archived item is preceded by a header that contains attribute and length fields. x_tar interprets each header and then skips over the remaining portion of the item. To parse the header, we use the String constructor to read a fixed number of characters from the byte array header[ ]. To convert these bytes into a Java String properly, we specify the character encoding used by web servers: 8859_1, which (for the most part) is equivalent to ASCII. Once we have a file's name, size, and time stamp, we accumulate the results (the file listings) in a StringBuffer—one line per file. When the listing is complete, getContent( ) returns the StringBuffer as a String object.

The main while loop continues as long as it's able to read another header record, and as long as the record's "name" field isn't full of ASCII null values. (The tar file format calls for the end of the archive to be padded with an empty header record, although most tar implementations don't seem to do this.) The while loop retrieves the name, size, and modification times as character strings from fields in the header. The most common tar format stores its numeric values in octal, as fixed-length ASCII strings. We extract the strings and use Integer.parseInt( ) to parse them.

After reading and parsing the header, x_tar skips over the data portion of the file and updates the variable count, which keeps track of the offset into the archive. The two lines following the initial skip account for tar's "blocking" of the data records. In other words, if the data portion of a file doesn't fit precisely into an integral number of blocks of RECORDLEN bytes, tar adds padding to make it fit.

As we said, the details of parsing tar files are not really our main concern here. But x_tar does illustrate a few tricks of data manipulation in Java.

It may surprise you that we didn't have to provide a constructor; our content handler relies on its default constructor. We don't need to provide a constructor because there isn't anything for it to do. Java doesn't pass the class any argument information when it creates an instance of it. You might suspect that the URLConnection object would be a natural thing to provide at that point. However, when you are calling the constructor of a class that is loaded at runtime, you can't easily pass it any arguments.

Using our new handler

When we began this discussion of content handlers, we showed a brief example of how our x_tar content handler would work for us. You can try that code snippet now with your favorite tar file by setting the java.content.handler.pkgs system property to learningjava.contenthandlers and making sure that package is in your class path.

To make things more exciting, try setting the property in your HotJava properties file. (The HotJava properties file usually resides in a *.hotjava* directory in your home directory or in the HotJava installation directory on a Windows machine.) Make sure the class path is set before you start HotJava. Once HotJava is running, go to the *Preferences* menu, and select *Viewer Applications*. Find the type *TAR archive*, and set its *Action* to *View in HotJava*. This tells HotJava to try to use a content handler to display the data in the browser. Now, drive HotJava to a URL that contains a tar file. The result should look something like that shown in Figure A-1.

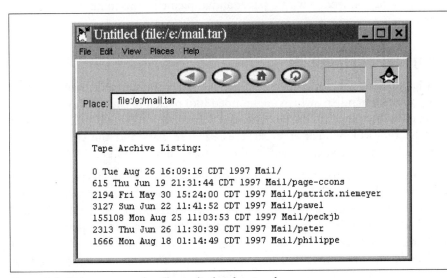

Figure A-1. Using a content handler to display data in a browser

We've just extended our copy of HotJava to understand tar files! In the next section, we'll turn the tables and look at protocol handlers. There we'll be building URLConnection objects; someone else will have the pleasure of reconstituting the data.

Writing a Protocol Handler

A URL object uses a protocol handler to establish a connection with a server and perform whatever protocol is necessary to retrieve data. For example, an HTTP protocol handler knows how to talk to an HTTP server and retrieve a document; an FTP protocol handler knows how to talk to an FTP server and retrieve a file. All types of URLs use protocol handlers to access their objects. Even the lowly "file" type URLs use a special "file" protocol handler that retrieves files from the local filesystem. The data a protocol handler retrieves is then fed to an appropriate content handler for interpretation.

While we refer to a protocol handler as a single entity, it really has two parts: a java.net.URLStreamHandler and a java.net.URLConnection. These are both abstract classes that we will subclass to create our protocol handler. (Note that these are abstract classes, not interfaces. Although they contain abstract methods we are required to implement, they also contain many utility methods we can use or override.) The URL looks up an appropriate URLStreamHandler, based on the protocol component of the URL. The URLStreamHandler then finishes parsing the URL and creates a URLConnection when it's time to communicate with the server. The URLConnection represents a single connection with a server and implements the communication protocol itself.

Locating Protocol Handlers

Protocol handlers are organized in a package hierarchy similar to content handlers. But unlike content handlers, which are grouped into packages by the MIME types of the objects that they handle, protocol handlers are given individual packages. Both parts of the protocol handler (the URLStreamHandler class and the URLConnection class) are located in a package named for the protocol they support.

For example, if we wrote an FTP protocol handler, we might put it in an learningjava.protocolhandlers.ftp package. The URLStreamHandler is placed in this package and given the name Handler; all URLStreamHandlers are named Handler and distinguished by the package in which they reside. The URLConnection portion of the protocol handler is placed in the same package and can be given any name. There is no need for a naming convention because the corresponding URLStreamHandler is responsible for creating the URLConnection objects it uses.

As with content handlers, Java locates packages containing protocol handlers using the java.protocol.handler.pkgs system property. The value of this property is a list of package names; if more than one package is in the list, use a vertical bar (|) to

separate them. For our example, we will set this property to include `learningjava.`
`protocolhandlers`.

URLs, Stream Handlers, and Connections

The URL, URLStreamHandler, URLConnection, and ContentHandler classes work together closely. Before diving into an example, let's take a step back, look at the parts a little more, and see how these things communicate. Figure A-2 shows how these components relate to each other.

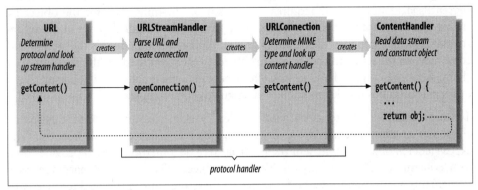

Figure A-2. The protocol handler machinery

We begin with the URL object, which points to the resource we'd like to retrieve. The URLStreamHandler helps the URL class parse the URL specification string for its particular protocol. For example, consider the following call to the URL constructor:

```
URL url = new URL("protocol://foo.bar.com/file.ext");
```

The URL class parses only the protocol component; later, a call to the URL class's getContent() or openStream() method starts the machinery in motion. The URL class locates the appropriate protocol handler by looking in the protocol-package hierarchy. It then creates an instance of the appropriate URLStreamHandler class.

The URLStreamHandler is responsible for parsing the rest of the URL string, including hostname and filename, and possibly an alternative port designation. This allows different protocols to have their own variations on the format of the URL specification string. Note that this step is skipped when a URL is constructed with the "protocol," "host," and "file" components specified explicitly. If the protocol is straightforward, its URLStreamHandler class can let Java do the parsing and accept the default behavior. For this illustration, we'll assume that the URL string requires no special parsing. (If we use a nonstandard URL with a strange format, we're responsible for parsing it ourselves, as we'll show shortly.)

The URL object next invokes the handler's openConnection() method, prompting the handler to create a new URLConnection to the resource. The URLConnection performs whatever communications are necessary to talk to the resource and begins to fetch data for the object. At that time, it also determines the MIME type of the incoming object data and prepares an InputStream to hand to the appropriate content handler. This InputStream must send "pure" data with all traces of the protocol removed.

The URLConnection also locates an appropriate content handler in the content-handler package hierarchy. The URLConnection creates an instance of a content handler; to put the content handler to work, the URLConnection's getContent( ) method calls the content handler's getContent( ) method. If this sounds confusing, it is: we have three getContent( ) methods calling each other in a chain. The newly created ContentHandler object then acquires the stream of incoming data for the object by calling the URLConnection's getInputStream( ) method. (Recall that we acquired an InputStream in our x_tar content handler.) The content handler reads the stream and constructs an object from the data. This object is then returned up the getContent( ) chain: from the content handler, the URLConnection, and finally the URL itself. Now our application has the desired object in its greedy little hands.

To summarize, we create a protocol handler by implementing a URLStreamHandler class that creates specialized URLConnection objects to handle our protocol. The URLConnection objects implement the getInputStream( ) method, which provides data to a content handler for construction of an object. The base URLConnection class implements many of the methods we need; therefore, our URLConnection needs to provide only the methods that generate the data stream and return the MIME type of the object data.

If you're not thoroughly confused by all that terminology (or even if you are), let's move on to the example. It should help to pin down what all these classes are doing.

The crypt Handler

In this section, we'll build a *crypt* protocol handler. It parses URLs of the form:

```
crypt:type://hostname[:port]/location/item
```

type is an identifier that specifies what kind of encryption to use. The protocol itself is a simplified version of HTTP; we'll implement the GET command and no more. We added the *type* identifier to the URL to show how to parse a nonstandard URL specification. Once the handler has figured out the encryption type, it dynamically loads a class that implements the chosen encryption algorithm and uses it to retrieve the data. Obviously, we don't have room to implement a full-blown public-key encryption algorithm, so we'll use the rot13InputStream class from Chapter 11. It should be apparent how the example can be extended by plugging in a more powerful encryption class.

The Encryption class

First, we'll lay out our plug-in encryption class. We'll define an abstract class called `CryptInputStream` that provides some essentials for our plug-in encrypted protocol. From the `CryptInputStream` we'll create a subclass called `rot13CryptInputStream`, that implements our particular kind of encryption:

```
//file: rot13CryptInputStream.java
package learningjava.protocolhandlers.crypt;
import java.io.*;

abstract class CryptInputStream extends InputStream {
    InputStream in;
    OutputStream out;
    abstract public void set( InputStream in, OutputStream out );
} // end of class CryptInputStream

class rot13CryptInputStream extends CryptInputStream {

    public void set( InputStream in, OutputStream out ) {
        this.in = new learningjava.io.rot13InputStream( in );
    }
    public int read( ) throws IOException {
        return in.read( );
    }
}
```

Our `CryptInputStream` class defines a method called `set( )` that passes in the `InputStream` it's to translate. Our `URLConnection` calls `set( )` after creating an instance of the encryption class. We need a `set( )` method because we want to load the encryption class dynamically, and we aren't allowed to pass arguments to the constructor of a class when it's dynamically loaded. (We noticed this same issue in our content handler previously.) In the encryption class, we also provide for the possibility of an `OutputStream`. A more complex kind of encryption might use the `OutputStream` to transfer public-key information. Needless to say, rot13 doesn't, so we'll ignore the `OutputStream` here.

The implementation of `rot13CryptInputStream` is very simple. `set( )` takes the `InputStream` it receives and wraps it with the `rot13InputStream` filter. `read( )` reads filtered data from the `InputStream`, throwing an exception if `set( )` hasn't been called.

The URLStreamHandler

Next we'll build our `URLStreamHandler` class. The class name is `Handler`; it extends the abstract `URLStreamHandler` class. This is the class the Java `URL` looks up by converting the protocol name (*crypt*) into a package name. Remember that Java expects this class to be named `Handler`, and to live in a package named for the protocol type.

```
//file: Handler.java
package learningjava.protocolhandlers.crypt;
import java.io.*;
```

```
import java.net.*;

public class Handler extends URLStreamHandler {

    protected void parseURL(URL url, String spec,
                            int start, int end) {
        int slash = spec.indexOf('/');
        String crypType = spec.substring(start, slash-1);
        super.parseURL(url, spec, slash, end);
        setURL( url, "crypt:"+crypType, url.getHost(),
            url.getPort(), url.getFile(), url.getRef() );
    }

    protected URLConnection openConnection(URL url)
      throws IOException {
        String crypType = url.getProtocol().substring(6);
        return new CryptURLConnection( url, crypType );
    }
}
```

Java creates an instance of our URLStreamHandler when we create a URL specifying the *crypt* protocol. Handler has two jobs: to assist in parsing the URL specification strings and to create CryptURLConnection objects when it's time to open a connection to the host.

Our parseURL() method overrides the parseURL() method in the URLStreamHandler class. It's called whenever the URL constructor sees a URL requesting the *crypt* protocol. For example:

```
URL url = new URL("crypt:rot13://foo.bar.com/file.txt");
```

parseURL() is passed a reference to the URL object, the URL specification string, and starting and ending indexes that show what portion of the URL string we're expected to parse. The URL class has already identified the simple protocol name; otherwise, it wouldn't have found our protocol handler. Our version of parseURL() retrieves our *type* identifier from the specification and stores it temporarily in the variable crypType. To find the encryption type, we take everything between the starting index we were given and the character preceding the first slash in the URL string (i.e., everything up to the colon in ://). We then defer to the superclass parseURL() method to complete the job of parsing the URL after that point. We call super. parseURL() with the new start index, so that it points to the character just after the type specifier. This tells the superclass parseURL() that we've already parsed everything prior to the first slash, and it's responsible for the rest. Finally we use the utility method setURL() to put together the final URL. Almost everything has already been set correctly for us, but we need to call setURL() to add our special type to the protocol identifier. We'll need this information later when someone wants to open the URL connection.

Before going on, we'll note two other possibilities. If we hadn't hacked the URL string for our own purposes by adding a type specifier, we'd be dealing with a standard URL specification. In this case, we wouldn't need to override parseURL( ); the default implementation would have been sufficient. It could have sliced the URL into host, port, and filename components normally. On the other hand, if we had created a completely bizarre URL format, we would need to parse the entire string. There would be no point calling super.parseURL( ); instead, we'd have called the URLStreamHandler's protected method setURL( ) to pass the URL's components back to the URL object.

The other method in our Handler class is openConnection( ). After the URL has been completely parsed, the URL object calls openConnection( ) to set up the data transfer. openConnection( ) calls the constructor for our URLConnection with appropriate arguments. In this case, our URLConnection object is named CryptURLConnection, and the constructor requires the URL and the encryption type as arguments. parseURL( ) put the encryption type in the protocol identifier of the URL. We recognize it and pass the information along. openConnection( ) returns the reference to our URLConnection, which the URL object uses to drive the rest of the process.

The URLconnection

Finally, we reach the real guts of our protocol handler, the URLConnection class. This is the class that opens the socket, talks to the server on the remote host, and implements the protocol itself. This class doesn't have to be public, so you can put it in the same file as the Handler class we just defined. We call our class CryptURLConnection; it extends the abstract URLConnection class. Unlike ContentHandler and StreamURLConnection, whose names are defined by convention, we can call this class anything we want; the only class that needs to know about the URLConnection is the URLStreamHandler, which we wrote ourselves:

```
//file: CryptURLConnection.java
  import java.io.*;
  import java.net.*;

class CryptURLConnection extends URLConnection {
    static int defaultPort = 80;
    CryptInputStream cis;

    public String getContentType( ) {
        return guessContentTypeFromName( url.getFile( ) );
    }

    CryptURLConnection ( URL url, String crypType )
      throws IOException {
        super( url );
        try {
            String classname = "learningjava.protocolhandlers.crypt."
                + crypType + "CryptInputStream";
            cis = (CryptInputStream)
                    Class.forName(classname).newInstance( );
        } catch ( Exception e ) {
```

```
                throw new IOException("Crypt Class Not Found: "+e);
        }
    }

    public void connect() throws IOException {
        int port = ( url.getPort() == -1 ) ?
                        defaultPort : url.getPort();
        Socket s = new Socket( url.getHost(), port );

        // Send the filename in plaintext
        OutputStream server = s.getOutputStream();
        new PrintWriter( new OutputStreamWriter( server, "8859_1" ),
                            true).println( "GET " + url.getFile() );

        // Initialize the CryptInputStream
        cis.set( s.getInputStream(), server );
        connected = true;
    }

    public InputStream getInputStream() throws IOException {
        if (!connected)
            connect();
        return ( cis );
    }
}
```

The constructor for our CryptURLConnection class takes as arguments the destination URL and the name of an encryption type. We pass the URL on to the constructor of our superclass, which saves it in a protected url instance variable. We could have saved the URL ourselves but calling our parent's constructor shields us from possible changes or enhancements to the base class. We use crypType to construct the name of an encryption class, using the convention that the encryption class is in the same package as the protocol handler (i.e., learningjava.protocolhandlers.crypt); its name is the encryption type followed by the suffix CryptInputStream.

Once we have a name, we need to create an instance of the encryption class. To do so, we use the static method Class.forName() to turn the name into a Class object and newInstance() to load and instantiate the class. (This is how Java loads the content and protocol handlers themselves.) newInstance() returns an Object; we need to cast it to something more specific before we can work with it. Therefore, we cast it to our CryptInputStream class, the abstract class that rot13CryptInputStream extends. If we implement any additional encryption types as extensions to CryptInputStream and name them appropriately, they will fit into our protocol handler without modification.

We do the rest of our setup in the connect() method of the URLConnection. There, we make sure we have an encryption class and open a Socket to the appropriate port on the remote host. getPort() returns -1 if the URL doesn't specify a port explicitly; in that case we use the default port for an HTTP connection (port 80). We ask for an OutputStream on the socket, assemble a GET command using the getFile() method to discover the filename specified by the URL, and send our request by writing it into the OutputStream. (For convenience, we wrap the OutputStream with a PrintWriter and call println( ) to send the message.) We then initialize the CryptInputStream class by calling its set( ) method and passing it an InputStream from the Socket and the OutputStream.

The last thing connect( ) does is set the boolean variable connected to true. connected is a protected variable inherited from the URLConnection class. We need to track the state of our connection because connect( ) is a public method. It's called by the URLConnection's getInputStream( ) method, but it could also be called by other classes. Since we don't want to start a connection if one already exists, we check connected first.

In a more sophisticated protocol handler, connect( ) would also be responsible for dealing with any protocol headers that come back from the server. In particular, it would probably stash any important information it deduced from the headers (e.g., MIME type, content length, time stamp) in instance variables, where it's available to other methods. At a minimum, connect( ) strips the headers from the data so the content handler won't see them. We'll be lazy and assume we'll connect to a minimal server, such as the modified TinyHttpd daemon (discussed in the next section), which doesn't bother with any headers.

The bulk of the work has been done; a few details remain. The URLConnection's getContent( ) method needs to figure out which content handler to invoke for this URL. In order to compute the content handler's name, getContent( ) needs to know the resource's MIME type. To find out, it calls the URLConnection's getContentType( ) method, which returns the MIME type as a String. Our protocol handler overrides getContentType( ), providing our own implementation.

The URLConnection class provides a number of tools to help determine the MIME type. It's possible that the MIME type is conveyed explicitly in a protocol header; in this case, a more sophisticated version of connect( ) would have stored the MIME type in a convenient location for us. Some servers don't bother to insert the appropriate headers, though, so you can use the method guess-ContentTypeFromName( ) to examine filename extensions, like .gif or .html, and map them to MIME types. In the worst case, you can use guessContent-TypeFromStream( ) to intuit the MIME type from the raw data. The Java developers call this method "a disgusting hack" that shouldn't be needed, but that is unfortunately necessary in a world where HTTP servers lie about content types and extensions are often nonstandard. We'll take the easy way out and use the guessContentTypeFromName( ) utility of the URLConnection class to determine the MIME type from the filename extension of the URL we are retrieving.

Once the URLConnection has found a content handler, it calls the content handler's getContent( ) method. The content handler then needs to get an InputStream from which to read the data. To find an InputStream, it calls the URLConnection's getInputStream( ) method. getInputStream( ) returns an InputStream from which its caller can read the data after protocol processing is finished. It checks whether a connection is already established; if not, it calls connect( ) to make the connection. Then it returns a reference to our CryptInputStream.

A final note on getting the content type: the URLConnection's default getContentType( ) calls getHeaderField( ), which is presumably supposed to extract the named field from the protocol headers (it would probably spit back information connect( ) had stored away). But the default implementation of getHeaderField( ) just returns null; we would have to override it to make it do anything interesting. Several other connection attributes use this mechanism, so in a more general implementation, we'd probably override getHeaderField( ) rather than getContentType( ) directly.

Trying it out

Let's try out our new protocol! Compile all the classes and put them in the learningjava.protocolhandlers package somewhere in your class path. Now set the java.protocol.handler.pkgs system property in HotJava to include learningjava.protocolhandlers. Type a "crypt" style URL for a text document; you should see something like that shown in Figure A-3.

Figure A-3. The crypt protocol handler at work

This example would be more interesting if we had a rot13 server. Since the *crypt* protocol is nothing more than HTTP with some encryption added, we can make a rot13 server by modifying one line of the TinyHttpd server we developed in Chapter 12, so

that it spews its files in rot13. Just change the line that reads the data from the file—
replace this line:

```
f.read( data );
```

with a line that reads through a rot13InputStream:

```
new learningjava.io.rot13InputStream( f ).read( data );
```

We'll assume you placed the rot13InputStream example in a package called
learningjava.io, and that it's somewhere in your class path. Now recompile and run
the server. It automatically encodes the files before sending them; our sample application decodes them on the other end.

We hope that this example has given you some food for thought. Content and protocol handlers are among the most exciting ideas in Java. It's unfortunate that we have
to wait for future releases of HotJava and Netscape to take full advantage of them.
But in the meantime, you can experiment and implement your own applications.

APPENDIX B

BeanShell: Simple Java Scripting

In this book, we (in this case, I, Pat) have avoided talking about many third-party tools that aren't part of the standard SDK. I'm going to make an exception here to mention a nifty, free Java tool called BeanShell. As its name suggests, BeanShell can be used as a Java "shell." It allows you to type standard Java syntax—statements and expressions—on the command line and see the results immediately. With Bean-Shell, you can try out bits of code as you work through the book. You can access all Java APIs and even create graphical user interface components and manipulate them "live." BeanShell uses only reflection, so there is no need to compile class files.

I wrote BeanShell while developing the examples for this book, and I think it makes a good companion to have along on your journey through Java. BeanShell is an open source software project, so the source code is included on the CD-ROM that accompanies this book. And you can always find the latest updates and more information at its official home: *http://www.beanshell.org*. In recent years BeanShell has become fairly popular. It is included with Emacs as part of the Java Development Environment (the JDE), with the NetBeans and Forte IDEs, and with BEA's WebLogic application server. I hope you find it both useful and fun!

Running BeanShell

All you need to run BeanShell is the Java runtime system (Version 1.1 or greater) and the *bsh* JAR file. Under Windows you can launch a graphical desktop for BeanShell by simply double-clicking the JAR file icon. More generally, you can add the JAR to your classpath:

```
Unix:      export CLASSPATH=$CLASSPATH:bsh.jar
Windows:   set classpath %classpath%;bsh.jar
```

Or just drop the JAR file in the *jre/lib/ext* directory of your Java installation. You can then run BeanShell interactively in either a GUI or command-line mode:

```
java bsh.Console       // run the graphical desktop
java bsh.Interpreter   // run as text-only on the command line
```

Running BeanShell with the GUI console brings up a simple, Swing-based, desktop that allows you to open multiple shell windows with basic command history, line editing, and cut-and-paste capability. There are some other GUI tools available as well, including a simple text editor and class browser. Alternately, you can run Bean-Shell on the command line, in text-only mode.

You can run BeanShell scripts from files, like so:

```
% java bsh.Interpreter myfile.bsh
```

Within the NetBeans and Forte IDEs, you can create BeanShell script files using the *New File* wizard or run any file with a *.bsh* extension just as you would execute Java code.

Java Statements and Expressions

At the prompt, you can type standard Java statements and expressions. Statements and expressions are all of the normal things that you'd include in a Java method: variable declarations and assignments, method calls, loops, and conditionals.

You can type these exactly as they would appear in Java. You also have the option of working with "loosely typed" variables and arguments. That is, you can simply be lazy and not declare the types of variables that you use (both primitives and objects). BeanShell will still give you an error if you attempt to misuse the actual contents of the variable. If you do declare types of variables or primitives, BeanShell will enforce them.

Here are some examples:

```
foo = "Foo";
four = (2 + 2)*2/2;
print( foo + " = " + four );    // print( ) is a bsh command
// do a loop
for (i=0; i<5; i++)
    print(i);
// pop up an AWT frame with a button in it
button = new JButton("My Button");
frame = new JFrame("My Frame");
frame.getContentPane( ).add( button, "Center" );
frame.pack( );
frame.setVisible( true );
```

If you don't like the idea of "loosening" Java syntax at all, you can turn off this feature of BeanShell with the following command:

```
setStrictJava( true );
```

Imports

By default, BeanShell imports all of the core Java packages for you. You can import your own classes using the standard Java import declaration:

```
import mypackage.*;
```

BeanShell can even automatically import all classes in your classpath, using the following special declaration:

```
import *;
```

But this can take quite some time if there are a lot of directories in your path.

BeanShell Commands

BeanShell comes with a number of useful built-in commands in the form of Java methods. These commands are implemented as BeanShell scripts, and are supplied in the *bsh* JAR file. You can make your own commands by defining methods in your own scripts or adding them to your classpath. See the BeanShell user's manual for more information.

One important BeanShell command is print(), which displays values. print() does pretty much the same thing as System.out.println() except it ensures the output always goes to the command line (if you have multiple windows open). print() also displays some types of objects (such as arrays) more verbosely than Java would. Another very useful command is show(), which toggles on and off automatic printing of the result of every line you type. (You can turn this on if you want to see every result value.)

Here are a few other examples of BeanShell commands:

source(), run()
> Reads a *bsh* script into this interpreter, or runs it in a new interpreter

frame()
> Displays an AWT or Swing component in a frame

load(), save()
> Loads or saves serializable objects (such as JavaBeans)

cd(), cat(), dir(), pwd(), *etc.*
> Unix-like shell commands

exec()
> Runs a native application

addClassPath(), reloadClasses()
> Modifies the classpath or reload classes

See the BeanShell user's manual for a full list of commands.

Scripted Methods and Objects

You can declare and use methods in BeanShell, just as you would inside a Java class:

```
int addTwoNumbers( int a, int b ) {
    return a + b;
}
sum = addTwoNumbers( 5, 7 );  // 12
```

BeanShell methods may also have dynamic (loose) argument and return types.

```
add( a, b ) {
    return a + b;
}
foo = add(1, 2);              // 3
foo = add("Hello ", "Kitty");  // "Hello Kitty"
```

In BeanShell, as in JavaScript and Perl, method *closures* take the place of scripted objects. You can turn the context of a method call into an object reference by having the method return the special value this. You can then use the this reference to refer to any variables that were set during the method call. To be useful, an object may also need methods; so in BeanShell, methods may also contain methods at any level. Here is a simple example:

```
user( n ) {
    name = n;
    reset( ) {
        print( "Reset user:"+name );
    }
    return this;  // return user as object
}
bob = user("Bob" );
print( bob.name ); // "Bob"
bob.reset( );       // prints "Reset user: Bob"
```

This example assigns the context of the user() method to the variable bob and refers to the field bob.name and the method bob.reset().

If you find this strange, don't worry. The most common reason you'd want to script an object is to implement a Java interface, and you can do that using the standard Java anonymous inner class syntax, as we'll discuss next.

Scripting Interfaces and Adapters

One of the most powerful features of BeanShell is that you can "script" any interface type (provided you are running Java 1.3 or greater). BeanShell-scripted objects can automatically implement any required interface type. All you have to do is implement the necessary method (or at least the ones that are going to be invoked). You can use this feature either by explicitly referring to a BeanShell script using a this style reference as described earlier, or by using the standard Java anonymous inner class syntax. Here is an example:

```
actionPerformed( event ) { print( event ); }
button = new JButton("Press Me!");
button.addActionListener( this );
frame( button );
```

You can type this code right on the command line and press the button to see the events it generates. In this case the `this` reference refers to the current context, just as in a method. BeanShell automatically implements the `ActionListener` interface and delegates calls to its `actionPerformed()` method to our scripted method.

Alternately, we could use the anonymous inner class syntax to create an `ActionListener` for our button:

```
button = new JButton("Press Me!");
button.addActionListener( new ActionListener() {
    actionPerformed( event ) { print( event ); }
} );
frame( button );
```

In this case the "anonymous inner class" is actually a BeanShell script that implements the `ActionListener` interface for us in the same way as the previous example.

One more thing: we hinted earlier that you only have to implement those methods of the interface that you want to use. If you don't script a method, it's okay as long as it's not invoked (in which case you'd get an exception). For convenience in implementing a large interface, you can define the special `invoke()` method, which handles calls to scripted methods that don't exist:

```
invoke( name, args ) { print("Method: "+name+" invoked!"); }
```

This `invoke()` method will handle method calls for methods that are not defined and simply print their names. See the user manual for more details.

Changing the Classpath

Within BeanShell you can add to your classpath and even reload classes:

```
addClassPath("mystuff.jar");
addClassPath(http://examples.oreilly.com/learnjava/magicbeans.jar);
```

To reload all classes in the classpath simply use:

```
reloadClasses();
```

You can do more elaborate things as well, such as reloading individual classes, if you know what you're doing. See the user manual for more details.

Learning More ...

BeanShell has many more features than I've described here. You can embed Bean-Shell into your applications as a lightweight scripting engine, passing live Java objects into and out of scripts. You can even run BeanShell in a remote server mode, which lets you work in a shell inside your running application, for debugging and experimentation. There is also a BeanShell servlet that can be used for running scripts inside an application server.

BeanShell is small (only about 200 KB) and it's free, licensed under the GNU Library General Public License and the Sun Public License. You can learn more by checking out the full user's manual and FAQ on the web site. If you have ideas, bug fixes, or improvements, please consider joining the developer's mailing list.

As a final caveat, I should say that you do get what you pay for, and BeanShell is still somewhat experimental. So you will certainly find bugs. Please feel free to send feedback, using the book's web page, *http://www.oreilly.com/catalog/learnjava2*. Enjoy!

Glossary

abstract

The abstract keyword is used to declare abstract methods and classes. An abstract method has no implementation defined; it is declared with arguments and a return type as usual, but the body enclosed in curly braces is replaced with a semicolon. The implementation of an abstract method is provided by a subclass of the class in which it is defined. If an abstract method appears in a class, the class is also abstract.

API (Application Programming Interface)

An API consists of the functions and variables programmers use in their applications. The Java API consists of all public and protected methods of all public classes in the java.applet, java.awt, java.awt.image, java.awt.peer, java.io, java.lang, java.net, and java.util packages.

applet

An embedded Java application that runs in the context of an applet viewer, such as a web browser.

\<APPLET\> tag

An HTML tag that specifies an applet run within a web document.

appletviewer

Sun's application that implements the additional structure needed to run and display Java applets.

application

A Java program that runs standalone; i.e., it doesn't require an applet viewer.

assertion

A language feature used to test for conditions that should be guaranteed by program logic. If a condition checked by an assertion is found to be false, a fatal error is thrown. For added performance, assertions can be disabled when an application is deployed.

AWT (Abstract Window Toolkit)

Java's platform-independent windowing, graphics, and user interface toolkit.

Boojum

The mystical, spectral, alter-ego of a Snark. From the Lewis Carroll poem "*The Hunting of the Snark*," 1876.

boolean

A primitive Java data type that contains a truth value. The two possible values of a boolean variable are true and false.

byte

A primitive Java data type that's an eight-bit two's-complement signed number (in all implementations).

callback

A behavior that is defined by one object and then later invoked by another object when a particular event occurs.

cast

A technique that explicitly converts one data type to another.

catch

The catch statement introduces an exception-handling block of code following a try statement. The catch keyword is followed by an exception type and argument name in parentheses and a block of code within curly braces.

certificate

An electronic document used to verify the identity of a person, group, or organization. Certificates attest to the identity of a person or group and contain that organization's public key. A certificate is signed by a certificate authority.

certificate authority (CA)

An organization that is entrusted to issue certificates, taking whatever steps are necessary to verify the identity for which it is issuing the certificate.

char

A primitive Java data type; a variable of type char holds a single 16-bit Unicode character.

Collections API

Classes in the core java.util package for working with and sorting structured collections or maps of items. This API includes the Vector and Hashtable classes as well as newer items such as List and Map.

class

a) An encapsulated collection of data and methods to operate on the data. A class may be instantiated to produce an object that's an instance of the class.

b) The class keyword is used to declare a class, thereby defining a new object type. Its syntax is similar to the struct keyword in C.

class loader

An object in the Java security model that is responsible for loading Java binary classes from the network into the local interpreter. A class loader keeps its classes in a separate namespace, so that loaded classes cannot interact with system classes and breach system security.

class method

A method declared static. Methods of this type are not passed implicit this references and may refer only to class variables and invoke other class methods of the current class. A class method may be invoked through the class name, rather than through an instance of the class.

classpath

The directory path specifying the location of compiled Java class files on the local system.

class variable

A variable declared static. Variables of this type are associated with the class, rather than with a particular instance of the class. There is only one copy of a static variable, regardless of the number of instances of the class that are created.

client

The application that initiates a conversation as part of a networked client/server application. See also *server*.

compilation unit

The source code for a Java class. A compilation unit normally contains a single class definition and, in most current development environments, is simply a file with a *.java* extension.

compiler

A program that translates source code into executable code.

component architecture

A methodology for building parts of an application. It is a way to build reusable objects that can be easily assembled to form applications.

composition

Using objects as part of another, more complex object. When you compose a new object, you create complex behavior by delegating tasks to the internal objects. Composition is different from inheritance, which defines a new object by changing or refining the behavior of an old object. See also *inheritance*.

constructor

A method that is invoked automatically when a new instance of a class is created. Constructors are used to initialize the variables of the newly created object. The constructor method has the same name as the class.

content handler

A class that is called to parse a particular type of data and that converts it to an appropriate object.

datagram

A packet of data sent to a receiving computer without warning, error checking, or other control information.

data hiding

See *encapsulation*.

deep copy

A duplicate of an object along with all of the objects that it references, transitively. A deep copy duplicates the entire "graph" of objects, instead of just duplicating references. See also *shallow copy*.

DOM (Document Object Model)

An in-memory representation of a fully parsed XML document using objects with names like Element, Attribute, and Text. The Java XML DOM API binding is standardized by the World Wide Web Consortium (W3C).

double

A Java primitive data type; a double value is a 64-bit (double-precision) floating-point number.

DTD (Document Type Definition)

A document containing specialized language that expresses constraints on the structure of XML tags and tag attributes. DTDs are used to validate an XML document and can constrain the order and nesting of tags as well as the allowed values of attributes.

encapsulation

An object-oriented programming technique that makes an object's data private or protected (i.e., hidden) and allows programmers to access and manipulate that data only through method calls. Done well, encapsulation reduces bugs and promotes reusability and modularity of classes. This technique is also known as *data hiding*.

event

A user's action, such as a mouse-click or key press.

exception

A signal that some unexpected condition has occurred in the program. In Java, exceptions are objects that are subclasses of Exception or Error (which themselves are subclasses of Throwable). Exceptions in Java are "raised" with the throw keyword and received with the catch keyword. See also *catch, throw*, and *throws*.

exception chaining

The design pattern of catching an exception and throwing a new, higher level, or more appropriate exception which contains the underlying exception as its *cause*. The "cause" exception can be retrieved if necessary.

extends

A keyword used in a class declaration to specify the superclass of the class being defined. The class being defined has access to all the public and protected variables and methods of the superclass (or, if the class being defined is in the same package, it has access to all non-private variables and methods). If a class definition omits the extends clause, its superclass is taken to be java.lang.Object.

final

A keyword modifier that may be applied to classes, methods, and variables. It has a similar, but not identical, meaning in each case. When final is applied to a class, it means that the class may never be subclassed. java.lang.System is an example of a final class. When final is applied to a variable, the variable is a constant; i.e., it can't be modified.

finalize

A reserved method name. The finalize() method is called when an object is no longer being used (i.e., when there are no further references to it) but before the object's memory is actually reclaimed by the system. A finalizer should perform cleanup tasks and free system resources not handled by Java's garbage-collection system.

finally
A keyword that introduces the `finally` block of a try/catch/finally construct. `catch` and `finally` blocks provide exception handling and routine cleanup for code in a try block. The `finally` block is optional and appears after the try block, and after zero or more catch blocks. The code in a `finally` block is executed once, regardless of how the code in the try block executes. In normal execution, control reaches the end of the try block and proceeds to the `finally` block, which generally performs any necessary cleanup.

float
A Java primitive data type; a `float` value is a 32-bit (single-precision) floating-point number represented in IEEE 754 format.

garbage collection
The process of reclaiming the memory of objects no longer in use. An object is no longer in use when there are no references to it from other objects in the system and no references in any local variables on the method call stack.

graphics context
A drawable surface represented by the `java.awt.Graphics` class. A graphics context contains contextual information about the drawing area and provides methods for performing drawing operations in it.

GUI (graphical user interface)
A GUI is constructed from graphical push buttons, text fields, pull-down menus, dialog boxes, and other standard interface components.

hashcode
An arbitrary-looking identifying number used as a kind of signature for an object. A hashcode stores an object in a hashtable. See also *hashtable*.

hashtable
An object that is like a dictionary or an associative array. A hashtable stores and retrieves elements using key values called hashcodes. See also *hashcode*.

hostname
The name given to an individual computer attached to the Internet.

HotJava
A web browser written in Java, capable of downloading and running Java applets.

HTTP (Hypertext Transfer Protocol)
The protocol used by web browsers or other clients to talk to web servers. The simplest form of the protocol uses the commands GET to request a file and POST to send data.

implements
A keyword used in class declarations to indicate that the class implements the named interface or interfaces. The `implements` clause is optional in class declarations; if it appears, it must follow the extends clause (if any). If an `implements` clause appears in the declaration of a non-abstract class, every method from each specified interface must be implemented by the class or by one of its superclasses.

import
The `import` statement makes Java classes available to the current class under an abbreviated name. (Java classes are always available by their fully qualified name, assuming the appropriate class file can be found relative to the CLASSPATH environment variable and that the class file is readable. `import` doesn't make the class available; it just saves typing and makes your code more legible.) Any number of `import` statements may appear in a Java program. They must appear, however, after the optional package statement at the top of the file, and before the first class or interface definition in the file.

inheritance
An important feature of object-oriented programming that involves defining a new object by changing or refining the

behavior of an existing object. That is, an object implicitly contains all the non-private variables of its superclass and can invoke all the non-private methods of its superclass. Java supports single inheritance of classes and multiple inheritance of interfaces.

inner class

A class definition that is nested within another class. An inner class functions within the lexical scope of another class.

instance

An object. When a class is instantiated to produce an object, we say the object is an instance of the class.

instance method

A non-static method of a class. Such a method is passed an implicit this reference to the object that invoked it. See also *class method* and *static*.

instanceof

A Java operator that returns true if the object on its left side is an instance of the class (or implements the interface) specified on its right side. instanceof returns false if the object isn't an instance of the specified class or doesn't implement the specified interface. It also returns false if the specified object is null.

instance variable

A non-static variable of a class. Copies of such variables occur in every instance of the created class. See also *class variable* and *static*.

int

A primitive Java data type that's a 32-bit two's-complement signed number (in all implementations).

interface

A keyword used to declare an interface. More generally, an interface defines a list of methods that enables a class to implement the interface itself.

internationalization

The process of making an application accessible to people who speak a variety of languages. Sometimes abbreviated I18N.

interpreter

The module that decodes and executes Java bytecode.

introspection

The process by which a JavaBean provides additional information about itself, supplementing information learned by reflection.

ISO 8859-1

An eight-bit character encoding standardized by the ISO. This encoding is also known as Latin-1 and contains characters from the Latin alphabet suitable for English and most languages of western Europe.

ISO 10646

A four-byte character encoding that includes all the world's national standard character encodings. Also known as UCS. The two-byte Unicode character set maps to the range 0x00000000 to 0x0000FFFF of ISO 10646.

JavaBeans

A component architecture for Java. It is a way to build interoperable Java objects that can be manipulated easily in a visual application builder environment.

JavaBeans

Individual JavaBeans are Java classes that are built using certain design patterns and naming conventions.

JavaScript

A language developed by Netscape for creating dynamic web pages. From a programmer's point of view, it's unrelated to Java, although some of its capabilities are similar. Internally, there may be a relationship, but even that is unclear.

JAXB (Java API for XML Binding)

A Java API that allows for generation of Java classes from XML DTD or Schema descriptions and the generation of XML from Java classes. JAXB includes a binding schema that maps names and structures in the Java classes to XML tags and vice versa.

JAXP (Java API for XML Parsers)

The Java API that allows for pluggable implementations of XML and XSL engines. This API provides an implementation-neutral way to construct parsers and transforms.

JDBC (Java Database Connectivity)

The standard Java API for talking to an SQL (structural query language) database.

JDOM

A native Java DOM created by Jason Hunter and Brett McLaughlin. JDOM is easier to use than the standard DOM API for Java. It uses the Java collections API and standard conventions. Available at *http://www.jdom.org/*.

layout manager

An object that controls the arrangement of components within the display area of a container.

Latin-1

A nickname for ISO 8859-1.

lightweight component

A Java component that has no native peer in the AWT.

local variable

A variable that is declared inside a single method. A local variable can be seen only by code within that method.

Logging API

The Java API for structured logging and reporting of messages from within application components. The Logging API supports logging levels indicating the importance of messages, as well as filtering and output capabilities.

long

A primitive Java data type that's a 64-bit two's-complement signed number (in all implementations).

message digest

A long number computed from a message, used to determine whether the message's contents have been changed in any way. A change to a message's contents will change its message digest. It is almost impossible to create two similar messages with the same digest.

method

The object-oriented programming term for a function or procedure.

method overloading

Providing definitions of more than one method with the same name but with different argument lists or return values. When an overloaded method is called, the compiler determines which one is intended by examining the supplied argument types.

method overriding

Defining a method that exactly matches (i.e., same name, same argument types, and same return type) a method defined in a superclass. When an overridden method is invoked, the interpreter uses "dynamic method lookup" to determine which method definition is applicable to the current object.

Model-View-Controller (MVC) framework

A user-interface design that originated in Smalltalk. In MVC, the data for a display item is called the "model." A "view" displays a particular representation of the model, and a "controller" provides user interaction with both. Java incorporates many MVC concepts.

modifier

A keyword placed before a class, variable, or method that alters the item's accessibility, behavior, or semantics. See also *abstract, final, native, private, protected, public, static,* and *synchronized*.

NaN (not-a-number)

This is a special value of the double and float data types that represents an undefined result of a mathematical operation, such as zero divided by zero.

native

A modifier that may be applied to method declarations. It indicates that the method is implemented (elsewhere) in C, or in some other platform-dependent fashion. A native method declaration should end with a semicolon instead of a brace-enclosed code block. A native method cannot be abstract, but all other method modifiers may be used with `native` methods.

native method
A method that is implemented in a native language on a host platform, rather than being implemented in Java. Native methods provide access to such resources as the network, the windowing system, and the host filesystem.

new
`new` is a unary operator that creates a new object or array (or raises an `OutOfMemoryException` if there is not enough memory available).

NIO
The Java "new" I/O package. A core package introduced in Java 1.4 to support asynchronous, interruptible, and scalable I/O operations. The NIO API supports nonthread-bound "select" style I/O handling.

null
`null` is a special value that indicates a variable doesn't refer to any object. The value `null` may be assigned to any class or interface variable. It cannot be cast to any integral type, and should not be considered equal to zero, as in C.

object
An instance of a class. A class models a group of things; an object models a particular member of that group.

\<OBJECT\> tag
A proposed HTML tag that may replace the widely used but nonstandard \<APPLET\> tag.

package
The package statement specifies which package the code in the file is part of. Java code that is part of a particular package has access to all classes (public and non-public) in the package, and all non-private methods and fields in all those classes. When Java code is part of a named package, the compiled class file must be placed at the appropriate position in the `CLASSPATH` directory hierarchy before it can be accessed by the Java interpreter or other utilities. If the package statement is omitted from a file, the code in that file is part of an unnamed default package. This is convenient for small test programs, or during development because it means the code can be interpreted from the current directory.

\<PARAM\> tag
An HTML tag used within \<APPLET\> ... \</APPLET\> to specify a named parameter and string value to an applet within a web page.

plug-in
A modular application component for a web browser designed to extend the browser's capabilities to handle a specific type of data (MIME type). The Java Plug-in supports Java applets in browsers that do not have up-to-date Java runtime support.

Preferences API
The Java API for storing small amounts of information on a per-user or systemwide basis across executions of the Java VM. The Preferences API is analogous to a small database or the Windows registry.

primitive type
One of the Java data types: `boolean`, `char`, `byte`, `short`, `int`, `long`, `float`, `double`. Primitive types are manipulated, assigned, and passed to methods "by value" (i.e., the actual bytes of the data are copied). See also *reference type*.

private
The private keyword is a visibility modifier that can be applied to method and field variables of classes. A private field is not visible outside its class definition.

protected
A keyword that is a visibility modifier; it can be applied to method and field variables of classes. A protected field is visible only within its class, within subclasses, or within the package of which its class is a part. Note that subclasses in different packages can access only protected fields within themselves or within other objects that are subclasses; they cannot access

protected fields within instances of the superclass.

protocol handler

Software that describes and enables the use of a new protocol. A protocol handler consists of two classes: a `StreamHandler` and a `URLConnection`.

public

A keyword that is a visibility modifier; it can be applied to classes and interfaces and to the method and field variables of classes and interfaces. A `public` class or interface is visible everywhere. A non-public class or interface is visible only within its package. A `public` method or variable is visible everywhere its class is visible. When none of the private, protected, or `public` modifiers are specified, a field is visible only within the package of which its class is a part.

public key cryptography

A cryptographic system that requires a public key and a private key. The private key can decrypt messages encrypted with the corresponding `public` key, and vice versa. The `public` key can be made available to the public without compromising cryptographic security.

reference type

Any object or array. Reference types are manipulated, assigned, and passed to methods "by reference." In other words, the underlying value is not copied; only a reference to it is. See also *primitive type*.

reflection

The ability of a programming language to interact with structures of the language itself. Reflection in Java allows a Java program to examine class files at runtime to find out about their methods and variables, and to invoke methods or modify variables dynamically.

regular expression

A compact yet powerful syntax for describing a pattern in text. Regular expressions can be used to recognize and parse most kinds of textual constructs allowing for wide variation in their form.

Regular Expression API

The core `java.util.regex` package for using regular expressions. The regex package can be used to search and replace text based on sophisticated patterns.

Remote Method Invocation (RMI)

RMI is a native Java distributed object system. With RMI, you can pass references to objects on remote hosts and invoke methods in them as if they were local objects.

root

The base of a hierarchy, such as a root class, whose descendants are subclasses. The `java.lang.Object` class serves as the root of the Java class hierarchy.

SAX (Simple API for XML)

SAX is an event-driven API for parsing XML documents in which the client receives events in response to activities such as the opening of tags, character data, and the closing of tags.

Schema

XML Schema are a replacement for DTDs. Schema are an XML-based language for expressing constraints on the structure of XML tags and tag attributes, as well as the structure and type of the data content.

SDK (Software Development Kit)

A package of software distributed by Sun Microsystems for Java developers. It includes the Java interpreter, Java classes, and Java development tools: compiler, debugger, disassembler, applet viewer, stub file generator, and documentation generator.

SecurityManager

The Java class that defines the methods the system calls to check whether a certain operation is permitted in the current environment.

serialize

To serialize means to put in order or make sequential. A serialized object is an object that has been packaged so that it can be stored or transmitted over the network. Serialized methods are methods that have been synchronized so that only one may be executing at a given time.

server

The application that accepts a request for a conversation as part of a networked client/server application. See also *client*.

servlet

A Java application component that implements the javax.servlet.Servlet extension API allowing it to run inside a servlet container or web server. Servlets are widely used in web applications to process user data and generate HTML or other forms of output.

servlet context

In the Servlet API, the web application environment of a servlet that provides server and application resources. The base URL path of the web application is also often referred to as the servlet context.

shadow

To declare a variable with the same name as a variable defined in a superclass. We say the variable "shadows" the superclass's variable. Use the super keyword to refer to the shadowed variable or refer to it by casting the object to the type of the superclass.

signature

A combination of a message's message digest, encrypted with the signer's private key, and the signer's certificate, attesting to the signer's identity. Someone receiving a signed message can get the signer's public key from the certificate, decrypt the encrypted message digest, and compare that result with the message digest computed from the signed message. If the two message digests agree, the recipient knows that the message has not been modified and that the signer is who he or she claims to be.

signed applet

An applet packaged in a JAR file signed with a digital signature, allowing for authentication of its origin and validation of the integrity of its contents.

signed class

A Java class (or Java archive) that has a signature attached. The signature allows the recipient to verify the class's origin and that it is unmodified. The recipient can therefore grant the class greater runtime privileges.

shallow copy

A copy of an object that duplicates only values contained in the object itself. References to other objects are copied as references and are not duplicated. See also *deep copy*.

short

A primitive Java data type that's a 16-bit two's-complement signed number (in all implementations).

socket

An interface that listens for connections from clients on a data port and connects the client data stream with the receiving application.

spinner

A GUI component that displays a value and a pair of small up and down buttons that increment or decrement the value. The Swing JSpinner can work with number ranges and dates as well as arbitrary enumerations.

static

A keyword that is a modifier applied to method and variable declarations within a class. A static variable is also known as a class variable as opposed to non-static instance variables. While each instance of a class has a full set of its own instance variables, there is only one copy of each static class variable, regardless of the number of instances of the class (perhaps zero) that are created. static variables may be accessed by class name or through an instance. Non-static variables can be accessed only through an instance.

stream

A flow of data, or a channel of communication. All fundamental I/O in Java is based on streams.

String

A class used to represent textual information. The String class includes many methods for operating on string objects. Java overloads the + operator for string concatenation.

subclass

A class that extends another. The subclass inherits the public and protected methods and variables of its superclass. See also *extends*.

super

A keyword that refers to the same value as this: the instance of the class for which the current method (these keywords are valid only within non-static methods) was invoked. While the type of this is the type of the class in which the method appears, the type of super is the type of the superclass of the class in which the method appears. super is usually used to refer to superclass variables shadowed by variables in the current class. Using super in this way is equivalent to casting this to the type of the superclass.

superclass

A class extended by some other class. The superclass's public and protected methods and variables are available to the subclass. See also *extends*.

synchronized

A keyword used in two related ways in Java: as a modifier and as a statement. First, it is a modifier applied to class or instance methods. It indicates that the method modifies the internal state of the class or the internal state of an instance of the class in a way that is not thread-safe. Before running a synchronized class method, Java obtains a lock on the class, to ensure that no other threads can modify the class concurrently. Before running a synchronized instance method, Java obtains a lock on the instance that invoked the method, ensuring that no other threads can modify the object at the same time.

Java also supports a synchronized statement that serves to specify a "critical section" of code. The synchronized keyword is followed by an expression in parentheses and a statement or block of statements. The expression must evaluate to an object or array. Java obtains a lock on the specified object or array before executing the statements.

TCP (Transmission Control Protocol)

A connection-oriented, reliable protocol. One of the protocols on which the Internet is based.

this

Within an instance method or constructor of a class, this refers to "this object"— the instance currently being operated on. It is useful to refer to an instance variable of the class that has been shadowed by a local variable or method argument. It is also useful to pass the current object as an argument to static methods or methods of other classes.

There is one additional use of this: when it appears as the first statement in a constructor method, it refers to one of the other constructors of the class.

thread

A single, independent stream of execution within a program. Since Java is a multi-threaded programming language, more than one thread may be running within the Java interpreter at a time. Threads in Java are represented and controlled through the Thread object.

throw

The throw statement signals that an exceptional condition has occurred by throwing a specified exception object. This statement stops program execution and resumes it at the nearest containing catch statement that can handle the specified exception object. Note that the throw keyword must be followed by an exception object, not an exception class.

throws

The throws keyword is used in a method declaration to list the exceptions the method can throw. Any exceptions a method can raise that are not subclasses of Error or RuntimeException must either be caught within the method or declared in the method's throws clause.

try

The try keyword indicates a block of code to which subsequent catch and finally clauses apply. The try statement itself performs no special action. See also *catch* and *finally* for more information on the try/catch/finally construct.

UCS (universal character set)

A synonym for ISO 10646.

UDP (User Datagram Protocol)

A connectionless unreliable protocol. UDP describes a network data connection based on datagrams with little packet control.

Unicode

A universal standard for text character encoding, accommodating the written forms of almost all languages. Unicode is standardized by the Unicode Consortium. Java uses Unicode for its char and String types.

UTF-8 (UCS transformation format 8-bit form)

An encoding for Unicode characters (and more generally, UCS characters) commonly used for transmission and storage. It is a multibyte format in which different characters require different numbers of bytes to be represented.

vector

A dynamic array of elements.

verifier

A theorem prover that steps through the Java bytecode before it is run and makes sure that it is well-behaved. The bytecode verifier is the first line of defense in Java's security model.

WAR file (Web Applications Resources file)

A JAR file with additional structure to hold classes and resources for web applications. A WAR file includes a *WEB-INF* directory for classes, libraries, and the *web.xml* deployment file.

web application

An application that runs on a web server or application server, normally using a web browser as a client.

XML (Extensible Markup Language)

A universal markup language for text, using *tags* to add structure and meta-information to the content.

XSL/XSLT (Extensible Stylesheet Language/XSL Transformations)

An XML-based language for describing styling and transformation of XML documents. Styling involves simple addition of markup, usually for presentation. XSLT allows complete restructuring of documents, in addition to styling.

Index

We'd like to hear your suggestions for improving our indexes. Send email to *index@oreilly.com*.

B

\B (nonword) boundary, 241
\b (word) boundary, 241
back key navigation, 511
backing store (for preferences), 278
BackingStoreException, 278
BadExpression exception, 524
base classes (C++), fragility of, 12
base directory, URL name and, 363
base type, 87
  of arrays, 110
base URL, 378
  finding, 312
  HTML documents, 669
baselines of fonts, 580
BasicStroke class, 565, 575
BeanBox development environment, 641
BeanBuilder development environment, 641
BeanContext class, 651
BeanContextServices class, 651
BeanInfo interface, 622, 642–645
  properties information, getting, 642–645
Beans class, 646
beans (see JavaBeans)
BeanShell script, 188, 623, 730–735
  classpath, changing, 734
  commands, 732
  importing classes, 732
  interfaces and adapters, 733
  methods and objects, 733
  online user's manual and FAQ, 735
  running, 730
  statements and expressions in, 731
big endian, 324
BigDecimal class, 256
BigInteger class, 256
binary files, text vs., 684
bind()
  Naming class, 361
  ServerSocketChannel class, 375
binding properties, 631–633
binding XML to Java classes, 705
bitwise left-shift (<<) operator, 608
block comments in Java, 81
<body> tag, HTML, 688
booleans, 42
  blinkState variable, 61
  Boolean class, 230
    system property, getting, 276
  boolean data type, 83, 737
  parsing, 230
  property values, 636

BorderLayout layout manager, 440, 539–542
  sizing components in, 540
borders, Swing components, 474–476
  Border interface, 474
    implementation classes, 474
  BorderFactory class, 474
  Borders class (example), 475
bound properties, 642
Box class, 500
  methods for component layout, 542
BoxLayout layout manager, 542
break statements, 90, 106
browsers, 6
  applets
    access to user filesystem, 311
    displaying, 21
    driving browser with, 662
    running in context of, 656
    security restrictions on, 20
    support for, 654
  building, using JEditorPane HTML
    display, 506–508
  caching, 137
  certificate authority certificates, 677
  content and protocol handlers, 381–383,
    719
  HotJava, 381, 740
  HotJavaBrowser Bean, 620
  Java, support for, 27, 671
  lacking cookie support, rewriting URLs
    for, 403
  passing information to servlet or CGI
    program, 397
  redirecting to different URL, 396
  responding to unknown tags, 667
  SecurityManager class, 659
  XML and, 685
  XSL in, 710
bubbling up (exceptions), 100
BufferedImage class, 604
  converting Image to, 614
  creating from ARGB pixel values
    array, 607
  Rasters and ColorModels, 605
  updating, 608–611
BufferedImageOp interface, 611, 614
  filter(), 615
buffering
  double buffering images, 584, 586
  input/output streams, 291
    BufferedInputStream class, 295
    BufferedReader class, 294

encryption
  public-key techniques, using over
      SSL, 388
  type, specifying in URLs, 722
encryption keys, 680
end styles for lines, 565, 575
endElement() (ContentHandler), 690
end-of-line characters, matching in regular
      expressions, 245
endsWith() (String), 225, 226
Enterprise JavaBeans (EJB), 26, 652
  Java 2 Enterprise Edition (J2EE)
      platform, 653
entities, XML, 687
Entity Beans, 652
enumerate(), 215
enumerations
  Enumeration interface, 229, 266
  property names, 274
environment variables
  classpath, 68
  host operating system, Java access to, 67
  system, 275
EOFException class, 310, 355
equality
  == operator, 92, 223
  equivalence and, 174
  identity vs., 53
equals()
  Color class, 574
  comparing has code keys, 269
  Object class, 174, 270
  String class, 223, 226
  UnicastRemoteObject class, 358
equalsIgnoreCase() (String), 223, 226
equations, parsing in spreadsheet, 522
equivalence
  comparing strings for, 223
  of hash code keys, 269
error messages, formatting with
      ChoiceFormat, 236
errors
  classes for, 97
  compile-time, unreachable statements
      as, 91
  Error class, 98
      unchecked exceptions and, 102
  handling with exceptions, 13
  HTTP error codes, 396
  image preparation, testing for, 600
  runtime exceptions, 101
  System.err objects, 292

(see also exceptions)
escape sequences, Unicode characters, 81
event handlers, anonymous adapter classes
      as, 170
EventHandler class, 649–651
EventListener interface, 446
events, 44–45, 445–459, 739
  action, 52
  ActionEvent class, 446, 462
  adapter classes implementing listener
      interfaces, 456–459
  AWTEvent class, 445
  calculator application (example), 559
  checkbox, 466
  classes for, 44
  delivery of, 449
  Dial component (example), 530, 532
  EventObject class, 445
  focus, 452
  generating for components, 529
  HyperlinkEvent class, 506, 508
  input, generating with AWT Robot
      class, 459
  InternalFrameEvent class, 526
  JavaBeans
      bound properties and, 631–633
      connecting Molecule Bean to
          Timer, 630
      getting information about, 643
      hookups and adapters, 627–631
      runtime event hookup with
          reflection, 649–651
  listeners for, in MVC framework, 435
  mouse, 446
  players, realizing, 619
  preference changes, notifying of, 279
  receivers and listener interfaces, 446
  SAX, 691, 695
  scrollbar and slider, 489
  sources of, 447
      design pattern, 449
  Swing GUI
      components, notification of, 433
      summary of, 453–455
  tree selection, 516
  trees, 513
  types of, 450
EventSetDescriptor class, 643
Exception class, subclassing, 99
exception handling, 98

exceptions, 13, 62, 96–107, 739
    bubbling up, 100
    checked and unchecked, 101
    classes for, 97
    handling with try/catch statements, 62,
        738
        finally clause, 106
    overridden methods and, 145
    parsing streams, 297
    performance and, 106
    runtime, 102
    servlet, 395
    stack traces for, 101
    throwing, 102–104
        chaining exceptions, 104
        messages with, 103
    try creep, 105
exclusive file locks, 328
executables, building from source code, 10
execute()
    MyCalculation class (example), 353
    MyClient class (example), 367
    RMI server (example), 360
exists() (File), 307
exit() (System), 198
expanding and collapsing nodes, 513
explicit casting, 147
exportNode() (Preferences), 279
exportObject() (UnicastRemoteObject), 358
exportSubtree() (Preferences), 279
expressions, 92–96
    assertion, evaluating, 108
    assignment, 93
    BeanShell, using in, 731
    creating and evaluating in spreadsheet
        table, 524
    grouping with comma (,) operator, 90
    method invocation, 94
    null values in, 94
    operators in, 92
        instanceof operator, 95
        object creation, 95
    order of evaluation, 88
extending
    classes, 35, 47
    interfaces, 155
extends keyword, 35, 739
Extensible Markup Language (see XML)
Extensible Stylesheet Language (see XML,
        XSL/XSLT)
extent (JScrollBar), 489

extra path, 397
extracting files from archive, 76

F

-f (file) option (jar utility), 76
face (or font) names, 575
    retrieving, 576
factory patterns, 690
false values, 42, 84
family names (fonts), 575
Field class, 180, 183
fields, 31
    HTTP headers, checking for response
        MIME type and encoding, 387
fields, class, 180
    accessing, 181, 183
file locking, 320
file types (images), 580
FileChannel class, 326–330
    concurrent access, 327
    direct data transfer, 329
    file locking, 328
    MapMode static inner class, 329
    memory-mapped files, 328
    transferTo(), 376
FileHandler class, 281
files
    applets and, 311
    compression (JAR files), 75
    content type, guessing from name, 727
    file selection dialog, 492–494
    FileNotFoundException, 308
    FileOutputStream class, 309
    FileReader class, 308
    input/output, 303–313
        File class, 303–307
    input/output streams, 307–310
    input/output streams for, 291
    listing contents of, 308
    localizing path with JFileDialog class, 304
    manifests (JAR), 77
    nonexistent on server, 381
    RandomAccessFile class, 310
    restricting access to, 344
    source code, .java extension, 73
    uploading and removing with HTTP, 394
fill constraints (GridBagLayout), 548, 551
fill() (Graphics2D class), 564
filling shapes, 566, 572, 573–575
    color gradients, using, 573
    desktop colors, 574

mouse wheels, scrolling with, 451, 483
mouseClicked() methods, 482
mouseDragged(), 44, 47, 586
    drawing to offscreen buffer, 592
    eliminating unnecessary image update
        actions, 589
mouseMoved(), 44, 47
mousePressed(), 482
mouseReleased(), 482
MouseWheelListener interface, 451
movies, working with, 617–619
    URLs for movies, passing in command
        line, 619
Mozilla browsers
    XML support, 685
    XSL support, 710
multicast sockets, 333
multidimensional arrays, 115–116
multiline mode, regular expression
        matching, 245
multiline text editor, 496
multimedia, 22
    Java Sound API, 616
    JMF (Java Media Framework), 617–619
multiple inheritance, 139
Multipurpose Internet Mail Extensions
        (see MIME types)
multithreading, 58
    requests, servlet handling of, 393
    Swing components and, 459–461
music files, playing, 616
MutableTreeNode interface, 513
MVC (see Model-View-Controller
        framework)

N

Nagle's algorithm, turning off, 345
name attribute (HTML), 669
names
    anonymous inner classes, 169
    applets
        code attribute, specifying with, 669
        name attribute of <APPLET> tag, 663
    dot-separated hierarchy (properties), 274
    files, localization of, 304
    fonts, 575
    HTML frames for displaying
        documents, 663
    inner classes, 167
    Naming class, 359
        binding/rebinding names to
            registry, 360

    packages, 157
    remote interfaces, 360
namespaces, 688
    XSL, 706
naming conventions
    constants, 122
    constructor methods, 42
    interfaces, 152
    JavaBeans, naming and design patterns,
        JavaBeans, 23
    packages, 38
    Swing components, 48
    Swing event listener interfaces and
        handler methods, 447
NaN (not-a-number), 255, 742
narrowing
    object types, 265, 267
    reference types, 147
native methods, 6, 742
native threads, 214
nativeOrder() (ByteOrder), 324
navigation
    applets, over multipage documents, 664
    keyboard focus, 511
NavigationFilter interface, 500
negative infinity, 255
negative lookahead operator (?!), 247
nested expressions, parsing, 524
nesting
    character classes, 241
    classes, 164
    comments, 81
    XML tags, 686
NetBeans IDE, 23, 622–625
    Bean Patterns wizard, using, 693
    get and set method patterns, recognition
        of, 637
    installing and running, 623–625
Netscape
    applets, history of use, 654
    JavaScript, 741
    Navigator
        certificate authority (CA)
            certificates, 677
        encryption keys, managing with
            KEYGEN, 678
        HTML tags for, 672
        Java, support for, 27, 671
        plug-in mechanism, 671
        signed applets, 679
        user certificates, 678
        viewing Plug-in applets with, 673

assignment, 93
comma (,) in C, 90
dot (.), 94
image operators, 611
instanceof, 95
Java, listing of, 92
new, 93, 743
not (!) operator, 61
overloaded, 87, 130, 222
precedence, maintaining in
    spreadsheet, 524
precedence of, 524
    in nested expressions, 524
string concatenation (+), 93
ternary operator, 61
optimizing code
    javac compiler, 144
    in JIT compilation, 6
option dialogs, 490
    examples, 491
order of evaluation, 88
order() (ByteArray), 324
OrientableFlowLayout layout manager, 560
out of bounds values, returning instead of
    throwing exceptions, 106
outgoing methods, mapping to incoming
    events, 457
output streams
    ByteArrayOutputStream class, 426
    DataOutputStream class
        network byte order, 339
    HttpServletResponse objects, 394
    ObjectOutputStream class
        order of creation, 355
        server response processing, 354
    objects, order of creation, 355
    OutputStream class, 289
    properties table, saving to, 275
    sockets, retrieving for, 335
    System.out and System.err, 292
    URL connections, 387
    writing preferences to, 278
overloading
    methods, 50, 129, 142, 742
        add(), 440
        append() (StringBuffer), 227
        casting and, 148
        constructors, 132
        equals(), 174
        overriding vs., 130, 143
    operators, 87, 130, 222

overriding methods, 35, 142–146, 742
    abstract methods, 151
    casting and, 148
    compiler optimizations for
        performance, 144
    component size, 536
    dynamic binding and, 143
    equals(), 174, 270
    exceptions and, 145
    final, performance and, 144
    hashCode(), 270
    method selection and, 145
    overloaded methods vs., 130
    static binding, 144
    subclasses, visibility and, 161

P

pack(), 536
    JFrame class, 444
packages, 10, 37, 743
    applet class files, locating on server, 670
    compilation units and, 156
    core, Java platform, 38
    cryptographic (JCE), 678
    drawing, classes for, 562
    enabling assertions for, 108
    event, 450
    importing, 38, 44
    Java API, 218
    java.lang, class hierarchy, 219
    java.text, 234–238
    naming, 157
    protocols handler, names for, 721
    scalability and, 14
    unnamed, 159
    user and system preferences for, 278
packing JAR files, 76
padding
    GridBagLayout, 553–555
        insets, relationship with, 555
    HTML attribute for, 668
    between lines of text, 580
Paint interface, 565
paint objects, 566
paint(), 436, 563, 572
    animation, use in, 604
    Component class, 564
    DrawPad class (example), 592
    image observers and, 582
    JApplet class, 656
    update() vs., 586

Runnable interface, 60, 190–195, 262
  anonymous inner class, implementing
      with, 194
  creating and starting threads, 191
  subclassing Thread, 192
running applications HelloJava
      (example), 30
runtime
  adaptive compiler, use of, 7
  typing (Java), 11
runtime interpreter, 4
runtime systems, 27
RuntimeException class, 63, 97
  unchecked exceptions and, 102

S

\S (nonspace character), matching in regular
      expressions, 240
s (single line mode), regular expression
      matching, 245
\s (space character), matching in regular
      expressions, 240
sameFile() (URL), 379
SampleModel class, 605, 610
save() (Properties), 275
saveFile() (Editor), 494
SAX (Simple API for XML), 685, 689–697
  Java object model, building from XML
      document, 691–697
  JAXP, accessing parser with, 690
  strengths and weaknesses of, 691
say(), 202
scalability of Java classes, 14
scalar types (C language), 83
scalar values, retrieving for numeric type
      wrappers, 257
scale() (Graphics2D), 565
scaleable I/O with NIO package, 368–376
  selectable channels, 369–371
scaling images, 583, 616
schedule() (Timer), 262
scheduling threads, 210
scientific algorithms, 256
scope
  application level in Java packages, 14
  declaring for classes, 163
  local variables, 124
  shadowed variables, 140
  this reference (inner classes), 171
scripting languages
  BeanShell, for Java (see BeanShell script)
  comparing to Java, 8

JavaScript, 8
  reflection API, using to integrate Java
      with, 188
scrollbars
  JScrollPane class, 471, 482–484
    scrollbar display policy, 483
  sliders, using with, 487–489
scrolling, mouse-wheel device, 451
SDK (Software Development Kit), 27, 65–79
  appletviewer, 337
  JAR (Java archive) files, 75–79
    jar utility, 76–79
  Java interpreter, 65–67
    system properties, access to, 67
  javac compiler, 73–75
  javap tool, 69
  policytool utility, 71–73
  Version 1.4, xii
    assertions, 107–110
    digital signatures for applets, 674–682
    exception chaining, 104
    focus in Swing components, 437, 511
    formatted text in Swing, 499–504
    Java Plug-in, using with
        applets, 671–673
    Java Web Start as alternative to
        applets, 673
    Logging API, 279–286
    mouse-wheel events in Swing, 451
    NIO (new I/O) package, 319–330,
        368–376
    overview of features, 25
    Preferences API, 276–279
    regular expressions, 238–253
    servlets and web
        applications, 390–428
    XML, 683–711
searching for substrings within strings, 225
security
  applets, restrictions on, 656
    reading/writing to files, 311
  digital signatures, using, 674–682
    certificates, 676, 682
  EventHandler class and, 650
  HTTP daemon server, 343
  inner classes and, 172
  Java design features, 9–14
    dynamic memory management, 12
    error handling, 13
    incremental development, 12
    scalability, 14
    simplicity of syntax, 10

Z

About the Authors

Patrick Niemeyer (*pat@pat.net*) became involved with Oak (Java's predecessor) while working at Southwestern Bell Technology Resources. He is an independent consultant and author in the areas of networking and distributed applications. Pat is the author of BeanShell, a popular Java scripting language, as well as various other free goodies on the Net. Most recently, Pat has been developing enterprise architecture for A.G. Edwards. He currently lives in the Central West End area of St. Louis with various creatures.

Jonathan Knudsen (*www.jonathanknudsen.com*) is the author of several books, including *Wireless Java, The Unofficial Guide to LEGO™ MINDSTORMS Robots, Java 2D Graphics*, and *Java Cryptography*. He is a technical writer at Sun's Wireless Developer web site, *http://wireless.java.sun.com/*.

Colophon

Our look is the result of reader comments, our own experimentation, and feedback from distribution channels. Distinctive covers complement our distinctive approach to technical topics, breathing personality and life into potentially dry subjects.

The animals on the cover of *Learning Java*, Second Edition, are a Bengal tigress and her cubs. The Bengal tiger (*Panthera tigris*) lives in Southern Asia where it has been hunted practically to extinction principally for its bone, which is reputed to have medicinal value. It now lives mostly in natural preserves and national parks where it is strictly protected. It's estimated that there are less than 3,000 Bengal tigers left in the wild.

The Bengal tiger is reddish orange with narrow black, gray, or brown stripes, generally in a vertical direction. Males can grow to nine feet long and weigh as much as 500 pounds; they are the largest existing members of the cat family. Preferred habitats include dense thickets, long grass, or tamarisk shrubs along river banks. Maximum longevity can be 26 years but is usually only about 15 years in the wild.

Tigers most commonly conceive after the monsoon rains; the majority of cubs are born between February and May after a gestation of three and a half months. Females bear single litters every two to three years. Cubs weigh under three pounds at birth and are striped. Litters consist of one to four cubs, with occasionally as many as six, but it's unusual for more than two or three to survive. Cubs are weaned at four to six months but depend on their mother for food and protection for another two years. Female tigers are mature at three to four years, males at four to five years.

Their white ear spots may help mothers and cubs to keep track of each other in the dim forests at night.

Mary Anne Weeks Mayo was the production editor, and Leanne Soylemez copy-edited select chapters for *Learning Java*, Second Edition. Matt Hutchinson and Jane

Ellin provided quality control. Phil Dangler provided production assistance. Ellen Troutman-Zaig wrote the index.

Hanna Dyer designed the cover of this book, based on a series design by Edie Freedman. The cover image is an original engraving from the book *Forest and Jungle: An Illustrated History of the Animal Kingdom* by P.T. Barnum (1899). Emma Colby produced the cover layout with QuarkXPress 4.1 using Adobe's ITC Garamond font. David Futato designed the CD-ROM label.

Melanie Wang designed the interior layout, based on a series design by David Futato. Neil Walls converted the files from Microsoft Word to FrameMaker 5.5.6 using tools created by Mike Sierra. The text font is Linotype Birka; the heading font is Adobe Myriad Condensed; and the code font is LucasFont's TheSans Mono Condensed. The illustrations that appear in the book were produced by Robert Romano and Jessamyn Read using Macromedia FreeHand 9 and Adobe Photoshop 6. The tip and warning icons were drawn by Christopher Bing. This colophon was compiled by Mary Anne Weeks Mayo.

Other Titles Available from O'Reilly

Java

Java Performance Tuning, 2nd Edition

By Jack Shirazi
2nd Edition January 2003 (est.)
600 pages (est.), ISBN 0-596-00015-4

Significantly revised and expanded, this second edition not only covers Java 1.4, but adds new coverage of JDBC, NIO, Servlets, EJB and JavaServer Pages. The book remains a valuable resource for teaching developers how to create a tuning strategy, how to use profiling tools to understand a program's behavior, and how to avoid performance penalties from inefficient code, making them more efficient and effective. The result is code that's robust, maintainable and fast!

Java Security, 2nd Edition

By Scott Oaks
2nd Edition May 2001
618 pages, ISBN 0-596-00157-6

The second edition focuses on the platform features of Java that provide security—the class loader, bytecode verifier, and security manager—and recent additions to Java that enhance this security model: digital signatures, security providers, and the access controller. The book covers in depth the security model of Java 2, version 1.3, including the two new security APIs: JAAS and JSSE.

Database Programming with JDBC and Java, 2nd Edition

By George Reese
2nd Edition August 2000
352 pages, ISBN 1-56592-616-1

This book describes the standard Java interfaces that make portable object-oriented access to relational databases possible, and offers a robust model for writing applications that are easy to maintain. The second edition has been completely updated for JDBC 2.0, and includes reference listings for JDBC and the most important RMI classes. The book begins with a quick overview of SQL for developers who may be asked to handle a database for the first time, and goes on to explain how to issue database queries and updates through SQL and JDBC.

Java Network Programming, 2nd Edition

By Elliotte Rusty Harold
2nd Edition August 2000
760 pages, ISBN 1-56592-870-9

Java Network Programming, 2nd Edition, is a complete introduction to developing network programs (both applets and applications) using Java, covering everything from networking fundamentals to remote method invocation (RMI). It includes chapters on TCP and UDP sockets, multicasting protocol and content handlers, and servlets. This second edition also includes coverage of Java 1.1, 1.2 and 1.3. New chapters cover multithreaded network programming, I/O, HTML parsing and display, the Java Mail API, the Java Secure Sockets Extension, and more.

Java Swing, 2nd Edition

By Marc Loy, Robert Eckstein, David Wood, James Elliott & Brian Cole
2nd Edition November 2002 (est.)
1296 pages (est.), ISBN 0-596-00408-7

This second edition of Java Swing thoroughly covers all the features available in Java 2 SDK 1.3 and 1.4. More than simply a reference, this new edition takes a practical approach. It is a book by developers for developers, with hundreds of useful examples, from beginning level to advanced, covering every component available in Swing. Whether you're a seasoned Java developer or just trying to find out what Java can do, you'll find Java Swing, 2nd edition an indispensable guide.

Java Pragramming with Oracle JDBC

By Donald K. Bales
1st Edition December 2001
496 pages, ISBN 0-596-00088-X

Here is the professional's guide to leveraging Java's JDBC in an Oracle environment. Readers learn the all-important mysteries of establishing database corrections; issuing SQL queries and getting results back; and advanced topics such as streaming large objects, calling PL/SQL procedures, and working with Oracle9i's object-oriented features. Also covered: transactions, concurrency management and performance. This is an essential tool for all Java Oracle developers who need to work with both technologies.

O'REILLY®

To order: 800-998-9938 • order@oreilly.com • www.oreilly.com
Online editions of most O'Reilly titles are available by subscription at safari.oreilly.com
Also available at most retail and online bookstores.

Java

Java Cookbook

By Ian Darwin
1st Edition June 2001
882 pages, ISBN 0-59600-170-3

This book offers Java developers short, focused pieces of code that are easy to incorporate into other programs. The idea is to focus on things that are useful, tricky, or both. The book's code segments cover all of the dominant APIs and many specialized APIs and should serve as a great "jumping-off place" for Java developers who want to get started in areas outside their specialization.

Java Enterprise Best Practices

By The O'Reilly Java Authors,
edited by Robert Eckstein
1st Edition December 2002 (est.)
304 (est.) pages, ISBN 0-596-00384-6

This book is for intermediate and advanced Java developers, the ones who have been around the block enough times to understand just how complex—and unruly—an enterprise system can get. Each chapter in this collection contains several rules that provide insight into the "best practices" for creating and maintaining projects using the Java Enterprise APIs. Written by the world's leading Java experts, this book covers JDBC, RMI/CORBA, Servlets, JavaServer Pages and custom tag libraries, XML, Internationalization, JavaMail, Enterprise JavaBeans, and performance tuning.

Java Message Service

By Richard Monson-Haefel &
David Chappell
1st Edition December 2000
238 pages, ISBN 0-596-00068-5

This book is a thorough introduction to Java Message Service (JMS) from Sun Microsystems. It shows how to build applications using the point-to-point and publish-and-subscribe models; use features like transactions and durable subscriptions to make applications reliable; and use messaging within Enterprise JavaBeans. It also introduces a new EJB type, the MessageDrivenBean, that is part of EJB 2.0, and discusses integration of messaging into J2EE.

Java Best Practices

By The O'Reilly Java Authors,
edited by Robert Eckstein
1st Edition January 2003 (est.)
304 (est.) pages, ISBN 0-596-00385-4

This book is for intermediate and advanced Java developers, the ones who have used the traditional Java APIs enough to know that some methods work much better than others. Each chapter contains several tips and tricks that offer valuable insight into using the Java APIs—essentially, "best practices" for creating and maintaining projects using Java SDK software. Written by some of the world's leading Java experts, this book covers networking, security, collections, NIO, Swing, 2D, Internationalization, Java Beans, and performance tuning.

Java Management Extensions

By J. StevenPerry
1st Edition June 2002
312 pages, ISBN 0-596-00245-9

Java Management Extensions is a practical, hands-on guide to using the JMX APIs. This one-of-a kind book is a complete treatment of the JMX architecture (both the instrumentation level and the agent level), and it's loaded with real-world examples for implementing Management Extensions. It also contains useful information at the higher level about JMX (the "big picture") to help technical managers and architects who are evaluating various application management approaches and are considering JMX.

Java RMI

By William Grosso
1st Edition November 2001
576 pages, ISBN 1-56592-452-5

Enterprise Java developers, especially those working with Enterprise JavaBeans, and Jini, need to understand RMI technology in order to write today's complex, distributed applications. O'Reilly's Java RMI thoroughly explores and explains this powerful but often overlooked technology. Included is a wealth of real-world examples that developers can implement and customize.

O'REILLY®

To order: 800-998-9938 • order@oreilly.com • www.oreilly.com
Online editions of most O'Reilly titles are available by subscription at safari.oreilly.com
Also available at most retail and online bookstores.

Java

Java Servlet Programming, 2nd Edition

By Jason Hunter with William Crawford
2nd Edition April 2001
780 pages, ISBN 0-596-00040-5

The second edition of this popular book has been completely updated to add the new features of the Java Servlet API Version 2.2, and new chapters on servlet security and advanced communication. In addition to complete coverage of the 2.2 specification, we have included bonus material on the new 2.3 version of the specification.

Java & XML, 2nd Edition

By Brett McLaughlin
2nd Edition September 2001
528 pages, ISBN 0-596-000197-5

New chapters on Advanced SAX, Advanced DOM, SOAP, and data binding, as well as new examples throughout, bring the second edition of *Java & XML* thoroughly up to date. Except for a concise introduction to XML basics, the book focuses entirely on using XML from Java applications. It's a worthy companion for Java developers working with XML or involved in messaging, web services, or the new peer-to-peer movement.

JavaServer Pages, 2nd Edition

By Hans Bergsten
2nd Edition August 2002
712 pages, ISBN 0-596-00317-X

Filled with useful examples and the depth, clarity, and attention to detail that made the first edition so popular with web developers, *JavaServer Pages*, 2nd Edition is completely revised and updated to cover the substantial changes in the 1.2 version of the JSP specifications, and includes coverage of the new JSTL Tag libraries—an eagerly anticipated standard set of JSP elements for the tasks needed in most JSP applications, as well as thorough coverage of Custom Tag Libraries.

Enterprise JavaBeans, 3rd Edition

By Richard Monson-Haefel
3rd Edition September 2001
592 pages, ISBN 0-596-00226-2

Enterprise JavaBeans has been thoroughly updated for the new EJB Specification. Important changes in Version 2.0 include a completely new CMP (container-managed persistence) model that allows for much more complex business function modeling; local interfaces that will significantly improve performance of EJB applications; and the "message driven bean," an entirely new kind of Java bean based on asynchronous messaging and the Java Message Service.

Java and XSLT

By Eric M. Burke
1st Edition September 2001
528 pages, ISBN 0-596-00143-6

Learn how to use XSL transformations in Java programs ranging from standalone applications to servlets. *Java and XSLT* introduces XSLT and then shows you how to apply transformations in real-world situations, such as developing a discussion forum, transforming documents from one form to another, and generating content for wireless devices.

How to stay in touch with O'Reilly

1. Visit our award-winning web site

http://www.oreilly.com/

★ "Top 100 Sites on the Web"—PC Magazine
★ CIO Magazine's Web Business 50 Awards

Our web site contains a library of comprehensive product information (including book excerpts and tables of contents), downloadable software, background articles, interviews with technology leaders, links to relevant sites, book cover art, and more. File us in your bookmarks or favorites!

2. Join our email mailing lists

Sign up to get email announcements of new books and conferences, special offers, and O'Reilly Network technology newsletters at:

http://elists.oreilly.com

It's easy to customize your free elists subscription so you'll get exactly the O'Reilly news you want.

3. Get examples from our books

To find example files for a book, go to:

http://www.oreilly.com/catalog

select the book, and follow the "Examples" link.

4. Work with us

Check out our web site for current employment opportunities:

http://jobs.oreilly.com/

5. Register your book

Register your book at:

http://register.oreilly.com

6. Contact us

O'Reilly & Associates, Inc.
1005 Gravenstein Hwy North
Sebastopol, CA 95472 USA
TEL: 707-827-7000 or 800-998-9938
    (6am to 5pm PST)
FAX: 707-829-0104

order@oreilly.com
For answers to problems regarding your order or our products. To place a book order online visit:

http://www.oreilly.com/order_new/

catalog@oreilly.com
To request a copy of our latest catalog.

booktech@oreilly.com
For book content technical questions or corrections.

corporate@oreilly.com
For educational, library, government, and corporate sales.

proposals@oreilly.com
To submit new book proposals to our editors and product managers.

international@oreilly.com
For information about our international distributors or translation queries. For a list of our distributors outside of North America check out:

http://international.oreilly.com/distributors.html

adoption@oreilly.com
For information about academic use of O'Reilly books, visit:

http://academic.oreilly.com

O'REILLY®

To order: *800-998-9938* • *order@oreilly.com* • *www.oreilly.com*
Online editions of most O'Reilly titles are available by subscription at *safari.oreilly.com*
Also available at most retail and online bookstores.